MURDER TRIALS IN IRELAND, 1836–1914

Murder Trials in Ireland, 1836–1914

W.E. VAUGHAN

FOUR COURTS PRESS
in association with
THE IRISH LEGAL HISTORY SOCIETY

Typeset in 10.5pt on 12.5pt EhrhardtMt by
Carrigboy Typesetting Services for
FOUR COURTS PRESS LTD
7 Malpas Street, Dublin 8, Ireland
www.fourcourtspress.ie
and in North America for
FOUR COURTS PRESS
c/o ISBS, 920 N.E. 58th Avenue, Suite 300, Portland, OR 97213.

© W.E. Vaughan and Four Courts Press 2009

ISBN 978-1-84682-158-5

Printed in England,
by MPG Books Ltd, Bodmin, Cornwall.

To the members of the Saturday Lunch Club

Contents

Abbreviations

The references in square brackets after English reports give the number of volumes in the series and the years covered

B & Ad	*Reports of cases argued and determined in the court of King's Bench* [5 vols, 1832–34]. By Richard Vaughan Barnewall and John Leicester Adolphus. In vol. 110 *English Reports*
B & Ald	*Reports of cases argued and determined in the Court of King's Bench* [5 vols, 1817–22]. By Richard Vaughan Barnewall and Edward Hall Alderson. In vol. 106 *English Reports*
Car & K	*Reports of cases argued and ruled at nisi prius, in the Courts of Queen's Bench, Common Pleas, & Exchequer; together with cases tried on the circuits, and in the Central Criminal Court* [3 vols, 1843–53]. By Frederick Augustus Carrington and Andrew Valentine Kirwan. In vols 174–5 *English Reports*
Car & P	*Reports of cases argued and ruled at nisi prius, in the Courts of Queen's Bench, Common Pleas, & Exchequer and on the circuit* [9 vols, 1823–40]. By F.A. Carrington and J. Payne. In vols 171–3 *English Reports*
Cl & Fin	*Reports of cases heard in the house of lords, on appeal and writs of error, and claims of peerage, and decided during the session* [12 vols, 1831–46]. By Charles Clarke and William Finnelly. In vols 6–8 *English Reports*
Cox CC	Edward W. Cox, *Reports of cases in criminal law, argued and determined in all the courts in England and Ireland*, 24 vols (London, 1843–1916)
Cr & Dix Abr	George Crawford & Edward Spencer Dix, *Abridged notes of cases argued and determined in the several courts of law and equity in Ireland, during the years 1837 and 1838; with some decisions at nisi prius and on the circuits. A table of cases, and index to the principal matters* (Dublin, 1839)
Cr & Dix	George Crawford & Edward Spencer Dix, *Reports of cases argued and ruled on the circuits, in Ireland, during the years 1839 and 1840; together with cases decided at the nisi prius sittings, and in the courts of criminal jurisdiction at Dublin, a table of cases, and an index to the principal matters*, vol. i (Dublin, 1841); vol. ii, *Reports of cases … during the years 1840, 1841, and 1842; together with cases decided at the nisi prius sittings, and in the courts of criminal jurisdiction at Dublin, a table of cases, and an index to the principal matters* (Dublin, 1843); vol. iii, *Reports of cases … during the years 1843, 1844, 1845, and 1846, together with notes of cases decided at the nisi prius sittings in Dublin, and in the courts of municipal revision* (Dublin, 1847)
Dears	*Crown cases reserved for consideration, and decided by the judges of England; selection of cases relating to indictable offences, argued and determined in the Courts of Queen's Bench and the Courts of Error* [1 vol., 1856–8]. By Henry Richard Dearsly. In vol. 169 *English Reports*
Eng Rep	*The English Reports* [covering the period 1210–1865], 176 vols (London, 1900–1930)

Exch | *The exchequer reports. Reports of cases argued and determined in the courts of Exchequer and Exchequer Chamber*, ed. by William Newland Welsby and Edwin Tyrrell Hurlstone (vols I–IX), and by Edwin Tyrrell Hurlstone and John Gordon (vols X, XI), 11 vols (London, 1849–56); contd by Edwin Tyrrell Hurlstone and J.P. Norman (London, 1857–62). In vols 154–8 *English Reports*

F & F | *Reports of cases decided at nisi prius and at the crown side on circuit; and decisions at chambers* [4 vols, 1856–67]. By Thomas Campbell Foster and William Francis Finlason. In vols 175–6 *English Reports*

Fost | *A report of some proceedings on the commission for the trial of the rebels in the year 1746, in the county of Surrey; and of other crown cases; to which are added discourses upon a few branches of the crown law* ... (London, 1809). By Sir Michael Foster [1 vol.]. In vol. 168 *English Reports*

Holt | *A report of the cases determined by Sir John Holt, from 1688 to which time he was lord chief justice of England; containing many cases not printed, taken from an original manuscript of T. Farresley* ... (London, 1738). In vol. 17 *English Reports*

ICLR | *Common law reports, of cases argued and determined in the courts of Queen's Bench, Common Pleas, Exchequer Chamber, and Court of Criminal Appeal* [from 1850 to 1866], 17 vols (Dublin, 1852–67)

ILT & SJ | *Irish Law Times and Solicitors' Journal* (Dublin, 1867–)

ILTR | *Irish Law Times Reports* [supplement to *Irish Law Times and Solicitors' Journal* (Dublin, 1867–)]

IR | *The Irish reports* (Dublin, 1894–)

IR ... CL | *The Irish reports, published under the control of the Council of Law Reporting in Ireland, containing reports of cases argued and determined in the superior courts in Ireland* [from Hilary term 1867 to Michaelmas term 1878], 11 vols (Dublin, 1868–79)

Ir Cir Rep | *Reports of cases argued and determined on six circuits in Ireland taken during the assizes, in the years 1841, 1842, 1843* ... (Dublin, 1843)

Ir Jur Rep | *The Irish Jurist*, 17 vols (Dublin, 1849–65)

Ir LR | *Irish law reports, particularly of points of practice, argued and determined in the courts of Queen's Bench, Common Pleas, and Exchequer of Pleas, from Michaelmas term 1838*, 13 vols (Dublin, 1839–52)

Jebb Rep | Robert Jebb, *Cases, chiefly relating to the criminal and presentment law, reserved for consideration, and decided by the twelve judges of Ireland, from May 1822, to November 1840* (Dublin, 1841)

Le & C | *Crown Cases reserved for consideration, and decided by the judges of England* [1 vol., 1861–5]. By Edward Chandos Leigh and Lewis William Cave. In vol. 169 *English Reports*

Leach | *Cases in crown law, determined by the twelve judges, by the court of King's Bench; and by commissioners of oyer and terminer, and general gaol delivery* ... [2 vols, 1730–1814]. By Thomas Leach. In vol. 168 *English Reports*

LR Ir | *The law reports (Ireland), published under the control of the Council of Law Reporting in Ireland, containing reports of cases argued and determined in the Court of Appeal, the High Court of Justice, and the Court of Bankruptcy, in Ireland*, 20 vols (Dublin, 1879–93)

Acknowledgments

I wish to acknowledge the following for permission to quote from manuscripts in their possession: the Director of the National Archives of Ireland, the Director of the National Gallery of Ireland, and the Board of Trinity College Dublin. I also wish to thank Fr Christy O'Dwyer for providing me with a xerox copy of Judge Keogh's notebook.

I wish to thank Elizabeth Gleeson and Mary Higgins of the Library of Trinity College, Dublin, for all the help they have given with the collections in their care. I also wish to thank the staff of the Department of Early Printed Books, Trinity College, Dublin, for creating the most cheerful reading room that I have ever worked in, and the staff of the National Archives of Ireland for their assiduous searching for files and their punctual attention to my requests for xeroxing.

To Professor Desmond Greer, who read my TS, made numerous suggestions, and gave me his notes and xeroxes of his research on nineteenth-century criminal law, my debt is enormous; his reading of my TS was meticulous, his suggestions were economical and relevant, and his encouragement was as necessary as it was welcome. The highest compliment I can pay him is to say that the care he lavished on my TS reminded me of the late T.W. Moody.

I thank Edward McParland for help in designing the dust-jacket. I also thank the Board of Trinity College Dublin for allowing me to base the dust-jacket design on Hubert von Herkomer's portrait of Lord Chief Baron Palles and Sarah Purser's portrait of Samuel Haughton. I thank Brendan Dempsey for providing me with photographs of the two portraits.

Finally, I wish to acknowledge the happy coming into existence of the websites, *justis* and *heinonline*, which together make the checking of UK acts of parliament and English reported cases so easy a matter.

25 Trinity College
Dublin 2

CHAPTER ONE

Murder trials, 1836–1914

THE SCOPE OF THE STUDY

THERE IS NO DEFINITIVE examination of the working of the criminal process in nineteenth-century Ireland. The aim of this study is to use murder trials between 1836 and 1914 to illustrate how prisoners charged with serious offences were brought to trial, how such trials were conducted, and how those found guilty were punished. Why take murder trials as the means of studying how trials were conducted? There are a number of reasons. First, they represented the actual working of the criminal justice system at its most elaborate, careful, and strained. Secondly, they were well documented in the National Archives' Convict Reference Files, which contain not only the judges' notes, but petitions on behalf of prisoners and complaints about how their trials were conducted. Thirdly, murders generated a considerable proportion of the criminal cases in the law reports – a capital trial seems to have given barristers an opportunity, if not a pretext, to raise legal issues. Fourthly, some limitation of scope is necessary to pursue a pioneering study of the criminal justice system because any study that was not so limited would end up more compendious than Hayes or Purcell.[1] It has to be admitted, however, that there are other ways of studying trials that would narrow the subject to a convenient compass and yet be rewarding. The trials connected with the political upheavals of the nineteenth century, for example, whether O'Connell's trial in 1844, or those of William Smith O'Brien and his associates in 1848, or of the fenians in the 1860s, would allow the historian to explore problems associated with the framing of indictments, the empanelling of juries, the law of evidence, and the reception of approvers' evidence. Yet political cases were not as numerous as murder trials, and they do not represent the routine of forensic procedure; nor do they have the variety of evidence displayed in murder trials, or the pathos of the prisoners' petitions and their mundane complaints.

---

1 Edmund Hayes, *Crimes and punishments, or a digest of the criminal statute law of Ireland, alphabetically arranged, with ample notes, in which are discussed the powers and authorities of the several courts of criminal jurisdiction in Ireland; the duties, responsibilities, and privileges of magistrates, coroners, constables, and other officers, in bringing criminals to justice, and also the practice of the courts in punishing offences upon indictment*, 2 vols (2nd ed., Dublin, 1842) and Theobald A. Purcell, *A summary of the general principles of pleading and evidence, in criminal cases in Ireland: with the rules of practice incident thereto* (Dublin, 1849).

The Convict Reference Files, which began as a series in 1836, contain thousands of petitions from prisoners, of which those sentenced to death were a small but conspicuous minority. In 1836, for example, there were over 40 petitions from prisoners sentenced to death, which was a small proportion of the 175 who were actually sentenced to death for all capital offences in 1836, but a substantial number compared with 22 who were sentenced to death for murder in that year. The number of petitions in capital cases fell rapidly from their high point in 1836 to about 25 in 1841 and to about a dozen in 1845. From 1850 there was only a handful each year, coinciding with the small number of death sentences pronounced. From these files, which amount to over 300 for the period from 1836 to 1914, about half were selected for inspection. From these in turn the most heavily documented files were chosen for various purposes such as examining the evidence presented at the trials or the complaints made about the conduct of trials. In the end the harvest was not as heavy as the large number of files might have suggested: about 85 of the files chosen yielded either useful petitions or judges' notes. In addition to the Convict Reference Files, other collections in the National Archives were used, such as the Outrage Papers, the Irish Crime Records, and the Registered Papers. Apart from these, and the Larcom Papers in the National Library of Ireland, the most useful sources were newspapers, law reports, parliamentary papers, and legal textbooks. The Larcom Papers were particularly useful in yielding cases where either the police or the courts were baffled in their efforts to detect and punish criminals.

The choice of 1836 and 1914 as terminal dates can be justified in the unsatisfactory way that such dates usually are justified: 1836 was the year of the prisoners' counsel act, which had a profound effect on felony trials because it gave prisoners' counsel the right to make a speech on their behalf; it was also the year of far-reaching changes in the organization of the Irish police and of stipendiary magistrates; more important in practice than either of these was the fact that 1836 marked the beginning of the Convict Reference Files as a separately catalogued collection in the National Archives. The choice of 1914 was simpler: 1914 is a good terminal date for practically any subject, especially for one that covers the nineteenth century; 1921 could have been chosen with equal propriety, except it might imply that the work contained some matter relevant to the 1916 rising or the war of independence. In fact, murder trials in the ordinary sense in which they are treated in this study were rare during the first world war, amounting to about a dozen, and none of those convicted was hanged. The problem with these dates, especially 1836, is that it is impossible to discuss the subject without going back before 1836 or referring to events after 1914. It is impossible, for example, to describe the steps by which capital punishment was curtailed without referring to legislation before 1836.

What follows is largely confined to the murder of one adult by another. Infanticide is referred to but not pursued systematically. Cases that started as murder and subsided into manslaughter or assault, or involved insanity are mentioned and used as examples, but left by the way in order to pursue murder cases to their conclusion in a verdict of guilty or not guilty. As a result many interesting subjects are left unexplored, some of which merit a monograph of their own: the crown solicitors, the social background of jurors, and the role of newspapers in reporting crime, to name only three, merit detailed study, but they are treated here as collateral questions.

THE LEGAL CONTEXT

It is easy enough to make an outline of the procedures that began when any serious crime, including murder, occurred. First, there were the pre-trial procedures: an information was sworn against the suspected perpetrator, who was then arrested and brought before a magistrate; the magistrate's function was to decide if there was a strong enough case to justify sending him for trial, either by committing him to gaol or by releasing him on bail. The second stage began at the assizes when a grand jury considered the case against the accused and, if satisfied that there was sufficient evidence, put him on trial by finding a bill of indictment against him. The prisoner was then arraigned, pleaded guilty or not guilty; if he pleaded not guilty, a petty jury was empanelled. It was at this point that the actual trial began: the crown counsel made an opening speech and called witnesses, the prisoner's counsel made a speech and called witnesses; the judge summed up, the jury delivered its verdict, and the judge passed sentence, or discharged the prisoner. If the accused was found guilty of murder, the sentence was death by hanging. The final stage to some extent depended on the prisoner, who might petition the lord lieutenant for mercy, or in certain circumstances, take his case by means of a writ of error to the Court of Queen's Bench or even to the house of lords. If an important legal point had been raised at the trial, the trial judge might reserve the case for the consideration of the twelve common law judges, or to the Court for Crown Cases Reserved, which in 1848 replaced the twelve judges as the arbiter of legal points. Should the convicted murderer be unsuccessful in relation to any of these procedures, he spent a short time in prison before being hanged.

It has been possible to outline the procedures in non-technical words. 'Writ of error' and 'swearing an information' are the only terms that require explanation. The former was simple because it was used when there was a legal defect or *error* in the trial procedure, but it had nothing to do with mistakes in the evidence against the prisoner. The latter was more complicated because its meaning in this context is different from its more familiar one: it was a complaint, made before a magistrate, that a crime had been committed. The witness who swore the information was known as the 'informer', which was a specialized use of a word commonly used to describe spies, sneaks and mercenary rascals in the higher ranks of a patriotic movement.[2]

2 'Informer' was also used as a synonym for an 'approver', who was an accomplice accepted by the

The impression of simplicity is enhanced by the familiarity of the procedures, some of which had remained unchanged in principle for centuries, such as committal by a magistrate, indictment by a grand jury, arraignment, and trial by a petty jury. Continuity of practice and familiarity are deceptive guides to the working of the nineteenth-century criminal justice system, however. First, they conceal the fact that many changes took place. Secondly, they conceal the fact that the nineteenth-century courts were neither simple nor familiar when looked at closely. The very technical terms used in criminal trials are enough to dispel any notion of simplicity: writs of *certiorari*, writs of *venire de novo*, criminal informations, official informations, pleas in abatement, pleas of *autrefois acquit* and *puis darrein continuance*, challenges to the array, peremptory challenges, arrests of judgment, general verdicts, and special verdicts, to mention only a few of the arcana that might be more familiar to medieval than to modern historians.

The courts that dealt with crime were apparently a single hierarchy based on the seriousness of the crimes they dealt with. The most serious cases, including all murders, were heard at the assizes, where the trial was initiated by an indictment brought in by the grand jury, and where the trial was presided over by one or two senior judges, and the accused was found guilty or not guilty by a petty jury. Indictment by a grand jury and trial by a petty jury also took place at the quarter sessions, where a court consisting of an assistant barrister (an office that later became that of county court judge) and a number of magistrates dealt with less serious offences. The petty sessions, which dealt with an ever-increasing number of minor offences, did not have juries – the assembled magistrates decided on questions of law, on the guilt or otherwise of the accused, and passed sentence. The petty sessions also had the important function of determining whether the Crown had made out a case to answer against a person accused of a serious offence, and if so satisfied the court sent the accused for trial at the quarter sessions or assizes. The power to commit was not exclusive to the petty sessions because magistrates acting on their own could send the accused for trial. In practice the committing magistrates reserved the most serious cases, including all murders, for the assizes or the Dublin Commission, and the less serious ones for the quarter sessions. This comprehensible distinction between serious and less serious cases, however, did not always apply, because even minor cases that would normally have been tried at quarter sessions were brought before the judges of assize when the assizes anticipated the next quarter sessions. The simplicity of the hierarchy of the criminal courts is slightly disturbed by the fact that the assizes for the county of Dublin and for the county of the city of Dublin were known as the Dublin Commission Court, which sat at Green Street; there were also special commissions appointed, from time to time, with the same jurisdiction as assizes, to try cases in particular counties or counties of cities and towns. At the top of the

Crown as a witness to give evidence against his confederates in return for a pardon. For two examples of this usage see Jarlath Waldron, *Maamtrasna: the murders and the mystery* (Dublin, 1992), pp 183, 194.

whole structure was the Court of Queen's Bench, which was the most senior of the criminal courts in Ireland. Its antiquity showed itself in little details. When Mary M'Mahon's case came before the court in 1875, the report of the case described her as 'coming before the Queen herself at Dublin'.[3] The Queen's Bench had a number of different functions.[4] It was in theory the venue for all indictments found in the county of Dublin and in the county of the city of Dublin, but in practice these were tried by the commission in Green Street. The court could also try misdemeanours committed anywhere in Ireland if they were prosecuted by information rather than indictment; but in practice its most important function was to examine the proceedings of any inferior court, including petty sessions, if the case was removed to the Queen's Bench by a writ of *certiorari* before sentence was passed or by a writ of error after sentence.

The rebarbative nature of court procedure was demonstrated by a distinction that informed every trial in this period: the difference between felony and misdemeanour. Felonies were the more serious crimes, such as murder, manslaughter, rape, burglary, robbery, and arson. According to Hayes, 'the definition of felony seems to be, an offence which occasions a total forfeiture of either lands or goods, or both, at the common law, and to which capital or other punishment may be superadded, according to the degree of guilt.'[5] Not all felonies were capital, but 'all offences, which by the common law were capital, come generally, under the title of felony', and every capital offence created by an act of parliament was a felony. The only indispensable attribute of felony, therefore, was forfeiture of goods and property, a consequence that had begun to die out by the early nineteenth century. From the late 1820s as capital punishment was abolished for many offences, non-capital felonies became the norm.

Misdemeanours were apparently less serious: they were crimes such as criminal libel, common assault, and attempted rape. They were punished by fine or imprisonment, or both, but not by death and forfeiture. They were created either by the common law or by act of parliament. According to Hayes, misdemeanour was 'the lowest class of offence punishable by indictment. In fact, any such offence which does not amount to felony must be a misdemeanour.'[6] Examples of misdemeanours included 'obstructing an officer of justice in the lawful apprehension of a person', 'a combination of workmen, for the purpose of dictating to masters what workmen they shall employ', and 'undressing and bathing in an exposed place on the seashore and near to inhabited houses'. There was nothing trivial about misdemeanours; some could be punished severely; misprision of treason, for example, was punishable with life imprisonment.

If the distinction between felonies and misdemeanours had been only one of punishment, it would have been no more than a survival of ancient nomenclature

---

3   IR 9 CL 309, at p. 312.
4   Hayes, op. cit., ii, 732–4; John G. Thompson, *The law of criminal procedure in Ireland* (Dublin, 1899), pp 3–5.
5   Hayes, op. cit., i, 280.   6   Ibid., ii, 556–60.

and no more anachronistic than benefit of clergy, right of sanctuary, hue and cry, and the *posse comitatus*, all of which still appeared in legal textbooks of the 1830s and 1840s. The distinction, however, went beyond punishment, and extended to how prosecutions were initiated and how trials were conducted. The prosecution of felonies could be initiated only at the assizes and by means of a bill of indictment; the prosecution of misdemeanours could be initiated by indictment just like felonies, but they could also be initiated by informations granted by the Court of Queen's Bench, which by-passed the grand jury. Those committed for trial for felonies and misdemeanours were treated differently: the former could have bail only as a matter of discretion, but the latter had bail as of right. At their trials they were treated differently: those tried for felony had to stand in the dock, they were tried at the next assizes or sessions after their committal, and they had to be present in court; those tried for misdemeanour did not have to stand in the dock, they did not even have to be present in court, and they could in certain circumstances have their trials postponed to the next assizes, or 'traverse', as it was called, which explains why some defendants were called 'traversers' and not 'prisoners'.

Even the juries employed were different: those tried for felonies were tried by 'common' juries, those tried for misdemeanours could in certain circumstances be tried by 'special' juries. The jury at a trial for felony could not separate during the trial, but the jury at a trial for misdemeanour could separate. In certain cases misdemeanants could have a new trial, while the verdict of the jury in a felony trial was final. The most important distinction between trials for felony and misdemeanour was probably the accused's right to challenge jurors peremptorily: those tried for capital felonies had the right to twenty peremptory challenges during the whole period, those tried for non-capital felonies had the same right from 1844,[7] but those tried for misdemeanours had no right of peremptory challenge until 1876 when they were given six peremptory challenges.[8]

By the early twentieth century the distinction between felony and misde-meanour had become blurred, certainly in terms of punishment. 'The word "felon" will doubtless never lose its hold on the popular imagination,' R.M. Hennessy wrote in 1910. 'Nowadays, however, some felonies are the most trivial offences imaginable. Some of the gravest and most serious offences against modern society are statutory misdemeanours.'[9]

The apparent stability of criminal procedure in the nineteenth century is misleading because important changes were made by legislation throughout the period: a series of acts of parliament in the 1830s and 1840s restricted the use of capital punishment; Perrin's jury act of 1833 defined the qualifications for jurors

7   For the Gray case, which decided that those tried for non-capital felonies should be allowed twenty peremptory challenges, see below, pp 145–6.
8   Below, p. 148.
9   R.M. Hennessy, *The justice of the peace for Ireland: a treatise on the powers and duties of magistrates in Ireland, in cases of summary jurisdiction, and in other matters, founded partly on Molloy's Justice of the Peace; with an appendix of statutes* (Dublin, 1910), p. 37.

in criminal cases; the Prisoners' Counsel Act of 1836 allowed the prisoner's counsel to make a speech and gave prisoners the right to have a copy of depositions made at their committals; Lord Campbell's act of 1851 simplified indictments; an act of 1865 gave prisoners' counsel the right to make a second speech; O'Hagan's jury act of 1871 increased the number of qualified jurors and obliged the sheriffs to summon jurors in a random manner; the winter assize act of 1877 established groups of counties as single assize counties.

Acts of parliament were the major instruments of procedural change, but they were not the only ones. The case law, declared by the judges, which in theory was a declaring of what the law always had been, affected the courts' procedure by interpreting acts of parliament and by changing decisions already made by other judges. All through the century there was an ebb and flow of judicial decision-making; sometimes there was a line of Irish cases that carried weight in Ireland, such as those on police questioning;[10] sometimes there was an eclectic mix of English, Irish, and colonial cases, such as those on abortive trials.[11] Some of these judicial decisions were as abrupt in their effects on the courts as acts of parliament. The decision of the house of lords in *Gray*, for example, to allow prisoners charged with non-capital felonies to have twenty peremptory challenges, was as immediate in its effects on the Irish courts as an act of parliament.[12] The effects of *Johnston*, on the other hand, which seemed to reverse a whole line of Irish cases on police questioning, were not as radical as those of *Gray* because it did not lead to an outbreak of police questioning.[13]

As a result of allowing the judges, especially when sitting in the Court for Crown Cases Reserved, to declare what the law was, there was constant change. Hayes might capture the law as it stood in 1842 when he published his two volumes of *Crimes and punishments,* and Purcell did the same in 1849 when he published *A summary of the general principles of pleading and evidence,* but in practice the law changed slightly from assize to assize. Tracing the main lines of those changes, however, is not beyond the wit of man: the digests of Thomas Brunker, of R.D. Murray and G.Y. Dixon, and of T. Henry Maxwell guide the historian to Irish reported cases right up to 1918,[14] and the websites *justis* and *heinonline*, which provide instant reference to English reported cases all through the nineteenth century, are splendid and agile supplements to the monumental *English Reports*, published in 176 volumes and covering English reported cases up to 1865. An even more powerful agent of change than the decisions of the judges, and more powerful probably even than acts of parliament, was what went on outside the courts, especially the effects of a centrally controlled and numerous constabulary and the growing number of crown solicitors and crown counsel, operating under the supervision of the attorney general, all of which led to more systematic prosecution and more elaborately prepared cases.

10 Below, pp 190–2. 11 Below, pp 267–73.
12 *Gray v. The Queen* (1844) 6 Ir LR 482; 11 Cl & Fin 427, 8 Eng Rep 1164.
13 (1864) 15 ICLR 60. 14 For full references see Bibliography, p. 403 below.

CAPITAL PUNISHMENT

Throughout the period covered by this study those who were found guilty of murder were sentenced to death. The Offences Against the Person Act 1829, for example, which repealed many of the Irish capital statutes of the previous century relating to crimes against the person, not only made the death sentence mandatory for murder, but actually prescribed in detail how and when sentences were to be executed: the sentence was to be carried out on 'the day next but one after that on which the sentence shall be passed', and the judge had to say whether the prisoner's body would be hung in chains or given to the surgeons for dissection.[15] Hanging in chains and dissection were abolished in 1834.[16] Even the Offences Against the Person Act 1861, which came at the end of a long period when capital punishment had been progressively abolished for numerous offences, made death by hanging the mandatory sentence for murder.[17] The eighteenth century had done things more laconically; when parliament created new capital offences or made existing offences capital, the stock formula was that the prisoner was to be found guilty of felony, without benefit of clergy.[18]

In 1836 when this study begins many offences other than murder were capital. The Offences Against the Person Act 1829 made death the mandatory sentence for murder, and for conspiracy to murder, solicitation to murder, and attempted murder. Attempted murder was defined by section 14 as 'unlawfully and maliciously' administering poison to any person, attempting to drown, suffocate or strangle any person, shooting at any person, cutting or stabbing any person, or throwing corrosive liquid at any person 'with intent in any of the cases aforesaid to murder such person'. Section 15 went even further and made shooting, stabbing, and throwing corrosive liquid capital offences if they were done 'with intent … to maim, disfigure, or disable such person, or to do some other grievous bodily harm to such person, or with intent to resist the lawful apprehension or detainer of the party so offending.' In addition to these the following offences against the person were defined as capital by the act of 1829: sodomy, rape, having carnal knowledge of a girl under ten, the forcible abduction of women, and administering poison or using instruments to procure a miscarriage (sections 16–22). In addition, other acts retained the death penalty for offences against property, such as burglary, robbery, and arson.[19] The fact that 175 death sentences were pronounced in 1836 (see Table 1.1) shows the extent to which capital punishment had survived the reforms of 1829 and the early 1830s.

As the period opened, however, two great assaults on capital punishment were about to take place. In 1837 six acts further reduced capital punishment. The first

---

15   10 Geo. IV, c. 34, s. 5 (4 June 1829).   16   4 & 5 Will. IV, c. 26 (25 July 1834).
17   24 & 25 Vict., c. 100 (6 Aug. 1861).
18   See, for example, 17 Geo. II, c. 5 (I), which made cattle stealing capital.
19   For more detail on the history of abolition in Ireland, see Appendix 2, below, pp 380–5.

of them amended the Offences Against the Person Act 1829, retaining capital punishment for murder, attempted murder, conspiracy to murder, and soliciting to murder.[20] It did, however, restrict capital punishment in the case of attempted murder to incidents where actual injury was caused: if the poisoning, shooting, drowning, suffocating strangling did not cause any injury, the crime was not capital. It abolished capital punishment for shooting or stabbing 'with intent ... to maim, disfigure, or disable such person, or to do some other grievous bodily harm to such person, with intent to resist or prevent the lawful apprehension or detainer of any person'. The act also abolished capital punishment for procuring a miscarriage, but retained it for sodomy, rape, having carnal knowledge of a girl under ten, and the forcible abduction of women. The Capital Punishment (Ireland) Act 1842 made rape, having carnal knowledge of girls under ten, and abduction non-capital.[21] It did not touch murder, attempted murder, solicitation to murder, conspiracy to murder, sodomy, 'unnatural offences', burglary with violence, arson of dwelling houses, and robbery with violence, all of which remained capital until 1861, when seven acts of parliament established what was in practice a new penal code, in which the only capital crime apart from high treason was murder.[22]

The number of hangings fell between the 1820s and the 1840s. In the seven years 1822–8 there were on average 271 death sentences a year and 47 hangings; in the four years 1843–6 there were only 16 death sentences a year and 6 hangings. In the 1850s there were years when there were no hangings.[23] Even before the changes in the law that reduced the number of capital offences, there had been dramatic changes; in 1824 there were 60 hangings, in 1825 only 18; in 1826 the number went up again, but not to the high figures of the early 1820s.[24] The number of death sentences before and after 1825 did not fall to the same extent as hangings; in the three years 1822–4 there were 877, and in 1825–7 there were 808, which suggests the fall was caused by the exercise of the royal prerogative. There was no corresponding fall in hangings in England in 1825.

20 7 Will. & 1 Vict., c. 85 (17 July 1837).   21   5 Vict., c. 28 (18 June 1842).

22 24 & 25 Vict., cc 94, 95, 96, 97, 98, 99, 100. The acts covered offences against the person, malicious injuries to property, larceny, forgery, and offences against the coinage. Only s. 1 of 24 & 25 Vict. c. 100 (6 Aug. 1861), which dealt with offences against the person, prescribed death.

23 *Summary statements of the number of persons charged with criminal offences, who were committed to the different gaols in Ireland for trial at the assizes and sessions held in the several counties, cities, towns, and liberties therein, during the last seven years ... 1822–8*, pp 8–9, HC 1829 (256), xxii, 434–5. See Appendix 1, below, pp 376–7.

24 For a discussion of the circumstances that accompanied this decline, see Stanley H. Palmer, *Police and protest in England and Ireland, 1780–1850* (Cambridge, 1988), pp 237, 269, 271, 338. The circumstances included a modest increase in agricultural prices, more active police, more courageous magistrates, the insurrection act, and the distraction provided by the Catholic Association; but Palmer notes that the homicide rate actually increased in the mid–1820s and peaked in 1824.

Table 1.1 shows that the acts of 1828 and 1829, of which the Offences Against the Person Act 1829 was one, did not reduce either the number of death sentences or the number of hangings; in fact the former increased until 1832 and, what is even more remarkable, the number of hangings for offences other than murder increased in the years after 1828 and remained substantial until 1835.[25]

TABLE 1.1

DEATH SENTENCES AND HANGINGS, 1824–45

years	sentenced for murder	total sentenced to death	executed for murder	total executed for all offences
1824	49	295	41	60
1825	17	181	9	18
1826	28	281	17	34
1827	22	346	12	37
1828	33	211	16	21
1829	28	224	21	38
1830	28	262	14	39
1831	27	307	25	37
1832	19	319	17	39
1833	38	237	26	39
1834	49	197	31	43
1835	31	179	19	27
1836	22	175	12	14
1837	21	154	10	10
1838	8	39	3	3
1839	30	66	15	17
1840	15	43	0	0
1841	17	40	5	5
1842	11	25	4	4
1843	12	16	4	5
1844	19	20	8	9
1845	9	13	3	3

The legislation of 1832, 1833, and 1835 did indeed reduce the number of death sentences, but it did not greatly affect the number of hangings until 1836. In practice it was the 1837 acts that produced years with small numbers of death sentences and years when hangings were in single figures; from 1840, a year when there were no hangings at all, hangings were in single figures in every year except in 1847, 1848, and 1883. Table 1.1 also shows that although murder and crimes

25   The figures in Table 1.1 are taken from Appendix 1, below, pp 376–7.

close to murder were still considered too serious to be included in the abolishing acts, the sentences of those who were sentenced to death for murder were more frequently commuted as the curtailment of hanging for other offences progressed. In the early 1820s 65% of those sentenced to death for murder were hanged; in the years 1841–5, only 35% were hanged.

Between 1844 and 1852 226 sentences of death were passed in Ireland, of which 172 were for murder; the rest were for attempted murder, solicitation to murder, conspiracy to murder, burglary, arson, high treason, and bestiality.[26] There were death sentences for burglary as late as 1849, for bestiality in 1856, and for arson in 1861.[27] Neither the burglar, the arsonist nor the abuser of animals was hanged, but, on the other hand, the retention of capital punishment for attempted murder, solicitation to commit murder, and conspiracy to murder until 1861 was not for ornamental purposes. Between 1844 and 1852 there were 88 hangings, of which 81 were for murder; the remaining 7 were for attempted murder (4), conspiracy to murder (2), and solicitation to murder (1). In 1852, for example, Patrick McCooey and James Kirk were hanged at Dundalk for the attempted murder of James Eastwood JP.[28] In England, on the other hand, there were no hangings except for murder after 1841.[29]

The last hanging before the first world war was in 1911, and by 1914 it could have been said that capital punishment was practically obsolete in Ireland. The decline in hangings was eventually noted by the newspapers: 'The black cap, the symbol of the culprit's doom, is seldom seen shading the judge's brow in our day … That functionary more frequently "sports" – the word, under the circumstances, is not inappropriate, notwithstanding its levity in its ordinary acceptation – a pair of white gloves, as emblematical of the purity of the county.'[30]

WHAT WAS MURDER?

Murder is probably one of the least complicated crimes, yet its definition and accompanying specimen indictments ran to thirty-two pages in the 1834 edition of *Archbold's Pleading and Evidence*.[31] *Archbold* in his various editions is as good a

---

26 *Thom's Directory, 1846, 1850, 1854.*

27 For the case of Ellen Ryan, against whom sentence of death was recorded in 1861, see below, p. 295.

28 *Belfast Newsletter*, 2 Aug. 1852. Appendix 1, below, p. 377, shows that in nearly every year from 1842 to 1856 there were hangings for offences other than murder.

29 There were 152 hangings In England between 1838 and 1852; 148 were for murder and only 4 for attempted murder (*'Return of the number of persons capitally convicted in England and Wales from the year 1838 to 1852, both inclusive; specifying the offences and sentences, and whether and how carried into effect by execution or otherwise'*, HC 1852–3 (386), lxxxi, 277). See also Gatrell, *Hanging tree*, p. 619 where it is stated that in England after 1841 only murderers were hanged.

30 Larcom Papers (NLI, MS 7620 [*Chronicle*, 25 Oct. 1860]).

31 *Of the law relative to pleading and evidence in criminal cases: with precedents of indictment, &c. and*

guide to the definition of murder in Ireland as any other, although his is an English textbook. Hayes used him as his authority when defining murder, justifiable homicide, etc.;[32] Thomas Lefroy used him in his *An analysis of the criminal law of Ireland*, published in 1849.[33] The distinctions made by Archbold and the same Latin phrases are found in Hayes and Lefroy. The advantage of *Archbold* as a guide, compared with indigenous Irish authorities, such as Hayes and Lefroy, or even Richard R. Cherry,[34] is that he is far more detailed than they are. The other advantage of *Archbold* is his successive editions, which make it possible to trace definitions of murder through the decades.

The difficulty in defining murder is to separate it from other homicides, of which manslaughter is the most obvious but not the only example. Archbold laid down four conditions that must be fulfilled to make homicide murder: first, the killing must be committed with 'malice aforethought'; secondly, it must be unlawful killing, 'not excusable or justifiable'; thirdly, 'it must be committed by a person of sound memory and discretion – it cannot be committed by an idiot, lunatic, or infant, unless indeed, he shew a consciousness of doing wrong, and of course a discretion or discernment between good and evil'; fourthly, 'the person killed must be a reasonable creature in being, and under the King's peace.'[35] The main application of this last condition was to unborn children because 'to kill a child in its mother's womb is no murder; but if the child be born alive, and die by reason of the potion or bruises it received in the womb, it is murder in the person who administered or gave them.'

The law presumed any killing to be murder 'until the contrary appears', and the prosecutor was not 'bound to prove malice, or any facts or circumstances, besides the homicide, from which the jury may presume it.'[36] The defendant, however, could counter the presumption of malice 'by proving that the homicide was *justifiable*, or *excusable*, or that at most it amounted to *manslaughter* only, and not to *murder*' (Archbold's italics). There were three kinds of justifiable homicide: first, where a criminal is put to death 'in strict conformity with his sentence'; secondly, where an officer of justice 'in the legal exercise of a particular duty kills a person who resists or prevents him from executing it'; thirdly, 'where the homicide is committed in prevention of a forcible and atrocious crime; as, for

---

*the evidence necessary to support them (*5th ed. by John Jervis, London, 1834), pp 314–45. As the years passed the space occupied by murder in Archbold did not become much greater, which is unexpected. See, for comparison, *Archbold's pleading and evidence in criminal cases; with statutes, precedents of indictments, &c., and the evidence necessary to support them by John Jervis* (20th ed. by William Bruce, London, 1886), pp 704–38.

32   Hayes, op. cit., i, 202.

33   *An analysis of the criminal law of Ireland, giving in alphabetical order all indictable offences, with their respective punishments and the statutes relating thereto, together with explanatory observations and notes; also an appendix of forms for the use of magistrates* (Dublin, 1849), pp 195–7.

34   *An outline of the criminal law as regards offences against individuals* (London, 1892), pp 35–48.

35   Archbold, op. cit. (1834), pp 319–20.

36   Ibid., pp 317–18.

instance, if a man attempt to rob or murder another, and be killed in the attempt, the slayer shall be acquitted and discharged.' Excusable homicide was of two kinds. First, 'where a man, doing a *lawful* act, without any intention of hurt, by accident kills another; as, for instance, where a man is working with a hatchet, and the head by accident flies off and kills a person standing by. This is called homicide *per infortunium*, or by misadventure'. Secondly, 'where a man kills another upon a sudden rencounter, merely in his own defence, or in defence of his wife, child, parent, servant, and not from any vindictive feeling, which is termed homicide *se defendo*.'[37] Justifiable and excusable homicide in practice led to the prisoner's acquittal or discharge. Manslaughter was different from these because it was 'the unlawful and felonious killing of another, without any malice either expressed or implied.'[38] It was of two kinds: 'involuntary manslaughter, where a man doing an *unlawful* act not amounting to felony, by accident kills another'; secondly, 'voluntary manslaughter, where, upon a sudden quarrel two persons fight, and one of them kills the other; or where a man greatly provokes another, by some personal violence, &c., and the other immediately kills him.' As we shall see, involuntary manslaughter turned into murder if the unlawful act that was done was a felony.

Malice aforethought, whose presence was the necessary ingredient of murder and whose absence was the characteristic of manslaughter, could be either 'express' or 'implied'. The former was 'when one, with a sedate and deliberate mind, and formed design, doth kill another; which formed design is evidenced by external circumstances discovering that inward intention; as lying in wait, antecedent menaces, former grudges, and concerted schemes to do him some bodily harm.'[39] Implied malice was where no malice was expressed or 'openly indicated', but where the law discerned its existence: 'where a man wilfully poisons another – in such a deliberate act the law presumes malice, though no particular enmity can be proved'; or where 'a man kill another suddenly, without any, or without a considerable, provocation'; or 'if he kill an officer in the legal execution of his duty'; or 'if, intending to do another felony, he undesignedly kill a man.' This last rule, which made the distinction between murder and manslaughter depend on the increasingly anachronistic distinction between felony and misdemeanour, was remarkable: if a man shot at a domestic duck in order to steal it, he was guilty of murder if he accidentally shot its owner; if he intended to shoot the duck but not to steal it, he was guilty of manslaughter; if he shot at his own pet duck but accidentally shot the postman, he committed excusable homicide.

Archbold admitted that 'there are many very nice distinctions ... upon this subject of malice prepense, express, and implied.' Whether killing was murder, manslaughter, or excusable homicide in the following circumstances was discussed in detail by Archbold: killing by poison, killing by fighting, killing upon

37 Ibid., p. 318.   38 Ibid., pp 318–19.   39 Ibid., p. 320.

provocation, killing by correction, killing in defence of property, killing without intention, killing officers of justice, killing by officers of justice.[40] Each circumstance produced a list of cases. Administering poison was given above as an example of implied malice, for example, but in practice a distinction had to be made for fatal doses administered by medical practitioners: if a physician or a surgeon gave a patient a dose to cure him, but 'contrary to expectation kills him, this also is neither murder nor manslaughter but misadventure.'[41] A distinction was made, moreover, between a regular physician and 'one who is not so, and the death in the latter case is said to be manslaughter at the least.' This distinction, however, seems to have been superseded by the rule that 'if a person, whether he be a regular practitioner or not, honestly and *bona fide* perform an operation which causes the patient's death, he is not guilty of manslaughter.'

'Killing upon provocation' also offered interesting distinctions. 'No provocation whatever can render homicide justifiable, or even excusable,' Archbold wrote. 'The least it can amount to is manslaughter.'[42] The weapon used was as important as the provocation: 'if it were effected with a deadly weapon, the provocation must be great indeed to extenuate the offence to manslaughter; if with a weapon or other means not likely or intended to produce death, a less degree of provocation will be sufficient; in fact, the mode of resentment must bear a reasonable proportion to the provocation to reduce the offence to manslaughter.' The speed of the reaction was also important: 'to reduce a homicide upon provocation to manslaughter, it is essential that the battery or wounding, &c. appear to have been inflicted immediately upon the provocation being given; for, if there be a sufficient cooling time for passion to subside and reason to interpose, and the person so provoked afterwards kills the other, this is deliberate revenge, and not heat of blood, and accordingly amounts to murder.'[43] Some of the examples given, however, were curious: 'if a man pull another's nose, or offer him any other great personal indignity, and the other thereupon immediately kill him, it is manslaughter only'; 'where a mob threw a pickpocket into a pond, for the purpose of ducking him, but he was unfortunately drowned: this was holden to be manslaughter.' Examples such as these gave some colouring to James Fitzjames Stephen's statement to the capital punishment commission in 1866 that

> there has never been any attempt made in this country to define murder in a systematic or scientific manner, but that the law upon the subject has been made bit by bit to meet particular cases as they arose … The definition has always remained the same, and a different meaning has been assigned to it as cases arose. That is the same as saying that there never was any real definition … The loose term 'malice' was used, and then when a particular

40   Ibid., pp 320–35.   41   Ibid., p. 321.   42   Ibid., p. 324.
43   Ibid., pp 325–6.

state of mind came under their notice the judges called it 'malice' or not according to their view of the propriety of hanging particular people.[44]

How much had changed in *Archbold* by the 1880s?[45] There was no change in the remarkable 'felony' murder rule, which treated accidental killing as murder if it were done while committing another felony.[46] The definition of manslaughter, on the other hand, seems to have expanded slightly to include the situation 'where a man, *by culpable neglect of a duty* imposed upon him, is the cause of the death of another.' There was still much that was familiar: there was the proportionality between weapons and provocation, there was the need to act on the spur of the moment, the pulling of a man's nose was still enough provocation to reduce murder to manslaughter, and the fatal ducking of the unhappy pickpocket was still manslaughter. A new source of provocation had, however, appeared: if a father see a person 'in the act of committing an unnatural crime with his son, and instantly kill him, it is manslaughter only; but, if hearing of it, he go in quest of the party and kill him, it is murder.'[47]

Although Archbold dealt with homicide at length, he did not mention infanticide as a form of homicide, which is not surprising because the law made no distinction between the murder of an adult and the murder of a newly-born child. The nearest that Archbold came to recognizing infanticide as a separate offence was to give a specimen form of indictment against a woman for the murder of her child. The words used left no doubt of the seriousness of the deed: she 'feloniously, wilfully, and of her malice aforethought, did make an assault.'[48] Archbold pointed out, however, how a jury could avoid bringing in a verdict of murder:

> if the defendant be acquitted of the murder, (and the jury find that she was delivered of a child, and it appear in evidence that she did, by secret bury-ing, or otherwise disposing of the dead body of such child, endeavour to conceal the birth thereof), the jury may find her guilty of the concealment, and she shall thereupon be imprisoned with or without hard labour.[49]

44   *Report of the capital punishment commission, with minutes of evidence, and appendix*, p. 279 [3590], HC 1866, xxi, 331.

45   Archbold, op. cit. (1886), pp 710–16.   46 Ibid., p. 715.   47 Ibid., p. 722.

48   Archbold, op. cit. (1834 ed.), pp 339–40. For a discussion of twentieth-century legislation on infanticide, which turned child murder into an offence 'akin to manslaughter', see Karen Brennan, 'Beyond the medical model: a rationale for infanticide legislation' in *Northern Ireland Legal Quarterly*, 58:4 (winter 2007), 505–35. For an interesting discussion of infanticide in a different legal milieu see the same author's 'Evidence of infanticide and exposure in antiquity: tolerated social practice, uncontrolled phenomenon or regulated custom?' in *University College Dublin Law Review*, 2 (2002), 92-119.

49   10 Geo. IV, c. 34, s. 17 (4 June 1829) made the same provision for Ireland, and made 'the secret burying or otherwise disposing of the dead body of the said child' a misdemeanor.

The problem for the prosecution in cases of child murder was to prove that the child had been born alive, which was not easy, for as Archbold noted 'putting the lungs of the child into water was formerly a very usual test whether the child was born alive or not: if the lungs floated, it was presumed that the child was born alive; otherwise, if they sunk; at present, however, very little confidence is placed in this test.' An indictment for concealment of birth, as well as offering a humane alternative, was easier to prosecute: the prosecution had to prove only that a woman had been 'big with child', that the child had been born alive, and had 'then and there instantly died.'

In a sense a homicide did not become a murder until the end of the trial when the jury found the prisoner guilty of murder. This statement can be qualified in various ways: first, the prisoner's acquittal did not exclude the fact that somebody else had perpetrated the murder; secondly, the jury may have perversely acquitted the prisoner, or found him guilty only of manslaughter. In spite of these qualifications, the fact remains that very few reported murders were eventually and incontrovertibly translated into verdicts of murder. In the *Judicial Statistics* for 1871 the registrar general made this point when he noted that out of a sample of 262 'murder' cases, excluding infanticides, 310 persons were committed for trial; of these, only 31 were convicted of murder, 63 were acquitted or discharged, 15 were found not guilty but insane, and in 8 cases the juries disagreed.[50] Those who were actually put on trial for murder accounted for only 117 of the 310 committed. What became of the other 193? The registrar general was able to account for some of them: 14 were found insane before they were tried, 3 died before trial, 103 were convicted of lesser offences, and in 23 cases the grand juries threw out the bills. This left 50 persons, committed to stand trial for murder, but neither acquitted, nor convicted, nor found insane, nor convicted of a lesser offence. The registrar general did not explain what happened to them but a plausible explanation is that some of them can be accounted for by those who were returned for trial for manslaughter, instead of murder, but acquitted of manslaughter, or found insane, and not included, therefore, in the registrar general's category of those *convicted* of lesser offences. The remarkable fact revealed by these figures is that two-thirds of cases that began as murder investigations were transformed into lesser offences or disappeared from the criminal system before they came into court.

There was nothing in Archbold, or indeed in Hayes or Lefroy, about 'agrarian' homicides, which were one of Ireland's most characteristic crimes.[51] Like infanticide, the term was used with confidence by contemporaries, as if it were a crime apart, but agrarian murder was in the eyes of the law a murder like any

---

50   *Judicial statistics (Ireland), 1871*, p. 26 [C 674], HC 1872, lxv, 260. The registrar general also
      noted that out of 106 cases of persons committed for trial for infanticide, grand juries threw out
      the bills in 9 cases, there were acquittals and discharges in 39 cases, and there were convictions
      for lesser offences than murder in 42; there no convictions for murder.
51   W.E. Vaughan, *Landlords and tenants in mid-Victorian Ireland* (Oxford, 1994), pp 147–50.

other murder. There were no special arrangements for trying agrarian homicides; they were tried like any other murder or manslaughter, although they were often tried at special commissions. In Ireland in this period the appointment of a special commission almost invariably meant that there had been an outbreak of agrarian disorder, but special commissions could be used to deal with any outbreak of crime that was too dangerous to be left unpunished until the ordinary assizes occurred.

The coercion acts that were passed to deal with agrarian crime did not, with one possible exception, set up special courts to try agrarian cases, although they did occasionally make special arrangements for dealing with homicides and other serious crimes. The first of these acts, the Crime and Outrage Act 1847,[52] was renewed until 1856, when it was replaced by the Peace Preservation Act,[53] which was in turn renewed until 1870. The main provision of these acts was the power of the lord lieutenant to 'proclaim' a district where certain crimes had been perpetrated. When the lord lieutenant proclaimed a district, firearms had to be licensed and the government could bring in extra police, whose cost had to be paid for by the ratepayers of the district. As far as murder was concerned, it was expressly stipulated that accessories after the fact 'to any murder committed may be tried and punished, although the principals may not have been convicted or taken.'[54] The Peace Preservation Act 1870, which introduced a new generation of coercive legislation that was to last until 1880, made it necessary for the inhabitants of a proclaimed district not only to have licences for firearms but to have special licences for revolvers; the act also provided that houses could be searched for evidence of the handwriting of persons suspected of writing threatening letters, that public houses could be closed, that strangers could be arrested and made to account for themselves, that those out at night under suspicious circumstances could be arrested, and that newspapers containing treasonable articles could be confiscated.[55] The act also made changes that affected the investigation and trial of crimes committed in proclaimed districts. First, the attorney general could apply to the Queen's Bench to have the venue changed to another county.[56] Secondly, when any felony or misdemeanour was committed, 'any justice of the peace in such district, although no person may be charged before him with the commission of such offence, shall have full power and authority to summon ... any person within his jurisdiction who, he shall have reason to believe, is capable of giving material evidence concerning any such felony or misdemeanour, and to examine such person on oath.'[57] This change enhanced the magistrate's power: before 1870 they could not compel witnesses to give evidence until someone had actually been accused of the crime by means of a sworn information. The new act allowed grand juries to award compensation

---

52 11 Vict., c. 2 (20 Dec. 1847).   53 19 & 20 Vict., c. 36 (30 June 1856).
54 11 Vict., c. 2, s. 18.
55 33 & 34 Vict., c. 9, ss 6, 7, 15, 23, 24, 25, 30 (4 Apr. 1870).
56 Ibid., s. 29.   57 Ibid., s. 13.

'where it shall appear that any person had been murdered, maimed, or otherwise injured in his person, and that such murder, maiming, or injury is a crime of the character commonly known as agrarian, or arising out of any illegal combination or conspiracy.'[58]

The act of 1870 was quickly followed by the Protection of Life and Property in Certain Parts of Ireland Act 1871, which applied to Westmeath and to the adjoining parts of Meath and the King's County.[59] The act allowed the lord lieutenant to detain without trial suspected Ribbonmen and those suspected of being in league with them. The act obviously did not affect the conduct of trials or even the investigation of crime, but the way the government dealt with those who were imprisoned demonstrated how Ireland might have been governed under an arbitrary form of government of the Continental kind.[60] After this draconian interlude, which lasted until the act's expiry on 1 June 1873, the successors of the Peace Preservation Act 1870 held sway until 1 June 1880, when for the first time since 1847 Ireland was without any coercive legislation to deal with agrarian crime. The violence of the land war, which had begun even before 1 June, soon changed that: in 1881 parliament passed the Protection of Person and Property Act,[61] which enabled the lord lieutenant to detain without trial, a power that applied to the whole country and not just to the proclaimed districts that had always been a restrictive feature of the earlier acts. Parliament also passed a new peace preservation act to regulate the possession of arms in proclaimed districts.[62] It was the Phoenix Park murders, however, and not agrarian crime, that led to the most radical of these acts, the Prevention of Crime (Ireland) Act 1882,[63] which also applied to the whole country. The most remarkable provision of this act was that it abolished trial by jury in certain cases and enabled the lord lieutenant to appoint special commissioners to try cases of treason, treason-felony, murder, manslaughter, attempted murder, aggravated violence, arson, and attacks on dwelling houses, 'whenever it appears to the lord lieutenant that in the case of any person committed for trial for any of the said offences a just and impartial trial cannot be had according to the ordinary course of law.'[64] The special commission was to consist of three judges of the Supreme Court of Judicature, and a person tried by them 'shall be acquitted unless the whole court concur in his conviction.'[65]

---

58   Ibid., s. 39. For a history of compensation awarded as a result of criminal actions, see Desmond Greer, *Compensation for criminal injury* (Belfast, 1990), pp 1–18. The Grand Jury (Ireland) Act, 1836 (6 & 7 Will. IV, c. 116, s. 106 (20 Aug. 1836)) gave grand juries the power to award compensation in certain circumstances: where witnesses had been murdered or maimed as a result of giving information against persons charged with offences against the public peace, and where magistrates or peace officers had been murdered or maimed as a result of their efforts to bring disturbers of the peace to justice.

59   34 & 35 Vict., c. 25 (16 June 1871).

60   Vaughan, *Landlords and tenants in mid-Victorian Ireland*, pp 170–3.

61   44 & 45 Vict., c. 4 (2 Mar. 1881).   62   44 & 45 Vict., c. 5 (21 Mar. 1881).

63   45 & 46 Vict., c. 25 (12 July 1882).   64   Ibid., s. 1(1).

65   Ibid., s. 1(2,4).

The special commissions were never used, and of far more importance were sections 4 and 6, which allowed either the attorney general or the prisoner to ask for a special jury in felony trials, and allowed the attorney general to apply for a change of venue. Section 16 followed section 13 of the 1870 Peace Preservation Act and provided that 'where a sworn information has been made that an offence has been committed, any resident magistrate in the county or place in which the offence was committed, although no person may be charged before him with the commission of such offence, may summon to appear before him ... any person within his jurisdiction whom he has reason to believe to be capable of giving material evidence concerning such offence, and he may examine on oath and take the deposition of such person.' The act also contained some other provisions of the Peace Preservation Act of 1870, such as allowing the arrest of suspicious strangers, the confiscation of newspapers, searches for arms and documents; it also allowed the lord lieutenant to award compensation, leviable on a particular district, for agrarian murders and maimings.[66]

The act, however, was a temporary one, section 37 providing that it 'shall continue in force until the expiration of three years next after the passing thereof, and to the end of then current session of parliament.' Two years after its expiry much of the act was replaced by the new Criminal Law and Procedure (Ireland) Act 1887, which was to be a permanent part of the criminal law and not merely renewable at certain intervals like the coercion acts. The new act did not resurrect the lord lieutenant's power to replace jury trials, but it retained the special jury, the attorney general's power to apply for a change of venue, and it allowed him to 'direct a resident magistrate, of whose legal knowledge and legal experience the lord chancellor shall be satisfied, to hold an inquiry ... although no person may be charged before him with the commission of such crime.'[67] These powers, however, could be exercised only in proclaimed districts. Henry Humphreys was under no illusions about the significance of the power given to the attorney general and the resident magistrates by section 1: 'the holding of such inquiries, where no accused person is present, and compelling witnesses to disclose what they know, is a serious departure from constitutional usage.'[68] This could have been said about this particular power at any time since it first appeared in 1870, but its potential as an instrument of tyranny was somewhat limited in 1887 because a witness compelled to give evidence was protected against self-incrimination and 'even in felonies any confession or answer to a question cannot be used afterwards against the witness, or the husband or wife of such person.'

The definitions of murder, manslaughter, and justifiable and excusable homicide determined how prisoners were charged, how the case against them was

---

66 Ibid., ss 12, 13, 14, 19.

67 50 & 51 Vict., c. 20, ss 1, 3, 4 (19 July 1887).

68 Henry Humphreys, *The Criminal Law and Procedure (Ireland) Act, 1887. 50 & 51 Vict., cap. 20 with a review on the general outline, scope, and provisions of the act; notes on the several sections, and offences to which is extended summary jurisdiction, with an appendix* (2nd ed., Dublin, 1887), p. 16.

constructed, and how they were defended. It was a comforting aspect of the law that prisoners were presumed to be innocent until they were proved guilty, but that comfort was limited in murder cases by the fact that the law presumed that any killing was murder until the prisoner proved that he was provoked, or attacked, or that he was the perpetrator of an accident.[69] The prisoner could also defend himself by proving that he was insane. As with manslaughter and justifiable and excusable homicide, the onus was on the prisoner to prove insanity because the law presumed him to be sane until he could prove he was not.

The degree of mental derangement that was required to establish insanity was great. In 1843 at Daniel M'Naghten's trial for the murder of Edward Drummond, who had been Sir Robert Peel's secretary, his medical witnesses had maintained:

> that persons of otherwise sound mind, might be affected by morbid delusions: that the prisoner was in that condition, that a person labouring under a morbid delusion, might have a moral perception of right and wrong, but that in the case of the prisoner it was a delusion which carried him away beyond the power of his own control, and left him no such perception; and that he was not capable of exercising any control over acts which had connexion with his delusion, that it was of the nature of the disease with which the prisoner was affected, to go on gradually until it had reached a climax, when it burst forth with irresistible intensity; that a man might go on for years quietly, though at the same time under its influence, but would all at once break out into the most extravagant and violent paroxysms.[70]

When M'Naghten was found not guilty but insane, the house of lords asked the judges what the law was 'respecting alleged crimes committed by persons afflicted with insane delusion, in respect of one or more particular subjects or persons: as, for instance, where at the time of the commission of the alleged crime, the accused knew he was acting contrary to law, but did the act complained of with a view, under the influence of insane delusion, of redressing or revenging some supposed grievance or injury, or of producing some supposed public benefit?'[71] Lord Chief Justice Tindal replied on behalf of the judges:

> assuming that your lordships' inquiries are confined to those persons who labour under such partial delusions only, and are not in other respects

---

69   See below, pp 223–4 for a case where the prisoner's counsel argued that the onus of proof was different in manslaughter cases. See also David Bentley, *English criminal justice in the nineteenth century* (London and Rio Grande, 1998), pp 205–8 for a discussion of the burden of proof.

70   *M'Naghten* (1843) 10 Cl & Fin 200, at pp 201–2; 8 Eng Rep HL 718, at p. 719. See Purcell, op. cit., pp 10–13 where the resolutions of the judges are reproduced. See also Finbarr McAuley, *Insanity, psychiatry and criminal responsibility* (Dublin, 1993), pp 18–34.

71   *M'Naghten* (1843) 8 Eng Rep HL 718, at p. 720.

insane, we are of opinion that, notwithstanding the party accused did the act complained of with a view, under the influence of insane delusion, of redressing or revenging some supposed grievance or injury, or of producing some public benefit, he is nevertheless punishable according to the nature of the crime committed, if he knew at the time of committing such crime that he was acting contrary to law.[72]

Tindal went on to state, in words that long remained the definition of insanity, that at criminal trials

the jurors ought to be told in all cases that every man is to be presumed to be sane, and to possess a sufficient degree of reason to be responsible for his crimes, until the contrary be proved to their satisfaction; and that to establish a defence on the ground of insanity, it must be clearly proved that, at the time of the committing of the act, the party accused was labouring under such a defect of reason, from disease of the mind, as not to know the nature and quality of the act he was doing; or, if he did know it, that he did not know he was doing what was wrong.

On the actual problem posed by M'Naghten's medical witnesses ('if a person under an insane delusion as to existing facts, commits an offence in consequence thereof, is he thereby excused?') Tindal replied that

if he labours under such partial delusion only, and is not in other respects insane, we think he must be considered in the same situation as to responsibility as if the facts with respect to which the delusion exists were real. For example, if under the influence of his delusion he supposes another man to be in the act of attempting to take away his life, and he kills that man, as he supposes, in self-defence, he would be exempt from punishment. If his delusion was that the deceased had inflicted a serious injury to his character and fortune, and he killed him in revenge for such supposed injury, he would be liable to punishment.[73]

HOW MANY BODIES?

Homicides accounted for only a small fraction of those whose deaths were the subject of inquests, which were held in 'any case of sudden death, or of death attended with suspicious circumstances'.[74] In 1841 there were 1,984 inquests in the whole country; but in the five years 1837–41 the constabulary in the Irish Crime Records annually returned on average only 180 homicides (murders and

72 Ibid., p. 722.   73 Ibid., p. 723.   74 Below, p. 40.

manslaughters) and 93 infanticides (the killing of children aged less than one year), which suggests that homicides and infanticide accounted for only 14% of all the inquests held.[75] In 1841 the three counties with the fewest inquests were Antrim, Dublin, and Donegal; the three with most were the King's County, Tipperary, and Wicklow. The contrast between Antrim (with 3.2 inquests per 100,000 population) and Wicklow (with 49 per 100,000) was so great that they could have been in different countries. The contrast between the county and the county of the city of Dublin was just as great: the latter had 53 inquests per 100,000 population, the former had only 3.6, which might have suggested to a cynical administrator that the people of the county dragged their mangled corpses into the city.

Inquests increased after the Famine in spite of the fall in population. In 1871, for example, there were 2,894, an increase that may have been caused either by greater punctiliousness on the part of coroners, police, and public, or by the occurrence of more fatal accidents.[76] The increase was certainly not caused by homicides, which had sporadically declined since the 1840s: they fell from 230 in 1837 to 106 in 1842, and fluctuated from 1843 to 1850, reaching a new high of 212 in 1847, which is not surprising given the onset of famine. After the Famine they fell steadily to 88 in 1859 and from then on remained below one hundred a year. The figures for infanticides also fluctuated, but did not fall to the same extent as those of homicides: in the five years 1866–70 the police returned an average of 69 a year, which is lower than the 93 a year returned in 1837–41.

An average of 180 homicides and 93 infanticides a year in the five years 1837–41 produced a homicide rate of 2.20 per 100,000 population and an infanticide rate of 1.14. In the five years 1866–70 the annual rate for homicides was 1.27 per 100,000 population, which was much lower than the rate in 1837–41; the rate for infanticides was 0.93.[77] By 1914 the annual homicide rate had fallen to about half of its 1860s figure.[78] In spite of homicide rates falling, strong contrasts between different parts of the country persisted. In the decade 1866–75, for

75 *A return of the number of inquests held by the several coroners of the counties and counties of cities in Ireland, in each month, during the year 1841; specifying the date, place, name of coroner before whom held, and finding of each inquiry*, HC 1842 (206), xxxviii, 185.

76 *Judicial statistics (Ireland), 1871*, pp 144–5 [C 674], HC 1872, lxv, 378–9.

77 The figures for homicides are taken from NAI, Irish Crime Records. See also *A return of outrages reported by the constabulary in Ireland during the years 1837, 1838, 1839, 1840, and 1841; a like return of outrages during each month of the year 1842 and for the months of January, February, and March, 1843* [460], HC 1843, li, 149; *Return of outrages reported to the Royal Irish Constabulary Office from 1 January 1844 to 31 December 1880* [C 2756], HC 1881, lxxvii, 887.

78 William Wilbanks, 'Homicide in Ireland' in *International Journal of Comparative and Applied Criminal Justice*, 20:1 (spring 1996), 65–6. According to Dr Wilbanks there was a 'rather sharp downward trend in homicide rates in Ireland over the 158-year period from 1837–1994'; his estimates suggest that the rate in the 1990s was about a quarter of that in the late 1830s (ibid. p. 67). For a fascinating survey that stretches from the eighteenth century to the end of the twentieth and covers many countries, including Ireland, see Ian O'Donnell, 'Unlawful killing past and present' in *Ir Jur*, n.s., 37 (2002), 56–90.

example, there were no murders in Carlow, but 17 in the north riding of Tipperary and 26 in the south riding.[79] Carlow might have been placed among the quietest of the Home Counties without enhancing their death rate. The two Tipperarys might have passed unremarked in the Kingdom of the Two Sicilies.[80]

The most comprehensive annually published series of Irish crime statistics were the returns of committals made by the clerks of the crown and peace (first published as a parliamentary paper in 1812 and continued until 1852), the annual reports of the inspectors of prisons (published from 1823 to 1852), the tables of offenders (published from 1846 to 1863), the constabulary's outrage returns in the Irish Crime Records, which began in 1837, and the *Judicial Statistics*, which began in 1863).[81] The fourth series mentioned here, the constabulary's outrage returns in the Irish Crime Records, were printed but not regularly published, although extracts from them appeared from time to time in parliamentary papers. Their value as a long, continuous, and coherent series is diminished by two short-comings: they did not include the Dublin Metropolitan Police district, and they did not divide homicides into murders and manslaughters until 1865. In the 1830s, moreover, it was claimed that the constabulary tended to under-estimate the number of crimes perpetrated. Indeed it was even claimed that they actually 'suppressed' crimes.[82]

The difficulties with the constabulary returns are as nothing compared to the problems created by the first two sources mentioned above, the returns of committals, which ran from 1812 to 1852, and the reports of the inspectors of prisons, which ran from 1823 to 1852. The figures in Table 1.2 are taken from a table constructed by Desmond Greer, using the committal returns and the prison inspectors returns for 1837.[83]

Professor Greer's reaction to these figures, which purported to measure the same thing, was a mild one: 'it is just possible that the figures can be reconciled'. The reaction of Jeffries Kingsley, who wrote in 1839, was less mild. 'There is not a criminal return,' he wrote, 'in which some omission, some evasion, or error, or

79   For references to the *Judicial Statistics* from which these figures were taken, see Bibliography, below pp 401–2.

80   For more on Tipperary, including the statement that 'no county was more lethal than Tipperary', see Palmer, op. cit., pp 372–3. It is doubtful, however, if even the area around Thurles, with its 20 murders in 1839, was as bad as the town of Corleone (in the former Kingdom of the Two Sicilies), which had 153 murders in the four years 1944–8 (Norman Lewis, *The honoured society* (London, 2003), p. 95).

81   All of these, except the Irish Crime Records, were published annually as parliamentary papers. There is also a large body of statistics relating to crime to be found in individual volumes of parliamentary papers. See Bibliography, below, pp 394–9.

82   Jeffries Kingsley, *Preparations for the session of 1839: on the criminal returns of Ireland* (Dublin, 1839), p. 41.

83   Desmond Greer, 'Crime, justice and legal literature in nineteenth-century Ireland' in *Ir Jur*, n.s., 37 (2002), 254.

TABLE 1.2

COMMITTALS, CONVICTIONS, AND ACQUITTALS, 1837

	clerks' returns	inspectors' returns
numbers committed	27,422	14,804
convicted	10,799	9,536
acquitted	7,034	3,011

mystification, cannot be detected.'[84] In practice the two sets of figures did not measure the same thing. First, the clerks' committals included prisoners committed to all gaols in the counties, but the prison inspectors' committals included only those committed to the county or city gaols. Secondly, the clerks' convictions included only those convicted at the assizes and quarter sessions, but the prison inspectors included those sentenced to terms of imprisonment at the petty sessions as well as those sentenced at the assizes and quarter sessions.[85] In short, the prison inspectors under-estimated committals and over-estimated convictions. Table 1.3 gives the clerks' and inspectors' returns of those committed for murder and convicted or acquitted in six counties in 1841.[86] Taking murders rather than

TABLE 1.3

COMMITTALS, CONVICTIONS, AND ACQUITTALS IN SIX COUNTIES, 1841

	clerks' returns	inspectors' returns
numbers committed	66	28
convicted	9	9
acquitted	9	7

all offences at least removes the disturbing element of those sentenced at the petty sessions. The results, however, are not reassuring: the table shows that the only point where the two sources coincided was at convictions, which is some comfort. It is

84   Kingsley, op. cit., p. 11.

85   William Yielding, *Observations on the alleged 'discrepancies' between returns made to parliament, by the clerks of the crown and peace respectively, and by the inspectors general of prisons, of the number of persons committed for trial, and convicted on trial, in Ireland, and upon the constabulary returns made to the lord lieutenant of the number of offences committed there, alluded to in the debates on the earl of Roden's motion, on the 27th November, 1837 ...* (London, n.d. [1838]), pp 6–8.

86   *Returns from the clerks of the crown, and clerks of the peace, of the several counties, &c. in Ireland, of the number of persons committed to the different gaols thereof for trial, in the year 1841,* HC 1842 (91), xxxii, 435; *Twentieth report of the inspectors general on the general state of the prisons of Ireland, 1841; with appendices* [377], HC 1842, xxii, 117.

possible, however, with a little juggling, to reconcile the figures for acquittals, but the figures for committals are still far apart and apparently irreconcilable.

These two sources show how difficult it is to reconcile two sets of statistics that purported to measure the same thing. It is hardly surprising, therefore, that the use of crime statistics to compare one period with another, or to compare one country with another, is difficult. Gatrell and Hadden recognized the fact that many crimes went unreported and that administrative and legal changes affected the discrepancy between officially recorded crime and actual crime, although they argued that trends and fluctuations through a period of time 'are not random phenomena' and that statistics are a better guide to actual crime than the anecdotes of interested observers.[87] Sean Connolly admitted that 'attempts to chart movement over time are ... hampered by the impossibility of distinguishing real changes in behaviour from changes in the efficiency of crime detection or in the propensity of victims to prosecute'. He also noted that 'variable assumptions and attitudes' affected 'the proportion of deaths categorized as manslaughter and as murder', which is an important shortcoming in homicide statistics.[88] Howard Taylor went even further and dismissed crime statistics in England as bureaucratic window-dressing. A few statements from his article will show his scepticism: 'it was an open secret that most murders went uninvestigated'; 'chief constables were forced to cover up and do nothing about the true extent of crime in their localities'; 'the instructions issued to the police for recording crimes ensured that little crime could be reported above the small amount that was actually prosecuted'; 'there is no evidence that the new police, whose numbers doubled between 1857 and the end of the century, had an ever-strengthening determination to extend the arm of the law ever more deeply into the dark area of crimes actually committed.'[89] The foundation of his case is that neither the Home Office nor local authorities in England wanted to pay more for law enforcement, and 'consequently, salaried and waged officers, including police officers of all ranks, maintained the average level of output that they were paid for.'

Taylor's reservations about public prosecution in England and the inertia of the new police forces do not apply to Ireland, where the number of crown solicitors, crown counsel, and constabulary increased, even though the population was falling from the 1840s. The figures given for the increase in inquests above, for example, do not suggest bureaucratic inanition. The fact that every hundred murders in Ireland in the years 1866–75 led to 86 committals, while every hundred murders in England led to only 43 committals, suggests the Irish police

87 V.A.C. Gatrell & T.B. Hadden, 'Criminal statistics and their interpretation' in E.A. Wrigley (ed.), *Nineteenth-century society: essays in the use of quantitative methods for the study of social data* (Cambridge, 1972), p. 337.

88 S.J. Connolly, 'Unnatural death in four nations: contrasts and comparisons' in Connolly (ed.), *Kingdoms United* (1999), p. 202.

89 Howard Taylor, 'Rationing crime: the political economy of criminal statistics since the 1850s' in *Econ Hist Rev*, 51:3 (1998), 586, 580, 578, 582.

were much more active than the English.[90] The ability of the Irish police to cope with the waves of crime that occurred during the Famine and the land war did not suggest exhaustion, but rather implied considerable reserves of strength, whose existence was further demonstrated by the Irish government's imposing new duties on the constabulary that went beyond the investigation of crime, such as the collection of the agricultural statistics. The fact that the constabulary were often anxious to take on new duties such as the registration of births, deaths, and marriages even when the government had other plans, suggests the constabulary itself felt under-employed. If anything the Irish constabulary and the Dublin Metropolitan Police gave the impression of being zealous to the point of making a nuisance of themselves. Although Taylor's strictures do not apply to the Irish constabulary, the important limitations of crime statistics, noted by Gatrell and Hadden and by Connolly, remain: the 'dark figure' of crimes that were unknown to the police, and the problems of taxonomy that were created as soon as the police tried to categorize what was reported. Homicides may have been more difficult to conceal from the police than many other crimes, and their fictitious existence may have been difficult to fabricate, but it would be hard to deny that the categorization of homicide created problems that have to be kept in mind when using statistics.[91]

In spite of these reservations, Irish historians might be tempted to congratulate themselves on having the constabulary's figures for homicides going back in a uniform series to 1837 and printed in the Irish Crime Records. Similar returns were not made for England until 1857. The constabulary's figures seem to represent their early rather than their matured view of incidents; according to a parliamentary return in 1843, for example, 'the outrages included in this return were all ... specially reported in detail to this office at or about the time of their occurrence.'[92] This recording of the first, fine, careless rapture would have pleased Gatrell and Hadden, who preferred their statistics to be created in the early stages of an investigation. 'The further the record is removed from the actual commission of the offence, ...' they wrote, 'the less directly and accurately it will reflect the incidence of a particular form of criminal activity, rather than the nature of the processes of law enforcement.'[93]

The problem of using crime statistics, including the constabulary's returns, is demonstrated by Table 1.4, which shows the number of murders, manslaughters, and infanticides obtained from different sources for the years 1866–70. The

90   For references to the *Judicial Statistics* from which these figures on murders and committals were taken, see Bibliography, below, pp 401–2.
91   For a discussion of police taxonomy in relation to agrarian crime see Vaughan, *Landlords and tenants in mid-Victorian Ireland*, pp 147–50.
92   *A return of outrages reported by the constabulary in Ireland during the years 1837, 1838, 1839, 1840, and 1841; a like return of outrages during each month of the year 1842 and for the months of January, February, and March, 1843*, p. 4 [460], HC 1843, li, 152.
93   Gatrell & Hadden, op. cit., p. 351.

column headed Irish Crime Records are the constabulary returns already referred to in the preceding paragraph. The second column shows the number of murders, manslaughters, and infanticides returned by the police for the *Judicial Statistics*, which were published annually from 1864.[94] The 'police' in this context were the Irish constabulary *and* the DMP. The third column shows the numbers returned by the coroners, also returned for the *Judicial Statistics*. The proper reaction to

TABLE 1.4

MURDERS, MANSLAUGHTERS, AND INFANTICIDES, 1866–70

offence	Irish Crime Records	police figures in the Judicial Statistics	from coroners
murders	119	142	145
manslaughters	226	289	215
infanticides	252	170	198
total	597	601	558

this table is probably despair tempered by resignation. First, the police seem to have returned two different sets of figures, a total of 597, excluding Dublin, and a total of 601, including Dublin, which precludes the comforting argument that the difference between the two figures was caused by Dublin. Secondly, both police figures are higher than those of the coroners, although some comfort can be taken from the closeness of the second police figure (601) to that of the coroners (558). Thirdly, the incidence of murder, manslaughter, and infanticide changes from column to column; infanticide is the biggest offence in the first police figures, and manslaughter is the biggest in the second police figures and in the coroners' figures.

Some comfort is to be taken from this table, nevertheless. First, the figures are of the same order of magnitude: all three totals are in hundreds, which is less worrying than if one had been in thousands and the other two in hundreds; all are in the region of five or six hundred, and the difference between the highest and the lowest is about 10%. Secondly, the difference between the figures for murders and manslaughters in the two sets of police figures is not great and might be explained by the inclusion of Dublin in the second set of figures. Thirdly, the figures for murders and manslaughters combined are not all that great from column to column (345 in the first police figures, 431 in the second, and 360 in the coroners). The vagaries of the table, therefore, seem to be caused mainly by infanticides and to a lesser extent by the problem of defining homicide as murder or manslaughter.

94 For references see Bibliography, below, pp 401–2.

How high were homicide rates revealed by these different sources? Is the annual rate given above for 1837–41, 3.34 per 100,000 population, a high rate for murders, manslaughters, and infanticides combined? It probably implies a lower homicide rate than Neal Garnham's rates for Armagh and Tyrone in the 1790s, which were 4.2 and 2.3 indictments for murder per 100,000 of population.[95] The average of these two figures is 3.3, but since Garnham's rates are based on the number of indictments, they will necessarily yield a lower rate than a return of homicides made at an earlier stage of the investigation, which suggests that homicide rates had fallen in Ireland since the 1790s. Connolly in a wide-ranging article on 'unnatural' death in Ireland refers to T.R. Gurr, whose research suggests that homicide rates in England fell from around 20 per 100,000 in the thirteenth century, to around 10 in the sixteenth century, to 'below five' in the seventeenth century, and to 'around two' in the late eighteenth century.[96] Assuming that English homicide continued to decline after 1800 and reached about 1.5 homicides per 100,000 of population in the 1850s and 1860s, this would imply that homicide was much lower in England than in Ireland in the 1830s.[97] This result is reassuringly close to Connolly's conclusion 'that the homicide rate in Ireland between 1835 and 1850 was two-and-a-half that recorded in England and Wales in the 1850s and 1860s.'[98] Yet even this apparently comfortable margin of difference between the two countries can be reduced to ambiguity. The years chosen, 1837–41, which produced the rate of 3.34, suit the dates of this study, but they may actually straddle two eras in Irish homicide. According to Palmer, 'the murder rate, high until 1838, was halved from 1835–8 (239 cases) to 1839–42 (131).'[99] A measurement made after 1838, therefore, would have brought Ireland closer to England; if made earlier, it would put the two countries even further apart.

A parliamentary return made in 1841 gives a vignette of the United Kingdom that supports the argument that Ireland had a higher homicide rate than England. In the years 1838-40 there were 56 convictions for murder in England and Wales, and 55 in Ireland, which suggests that there were twice as many murders in Ireland as in England. There was a greater contrast in committals for murder: 175 in England and Wales, and 610 in Ireland, which suggests that there were seven times as many murders in Ireland as in England![100] It may be argued that

95   Neal Garnham, *The courts, crime and the criminal law in Ireland 1692–1760* (Dublin, 1996), p. 179.
96   Connolly, op. cit., p. 202.
97   The figure of 1.5 homicides per 100,000 is based on Connolly's Table 1, ibid., p. 204.
98   Ibid., p. 206.
99   Palmer, op. cit., p. 372; see also the tables at pp 371, 473.
100 *An abstract of the aggregate number of persons committed for criminal offences in England, Scotland and Ireland, in each of the three past years* [1838–40], p. 2, HC 1841 (345), xviii, 544. The figures for convictions for murder given in this report are slightly different from the number of death sentences for murder in Appendix 1, below, p. 376, but the point they make is not invalidated by that.

committals for murder are not a good basis for comparison because a more active police force probably produced those, but it is difficult to see how such a high conviction rate for murder in Ireland did not imply an equally high homicide rate. A very high conviction rate for murder and a relatively low murder rate would have required Ireland not only to have had a very efficient police force, but to have also had those things that are conducive to high conviction rates, such as a cloud of eager but credible witnesses, stern jurors, and determined judges.

An additional piece of evidence that also suggests Ireland had a higher murder rate than England in the early part of the period is the fact that Ireland had relatively more sentences of death and more hangings for murder than England. Table 1.5 gives the number of death sentences for murder and the number of hangings for murder per million of population per year.[101] If death sentences and

TABLE 1.5

SENTENCES OF DEATH AND HANGINGS FOR MURDER PER 1,000,000 POPULATION, 1822–60

years	sentenced to death for murder		hanged for murder	
	Ireland	*England*	*Ireland*	*England*
1822–30	4.27	1.11	2.90	0.98
1831–40	3.26	1.11	1.98	0.71
1841–50	2.16	1.08	0.92	0.63
1851–60	1.12	0.91	0.37	0.53

hangings for murder are plausible surrogates for reliable murder statistics, murder seems not only to have been very much higher in Ireland from the 1820s to the 1840s than in England, but it also declined more rapidly in Ireland between the 1820s and the 1850s than in England. In Ireland in the 1850s the rate for death sentences was just slightly more than a quarter of the 1820s rate, but in England the rate had fallen only from 1.11 to 0.91. It was in hanging, however, that the change was greatest: in the 1820s the Irish rate was almost three times that of England, but by the 1850s it was lower than England's.[102]

The homicide figures in the Irish Crime Records suggested that the Irish homicide rate fell between the late 1830s and the late 1850s. Did this improvement enable Ireland to catch up on England, as the sentences of death for murder and

101 The table is based on information from NAI, OP (MA) 146/6 [1864] and *Report of the capital punishment commission, together with the minutes of evidence, and appendix*, pp 612–13, 656–7 [3590], HC 1866, xxi, 664–5, 708–9. See also Table 7 in Connolly, op. cit., p. 213 where rates for death sentences of all kinds are given.

102 Connolly, op. cit., p. 213 shows that this trend continued until the 1880s when Ireland drew slightly ahead of England.

hangings in the last table suggest? Table 1.6, which covers the years 1866–75, is able to compare the number of murders returned by the police in Ireland and in England because such figures became available for England from 1857. If it is assumed that the population of England and Wales was just over four times that

TABLE 1.6

MURDERS AND INFANTICIDES IN IRELAND AND ENGLAND, 1866–75

offence	Ireland	England
murders	302	nr
infanticides	268	nr
total	570	1324

of Ireland in 1871, there were far more murders returned by the police in Ireland than in England and Wales. This is supported by the Irish registrar general's calculations in 1866 'as to murder' in the two countries, which suggested that Ireland's murder rate was about 80% higher than England's.[103] A calculation of murder rates in the two countries based on Table 1.6 suggests that Ireland had a murder rate of 10.53 murders per 100,000 in the ten-year period and that England had a rate of 5.83, which is just a more cumbersome way of saying the same thing as the registrar general.

There seems to be little doubt that in spite of the change suggested by a fall in sentences of death and hangings, Ireland still had a higher murder rate than England in the second half of the nineteenth century. The rates for murders per million of population in Table 1.7 are taken from a table compiled by Sean Connolly, which shows that the difference between Ireland and England persisted: in the 1870s the Irish murder rate was 75% above England's and in the 1880s and 1890s it was twice as big.[104] Connolly argued that the figures in this table 'leave little doubt that the common perception of Ireland as a more violent society than other parts of the United Kingdom was firmly based in fact.'[105]

A note in the Irish *Judicial Statistics*, however, calls even this modestly comfortable conclusion into doubt. 'The police statistics as to murder show 66 in Ireland, as compared with 36 for the corresponding population in England and Wales in 1865,' the Irish registrar general wrote in 1866, which is fair enough because that is the 80% difference mentioned above, but he went on to add that

---

103 *Judicial statistics (Ireland), 1866*, p. 15 [3930], HC 1867, lxvi, 749. The figures actually used by the Irish registrar general were those for Ireland in 1866 and those for England and Wales in 1865.

104 Connolly, op. cit., p. 204.   105 Ibid., p. 205.

TABLE 1.7

MURDERS PER 1,000,000 OF POPULATION IN IRELAND,
ENGLAND AND SCOTLAND, 1871–1900

years	Ireland	England	Scotland
1871–80	9.3	5.3	5.7
1881–90	11.2	5.6	4.7
1891–00	8.8	4.4	nr

'the coroner's statistics, which as to the number of crimes affecting life *appear to be more reliable than those returned by the police*, show 64 verdicts of wilful murder in Ireland and ... 106 as the number of murders in a portion of the population in England equal to that of Ireland, which is a very much larger proportion than in Ireland'[106] (Author's italics). The registrar general, therefore, is suggesting that the coroners' returns change the relative position of the two countries: the police returns made Ireland's rate 80% higher than England's, but the coroners' returns made England's murder rate 60% higher than Ireland's! Table 1.8, which gives the number of murders returned in the *Judicial Statistics* by the coroners in Ireland and in England in the ten years 1866–75, demonstrates the registrar general's point, if it is remembered that in 1871 the population of England and Wales was just over four times that of Ireland's. These figures reverse the positions of Ireland and England, not by reducing the Irish murders, but by greatly increasing the English ones. The coroners' figures suggest Ireland had 0.53 murders per 100,000 of population, and England 1.06; that Ireland had 0.53 infanticides per 100,000, and England 0.64. The difference between the English police's figures and those of the English coroners seems to have been caused by

TABLE 1.8

MURDERS AND INFANTICIDES RETURNED BY CORONERS IN IRELAND
AND ENGLAND, 1866–75

offence	Ireland	England
murders	289	2404
infanticides	289	1449
total	578	3853

106 *Judicial statistics (Ireland), 1866*, p. 15.

the time at which the returns were made: the coroners' results were based on early impressions of the deaths inquired into, while the police figures were adjusted retrospectively in the light of inquiries made after the discovery of the homicide, when many homicides that had started as murders were shown to have been something less than murder.[107] Taylor confirms this when he writes that a homicide 'was not recorded as a murder "known to the police" until the outcome of the investigation or trial was known.'[108] The fact that the Irish police's figures were close to those of the Irish coroners suggests that they were returning figures compiled at the early stages of their investigations, which means that their figures are not comparable with those of the English police. The choice seems, therefore, to be between a comparison of the first impressions of the coroners in both countries and a comparison of the first impressions of the police in Ireland with the mature recollection of the police in England.

Which should be preferred? To compare the police figures in Ireland with those in England is not to compare like with like. Gatrell and Hadden would have preferred the coroners, since they were closer to the events they purported to describe; they would also have preferred the Irish police's figures to the English ones. If the coroners are accepted, therefore, Ireland had a much lower rate of murder than England by the 1860s, which suggests that Ireland had caught up with and passed England. Even if the unsatisfactory course of assuming that the least degree of falsehood probably lies somewhere between two less than satisfactory estimates, Ireland and England came close to each other in the 1860s, which at least implies that Ireland had caught up with England. Connolly thought that Ireland gradually gained on England, but remained behind. 'Where Irish homicide rates in the first half of the nineteenth century had recalled those of England a century and a half before,' he wrote, 'those recorded during 1900–14 were comparable to the England of the 1860s and 1870s.'[109] The convergence came more quickly than that, if the doubts of the Irish registrar general had any foundation.

Even the widest possible difference between Ireland and England in these calculations was small in international terms. Around 1880 England, Scotland, Germany, and France had the lowest rates for homicide convictions in Europe, with England having 0.60 per 100,000 of population, Scotland, 0.68, Germany 0.94, and France 1.49. At the other extreme were Romania with 5.3, Spain with 5.5, Italy with 9.9, and Servia with 10.5.[110] Even the high figure for Ireland in the 1880s in Table 1.7 above would have put Ireland between Germany and France

---

107 For a discussion of why the police and the coroners arrived at different figures for manslaughters, infanticides, and murders see *Judicial statistics 1866. England and Wales:* pt i, *Police, criminal proceedings, prisons;* pt ii, *Common law, equity, civil and canon law*, p. xviii [3919], HC 1867, lxvi, 540.

108 Taylor, op. cit., p. 586.

109 Connolly, op. cit., p. 208.

110 Jean-Claude Chesnais, *Histoire de la violence en occident de 1800 à nos jours* (Paris, 1981), p. 64.

rather than with Spain, Italy, and Servia. In the late 1980s and early 1990s Colombia had 89.5 murders per 100,000 of population and the USA had 10.1, both of which are enormous compared with even the highest figure for nineteenth-century Ireland.[111] According to David Johnson, 'in the second half of the nineteenth century, by contemporary standards, Ireland was a violent society. The number of assaults per head of the population was double that in England and Wales and it is highly unlikely that this was caused by difference in police arresting practice between the two countries.'[112] Johnson also argued that 'figures for homicides, generally regarded as the most reliable of all indicators of violence as few went undetected, corroborate the evidence gleaned from assault statistics.' The difference, however, between the homicide rates for Ireland and England that Johnson produced suggests the difference was negligible in international terms – a rate of 2 per 100,000 for Ireland for 1863–9 and 1.8 for England and Wales. Even the rates that he produced for the 1880–89, 2.6 for Ireland, 1.5 for England and Wales, do not suggest that Ireland was violent by contemporary standards unless contemporary standards mean standards set by only England and Wales.

How many dead bodies were not discovered? All that can be said with certainty is that some were discovered only because murderers were remarkably careless. In 1841 Sub-Inspector Hannyngton reported from Glaslough, Co. Monaghan, that 'a coffin containing the body of a young woman was found in the churchyard of Errigal laid beside the wall and covered with earth and stone about four inches deep. The circumstances of its not being properly buried excited suspicion. Upon opening the coffin they perceived a large cut upon the deceased's temple.' Although the constabulary made 'strict inquiry to ascertain if any person has been missed in the neighbourhood', they found nothing. The sub-inspector concluded 'that the unfortunate girl has been seduced and murdered by some person to avoid further trouble.'[113] The body of Anne Hayes would not have been discovered if her husband, Thomas Hayes, had not taken the police to the spot where he had buried her body.[114] Hayes summoned the curate of Attanagh, T.B. Wills, to the bridewell (Hayes was a member of the Irish church) and told him that he had tried to kill himself by cutting his throat with a piece of iron, 'but that as he was about to commit the deed, the Lord Jesus whispered in his ear not to do so, as he had done enough already.' The curate warned him not to speak, because he would be 'bound to make a communication to the authorities if he told him any more', but Hayes persisted, and offered to show where he had buried his wife's body. Escorted by the curate, the RM, and the constabulary, Hayes 'crossed several drains and traversed a good deal of ground until he came to a small gangway across a drain which had recently been cleared up, and then he stopped, raising

111 *Economist*, 8 Mar. 1997, p. 50.
112 D.S. Johnson, 'Trial by jury in Ireland 1860–1914' in *Journal of Legal History*, 17:3 (Dec. 1996), 278–9.
113 NAI, Outrage Papers/Monaghan/1841.
114 *Irish Times*, 27 May 1865, from a special edition of the *King's County Chronicle*.

his haggard face and lack-lustre eyes to Heaven, he pointed to the place, exclaiming – "Before God, Mr Curran, there she is!"[115] Hayes had been 'continually' quarrelling with the dead woman, who had spread stories of an 'improper intimacy between the prisoner and his own daughter by a previous marriage, resulting in his having to send the daughter to Liverpool, where she has been confined of a child, which is reported to have since died. It seems to have been notorious in the neighbourhood that the prisoner occupied the same bed with his daughter.' Hayes said the gossip had 'driven him frantic'. He was hanged at Tullamore on 23 August 1865.

The discovery of mutilated corpses was often recollected in tranquillity.[116] Patrick Tynan, 'a fat, quiet, heavy-looking boy, of about eighteen years of age', found the body of Alfred Lynch in a lime-kiln near Milltown, Co. Dublin. 'I thought from the smell that some of the boys might have been roasting a duck, as the smell was partly like that of burning feathers,' Tynan told the coroner. 'When I saw the body I thought at first that it was a log of wood until I saw that the arm was raised up ... When I helped to pull out the body I did not perceive the throat cut, and did not hear of there being a wound on the throat until breakfast time.'[117] A lethal attack, even when closely observed, did not appear to amount to much. Bernard Smith saw Laurence Smith attacking Patrick Lynch: 'I considered they were both stooped as if pouncing [*sic*] or shaking each other. I didn't see them lying at all on the road. It appeared to me that neither was undermost ... They both stood upright. The prisoner went his way home. Lynch then walked a step or two and fell, as if towards my gate.'[118] At the assizes the dispensary doctor described what Smith had done to Lynch: 'I found eighteen wounds on the body altogether. One contused wound on the left temple might be caused by a fall, or blow of a blunt instrument. One incised on left knee. These two were minor wounds. Sixteen wounds on the trunk that is to say, eight in abdomen, two on left side and six on the back of body. Seven of the eight were penetrating wounds. Five of these seven penetrated and injured some of the intestines ... These five were fatal wounds, and would cause death to five different people.'[119]

115 'Mr Curran' was Henry Grattan Curran RM, of Parsonstown.
116 There was a saying in rural Ireland that 'a wise man never finds a dead man' (Éanna Hickey, *Irish law and lawyers in modern folk tradition* (Dublin, 1999), p. 102).
117 Larcom Papers (NLI, MS 7519 [*Weekly Freeman*, 24 Dec. 1842]).
118 NAI, CRF/1873/Smith/18.
119 See Appendix 3, below, pp 386–92 for a description of weapons, motives, and the people involved in homicide cases.

CHAPTER TWO

Apprehending a suspect

'VIOLENT AND UNNATURAL DEATH'

WHEN A BODY WAS FOUND, four functionaries usually turned up: a coroner, a policeman (usually a sub-inspector of constabulary), a stipendiary magistrate, and possibly, but not always, an ordinary magistrate. The coroner was an independent, local official: he was paid by the grand jury and not by the central government; he held office for life; he was unique among law-enforcement officials in that he was elected. The sub-inspector of constabulary was a salaried officer who was a member of an administrative hierarchy that included the inspector general of constabulary, the under-secretary, the chief secretary, and possibly even the lord lieutenant; he could be dismissed, or transferred, and he looked to his superiors for promotion. He was a sub-inspector either because he had done well in the lower ranks of the constabulary, or because he had the necessary combination of education and ambition to get a constabulary cadetship. The stipendiary magistrate, who became officially known as a 'resident magistrate' only as late as 1853, was a full-time official, who probably owed his appointment to political influence.[1] His legal knowledge might be meagre. When Christopher Lynch-Robinson, who was an RM in Co. Donegal, took the depositions in a case of conspiracy to murder, he admitted that 'my knowledge of the law was merely what I could mug up in the only books I possessed on the subject, O'Connor's *Irish justice of the peace*, Stephen's *Digest of the law of evidence*, and Kenny's two books on criminal law.'[2]

The ordinary magistrates, who were mainly resident landlords, turned up because they lived nearby, which meant that they probably owned the murder scene. They were unpaid, and probably had nothing more than a smattering of legal knowledge. They did not have to turn up; their doing so was a sign that they took their duties seriously. Most of their magisterial work had nothing to do with serious crime. In 1871, for example, they tried 220,179 persons at the petty sessions, but in the same year they returned only 4,485 persons for trial at the

---

1 16 & 17 Vict., c. 60 (4 Aug. 1853) used the term 'resident magistrate' in its title. See also Penny Bonsall, *The Irish RMs: the resident magistrates in the British administration of Ireland* (Dublin, n.d. [1977]), p. 12.

2 Sir Christopher Lynch-Robinson, *The last of the Irish RMs* (London, 1951), pp 110–11. Courtney Stanhope Kenny was author of *A selection of cases illustrative of English criminal law* (Cambridge, 1901) and *Outlines of criminal law* (Cambridge, 1902). See also Bonsall, op. cit., p. 75.

assizes and quarter sessions.[3] When they issued warrants or committed prisoners, they were described as acting *ministerially*, as opposed to *judicially* when they acted as judges at the petty sessions. Their contribution was a complicated one: they probably had a good knowledge of their own locality; their presence gave an authority to the proceedings.

The powers of the stipendiaries and the ordinary JPs were roughly the same: both could issue warrants and summonses; both could remand suspects for short periods; both could commit suspects for trial; both could secure the attendance of witnesses at the assizes, either by making them enter into recognizances or by committing them to prison. The practical difference between ordinary magistrates and RMs was reflected by the fact that the Constabulary Code seemed to contradict itself on the part to be played by ordinary magistrates and RMs.[4] Section 77 stated that when an outrage occurred the constabulary officer was to report to the nearest magistrate 'whether local or stipendiary'. On the other hand, section 207 seemed to give the RM precedence: 'on the occurrence of any serious outrage especially where life has been taken or attempted the officer, head or other constable in charge nearest to the scene, will make a point of sending without a moment's loss of time, an intimation thereof to the nearest resident magistrate, in doing which he is to employ the readiest means at command whether telegraph, railway, car, or other conveyance.' The difference here was one of practice, but gradually legislation made a legal distinction between ordinary magistrates and RMs. The Peace Preservation (Ireland) Act 1870, for example, allowed single RMs and Dublin police magistrates to 'do alone all acts by this part of this act authorized to be done by justices of the peace at petty sessions', which meant that the stipendiaries could sit alone as judges in certain cases where an ordinary magistrate could not.[5] The act, however, allowed ordinary magistrates as well as RMs to examine witnesses in cases where nobody had been actually accused of committing a crime, which was a considerable enhancement of their power;[6] but section 16 of the Prevention of Crime (Ireland) Act 1882 granted this power only to RMs,[7] a distinction that was made permanent by section 1 of the Criminal Law Procedure (Ireland) Act 1887.[8]

There had been a time when the gentry acting as JPs had had a virtual monopoly of the investigation of crime. In William Henry Curran's account of the murder of Ellen Hanly, whose body was found washed ashore near Kilrush in July 1819, the magistrates did everything, including identifying Hanly's body by

---

3	*Judicial statistics (Ireland), 1871*, pp 149, 20 [C 674], HC 1872, lxv, 383, 254.
4	Larcom Papers (NLI, MS 7618, item 78). See Ian Bridgeman, 'The constabulary and the criminal justice system in nineteenth-century Ireland' in *Criminal Justice History*, 15 (1994), 103–4. See Jim Herlihy, *The Royal Irish Constabulary: a short history and genealogical guide* (Dublin, 1997), p. 242 for a list of guides, manuals, and regulations issued to the constabulary.
5	33 & 34 Vict., c. 9, s. 28 (4 Apr. 1870).
6	Ibid., s. 13.	7	45 & 46 Vict., c. 25 (12 July 1882).
8	50 & 51 Vict., c. 20 (19 July 1887).

means of her teeth. According to Curran, who was called to the bar in 1816, 'the task could not have devolved upon a more competent class of men. Whatever other failings may have been imputed to the Irish country gentlemen, indifference or inexpertness in the detection of criminals has not been among them. Time out of mind, the political and social anomalies of Ireland have kept that body continually on the alert for the protection of their lives and properties.'[9] Even a superficial study of the Outrage Papers in the National Archives of Ireland shows, however, that the constabulary and the stipendiary magistrates had largely supplanted the ordinary magistrates by 1830s and 1840s. One of many such reports, taken at random, that of Patrick C. Howley, a stipendiary magistrate in Co. Longford in 1844, showed him going to the scene of the crime, taking the dying man's declaration, and with the sub-inspector of constabulary, taking the depositions of witnesses, all without mentioning the presence of a local magistrate.[10]

Although the constabulary's prominence is one of the most important facts of the history of law enforcement in nineteenth-century Ireland, they did not move to the centre of the stage all at once. In 1836 George Robert Dawson, who lived at Moyola Park, Castledawson, could describe a murder investigation without ever mentioning the constabulary or the stipendiary magistrates: 'I, my agent (to whom the clear detail of the evidence is chiefly due) my own tenants and all the neighbourhood worked night and day until we had unravelled the whole business, and established the nicest chain of circumstantial evidence upon which the men were found guilty. We spared neither time, exertion, nor money. We hunted the men through all their manoeuvres, like blood-hounds, and we never ceased until we had them condemned under the sentence of the law.' Dawson was MP for Co. Londonderry, brother-in-law of Sir Robert Peel, and had just resigned as secretary of the admiralty.[11] John Cunningham has described a fascinating case in Co. Fermanagh in 1845 when local JPs not only excluded the local constabulary from the investigation of an attempted murder, but actually called in Inspector Benjamin B. Tydd, a detective from the DMP, to assist them.[12] Fourteen years later, when John Holden murdered Sergeant McClelland in Dungannon in December 1859, the search for his murderer was led by local JPs and 'many other persons of respectability from the town'. The JPs concerned were country gentlemen: Basil Brooke, Edward Robert Evans, Alexander Lyle,

---

9   William Henry Curran, *Sketches of the Irish bar; with essays, literary and political*, 2 vols (London, 1855), i, 300. The story of Ellen Hanly was the basis of Gerald Griffin's *The Collegians*, which appeared in 1829, and of Dion Boucicault's *The Colleen Bawn*, which was first performed in public in New York in 1860. Benedict's opera *The Lily of Killarney* was produced at Covent Garden in 1862.

10 NAI, Outrage Papers/Longford/1844.   11 Ibid., CRF/1836/Agnew/3.

12 John B. Cunningham, 'The investigation into the attempted assassination of ffolliot Warren Barton near Pettigo, on 31 October 1845' in *Clogher Record*, 13:3 (1990), 125–45. See also Henry John Brownrigg, *Examination of some recent allegations concerning the constabulary force in Ireland, in a report to his excellency the lord lieutenant* (Dublin, 1864), p. 26 for a reference to 'a first rate officer' from England being sent over to investigate a 'barbarous murder' in Ireland.

and the Hon. Major William Knox (MP for Dungannon, deputy lieutenant of Tyrone, and uncle of the third earl of Ranfurly). Brooke took command: he 'despatched Sub-Constable Farrell to Cookstown, Acting-Constable Kearns to Dublin, Sub-Constable Ritchie to Belfast, and Sub-Constable Gallaher to Derry, in pursuit of Holden.'[13] R.D. Coulson, the Tyrone RM, was not mentioned at this stage, although he was later identified as the official most determined to see Holden hanged.[14] The fact that Coulson was stationed in Omagh may have explained his initial absence from Dungannon.

The main lines of change from the 1830s to the early years of the twentieth century can be discerned easily enough: the constabulary moved from a position of predominance to a position almost of monopoly, having supplanted the ordinary magistrates, the coroners, and even, to some extent, the RMs. When James Doherty was arrested in 1902 for the murder of his son, he was brought before the RM in Carrick-on-Shannon – but meanwhile the constabulary arranged to have a model made of the house where the murder had occurred, they arranged to have photographs taken, they asked for the crown solicitor to conduct the case before the magistrate, and they offered advice on what the prisoner's defence was likely to be.[15] At Doherty's trial, moreover, in December 1902 they appeared as witnesses and gave important evidence not only about the scene of the crime and the arrest of the prisoner, which was what they had always done at trials, but also about the background of the case. In spite of examples given in the previous paragraph, the activity of the ordinary magistrates may be seen as an occasional irruption rather than a persistent current. Two things, however, need to be remembered. First, the ordinary magistrates were not supplanted because of any formal change in their legal powers, which remained substantially the same throughout the whole period. Secondly, the constabulary and the RMs wrote most of the reports that have survived in the National Archives. Their predominance at any period of time, therefore, is likely to appear greater than perhaps it was in practice.

The dominance of the constabulary was made possible by Dublin Castle's control of their routine, which established uniform methods of proceeding and some accumulation of experience. The extent to which Dublin Castle was involved in investigations was remarkable. After Thomas Bateson's murder in Co. Monaghan in December 1851, for example, the correspondence between the under-secretary and the constabulary showed the under-secretary sanctioning the proclamation of the district and the provision of money to offer a reward, which was a substantial degree of interest even considering that Bateson was related to Thomas Bateson, MP for Co. Londonderry, 1844–57.[16] The constabulary's

---

13   Larcom Papers (NLI, MS 7620 [*Evening Mail*, 7 Dec. 1859]).
14   NAI, CRF/1860/Holden/26.   15   Ibid., CRF/1902/Doherty/69.
16   Ibid., CSO LB 459, Resident Magistrates Letter Books (23 June 1848–28 Dec. 1857). For an enumeration of the outrages in Cos Armagh, Monaghan, and Louth, including Bateson's murder, see *A return 'of the number of murders, waylayings, assaults, threatening notices, incendiary fires, or other*

dominance also depended on their numbers. In 1871, for example, the constabulary had an establishment of 12,714, or 24 policemen per 10,000 of the population outside Dublin, which was almost twice England's density of policing.[17] The force was not evenly distributed over the whole country: Down had only 9 policemen per 10,000 population, in the middle of the county league was Carlow with 25, and at the bottom were Westmeath with 50 and North Tipperary with 51. Even in a county with an average police establishment, the constabulary outnumbered the ordinary magistrates; in Carlow, for example, there were about 126 constabulary officers in 1871; at the same time there were only 40 ordinary magistrates, some of whom were old, some of whom were lazy, and some of whom had less important things to do. The impression of central control is enhanced when it is remembered that Carlow had an RM devoted entirely to the county, a sessional crown solicitor also devoted to the county, and a crown solicitor shared with the Queen's County.

For decades the ordinary JPs resented their subordination to the constabulary. In 1862 their resentment turned to anger when three landlords were murdered one after the other: Gustavus Thiebault in April, Francis Fitzgerald in May, and Walter Braddel in July. The constabulary did well in the Fitzgerald case: Fitzgerald was murdered in May, and his murderer, Thomas Beckham, was hanged in July; an accessory, Denis Dillane, was hanged in April 1863. Nobody was made amenable in the other two cases, however. Grand juries passed angry resolutions, questions were asked in parliament, and pamphlets were written. The gentry who had for nearly three decades felt a sense of forensic inferiority to the constabulary now retaliated by demanding from the constabulary an impossibly high standard of competence, which was an unintended compliment. The constabulary, nevertheless, felt slighted. When Lt. Col. Samuel Dickson (JP and DL for Co. Limerick and tory MP for the county, 1859–65) attacked the constabulary in the house of commons, his attack did not go unnoticed. According to Sir Henry Brownrigg (inspector general, 1858–65), 'those slighting remarks are read in every police barracks in Ireland almost as soon as they are spoken, and so far from stimulating the members of the force, whether officers or men, to exertion, they are eminently calculated to impair their efficiency and make them indifferent to their duties.'[18] The inspector general went into print to defend his men.[19]

---

crimes of an agrarian character reported by the constabulary, within the counties of Louth, Armagh, and Monaghan, since 1 Jan. 1849 [to 28 Mar. 1852], distinguishing by name the persons murdered and waylaid; also stating the numbers arrested for each offence; whether informations have been sworn in the case, and the result of any trial of the same', HC 1852 (448), xlvii, 465.

17 *Judicial statistics (Ireland), 1871*, p. 113 [C 674], HC 1872, lxv, 347.

18 Larcom Papers (NLI, MS 7618 [Brownrigg's *Observations concerning the constabulary force*]). See also Vaughan, *Landlords and tenants in mid-Victorian Ireland* (Oxford, 1994), pp 151, 188–9 and Virginia Crossman, *Politics, law and order in nineteenth-century Ireland* (Dublin, 1996), pp 97–8.

19 Brownrigg, *Examination of some recent allegations concerning the constabulary force in Ireland, in a report to his excellency the lord lieutenant* (Dublin, 1864). See also Vaughan, *Sin, sheep and Scotsmen: John George Adair and the Derryveagh evictions, 1861* (Belfast, 1983), pp 25–6. When

The gentry's attack on Dublin Castle failed, and a second attack became unthinkable when the fenian crisis led to the constabulary's apotheosis. The debate in the early 1860s showed what Dublin Castle thought of the gentry acting as JPs: that they liked the dignity of the bench and the seat on the poor law board that went with it, but they did not like attending the petty sessions, and they left the RMs to do the dirty work of attending fairs, suppressing riots and faction fights, and going out on patrol at night. 'An unpaid magistracy is a beautiful thing,' wrote Sir Robert Peel. 'It indicates a united people, & mutual confidence and esteem between the different classes of society, but cannot exist under other circumstances, & certainly we have them not in Ireland.'[20] The gentry were mainly tories; the highest Castle officials from the 1830s were often whigs whose partiality was sustained by hundreds of reports from the RMs and senior constabulary officers who were quick to point out the JPs' faults. Patrick C. Howley RM, for example, writing from Co. Monaghan in 1851 when agrarian murders were common in the county, deplored the 'unhappy division' among the magistrates near Carrickmacross: they refused to cooperate with one of their number, James Bashford (of Donamine, Carrickmacross), 'who is certainly a very bad specimen, and he on the other hand animadverts publicly on their acts as I have heard him before the people.'[21] Howley also deplored the JPs' unpunctual behaviour: eight of them asked him to be present at the investigation of the attack on William Henry Kenny JP, of Rocksavage, Carrickmacross, but only one turned up. He deplored their technical incompetence: they discharged a prisoner against whom there was 'quite conclusive' evidence; they were not able to draw up an information. 'I never saw such an unbusinesslike document as this information taken by those justices,' he wrote. 'There's neither the name of one of them or the witness to it, and on those grounds I think it might be laid aside as if no such document ever existed.'

THE INQUEST

The constabulary were obliged to inform the coroner of 'any case of sudden death, or of death attended with suspicious circumstances', but the coroner issued his precept only if 'he shall deem it necessary to hold an inquest upon such dead body.'[22] The inquest usually took place near where the body had been found. The Coroners (Ireland) Act 1846 explicitly gave the coroner the power to 'order that

Brownrigg retired in 1865 he advised the constabulary to obey the magistrates at all times 'with a respectful alacrity' (TNA (UK), HO 184/113, Circular 183).

20   Larcom Papers (NLI, MS 7618 ['Memorandum on Sir Robert Peel's letter of 20th May 1862'])
21   NAI, Outrage Papers/Monaghan/1851.
22   9 & 10 Vict., c. 37, s. 22 (27 July 1846). See also Edmund Hayes, *Crimes and punishments, or a digest of the criminal statute law of Ireland, alphabetically arranged, with ample notes, in which are discussed the powers and authorities of the several courts of criminal jurisdiction in Ireland; the duties, responsibilities, and privileges of magistrates, coroners, constables, and other officers, in bringing*

such dead body shall be brought into the nearest convenient tavern, public house, or house licensed for the sale of spirits', and the coroner could fine a publican who refused to allow his premises to be used.[23] The inquest on the body of Margaret Gilroy, found near Lavey in Co. Cavan, was held 'at the house of Mr John Lee, formerly known as the New Inn, midway between Cavan and Virginia, a roadside and respectable inn, adjacent or abutting the high or mail coach road between these towns.'[24] Inquests were often held in private houses: the inquest on Thomas Graham's body was held in his father's house on the Lisburn to Saintfield road.[25] The householder could be paid 'any sum not exceeding, *per diem* 3s. 6d.'[26]

The coroner, who was the only elected official in local government, had the same powers as the magistrates: he could issue warrants, commit the prisoner for trial, and bind over witnesses to appear at the assizes.[27] Andrew Carr, for example, hanged in the Richmond Bridewell in Dublin in 1870, had been committed on a coroner's warrant 'charged with having caused the death of a certain Margaret Murphy'.[28] The coroner's 'inquisition' could put the prisoner on trial without the intervention of a committing magistrate and without indictment by the grand jury. The coroner's functions, on the other hand, could be performed by magistrates if he failed to act within two days of the finding of the body. According to Hayes, writing in 1842, this practice was illegal, which implies that the coroners act of 1846 made it legal for the first time,[29] but it is worth noting the grand jury act of 1837 referred to two magistrates ordering the payment of medical witnesses at inquests when they held an inquest 'in the absence of the coroner'.[30] This curious duplication of powers existed because the JPs, RMs, coroners, and the policemen who conducted the pre-trial proceedings were an amalgam of old and new, which also partly explains why in practice their progress might be only intermittently parallel. Not the least of these anachronistic inconsistencies was the fact that the coroner had a jury and the committing magistrates did not.

The office of coroner was subjected to considerable legislative change from the 1820s on. It is probably fair to say that no other institution connected with the investigation of murder was more legislated for, except possibly the petty jury. According to Farrell, 'between 1829 and 1908 there were nine acts dealing specifically with the office of coroner, with sections on coroners in at least seven other enactments.'[31] The main legislative changes make an impressive list, even

criminals to justice, and also the practice of the courts in punishing offences upon indictment, 2 vols (2nd ed., Dublin, 1842), i, 196.

23 9 & 10 Vict., c. 37, s. 36.   24 *Irish Times*, 13 June 1861.

25 NAI, CRF/1866/Logue/6.   26 9 & 10 Vict., c. 37, Schedule C.

27 Hayes, op. cit., i, 194.   28 NAI, CRF/1870/Carr/16.

29 Hayes, op. cit., i, 197; 9 & 10 Vict., c. 37, s. 44 (27 Aug. 1846).

30 7 Will. IV & 1 Vict., c. 2, s. 6 (24 Feb. 1837).

31 Brian Farrell, *Coroners: practice and procedure* (Dublin, 2000), p. 21. For another historical survey of the office of coroner, see John L. Leckey & Desmond Greer, *Coroner's law and practice in Northern Ireland* (Belfast, 1998), pp 1–14.

when it is remembered that they were spread over nearly sixty years. Four acts laid
the foundations for most of the nineteenth century: an act of 1828, which dealt
with magistrates as well as coroners, obliged them to forward informations,
depositions, and inquisitions in murder and manslaughter cases 'to the proper
officer of the court in which the trial is to be';[32] an act of 1829 provided that
coroners were to be elected by parliamentary electors and that they could pay
witnesses;[33] an act of 1836 empowered them to summon medical witnesses and to
order *post-mortem* examinations and an analysis of the contents of stomachs and
intestines.[34] The fourth act, the Coroners (Ireland) Act 1846, which was by far the
most comprehensive of these acts, retained the election of coroners by parliamentary electors, and continued their power to pay witnesses (including medical
witnesses),[35] to order an analysis,[36] and to pay for *post-mortem* examinations.[37]
This act broke new ground by dividing the counties into districts, each of which
was to have its own coroner. The existing coroners were to be appointed to the
new districts and were obliged to live in them.[38] The jury in future was to consist
of 'such persons as shall be resident within the district and rated to the relief of
the poor in a sum of not less than four pounds.'[39] Two further points about this
act are worth noting because they represented an affirmation of the power of the
coroner: there was to be an inquest only when 'he shall deem it necessary to hold
an inquest', and he had the power 'to issue a summons for every witness whom he
shall deem necessary to attend such inquest.'[40]

The two most important changes in the last decades of the century came
in 1881 and 1898. The 1881 act provided that coroners should be medical
practitioners, barristers, solicitors, or JPs of five years' standing, that they should
be paid salaries instead of fees, that persons against whom verdicts of murder or
manslaughter were found 'shall be entitled to have, from the coroner ... copies of
the depositions', and that if twelve of the jury could not agree the coroner could
discharge them and summon a new jury.[41] The Local Government (Ireland) Act
1898 abolished elections and gave the power of appointment to the new county
councils.[42]

The coroner's first task was to empanel a jury of at least 12, and not more than
23. When the jury was sworn they 'proceed to examine the body, and the coroner
makes such observations as occur to him, at the time drawing their attention to
the appearances which elicit his remarks. The whole body ought, if possible, to be

---

32   9 Geo. IV, c. 54, s. 4 (15 July 1828).   33   10 Geo. IV, c. 37, ss 2, 3 (4 June 1829).
34   6 & 7 Will. IV, c. 89 (17 Aug. 1836).   35   9 & 10 Vict., c. 37, s. 28 (27 July 1846).
36   Ibid., s. 31.   37   Ibid., schedule C.
38   Ibid., ss 3, 21.
39   Ibid., s. 23. Before 1846 'no particular qualification is required for a coroner's juror, further than
     that he must be a *good and lawful man*' (Hayes, op. cit., i, 197).
40   9 & 10 Vict., c. 37, s. 22.   41   44 & 45 Vict., c. 35 (11 Aug. 1881).
42   61 & 62 Vict., c. 37, s. 14(1) (12 Aug. 1898).

seen and examined.'[43] When the body had been 'viewed', the coroner examined the witnesses, wrote down their evidence, read it over to them, and made them sign it.[44] Then he addressed the jury, stating his 'view of the law as applicable to the facts deposed to'. If the jury could not reach a unanimous verdict, the coroner 'collects the voices, beginning from the bottom of the panel, and according to the opinion of the majority, (which, however, must consist of twelve), the verdict is taken.'[45] The jury's verdict was 'recorded in the inquisition, which is a statement, in writing, of the verdict or finding of the jury, ingrossed on parchment, indented.'[46] The inquisition might include an accusation against the perpetrator, which 'must be set forth with legal certainty.' The verdicts included suicide, murder, manslaughter, justifiable homicide, or killing 'by an irrational agent', but these homicidal verdicts were only a minority of all verdicts.[47] If twelve jurors could not agree, the coroner could adjourn the inquest to the next assizes.[48] The act of 1881 allowed the coroner to discharge the jury and to summon another one.[49]

From 1836 the coroner could order a medical practitioner to make a *post-mortem* examination and an 'analysis of any matter or thing' connected with the dead body.[50] The jury could call a second medical practitioner 'whenever it shall appear to the majority of the jurors upon any inquest, that the cause of death has not been satisfactorily explained by the evidence of [the first] such medical practitioner, or of the witness or witnesses who shall have been examined at such inquest.' The coroner could order the disinterment of bodies.[51] On 21 May 1837,

---

43 Hayes, op. cit., i, 198. 9 & 10 Vict., c. 37, s. 46 provided that inquisitions would not be quashed 'because the coroner and jury did not all view the body at one and the same instant, provided they all viewed the body at the first sitting of the inquest'.

44 Hayes, op. cit., i, 199–200.

45 Ibid., p. 205. See also Edward Parkyns Levinge, *The justice of the peace for Ireland; comprising the practice in indictable offences, and the proceedings preliminary and subsequent to convictions; with an appendix of the most useful statutes, and an alphabetical catalogue of offences* (2nd ed., Dublin, 1862), pp 249, 257 and Joseph Gabbett, *A treatise of the criminal law; comprehending all crimes and misdemeanors punishable by indictment; and offences cognizable summarily by magistrates; and the modes of proceeding upon each*, 2 vols (Dublin, 1843), ii, 60.

46 Gabbett, op. cit., ii, 64, 66; Hayes, op. cit., i, 206.

47 For verdicts in 861 cases see Michelle McGoff-McCann, *Melancholy madness: a coroner's casebook* (Dublin, 2003), pp 341–57, where details of William Charles Waddell's casebook for 1856–76 are reproduced. When Waddell compiled this casebook he was coroner for the northern part of Co. Monaghan. See also Hayes, op. cit., i, 200; Huband, op. cit., p. 258.

48 Hayes, op. cit., i, 205.

49 44 & 45 Vict., c. 35, s. 6 (11 Aug. 1881).

50 9 & 10 Vict., c. 37, ss 31, 33 (27 July 1846).

51 Hayes, op. cit., i, 217. Not even the lord lieutenant could order an exhumation. In 1852 when Professor Thomas. G. Geoghegan wanted an exhumation to enable him to perform an autopsy, he was told that 'his excellency has no power to order the exhumation of the body' (NAI, CSO LB 41, the earl of Clarendon's country letters no. 5 (2 Jan. 52 to 23 Dec. 53), p. 87). In 1909 when it was proposed to exhume the bodies of the Cormack brothers (hanged at Nenagh in 1858), the solicitor general decided that the lord lieutenant did not have the power to *order* the

for example, a man named Thomas Walsh died in Listowel 'from inflammation of the brain caused by the effect of a fall he got off the steps leading to John Sullivan's house while looking at a riot on the 15th of last March.'[52] The chief constable in Listowel wrote to James McGillycuddy, the coroner, who lived at Tralee, but got no answer. The local magistrates did not step in, and 'the people would not wait and buried the body since which nothing has been done.' The coroner eventually appeared on 2 June, which was almost a fortnight after Walsh's death. He ordered the disinterment of Walsh's body, and the jury decided that Walsh 'came to his death by means of an accidental fall off the steps leading to Sullivan's house while looking at a riot, and, pushed by Thomas Brosnahan.' Chief Constable McDonagh thought that 'the holding of the inquest has had a good effect and prevents future interments in similar cases until inquests are held.'

In a case in Co. Louth, Sub-Inspector Edmund Kilroy reported that an RM had 'ordered the coroner to proceed to Richardstown where the body was interred, and have it exhumed, and hold an inquest on it', which suggests that the constabulary occasionally regarded the coroner as a creature of the RM.[53] An example of the trouble the coroner's absence could cause occurred when William Graham, who died near Ballymahon in September 1844, was buried without an inquest. His brother, who lived fifty miles away, memorialized the lord lieutenant, alleging that 'the said William Graham deceased has frequently said to the minister that he had been *poisoned*.' The brother tried to throw suspicion on his sister-in-law, who had inherited William's house and garden. After a fuss that involved the lord lieutenant, the Longford constabulary, and the medical practitioner who had performed the *post-mortem* examination, the affair was dismissed. The county inspector of Longford lamented the coroner's absence: 'there has not been a coroner for the last two years, which throws the whole onus for such enquiries upon the magistrates.'[54]

Coroners' juries survived as a remnant of local independence and occasionally asserted themselves as the *vox populi*. When soldiers of the 31st Regiment of Foot fired on an election crowd at Sixmilebridge on 22 July 1852, verdicts of wilful murder were returned against eight soldiers and a justice of the peace.[55] In November 1875 when the agent of the Berridge estate near Oughterard brought

disinterment of a corpse, but he could 'direct that it be disinterred' (Nancy Murphy, *Guilty or innocent? The Cormack brothers: trial, execution and exhumation* (Nenagh, Co. Tipperary, 1998), p. 131).

52   NAI, Outrage Papers/Kerry/1837.
53   Ibid., Outrage Papers/Louth/1840.
54   Ibid., Outrage Papers/Longford/1844.
55   *Copies of the several inquisitions removed from the Court of Queen's Bench in Ireland, in the month of January last, and transferred to the county of Clare … in relation to any of the cases of homicide, riot, unlawful assembly or other criminal offence alleged to have been committed at the town of Sixmilebridge, in the month of July last, at the time of the general election …*, pp 3–7, HC 1852–3 (313), xciv, 65–9.

an ejectment against tenants whose leases had expired, John Sullivan, who seemed 'to be in apparently good health, ... took suddenly ill and expired shortly after.'[56] At the inquest the jury brought in a unanimous verdict of manslaughter against Berridge's bailiff, Bartly Murphy. The coroner did nothing to make Murphy 'amenable': the dead man was aged 85, he had received no ill-treatment from Murphy, and some of the jurors, including the foreman, were related to him. The bailiff Murphy was described as 'a most respected humane man'.

The jurors were often from the very townland where the body had been found. At least 6 of the 12 jurors that inquired into the death of Daniel O'Fee, who had been a farmer near Rasharkin, were from the same townland as O'Fee.[57] At the inquest on John Ellis, who was shot dead near Templemore on 22 October 1857, the connection was even more intimate because one of the jury was William Cormack, who with his brother Daniel, was hanged for Ellis' murder on 11 May 1858.[58] The property qualification should have kept out the poorest people from 1836, but often there were not enough fully qualified jurors to constitute a jury. At the inquest on the body of James Stapleton, of Ballymacmurragh, only 7 of his neighbours in Ballymacmurragh were qualified, and in the neighbouring town of Kinnity only 13 of the 37 householders were qualified.[59]

The coroner's court was relatively informal, allowing the jurors and by-standers to intervene in a way that would have been unthinkable at the assizes. The coroner's court, 'being a court of record', was 'generally speaking open to the public', although 'as the ends of public justice or public decency may frequently require it, ... the coroner has authority, if he see fit (and of such fitness he is the best and only judge), to exclude either the public generally, or any individual in particular.'[60] According to the English authority on coroners, John Jervis, the coroner was bound by the law of evidence. 'The general rules of evidence are applicable alike to civil and criminal proceedings ...,' he wrote. 'It will, therefore, be unnecessary to do more than refer the reader to the established treatises upon this subject, and to observe that the inquiry of the coroner is not fettered by any stated allegations in pleading, which require particular proof.'[61] The coroner was not 'fettered by any stated allegations in pleading' because in the early stages of the inquest at least there was often no accused; if the accused were present his latent guilt might develop only in the course of the proceedings.

56 NAI, RP/1875/17,226. See also Vaughan, *Landlords and tenants*, pp 37–8.
57 NAI, Outrage Papers/Antrim/1836.   58 Murphy, *Guilty or innocent?*, p. 15.
59 *General valuation of rateable property in Ireland. King's County. Valuation of the several tenements in the union of Parsonstown* (Dublin, 1854), pp 49–51.
60 Hayes, op. cit., i, 207; Constantine Molloy, *The justice of the peace for Ireland: a treatise on the powers and duties of magistrates in Ireland, in cases of summary jurisdiction, in the prosecution of indictable offences, and in other matters. Founded partly on Levinge's Justice of the Peace; with an appendix of statutes and notes and decisions thereon, and a catalogue of offences alphabetically arranged* (Dublin, 1890), p. 365.
61 John Jervis, *A practical treatise on the office and duties of coroners: with forms and precedents* (2nd. ed. by W.N. Welsby, London, 1854), p. 264. Cf. Leckey & Greer, op. cit., p. xv where it is stated

This freedom to range at will probably explains the apparent and erratic discursiveness of many inquests. When the body of a young woman was found in a bog in Co. Cavan in 1861, the neighbourhood believed it was the body of Margaret Gilroy, who had disappeared about three years before when she had been John Smith's servant.[62] Although suspicion 'attached' itself to Smith, Thomas Mawhinny's medical evidence suggested that the body was not Margaret Gilroy's because it been buried for at least ten years; the bones showed 'from their pliability and lightness, as they all floated in water, owing to the absence or absorption of their earthy matter, the deceased must have been more than ten years dead.' At this point a member of the public, Philip Smith, interrupted Mawhinny and asked for the recall of the boy who had found the body. The boy, Thomas Kearns, when recalled, said that 'he found the remains about six inches under the surface of the peat moss.' Smith asked Mawhinny, 'Are you still of opinion that the body was there for ten years?' Mawhinny admitted that three years might be closer to the truth than ten, 'on account of the ready admission of atmospheric air, and it might present the appearance it had, although in the ground for only that length of time.' At the inquest on the body of Alfred Lynch, in Co. Dublin, the coroner, James McCarthy, suggested that 'it would be better if ... they took the statement of the dairy-boy who was to give evidence, and postpone putting him on his oath until another day.'[63] The jurors objected; one said 'the boy might vary in the statement which he would make after being sworn to what he would first tell on his word'; another insisted 'it would be much better to proceed in the usual way, and swear the witnesses in the first instance.' The jurors' assertiveness persisted during the proceedings, which lasted from Monday to Friday: they asked questions, they offered advice to the coroner, and they heckled witnesses.

How were suspects treated at inquests? By the 1840s it was accepted that they could call witnesses. According to Gabbett, 'it seems now to be agreed, that the coroner's inquest must, in all cases, hear evidence, on oath, as well for the party accused or suspected, as for the king, if it be offered to them.'[64] But could the accused be allowed, or even compelled, to incriminate himself?[65] According to

that the inquest is 'inquisitorial in form, in contrast to the more traditional adversarial nature of civil and criminal proceedings. There are no "parties", it is the coroner who decides which witnesses will testify and what other evidence will be adduced; the formal rules of evidence do not apply, and the coroner generally assumes a more dominant role in the proceedings.'

62   *Irish Times*, 13 June 1861.
63   Larcom Papers (MS 7519 [*Weekly Freeman*, 24 Dec. 1842]).
64   Gabbett, op. cit., ii, 60. See also Hayes, op. cit., i, 200 and Huband, op. cit., p. 250. According to Levinge, the coroner could listen to the suspect's witnesses but he could not bind them over to appear at the trial (Levinge, *Justice of the peace*, p. 257).
65   For a discussion of the interpretation of *Wakley v. Cooke* (1849) 4 Exch 511, 154 Eng Rep 1316, see Leckey & Greer, op. cit., pp 186–7. In the course of *Wakley*, Baron Parke had stated 'it is quite clear that the evidence of a man ought never to be excluded in an investigation before a coroner, on the ground that he may criminate himself, for it is not right to assume that he is

Hayes, 'no person who appears to be implicated by the previous evidence ought to be examined on oath. He may, however, be allowed to make a statement not on oath.'[66] In *Reardon* and *Marshall* Judge Fitzgerald stated that the accused, even if they were prisoners, could give evidence, but only 'if they wished and if the coroner were prepared to receive it.'[67] Practice seems to have varied from case to case. William Burke Kirwan 'took an active part' at the inquest on the body of his wife: he interrupted witnesses, he examined witnesses, and in turn he was examined ('the jury wished Mr Kirwan to be examined, and he was accordingly examined at their request').[68] At his trial at the Dublin Commission Court in September 1852 his deposition before the coroner was read out as part of the Crown's case. At the inquest on the body of Owen Murphy, on the other hand, Sam Gray was not allowed to say anything. At Gray's trial 'the coroner stated that, by the advice of two magistrates, who were present at the inquest, he did not permit the prisoner to go into any defence, nor did he take any depositions after he had conceived a case for the Crown was made out.'[69] The silence of the accused at inquests is an example of the varying degrees of silence that was imposed on the accused at every point in the investigation of crime. Their silence before the coroner, however, was different from their silence on other occasions: they spoke before the coroner if they wanted to and if he allowed them to; they spoke to policemen and to the magistrates if they wanted to, but only after they had been warned not to; at their trial at the assizes, they did not speak at all, although they could speak after they were convicted and before they were sentenced.

Suspects were occasionally legally represented, but this was not an absolute right. At inquests, according to Hayes, 'no person, whether barrister or attorney, has a right to interfere in the proceedings of this court, as by examining witnesses, addressing the court, or the like, without the leave of the court; which is also requisite before its proceedings can be lawfully published. Such permission, however, would not sanction the publication of even an impartial statement of the occurrences, if that publication were libellous towards an individual.'[70] This was repeated by Molloy more than forty years later, but in practice, barristers and attorneys were often present at inquests.[71] Joseph Lynch was represented by John

---

guilty, and the witness may guard his own interests in giving his evidence' (154 ER 1316, at p. 1318).

66 Hayes, op. cit., i, 199.

67 *Re Reardon* (1873) 7 ILTR 193; *Re Marshall* (1874) 8 ILTR 1.

68 John Simpson Armstrong, *Report of the trial of William Burke Kirwan, for the murder of Maria Louisa Kirwan, his wife, at the island of Ireland's Eye, in the county of Dublin on the 6th September, 1852, before the Hon. Judge Crampton and the Rt Hon. Baron Greene, at the Commission Court, Green Street, on the 8th and 9th December, 1852* (Dublin, 1853), p. 41.

69 *Impartial Reporter*, 25 Mar. 1841.

70 Hayes, op. cit., i, 207. This restriction on publication was repeated as late as 1898 by Huband, op. cit., p. 289 (citing *Fleet* (1818) 1 B & Ald 379, 106 Eng Rep 140).

71 Molloy, op. cit., p. 365, note *t*.

Adye Curran at his brother's inquest, which strengthened the impression of his guilt and his family's complicity. 'If they were innocent,' Thomas Colby wrote, 'the employment of counsel was injudicious.'[72] The appearance of a barrister at an inquest was probably more likely in Dublin, where many barristers lived, than in the countryside. Stephen McKeown, arrested on 24 April 1876 for the murder of Mary McShane near Forkill, was represented at the inquest by Thomas Joseph Maginnis, a solicitor from Newry.[73] The inquest took place 'at the house of the deceased's mother', which raised the emotional temperature. The Crown could also be represented. At the inquest in Ballymote on the Callaghans and their servant girl, the Crown was represented by a solicitor, John Reynolds, who was neither crown solicitor nor sessional crown solicitor, but a solicitor in Ballymote.[74] At the Sixmilebridge inquest the crown solicitor attended.[75]

Although the 1846 act provided that the coroner could summon 'every witness whom he shall deem necessary to attend', the police tried to hold back witnesses.[76] In 1843 in Co. Waterford, Nicholas Kelly RM reported that he attended an inquest 'to prevent more witnesses being examined than was necessary to enable the jury to find a verdict'.[77] After 'the revolting and cruel murder' of James Stapleton of Ballymacmurragh in the King's County in 1844, the constabulary thought it 'injudicious' to produce three of their witnesses because of 'the spirit of intimidation that prevails'.[78] Not all coroners were the constabulary's supine assistants. Atavistic impulses occurred. Andrew Hosty, wrote from Milltown in Co. Galway to the constabulary in terms that showed that he was in charge. He had, he wrote, adjourned the inquest 'hopeing [*sic*] to procure evidence to bring it home to the savage perpetors [*sic*]'; he told the constabulary to make a 'dilligent' [*sic*] search for Roger and Patrick McDonagh; he also told them that he was about to write to the lord lieutenant to ask for a reward, being confident that 'government will give a most liberal reward.'[79]

There is no doubt that in the 1830s and 1840s the coroner was prominent in the actual arrest of suspects in spite of the ubiquity of the constabulary and the stipendiary magistrates. There are frequent references to the constabulary making arrests on coroners' warrants and to prisoners being committed by coroners.[80] In a competition with the police the coroners had certain advantages. On the one hand, the police could not ignore them because they had to be called; secondly, they were independent. On the other hand, they suffered from certain disadvant-

---

72   Larcom Papers (NLI, MS 7519 [Thomas Colby to Larcom, 29 Dec. 1842]).
73   NAI, CRF/1876/McKeown/22.
74   Larcom Papers (NLI, MS 7620 [*Freeman's Journal*, 14 Jan. 1861]).
75   Below, p. 92.   76   9 & 10 Vict., c. 37, s. 22.
77   NAI, Outrage Papers/Waterford/1843.
78   Ibid., Outrage Papers/King's County/1845.
79   Ibid., Outrage Papers/Galway/1836.
80   For examples see NAI, Outrage Papers/Monaghan/1851; ibid., Armagh/1837; ibid., Carlow/1838.

ages. Few had either the legal or medical training that would have given them a strong countervailing power to balance the experience of the constabulary.[81] Of 91 coroners in 1870, for example, only 18 were solicitors and only 18 had medical degrees or diplomas.[82] This situation was changed by the 1881 act, which required future coroners to be qualified medical practitioners, barristers, solicitors, or justices of the peace of five years' standing.[83] The fact that the coroner's functions could be exercised by two magistrates, if he failed to act within two days of the finding of a body, made him a sort of legal hermaphrodite.[84] He was expected to be a passive hermaphrodite because he 'should, in general, wait until he is sent for by the peace officers of the place.'[85] An officious coroner was regarded as a constitutional nuisance. In 1859 a 'Mr Irwin' complained that F.G. Long, of Manorcunningham, coroner for the barony of Raphoe, had held unnecessary inquests; one case was an 'overlaid' child and the other a child 'scalded to death'.[86] The coroner defended himself against 'Mr Irwin', in terms that showed he knew his place: 'I am well aware that we (coroners) are a body of officers, not very much beloved by some, from the office which we hold, this however, does not deter me as one of the body from the faithful discharge of my duty.' The grand jury, he pointed out, had a remedy for officiousness: when they 'consider that an inquest has been unnecessarily held, or where the cause of death was totally devoid of all suspicion, they refuse to make any presentment whatever for the same.'

The supplanting of the coroner by the constabulary is slightly easier to document than their supplanting of the ordinary magistrates because it can be traced to a legal decision by the law officers of the crown that led eventually to coroners confining themselves to establishing the cause of death rather than helping to apprehend suspects. In 1873 the law officers decided that it was illegal for magistrates to issue warrants to bring before the coroners prisoners whom they had already committed. The under-secretary, T.H. Burke, explained the change in a letter in October 1873 to the senior coroner of the city of Dublin:

> it having been lately brought under the notice of the government that instances had occurred in which persons in custody charged with murder or manslaughter had been produced at coroners' inquests in obedience to the orders or warrants of coroners or magistrates, the matter was referred to the law officers of the Crown for their opinion as to this course of procedure. The law officers were of opinion that the practice referred to was illegal,

---

81 9 & 10 Vict., c. 37, s. 16 referred to the coroner's qualifications, but these related to property and not to medical or legal diplomas.

82 *Thom's Directory, 1870*, passim.

83 44 & 45 Vict. c. 35, s. 2 (11 Aug. 1881). The Coroners (Dublin) Act (39 & 40 Vict., c. xciii) had required future Dublin coroners to be medical practitioners, barristers, or solicitors. See also Farrell, op. cit., pp 27–8.

84 Above, p. 41.   85 Gabbett, op. cit., ii, 56.

86 NAI, RP/1859/959.

and that the only legal mode of taking before a coroner a person who was in custody under a justice's warrant was by writ of habeas corpus, in case the Court of Queen's Bench should think proper to issue such a writ. This view of the law has been communicated to the chief commissioner of the Dublin Metropolitan Police, and to the inspector general of the Royal Irish Constabulary.[87]

This decision made the concurrent jurisdiction of magistrates and coroners cumbersome, to put it mildly. It also allowed the police, especially in the towns and cities, to opt for the administrative simplicity of taking all cases to the magistrates. The *Irish Law Times* complained in 1873, for example of a sub-constable 'acting on his veritable or supposed instructions from the Castle, who refuses, as in the Marron case at Belfast, to receive the coroner's warrant to bring up the suspected person, until he obtains his superior officer's permission, and, that having been graciously accorded, perfunctorily deposits the warrant in his pocket and takes it upon himself to pronounce it a dead letter.'[88] The obvious solution to the duplication of powers was to confine the coroner to inquiring into the cause of death and to adjourn the inquest as soon as a suspect was identified or committed.

In two cases that came before the Queen's Bench, *Reardon* and *Marshall*, both of which were heard by Judge Fitzgerald, writs of habeas corpus were granted, and the right of the prisoners to give evidence to the coroner was upheld, but only if they wished to and if the coroner were prepared to receive it.[89] In *Reardon* the prisoner, Patrick Reardon, had been remanded by the Dublin police magistrate, E.S. Dix, on a charge of having murdered Kate Pyne. Reardon's solicitor told the coroner that Reardon objected to the reception of evidence against him in his absence; the coroner adjourned the case, and the prisoner applied for a writ of habeas corpus, based on his solicitor's affidavit, stating that 'the prisoner himself desires to be present; otherwise, in his absence a verdict of wilful murder may be returned against him. He wishes to hear the evidence affecting him, and it is necessary that he should be present, in order that he himself may be tendered as a witness, or that, even if not sworn, he may make a statement.'[90] Fitzgerald noted that 'the difficulty in this case arises from the circumstance that the suspected person has been brought before and committed by the magistrate, instead of being detained and brought before the coroner, whose court ought, in the first instance, to have charge of the preliminary inquiry', which was an interesting affirmation of the coroner's primacy.[91] Fitzgerald upheld the prisoner's right to be present, stating 'it would be a strange anomaly, if, in the coroner's court, the person

87   'Coroners and the Crown' in *ILT & SJ*, 7 (1873), 506.
88   'The production of prisoners at coroners' inquests' in *ILT & SJ*, 7 (1873), 534.
89   *Re Reardon* (1873) 7 ILTR 193; *Re Marshall* (1874) 8 ILTR 1.
90   *Re Reardon* (1873) 7 ILTR 193, at p. 194.   91   Ibid., p. 196.

suspected in relation to the matter of the inquiry, and desirous of being present on the hearing, should be by law excluded.' On the other hand, he also upheld the right of the coroner to proceed even if the prisoner was absent: 'it is not at all of necessity that he should be present at the inquest. And it would be a grave mistake to suppose that, in his absence, evidence could not be gone into, or that, if affecting him, such evidence ought not to be received, for the evidence is not given technically upon a charge against any person, but merely for information in relation to the inquiry.'

Remarkable arguments for the coroner's primacy were rehearsed. The *Irish Law Times* argued that the coroner's court was the superior one and that 'traditional usage' should not be 'ousted and overridden by sudden reformations, without recourse to the legislature.'[92] In *Marshall*, which arose out of Anne Wyndford Marshall's having been charged with poisoning Colin Donaldson, of the Royal Artillery, it was argued that the prisoner should be able to cross-examine witnesses, that 'important suggestions of guilt or innocence may be derived from the very demeanour of the accused when face to face with the corpse, even without the obsolete ordeal of touch',[93] and that 'it would work hardly on an accused person to substitute the discretion of a single police magistrate for that of a jury of twelve or twenty-three men.'[94] The Crown's case in *Marshall* was more practical: 'the prisoner, in the present instance, refused to make any statement before the magistrate, and all the probabilities are that she has no *bona fide* intention of tendering her evidence at the inquest.'[95]

Although *Reardon* and *Marshall* vindicated the ancient primacy of the coroner, they did not dispense with the need for a writ of habeas corpus to bring the prisoner before the coroner. In practice it was unlikely that prisoners were going to go to the expense of applying for a writ of habeas corpus just for the privilege of appearing before the coroner. The Crown, for whom expense was less of a problem, might chose to bring the prisoner before the coroner by means of habeas corpus. In *Claffey*, for example, which occurred just after *Marshall*, on 20 January 1874, a police magistrate in Dublin remanded Eliza Claffey for one week, 'charged before him with the crime of infanticide'. On the very same day the coroner began his inquest but 'declined to proceed with the inquest in her absence'. The under-secretary instructed the crown and treasury solicitor to apply for a writ of habeas corpus, and the Queen's Bench issued it.[96]

It was highly unlikely that such a cumbersome procedure would become routine, and given the preference of the police for bringing the accused immediately before a magistrate, which was one of the causes of this whole dispute, it was unlikely that coroners would maintain their role in establishing the identity of the perpetrator. The *Irish Law Times* admitted that change was

---

92 'The production of prisoners at coroners' inquests' in *ILT & SJ*, 7 (1873), 533.
93 *Re Marshall* (1874) 8 ILTR 1, at p. 2.   94 Ibid., p. 4.
95 Ibid., p. 2.   96 8 ILTR 20, at p. 21

desirable: 'we are inclined to think that the coroner's jurisdiction needs reform, and that the question upon every inquest should merely be, Whether death was occasioned by violence or by natural causes? The present state of the law is certainly anomalous and unsatisfactory, whether the jurisdiction to be exercised be the limited one suggested, or the more enlarged one actually existing; and, in any case, therefore, we hold that reform is needed.'[97] Judge Fitzgerald admitted in *Marshall* that 'the present mode of proceeding presents to the public rather an unseemly aspect.'

The end of the virtually concurrent operation of the coroners and the committing magistrates was confirmed in a characteristic way. In the *Judicial Statistics* for 1878, the registrar general noted that

> The statistics as to coroner's inquests has [*sic*] been entirely omitted. The information is presented to parliament in the reports of the registrar general as to deaths. As the great majority of the cases belong to accidental deaths, in no way connected with crime, they more properly belong to the registrar general's department than to the criminal statistics. Then the practice, introduced in recent years, in consequence of the system of public prosecutor [*sic*], which is completely established in Ireland, of not producing the accused person before a coroner's jury, has, as pointed out in previous reports, destroyed the value of coroners' verdicts as an indication of crime. In many plain cases of crime coroners' juries, from the absence of the prisoner, confine their verdict to the medical cause of death.[98]

If the *Judicial Statistics* noted a historical turning-point, the course of history had been accurately predicted in the constabulary's *Standing Rules* in 1860 when policemen were warned that 'it is the duty of the constabulary to inform the coroner of all cases of sudden death, although from the notoriety of certain facts it may appear that an inquest may be nothing more than matter of form; but still it is form, the regular observance of which is equally required by law and policy.'[99] The changes in the role of the coroner in the 1870s did not put an end to the coroner's jury as the *vox populi*: they did not prevent the outburst of the coroner's jury at Oughterard,[100] nor did they prevent the controversial inquests at Edenderry into the death of two children who died after their parents were evicted in 1882 near Rhode,[101] nor the Mitchelstown or Ardee controversies, the

---

97 'The office of coroner' in *ILT & SJ*, 7 (1873), 484.

98 *Judicial Statistics (Ireland), 1878*, p. 13 [C 2389], HC 1878–9, lxxvi, 291.

99 Henry John Brownrigg, *Standing rules and regulations for the government and guidance of the constabulary force in Ireland; revised edition, as approved by his excellency the lord lieutenant* (Dublin, 1860), p. 44.

100 Above, pp 44–5.

101 *Copy 'of report by Mr Richard Bourke, inspector of the Local Government Board, of the result of his inquiry into the circumstances connected with the deaths of two children named Kavanagh, whose*

former arising out of a riot during the Plan of Campaign and the latter out of an eviction at Belpatrick, near Ardee.[102]

THE POLICE AS DETECTIVES

There were few full-time 'detectives' in the RIC and the DMP. Most murders were investigated by ordinary policemen and RMs who used their eyes and their ears, without any technical aids or even any particular experience. When James Scully's body was found near his home, Kilfeacle House, Captain John Macleod RM noted that Scully's gold watch had not been taken, that he had been shot from behind as well as from in front, and that he had been shot at close range ('as the hair and skin round the aperture were scorched with gun powder').[103] Macleod not surprisingly concluded that 'from the determined character of the deceased who was a powerful young man, and his being so well armed at the time, it may be inferred that the assassins must have got close behind him without being perceived, and had actually fired at him through the back before he had any intimation of their approach; that the other wounds were subsequently inflicted when he was lying helpless at their mercy.' At Sixmilebridge in 1852 when a military detachment fired on an election crowd, Louis Cronin RM inspected the soldiers' muskets:

> I put my finger into each barrel, and I found each barrel soil my finger with powder recently discharged. I said to the soldier, 'You have fired, have you not?' The reply was, 'Yes, I did.' This was in every instance where I discovered a trace of powder; there were ten such instances ... On examining each musket I asked each man whose gun soiled my finger his name, which he gave me. I wiped my finger after each examination.[104]

Occasionally the constabulary rose to something in the Sherlock Holmes line. At the trial of Jeremiah Moore (hanged at Maryborough on 19 April 1862), Lord

parents lived at Rhode, in the King's County, together with the minutes of evidence taken at the inquiry', HC 1882 (341), liv, 181.

102 Farrell, op. cit., pp 31–2; Huband, op. cit., p. 269.

103 NAI, Outrage Papers/Tipperary/1842. For the Scully family as landlords in Ireland and the USA, see Homer E. Socolofsky, *Landlord William Scully* (Lawrence, KA, 1979). Captain Macleod was murdered in Co. Leitrim in January 1845 (*A return 'of all murders that have been committed in Ireland since the 1st day of January 1842; specifying the county, and the barony of the county where such murder had been committed; the name and condition of the person so murdered; also, a return of the rewards offered in each such instance; where such rewards have been claimed; and where conviction has followed ...'*, p. 6, HC 1846 (220), xxxv, 298).

104 *Copies of the several inquisitions removed from the Court of Queen's Bench in Ireland, in the month of January last, and transferred to the county of Clare ... in relation to any of the cases of homicide, riot, unlawful assembly or other criminal offence alleged to have been committed at the town of Sixmilebridge, in the month of July last, at the time of the general election ...*, p. 26, HC 1852–3 (313), xciv, 88.

Chief Justice Monahan noted that two policemen, one of whom he described as 'a very intelligent young man, a sub-inspector', had demonstrated that footprints at the scene of the murder matched the nails on the prisoner's shoes, which 'were very remarkable, 4 rows of nails in one shoe, 5 on the other and in some instances several nails wanted.'[105] These three examples are slightly misleading if they suggest that the scene of the murder was a rich source of evidence: out of 1029 pieces of evidence generated by 54 trials, for example, only 50 pieces came from policemen's observations of the scene.[106]

There were no technical innovations in detection in the nineteenth century to justify a separate forensic establishment. John Lentaigne, who succeeded Walter Crofton as inspector general of prisons, was 'an early and enthusiastic advocate of photography as a method of criminal identification.'[107] Finger-printing came in at the end of the period.[108] Maps, the electric telegraph, and the railways were probably the nineteenth century's most important advances in forensic technique.[109] Until the use of finger-prints, ballistic analysis, and accurate pathology, magistrates and policemen were not much better off than Sir Walter Scott's sheriff depute, Paulus Pleydell, whose unravelling of a murder mystery is described in detail in *Guy Mannering.*[110]

In April 1869, after a series of murders, including the affray at Ballycohey when a policeman and a bailiff were killed, the inspector general, Colonel John Stewart Wood, admitted that while the Irish constabulary 'are generally held to be, as a body, the best police force in the world … yet it is widely felt, and with too

---

105 NAI, CRF/1862/Moore/8.

106 See below, pp 207–8.

107 R.B. McDowell, *The Irish administration 1801–1914* (London and Toronto, 1964), p. 156. For an exhaustive study of the uses of photography by the police in Ireland see, Peadar Slattery, FRPS, 'The uses of photography in Ireland 1839–1900' (PhD thesis, 3 vols, Dublin University, 1991), i, 223–80. See ibid., iii, plates 88–106 for examples of forensic photography. Plates 101–2 relate to the murder of James Donovan in 1894, which played a prominent part in A.M. Sullivan's memoirs. See also Palmer, op. cit., p. 533.

108 For a thief leaving his finger-prints on a bottle see Georgina O'Brien, *The reminiscences of the Right Hon. Lord O'Brien (of Kilfenora) lord chief justice of Ireland*, edited by his daughter Hon. Georgina O'Brien (London, 1916), p. 135. See Tim Carey, *Mountjoy: the story of a prison* (Cork, 2000), p. 120 where it is stated that Irish officials, including a clerk from Dublin Castle, went to Scotland Yard in 1903 to learn about finger-printing. There is a reference to Bertillon in NAI, NA 999/731.

109 'Modern improvements in the mode of lighting towns and their suburbs, following the introduction of gas, must be reckoned among the most effectual preventives of robbery by night. Telegraphs aid not a little in the detection of offenders after a crime has been committed, and photography has often done most important service in proving the identity of a criminal' (Luke Owen Pike, *A history of crime in England illustrating the changes of the laws in the progress of civilization written from the public records and other contemporary evidence*. ii, *From the accession of Henry VII, to the present time* (London, 1876), p. 467).

110 Sir Walter Scott, *Guy Mannering*, preface and glossary by W.M. Parker (London, Everyman's Library, 1906; reprint, 1968), pp 73, 75–8.

much truth, that it fails to a great extent in the detection of certain classes of serious offenders.'[111] Samuel Waters remembered the limited effects of Wood's efforts to improve the force's detective abilities. When Lt. Col. George Hillier inspected Grange sub-district, Head Constable Lindley was found wanting: 'In those days Col. Sir John Stewart Wood, the inspector general, had issued a special memorandum on detective duties which all ranks were required to study carefully. I had never even heard of it as Lindley had carefully put it aside as of no importance. Hillier called on the head constable to examine the men in their knowledge of this memorandum. He was speechless, and the men had never seen this document. Hillier called for the inspection book and wrote this minute – "This is the worst district I ever inspected. There is no drill known here and no police duties!"'[112]

When Wood wrote of the constabulary's shortcomings as detectives, the only detectives in the constabulary were a body of plainclothes 'disposable' constables in every county, who were 'disposable' in the sense that they could be moved from county to county, and their numbers 'enlarged *ad libitum*'.[113] They were, according to Sir Henry Brownrigg, 'always ready to mount the frieze, to assume the short pipe, to converse (many of them) in the Irish language, and to employ devices, as an Irishman knows how, to come at the knowledge they are in quest of.' In December 1869 the Irish government appointed a detective director for the RIC.[114] The next advance came in September 1882 after a summer of great tension in Dublin, which included the Phoenix Park murders, when Edward Jenkinson established a criminal investigation department and selected seven police officers 'to undertake special police work and break up agrarian secret societies.'[115] In October 1883 the department was divided into 'ordinary' and 'special' branches.[116]

111 TNA (UK), HO 184/114, Memorandum III, 1 Apr. 1869, quoted by Vaughan, 'Ireland, *c.*1870', in Vaughan (ed.), *A new history of Ireland*, v, *Ireland under the union I, 1801–70* (Oxford, 1989), p. 770. See also Virginia Crossman, *Politics, law and order in nineteenth–century Ireland* (Dublin, 1996), p. 95. Neglect of detective work went back to the very origins of the Irish constabulary (Palmer, op. cit., pp 252, 367, 374).

112 Samuel Waters, *A policeman's Ireland: recollections of Samuel Waters, RIC*, ed. Stephen Ball (Cork, 1999), p. 30.

113 Henry John Brownrigg, *Examination of some recent allegations concerning the constabulary force in Ireland, in a report to his excellency the lord lieutenant* (Dublin, 1864), p. 21. For the formation and organization of the 'disposables' see Elizabeth Malcolm, 'Investigating the "Machinery of Murder": Irish detectives and agrarian outrages, 1847–79' in *New Hibernia Review*, 6:3 (autumn 2002), 73–91.

114 Vaughan, 'Ireland *c.*1870', pp 770–1.

115 Waters, op. cit., p. 12. See also Bridgeman, op. cit., pp 108–15.

116 Waters, op. cit., p. 96 (based on NAI, RP/1883/22,072): 'Hitherto the RIC had no full-time detectives outside Belfast, while the DMP had its own detective force. In October 1883, when the divisional system was reorganized, the Crime Ordinary Branch handled "all the reports' relating to outrages, the ordinary investigation of crime, the preservation of the peace, illegal assemblies and personal protection", while the Crime Special Branch collected and transmitted

The limited usefulness of detectives, even after 1869, was demonstrated in the case of Humphrey Davis, a landlord's bailiff, who was murdered near Ballina in 1871. A constable, Francis Cottrell, was sent to work under cover as a groom for Standish O'Grady McDermott JP, of Clongee, near Foxford.[117] Cottrell's mission came to an abrupt end in July 1871 when the Chief Secretary's Office received a document entitled 'The humble petition of the inhabitants of Ballina in the county of Mayo', which denounced Arthur M. Mitchell, the RM in charge of the case:

> Mr Mitchell has a brother of very drunken and intemperate habits living with him and who at any time of the day will drink with the meanest of the people. And this brother living with him in the same house and having uninterrupted access to where the RM keeps the correspondence of the government removed several important official documents therefrom. Amongst some of those removed by the drunken brother was one from the 'detective department Castle Dublin' referring to the groom, his pretended employment and real occupation. This letter was found on the streets of Ballina and read and profited by the several enemies of her majesty's government. Its contents were communicated to persons residing in Foxford and in consequence the groom to save his life was coerced to leave Foxford.

Mitchell defended himself, demonstrating how seriously undercover work was taken: 'this letter was torn up by me and some fragments of it were found in a yard at the back of my premises some six weeks since. Having heard a rumour of the finding I instituted inquiries and ascertained from the party who found it that he had destroyed the fragments by lighting his pipe with them.'

The best detectives were to be found in the DMP's G Division, led by Daniel Ryan (superintendent of G Division, 1869–74) and John Mallon (superintendent, 1874–83, and assistant commissioner of the DMP, 1893–1902).[118] Mallon's

---

"all secret information" and in very special cases assisted the local Constabulary inquiries into cases of serious outrages.' For the establishment of the Special Irish Branch by the London Metropolitan Police on 17 March 1882 see Jim Herlihy, *The Dublin Metropolitan Police: a short history and genealogical table* (Dublin, 2001), pp 136–7.

117 NAI, RP/1871/14,028.

118 For G Division see Herlihy, op. cit., pp 125–9. For Mallon's career see ibid., pp 137–47. See also Nigel I. Cochrane, 'The coming of the G Men: the birth of the Dublin detective division 1838–45' in *Police Journal*, 61 (1988), 42–52. (I am indebted to Professor Desmond Greer for this reference.) For Daniel Ryan's work, as revealed by the expenses he claimed during January 1859, a period that included the investigation of a suspected murderer, Thomas Black, see NAI, RP/1859/976. Ryan's reimbursements included paying for the forensic examination of Black's clothes, paying for new clothes for Black, paying for an analysis of bloodstains found on Black's clothes, and paying for Black's 'support'. Ryan's reimbursements also included payment 'to services rendered whipping boys convicted of larceny'.

handling of the Phoenix Park murders was one of the most patient, determined, and meticulous investigations of the nineteenth century. His methods were not original: he gave his clients the impression that he was omniscient (he 'would blurt out a positive declaration in the form of query').[119] He was skilful 'in sandwiching the witnesses, one between certain others, so as to create alarm by the very sequence in which they were called'. He was not too grand to eavesdrop; in Kilmainham Michael Kavanagh and Peter Carey were called for a medical examination; part of a sheet of oak panelling was replaced by a sheet of perforated zinc; Mallon 'metaphorically glued his ear to the perforated zinc'. He also 'verified' his stories. When Michael Kavanagh, who had been one of the car-drivers on the fatal 6 May 1882, turned approver, Mallon took him 'out of prison, put him in a trap, and drove him over the whole route he had taken on the day of the murders, from the time he left his stables in the morning until he returned to them in the evening. The object of this was to test him as thoroughly as possible, to piece his statement together in sequential order, and to gather material for picking up whatever tiny threads of corroboration there might be available.' Verification seems to have been a routine of police work. William Deery, a discharged soldier who had served in the Crimea, told the constabulary in Donegal the names of those who had murdered James Murray, John George Adair's steward. When the constabulary took Deery to the scene of the crime he could not identify the spot where Murray was attacked; he got Murray's hat wrong, saying it was a 'Tom and Jerry' when it was in fact a cap. When the constabulary examined Deery's most promising suspect he was able to prove that he had been respectably employed in Glasgow at the time of the attack on Murray.[120]

The constabulary's detection rate was not as bad as their critics made out. Agrarian homicides, especially the assassination of landlords and their agents, were supposed to be the constabulary's Achilles heel. Assuming that homicides caused by the landlords' actions accounted for a small fraction of all homicides,

---

119 Frederick Moir Bussy, *Irish conspiracies: recollections of John Mallon (The Great Detective) and other reminiscences* (London, 1910), pp 84–92, 157. Sir David Harrell described another nice bit of snooping in his memoirs. An anonymous letter warned Lord Spencer about two men from the USA who were coming to assassinate him. A detective went to Richard Pigott's house in Kingstown: 'While Pigott was out of the room making some enquiries from his landlady, the detective went through his papers and obtained specimens of handwriting as well as a half sheet of notepaper which was blank. On comparing this half sheet with the note sent to His Excellency, the marks of tearing fitted exactly. This and the specimens of handwriting left no doubt that Pigott was the writer of the anonymous letter to the lord lieutenant' (Sir David Harrell, Recollections and Reflections, pp 104–6 (typescript in Department of Early Printed Books, TCD); 25 copies produced 'for private circulation'; dated Apr. 1926).

120 NAI, RP/1861/7273 and Vaughan, *Sin, sheep and Scotsmen: John George Adair and the Derryveagh evictions, 1861* (Belfast, 1983), pp 37–8. See also NAI, Outrage Papers/Wicklow/1852 for the revelations of Charles Harris, a self-confessed assassin; the constabulary, who were initially impressed by his stories, checked them and decided he was an impostor.

the constabulary's achievement, measured by the number of agrarian assassins who were hanged was not unimpressive. In 1852 James Kirk and Patrick McCooey were hanged in Monaghan for the attempted murder of James Eastwood JP, and Francis Berry in Armagh for the attempted murder of Merideth Chambré; in 1853 Thomas Hodgens and Patrick Breen were hanged in Monaghan for conspiring to murder William Steuart Trench; in 1854 Neal Quin, Bryan Grant, and Patrick Coomey were hanged for the murder of Thomas Bateson, which had occurred three years before in December 1851; in 1856 Thomas Dunn and James Murphy were hanged in Cavan for the murder of Charlotte Hinds; in 1858 Daniel and William Cormack were hanged in Nenagh for the murder of John Ellis. In the years 1852–8 there were 26 hangings in Ireland; 12 of those hanged were agrarian assassins. In the same seven years there had been only 34 agrarian homicides, which were a very small percentage of the 772 ordinary homicides that occurred in the same years. The landlords may have felt that the constabulary did not meet their needs, that Dublin Castle ignored them, and that a whig-dominated parliament was unsympathetic to them. Those who died on the gallows might reasonably have thought otherwise.

The Irish constabulary impressed those who confronted them in court. Alexander Sullivan remembered their machine-like perseverance:

> At assizes the defence would probably be an alibi. It was the duty of the constabulary to be able to foretell with regard to each potential criminal what would be his defence when he had accomplished his crime. Intelligent anticipation of the possible inventions of minds trained to deception, and genius to defeat them, were developed in the force to an uncanny point. Had GHQ been staffed by RIC the [first world] war would have been won in weeks. Before the offenders' friends had constructed an alibi, indeed before he arrested or charged anybody, the sergeant would have reviewed all possible alibis and would have secured signed statements as to their movements at the crucial period from all persons who were liable to become witnesses for the defence. In the same way other defences would be anticipated and blighted by some constable getting unwary persons to tell the truth before other people were ready with suggestions of falsehood. To circumvent this phase of official activity, in the graver conspiracies of agrarian crime, the alibis were prepared and their supporters trained before the event.[121]

121 A.M. Sullivan, *The last serjeant: the memoirs of Serjeant A.M. Sullivan QC* (London, 1952), p. 109. There were some predictable anecdotes about the constabulary's skill. Maurice Healy told the story of Patrick Ryan, whose hand-made boots gave him away because a police officer noticed 'little shamrock-shaped groups of hobnails' in the soles (*The old Munster circuit. A book of memories and traditions* (London, 1939), p. 235). Peter O'Brien told the story of a dog called Sam, whose presence at the scene of the crime was used by a sub-inspector and an RM to corroborate an approver's evidence (Georgina O'Brien, op. cit., pp 33–4).

ARRESTS, WARRANTS, AND SWEARING INFORMATIONS

An arrest was 'the apprehending or detaining of a person in order that he may be forthcoming to answer an alleged or suspected crime.'[122] According to Gabbett, 'to constitute an arrest, whether with or without a warrant, the party must either be actually touched by the officer, or restrained of his liberty – as by confining him in a room; or else he must submit himself, by words or actions, to be in custody.'[123] Occasionally the arrest told the whole story. As Lord Leitrim was walking along the main street of Mohill in September 1860, James Murphy tried to shoot him: 'two of the constabulary who were on duty in the street at the time, on observing smoke issue from the window of Murphy's shop, they forced an entrance, and arrested Murphy, with a large blunderbuss in his hand, just as he was making his escape by the rere.'[124]

There were four kinds of arrest: by a policeman with a warrant, by a policeman without a warrant, by a private citizen without a warrant, and by hue and cry.[125] Of these four, the first two were the most likely in practice, and the fourth had long fallen into abeyance. The third was uncommon but not unknown. When some men threw stones at James Meegan's house in Drumboat, Co. Monaghan:

> James Meegan immediately returned into the house and brought out a pistol and repeatedly desired them to stand off and he observed three of the assailants approach to the end of the house after which he fired a shot at them and then a second shot was fired at them by s[ai]d Meegans, on which they ran off as fast as they could while the Meegans pursued them and arrested one of them named James Plunkett who has received a wound on the chin supposed to be from the shots fired by said Meegans.[126]

A policeman could arrest without a warrant, if he saw a person committing a felony, or if he had 'reasonable cause to suspect that treason or felony has been committed, or a dangerous wound given.'[127] He was also justified, if 'upon the reasonable charge and information of another', he arrested 'any one supposed to be guilty of treason or felony, or inflicting a dangerous wound, even though it should afterwards turn out that the party was not guilty, or in fact, that no such crime had been committed.' This was the only respect in which a policeman

---

122 Levinge, *Justice of the peace*, p. 39.
123 Gabbett, op. cit., ii, 144.
124 Larcom Papers (NLI, MS 7620 [*Express*, 18 Sept. 1860]).
125 Hayes, op. cit., i, 64, 73–8; John G. Thompson, *The law of criminal procedure in Ireland* (Dublin, 1899), pp 27–33.
126 NAI, Outrage Papers/Monaghan/1838.
127 Hayes, op. cit., i, 73–4. See also R.M. Hennessy, *The justice of the peace for Ireland: a treatise on the powers and duties of magistrates in Ireland, in cases of summary jurisdiction, and in other matters, founded partly on Molloy's Justice of the Peace; with an appendix of statutes* (Dublin, 1910), pp 34–6.

enjoyed a more privileged position than an ordinary citizen, who could act safely only when a felony had actually been committed. If an ordinary citizen broke into a building and made an arrest, 'his conduct will not only be excusable, but laudable', but 'should it turn out, however, that no such crime has been committed, or that the doors of an innocent third party are broken in a fruitless search after the suspected criminal, or that the party has acted on the suspicions of another, rather than his own, it is clear, that the party will not be justified.'[128] The distinction between the officer and the ordinary citizen did not change over time. Thompson, for example, wrote in 1899 that 'there is this distinction between the case of a private individual and a constable; in order to justify the former he must not merely show a reasonable ground of suspicion, but must also prove that a felony has actually been committed, while a constable is protected if he had reasonable ground for suspecting that a felony had been committed, whether in fact it has been committed or not.'[129]

Warrants could be issued by the privy council, by a secretary of state, by judges of assize, by judges of the Queen's Bench, by coroners, and by justices of the peace.[130] In practice, the justices of the peace were the most important issuers of warrants, although coroners played their part, especially in the early part of the period. The warrant, which was a command to an officer to bring a particular person before him, protected the citizen from arbitrary arrest by policemen, and protected policemen from being sued because 'an arrest for a criminal cause, without express warrant is a false imprisonment' – unless, of course, the policeman had good grounds for arresting without a warrant.[131] Before a magistrate could issue a warrant, an information had to be sworn before him. The word 'information', which was usually the first step on the prisoner's road to the gallows, had a meaning in this context that was different from its familiar one: it was a complaint, made before a magistrate, that a crime had been committed.

Swearing an information ignited the blue touch-paper that made the magisterial firework go off with a reassuring bang or fizzle out in dampness and disappointment. It was the necessary prelude to action because the magistrate could not compel witnesses to give evidence until some particular party was actually accused.[132] The magistrate was obliged to examine the informer and his witnesses 'on oath or solemn affirmation, and to take down, in writing, the particulars of their statements. This is called the *information* of the party.'[133] Even when an information had been sworn, the magistrate was not obliged to issue a warrant. According to Hayes, he had to exercise his discretion because if he issued a warrant 'maliciously, or without a statement on oath or affirmation, of

128 Hayes, op. cit., i, 77.   129 Thompson, op. cit., p. 32.
130 Hayes, op. cit., i, 64, 194; Thompson, op. cit., p. 27.
131 Hayes, op. cit., i, 64.
132 See above, pp 17–19 for changes that allowed magistrates to examine witnesses before anybody had actually been accused of an offence.
133 Hayes, op. cit., i, 65.

circumstances affording a reasonable suspicion of guilt, and the party prove to be innocent, he will be liable to an action of trespass at the suit of the party grieved.'[134] Fifty years after Hayes, Constantine Molloy was insistent that 'it is the duty of the magistrate, and not of the officer, to judge of the ground of suspicion' and warned that the magistrate 'will be liable for an action for issuing it groundlessly or maliciously and without such probable cause as would induce a candid and impartial man to suspect the party accused, or without taking duly into consideration all the circumstances in his power to investigate the case.'[135]

The issuing of a warrant was not prohibitively cumbersome. A policeman could swear an information if no member of the public was willing to do so. Dr Thomas Courtenay was arrested after Head Constable Arthur Jackson swore an information that was not weighed down with relevant facts: 'whereas complaint has been made on oath and in writing that Arthur Jackson Head Constable at Ballymena had strong suspicion and did suspect that the defendant was accessory to the death of one Amelia Carey whose body has been recently exhumed and in which case the coroner has held and commenced an inquest but adjourned the same until the 22nd January 1863 and evidence having transpired on the 1st day of said inquest on the 8th January 1863 implicating the said Thomas Courtenay the doctor in attendance to said Amelia Carey prior to her death.'[136] Head Constable Jackson's 'strong suspicion' was enough to allow him to become an 'informer' and to allow the magistrate to issue a warrant.

As late as 1842 Hayes could speak in almost archaic terms of justices directing warrants not only to constables, whom he distantly describes as 'the known officers of justices of the peace', but also to 'any indifferent person who is not an officer; for a justice may authorize any one whom he pleases to be his officer.'[137] In fact since the constabulary act of 1836 warrants were directed by law to members of the constabulary.[138] Hamilton Smythe wrote of warrants being given to a head constable, or to a sub-constable who was supposed to show them to 'the chief constable under whose immediate command he is'.[139] The Petty Sessions Act of 1851 provided that 'in any case which shall appear to the justice by whom any warrant shall be issued, to be a case of emergency, he may address such warrant to any constable of the county.'[140] To protect themselves the constabulary kept a careful note of what they did with warrants: 'the dates of the receipt and execution of all warrants, and by whom executed must be punctually endorsed thereon; and such documents are to be numbered and carefully preserved by the sub-inspector, head or other constable by whom they shall have been executed, as a safeguard against any proceedings which may be taken against them.'[141]

---

134 Ibid.
135 Molloy, op. cit., pp 68, 66.
136 NAI, RP/1863/10,102.
137 Hayes, op. cit., i, 68–9.
138 6 Will. IV, c. 13, s. 16 (20 May 1836).
139 Hamilton Smythe, *Justice of the peace in Ireland* (Dublin, 1841), p. 196.
140 14 & 15 Vict., c. 93, s. 26 (7 Aug. 1851).
141 Henry John Brownrigg, *Standing rules and regulations for the government and guidance of the*

The power to arrest was occasionally used to round up suspects against whom there was little evidence. When a young man named Edward Byrne was murdered in 1841, the RM at Maryborough, F.B. Haly, was at a loss because no one could identify the assassin. Haly quickly discovered the background: 'the Byrnes had lately got possession of the land from which a family of the Moores who live on the spot have been recently evicted and to this cause the murder is attributed.'[142] Being weak on means and opportunity, Haly relied on motive: 'I have all the Moores with the exception of one member arrested and placed under the care of the police until tomorrow when I shall commence the inquiry after the inquest.' The *Judicial Statistics*, however, do not suggest that there were massive round-ups of suspects. In the ten years 1866–75, for example, the police returned 570 murders, including infanticides; 773 persons were arrested in connection with these, and of these 372 were committed for trial.[143]

The electric telegraph, combined with a countrywide network of constabulary barracks, gave the constabulary a long reach and an enormous trawling power. Constable O'Neill of the DMP was murdered in Dublin in 1866. A man called Kearney was suspected. His description was circulated, and a reward of £50 offered. In Donoughmore, Co. Cork, Constable Scanlon, 'whose usual intelligence and vigilance were, no doubt, sharpened by the prospect of earning a reward, saw a man pass through the village who bore a marked resemblance to the fugitive, his appearance corresponding with singular closeness to the published description of Kearney.'[144] The man's description must have fitted many working men wandering about looking for work: he was 'about 25 years of age, about 5½ feet high, with a fair complexion, a tuft of beard on his chin, and of dirty appearance, probably to be in some degree attributed to his avocation of blacksmith.' Donoughmore is 182 miles from Dublin. Constable Scanlon, therefore, was perfectly right when he noticed that 'the man seemed to have walked a considerable distance, and this circumstance with the more particular peculiarities of his appearance, sufficiently excited the constable's suspicion to lead him to arrest the man.' The constable brought the prisoner before George Washington Braziere Creagh JP (of Firmount, near Blarney) and swore an information 'stating the grounds which he believed he had for thinking him to be Kearney, and praying a remand till the fact should have been ascertained.' The magistrate warned the prisoner 'not to say anything that would tend to criminate himself, but stated that if he desired to make any statement he would take it down in writing.' The prisoner treated the caution as an invitation to say 'that his name was Foley, that he was a blacksmith, that he had a short time since been arrested at Bruree, Co. Limerick, also on suspicion of being Kearney; but that on one of the

constabulary force in Ireland; revised edition, as approved by his excellency the lord lieutenant (Dublin, 1860), p. 273.

142 NAI, Outrage Papers/Queen's County/1841.

143 These figures are taken from the *Judicial Statistics*; for full references see below, 401–2.

144 Larcom Papers (NLI, MS 7592 [*Freeman's Journal*, 18 Aug. 1866]).

witnesses of the murder being brought from Dublin to see him, he was found not to be the fugitive, and that he was then discharged by Mr Franks RM.'[145] Foley had been arrested on Saturday morning. On Sunday he was remanded to the county gaol, where he was held until Creagh checked his story. 'Mr Creagh put himself in communication with the authorities in Dublin, and also with Mr Franks RM, Co. Limerick, as well as with the constabulary at Sneem. From all three places he has received replies which fully bear out the prisoner's statements.' Foley was discharged.

Until *Johnston* in 1864, which admitted as evidence replies made to questions asked by a policeman, many Irish judges expressed their disapproval of policemen questioning those whom they arrested.[146] The judges' disapproval was reflected by the textbooks. Nun and Walsh in 1841 warned that 'constables should abstain not only from tampering with or holding out any inducement to prisoners to confess, which is a gross violation of their duty, but it seems also that, in general, they should not question the prisoner respecting the charge.'[147] Hayes warned that 'police constables, and all other persons having access to a prisoner under arrest on a criminal charge, whether before or after examination by a magistrate, ought to be most careful that, in their conversation with the prisoner, nothing should be said on their part which can be in anywise construed into a threat or promise to extort a confession.'[148] Hayes also referred to the constable giving the prisoner 'a suitable caution', but if after being cautioned, the prisoner wanted to speak 'he ought to caution him on the subject, and tell him that he should expect no advantage from it.'[149] Nun and Walsh thought the caution ought to be given as soon as there was a 'reasonable suspicion' against the accused, 'to apprize him, that any statement made by him may be produced in evidence against him at his trial.'[150] Levinge seemed to exclude any questioning by the police, certainly not before the suspect was cautioned: 'the practice of questioning prisoners by police officers is entirely opposed to the spirit of our law, for by the law of this country no person ought to be made to criminate himself; if there is evidence of an offence, a police officer is justified, after a proper caution, in putting to a suspected person interrogatories, with a view to ascertaining whether or not there are fair and reasonable grounds for apprehending him.'[151]

There was, however, a loophole, which some judges allowed even before *Johnston* in 1864. If a conversation sprang up between the policeman and the prisoner, the policeman could keep the ball rolling. 'It is not the duty or the

---

145 D.B. Franks, of Bruff.
146 *R. v. Mary Johnston* (1864) 15 ICLR 60.
147 Richard Nun & John Edward Walsh, *The powers and duties of justices of the peace in Ireland, and of constables as connected therewith; with an appendix and statutes and forms* (Dublin, 1841), p. 336.
148 Hayes, op. cit., i, 70.
149 Ibid., p. 71.
150 Nun & Walsh, op. cit., p. 333.
151 Levinge, *Justice of the peace*, p. 54 (referring to *Berriman* (1854) 6 Cox CC 388, at p. 389).

province of a constable to put questions which are to be used afterwards against the prisoner but if questions grow out of conversation I see no objection to using them,' Crampton stated at Armagh summer assizes in 1841 at the trial of Patrick Woods. 'On the Munster circuit this question has arisen two or three times, and been so decided.'[152] The promising possibilities of the conversational approach were demonstrated when in August 1864 Sergeant Archibald McClaughan arrested John McLoughlin, who had just attacked the solicitor John McCrossan. The sergeant approached McLoughlin in a reassuring way (the quoted passage is from the judge's notes):

> I said to the prisoner, 'John! I am sorry for the position you have placed yourself in.' He said 'I was in defence of my life.' I said 'You must consider yourself a prisoner.' Later in his account of McLoughlin's arrest, he mentioned cautioning him. 'I cautioned him when I brought him to the strong room in the barrack, not to say anything as it might be used against him. I heard him afterwards cautioned by Mr Coulson.'[153]

It is worth noting that the sergeant apparently did not caution McLoughlin until they went to the barracks. Even after being cautioned by the policeman and the magistrate, McLoughlin could not contain himself: 'in going to the gaol we passed by McCrossan's house. In passing it the prisoner shouted out "The robbing rascal – it was not enough to come & take all my money – but he must come to take away my wife."'[154]

The conversational approach worked wonders with Laurence Smith, a blind man who stabbed Patrick Lynch, known as the 'Yankee'. At Smith's trial the court heard of disputes between the two men, leading to actions for slander and trespass, to the execution of a writ of *capias ad satisfaciendum*, and to the forced sale in 1869 of a piece of land belonging to the prisoner. Sub-Inspector Ware set out from Ballyjamesduff, looked at the Yankee's body, and arrested three of the Smiths, including Laurence, telling them he was arresting them for Lynch's murder. In spite of the caution, Laurence spoke: 'I do not consider myself an assassin. What I did, I did in my own defence. I look upon myself as a soldier defending myself … Lynch drew the knife first.'[155] Laurence then showed the sub-inspector how he had taken the knife off Lynch. So far Smith had done himself no harm: he was blind, he had tried to exonerate his family, and he had been attacked by Lynch with a knife. Then things started to go wrong for Smith. He asked for a drink. The sub-inspector told the court how the bringing of the drink illuminated the case: 'One of the people brought it and handed it to him. He

152 NAI, CRF/1841/Woods/26.
153 Ibid., CRF/1885/McLoughlin/18.
154 The murder of 'Torney' McCrossan was still remembered in Omagh in the 1930s (Benedict Kiely, *Drink to the bird. A memoir* (London, 1992), p. 20).
155 NAI, CRF/1873/Smith/18.

said, "Thank you Tom." I said it was a curious thing, you knew this man. *He said, he knew him by his step, for when providence takes away one sense he strengthens the other senses'* (Author's italics).

The best course for a policeman who was confronted with a talkative suspect was to incite volubility by scepticism. Richard Maguire, of the DMP, confronted with Patrick Kilkenny, who was later hanged for the murder of Margaret Forker, showed how it could be done:

> He asked me if I found the girl. I said 'yes'. I told him to ask me no questions as anything he would say would appear in evidence against him. In the house we went into in Mabbot St on Saturday morning I asked him if he would take a glass of grog. He said 'yes'. I called for a glass & a half. I again asked him what was the matter. He told me I'd have the heaviest job I ever had in my life. I asked what did he do. He said he murdered Marg[are]t Forker. I said it could not be. She mightn't be dead. He said she was – he did it yesterday evening before sunset ... I asked him did any one see him. I asked him did anyone know it. He said there did not but one. I asked him who it was. He said it was Paddy Fitzpatrick.[156]

It is worth noting that these three cases (McLoughlin, Smith, and Kilkenny) occurred after *Johnston*, which had admitted as evidence replies made to police questions.

Even if the prisoner said nothing, the policeman could describe the arrest, which might add a little to the Crown's case. Sam Gray's arrest at Ballybay was almost genteel, but provocative of suspicion. Constable James King, having failed to find Gray at home, 'then went to the York Hotel, kept by his son, and found him in bed. When he asked me what was the matter, and I replied he had shot a man, and must get up. He then said, "Oh, it's all nonsense, it could not be," but I insisted he should get out of bed as he was my prisoner; I then asked for his pistols, and he said they were in Dublin, but I would not be positive to the words; when he got up and came down stairs he refused to leave the house until he got his tea; I then laid hold of him, and his wife laid hold of me but he came away shortly after.'[157]

If the prisoner were arrested in bed the gratuitously suspicious effect of an arrest might be enhanced. Constable Patrick Smith, examined by the attorney general at Charles McCormick's trial at the summer assizes in Longford in 1863, described how he searched Michael McCormick's house, where he thought Charles was hiding. The constable could not at first find Charles, but eventually he directed his attention to Michael's wife, who was still in the bed:

156 Ibid., CRF/1865/Kilkenny/10.
157 *Impartial Reporter*, 25 Mar. 1841.

I asked her had she anyone inside; she said not, but the child. I requested her to let me try, at the same time catching hold of the clothes, which she firmly grasped round her neck; I then begged her to let me try; I then saw the prisoner's head under her arm-pit, and the woman lying over him; I then told him I had him at last, and called down my men to see the position in which he was; the prisoner then got up and dressed himself in bad, torn clothes, which I think were not his own.[158]

The exchange with Mrs McCormick, whom the constable referred to as 'Mrs Mick', would have given Percy French a chorus. The discovery of McCormick in such a position was only a small part of the case against him: his identification by the murdered man's father and the discovery of the peculiar murder weapon, a bull's pizzle, were what hanged him, but his arrest added a little colour to the case.

An arrest was usually accompanied by a search not only of the prisoner but also of his surroundings.[159] After Constable Patrick Fogarty arrested Matthew Phibbs at the door of Pat Conway's pub in Riverstown, he brought him to the barracks and searched him. 'I found money on him (£17. 17s. 3¼d.) in notes, gold, silver, & copper,' he later testified. 'I found 3 razors on him, also a watch-key, which I produce. I also produce the coat he had on when arrested, a blue frock coat.'[160] Fogarty had 'previously cautioned Phibbs against criminating himself.' Constable John Russell, who arrested Daniel Ward, combined a search of the prisoner with the conversational approach, calling the prisoner by his first name: 'I arrested him in his own house on the 13 May. When I arrested him I said, "Dan, C[harles] Wilgar has been missing since Saturday evening last. As you were the last person seen in his company I now arrest you on suspicion of making away with him. You need not say anything to me unless you choose yourself least anything you do say may appear in evidence against you." ... I searched his person in the loaning after coming out of his house. I found the £1 note (produced) & half a crown, 2 single shillings, one penny, & 5 half pence. The money was in his pocket. I found a tobacco box also.'[161] The police searched Ward's house, finding a hammer, a hatchet, and a saw, which were brought to the inquest. They were not the murder weapons, but they added a nice touch to the case.

According to Hamilton Smythe, writing in 1841, when the policeman arrested the prisoner, he was supposed to take him 'with convenient speed' before a magistrate, but 'if it be late in the evening, and no justice of the peace sitting in his public capacity, it is not reasonable, unless in crimes of a heinous nature, or under very peculiar circumstances, that a justice should be called on immediately to examine into the charge, and the party may in the mean time be kept in a secure place.'[162]

158   *Irish Times*, 3 July 1863.
159   Hayes, op. cit., i, 70; Levinge, *Justice of the peace*, pp 54–5; Hennessy, op. cit., pp 29–30.
160   NAI, CRF/1861/Phibbs/5. See below, p. 208, for the part that such searches played in the Crown's case.
161   NAI, CRF/1863/Ward/5.   162   Smythe, op. cit., p. 207.

In 1842 Hayes pointed out that a warrant ought never to specify the time at which the prisoner should be brought before a justice because 'the law has already fixed the time, by requiring that the officer should carry his prisoner before the magistrate with all reasonable expedition.'[163] This had not changed much by 1890 when Molloy wrote that the policeman was to take the prisoner 'with all reasonable expedition' before a magistrate.[164] After arrest, the prisoner was in the custody of the policeman even when he brought him before the magistrate; indeed, his responsibility did not end 'till the justice either discharge or bail him, or till he be actually committed to the gaol by warrant of the justice.'[165]

When the prisoner was not taken promptly before a magistrate strange things could happen. In early November 1838 near Myshall in Co. Carlow, a farmer named Nolan, his wife, and their eldest daughter went to dig potatoes. According to Charles H. Tuckey RM, 'at midday the eldest little girl was sent home in order to have the dinner prepared, and on reaching the house she found both her grandmother Catherine Donoghue aged 90 years, and her sister barbarously murdered. The body of the child Bridget had been put on the fire and consumed with the exception of the feet and skull, and the poor old women's remains had been partially burned but not to the same extent.'[166] The remainder of the RM's report reveals the apparent simplicity of murder investigations. First, a motive was established: 'Nolan and his wife returned home. On minute search they found that the door of an inner room which had been carefully locked had been forced and a box in the apartment broken open and robbed of one pound note, a 30 shilling note and 5 shillings in silver.' Secondly, suspicion was acted on: 'The brother of Nolan lived next door and had a son (John) of bad character who was suspected of this double crime. The police promptly arrested him.' Thirdly, John Nolan's arrest produced results that were satisfying: 'as they were bringing him into the police barrack at Myshall the sub-constable observed the prisoner take a small book out of his bosom and throw it behind the door. He immediately took it up and on examination found a £1. 10s. note concealed in it which was defective in one of the corners.'

If the police had left well alone this case might have passed off without fuss. According to their own report, while Nolan was in their custody, 'the unfortunate wretch in the course of the night made a voluntary confession to the sub-constable and stated that *he alone* perpetrated the foul deed; he said he knocked the old woman and little girl down with a stick and put the latter on a large turf fire that was at the time lighting; the old woman had only been stunned but he finished her by repeated blows of a shovel and then drew her close to the fire when he forced the door of the room and lid of the box and took the money.' When Nolan was tried at Carlow spring assizes in 1839 one of the policemen gave a slightly different picture of Nolan's night in Myshall barracks:

163 Hayes, op. cit., i, 67.
165 Ibid., p. 72.
164 Molloy, op. cit., p. 68.
166 NAI, Outrage Papers/Carlow/1838.

the prisoner fell asleep by the fire in the police barracks, but slept uneasily, and talked incoherently in his sleep; that upon his awaking, witness informed him of the state he had been in, and asked him why he was so much disturbed; that the prisoner replied that it was no wonder he should be disturbed after what he had done, and that he would wish to have his clergy to unburthen his mind to before he went to Carlow; that witness told the prisoner that he could have his clergy if he wished it, but advised him not to tell witness any thing that would criminate himself, (the prisoner,) as witness would bring it all against him; that witness mentioned to him that he had heard that his (prisoner's) father had been charged by the neighbours with the murder … that the prisoner thereupon said he hoped nobody would be charged with the crime but himself, as no other person had act, part, or knowledge of it; that he (the prisoner) beat out the brains of the deceased with a shovel-handle, and then, after they were dead, threw the bodies into the fire.[167]

The prisoner's counsel objected to this statement because 'an admission made under a threat that his father would be accused of the crime of murder is not a free or voluntary admission.' A question from the judge to the policeman elicited the embarrassing fact that 'he could not positively swear whether it was before or after the caution, that witness mentioned the fact of the prisoner's father having been accused by the neighbours.' The prisoner's counsel pressed their advantage by saying they were 'instructed that the prisoner was intoxicated at the time when he made the declaration to the last witness; and, that the fact of such, the prisoner's intoxication, and also the fact that a large quantity of spirits was brought into the police barrack, and given to the prisoner while he was in charge of the constable, Boylan, can be proved by three witnesses.' The judge, Doherty, refused to let the three witnesses give evidence because the spirits were a collateral issue. On the admissibility of the confession, he decided that the fact that the father had been accused of murder was 'likely to act' on the prisoner's feelings, but said 'I do not think that upon that ground, I would be warranted in refusing to receive the confession in evidence.' Nolan was found guilty.

167 1 Cr & Dix 74, at pp 74–5. For *Nolan* and similar cases, see Henry H. Joy, *On the admissibility of confessions and challenge of jurors in criminal cases in England and Ireland* (Dublin and London, 1842), pp 5–22.

CHAPTER THREE

Committal, indictment, and arraignment

COMMITTAL

WHEN A POLICEMAN ARRESTED a suspect, he brought him before a magistrate, either an ordinary one or an RM, who had to decide whether to commit him for trial, or to release him on bail, or to discharge him. The aim of the proceedings before the magistrate was to discover if there was a *prima facie* case against the accused. A *prima facie* case had two characteristics. First, the evidence for the prosecution was to be considered on its own, regardless of what evidence the prisoner produced or what arguments were put forward on his behalf. According to Molloy, 'magistrates in the performance of this part of their duty should not balance the evidence and decide according as it preponderates, for this would in fact be taking upon themselves the functions of the petty jury.'[1] Secondly, there should be enough evidence to convince a jury of the prisoner's guilt. Again, according to Molloy, magistrates

> should ask themselves whether or not the evidence as it stands makes out a strong or probable case of guilt, in which case they will do right in committing the party to trial. If from the slender nature of the evidence they feel that the case is not sustained, and that if they committed a verdict of acquittal must be the necessary consequence, they should at once discharge the accused.

Coroners as well as magistrates could commit prisoners for trial; indeed, the coroner's inquisition could put the prisoner on trial at the assizes for murder and manslaughter without the intervention of a committing magistrate or of the grand jury.[2] The parallel activity of the coroner and the magistrate in murder and manslaughter cases and the need for swearing an information in the first place meant that witnesses frequently gave their evidence more than once. After the murder of Charlotte Hinds near Ballyconnell in October 1855, for example, her servant boy, James McKeown, told his story to a local magistrate, James Benison (of Garvarry Lodge, Ballyconnell), to the coroner at the inquest a fortnight later,

---

1 Constantine Molloy, *The justice of the peace for Ireland: a treatise on the powers and duties of magistrates in Ireland, in cases of summary jurisdiction, in the prosecution of indictable offences, and in other matters. Founded partly on Levinge's Justice of the Peace; with an appendix of statutes and notes and decisions thereon, and a catalogue of offences alphabetically arranged* (Dublin, 1890), p. 136.
2 Below, p. 107.

and to Nicholas Kelly RM and Theophilus Thompson JP, when they committed James Murphy in January 1856.[3]

There were three kinds of committal by magistrates: committals for safe custody, for re-examination, and for contumacy. The first applied to those who were to be put on trial at the assizes or quarter sessions and to those who had been accepted as approvers; the second applied to those who were remanded for re-examination, and the third to witnesses who refused to give evidence or to be bound over to prosecute.[4] A single magistrate could act alone at committal proceedings, although the Criminal Law (Ireland) Act 1828 put an ostensibly inconsistent limit on his power: he could commit prisoners for trial, or he could discharge them, but he could not admit them to bail until another justice had heard the evidence: 'if there shall be only one justice present, and the whole evidence given before him shall be such as neither to raise a strong presumption of guilt, nor to warrant the dismissal of the charge, such justice shall order the person charged to be detained in custody, and such person shall be taken before two justices at the least.'[5] The Indictable Offences (Ireland) Act 1849 and the Petty Sessions (Ireland) Act 1851 used the word 'justice' in the singular, which ended the strange arrangement of 1828.[6] One magistrate might be enough, but more than one might be present. Even before John Holden was brought back to Dungannon after his arrest, for example, the local magistrates, the RM from Omagh, the coroner, and the county inspector had gathered to deal with him.[7] Witnesses might be examined by the magistrates who attended the petty sessions. In the case of the murder of Owen Rice near Clontibret in 1851, the case against the accused was heard by the full bench of magistrates at Monaghan.[8]

The magistrate's examination of witnesses had to be made subject to the laws of evidence. Nun and Walsh, for example, explained the rules on the admissibility of confessions and dying declarations,[9] and the Petty Sessions (Ireland) Act 1851

3   NAI, CRF/1856/Dunn/26.
4   Edmund Hayes, *Crimes and punishments, or a digest of the criminal statute law of Ireland, alphabetically arranged, with ample notes, in which are discussed the powers and authorities of the several courts of criminal jurisdiction in Ireland; the duties, responsibilities, and privileges of magistrates, coroners, constables, and other officers, in bringing criminals to justice, and also the practice of the courts in punishing offences upon indictment*, 2 vols (2nd ed., Dublin, 1842), i, 161.
5   9 Geo. IV, c. 54, s. 1 (15 July 1828).
6   12 & 13 Vict., c. 69, s. 17 (28 July 1849); 14 & 15 Vict., c. 93, s. 14 (7 Aug. 1851), but see James O'Connor, *The Irish justice of the peace: a treatise on the powers and duties of justices of the peace in Ireland, and certain matters connected therewith* (Dublin, 1911), p. 13 where he wrote that 'any one justice may conduct the inquiry' but he also referred to 9 Geo. 4, c. 54, s. 1, and concluded that 'in doubtful cases of felony one justice alone should not act'.
7   Larcom Papers (NLI, MS 7620 [*Evening Mail*, 7 Dec. 1859]).
8   NAI, Outrage Papers/1851/Monaghan/156.
9   Richard Nun & John Edward Walsh, *The powers and duties of justices of the peace in Ireland, and of constables as connected therewith; with an appendix and statutes and forms* (Dublin, 1841), pp 348–55. According to James Fitzjames Stephen committal proceedings were 'subject to all the rules of evidence' ('The characteristics of English criminal law' in *Cambridge essays, contributed by members of the university, 1857* (London, [1857]), 39).

referred to admissions, confessions, and statements 'which would be admissible by law as evidence.'[10] The police, in making their investigations, may have relied on gossip, the suspect's bad character, and on hearsay, but in the end their case against the prisoner had to depend on evidence that would be admissible in court, and that generally excluded gossip, the prisoner's bad character, and hearsay. The proceedings before the magistrate 'may be either public or private: but it may be observed, that all proceedings must be in the presence and hearing of the accused.'[11] The Petty Sessions (Ireland) Act 1851 seems to have left the magistrate his power to exclude the public in certain circumstances, stating that 'the place in which any justice or justices shall sit to take any examination or statement relating to any such offences shall not be deemed an open court for that purpose.'[12] The prisoner's right to be legally represented was not clearly established, 'this being only a preliminary investigation, all professional assistants may be excluded, if the magistrate think right.'[13] In practice those who could afford to be represented could employ either solicitors or barristers.

The constabulary managed the prosecution, although the crown solicitor or sessional crown solicitor might appear in very exceptional cases, such as that of the scandalous death of Amelia Carey in Ballymena.[14] In some cases the Crown might be represented by a local solicitor. At the committal of Patrick McPhillips in January 1888 at Clones, 'Mr Bailey, of Castleblayney, prosecuted for the Crown, and Mr Knight, of Clones, appeared for the defence.'[15] As late as 1884, at a time when crown solicitors were beginning to appear at committal proceedings, the attorney general told the select committee on public prosecutors that 'in the ordinary run of cases ... the police or the constabulary conduct the prosecution in the first instance before the magistrates.'[16] It might, however, be more accurate to say that in many cases, the 'constabulary' included the RM, even if he apparently acted in a judicial capacity. There was no doubt, for example, of the vigorous ubiquity of Charles Hunt RM in organizing the case against Daniel Ward.[17] When policemen had to give evidence, the constabulary's *Standing Rules* laid down that they 'should give their testimony in a manly straight-forward manner without caring, or appearing to care, about the effects of it.'[18]

10   14 & 15 Vict., c. 93, s. 14(2) (7 Aug. 1851).   11   Hayes, op. cit., i, 250.

12   14 & 15 Vict., c. 93, s. 9(2) (7 Aug. 1851). See also 12 & 13 Vict., c. 69, s. 19 (28 July 1849), which had stated the same thing.

13   Hayes, op. cit., i, 250. Even in the early twentieth century the accused's right to be represented before the magistrates was not unquestioned (Courtney Stanhope Kenny, *A selection of cases illustrative of English criminal law* (Cambridge, 1901), p. 446). But see John G. Thompson, *The law of criminal procedure in Ireland* (Dublin, 1899), p. 34 where it is stated that the justice may exclude anyone, 'the counsel or solicitor of any prisoner only excepted'.

14   NAI, RP/1863/10,102.   15   *Impartial Reporter*, 17 Jan. 1888.

16   *Report of the committee appointed to inquire into the office of public prosecutor with minutes of evidence and appendix*, p. 31 [C 4016], HC 1884, xxiii, 309.

17   NAI, CRF/1863/Ward/5.

18   Henry John Brownrigg, *Standing rules and regulations for the government and guidance of the*

The magistrate himself was supposed to be the moving force at the actual committal proceedings. The Petty Sessions (Ireland) Act 1851, for example, actually stated that the justice shall take the depositions.[19] At the very least everything was supposed to be done in his immediate presence, even if it were his clerk who actually kept things moving. When James O'Shaughnessy, a magistrate of the city of Limerick, took a deposition from John Hickie in a room in Barrington's Hospital, the clerk of the petty sessions, E.M. Beauchamp, seemed to do everything, but this was perfectly in order because Beauchamp 'swore and examined Hickie in the presence of the magistrate; wrote out the information in the magistrate's presence; and wrote out the cross-examination of the prisoners in his presence also.'[20] O'Shaughnessy may have been a passive spectator, but 'he was present, and within hearing of everything that was said, and within sight of everything that was done, throughout the whole transaction.' The examination of Hickie gives a vignette of the actual examination of a witness before a magistrate; Beauchamp is describing what happened:

Hickie was then in bed. The information was written out by me. Mr O'Shaughnessy, the head constable, the three prisoners, and some others, were present in the room the entire time that I was writing the information. I had gone into the room with Mr O'Shaughnessy and the three prisoners, up to the bed where Hickie was. I then swore Hickie, in the presence of and before Mr O'Shaughnessy, that the evidence he would give before the magistrates in the charge he had against the prisoners should be the truth, the whole truth, and nothing but the truth, but I did not mention what the charge was. I then asked Hickie certain questions, and I took down his answers truly, and read over each answer to him after I had taken it down, as I went on. I did that with all the questions that I put, and the answers, and, when I had taken down the whole of his answers to my questions, I read the whole over to him truly; and I told the three prisoners that they were at liberty to cross-examine him, and ask him any questions they liked … The prisoners, M. Farrell and Thomas Galvin sen. then cross-examined Hickie, and I took down truly the answers he gave to their questions, and I read them truly for Hickie, in the presence and hearing of the prisoner; and when those answers were taken down, I then read over truly the entire information again for Hickie, in the presence and hearing of the prisoners. After that was done, I put the paper before Hickie, and gave him a pen: he held the pen, with which I put his mark while he held it; he then acknowledged it to be his mark.[21]

---

constabulary force in Ireland; revised edition, as approved by his excellency the lord lieutenant (Dublin, 1860), p. 278.

19   14 & 15 Vict., c. 93, s. 14(1) (7 Aug. 1851). See also 12 & 13 Vict., c. 69, s. 17 (28 July 1849).
20   *Galvin* (1865) 16 ICLR 452, at p. 461.   21   Ibid., p. 454.

The procedure at committal proceedings under the 1828 act, as described by Hayes, seems to have put a new emphasis on writing: what the witnesses said had to be taken down in writing 'in a plain and intelligible manner, and as nearly as possible in the language in which the first narrative was delivered'; all that was necessary to prove the offence ought to be noted 'in order that the witnesses may be thereby tied down to their narrative, and not left open to subsequent influence'; the deposition should ideally be 'taken in the first person'.[22] This concern with writing everything down was not merely to capture evidence at a time when it was still clear in the witness' memories, but it also provided for the perpetuation of their testimony if they died or were otherwise unavoidably absent from the trial at the assizes or quarter sessions.[23]

The prisoner was not expected to be a mere passive spectator at his committal. He was entitled to cross-examine witnesses. His cross-examination was important not only because it might elicit something useful, but also because 'the depositions cannot be read on the trial where the witness has died since the examination, unless the depositions in cross-examination have been correctly taken.'[24] When the prosecution witnesses had given their evidence, 'the prisoner should then be called on for his defence. If he wish to bring forward witnesses the magistrate will consider of the propriety of allowing it, as in cases of felony he need not do so unless he think it conducive to the ends of justice.'[25] If there was 'even a slight case of suspicion' against the prisoner, the magistrate was supposed to ask him if he had anything to say, and 'to caution him before he commences his statement, that anything which he says will be reduced to writing and may afterwards be made use of against him upon his trial; and that he ought not to expect any favour, though he should confess himself guilty of the crime charged.'[26] If the prisoner spoke, 'he ought not to be pressed to answer questions like a witness; but should be left at liberty to speak or be silent', nor was he to be sworn because a statement on oath was not voluntary and therefore not admissible at the trial.[27] The prisoner's statement was to be written down, read over to him, and he was to be asked if it was correct, and to sign it, if it was correct; if he refused to sign, it could not be read out at the trial, but it could be used at the trial 'as a document to refresh the memory of the magistrate, or his clerk'.[28]

Neither the short-lived Indictable Offences (Ireland) Act 1849[29] nor the Petty Sessions (Ireland) Act 1851[30] made great changes in how committal proceedings were conducted, apart from the fact that they sealed up irrevocably any loophole that allowed justices to question prisoners. Hayes had warned in 1842 that

---

22   Hayes, op. cit., i, 251–2.
23   In *Galvin* (1865) 16 ICLR 452, at pp 474–5 Baron Fitzgerald gave a history of the perpetuation of dead deponents' evidence, starting with 10 Car., sess. 2, c. 18 and ending with the Petty Sessions (Ireland) Act, 1851.
24   Hayes, op. cit., i, 253.   25   Ibid., p. 254.   26   Ibid.   27   Ibid., p. 255.
28   Ibid., p. 256.   29   12 & 13 Vict., c. 69 (28 July 1849).
30   14 & 15 Vict., c. 93 (7 Aug. 1851).

prisoners should not be questioned like witnesses, but he had admitted it was 'no objection to the statement of a prisoner, that it has been elicited by questions put by a magistrate.'[31] In 1849 Purcell had written that 'it was formerly held that a prisoner ought not to be questioned by a magistrate; but it is now settled that it is no objection to the admissibility of an examination that it was by way of question and answer, if it appears to be free from any other objection.'[32] The case Purcell cited in support of questioning was *Glennon, Toole, and Magrath.*[33] When Thomas Glennon and John Toole were tried at Westmeath spring assizes in 1840 for the murder of Patrick Branagan their counsel had objected to the reception of statements they had made to the magistrate who committed them because they had been 'elicited by interrogatories'. They referred to the English case, *Wilson*, which was venerable by this time, and in which the English chief baron had stated that 'an examination of itself imposes an obligation to speak the truth. If a prisoner will confess, let him do so voluntarily. Ask him what he has to say? But it is irregular in a magistrate to examine a prisoner in the same manner as a witness is examined.'[34] In spite of this, Chief Justice Doherty decided that while questioning by policemen and others was not permitted, 'in this case it was the duty of the witness and the other gentlemen before whom the statements were made, as magistrates, to ask certain questions of the persons brought before them; and I do not see how an examination could be carried on, or a committal take place, without some sort of interrogation.'[35]

In spite of the tendency noted by Hayes in 1842 and Purcell in 1849, and of Doherty in *Glennon*, the acts of 1849 and 1851 established that the only question the magistrates could now ask a prisoner was whether he wished to say anything. The act of 1849 actually prescribed the words of the question: 'Having heard the evidence, do you wish to say anything in answer to the charge? You are not obliged to say anything unless you desire to do so, but whatever you say will be taken down in writing, and may be given in evidence against you upon your trial.'[36] The 1851 act described the procedure in detail but did not repeat the words of the question used in 1849 act: 'the justice or one of the justices present shall … read or cause to be read to the person accused the several depositions, and then take down in writing the statement of such person (having first cautioned him that he

---

31   Hayes, op. cit., i, 255.
32   Theobald A. Purcell, *A summary of the general principles of pleading and evidence, in criminal cases in Ireland: with the rules of practice incident thereto* (Dublin, 1849), p. 311.
33   (1840) 1 Cr & Dix 359.
34   (1817) Holt 597, at pp 597–8; 17 Eng Rep 353, at p. 353. In the 1820s and 1830s some English judges questioned *Wilson* and upheld the right of magistrates to examine prisoners; in England Jervis' act in 1848 tipped the balance back again and 'the only question the magistrate was to be permitted to ask [the prisoner] was whether he wished to make a statement or to call any witness' (David Bentley, *English criminal justice in the nineteenth century* (London and Rio Grande, 1998), pp 29–31).
35   1 Cr & Dix, 359, at pp 362–3; for more details see NAI, CRF/1840/Glennon/4.
36   12 & 13 Vict., c. 69, s. 18.

is not obliged to say anything unless he desires to do so, but that whatever he does say will be taken down in writing, and may be given in evidence against him on his trial.'[37] In *Johnston*, James O'Brien stated that 'these enactments show that the intention of the legislature was to give the prisoner an opportunity of making any statement he desired; but not to allow the magistrates to interrogate him, save by asking him, in general terms, if he desired to say anything in answer to the charge.'[38] If the prisoner decided to speak, Levinge warned that the magistrate 'ought not to press [him] with questions as to any matters bearing upon the charge upon which he is brought before them.'[39] If the prisoner was asked a question before he was cautioned by the magistrate, his answer was 'not admissible against him on his trial'.[40] A nice distinction was made at this point because, if the prisoner said anything *without* being questioned, but *before* he was cautioned, what he said 'is admissible in evidence, although no caution has been given by the magistrate; such observation, therefore, if material, should be taken down in the depositions.'[41] O'Connor, writing in 1911 said the same things: 'if the accused voluntarily interposes a statement during the hearing, it should be taken down, and, if so taken down, is admissible in evidence at the trial; but, if not so taken down, it is not admissible … A statement made by the accused in answer to a question put to him by a justice, without previous caution, is not admissible.'[42] Both Levinge and O'Connor based their rule on three English cases, which had prevailed since the 1850s.[43] There was a lot to be said, therefore, for keeping quiet, which is what most prisoners did.

The standard of proof at committal proceedings was higher than that required for a warrant, which was 'probable cause' for suspecting that the accused had committed the crime.[44] According to the Criminal Law (Ireland) Act 1828, those arrested on charges of felony were not to be committed unless 'the charge shall be supported by positive and credible evidence of the fact, or by such evidence as if not explained or contradicted shall, in the opinion of the justice or justices, raise a strong presumption of the guilt of the person charged.'[45] The Petty Sessions (Ireland) Act 1851 laid down that 'if in the opinion of such justice or justices such evidence is sufficient to put such person on his trial, or if such evidence raises a

---

37   14 & 15 Vict., c. 93, s. 14(2). See also Edward Parkyns Levinge, *The justice of the peace for Ireland; comprising the practice in indictable offences, and the proceedings preliminary and subsequent to convictions; with an appendix of the most useful statutes, and an alphabetical catalogue of offences* (2nd ed., Dublin, 1862), p. 86.

38   (1864) 15 ICLR 60, at p. 89.

39   Levinge, *The justice's manual, containing the justices' protection act, 1851, the summary jurisdiction act, 1851, the petty sessions act, 1851, and the law of evidence amendment act; with notes, comments, and copious index* (Dublin, 1853), p. 144.

40   Levinge, *Justice of the peace*, p. 86.   41   Ibid., p. 87.

42   O'Connor, op. cit., p. 23.

43   *Weller* (1846) 2 Car & K 223, 175 Eng Rep 93; *Stripp* (1856) Dears 648, 169 Eng Rep 882; *Pettit* (1850) 4 Cox CC 164.

44   Above, p. 61.   45   9 Geo. IV, c. 54, s. 1 (15 July 1828).

strong or probable presumption of guilt, then such justice or justices shall either by warrant ... commit him to gaol, to be there kept until his trial for the said offence, or shall admit him to bail.'[46] The 1851 definition persisted for the rest of the period. In 1890, for example, Constantine Molloy wrote that 'the justice is clearly bound, in the exercise of a sound discretion, not to commit anyone unless a *prima facie* case is made out against him by witnesses entitled to a reasonable degree of credit.'[47] In 1899 Thompson wrote of 'a strong or probable presumption of guilt', which is probably as good a guide as any.[48] In the ten years 1866–75, only 244 of the 372 committed to stand trial for murder were returned for trial, which suggests that in 128 cases, or 34% of cases, the magistrates had opted for a presumption that was probable rather than strong.[49] This picture of magisterial prodigality, however, is altered by the fact that it is arguable that many of the 128, possibly as many as 99, who were not put on trial for murder, were put on trial for manslaughter or some lesser offence.[50]

The accused's right to call his own witnesses was not clearly established even by the early years of the twentieth century. The act of 1828 did not 'require any such justice or justices to hear evidence on behalf of any person so charged ... unless it shall appear to such justice or justices to be meet and conducive to the ends of justice to hear the same.'[51] Hayes agreed that the magistrate did not need to examine the prisoner's witnesses 'unless he think it conducive to the ends of justice.'[52] There was no mention of such a right in the Irish Petty Sessions (Ireland) Act 1851, which mentioned prosecution witnesses but not the prisoner's.[53] Many benches of magistrates in England refused to hear the prisoner's witnesses, if a *prima facie* case had been made by the Crown.[54] Greaves' report on criminal procedure in 1856, however, deplored such exclusion as 'an error'.[55] Levinge followed Greaves and advised Irish magistrates to examine the prisoner's witnesses, quoting Lord Denman at the Somerset spring assizes in 1849 when he advised magistrates to examine the accused's witnesses 'if they are in attendance at the time of the examination.'[56] As late as 1911 James O'Connor

---

46   14 & 15 Vict., c. 93, s. 15(1) (7 Aug. 1851).   47   Molloy, op. cit., pp 135–6.

48   Thompson, op. cit., p. 35.   49   Below, p. 93.

50   Below, pp 279–80.   51   9 Geo. IV, c. 54, s. 1 (15 July 1828).

52   Hayes, op. cit., i, 254.   53   See 14 & 15 Vict., c. 93, s. 14(2) (7 Aug. 1851).

54   Stephen, *A general view of the criminal law of England* (London and Cambridge, 1863), p. 175.

55   *A report on criminal procedure to the lord chancellor; by Charles Sprengal Greaves, Esq., one of her majesty's counsel*, pp 10–12 [456], HC 1856, l, 88–90. Greaves gave four reasons for hearing the prisoner's witnesses: (1) 'it is difficult to imagine a greater act of injustice' than their exclusion; (2) 'the prosecutor may before the trial investigate the accuracy of their statements, and be prepared at the trial with evidence to contradict them, if false'; (3) their exclusion was inconsistent because justices had to note any evidence in the prisoner's favour 'elicited from the witnesses for the prosecution on their cross-examination'; (4) 'the present system also affords prisoners every facility for fabricating whatever defence may seem at the last moment best calculated to serve their purposes.'

56   Levinge, *Justice of the peace*, p. 87. For similar advice see Molloy, op. cit., p. 133. In 1867 Russell Gurney's act (30 & 31 Vict., c. 35, s. 3 (20 June 1867)) obliged magistrates to 'take the statement

went no further than his mid-nineteenth-century predecessors: 'there is no absolute obligation on the justices to take the depositions of any witness whom the accused may tender', and he followed Levinge by repeating Lord Denman's advice, that 'in all cases in which prisoners charged with felony have witnesses and those witnesses are in attendance at the time of the examination before the magistrate, I should recommend that the magistrate should hear the evidence of such witnesses as the prisoner, on being asked, wishes to be examined in his defence ... and the depositions of the prisoner's witnesses, being taken and signed by them, should be transmitted together with the depositions in support of the charge.'[57]

Magistrates could remand prisoners until more evidence was obtained, 'but the time for which a prisoner may be remanded in custody must be always a reasonable time, to be determined by the circumstances of each particular case.'[58] Hayes mentioned three or four days, and the Petty Sessions Act 1851 fixed a limit of 'eight clear days' between appearances, which had also been the period prescribed by the Indictable Offences (Ireland) Act 1849.[59] A sworn statement by a policeman might be enough to enable a magistrate to remand a prisoner for successive eight-day periods. On 23 May 1883, Sub-Inspector William Hamilton applied for the remand of Patrick William Nally, who had been arrested on 15 May. Hamilton's statement was mere assertion:

> I have charge of a case in which all the above named defendants are charged with conspiracy to murder. I am at present engaged in inquiring into the facts of it, and procuring additional evidence against the accused. I believe that if a remand be granted I shall be able to procure important additional evidence, and I now apply for a further remand of eight days. That application is made *bona fide* and not for the purpose of delay, and I further believe that it would be in the interest of public justice that it should be granted.[60]

Nally was eventually convicted, and died in Mountjoy.[61] The power to remand was important in producing a case. Alexander Sullivan noted that it was only when John Twiss was remanded that the 'whispering' began: the murdered man's son identified Twiss, and a witness appeared with a story 'about statements under hallucination'.[62]

on oath or affirmation, both examination and cross-examination, of those who shall be so called as witnesses by such accused person', but it did not apply to Ireland. According to Bentley, Gurney's act made 'it possible for the first time for the evidence of defence witnesses who had died or were ill to be read at the trial' (Bentley, op. cit., p. 220).

57 O'Connor, op. cit., pp 23–4.   58 Hayes, op. cit., i, 257.
59 14 & 15 Vict., c. 93, s. 14 (7 Aug. 1851); 12 & 13 Vict., c. 69, s. 21 (28 July 1849).
60 NAI, NA Miscellaneous 999/2.
61 T.W. Moody, *Davitt and Irish revolution 1846–82* (Oxford, 1981), p. 285. See also Carey, *Mountjoy* (Cork, 2000), pp 170–1.
62 A.M. Sullivan, *The last serjeant*, p. 88.

The attendance of the prisoner at his trial was secured either by sending him to gaol or by releasing him on bail. Even in murder cases, bail was often granted, certainly in the 1830s and 1840s. In 1841, for example, John and James Power were admitted to bail, and being 'conscious of their innocence' of John Peters' murder, presented themselves for trial at the Clonmel summer assizes, where they were found guilty.[63] They were hanged on 4 September 1841. The attendance of the witnesses at trials was also secured by making them enter into recognizances, or by committing them to gaol. (A recognizance was a 'record, testifying that the recognizor owes a certain sum of money to the Queen, and conditioned for the performance of some particular act.')[64] Equally important was the police's ability to keep witnesses out of harm's way, either by committing them, or by keeping them in a special government guest-house. Frank Thorpe Porter referred to two houses in Ship Street, Dublin, where crown witnesses were lodged. The lodgers seem to have passed the time in self-improvement. According to Porter, 'the crown witnesses were accustomed to have their evidence rehearsed before an amateur judge, an improvised jury, and a couple of supposed counsel, one to prosecute and the other to defend. If a case failed, the witnesses were instructed as to their deficiencies, either in manner or matter; and they were drilled to avoid admissions of any nature calculated to weaken their testimony.' Having discovered this centre of excellence, Porter 'made such representations to the executive as produced the suppression of the Ship Street establishment.'[65] Later there was a similar establishment at Ballybough, which was succeeded by one at Kingscourt House.[66]

Many newspaper reports of committal proceedings were terse to the point of obscurity. Much was left unexplained, for example, in the *Newry Telegraph*'s report of the proceedings at Cabra Castle, near Kingscourt, Co. Cavan, 'relative to the mysterious murder of Mary Daley'. The magistrates who heard the evidence were a local JP (who seems to have been Joseph Armstrong, of Woodfort, Kingscourt) and the RM from Virginia, James Little. There was no mention of witnesses or of the circumstances of Mary Daley's death. The report ended blandly: 'from the result of the inquiry we have reason to believe that the report accusing a person of high rank and character were entirely removed, and probed [*sic*] to be without the slightest foundation.' The mention of a person of high rank and character suggested Lt. Col. Joseph Pratt, who lived at Cabra Castle and who owned nearly 30,000 acres in the counties of Cavan, Meath, and Mayo. The report referred to Colonel Pratt, but made the mystery more obscure in doing so: 'Colonel Pratt JP, although present, took no part as a magistrate in the investigation, but gave the other justices every possible assistance in procuring witnesses, to throw any light on this mysterious case, in which he made most laudable exertions.'[67]

63   NAI, CRF/1841/Power/13.   64   Hayes, op. cit., ii, 746.

65   *Gleanings and reminiscences* (Dublin, 1876), pp 197–8.

66   For use of the Ballybough establishment in 1882 see Jarlath Waldron, *Maamtrasna: the murders and the mystery* (Dublin, 1992), pp 158–9.

67   *Impartial Reporter*, 22 Apr. 1841. See also Larcom Papers (NLI, MS 7620 [*Express*, 4 Feb. 1860]).

The reasons for such obscurity may have been the fact that reports of *ex parte* proceedings were not privileged. It might be better to say, they were apparently not privileged because in *R. v. Gray* in 1865, when the fenian John O'Leary applied for a criminal information against Sir John Gray, the owner of the *Freeman's Journal*, Lord Chief Justice Lefroy was certain that proceedings before magistrates 'or any other similar tribunal' should be published:

> it is for the interest of the public that proceedings of this description should be published fully and at the same time fairly and correctly, for otherwise it would virtually amount to an investigation with closed doors, in which injury might result to the prisoner either from undue influence or some other cause. Now it is of the utmost importance for the public to know that the magistrates do their duty impartially and without influence of any sort, and that they exercised their duty fairly and correctly according to the evidence brought before them – not only to prevent them from making unfair orders against the prisoners, but also to prevent them from undue influence which might be ascribed to them as officers appointed by the Crown.[68]

In this account of committal proceedings and the earlier account of arrests and warrants, it will have become clear that those who investigated murder did so under certain disadvantages. First, the police were not allowed to question the prisoner either at his arrest, or before the magistrate, or during his imprisonment as he waited for trial. Secondly, for most of the period magistrates were not allowed to question the prisoner when he was brought before them for committal. Thirdly, the magistrate's examination of witnesses at committal proceedings, and apparently the coroner's examination at inquests, had to be made subject to the laws of evidence. Fourthly, magistrates, coroners, police, and witnesses usually acted in public, although the public's right to be present was not absolute. The prisoner's right to be legally represented at inquests and committal proceedings was not clearly established, but in practice those who could afford to be represented could employ either solicitors or barristers. The magistrates, coroners, and police were, moreover, legally accountable for what they did and said, unlike judges, jurors, and counsel at the assizes. Cases of police being sued for unlawful arrest are not hard to find.[69] A JP or RM could be sued in the ordinary way or prosecuted by means of a criminal information, filed in the Court of Queen's Bench, for 'criminally neglecting to act on any given occasion, as for misconducting himself in his office; and the party grieved may also apply to put him out of his commission.'[70] It was probably a comfort to some JPs to know that

68   10 Cox CC 184, at p. 189. See also Bentley, op. cit., p. 48 where it is stated that this matter was not resolved in England until 1878.

69   Vaughan, *Sin, sheep and Scotsmen* (Belfast, 1983), p. 20.

70   Levinge, *Justice of the peace*, p. 17. When D.B. Franks, RM, was sued as result of his conduct of a murder investigation, the solicitor general, John David Fitzgerald, appeared for the plaintiff,

'a mere display of ill-humour, or an error of judgment, will not induce the court to interfere.' Prosecutions, nevertheless, did take place. In 1863 the Ballymena physician, Dr Thomas Courtenay, applied for a criminal information in the Queen's Bench against Charles Hunt RM 'for having in his capacity of justice of the peace for the county of Antrim' investigated Courtenay's part in the death of Amelia Carey.[71] Hunt had suspected Courtenay of killing Amelia Carey while carrying out an abortion.

MANAGING DEPOSITIONS

The word 'information' tended to be used indiscriminately to describe all sworn statements made before magistrates and coroners but there was in fact a difference between 'depositions' and 'informations': 'the term "information" is applied to the statement grounding the charge, taken in the absence of the accused; the term "deposition" means each written and sworn statement taken at the inquiry in the presence of the accused.'[72] The typical information or deposition appeared to be a bit more than the gist of the witness' statement but less than a verbatim account of what was said, unless Irish witnesses were uncharacteristically laconic. The finished product looked like a précis, with a bit of ornamentation. In practice it is unlikely that depositions were a first, fine, careless rapture. A bitter struggle between a farmer called Dixon and D.B. Franks RM exposed the kind of manoeuvrings that sometimes created depositions, certainly when such statements started their existence as informations made in the absence of the prisoner.[73] Dixon, who had been a physician in Norwich, had taken a farm in 1848 in the Queen's County on the estate of the Revd William Lawrenson, the incumbent of Howth and a canon of St Patrick's cathedral, Dublin. When a row broke out between Dixon and a subtenant, Thomas Brophy, Dixon served Brophy with a notice to quit. At this point any observer of rural Ireland, whose knowledge was gleaned from *The Nation*, would have expected Brophy to have shot Dixon. In the event it was Dixon who tried to shoot Brophy, an event that even connoisseurs of the idiocy of rural life must have found improbable. Franks investigated the affair, arrested Dixon and his wife, and took their six-year-old son, Frank, into custody as a witness.

When Dixon sued Franks for the illegal imprisonment of his son and when that case was followed by an action for slander, Franks described in court how it took three meetings to produce young Frank Dixon's information: a preliminary interview on the evening of 20 February 1853, which seems to have gone over the boy's story at least twice; a second interview the next morning, which tried to

---

which did not suggest much official solidarity (Larcom Papers (NLI, MS 7576 [*Clare Freeman*, 5 Jan. 1856])).

71   NAI, RP/1863/10,102.   72   O'Connor, op. cit., p. 21 n3.
73   Larcom Papers (NLI, MS 7576 [*Clare Freeman*, 5 Jan. 1856]).

resolve contradictions in the boy's story by referring to the evidence of another witness; the final swearing of the information four days later, after Franks had consulted the attorney general, Abraham Brewster.[74] A sub-inspector of constabulary and the petty sessions clerk were present at the first two interviews. Although Franks did not swear the boy until the third interview, at the first session he had 'put some questions to him to ascertain whether he was conscious of a future state.'

Frank Dixon's information was not spontaneous, but it was a model of spontaneity compared with the Revd William Lawrenson's. Franks went to Howth to dine with Lawrenson. Before dinner they discussed the case and Franks used his notes to refresh Lawrenson's memory, which produced a flood of recrimination. According to Lawrenson, for example, Dixon 'was always either carousing in his own house with blackguards, or drinking with dubious characters in the Durrow, named Ford and Fletcher'. After dinner the two men settled down to compose the information. Lawrenson spoke and Franks wrote as Lawrenson spoke. 'I put in Brophy's rent (5*s.* per annum) at his request,' he recalled. 'It had been previously omitted as he said it would show for how small a sum Dixon would take away a man's life.' Two drafts were discarded. When the third was complete, Franks read it over, and Lawrenson, 'having sent his son for a Testament was sworn'. A comfortable gossip before dinner, two discarded drafts after dinner, and details put in for effect do not suggest spontaneity.

The Prisoners' Counsel Act 1836 gave prisoners the right to copies of the depositions made at their committal.[75] The commonsense implication of this was that the act intended to confer a benefit on prisoners and that benefit was the right to know the case against them before they were tried. The act gave rise to a number of questions. Were prisoners entitled to copies of statements made after their committal? Were they entitled to copies of statements made on their behalf at the committal proceedings, or even to copies of anything they had themselves said? Was the prosecution bound to produce all its witnesses at the committal proceedings? The judges' answers to these questions gave prisoners something that was much less than the right to know the full case against them. As soon as the act was passed, the English and Irish judges decided that prisoners had no right to statements made after their committal.[76] In *R. v. Connor*, an English case, Patteson decided that the act 'does not empower a judge to order the prosecutor to furnish the prisoner with all the evidence.'[77] There is no doubt that Patteson

---

74   For the difference between an information and a deposition see above, p. 80.

75   6 & 7 Will. IV, c. 114, s. 3 (20 Aug. 1836).

76   David J.A. Cairns, *Advocacy and the making of the adversarial criminal trial 1800–1865* (Oxford, 1998), p. 117; Hayes, op. cit., ii, 864.

77   (1845) 1 Cox CC 233, at p. 233. A slightly different question was the assumption that the Crown was obliged to pass on to the prisoner any information that might be valuable to him, which is the fourth item in Bentley's list of things that are necessary for a fair trial (Bentley, op. cit., p. xiv). In the case of Archibald Slye, a Protestant accused of murdering a priest and apparently

followed faithfully the very words of the act, which had quite explicitly referred to depositions made when the prisoner was committed. The words actually used in section 3 were 'copies of the examinations of the witnesses respectively upon whose depositions they have been held to bail or committed to prison.' In *R. v. Glennon, Toole, and Magrath*, an Irish case, Chief Justice Doherty decided that prisoners had no right to inspect or to take copies of their own statements made at their committal.[78] Again, Doherty followed the actual words of the act, which had not mentioned such statements. Parliament did not overrule the judges. Neither the Indictable Offences Act of 1849 nor the Petty Sessions Act of 1851 gave Irish prisoners the right to have copies of post-committal statements.[79]

Some lawyers had been prepared to contend, even before the act was passed, that evidence should not be taken against a prisoner in his absence. During the debates on the bill in the house of lords in 1836, for example, Lord Abinger protested against prisoners being allowed to have copies of depositions made after their committal: 'If, after committal, fresh proof should be adduced, who ever heard of the magistrate's clerk being compelled to send to the prisoner copies of any depositions that be sworn against him in his absence?' The lord chancellor, Henry Brougham, pounced on this commendation of magisterial zeal: 'It was no part of the duty of a magistrate to assist in getting up a prosecution. His duty was merely, upon *prima facie* evidence, to secure a prisoner's person against the day of trial ... That question once decided his jurisdiction ceases.' The duke of Richmond, who had probably in his time committed the occasional felon in the vicinity of Goodwood, expressed what was probably the plain man's view of the British constitution: 'What! Evidence taken against a man in his absence! He ... had never heard of such a thing! It was contrary to any principle of British law ... Taking depositions against a prisoner in his absence was more fitted for the meridian of Spain than to that of this free country.'[80]

Keeping back witnesses was actually commended by the former attorney general, Joseph Napier, when he told a select committee in 1854 that it 'requires a great deal of watching not to take down too many depositions, but only to take

the victim of a conspiracy, the crown solicitor of the home circuit, Piers Geale, made apparently contradictory statements about revealing such information. To the question, 'Did you communicate to the counsel for the prisoner, or the prisoner himself, or any body on his part, any suspicion that you might have of those witnesses?', he answered, 'Certainly not.' On the other hand, he later said, 'Every circumstance that can affect the prosecution I invariably communicate to the leading counsel ... I have known instances where we have discovered points favourable to the prisoner, and I have handed them over to the counsel for the prisoner' (*Report from the select committee of the house of lords, appointed to enquire into the state of Ireland in respect of crime, and to report thereon to the house; with the minutes of evidence taken before the committee, and an appendix and index*, pt II, evidence 27 May to 11 June, pp 678, 680, HC 1839 (486–II), xi, 684, 686).

78   (1840) 1 Cr & Dix 359, at p. 361; Bentley, op. cit., p. 37.

79   12 & 13 Vict., c. 69, s. 27 (28 July 1849); 14 & 15 Vict., c. 93, s. 14 (7 Aug. 1851).

80   *Hansard 3*, xxxv, 229–32 (15 July 1836).

so much as to start the case, as I may say.'[81] Bentley has a reference to an Irish case where the prisoners were refused even the names of the new witnesses.[82] Holding back witnesses had its risks. If they died before the trial, the written version of their evidence was not admissible if they had not been examined in the prisoner's presence.[83] The extent to which committing magistrates might go in keeping prisoners in the dark was demonstrated at the spring assizes at Nenagh in 1846 in *R. v. Rice and Hayes* where it appeared that

> The magistrate who took the examination had previously taken infor-
> mations, charging the prisoners with the offence for which they were tried.
> These informations were not taken in the presence of the prisoners, nor
> read over to them, neither were the prisoners apprized of their contents, or
> of the names of the persons by whom they had been sworn; but the prisoner
> Hayes was told by the magistrate that informations had been sworn
> charging him with being a party to a conspiracy to murder the late Mr
> Clarke, and he was then asked, with the usual form of caution, whether he
> wished to say any thing before he should be committed on the charge.[84]

In spite of this caution, the magistrate's question acted as an invitation rather than a warning:

> The prisoner thereupon proceeded to give an account (in detail) of the
> places where he had been, and the persons whom he had met or seen on the
> day of the murder; and this statement was so directly at variance with all the
> testimony given on the trial, that when read in evidence, it was felt to be
> conclusive of the prisoner's guilt. No objection was taken by the prisoner's
> counsel to the admission of the evidence, and the prisoner was found guilty
> and sentenced to death.

81 *Report from the select committee on public prosecutors; together with the proceedings of the committee, minutes of evidence, appendix and index*, p. 153, HC 1854–5 (481), xii, 161.
82 Bentley, op. cit., p. 37, referring to an English case, *R. v. Lacey, Cuffey, and Fay* (1848) 3 Cox 517, where the judges decided that a prisoner should not be allowed to have a list of the names of the witnesses, but 'he will be allowed to inspect the indictment for the purpose of seeing the names of such witnesses.' In the same case the judges refused to give a copy of the indictment to the prisoners although their counsel argued that in *R. v. Martin*, 'recently tried in Ireland, under the same statute, a similar application was made, and the judges at once acceded to it' (ibid., p. 518).
83 *R. v. Dingler* (1792) 2 Leach 561, 168 Eng Rep 383. For a discussion of *Dingler* see Bentley, op. cit., p. 29. The depositions of witnesses examined by the coroner in the prisoner's absence, however, seem to have been admissible (Sir William Oldnal Russell, *A treatise on crimes and misdemeanours*, 3 vols (4th ed. by Charles Sprengel Greaves, London, 1865), iii, 478).
84 Thomas Lefroy, *An analysis of the criminal law of Ireland, giving in alphabetical order all indictable offences, with their respective punishments and the statutes relating thereto, together with explanatory observations and notes; also an appendix of forms for the use of magistrates* (Dublin 1849), p. xlii.

The trial judge, Ball, reserved the case for the twelve judges, who found the conviction good.

In August 1856 when Mary Lydane was murdered, her husband Patrick was committed on the evidence of five witnesses who had been examined by the coroner. The Crown did not put him on trial at the spring assizes in 1857 nor at the summer assizes, 'altho' memorialist was all fully prepared for his trial.'[85] Between the summer assizes of 1857 and the spring assizes in March 1858 the Crown found nine new witnesses, but 'no further deposition was made either before the coroner or any magistrate.' At the spring assizes in 1858, therefore, 'memorialist was put upon his trial ... without having ever received any intimation that ... any other witness would be examined by the Crown except those who had made informations in the case and of which memorialist procured copies and placed them in the hands of his counsel with instructions for cross-examination.' Robert Blakeney, the prisoner's counsel, believed that if the magistrates 'who got up the additional evidence had reduced them to writing and returned them to the crown office, the result of the case might have been very different by enabling those defending him to know the case they had to meet.' 'Modern legislation requires that the evidence of witnesses should be reduced to writing at the time of the enquiry,' Blakeney argued. 'The accused then has a right to copies of those depositions and thus enabled to test the truth or accuracy of their contents.' Christian, who was the trial judge, denied that 'there is any ground for the assertion of the prisoner's counsel that he has not had a fair trial.' Yet Blakeney's complaint was one that carried weight. Blakeney could have pointed to the decision of Baron Cresswell in *R. v. Ward* in 1848[86] and to the words of Lord Denman, who declared that when a magistrate did not return a deposition, 'it did not give the prisoner what the law intended it should, viz. an account of the whole evidence against him given before the magistrate.'[87]

Blakeney could also have pointed to the practice of several Irish judges, including Perrin, who was referred to by Thomas O'Hagan at Vladimir Petcherini's trial at the Dublin Commission in 1855 when he objected to a witness being examined:

> the Crown has no right to produce a witness who has not made an information. There is a rule on the Munster circuit that ... it is not fair to

85   NAI, CRF/1858/Lydane/15.
86   2 Car & K 759, 175 Eng Rep 319.
87   Russell, op. cit., iii, 495. In Scotland, the prisoner 'is entitled to be served with a list of the witnesses proposed to be called against him, and also of the jury, fifteen days before trial'. By the same token, however, 'a pannel is bound, twenty-four hours before the trial, to give to the prosecutor a list of the witnesses he is to call' (James Paterson, *A compendium of English and Scotch law stating their differences: with a dictionary of parallel terms and phrases* (Edinburgh, 1860), pp 329–30). The prisoner's right to know the full case against him is listed by Bentley as one of the indispensable conditions of a fair trial (Bentley, op. cit., p. xiv).

an accused person that a witness should lie by or be kept back without making an information, and thus deprive a prisoner of means of cross-examination, or of making inquiries. Mr Justice Perrin, as I am informed, is in the habit of excluding such testimony, unless it can be shown why informations were not made, and his reason is, that otherwise the prisoner would be deprived of the benefit of the act which entitles him to copies of the informations.[88]

The judge at the Dublin Commission, Crampton, did not agree, saying he had 'been acting under the contrary rule for twenty-one years.' The correct procedure, certainly from the point of view of Blakeney and O'Hagan, seems to have been that followed by two magistrates when they committed Edward Walsh in Castlebar in 1873 for the murder of his wife.[89] The bulk of the case against Walsh was heard on 30 April 1870 when he seems to have been committed, but the magistrates examined witnesses on 3 May, 5 May, 9 May, and 5 June, and on 8 July, which was less than a fortnight before Walsh's trial at the assizes. The statements made after 30 April were, however, proper depositions, with all the particulars written down with the same detail and formality as those taken on 30 April.

Perrin was not the only judge who took a different view from Christian's and Crampton's. At Enniskillen assizes in March 1860, Chief Baron Pigot rejected the evidence of a policeman who was the Crown's last witness against Robert Richey, who was on trial for murdering his father. The policeman's evidence was important. He had searched Richey's house just after the body had been found; he had found a coat 'torn and soiled; there was a mark like blood on the left arm'. On a hedge near the house he found trousers that 'were quite wet, and had been washed.'[90] Pigot asked the policeman if he had sworn an information; the policeman answered that he 'never gave any information.' Pigot told the jury to ignore the policeman's evidence 'as this man must have come by surprise upon the prisoner.' He also rebuked the magistrates for their 'improper' behaviour in not taking the policeman's information. The jury had heard the policeman, in spite of Pigot, but they acquitted the prisoner.

The problem of witnesses appearing by surprise, in spite of the cases mentioned above, does not seem to have been a common one in Ireland. In the selection of cases discussed below[91] there were only three complaints about witnesses taking the prisoner by surprise. The first, Patrick Cain, complained that 'if the evidence given by said Thomas Hughes in said original memorial set forth had not come upon him by surprise he would have been enabled by most respectable and satisfactory evidence to establish the statement in his said original memorial in relation thereto and thereby (as memorialist is advised and submits) would have been entitled to a verdict of acquittal.' The other two who complained

88   7 Cox CC 79, at p. 82.   89   NAI, CRF/1873/Walsh/11.
90   Larcom Papers (NLI, MS 7620 [*Express*, 14 Mar. 1860]).
91   Below, pp 210–11.

were Patrick Lydane in 1858 and Daniel Ward in 1863.[92] The Ward case was the last complaint in the selection of cases, which suggests, but does not prove, that Irish practice silently followed English practice.[93] According to John Naish, attorney general, 1883–5, the practice was that

> all the preliminary informations and depositions taken before a magistrate, where a person is charged and returned for trial, are sent on to the clerk of the crown. So also, where the case is one of murder, are all the depositions taken before the coroner at the inquest. It is the business of the prisoner's solicitor to go to the Crown Office and procure copies of all of these for the purpose of making up his brief. It is not the business of the Crown, nor is it usual to furnish the prisoner's solicitor with copies of these any more than it is their business to prepare the prisoner's brief. In ordinary cases it is not done. As a matter of courtesy, where the Crown gets a long series of informations reprinted, a copy or copies are given to the prisoner's solicitor, for his convenience, if he chooses to ask for them.[94]

When Kenny's *Outlines* was published in 1902 the meridian of Spain had been left behind: 'modern practice concedes to every accused person the right to know, before his trial, what evidence will be given against him. Hence if any one who was not produced before the committing justice is to be called as a witness, full information should be furnished to the accused, both as to his name and as to the evidence he will give.'[95]

THE ASSIZES

Serious crimes, including murders, were tried at the spring and summer assizes, which took place in each county in the Hilary and Trinity vacations.[96] The county and the county of the city of Dublin had their own assizes, called the Dublin Commission, which met six times a year at Green Street.[97] In 1877 a winter assize was added to the two existing assizes. All of the counties, except the two Dublins, were formed into four groups 'corresponding practically to the four provinces',

92   NAI, CRF/1839/Cain/45; ibid. 1858/Lydane/15; ibid. 1863/Ward/5.
93   Bentley refers to three cases in England (in 1848, 1867, and 1870) where judges thought that the 'fair course' was for the Crown to tell the defence 'of the character of the additional evidence'. Some judges granted adjournments to enable prisoners to counter new evidence, but this was not established as a right until 1884 (Bentley, op. cit., pp 37–8).
94   Quoted in Waldron, *Maamtrasna* (Dublin, 1992), p. 225.
95   Kenny, op. cit., p. 472, fn. 3.
96   Hayes, op. cit., i, 59.
97   Joseph Gabbett, *A treatise of the criminal law; comprehending all crimes and misdemeanors punishable by indictment; and offences cognizable summarily by magistrates; and the modes of proceeding upon each*, 2 vols (Dublin, 1843), ii, 14; Thompson, op. cit., pp 8–9.

and 'the counties so united are deemed to be one county, and the winter assizes in and for the united county is deemed to be held in and for each of the constituent counties.'⁹⁸ The assize judges went in pairs to the county towns on each of the six circuits (five from 1885),⁹⁹ with the two judges alternating between civil and criminal cases as they moved from town to town.¹⁰⁰ If the judge who tried the civil cases (or nisi prius as it was sometimes called) got through them before his brother judge ('the judge in commission') had finished the criminal cases, he would try some of the crown cases.¹⁰¹

In addition to the assizes there were special commissions when two judges, who sat together, were appointed to deal quickly with outbreaks of local disorder, especially outbreaks of agrarian murder.¹⁰² Special commissions were different in important ways from the assizes: the government selected the judges, and the attorney general decided what cases would be tried, whereas at the assizes the

98 The Supreme Court of Judicature (Ireland) Act (40 & 41 Vict., c. 57, s. 63 (14 Aug. 1877)) extended an English act, 39 & 40 Vict., c. 57 (11 Aug. 1876), to Ireland; Thompson, op. cit., p. 11.

99 The six circuits were the home circuit, the north-east, the north-west, the Leinster, the Munster, and the Connacht. The home circuit included Carlow, the King's County, Kildare, Westmeath, the Queen's County, and Meath; the Leinster circuit included the rest of Leinster, the two ridings of Tipperary, and the county and city of Waterford; the north-east included Louth, Monaghan, Armagh, Down, and Antrim, and the towns of Drogheda and Carrickfergus; the north-west included Longford, Cavan, Fermanagh, Tyrone, Donegal, and the county and city of Londonderry; the Munster was the province of Munster, including the cities of Cork and Limerick, but minus Tipperary and Waterford; Connacht was actually Connacht (*Thom's Directory, 1881*, p. 870). From 1886 there were only five circuits; the six counties of the home circuit were distributed among the north-west (Westmeath), the north-east (Meath), the Leinster (Carlow, Kildare, Queen's County), and the Connacht (King's County) (ibid., 1886, p. 839).

100 For circuits, grand juries, and the judges' commissions in the eighteenth century see Neal Garnham, *The courts, crime and the criminal law in Ireland 1692–1760* (Dublin, 1996), pp 78–80.

101 *Minutes of evidence taken before the select committee of the house of lords appointed to enquire into the state of Ireland, since the year 1835, in respect of crime and outrage, which have rendered life and property insecure in that part of the empire*, pt III, *evidence 12 June to 19 July*, p. 877, HC 1839 (486–III), xii, 13.

102 For examples see James Mongan, *A report of trials before the Rt Hon. the Lord Chief Justice, and the Hon. Baron Sir Wm. C. Smith, bart at the special commission, at Maryborough, commencing on the 23rd May, and ending on the 6th June* [1832] (Dublin, 1832), John Simpson Armstrong, *A report of trials held under a special commission for the county of Limerick, held at Limerick, January 1848* (Dublin, n.d. [1849]), and R.W. Kostal, 'Rebels in the dock: the prosecution of the Dublin fenians, 1865–6' in *Éire–Ireland*, 34:2 (summer 1999), 76–8. For an account of the expenses of a special commission at Cork in 1829 see *Copy of the entry in the clerk of the crown's book, relative to the postponement from the last Cork assizes, of the trials of Leary, Magrath and others, charged with a conspiracy to murder*, HC 1830 (131), xxvi, 637. Crown counsel's fees were £1,386. 15s. 0d., witness' expenses were £556. 4s. 9d., the crown solicitor's costs were £331. 15s. 3d., and the fees of the two judges (Richard Pennefather and Robert Torrens) were £738. 9s. 2d. For an example of expenses in England see *Return of the expenses incurred by holding the special commission to try persons who were implicated in the disturbances during the last winter; distinguishing the amount paid to counsel and agents, from those paid to the witnesses*, HC 1831–2 (64), xxxv, 403.

judges were obliged to try all of the prisoners who had been committed for trial.[103] On rare occasions the two judges sat together at the ordinary assizes, or at least made it clear that they had deliberated together. At the trial of Patrick Lynch and John Conway at the summer assizes in Limerick in 1843 the jury was discharged 'with the concurrence of the two judges before whom the assizes were held.'[104] At the Dublin Commission, two judges presided.[105] When cases that had begun as criminal informations in the Queen's Bench were sent to the assizes for trial, they were tried before the judge who tried civil cases.[106] When the Queen's Bench sent back cases to the assizes that had been removed from them by *certiorari*, they were also tried on the civil side of the court. Sam Gray, for example, applied to the Queen's Bench for a change of venue; when that was refused, 'the proceedings were remitted to the county of Monaghan by *precedendo*. The prisoner was subsequently tried on the civil side of the court, and convicted.'[107]

The judges' authority to try cases came not from their position as common law judges but from a patent issued under the great seal directing them, 'from time to time, as need shall be, to deliver our gaols of the several counties ... of all prisoners and malefactors therein.'[108] The commission might be addressed not only to the twelve judges of the Queen's Bench, Common Pleas, and Exchequer, but to the three serjeants and to senior QCs, any of whom could become the 'going' judges of assize.[109] All of the available judges seem to have been simultaneously named for every circuit. At Galway summer assizes in 1873, for example, ten common law judges, the solicitor general, and the three sergeants were described in the Galway assize book as 'commissioners for Galway'.[110] Those named in the commission seem to have decided among themselves, according to their seniority, which circuits they would take.[111] Crampton, for example, 'contrived frequently to go the Connacht circuit, generally stopping at Cahermorris, his brother's place, near Headford, on the way from Castlebar to Galway.'[112]

103 Armstrong, *A report of trials held under a special commission for the county of Limerick*, p. 314; Mongan, *A report of trials before the Rt Hon. the Lord Chief Justice, and the Hon. Baron Sir Wm. C. Smith, bart at the special commission, at Maryborough*, pp 324–5.

104 7 Ir LR 149, at p. 188.   105 See below, p. 190.

106 *Minutes of evidence taken before the select committee of the house of lords appointed to enquire into the state of Ireland, since the year 1835, in respect of crime and outrage, which have rendered life and property insecure in that part of the empire*, pt III, *evidence 12 June to 19 July*, p. 871, HC 1839 (486–III), xii, 7.

107 *R. v. Conway* (1858) 7 ICLR 507, at p. 514. See also *R. v. Gray* (1842) 3 Cr & Dix 93 and *R. v. Gray* (1842) Ir Cir Rep 420.

108 Gabbett, op. cit., ii, 8–11. By the time Gabbett was writing the five commissions (of assize, of the peace, of oyer and terminer, of gaol delivery, and of nisi prius) had been consolidated into one.

109 See below, p. 263 for serjeants and QCs passing sentence of death at the assizes.

110 NAI, Crown Book at Assize, Co. Galway, 1873.

111 Hayes, op. cit., ii, 598; Thompson, op. cit., p. 9. John Alcock refers to the judges as 'selecting' their circuits (Alcock, *Observations concerning the nature and origin of the meetings of the twelve judges, for the consideration of cases reserved from the circuits* (Dublin, 1838), p. 20).

112 Oliver J. Burke, *Anecdotes of the Connaught circuit: from its foundation to close upon the present time* (Dublin, 1885), p. 300.

The assizes were busy affairs, especially in the 1830s. In 1833 at the Monaghan spring assizes, 171 persons were returned for trial; 95 of these were put on trial, 36 were convicted, 49 were acquitted, and in one case, involving 10 prisoners, the jury disagreed.[113] Of the 76 who were not put on trial, in 19 cases no bills were found, in 21 cases there was no prosecution, in 3 cases other courts assumed jurisdiction, and in 33 cases the trials were postponed – 26 on the application of the Crown and 7 on the application of the prisoner. Of the 36 who were convicted, 3 received recorded sentences of death, 9 were transported for seven years, one was imprisoned for one year, and the rest were fined or imprisoned for short periods. The 95 trials did not take long. The assizes began at noon on Saturday, 2 March, and ended on the following Thursday, when the judges left for Armagh, where they began business at 3 p.m. Assuming that the 'judge in commission' sat for thirty hours, each case took, on average, about twenty minutes. The relative decline of the assizes is shown by the fact that at Monaghan forty years later, in 1873, the two assizes and the four quarter sessions combined tried only 118 persons.[114]

The machinery that dealt with these cases when they came to court was kept going by the clerk of the crown, in whose hands all the informations, depositions, and recognizances were placed. During the assizes he appeared to combine the functions of stage-manager and prompter: he called on the prisoner to plead, he called over the names on the long panel, he charged the jury when they were sworn, he received their verdict, and he asked the convicted prisoner if he had anything to say. If necessary he compiled the formal 'record' of the trial for the Court of Queen's Bench.[115] His ancient importance was still recognized by the fact that he still formally conducted the prosecution. When Robert Henry O'Neill challenged the array at the spring assizes in Belfast, it was not the crown counsel who formally opposed him, but the clerk of the crown for Co. Antrim, 'the said Walter Bourne, coroner and attorney to our Lady the Queen, who for our said Lady the Queen in this behalf prosecuteth as aforesaid, comes and demurs to the challenge of the said Robert Henry O'Neill.'[116] The clerk of the crown, however, although he continued to be grandiloquently styled the Queen's coroner and attorney, gradually subsided after 1877 into merely local eminence, as in more and more counties his office was merged with that of the clerk of the peace, who had been stage-manager and prompter to the magistrates at the quarter sessions.[117] In the mid-1880s the two offices were combined in just over half of the counties; by 1914 they were combined in all.

113 *Return of persons for trial at last spring assizes in the counties of Monaghan, Armagh, Antrim and Down, and how disposed of; also, of the times appointed for opening the commission in those several counties, and of the times when the criminal business was actually commenced and proceeded upon in each ...*, pp 1–2, HC 1833 (402), xxix, 407–8.
114 *Judicial statistics (Ireland), 1873*, p. 155 [C 1034], HC 1874, lxxi, 405.
115 For more, see R.B. McDowell, *The Irish administration 1801–1914* (London and Toronto, 1964), pp 132–3. See below, pp 132, 167–8, 264, 275–6, 289.
116 (1854) 6 Cox CC 495, at p. 498.   117 McDowell, op. cit., p. 133.

The assizes were occasions of pageantry. Maurice Healy described the procession of the judges from their lodgings to the courthouse: 'First came a trumpeter and a mounted policeman riding abreast, then two policemen, then two troopers; then came the judges' carriage, with the military officer riding at one door and the police officer at the other; then two more troopers, followed by two more mounted police.'[118] At the opening of Cork assizes on 17 March 1875 John Ryan noted that the shamrock 'graced the county inspector's shako as well as the resident magistrate's Lincoln and Bennett, the country boy's caubeen and the cit's stovepipe.'[119] At Carrick-on-Shannon assizes Anthony Trollope remembered that 'all was bustle and confusion, noise, dirt, and distraction.'[120] The formal opening of the assizes brought to light nice points of ceremony and millinery. The judge who was to try the criminal cases ('the judge in commission') wore a full-bottomed wig and scarlet robes trimmed with ermine. The other judge wore a bob-wig and black robes trimmed with ermine and carried a three-cornered hat.[121] The significance of the judge's red robes was not difficult to spot.[122]

THE CROWN SOLICITOR AND CROWN COUNSEL

The crown solicitors and sessional crown solicitors were eponymous *rarae aves* in the legal profession because they were exactly what their title implied, solicitors who acted on behalf of the Crown, the former at the assizes and the latter at quarter sessions.[123] At first there was only one crown solicitor for each circuit, but

118 Healy, *The old Munster circuit*, p. 11.

119 Diary of John Ryan (TCD, MS 10350 (no. 4), p. 46).

120 *The MacDermots of Ballycloran*, ed. Robert Tracy (Oxford, 1989), p. 503. See also Peter Ingram, 'Law and lawyers in Trollope's Ireland' in Dawson, Greer & Ingram (eds), *One hundred and fifty years of Irish law* (1996), pp 125–43.

121 V.H.T. Delany, *Christopher Palles, lord chief baron of Her Majesty's Court of Exchequer in Ireland 1874–1916: his life and times* (Dublin, 1960), pp 37–8.

122 'Red signified the power of the state over the body of the subject' (Richard J. Evans, *Rituals of retribution: capital punishment in Germany 1600–1987* (Oxford, 1996), p. 69). The clergyman who preached the assize sermon at Castlebar in 1786 reminded the going judges, in case they had forgotten, 'that the scarlet and the violet had been the colours worn by the judges ever since the robes of Aaron were transferred to Eleazar, his son and successor' (Burke, *Anecdotes of the Connaught circuit*, p. 139).

123 There was an exception: Thomas Kemmis, who was the crown solicitor of the Leinster circuit, was a barrister (*Report from the select committee on public prosecutors; together with the proceedings of the committee, minutes of evidence, appendix and index*, p. 148, HC 1854–5 (481), xii, 156). Crown solicitors included in their ranks the socially prominent: Matthew Barrington, the crown solicitor of the Munster circuit in the early 1840s, was a baronet and the son of Sir Matthew Barrington Bt., who founded Barrington's Hospital in Limerick. By the 1860s crown solicitors were 'largely paid', receiving from £1500 to £2000 a year, in addition to 'handsome allowances' for clerks (Larcom Papers (NLI, MS 7620 [*Express*, 1 Nov. 1860])). From 1842 they were paid salaries instead of fees, 'the Treasury refusing to make an exception which was suggested in favour of fees for briefs and the examination of crown witnesses, "since in these two cases above all there

by the 1870s one crown solicitor usually served two counties, and some served a single large county such as Mayo. Their increasing numbers represented the replacement of private prosecution by public prosecution.[124] According to Desmond McCabe, public prosecution, which had at first been confined to 'cases of an insurrectionary nature', increased until the mid-1830s when 'nearly all murders and manslaughters, all agrarian crimes, robberies with violence, and most rapes and abductions were prosecuted by the Crown at assizes.'[125] In 1836 sessional crown solicitors were appointed in each county to prosecute at the quarter sessions in 'all cases of assault, riot and breaches of the peace', and by 1839 'only the simplest of larcenies and offences such as fraud or embezzlement, in which it was believed that large institutions capable of hiring counsel were involved, were left at assizes to private prosecution.' Private prosecution even for serious offences persisted, nevertheless. In 1847, for example, when John Kiernan was indicted at the summer assizes in Armagh for perjury, 'the prosecution was carried on by a private individual, and not by, or under the direction, of the attorney general.'[126]

The crown solicitors were the attorney general's agents: they referred cases to him, they acted on his instructions, especially in the setting aside of jurors, and they reported to him after the assizes.[127] They were not, however, his creatures. They did not give up office, for example, when a new administration came in.[128]

is the greatest temptation to swell, by undue prolixity or irrelevant matter, the cost of the pro-
ceedings'" (R.B. McDowell, 'The Irish courts of law, 1801–1914' in *IHS*, 10:40 (Sept. 1957), 380).
See also John F. McEldowney, 'Crown prosecutions in nineteenth-century Ireland' in Douglas Hay
& Francis Snyder (eds), *Policing and prosecution in Britain 1750–1850* (Oxford, 1989), pp 449–53.

124 Dr Crossman, who uses the word 'quiet' to describe this change, ascribes the extension of
crown prosecution to William Conyngham Plunket (attorney general, 1822–7), who extended
it to homicides, burglaries, and rapes (Virginia Crossman, *Politics, law and order in nineteenth-
century Ireland* (Dublin, 1996), p. 36). For the genesis of public prosecution in England and
Wales see Bentley, op. cit., pp 83–7.

125 Desmond McCabe, '"That part that laws or kings can cause or cure": crown prosecutions and
jury trial at Longford assizes' in Raymond Gillespie & Gerard Moran (eds), *Longford: essays in
county history* (Dublin, 1991), p. 158. For more on the history and duties of the crown solicitors
and sessional crown solicitors see R.B. McDowell, 'The Irish courts of law, 1801–1914' in *IHS*,
10:40 (Sept. 1957), 380; id., *The Irish administration, 1801–1914* (London and Toronto, 1964),
p. 122; John F. McEldowney, 'The case of *The Queen v. McKenna* (1869) and jury packing in
Ireland' in *Ir Jur*, n.s., 12 (1977), 339–53; id., '"Stand by for the Crown": an historical analysis'
in *The Criminal Law Review 1979*, 272–83; id., 'Some aspects of law and policy in the
administration of criminal justice in nineteenth-century Ireland' in McEldowney & O'Higgins
(eds), *The common law tradition* (1990), pp 117–55.

126 Thomas Lefroy, *An analysis of the criminal law of Ireland, giving in alphabetical order all indictable
offences, with their respective punishments and the statutes relating thereto, together with explanatory
observations and notes; also an appendix of forms for the use of magistrates* (Dublin 1849),
pp xlvi–xlvii. For another example of what seems to have been a private prosecution see *Farrell
and Moore* (1848) 3 Cox CC 139.

127 *Report from the select committee on public prosecutors* ..., pp 149, 154.

128 For the history of the office of attorney general see J.P. Casey, *The office of the attorney general
in Ireland* (Dublin, 1980), pp 15–32.

They were not resident officials, like the RMs and sessional crown solicitors; most of them had Dublin addresses, and for the most part they came to their counties only at the assizes. When Piers Geale, who had been a crown solicitor on the home circuit for twenty-two years, was asked by a house of lords committee in 1839 what he did between assizes, he mentioned 'generally taking informations where they are necessary, preparing for cases to come on in the ensuing assizes, providing for prosecutors at the last assizes, reporting on cases that were prosecuted, and a number of other duties.'[129] He did not mention supervising RMs and policemen. In the early part of the period crown solicitors did not usually concern themselves with the early stages of the case, such as appearing at the committal proceedings or at inquests. When a crown solicitor appeared at the Sixmilebridge inquests, for example, it was only because the attorney general had instructed him to do so.[130] In 1863 Alexander O'Rorke represented the sessional crown solicitor at the sensational proceedings before the magistrates in Ballymena after the death of Amelia Carey, but it is interesting that he represented the sessional crown solicitor, not the crown solicitor.[131]

When Joseph Napier (attorney general, 1852–3) gave evidence to the select committee on public prosecutors, he described how the magistrates sent informations and depositions either to the crown solicitor for trial at the assizes or to the sessional crown solicitor for trial or at the quarter sessions.[132] The crown solicitors received the more important cases for trial at the assizes, and in turn they sent them to the attorney general, who decided in each case whether it was a 'fit case for the Crown to prosecute'. If the attorney decided not to take up the case, a private prosecutor could still take it up, but 'it is not very usual, because it is considered that the case, having been rejected by the attorney general, he does not deem it a fit case, or one with sufficient materials for a prosecution.' Napier complained of the last-minute precipitancy of the crown solicitors when inflicting their cases on the attorney general:

129 *Report from the select committee of the house of lords, appointed to enquire into the state of Ireland in respect of crime, and to report thereon to the house; with the minutes of evidence taken before the committee, and an appendix and index*, pt II, *evidence 27 May to 11 June*, p. 676, HC 1839 (486–II), xi, 682. See also Desmond McCabe, '"That part that laws or kings can cause or cure": crown prosecutions and jury trial at Longford assizes', p. 159 and Ian Bridgeman, 'The constabulary and the criminal justice system in nineteenth-century Ireland' in *Criminal Justice History*, 15 (1994), 96–8.

130 *Hansard 3*, cxxiv, 317–18 (17 Mar. 1853).

131 NAI, RP/1863/10,102.

132 *Report from the select committee on public prosecutors; together with the proceedings of the committee, minutes of evidence, appendix and index*, p. 141, HC 1854–5 (481), xii, 149. See also Robert Evan Bell, 'The office of Director of Public Prosecutions in Northern Ireland' (PhD thesis, QUB, 1989), pp 13–21. (I am indebted to Professor Desmond Greer for drawing my attention to this passage.)

Sometimes, immediately before the assizes, they gather up a whole heap, and then send them all at once; whereas I thought that the right plan would be, that as informations are taken from time to time, they should be distributed properly between the assizes and the sessions, being first sent periodically to the attorney general.[133]

The number of cases rejected by the attorney general or the crown solicitor before the assizes is not easy to estimate. In the ten years 1866–75, for example, 39 of the 244 cases returned for trial for murder were 'not prosecuted', but the figure of 244 did not include those who were committed for murder but returned for trial for manslaughter or a lesser offence. The provenance of those who were returned for trial for murder or manslaughter presents interesting statistical problems, as Table 3.1, shows.[134] The category 'returned for trial' in the table is a

TABLE 3.1

NUMBERS COMMITTED AND RETURNED FOR TRIAL FOR MURDER
AND MANSLAUGHTER, 1866–75

offence	*committals*	*returned for trial*
murder	372	244
manslaughter	429	757
total	801	1001

curious one: it includes, in the case of murder, those who were convicted of murder, acquitted of murder, or acquitted as being insane, and those who were bailed, or who were 'not prosecuted', or against whom no bill was found. In other words, the category, which is taken from the *Judicial Statistics*, includes some who were not put on trial and *excludes* those who were found guilty of offences that did not amount to murder! The fact that committals for murder exceeded those returned for trial for murder suggests that many cases that were treated as murders at committal became manslaughter at the assizes. The most remarkable thing shown in the table, however, is that those returned for trial for manslaughter actually exceeded those committed for manslaughter, and that those returned for the two offences of murder and manslaughter combined actually exceeded those committed! These two figures suggest that manslaughter was used as a receptacle not only for crimes that had started out as murder but for many that had not even

133 *Report from the select committee on public prosecutors; together with the proceedings of the committee, minutes of evidence, appendix and index*, p. 149, HC 1854–5 (481), xii, 157.
134 These figures are taken from the *Judicial Statistics*; for full references see below, pp 401–2.

started out as manslaughter. While many murders were reduced in seriousness between committal and trial, many lesser offences were promoted to manslaughter and even to murder.

When the attorney general had 'marked' the cases he wanted to prosecute, the crown solicitor prepared them for the crown counsel, who represented the attorney general on each circuit.[135] There was a senior and a junior crown counsel, the former serving the whole circuit in the early part of the period and the latter attached to a county; the senior counsel was usually a QC.[136] The annually published lists of crown counsel in *Thom's Directory* in the 1850s showed how the crown counsel were distributed. In 1853, for example, Sir Thomas Staples QC was the senior for the north-east circuit and each county had a junior; the only junior who was a QC was Thomas McDonnell for Co. Down. There were also supernumerary counsel who sometimes got a 'stray' brief or two, especially when the two assize judges simultaneously tried criminal cases.[137] If the crown solicitor required 'any further directions on the circuit, he has the counsel of the circuit, who represents the attorney general, to direct proofs, or to make additional suggestions.'[138] The junior crown counsel prepared the indictments and saw 'that the evidence is all correct.'[139]

The crown solicitor and the crown counsel might be joined by counsel for the next of kin. When Patrick Woods was tried for murder at Armagh assizes in 1841, he complained that the murdered man's family had retained counsel who had assisted the crown counsel at his trial.[140] Whether the balance was tipped against Woods by George Tombe's assisting the crown counsel was debatable, but Tombe had every right to be there. The right survived long after the 1840s. In 1861, for example, the attorney general was willing to allow Lord Leitrim to be represented by his own counsel at the trial of James Murphy. 'The practice with which I have been many years familiar on the circuit with which I am best acquainted does not prevent me from permitting the employment of counsel to assist the counsel for the crown,' he wrote. 'If Lord Leitrim desires to do so, he may retain either of the gentlemen he names, to be associated in the conduct of the pending prosecution, and the crown solicitor will afford the counsel his lordship may select all necessary informations to enable him to aid in it effectively.'[141] In 1868 in *Rumble and Bonnello*, a case where two soldiers had killed a man in an election affray in Drogheda, the majority of the Queen's Bench were in favour of hearing counsel for the next of kin. Whiteside, however, was against hearing them because 'where the attorney general prosecutes, he has the whole conduct of the proceedings and no one else has a right to interfere.'[142] One of his observations showed he was aware of how far England and Ireland had diverged in the matter of public and private prosecution: 'the practice in England as to private prosecutions, as most

135 *Report from the select committee on public prosecutors* … p. 141, HC 1854–5 (481), xii, 149.
136 Ibid., p. 148.   137 Ibid., pp 145–6.   138 Ibid., p. 146.
139 Ibid., p. 148.   140 NAI, CRF/1841/Woods/26.
141 Larcom Papers (NLI, MS 7634, f. 70).   142 IR 3 CL 271, at p. 274.

there are, should not affect the practice as to prosecutions by the attorney general in this country.'

Crown counsel were paid according to the number of cases they conducted, although Napier thought it would be better to pay them salaries, which would presumably have made them more disinterested in the conduct of their cases.[143] 'It is important for the administration of the law that a case should not be unduly pressed,' he told the select committee on public prosecutors. 'There are often matters of right feeling and principle which require a man of a very high class, and he is considered as having the power of the attorney general; he has the power of entering a *nolle prosequi* upon the proceedings; he has a large and ample power over life and liberty, and a man in that position ought to be of a very high class, and they generally are so; but I think it a fearful thing to leave anything of that sort to mere private considerations.'[144]

The powers exercised by crown counsel as the attorney general's representatives were considerable, as Napier had pointed out.[145] Crown counsel could ask for the postponement of trials, for a change of venue, and they could make a concluding speech at trials, which was one of the attorney general's prerogatives. They could enter a *nolle prosequi*, which was a declaration that the Crown would not continue with a prosecution. This did not prevent the Crown prosecuting again, either for the same offence or one like it.[146] At the spring assizes in 1871, for example, 100 *nolle prosequis* were entered, which is a substantial number when compared with the 282 persons who were found guilty at those assizes or with the 225 persons who were acquitted.[147]

Perhaps their most important power was their power to make bargains with prisoners. A considerable number of those committed for murder were returned for trial for manslaughter. Some of these may have been due to the crown solicitor

143 Counsels' fees were not exorbitant. At the Dublin Commission in 1873, for example, the fees in 166 cases amounted to £1,135 (*Return 'for each county in Ireland, of the amount expended at each assizes for the last three years in fees to counsel in criminal prosecutions (excluding the amount of fees paid to special counsel), and the number of cases in which such fees were paid'; 'and, similar return, for the same period, for each commission at Green-street for the county of Dublin and the county of the city of Dublin, and for the session of the city of Dublin held before the recorder'*, p. 13, HC 1877 (40), lxix, 531).

144 *Report from the select committee on public prosecutors; together with the proceedings of the committee, minutes of evidence, appendix and index* p. 143, HC 1854–5 (481), xii, 151.

145 The fact that the crown counsel on each circuit represented the attorney general and exercised his powers was upheld in *R. v. M'Namara* at Cork spring assizes in 1843 (Ir Cir Rep 869, at pp 869–70).

146 For an example see below, p. 280.

147 *Returns 'from the clerks of the crown in each county in Ireland, of the number of criminal cases in each county tried before a jury at the spring assizes of the years 1871, 1872, and 1873, with a description of the crime charged, and the result of the trial, specifying in each case whether the prisoner was found guilty (and, if so, of what offence) or acquitted, or the jury disagreed'; 'of the number of cases postponed on the application of counsel for the Crown, or in which nolle prosequi was entered'; 'and, from the secretaries of the grand juries of Ireland respectively, of any resolutions adopted by any of the grand juries referring to the Juries Act (Ireland) of 1871'*, pp 2–4, HC 1873 (220), liv, 360–2.

deciding that the case was one of manslaughter, but others may have been due to plea bargaining, evidence of which occasionally came to light. Timothy Carew, who was charged with being an accessory to the murder of Michael Keeshan, was told, apparently by his own counsel, that 'his only chance of saving his life was to plead guilty, and that he might thereby get off with transportation', and the crown solicitor, Piers Geale, described how the deal had been made: 'the counsel for the prisoner intimated to counsel for the crown that the prisoner would plead guilty to the indictment on the terms of his being transported for life, the crown counsel acceded to the proposition, and the prisoner accordingly pleaded guilty.'[148] At Kildare spring assizes in 1856 Matthew Leary pleaded guilty of bestiality; the judge recorded sentence of death, noting that 'the advisers of the Crown were very properly most anxious to avoid the necessity of a public trial.'[149] A few years earlier the evidence of plea bargaining had been stated in even more detail in a similar case. When Thomas Wiggins was convicted at Wexford, William Kemmis, the crown solicitor, wrote to the under-secretary on 12 March 1849:

> I beg to inform you that at the recent assizes at Wexford a person of the name of Thomas Wiggins pleaded guilty to a capital offence (bestiality) and sentence of death was recorded by Judge Jackson. It is right however that govt should be informed that an assurance was given to the prisoner that his life would be spared on his pleading guilty – this course being adopted by directions of the attorney general who was desirous of avoiding a public trial of such a nature. I presume the usual direction will be given for the transportation of the prisoner for life.[150]

The attorney general and the solicitor general often appeared in person at the assizes. Both appeared, for example, at Charles McCormick's trial at Longford summer assizes in 1863.[151] Napier thought that the attorney's appearance 'shows the determination of the executive government'. In 1852 he appeared at the assizes in Armagh and Louth after a number of agrarian murders in those counties. 'I took a great deal of pains with the evidence; probably I did what I used to do when I was junior counsel, namely, to look carefully myself into the case,' he remembered. 'The result was, that we got verdicts in both counties without difficulty.'[152] Those found guilty of murder and attempted murder included James Kirk and Patrick McCooey, hanged at Dundalk in July 1852, and Francis Berry, hanged at Armagh in August.

A few briefs prepared by crown solicitors for crown counsel survive. The brief prepared for the trial of Edward Walsh at Castlebar summer assizes in 1873 for the murder of his wife, which was endorsed with the name of Myles Jordan, the

148 NAI, CRF/1840/Carew/52.   149 Ibid., CRF/1869/Leary/13.
150 Ibid., CRF/1858/Wiggins/17.   151 *Irish Times*, 3 July 1863.
152 *Report from the select committee on public prosecutors; together with the proceedings of the committee, minutes of evidence, appendix and index*, p. 149, HC 1854–5 (481), xii, 157.

crown solicitor of Mayo, ran to 40 pages of MS, consisting of informations and depositions, 19 in all, with notes of questions asked by the prisoner and his counsel, Charles O'Malley, at the inquest.[153] The brief seems not to have been completed until 8 July 1873, which was the date of the last deposition included. Walsh's trial began on 17 July, which shows that the Crown went on taking depositions until the assizes were imminent. The writing throughout is clear and regular, which suggests a humble hand, presumably that of a clerk. Inside the first page is the title 'Brief on behalf of the Crown'. If the word 'brief' had not been inserted, this collection of documents, which are not even arranged in chronological order, would have seemed to the layman to be nothing more than the raw material of the case. There were no arguments, no warnings about difficulties with witnesses, no suggestions of lines of questioning, no anticipation of the defence, and no suggestions about the order in which the witnesses might be called. Alexander Sullivan thought that an English brief was different from an Irish one: an English barrister was given 'minute instructions as to the points to be made and the method of conducting the case', but an Irish barrister conducted the case in his own way.[154] If this is true, the briefs prepared by the crown solicitors conformed to Irish rather than English standards. There was an example of the kind of 'English' brief envisaged by Sullivan, put together by Alexander O'Rorke, who stood in for the sessional crown solicitor of Co. Antrim at the inquiry into the death of Amelia Carey in 1863.[155] Thomas Courtenay was supposed to have killed Amelia Carey by giving her a dose of tartar emetic. O'Rorke took as his starting-point a list of the symptoms of poisoning by tartar emetic, which were described in Taylor's *Medical Jurisprudence*.[156] O'Rorke matched these with Carey's symptoms. His effort to produce a résumé of the case was not auspicious: the case against Courtenay collapsed.

The crown solicitor's preparations were not as perfunctory as the briefs implied, however. 'When the crown solicitor arrives at the assize town he is obliged to examine all the witnesses, and take down in writing what they can testify,' an RM told the house of lords committee in 1839. 'Those are called proofs, and directing counsel has then to decide whether the prosecution shall be

---

153 NAI, CRF/1873/Walsh/11.
154 Sullivan, *The last serjeant*, p. 281. Stephen made the same point when he implied that the depositions merely copied out were only a perfunctory brief (Stephen, *A general view of the criminal law of England* (London and Cambridge, 1863), p. 156). The brief in *R. v. Corder* has been preserved in the Suffolk County Record Office. It contains a connected narrative of the murder that made the Red Barn famous; it also contains the informations; but it does not contain the sort of instructions described by Sullivan. I am indebted to the Director of Suffolk County Record Office for supplying me with a microfilm of *R. v. Corder*, prosecution briefs 568/(Kelly) and 568/2 (Andrews). I am indebted for the reference to the Corder case to Cairns, op. cit., p. 202.
155 NAI, RP/1863/10,102).
156 Alfred Swaine Taylor, *The principles and practice of medical jurisprudence* (London, 1865), pp 247–54.

instituted or not, as he may deem right.'[157] The actual questioning of the witnesses seems to have been done by the crown solicitor's clerks, who usually arrived in the assize town before the crown solicitor. Occasionally this rehearsal was referred to in court. At Daniel Ward's trial in 1863, for example, an important and prevaricating witness, Jane McCullagh, told how a clerk had asked her 'to tell him all I knew about it'.[158] The clerks' questioning was often the end of the case. In the Outrage Papers for Co. Limerick in 1841 there is a reference to the examination of Ellen Lynch, who complained she had been raped by John Sheehy. According to the crown solicitor, Matthew Barrington, 'the case was taken up by the Crown, but on the examination of the prosecutrix in the office of the crown solicitor preparing for the trial she stated she did not cry out and that she was a long time on the night of the alleged rape in company with the prisoner and that she had been in the habit of meeting the prisoner in jig-houses.' Barrington let Ellen Lynch go before the grand jury 'but the grand jury on investigating the case ignored the bills and under the circumstances I submit this case does not call for any further investigation.'[159] Although crown solicitors' examining witnesses before the assizes suggests more preparation than was implied in the briefs, the fact remains that the Crown's case was prepared on the very eve of the assizes.

In the 1860s there was a movement to make the crown solicitor more active in the earlier stages of the investigation of serious crimes. In November 1860 the *Express* complained that the crown solicitor 'only arrives at the circuit town about the same time as the bar, and when he and some experienced clerks under him begin to examine the witnesses personally, links are often wanting that there is no opportunity of supplying at the moment.'[160] The remedy was clear: 'to require the crown solicitor and one of his expert staff to proceed at once to the locality where any outrage had been committed, to aid the magistrates in their investigations, to give them the benefit of his more mature knowledge.' A press cutting in the Larcom papers suggests that Larcom had taken the hint, or given it, about crown solicitors going to the scene of the crime. When James Murray, John George Adair's steward on his Co. Donegal estate, went missing in

157 *Report from the select committee of the house of lords, appointed to enquire into the state of Ireland in respect of crime, and to report thereon to the house; with the minutes of evidence taken before the committee, and an appendix and index*, pt I, *report, and evidence 22 Apr. to 16 May 1839*, p. 164, HC 1839 (486–I), xi, 168.

158 NAI, CRF/1863/Ward/5. Alfred Aylward, who was George Bolton's clerk, was a character in his own right: he was educated by the Jesuits, studied for the priesthood, fought for Garibaldi, became a fenian, fought for the Boers at Majuba, and worked as a telegraphist on the GNR (Eileen McCracken, 'Alfred Aylward: a fenian in South Africa' in *Irish Sword*, 12 (1975–6), 261–9). I am indebted to Dr David Murphy for this reference.

159 NAI, OP/Limerick/1841.

160 Larcom Papers (NLI, MS 7620 [*Express*, 1 Nov. 1860]). Press cuttings in the Larcom Papers often coincide with large and interesting files in the Chief Secretary's Office. The fact that three articles on crown solicitors were noted by Larcom in November 1860 suggests considerable official interest.

November 1860, a cutting from the *Freeman's Journal* noted that 'since Monday last, Mr Thomas Fitzgerald, the crown solicitor for the county, has been in the district, and has held several private investigations.'[161]

There was nothing new about crown solicitors going to the scene of the crime. When two men were arrested for the murder of Thomas Bateson in Co. Monaghan in November 1852, the lords justices ordered Maxwell Hamilton, the crown solicitor for the north-east circuit, 'to attend at Monaghan on Friday next 26 instant'.[162] In the Kirwan case in 1852, Butt accused 'the agents of the crown solicitor' of bringing the Crown's medical witness, George Hatchell, to Ireland's Eye 'to tutor and instruct him'.[163] Fitzgerald's example at Derryveagh was occasionally followed, but the crown solicitors in the 1860s did not become the equivalent of the Scottish procurators fiscal, probably because they did not want to be dragged down to their counties on wild goose chases. John Julian, the crown solicitor for the King's County and Westmeath, for example, was called down to Mullingar to examine a prisoner who 'is willing to give some *most important* information'. On his return to Dublin he reported that the prisoner's 'story is manifestly a fabrication undeserving of the slightest credit.'[164]

The crown solicitors were sometimes likened to the Scottish procurators fiscal, but there were important differences. The fiscals were local attorneys who lived in their counties, but crown solicitors lived in Dublin.[165] When a crime was discovered, the 'procurator fiscal proceeds to the spot, and commences an investigation by the examination of witnesses', but crown solicitors only occasionally went to the scene of the crime.[166] The sessional crown solicitors, on the other hand, more closely resembled the procurators fiscal. If the Scottish system had been extended to Ireland, the sessional crown solicitors would have been the obvious foundation of its extension.

When Andrew Marshall Porter (attorney general, 1883) described crown solicitors and crown counsel for yet another select committee on public prosecutors in England and Wales, he did not reveal anything that suggested major changes since the 1850s except in the numbers of those involved: there were still crown solicitors and sessional crown solicitors; crown solicitors still sent their cases to the attorney general, who 'in each case for the assizes directs whether the case is one to be prosecuted or not, and gives special directions when necessary.'[167]

---

161 Larcom Papers (NLI, MS 7620 [*Freeman's Journal*, 24 Nov. 1860]). For the part played by Fitzgerald in the Derryveagh affair see NAI, RP/1860/7273. See also Vaughan, *Sin, sheep and Scotsmen*.

162 NAI, CSO LB 459, resident magistrates letter books (23 June 1848–28 Dec. 1857), p. 176.

163 John Simpson Armstrong, *Report of the trial of William Burke Kirwan, for the murder of Maria Louisa Kirwan, his wife, at the island of Ireland's Eye, in the county of Dublin on the 6th September, 1852, before the Hon. Judge Crampton and the Rt Hon. Baron Greene, at the Commission Court Green Street, on the 8th and 9th December, 1852* (Dublin, 1853), p. 46.

164 NAI, RP/1863/4662.   165 *Thom's Directory, 1870*, p. 235.

166 Larcom Papers (NLI, MS 7620 [*Daily News*, 21 Nov. 1860]).

167 *Report of the committee appointed to inquire into the office of public prosecutor with minutes of*

There were still crown counsel allocated to each county but now there were usually two and sometimes three; the single senior counsel serving the whole circuit had been replaced by senior counsel in each county supported by a junior, and both received 'an appointment from the attorney general for the time being, and they continue in office.' When the attorney decided to prosecute, the crown solicitor instructed the crown counsel, and 'the junior crown counsel draws the indictments; the senior crown counsel receives a case to direct proofs. Each of them receives a brief in the case.'

The crown solicitor, when Porter described the office in 1884, was still not a local official involved in investigations in their early stages:

> In most instances, the crown solicitor has nothing to do with the case until it has been returned for trial by the magistrate; and in most cases no solicitor has seen it at all until that stage. ... He goes to the assize town (if he does not reside there) some days before the assize; he sees all the witnesses who have made depositions; he takes a fresh statement from each of them (or at least is supposed to do so), and makes such inquiries, and gives such directions, as he thinks right.[168]

But things were changing: 'if there be a case of exceptional importance the constabulary communicate with the assistant secretary in Dublin, who obtains permission for the sessional crown solicitor to attend before the magistrates in the first instance.' This, however, was still regarded as exceptional because 'in cases of any importance the constabulary in the district make careful inquiries in the district about the case under the direction of their own officers, and they communicate with the crown solicitor from time to time, if any fresh evidence turns up.'

Porter also told the committee of an inquiry that was about to be held in Dublin into the offices of crown solicitor and sessional crown solicitor 'with a view to see if they can be made more efficient and more economical.'[169] The effects of the inquiry can be clearly seen after the mid–1880s, when the offices of crown solicitor and sessional crown solicitor were more and more frequently filled by the same person. In the mid-1880s the offices were still distinct in all counties; in the mid-1890s they had been combined in several counties, and by 1910 amalgamation was almost complete. In that year there were in all only 38 crown and sessional crown solicitors compared with 55 in 1870. The reason for the reduction in the numbers of those engaged was not hard to discover. In the five years 1906–10, 2,152 cases were brought to trial annually at the assizes and quarter

evidence and appendix, pp 31–3 [C 4016], HC 1884, xxiii, 309. See also Thompson, op. cit., p. 67 where there is a brief description of how prosecutions were organized in the late 1890s, which shows that no formal changes had occurred since the mid-1880s.

168 *Report of the committee appointed to inquire into the office of public prosecutor* ..., p. 31.
169 Ibid.

sessions;[170] in the five years 1866–70, the figure had been 4,400 cases, a burden shared by 21 crown solicitors and the 34 sessional crown solicitors.[171]

Even in the early years of the twentieth century, the appearance of the crown solicitor was not routine. After the remand of James Doherty in 1902 for the murder of his son, the county inspector of Leitrim wrote to the inspector general asking for the crown solicitor's help because the district inspector 'does not feel competent to conduct the prosecution and as I, as county inspector, cannot conduct it, I request that the Crown Solicitor be authorized to do so. I will see to the preparation of the case for the court and can let the crown solicitor know when it is ready. The case seems clear but there are some points which should be distinctly brought out in evidence or a jury of this county may disagree.'[172] The problem was that 'the defence is likely to be that the deceased committed suicide and in order to illustrate the points of the evidence against the prisoner in a manner likely to influence a Leitrim jury (which is proverbially unreliable) it will be *necessary to have a model of the house where the murder was committed* and I request authority to get the model made by Sergt James Mallon, 45528, of Carrick station.'

When the assizes were over the crown solicitors reported on what they had achieved. After the Limerick spring assizes in 1841, Matthew Barrington was pleased with himself. 'Convictions were had in almost every case and particularly in those in the district in which so many outrages have been so recently committed,' he wrote. 'I have no doubt but the sentencing of 25 persons to transportation will tend much to the tranquillity of that district, as several of those persons were the leaders of gangs and most notorious offenders.'[173] Barrington's list of cases, which ran to three pages, was even more impressive than his words implied. There were nearly 50 prisoners involved in the 25 convictions; 3 prisoners, moreover, had been found guilty of murder, including Michael Fitzpatrick, found guilty of the murder of John Griffin in August 1840, 'arising out of the combination of trades'. Barrington's only failure to convict was in a murder case, where John Marnane and others escaped temporarily because the jury could not agree (Barrington noted that eleven jurors were for conviction). Barrington's list shows the amount of work done by the crown solicitor and crown counsel in a few days: 26 cases were brought on and 200 witnesses were examined.

The crown solicitor appraised, with the eye of a connoisseur, how the Crown's witnesses had conducted themselves at the assizes. In April 1841, Edward Hickman, the crown solicitor of the Connacht circuit, made a return 'of the several crown witnesses under the protection of the police on my circuit, with the remuneration or other disposal which I consider each of them entitled to.'[174] The

170 *Judicial statistics (Ireland), 1910*, p. xxxvii [Cd 5866], HC 1911, cii, 411.
171 Ibid., pp 158–9 [C 443], HC 1871, lxiv, 388–9.
172 NAI, CRF/1902/Doherty/69.
173 Ibid., Outrage Papers/Limerick/1841.
174 Ibid., Outrage Papers/Sligo/1841.

'manner in which they gave their evidence' was noted, each witness being commended as having given evidence 'in a satisfactory manner', or 'in a very satisfactory manner'. The return was made to Norman Macdonald, the under-secretary, which suggests that such returns were taken seriously by the government. The witness' remuneration included sums paid for emigration. Michael Reynolds of Mohill was not satisfied with the £5 he got to enable him to emigrate; he petitioned the lord lieutenant: 'memorialist having to buy clothing for himself and his family to the minutest article, humbly trusts that your excellency will be graciously pleased to order him so much more as your excellency in your wisdom, may deem sufficient.' The stipendiary magistrate in Sligo suggested that he should be given £10.

More ticklish was John Gallagher, who had to be held over to the next assizes, when he was expected to be the principal witness against two men and two women who were charged with murder. He had been kept in Sligo since December 1840, along with his wife and three children. He wanted more money; he begged the lord lieutenant 'to look to him and family with an eye of charity and to order him to be paid for the support of his son above named to enable him to clothe himself and family as he will not be able after the next assizes to show his face in his own country and after must leave Ireland and proceed to a strange place.' The stipendiary magistrate explained that Gallagher and his family had been getting £1. 2s. 2d. a week, which was wealth beyond the dreams of avarice for a small farmer or a cottier. The stipendiary did not think the allowance should be increased, although he was no doubt worried that Gallagher's discontent might lead him to be struck dumb before the next assizes or to suffer amnesia. In the end the parties kept faith with each other. Gallagher told his story satisfactorily. According to the crown solicitor, he 'fully supported his original information of the truth of which I have no doubt'. The prisoners were acquitted but Gallagher was not to blame, and the crown solicitor recommended 'that he may receive *ten pounds* on being discharged.' The practical arrangements for spiriting away unpopular crown witnesses were made by the RMs and the constabulary. After the conviction of the Phoenix Park murderers, for example, Sir David Harrel recollected that 'the safety and disposal of witnesses became the duty of the police and gave me a good deal of anxiety. All were successfully placed and dropped out of public notice, except James Carey who brought his death upon himself in a coasting steamer in South Africa.'[175]

175 Sir David Harrel, Recollections and Reflections, p. 77 (typescript, dated Apr. 1926 in Dept of Older Printed Books, Trinity College, Dublin). For Carey's murder see J.L. McCracken, 'The fate of an infamous informer' in *History Ireland*, 9:2 (summer 2001), 26–30. For a crown witness who did not discreetly vanish or conveniently die, but managed to run through £50 he had been given, see C.P. Crane, *Memories of a resident magistrate 1880–1920* (Edinburgh, 1938), pp 143–4. In 1871 the Treasury spent £44,051 on criminal prosecutions at assizes and commissions in Ireland; only part of this, however, would have been devoted to witness' expenses (*Judicial statistics (Ireland), 1871*, p. 69 [C 674], HC 1872, lxv, 303).

THE GRAND JURY

After the clerk of the crown had formally opened the assizes by reading out the judges' commission, he swore in the grand jury. The function of the grand jury was similar to that of the magistrates when they committed prisoners: to decide whether or not there was a *prima facie* case against them. The grand jury was supposed to consist of at least 12 members and not more than 23, chosen by the sheriff from among the 'resident freeholders' of the county, which meant in practice from among the landed gentry.[176] The foreman of the grand jury that indicted Sam Gray at the spring assizes in Monaghan in 1841 was Edward Lucas, who had been MP for the county since 1834, which implied local prestige and great landed wealth, or at least a strong family relationship with it. As well as Lucas, the grand jury included some small landlords such as Thomas Johnston JP, of Fort Johnston near Glaslough, who had an estate of about a thousand acres. It did not, however, include some of the biggest landlords in the county, such as the Hon. Henry Robert Westenra and Evelyn John Shirley.[177] MPs often served on grand juries. William Smith O'Brien and William Monsell served on the grand jury at the special commission in Limerick in 1848. Their labours were shared by the nominally advantaged Sir Vere de Vere Bt., The O'Grady, and the Knight of Glin, and they did not labour in vain because at the end of the commission, the chief baron noted that 'in the city of Limerick and in the town of Ennis, within eighteen miles of each other, eleven human beings will be left sentenced to suffer death for the crime of murder.'[178] O'Brien would find himself involved with another special commission and another grand jury nine months later in Clonmel, when he was put on trial for treason.

The grand jury had two functions: to arrange the county's finances[179] and to decide whether there was enough evidence to put prisoners on trial. There had been a connection between the financial business of the grand jury and the perpetration of murder since the Grand Jury (Ireland) Act 1836, and from 1870 section 39 the Peace Preservation (Ireland) Act 1870 gave grand juries power to award compensation in agrarian cases.[180] In such cases the grand jury had to do three things: (1) to decide that the crime was agrarian or 'arising out of any illegal combination or conspiracy'; (2) to fix the amount of compensation; and (3) to say which part of the county should pay it. At Westmeath spring assizes in 1871 the grand jury levied £375 on the parish of Mullingar 'in favour of Mrs Waters,

---

176 Not all were landed gentry. John McCrossan, who served on the Tyrone grand jury in the 1860s, was a solicitor in Omagh.

177 *Impartial Reporter*, 25 Mar. 1841.

178 Armstrong, *A report of trials held under a special commission for the county of Limerick, held at Limerick, January 1848* (Dublin, n.d. [1849]), pp 1, 310.

179 The grand jury arranged the county's finances by making 'presentments', which came into force when they received the judges' *fiat* (Virginia Crossman, *Local government in nineteenth-century Ireland* (Belfast, 1994), pp 25–41).

180 Above, pp 17–18. 33 & 34 Vict., c. 9, s. 39 (4 Apr. 1870).

mother of the late process server'.[181] Thomas Waters, who had been the Revd James Crofton's process server, had been shot after serving a notice to quit on 'Captain' Duffy, who was a leader of the Ribbonmen in Co. Westmeath. The ratepayers of Mullingar had retained Constantine Molloy, whose attack on the grand jury's proposal was predictable: 'first, that the amount awarded was excessive; and secondly, that under the Peace Preservation Act the grand jury had no power to assess the amount on a parish, but that it was incumbent on them to direct it to be levied on a barony or division of a barony.' The assize judge refused to 'interfere with the presentment, which was accordingly fiated.'

The main criminal function of the grand jury, however, was to consider the evidence against those who had been returned for trial. Grand jurors were supposed to act only 'upon *legal* evidence', which, if *uncontradicted* by evidence for the prisoner, 'would warrant a conviction before the petty jury.'[182] When they decided that there was enough evidence to put the accused on trial they returned an indictment, which 'was a written accusation of one or more persons of a crime, preferred to a grand jury and found or presented by them on oath.'[183] There were nice points of nomenclature associated with indictments: the accusation was called a bill when it was brought before the grand jury, but when they decided there was a case against the prisoner it became an indictment.[184] Bills were 'preferred' and indictments were 'found'. If the grand jury was satisfied, they found 'a true bill'; if not, the foreman subscribed it as 'no true bill', and 'threw it out' or 'ignored' it. The grand jury made its decisions by a majority, which had to include at least twelve of its members.[185]

Before the grand jurors retired to their room, the senior judge charged them. It was always the senior judge, regardless of whether he was the 'judge in commission' at that particular assize town or not.[186] At the Downpatrick spring assizes in 1866, for example, Baron Fitzgerald was the judge in commission but it was Judge Fitzgerald who delivered what was described as a 'luminous' charge.[187]

181 Larcom Papers (NLI, MS 7719 [*Express*, 2 Mar. 1871]). For Thomas Waters, 'Captain' Duffy, and the Revd James Crofton see Vaughan, *Landlords and tenants in mid-Victorian Ireland* (Oxford, 1994), pp 143, 171–3. See also NAI, OP 1872/3/15 and RP/1871/14,028.
182 Hayes, op. cit., i, 361.   183 Thompson, op. cit., p. 43.
184 Ibid., p. 66. See also Thomas Edlyne Tomlins, *A popular law-dictionary, familiarly explaining the terms and nature of English law; adapted to the comprehension of persons not educated for the legal profession, and affording information peculiarly useful to magistrates, merchants, parochial officers, and others* (London, 1838), p. 284.
185 The twelve grand jurors, who were the least number able to find a true bill, matched the twelve petty jurors who found the prisoner guilty, 'for so tender is the law of England of the lives of the subject, that no man can be convicted at the suit of the queen for any capital offence unless by the unanimous voice of twenty-four of his equals and neighbours' (Tomlins, op. cit., p. 285).
186 The King's Bench was the senior court, Common Pleas came next, and Exchequer third; the chief justices of the first two and the chief baron of the third were the three senior judges. The puisne judges' seniority depended on their date of appointment and on the court to which they were appointed.
187 NAI, CRF/1866/Logue/6. Baron Fitzgerald was appointed to the Court of Exchequer in 1859

The charge dealt briefly with the cases in the calendar. Torrens told the Monaghan grand jury in 1841 that 'nothing of importance, or requiring comment from him, appeared on the face of the calendar, with one exception.' The one exception was the charge of murder against the Orangeman, Sam Gray. Mary Ann McConkey, who was about to be tried for the murder of her husband, came under the heading 'nothing of importance'. Torrens' comments on Gray's case were not the austere, detached, non-committal expressions that might have been expected. 'If the several testimonies were sustained before them, they would have no difficulty in finding true bills against the accused of wilful murder,' he told the grand jurors. 'In the evidence, the individuality and identity of a person was fully stated, and the means and mode of perpetration made it appear a wilful and cold-blooded murder.'[188] Torrens might be dismissed as a judge of the old school (he was called to the bar in 1798). Yet thirty years later, in 1873, Judge Fitzgerald spoke roundly to the Mayo grand jury that was about to indict Edward Walsh for the murder of his wife. 'There will be no doubt upon your mind that she died from the injuries she received from shock and haemorrhage,' he told them. 'So far as the informations disclose there is nothing in the case to reduce the crime to manslaughter.'[189] To a juror with an open mind, but looking for a hint, here was a hint. When the judge addressed the grand jury, barristers were absent 'by custom'.[190]

When the grand jury retired to their room, they examined the Crown's witnesses *viva voce*.[191] They did not have to examine all the witnesses in a case. When a bill was preferred against George Davison and seven others at the Co. Monaghan summer assizes in 1851, 7 witness' names appeared on it; 6 attended, and the 'usual' oath was administered to them (their names were marked 'TVD', the initials of the foreman, Capt. the Hon. Thomas Vesey Dawson, MP for the county). The crown solicitor, however, reported that the grand jury had examined only 2 of the 6 witnesses (the 2 'who alone professed to have seen the murder committed & to have been enabled to identify Davison & the others as perpetrators').[192] The grand jury ignored the bill. They did not believe the two witnesses, 'the fact being that under circumstances under which they came forward to give information no reliance could be placed in their veracity. An

---

and Judge Fitzgerald to the Queen's Bench in 1860; the latter was senior to the former in spite of being appointed later.

188 *Impartial Reporter*, 25 Mar. 1841.
189 NAI, CRF/1873/Walsh/11 [*Mayo Ex.* 21 July 1873].
190 Delany, op. cit., p. 38.
191 Until 1816 the grand jury merely read the informations, but 56 Geo. III, c. 87 (26 June 1816) provided that no grand jury was to find a bill of indictment 'unless the same has been found by the jurors upon the evidence of one or more witnesses for the Crown, sworn in court and produced before them.' (See also W.N. Osborough, 'Law and the spread of literacy: millennial reflections on Boddington's plight': an inaugural lecture delivered at University College Dublin on 4 February 2000).
192 NAI, Outrage Papers/Monaghan/1851.

inquest was held on the body of Owen Rice on 23 February last & altho' McKenna and McGrory live in the immediate neighbourhood they did not attend the inquest & offer their depositions.' The attorney general had allowed the case to go forward, although he admitted that 'much discredit rests upon the testimony of those witnesses who did not come forward to give evidence for so long a period.' The crown solicitor, Maxwell Hamilton, had to accept that 'the indictment being ignored ... the traversers' bail [was] as a matter of course discharged & at present there does not appear to me to be any just grounds for taking any proceedings against them.'

Grand juries examined only the Crown's witnesses, and neither the prisoners, nor their counsel, nor their witnesses were present.[193] Whether the crown solicitor had actually been in the grand jury room at Monaghan is not clear because the grand jury's deliberations were supposed to be secret. According to Hayes, 'it is not usual for any person to be present, except the members of the jury, and the witness immediately under examination', although in cases of high treason 'any of the Queen's counsel may attend there, and prosecute on her behalf.'[194] There are hints, however, that officials attended at least on occasion. D.B. Franks RM, for example, recollected that he had not been in the grand jury room when an important witness was examined, which implied that it was not unheard of for officials to be present.[195] John Ryan described the grand jury at Cork in July 1875 in terms that suggested their deliberations were not private. 'Mr Smith Barry the foreman lolled at the top, occasionally signing a paper,' Ryan wrote. 'All round the table the grand jurors were amusing themselves with reading papers and cutting their nails.'[196] Ryan may have been describing the grand jurors' fiscal deliberations and not their criminal proceedings. The grand jury's deliberations seem to have been expeditious. The case at Monaghan summer assizes in 1851, referred to above, suggested not only speed but the fact that the case had been studied by someone, either the clerk of the crown or the foreman, before it came before the grand jury. Although the grand jury probably got through most of their business on the first day of the assizes, they remained in being through the assizes. At the

---

193   Hayes, i, 360; Thompson, op. cit., p. 66. See also Paterson, op. cit., p. 327.
194   Hayes, op. cit., i, 360.
195   Larcom Papers (NLI, MS 7576 [*Clare Freeman*, 5 Jan. 1856]). James Paterson, describing English grand juries, refers to a 'few persons' being present 'besides the grand jury' (Paterson, op. cit., p. 327). The foreman's oath implied that the crown solicitor or crown counsel could be present (William G. Huband, *A practical treatise on the law relating to the grand jury in criminal cases the coroner's jury and the petty jury in Ireland* (Dublin, 1896), p. 166, quoting Gabbett, op. cit., ii, 269). See also Huband, op. cit., p. 183 where *R. v. Coulter* (1839) 1 Cr & Dix 253, at p. 253 is cited to suggest that the crown counsel was present. For a description of a grand jury that shows that the public were excluded see *Minutes of evidence taken before the committee of the whole house, on the statement made by the attorney general of Ireland, in his place, on the 15th day of April last, respecting the proceedings on the trials of Forbes, Graham, and Handwich, and the conduct of the sheriff of the city of Dublin on that occasion*, p. 84, HC 1823 (308), vi, 545.
196   Diary of John Ryan (TCD, MS 10350 (no. 4), p. 97).

Tullamore spring assizes in 1860, for example, the grand jury returned a bill against George Dunne for perjury that he was supposed to have committed at a trial a day or two before at those assizes.[197] There was debate about whether the grand jury was bound by the laws of evidence. An English judge in 1872, for example, 'stated that the grand jury were not bound by any rules of evidence. They were a secret tribunal, and might lay by the heels in jail the most powerful man in the country, by finding a bill against him; and for that purpose might even read a paragraph from a newspaper.'[198]

The grand jury was not the only body that could put people on trial. Coroners' juries could put prisoners on trial without any proceedings before the grand jury, although crown prosecutors seem to have ignored coroners' inquisitions and to have preferred bills of indictment. After the Sixmilebridge massacre in 1852 Joseph Napier told the house of commons that 'with hardly one exception, the practice is to send up a bill of indictment, and not act on the coroner's inquisition, for experience has invariably shown that coroners' inquisitions obstruct rather than promote the ends of public justice.'[199] Napier's successor, however, found the coroner's inquisition a useful supplementary tool. When the Clare grand jury ignored the bills against the ten soldiers and a magistrate involved in the massacre, he used the coroner's inquisition to proceed with the trial.[200]

There were grander modes of putting people on trial than indictments and inquisitions. Misdemeanours, but not treasons or felonies, could be prosecuted through the Queen's Bench by means of an information, 'which differs from an indictment principally in this, that it is not presented to the court upon the oath of a grand jury, but by some authorized public officer on behalf of the crown.'[201] There were two kinds of information: *ex officio* informations were sought by the attorney general 'for offences so high and dangerous in the punishment or prevention of which a moment's delay would be fatal'; criminal informations were sought by ordinary citizens to deal with 'batteries, libels, and other immoralities, of an atrocious kind not peculiarly tending to disturb the government (for they are

---

197 Larcom Papers (NLI, MS 7639 [*Packet*, 8 Mar. 1860]).

198 Huband, op. cit., p. 183 (referring to *Bullard* (1872) 12 Cox CC 353, at p. 353). When a grand jury acted from their own knowledge and without any bill of indictment having been brought before them either by the clerk of the crown or the clerk of the peace, their accusation was known as a 'presentment' (Hayes, op. cit., i, 357).

199 *Hansard 3*, cxxiii, 205 (16 Nov. 1852). See also *Re Marshall* (1874) 8 ILTR 1, at p. 3 where Judge Fitzgerald said he had known a case where 'the party was put upon trial on a coroner's inquisition alone'.

200 *Copies of the several inquisitions removed from the Court of Queen's Bench in Ireland, in the month of January last, and transferred to the county of Clare ... in relation to any of the cases of homicide, riot, unlawful assembly or other criminal offence alleged to have been committed at the town of Sixmilebridge, in the month of July last, at the time of the general election ...*, HC 1852–3 (313), xciv, 63; Oliver Burke, *The history of the lord chancellors of Ireland from a.d. 1186 to a.d. 1874* (Dublin, 1879), p. 309.

201 Purcell, op. cit., p. 106.

left to the care of the attorney general) but which, on account of their magnitude or pernicious example deserve the most public animadversion.' The public officer who acted on behalf of ordinary citizens was the clerk of the crown in the Queen's Bench, also called the master of the crown office. Criminal informations could also be sought 'against ministerial officers for any act of oppression, or for any illegal act committed by them in the execution of their duties, from corrupt, vindictive, or other improper motives; but not where they act from ignorance or mistake merely.'[202] ('Ministerial' officers included justices of the peace.) In practice, the offences prosecuted by information tended to be the more genteel crimes. Even the language used was tentative. The procedure began in the Queen's Bench, for example, when a rule was obtained 'for liberty to file a criminal information'.[203] Even grander and more select as forms of prosecution were impeachment and bills of pains and penalties, where the prosecution took place in parliament.[204]

Most of the cases that came before the grand jury had already been dealt with by the magistrates, a fact that led to calls for its abolition. In 1871, when jury reform was a legislative possibility, George Malley QC suggested taking away the grand jury's criminal functions. Malley recognized the ancient pedigree of the grand jury, 'whose origin is contemporaneous with our language, confirmed by Magna Charta, re-enacted by the statutes of Henry IV, Henry VIII, and Charles I, and has been handed down to us by all the sanctity derivable from antiquity'.[205] In spite of this, however, he pointed out that the accused's case had been considered on at least three occasions before it came before the grand jury: first, before the committing magistrate where the accused was legally represented and able to cross-examine witnesses; secondly, when the informations were sent to the attorney general, who 'if he finds they do not set forth a sufficient case to warrant a prosecution, he directs it to be abandoned, irrespective of and uninfluenced by the fact that the committing magistrate had returned the informations for trial'; thirdly, on the eve of the trial, when the senior crown counsel examined the case before sending a bill to the grand jury. In spite of this three-fold scrutiny by magistrates, the attorney general, and the crown counsel, grand juries threw out bills, which suggests that the magistrates, the attorney general, and crown counsel did not examine some cases carefully. Between February 1850 and April 1851, for example, 6,077 bills were sent to grand juries, including quarter sessions' grand juries; 5,410 were found, 546 were not found, and 121 were not found 'by reason of non-attendance of witnesses', which means that nearly 700 prisoners were kept in custody or on bail on evidence that should have been rejected sooner.[206] In the ten

202 Ibid., pp 106–7, 114; Thompson, op. cit., p. 4.
203 *The Queen, at the prosecution of Richard Armstrong v. Francis Kieran* (1855) 5 ICLR 171.
204 See, for an example, Oliver MacDonagh, 'The last bill of pains and penalties: the case of Daniel O'Sullivan, 1869' in *IHS*, 19:74 (Sept. 1974), 136–55.
205 *ILT & SJ*, 5 (1871), 83.
206 *Return 'from the clerks of the crown and clerks of the peace of the several counties in Ireland, of the*

years 1866–75, 244 persons were returned for trial for murder; in 39 of these 244 cases, there was 'no prosecution', which seems to represent the third stage mentioned by Malley above. This left 205 cases, and in 32 of these, the grand juries ignored the bills, which was about 13% of those originally returned for trial for murder.[207]

INDICTMENT

When William Burke Kirwan was indicted in 1852 for murdering his wife, the language of the indictment smacked more of heraldry than of forensic rigour:

> The jurors for our Lady the Queen upon their oath do say and present that William Burke Kirwan, late of Howth in the county of Dublin gentleman not having the fear of God before his eyes but being moved and seduced by the instigation of the devil on the sixth day of September in the sixteenth year of our Sovereign Lady Queen Victoria with force and arms at Ireland's Eye in the county of Dublin did wilfully feloniously and of malice prepensed kill and murder one Maria Louisa Kirwan against the peace of our said Lady the Queen her Crown and dignity.[208]

Kirwan's indictment was exiguous on particulars. How Kirwan had killed Mrs Kirwan was not stated; neither weapon nor cause of death was mentioned; 'kill and murder' if it had appeared outside a legal document would have been a Hibernicism. The most notable achievement of Kirwan's indictment was to bring in God, the Devil, and Queen Victoria, and to call Kirwan a gentleman.[209] The apparently formulaic words, however, were significant. The words 'against the peace of our said Lady the Queen her Crown and dignity', for example, marked

---

number of bills of indictment sent up to the respective grand juries, between 20th day of February 1850 and the 5th day of April 1851; the number found, and the number ignored; and where such have not been found by reason of the non-attendance of witnesses, that the number be stated in the return', p. 3, HC 1851 (328), l, 319.

207 These figures are taken from the *Judicial Statistics*; for full references see below, pp 401–2.

208 Armstrong, *Report of the trial of William Burke Kirwan, for the murder of Maria Louisa Kirwan*, ..., p. 2. In 1842 Patrick Collings was indicted for killing 'one goat of the value of one pound'. Neither God nor the Devil was mentioned; but capricide affronted Queen Victoria just as much as uxoricide: her peace, crown, and dignity were mentioned (NAI, CRF/1842/Collings/5). English had replaced Latin in 1738 (Garnham, op. cit., p. 110).

209 Lesser crimes provoked more rousing language. John Farrell, who was convicted of indecent exposure in 1862, was indicted as 'being a scandalous and evil-disposed person, and devising, contriving, and intending the morals of divers liege subjects to debauch and corrupt, on a certain public and common highway situate at Rathgar-road, in the county of Dublin, in the presence of divers liege subjects, and within sight and view of divers other liege subjects through and on the said highway then and there passing, unlawfully, &c. did expose his person' (9 Cox CC 446, at p. 446).

the crime as one defined by common law and not by statute; the words 'wilfully feloniously and of malice prepensed' marked the crime as murder and not as manslaughter.[210]

Kirwan's indictment was not an archaic relic but the latest newly minted kind of indictment made possible by the Criminal Procedure Act 1851, often referred to as Lord Campbell's act, which had been passed in the previous year in an attempt to remove the complexity of indictments.[211] The silence of Kirwan's indictment on how he killed his wife, for example, showed the effects of section 4 of the act, which made the remarkable provision that in murder and manslaughter cases, 'it shall not be necessary to set forth the manner in which or the means by which the death of the deceased was caused.'[212] The brevity of Kirwan's indictment would have impressed those who had experienced the long indictments that were not uncommon before 1851. The indictment of Bridget Daly, for example, tried at the Roscommon spring assizes in 1840 for murdering her child, ran to two and a half pages of print. When she was convicted, her counsel moved in arrest of judgment 'on the ground of the insufficiency of the indictment; the first count being defective in not averring that the child was born alive, and the second in not properly describing the male child therein mentioned, either by name, or age, or otherwise, or saying that it was to the jurors unknown; and in being too general.'[213] The judge, Serjeant Greene, whose opinion was that 'the second count was bad, but that the first was good', reserved the case. Eleven judges upheld the conviction 'on the ground that the first count was good.'

The problem before 1851 was 'variance', which occurred when the evidence presented at a trial did not match the indictment in some detail and resulted in the quashing of the indictment, which might lead to the prisoner escaping untried. The prisoner's escape, however, might be only temporary because the quashing of an indictment for technical reasons was not an acquittal and the prisoner could be prosecuted again. Purcell gave two examples of variance: where the indictment named the murder weapon as a brick, but at the trial it turned out the dead man had been thrown to the ground and had hit his head on a brick; where the indictment named the murder weapon as a pistol loaded with powder and a lead bullet, but no bullet was found.[214] Before 1851 the trial judge could not amend the indictment even in trivial matters because it was the sworn statement of the grand jury, but Lord Campbell's act allowed the judge to order the indictment to be amended if he 'shall consider such variance not material to the merits of the case, and that the defendant cannot be prejudiced thereby in his defence on such merits.'[215]

---

210 Kenny, op. cit., p. 462. For offences created by statute, and not by the common law, see Tomlins, *A supplement to the crown circuit companion* ..., p. xxx.

211 14 & 15 Vict., c. 100 (17 Aug. 1851).   212 See also Purcell, op. cit., p. 260.

213 Jebb Rep 299, at pp 301–2.   214 Purcell, op. cit., pp 264–5.

215 14 & 15 Vict., c. 100, s. 1 (17 Aug. 1851).

From 1851 no indictment 'shall be held insufficient ... for want of or imperfection in the addition of any defendant.'[216] (Additions were names connected with a person's 'estate, or degree, or mystery'.)[217] From 1851 the judge could put right mistakes in Christian names, surnames, and titles. He could also put right mistakes about time 'in any case where time is not of the essence of the offence', and the venue did not have to be described in detail: 'the county, city, or other jurisdiction named in the margin thereof shall be taken to be the venue for all the facts stated in the body of such indictment.'[218]

The putative effects of the Criminal Procedure Act 1851 on the results of trials are shown in Table 3.2, where convictions are given as percentages of committals.[219]

TABLE 3.2

CONVICTIONS AS PERCENTAGES OF ALL COMMITTALS AND OF
COMMITTALS FOR MURDER, 1843–54

year	convictions % all committals	convictions % committals for murder
1843	46.60	13
1844	41.35	16
1845	42.53	14
1846	46.72	12
1847	48.81	21
1848	47.26	26
1849	50.49	19
1850	54.61	14
1851	58.24	15
1852	59.14	23
1853	57.54	23
1854	59.81	11

At first sight Table 3.2 shows that Lord Campbell's act had a substantial effect on trials and that 'the recurrent quashing of strong prosecution cases for technical flaws' was a thing of the past.[220] The years 1852, 1853, and 1854 had higher conviction rates for all offences and for murder than the years of the early 1840s.

216 Ibid., s. 24.
217 Purcell, op. cit., p. 66. 9 Geo. IV, c. 54, s. 30 (15 July 1828) had tried to deal with additions.
218 14 & 15 Vict., c. 100, ss 23, 24. See also Thompson, op. cit., pp 48–52.
219 The table is based on figures in *Tables of number of criminal offenders committed for trial, or bailed for appearance at the assizes and sessions in each county, 1849; with the result of the proceedings*, pp 5, 96–7 [1271], HC 1850, xlv, 533, 624–5; *Tables of number of criminal offenders ... 1854*, pp viii, xx–xxi [1930], HC 1854–5, xliii, 76, 88–9.
220 Desmond Greer, 'Crime, justice and legal literature in nineteenth-century Ireland' in *Ir Jur*, n.s., 37 (2002), 260–1.

The second column of Table 3.2 suggests that conviction rates rose from just over 40% in the early 1840s to almost 60% in the early 1850s. The rates for murders in 1852 and 1853 are also impressive compared with the early 1840s, although 1854 seems to suggest a reversion to the 1840s. The problem with ascribing these increases to Lord Campbell's act is that conviction rates began to improve *before* it was passed; indeed, the years 1846 and 1847 might be plausibly seen as the turning-point.

The act did not get rid of all the problems that had existed before 1851. The provision about venue, for example, did not solve the problem of defining the place where the murder occurred. When Laurence King was indicted in 1865 for the murder of Lt. James Henry Clutterbuck, the marginal note in his indictment named the King's County as the venue but no venue was named in the body of the indictment; at the trial it turned out that the attack had taken place in Co. Tipperary, but within 500 yards of the King's County.[221] Lefroy reserved the case, the Court for Crown Cases Reserved affirmed the conviction, and King was hanged. The complexity of the case was shown by the fact that proceedings in the Court for Crown Cases Reserved filled twenty-seven pages of the law reports. In spite of this example, it must be admitted that the act made indictments simpler. Section 4, for example, certainly made indictments in murder cases easier since the means of death could be left unspecified. Another sign of simplicity was the fact that Thompson took only 21 pages to describe indictments in 1899, while Purcell had taken 105 pages in 1849. The fact, however, that Thompson devoted nearly a fifth of his book to them showed that they still needed explanation. By the turn of the century it was possible to produce standardized forms of indictment. Murder and manslaughter were among the simplest, requiring the name of the county, the name of the accused, the name of the dead person, the date, and the formula that 'WILLIAM KING feloniously wilfully and of his malice afore-thought did kill and murder one JOHN BROWN: against the peace of Our Sovereign Lord the King, his Crown and dignity.'[222]

Indictments tended to be complicated because they tried to anticipate a variety of contingencies. At the special commission in Limerick in 1848 Michael Howard was indicted for the murder of Johanna Hourigan. The indictment contained three counts, which anticipated three eventualities: that Michael Rourke fired the shot, and 'the prisoner was feloniously aiding and abetting'; that Michael Howard himself fired the shot; and that 'a person unknown' fired the shot, and Howard was 'feloniously aiding and abetting'.[223] There was, however, a limit to the variety

221   16 ICLR 50, at p. 50.

222   George Hill Smith, *Forms of indictments (with special reference, where necessary, to the requirement of IRISH criminal laws)* (Dublin, 1903), p. 1.

223   John Simpson Armstrong, *A report of trials held under a special commission for the county of Limerick, held at Limerick, January 1848* (Dublin, n.d. [1849]), p. 257. For another example see id., *A report of trials under a special commission for the county of Clare, held at Ennis, January 1848* (Dublin [1849]), pp 1–2.

of counts because 'as a general rule, the defendant must not be charged in any one count of the indictment with having committed two or more distinct offences, otherwise the count will be bad for duplicity. Thus the same count cannot charge the defendant with murder, and a robbery, or the like; nor can two defendants be jointly charged with murder or manslaughter, by means of an injury done by one of them to the deceased on one day, and another injury done by the other of them on a different day.'[224]

The different counts, which were in practice distinct charges, on any one of which the prisoner could be found guilty, tried to grapple with different problems, one of which was the distinction made between principals and accessories. Occasionally it was a matter of niceness to decide whether a person was an accessory or a principal. Patrick Murphy was tried at Cork spring assizes in 1840 for soliciting James Barrett to murder his wife by poisoning her. When the Crown's case closed, the prisoner's counsel argued that the prisoner should have 'been indicted as an accessory before the fact, for administering poison with intent to murder, and not under the 9th section of 10 Geo. IV, c. 34 [Offences Against the Person Act 1829].'[225] The distinction in this case was an important one because section 9 of the 1829 act had made soliciting to murder a capital offence, but the Offences Against the Person Act 1837, which according to the prisoner's counsel 'impliededly repealed' section 9, made administering poison non-capital.[226] The evidence at the trial showed Murphy to have been guilty of both crimes, but since the attempt to poison had actually taken place (Barrett had bought two pints of porter, ordered the pint he had bought for Catherine Murphy 'to be well mulled and sweetened', and put two ounces of saltpetre into it), there was a good argument for bringing Murphy's crime under section 3 of the Offences Against the Person Act 1837. Murphy was found guilty of soliciting Barrett to murder, the judge, Louis Perrin, reserved the case, and 6 of the 10 judges decided that the conviction for solicitation was good. In the event, Murphy did not hang because Perrin recommended the commutation of his sentence to transportation for life.

Principals were divided into two classes, principals of the first degree ('one who hath actually and with his own hands committed the fact') and principals of the second degree ('one who is present, aiding and abetting, at the commission of the fact').[227] Accessories were more remote than principals of the second degree (an accessory was 'he who is not the chief actor in the offence, nor present at its performance, but is concerned therein, either before or after the fact committed').[228] An accessory before the fact 'is he that, being absent at the time of the felony committed, doth yet procure, counsel, command, or abet another to commit a felony'. An accessory after the fact 'is one who knowing a felony to have been committed by another, receives, relieves, comforts or assists the felon.'

224 Purcell, op. cit., p. 36.   225 Jebb Rep 315, at pp 317–18. Below, pp 381–2.
226 1 Vict., c. 85, s. 3 (17 July 1837).   227 Purcell, op. cit., pp 18–19.
228 Ibid., pp 24, 25, 28. For principals and accessories in the 1890s see Richard R. Cherry, *An outline of the criminal law as regards offences against individuals* (London, 1892), pp 28–32.

(There were no accessories in treason or misdemeanour, only in felonies.) The distinction between principals and accessories sometimes did not mean much in terms of guilt: 'if one command another to kill a third, both the agent and contriver are guilty as principals'; 'if several persons combine for an unlawful purpose, or for a purpose to be carried into effect by unlawful means, particularly if they have resolved to carry it into effect, notwithstanding any opposition which may be made to it ... and one of them, in the prosecution of it, kill a man, it is murder in all who are present, whether they actually aid and abet or not.'[229] In 1856 Thomas Dunn, for example was found guilty at a special commission at Cavan as an accessory before the fact of the murder of Charlotte Hinds. Dunn and James Murphy, the actual perpetrator, were hanged; the only distinction that the law made between them was that Murphy's body was buried inside Cavan gaol and Dunn's was given to his friends.[230]

Indictments also tended to be made more complicated by the fact that more than one prisoner could be included in the same indictment. According to Purcell, 'where the act is such that several may join in it, all the parties so co-operating, or any number of them, may be included in the same indictment, or may be indicted separately.'[231] Prisoners who were indicted together had no legal right to a separate trial,[232] although in practice if they refused to join in their challenges, the crown counsel might be obliged to put them on trial separately. The Crown could not promiscuously lump prisoners together because 'whenever two or more persons are indicted jointly for a single offence, the evidence must show it to have been the joint act of the accused, i.e. that they acted together in it.'[233]

The case of John Ahearne, Maurice Ahearne, and Patrick Power, who were indicted at Waterford spring assizes in 1852 for conspiracy to murder James Troy, illustrated the problem of trying a group of prisoners. The prisoners pleaded not guilty, refused to join in their challenges, and the Crown decided to try them separately. When John Ahearne, who was tried first, was found guilty, his counsel objected that 'he could not by law have been tried alone for the conspiracy, but that the other two persons named in the indictment being amenable and having pleaded, should have been tried along with him.'[234] The prisoner's counsel 'certified as to their opinion that the objection made was a serious one.' The judge, Moore, sentenced Ahearne to death but reserved the case. The prisoners' arguments before the judges were that 'a single person cannot be tried on a charge of conspiracy, unless the other persons concerned be not amenable to justice', that in this case 'there was no evidence to show that any other person besides those named in the indictment was engaged in the alleged conspiracy', and that 'if the

229 Purcell, op. cit., p. 22.
230 NAI, CRF/1856/Dunn/26; *Impartial Reporter,* 22 May 1856.
231 Purcell, op. cit., p. 33.
232 *A report on criminal procedure to the lord chancellor; by Charles Sprengal Greaves, Esq., one of her majesty's counsel,* p. 31 [456], HC 1856, l, 109. See also Purcell, op. cit. p. 174.
233 Ibid., p. 34.   234 2 ICLR 381, at p. 382.

other two persons were subsequently acquitted, Ahearne, who had been previously convicted, would be, *ipso facto*, acquitted.'[235] The Court for Crown Cases Reserved decided not to arrest judgment, and Lefroy summed up by saying that 'the verdict binds the man tried, not the other untried, and what difference is there, if he be the one outstanding and not the one appearing?'[236] The sentences of death passed on John and Maurice Ahearne were not carried out; both were transported for life. Power's name did not appear in the Death Book in 1852, which suggests that he was either acquitted or found guilty of a non-capital offence.[237]

Not only could an indictment include several counts and several prisoners, but the Crown could bring in several indictments against the same prisoner or group of prisoners. At Down summer assizes in 1851 Lawrence Hoy and Bernard Larkin were 'indicted under the statute 11 Vict., c. 2, s. 9 [the Crime and Outrage Act 1847], for, on the 23rd June last, having in their possession a certain pistol within a proclaimed district; and in a second indictment, with appearing in arms by night to the terror of Her Majesty's subjects.' Larkin's counsel, William McMechan, objected that Larkin could not be tried on both indictments at the same time. Sir Thomas Staples QC, who conceded with an easy grace that suggested a prior intention to pull the wool over somebody's eyes, 'elected to proceed on the first indictment, and called witnesses who proved the finding a pistol upon the prisoner Hoy on the night mentioned in the indictment; but the evidence only went to show that the prisoner Larkin was present, and no arms were found upon him.' Larkin was acquitted, Hoy was found guilty.[238]

The proposition that a prisoner, indicted for one crime, could be found guilty of a lesser one, was not always straightforward. Russell's *Treatise* yielded a nice pair of examples.[239] A prisoner indicted for murder could be found guilty of manslaughter, 'for the indictment contains all the allegations essential to that charge.' The principle here is easy to grasp ('it is necessary that the minor offence should be substantially charged in the indictment'). Having grasped this the reader then has to reconcile it with Russell's second example, 'where two prisoners were tried … on a charge of stealing five sheep, and upon the evidence they appeared to be lambs, the judges held that the prisoners could not be convicted, as the statute mentioned both sheep and lambs.' This edition of Russell's *Treatise* was published in 1865, which suggests that the Criminal Procedure Act 1851 had not cleared away all nice distinctions. Another nice distinction to be found in Russell was the statement that copulation with a chicken was not bestiality, 'a fowl not coming under the term "beast".'

235 Ibid., pp 381, 382, 384.   236 Ibid., p. 385.
237 Death Book, 1852–1932 (NAI, GPB/CN/5).
238 5 Cox CC 288, at p. 288. See also *Shea v. R* (1848) 3 Cox CC 141, at p. 144 where it was alleged that there were nine errors assigned to the 'record' of the trial; the errors seem to have originated in the wording of an indictment under 1 Vict., c. 85, s. 2.
239 Russell, op. cit., iii, 309–10, 313; i, 938.

ARRAIGNMENT

Those who were indicted enjoyed two ancient rights. First, they were to be tried 'within the jurisdiction in which the offence is committed'.[240] Secondly, those indicted of felony were 'bound to plead and submit to trial instanter', or, as Lawson said in *Poole*, 'the prisoner is entitled to have the case disposed of, and to force it on; and if the Crown do not wish to proceed, it is open to the prisoner to call on the Crown to proceed; and the judge must call on the Crown to say why they should not go on; and except for some good cause shown he cannot refuse to proceed.'[241] When the prisoner was brought into the dock, the clerk of the crown read the indictment to him and asked him if he was guilty or not guilty.

This was the arraignment, when the prisoner was 'called to a reckoning (*ad rationem*) by hearing the indictment read.'[242] Prisoners were not allowed copies of the indictment, except when indicted for treason. When John Mitchel was indicted at the Dublin Commission in 1848 for the new offence of treason-felony, the judges refused to allow him a copy of the indictment because 'it would be mischievous to break in upon a long-established practice, sanctioned by the highest authorities.'[243] The prisoner's only right, 'in accordance with the authorities and with universal practice', was 'that the indictment be read slowly over once, and once only.'[244] If more than one indictment had been found against the prisoner, the Crown could decide the order in which they were to be taken, or even if they were to proceed at all. At the special commission in Limerick in 1848 Patrick Bourke was indicted for firing at Christopher Miller with intent to murder him; he was also indicted for 'assaulting the habitation' of Miller. The Crown 'elected to proceed on the second charge.'[245] At the same commission, Denis Ryan faced three indictments; he pleaded guilty to the first two, and the Crown decided not to proceed with the third, which was a capital one, that he had shot at and wounded Michael Sullivan with intent to murder him.[246]

Judges were reluctant to accept pleas of guilty in capital cases. When Thomas Hayes, the serendipitous wife-murderer, tried to plead guilty at the King's County summer assizes in 1865, Lord Chief Justice Lefroy persuaded him to plead not guilty.[247] There was conscientious unease about the plea of not guilty. 'Many persons ... believe that a prisoner who is guilty cannot obtain a trial unless he

---

240 Purcell, op. cit., p. 101.

241 (1883) 14 LR Ir 14, at p. 22; Purcell, op. cit., p. 95.

242 Kenny, op. cit., p. 466.

243 *R. v. Mitchel* (1848) 3 Cox CC 1, at p. 6. See also Kostal, op. cit., 78–9. Stephen thought the importance of the prisoner's seeing the indictment was 'overrated' because 'a copy of the indictment would only have enabled prisoners to make little quibbles' (*A history of the criminal law of England,* 3 vols (London, 1883), i, 399).

244 *R. v. Dowling* (1848) 3 Cox CC 509, at p. 510.

245 John Simpson Armstrong, *A report of trials held under a special commission for the county of Limerick ... January 1848,* p. 46.

246 Ibid., p. 110.

247 NAI, CRF 1865/Hayes/21.

tells a falsehood by pleading that he is not guilty,' Charles Greaves wrote. 'Unfortunately this opinion prevails among chaplains of gaols as well as other persons, and strong remonstrances have been made by them against this form of plea.'[248] An attempted remedy that would have enabled the prisoner simply to say that he wished to be tried failed to get through parliament in 1851.[249]

The prisoner was not confined to pleading guilty or not guilty. He could object to the indictment by means of a motion to quash it or by demurrer. The former was rare because it required the indictment 'to be so defective on the face of it that no judgment can be given on it even should the defendant be convicted'. The latter admitted the facts of the case to be true, but argued that they did not 'in point of law constitute him guilty of an offence sufficiently charged against him.'[250] Demurrers were of two kinds: special demurrers, which were aimed at formal defects in the indictment, and general demurrers. After Lord Campbell's act the former became practically obsolete because 'many omissions in indictments which formerly rendered them the subject of special demurrer have become altogether immaterial.'[251] The prisoner took a risk when he demurred because if the judgment went against him it was not clear that he could retrace his steps and plead not guilty, which was known as 'pleading over'. According to Thompson, for example, writing as late as 1899, 'in case of felony it seems that a judgment for the Crown is final; though this has been doubted, and in some cases the defendant has been held entitled to plead over.'

Even demurrers did not exhaust the prisoner's repertoire. He could enter a plea in abatement, which was either a challenge to the composition of the grand jury or an objection to the indictment itself. At Tullamore in 1838, for example, in one case 'prisoners pleaded in abatement that the grand jury were returned by one who was not duly appointed as high sheriff', because the high sheriff, Michael Bernard Mullins, had not been appointed according to 'the ancient usage and custom of this realm'.[252] The prisoner could also enter a special plea in bar, which meant he claimed he had been already tried for the same crime, and had either been convicted, acquitted, or pardoned.[253] These special pleas retained their French names: *autrefois acquit* (the acquittal had to be by a petty jury); *autrefois convict* ('no man ought to be twice brought in danger for one and the same crime … but a plea of *autrefois convict* will not avail where the previous conviction has been reversed for error'). If the prisoner pleaded *autrefois acquit* 'a jury are sworn instanter to try the issue. If the judgment is for the Crown, this in misdemeanours

248 *A report on criminal procedure to the lord chancellor; by Charles Sprengal Greaves, Esq., one of her majesty's counsel*, p. 30 [456], HC 1856, l, 108.

249 *A bill intituled an act for further improving the administration of criminal justice*, p. 12, HC 1851 (366), i, 18.

250 Thompson, op. cit., pp 72–3. For an earlier and more detailed account see Purcell, op. cit., pp 126–46.

251 Thompson, op. cit., p. 73.

252 Huband, op. cit., p. 175 (citing *Minnock* (1838) Cr & Dix Abr 537).

253 Thompson, op. cit., pp 77–9.

is final; but in treason or felony the defendant may plead not guilty as well.' These special pleas were rare in practice, but they were not unknown. At Monaghan spring assizes in 1842 Sam Gray, having been acquitted of the murder of Owen Murphy at the spring assizes in 1841, pleaded *autrefois acquit* when he was indicted for shooting at James Cunningham because 'Owen Murphy was then and there feloniously killed and murdered by the same identical person by whom the said shot was fired at James Cunningham'. The case was eventually removed by *certiorari* to the Queen's Bench, which decided in May 1843 that the two offences were distinct felonies.[254]

Silence, which was a rare thing in legal proceedings, could intervene at arraignment. If the prisoner refused to say anything, a jury was empanelled 'to try whether the prisoner be mute of malice or by the visitation of God'. Mute of malice implied he would not speak, mute of God implied he could not speak.[255] If the prisoner were found to be mute by the visitation of God, the court was supposed 'to use such means as may be sufficient to enable the prisoner to understand the charge; and if this be found impracticable a plea of not guilty should be entered, and the trial proceed'. If the prisoner were found mute of malice, the court 'could order the proper officer to enter a plea of not guilty on behalf of such person.'[256] While demurrers and special pleas opened up interesting opportunities, the most common occurrence at arraignment, apart from pleas of not guilty, was that the prisoner was found to be insane. Insanity, by definition, meant that the prisoner could not be guilty, certainly not until the law was changed in 1883.[257] Out of 244 prisoners returned for trial in the ten years 1866–75, for example, 22 were found insane at arraignment. If the prisoner appeared to be insane, a jury was empanelled to decide whether he was fit to be tried. If he was found unfit, he could be put on trial when he recovered. At Galway summer assizes in July 1886, the issue paper given to such a jury had the words 'Your issue is to try and inquire whether Terence Benjamin Brodie is a person of sound mind and capable of pleading to the charge preferred against him.'[258] The jury decided he was not capable. At the next assizes, however, he was put on trial, his trial went through all its stages, and the petty jury found him 'guilty but was insane at the time he committed the action.'

The only consideration given to the case against a prisoner who pleaded guilty, apart from whatever may have passed between his counsel and the crown counsel, was the judge's reading of the informations. At the spring assizes in South

---

254 (1842) 3 Cr & Dix 93, at pp 95–6; (1843) 5 Ir LR 524, at pp 524, 533.

255 Thompson, op. cit., p. 74. For the Scottish procedure see Paterson, op. cit., p. 331. Prisoners who refused to plead had formerly been tortured by having heavy weights placed on their bodies. Garnham has found a case of 'pressing' at Kilkenny as late as 1740. Refusing to plead had been a way of avoiding the forfeiture of property that was one of the incidents of being found guilty of treason or felony (Garnham, op. cit., p. 111).

256 9 Geo. IV, c. 54, s. 8 (15 July 1828).   257 Below, p. 281.

258 NAI, Crown Book at Assize, Co. Galway, 1886.

Tipperary in 1853, Michael Rourke pleaded guilty to murder.[259] The judge, who was the first serjeant, John Howley, decided that Rourke's was not a case 'for exacting the capital punishment'. His explanatory letter to the lord lieutenant shed hardly any light on the case: 'the occurrence took place in a hayfield by night, where a number of disorderly characters boys & girls had assembled ... for the purpose of passing the night.' Apparently the murdered man's name was unknown, and the cause of the quarrel was unknown, but may have had something to do with the murdered man's believing Rourke was about to rob him. Howley did not mention a bargain between the Crown and the prisoner. His letter implied that he had groped his own way to the decision he had just made. After thirteen years in Mountjoy, Bermuda, and Spike Island, Rourke appealed to the lord lieutenant for release and revealed details that made some sense of the affair: 'In July 1852, there being a general election in this country for members of parliament, the "memorialist" was in company with several others, and had been drinking for three or four days consecutively, and on the night of the unfortunate occurrence, they had obtained a large quantity of whiskey, with which they agreed to pass the night in a neighbouring field. He states that the unfortunate man who was murdered on that night, was not of the company but, that in the night time he came into the field accompanied by four girls of disreputable character, in a state of intoxication and joined the party.' Rourke was released in December 1866.

259 Ibid., CRF/1866/Rourke/25.

CHAPTER FOUR

Empanelling the jury

THE LONG PANEL

THE FORMATION OF THE JURY was potentially the most complicated part of the trial. It could take a long time, it might involve dozens of persons, sometimes hundreds, and it might generate an enormous amount of friction and publicity. When a political or an agrarian case had to be tried, the formation of the jury might cause more controversy than any other aspect of the trial. Implicit in every discussion of nineteenth-century Irish juries was the belief that either the sheriff or the crown solicitor had packed them. 'Ireland during the nineteenth century was a period of great difficulty for the operation of jury trial,' John McEldowney wrote. 'Periods of violence and outbreaks of serious crimes placed the jury system under severe pressure.'[1] Speaking of the efforts of successive attorneys general to control the activities of crown solicitors, McEldowney concluded that 'despite these efforts allegations of jury-packing were made, although the extent of the practice and the number of cases which were proven are difficult to estimate.'[2]

Murder cases were less likely to produce complaints of jury-packing, if only because murder and high politics rarely coincided, one of the few exceptions during this period being the Phoenix Park murders. Agrarian murders, however, occurred regularly, and their trial was much more likely to cause complaint than ordinary murder trials. The trials of Francis Hughes and Patrick Woods, for example, at Armagh in 1841–2, not only stimulated a lively correspondence between the attorney general and the crown solicitor, but led to the prosecution of Charles Gavan Duffy, the proprietor of the *Belfast Vindicator*, for criminal libel.[3] There were cases where prisoners needed more protection from popular opinion than from the Crown, but these received less attention than contentious political cases. The Ireland's Eye case, for example, has never acquired the historical resonance enjoyed by the Maamtrasna murders or the Phoenix Park murders. William Burke Kirwan badly needed to be protected from the prejudices of respectable and credulous Dublin, but the first questioning of the verdict against him came largely from sources outside Ireland, such as *The Times*.[4]

---

1 John F. McEldowney, '"Stand by for the Crown": an historical analysis' in *Criminal Law Review* *1979*, 277.
2 Ibid., p. 279.   3 Below, p. 153.
4 Richard S. Lambert, *When justice faltered: a study of nine peculiar murder trials* (London, 1935), pp 205–9.

Juries at murder trials were taken from the ordinary, qualified jurors.[5] In other words they were the same kind of juries that tried less serious offences such as theft. There were special juries, which were called in intricate civil cases and in certain cases of misdemeanour, but they played no part in felony trials. According to Purcell, a special jury was grantable only 'in the case of a misdemeanour and where the prosecution is depending in the Queen's Bench'.[6] When O'Connell and eight others were indicted in November 1843 for 'conspiracy and other misdemeanours', they were tried by a special jury: 48 names were taken from the long panel; the Crown and the traversers struck off 12 each; the first 12 of the remaining 24 became the petty jury. According to Oliver J. Burke, 'so well did the sheriff carry out the views of the government, and so well did he manage the list, that out of the 48 there were just 11 Catholics, and these 11 names were struck off, and a jury whose principles could be relied on was secured.'[7]

Nineteenth-century lawyers had inherited a number of ancient devices for producing impartial juries, or at least juries from which some gross imperfections had been removed. Prisoners could not only challenge individual jurors, they could also challenge the whole list summoned by the sheriff. The Crown could ask jurors to 'stand by', which was a form of temporary challenge. These devices were employed at the trial itself, but even before the trial took place other methods of selection were at work: acts of parliament defined the qualifications of those who were to be called for jury service and determined how their names were to be entered in the jurors books; the same acts prescribed how the sheriffs were to select names of those qualified from the jurors books to attend the assizes and quarter sessions. From 1833 to 1871 Perrin's act defined jurors' qualifications, the compilation of the jurors books, and the means by which the sheriffs were to select their 'long panels' to attend the assizes and quarter sessions.[8] In 1871 O'Hagan's act replaced much of Perrin's act.[9]

Under Perrin's act, which was in force from 1833 to 1871, jurors had to be 'between the ages of 21 years and 60 years', and they had to have property.[10] The more secure their tenure, the less property they had to have: if it were freehold (fee simple, fee tail, 'or for the life of himself or some other person or persons'), it had to be worth £10 'by the year above reprizes in lands or tenements or in rents issuing out of any lands or tenements'.[11] If their property were leasehold 'for a term not less than 21 years', it had to be worth £15 a year. In the cities, towns, and

5   For the change that took place in 1882, see below, p. 129.
6   Theobald A. Purcell, *A summary of the general principles of pleading and evidence, in criminal cases in Ireland: with the rules of practice incident thereto* (Dublin, 1849), p. 161.
7   *The history of the lord chancellors of Ireland from a.d. 1186 to a.d. 1874* (Dublin, 1879), p. 254.
8   3 & 4 Will. IV, c. 91 (28 Aug. 1833).
9   34 & 35 Vict., c. 65 (14 Aug. 1871).
10   3 & 4 Will. IV, c. 91, s. 1 (28 Aug. 1833).
11   'Above reprizes' meant 'clear of all incumbrances and charges' (*First, second, and special reports from the select committee on juries (Ireland); together with the proceedings of the committee, minutes of evidence, and appendix*, p. 2, HC 1873 (283), xv, 406).

boroughs, 'every resident merchant, freeman, and householder' was qualified if he had a house 'of the clear yearly value of £20' or 'lands or tenements or personal estate of the value of one hundred pounds'.

This was a very restrictive property qualification. It was not so much the value of the property required, as the tenure, that excluded the great mass of agricultural tenants. The average agricultural tenant's farm after the Famine had a valuation of about £20, but only about 20% of tenants were leaseholders.[12] Even in the towns there were not many resident townsmen who were qualified. In 1857 in Main Street, Cavan, for example, out of 83 tenements only 9 exceeded a valuation of £20.[13] As a result of the restrictive property qualification, the number of jurors returned as qualified was small. In 1871 in the counties the high constables returned 44,073, and in the counties of cities and towns, they returned 11,327; of the former figure, the most numerous categories were freeholders (10,962), leaseholders (17,137), and householders (9,530).[14] Only 142 qualified because they possessed personal property worth £100. It had been pointed out in the 1850s that part of the problem was that high constables and cess collectors had no means of discovering the tenure of occupiers. It was even hinted that they took bribes to keep people off the lists.[15]

The property qualifications for the parliamentary franchise were apparently more generously framed than those for jurors. The Representation of the People (Ireland) Act 1832 gave the vote in the counties to two kinds of leaseholders, depending on the length of their leases: those with property worth £10 and more 'over and above all rent and charges' held on a lease for 60 years, and those with property worth £20 and more held on a lease of 14 years.[16] The act also gave the vote to those in counties of cities and counties of towns who 'shall hold and occupy within such city or town, as tenant or owner, any house, warehouse, counting-house, or shop which ... shall be *bôna fide* of the clear yearly value of not less than 10 pounds.' The 1832 act created an electorate of 92,141 in the 1830s.[17] The Parliamentary Voters (Ireland) Act 1850, which gave the vote in the counties

12   Vaughan, *Landlords and tenants in mid-Victorian Ireland* (Oxford, 1994), p. 7.

13   *General valuation of rateable property in Ireland. County of Cavan. Valuation of the several tenements comprising that portion of the union of Cavan, situate in the county above named* (Dublin, 1857), pp 341–2.

14   *Judicial statistics (Ireland), 1871*, pp 242, 245 [C 674], HC 1872, lxv, 476, 479.

15   *Report from the select committee on outrages (Ireland); together with proceedings of the committee, minutes of evidence, appendix and index*, pp 221, 224, HC 1852 (438), xiv, 239, 242.

16   2 & 3 Will. IV, c. 88, ss 1, 5 (7 Aug. 1832). For a discussion of the complexities of defining property qualifications for the parliamentary franchise under the 1832 act, see Desmond Greer, 'Lawyers or politicians? The Irish judges and the right to vote, 1832–1850' in Caroline Costello (ed.), *The Four Courts: 200 years: essays to commemorate the bicentenary of the Four Courts* (Dublin, 1996), pp 126–58.

17   The figures for the size of the electorate at different times are taken from B.M. Walker, 'Parliament of the United Kingdom of Great Britain and Ireland, 1801–1918' in T.W. Moody, F.X. Martin, and F.J. Byrne (eds), *A New History of Ireland*, ix, *Maps, genealogies, lists. A companion to Irish history*, p. 635.

to occupiers with a valuation of £12 and more, regardless of tenure, and in the cities and towns to occupiers with a valuation of £8 or more, created an electorate of 165,246.[18] The Representation of the People (Ireland) Act 1868, which extended the vote in cities and towns to those with tenements valued at £4 and more and to lodgers with rooms worth £10 or more, created an electorate of 225,551, which was more than four times the number of jurors in the country in 1871.[19]

Perrin's act required the clerk of the peace to instruct the high constables and cess collectors to make lists of those qualified.[20] These lists were left in the clerk's office for three weeks to be inspected by the public 'without any fee or reward'.[21] A special sessions of magistrates, which took place after the October quarter sessions, scrutinized the lists, and amalgamated them into 'one general list ... containing the names of all persons whose qualification shall have been so allowed, arranged according to rank and property.'[22] The magistrates sent their list to the clerk of the peace, who copied it into a book, 'in the same order'. This book, which was known as 'the jurors book for the year', came into force on 'the first day of January after it shall be so delivered by the clerk of the peace to the sheriff or his under sheriff.'

The sheriff had to choose the jurors from these jurors books. His selection, known as the long panel, was 'not to be less than 36 nor more than 60, unless by the direction of the judges appointed to hold the assizes.'[23] The sheriff, moreover, had to act in public: he had to make his long panel public 'for seven days at least before the sitting of the next court of assize' and to allow parties and their attorneys to inspect it 'without any fee or reward to be paid for inspection'.[24] Subject to these restraints, however, he could choose any names he liked for his long panel, subject only to the requirements that he took them from the jurors book of the year,[25] and that he arranged them 'according to rank and property',[26] which meant that the names of gentry came before those of their social inferiors and that the foremen of petty juries would be those with the highest rank. The long panel included, on some occasions at least, jurors from a wide range of backgrounds. At the Mayo spring assizes in 1851, for example, the long panel,

18   13 & 14 Vict., c. 69, ss 1, 5 (14 Aug. 1850).   19   31 & 32 Vict., c. 49, s. 3 (13 July 1868).
20   3 & 4 Will. IV, c. 91, s. 4.   21   Ibid., s. 8.
22   Ibid., s. 9.
23   Ibid., s. 12. See below, p. 160 for an example of a very long panel, with over a hundred jurors, called at the trial of Thadeus Derrig. The sheriffs seem to have returned two long panels, one for civil cases, and one for criminal cases. After the passage of the Common Law Procedure Act 1853 sheriffs returned only one panel (Constantine Molloy, 'Observations on the law relating to the qualification and selection of jurors, with suggestions for its amendment' in *Journal of the Statistical and Social Inquiry Society of Ireland*, 4:30 (July 1865), 191–2).
24   3 & 4 Will. IV, c. 91, s. 14.   25   Ibid., s. 11.
26   Ibid., s. 9. See Purcell, op. cit., p. 188 where it is stated that the first juror called was to be 'the juryman who stands highest on the panel.' See also *Carroll* (1840) 1 Cr & Dix 337, at pp 337–8 where the prisoner's counsel suggested selecting the names from the long panel by ballot, but the judge decided that in a criminal case this could be done only with the consent of the Crown.

which had 159 names,[27] began with 10 esquires; Edward Howley JP, of Belleek Castle, Ballina, was the first name on the list.[28] The next 11 were gentlemen, beginning with Charles Coyne of Castlehill, who was not a JP.[29] After the gentlemen came the farmers and shopkeepers, who were the two biggest categories on the panel.[30]

The Mayo long panel was demotic when compared with the long panel at the spring assizes at Nenagh in 1840, which consisted exclusively of 200 esquires and gentlemen, including county grandees such as Lt. Col. Henry Dwyer, of Ballyquirk; William Smithwick, of Youghal; William Tibeado, of Clonakillyduff; and Terence Alt, of Ringroe, who had obviously mended his manners and subsided into respectability.[31] Both of these long panels were for the ordinary assizes and not for special commissions where it was not unusual for the sheriff to

27   *A return 'of the jury panel in the criminal court at the last assizes for the county of Mayo, stating the names of the jurors empannelled and sworn in the case of* The Queen *versus* Thadeus Derrig and others; *the order in which the persons on said panel were called; the names of those ordered on the part of the Crown to stand by, and the names of the counsel engaged in said prosecution'*, HC 1850 (235), l, 655.

28   According to Levinge, 'esquires in law' were (1) 'the sons of all the peers and lords of parliament in the lives of their fathers; the eldest sons of the younger sons of peers, and their eldest sons in perpetual succession; and consequently the younger sons of peers after the death of their fathers'; (2) 'all the noblemen of other nations, and Scotch and Irish peers if they be not knights. The eldest sons of baronets; the eldest sons of knights, and their eldest sons for ever.' This list, which threatened to go on forever, had formerly included 'esquires created expressly with a collar of SS and spurs of silver, *of which at present there are none*' (Edward Parkyns Levinge, *The game laws of Ireland* (Dublin, 1858), pp 23–4).

29   A gentleman was less than an esquire: 'whosoever studieth the law of the realm, who studieth in the universities, who professeth the liberal sciences, and (to be short) who can live idly, and without manual labour, and will bear the part, charge and countenance of a gentleman, he shall be called master, and taken for a gentleman' (James Whishaw, *A new law dictionary; containing a concise exposition of the mere terms of art, and such obsolete words as occur in old legal, historical and antiquarian writers* (London, 1829), p. 134). For a case in Galway in 1845 where the issue was the plaintiff's being a gentleman, see Oliver J. Burke, *Anecdotes of the Connaught circuit: from its foundation to close upon the present time* (Dublin, 1885), pp 262–3.

30   The following were specifically excluded from jury service: peers, clergymen, 'all persons who shall teach or preach in any religious congregation', medical practitioners, officers of the army and navy on 'full pay', officers of the customs and excise, post-office employees, treasurers and secretaries of grand juries. Nearly all who were involved with the administration or the enforcement of the law were also excluded: judges, serjeants, barristers, assistant barristers, and judges of the ecclesiastical courts, advocates in the ecclesiastical courts, attorneys, solicitors, proctors, all officers of the courts, notaries, coroners, jailers, keepers of houses of correction, sheriff's officers, and police constables (3 & 4 Will. IV, c. 91, s. 2). Aliens, and those convicted of treason or felony, or of 'any crime that is infamous', and those outlawed or excommunicated were also excluded (ibid., s. 3).

31   *A list of the names of all persons qualified to serve as jurors in the northern division of the county of Tipperary, returned by the collectors of jury cess to the clerk of the peace, submitted by him to the magistrates at special sessions, agreeably to the Act 3 & 4 Will. 4, c. 91, commencing spring assizes 1839, and ending spring assizes 1844; also, a return, for the same period, of the long panel of the above county, from which petty juries are selected*, pp 15–16, 27–9, HC 1844 (380), xliii, 175–6, 187–9.

summon a long panel composed of gentry.[32] In spite of these examples and others where a smattering of gentlemen can be found,[33] however, farmers and shopkeepers predominated on juries. In *R. v. Fay* Judge Fitzgerald deplored long panels chosen from a narrow social group:

> I am amazed to hear that the practice in Cavan has been, that the panel summoned to try criminal cases has always been selected from the humblest class of jurors. Now, I do not wish to say one word that would interfere with the proper discretion of sheriffs, as to the manner in which they should summon juries; but I must express my opinion, that if the panel has been selected from the lowest grade of jurors, the sheriff's discretion has been most erroneously exercised. I do not say that it ought to be taken from the highest, but from all, both high and low, impartially.[34]

The sheriff was the holder of an ancient office, which he served for only one year, a year that was one of ceremony and hospitality. He was not appointed directly by the government, unlike the crown solicitors or RMs; he did not act under the instructions of the lord lieutenant or the attorney general; his powers did not come from the government, but from the law.[35] Most of his work was done for him by the sub-sheriff, whom he appointed.[36] The sub-sheriffs' local knowledge was supposed to be an advantage in compiling the long panel. 'They are men who know the county thoroughly; the very nature of their duties, the execution of civil-bill processes, and the various duties that they have to discharge, make them thoroughly acquainted with almost every character in the county,' James Hamilton QC told the Hartington committee: 'If there is an agrarian case to be tried, or a Ribbon case to be tried, or an Orange case to be tried, they will omit from their panel ... the names of men whom they know right

32   For more on 'special' jurors at special commissions, see below, p. 129.
33   For gentry serving on the two juries that tried William and Daniel Cormack at Nenagh spring assizes in 1858, see Nancy Murphy, *Guilty or innocent? The Cormack brothers: trial, execution and exhumation* (Nenagh, Co. Tipperary, 1998), pp 40–1, 59.
34   (1872) IR 6 CL 436, at p. 448.
35   On the appointment of sheriffs and the government's interference with the judges' powers to appoint them, see John F. McEldowney, 'The appointment of sheriffs and the administration of justice in nineteenth-century Ireland' in Richard Eales & David Sullivan (eds), *The political context of law. Proceedings of the seventh British Legal History Conference Canterbury 1985* (London and Ronceverte, 1987), pp 128–31. See also [Henry H. Joy], *Letter to the Right Honorable Lord Lyndhurst, on the appointment of sheriffs in Ireland, under the earl of Mulgrave by a barrister* (London, 1838).
36   According to George Battersby QC, 'The sub-sheriff is the sheriff for all purposes. The high sheriff never interferes; he does nothing but attend the judges' (*First, second, and special reports from the select committee on juries (Ireland) ...*, p. 100, HC 1873 (283), xv, 504). For sheriffs' hospitality at the assizes and for their hiring of javelin men, see *Report from the select committee of the house of lords on high sheriffs; together with the proceedings of the committee, minutes of evidence, and appendix*, pp 71–2, HC 1888 (257), xii, 287–8.

well to be Orangemen, Ribbonmen, fenians, or persons who have a sympathy with agrarian crime.'[37] The sub-sheriffs' local knowledge, however, tended to confine jury service to those whom they knew. 'The same jurors were generally selected from year to year,' William Henry McGrath, the crown solicitor for Tyrone and Fermanagh, pointed out. 'The sub-sheriff selected men who were, as he knew, acquainted with the duties, and were on the spot.'[38] This practice aroused suspicions of partiality, but Hamilton thought the sub-sheriff's dependence on a succession of high sheriffs 'of the most different views, political and religious' counteracted his partiality because if 'he acts as a violent partisan under one sheriff he would be certain to be dismissed under the next, who was a person of opposite views.'[39]

There were attempts to reform the jury laws in the 1850s and 1860s. Nine private members' bills were introduced into the commons between 1852 and 1869. Reform was frequently advocated. In 1852 John Major QC, when giving evidence to a select committee, suggested a qualification based on rateable valuation.[40] In 1861 Arthur Houston, in an address on jury reform to the Statistical and Social Inquiry Society of Ireland, called for the payment of jurors, majority verdicts, and greater efforts 'to see that none but those duly qualified are returned, and that none who are so qualified evade the responsibility.'[41] By the late 1860s a change in the law had become 'absolutely necessary', according to Constantine Molloy, who drafted O'Hagan's act, 'owing to the small number of persons who were qualified, so that the prisoner, if he wished to postpone his trial, had the means of doing it simply by exhausting the panel by his challenges for want of qualification, or by his peremptory challenges.'[42] The barony of Geashill in the King's County was probably an extreme example of juror scarcity, but it was a telling one: 151 persons had a rateable valuation of £20, but in 1858 only 28 made their way into the jurors book, and in 1859 only 3 made their way in.[43]

37   *First, second, and special reports from the select committee on juries (Ireland)* ..., p. 66, HC 1873 (283), xv, 470.

38   Ibid., p. 124. Accommodation in most county towns was scarce. In 1880, Enniskillen, which was bigger than assize towns such as Lifford or Carrick-on-Shannon, had only four hotels (Henry N. Lowe, *County Fermanagh 100 years ago: a guide and directory 1880* (Belfast, 1990), p. 73).

39   *First, second, and special reports from the select committee on juries (Ireland)* ..., p. 74, HC 1873 (283), xv, 478.

40   *Report from the select committee on outrages (Ireland); together with proceedings of the committee, minutes of evidence, appendix and index,* pp 224–5, HC 1852 (438), xiv, 242–3.

41   'Observations on trial by jury, with suggestions for the amendment of our present system' in *Journal of the Statistical and Social Inquiry Society of Ireland,* 3 (May 1861), 109.

42   *First, second, and special reports from the select committee on juries (Ireland)* ..., p. 103, HC 1873 (283), xv, 507.

43   *Returns 'stating the area and population of Geashill barony, in the King's County, Ireland; ... of the number of persons who have been summoned from said barony to serve as petty jurors at each assizes and quarter sessions respectively during the years 1857, 1858, 1859, 1860, 1861, and 1862; and also the number of persons from the said barony whose names have been returned on the jurors' books for those years',* pp 2–3, HC 1863 (337), l, 685–6.

Lord O'Hagan made the same point in 1871 when he introduced his bill in the house of lords: 'numerous social and economic changes had revolutionized the different classes of Ireland, and the old qualification of freeholders and lease-holders had become so obsolete that there were now none who could now constitute a jury in Ireland; while in some counties 45 and even 55 and 66 per cent of persons as well qualified in regard to property to serve as those who actually did serve, were excluded from the lists by their not possessing the legal qualification.'[44] The catalyst seems to have been the McKenna case in Co. Monaghan in 1869, which, according to John McEldowney, 'had the major importance of expediting the reform of the jury system in Ireland. Lord O'Hagan's act was a genuine attempt to end the packing of juries by the sheriff and prevent a recurrence of the McKenna case.'[45]

O'Hagan's act abandoned distinctions based on tenure and opted for a qualification based on rateable valuation. All occupiers whose net annual valuation was £20 and above were to be qualified, regardless of whether they were freeholders or leaseholders.[46] A lower net annual value of £15 was set for the county of Leitrim, the city of Kilkenny, and the towns of Carrickfergus, Drogheda, and Galway. The act also took away the sheriff's power to select the long panel as he pleased. From 1873,[47] when the act came into effect, the sheriff had to select the long panel on an alphabetical system from the jurors book 'by returning one name from each letter in succession, beginning with the first letter, and so proceeding regularly through the letters of the alphabet from first to last as often as may be necessary, and so far as the number of names in each letter will admit, until a sufficient number of names shall have been placed on the panel.'[48] The sheriff could no longer form a pool of familiar and experienced jurors because 'in preparing any subsequent panel ... the return shall commence with the letter next following that from which the last name in the preceding panel was taken, and shall proceed in like manner through the letters, taking the names of the persons not already summoned during the current or next two preceding years.'

The first names called under this new arrangement were not those 'highest in position and highest in fortune', but those whose names came earliest in the alphabetical sequence, which meant that the gentry and the better off did not

44 *Hansard 3*, ccvi, 1032 (19 May 1871).
45 John F. McEldowney, 'The case of the *Queen v. McKenna* (1869) and jury packing in Ireland' in *Ir Jur*, n.s., 12:2 (winter 1997), 352. See below, pp 134–5.
46 34 & 35 Vict., c. 65, fourth schedule.
47 Section 8 fixed 1 July in every year as the date when the clerk of the peace was to start compiling the jurors book for the next year; since the act received the royal assent on 14 August, 1871, the first jurors books would not have been ready until the beginning of 1873, which partly explains why the act did not come into effect for practically two years. In practice, a new act, 35 & 36 Vict., c. 25 (27 June 1872), actually fixed 30 June 1872 as the date when the new system 'shall come into operation'.
48 34 & 35 Vict., c. 65, s. 19.   49 Ibid., s. 18.

come at the top of the long panel as they had under Perrin's act.[49] At Galway spring assizes in 1873, for example, a publican, a hotelkeeper, and a draper were the first names on the long panel.[50] O'Hagan's act did not make any change in how the clerk of the crown was to call the names from the long panel in criminal trials, although it made arrangements for selecting jurors by ballot from the long panel 'in any court of assize or nisi prius', which confined balloting to civil trials.[51] The Juries Act, 1876, however, provided that

> the name of each man, who shall be summoned and empanelled as a juror in any court for the trial of criminal issues ... shall be written on a distinct piece of card, such cards being all as nearly may be of an equal size, which shall be delivered unto the proper officer by the sheriff or other officer returning the process, and the same shall, under the direction and care of such officer, be put together in a box to be provided for that purpose and shall be shaken together; and when any criminal issue shall be brought on to be tried, such officer shall in open court draw out the said cards, one after another, and shall call out the name and number upon each such card as it is drawn, until such a number have answered to their names as in the opinion of the court will probably be sufficient, after allowing for challenges of jurors and directions to stand aside, to provide a full jury.[52]

The new long panels tended to be rather long. At the Galway summer assizes in 1873, for example, there were 163 names on the long panel. There was no restriction on the length of the long panel as there had been in Perrin's act because section 18 of O'Hagan's act merely required the sheriff to 'select a sufficient number of names from the "general jurors book"'. The sheriffs may have called more jurors simply because they had more to call, or because they felt obliged to go through all of the letters of the alphabet. Very long panels, as we shall see, upset the balance between the Crown and the prisoner.

These acts of the 1870s also produced new qualifications for special jurors. To the baronets, knights, magistrates, and sons of peers, who had been special jurors before 1871, O'Hagan's act added those possessing landed property of a certain valuation, whose amount depended on the county where it was held. A net annual valuation of £100 was set for seven counties (Cork, Down, Kildare, Limerick, Meath, Tipperary, and Westmeath), and £50 for the remainder (with the exception of Leitrim where it was £30, the county of the city of Limerick where it was £40, and the cities of Waterford and Kilkenny, and the towns of Carrickfergus, Drogheda, and Galway where it was £30).[53] In the act of 1873 new qualifications were established, the most important of which was that the highest was £150, not £100, and the lowest £50, not £30.[54] In 1876 special jurors were

50   NAI, Crown Book at Assize, Co. Galway, 1873.
51   34 & 35 Vict., c. 65, s. 41.   52   39 & 40 Vict., c. 78, s. 19 (15 Aug. 1876).
53   34 & 35 Vict., c. 65, fifth schedule.   54   36 & 37 Vict., c. 27, second schedule (16 June 1873).

reinforced by, among others, those 'who shall be a director or manager of any banking, railway, insurance, steamship, shipping, or other company incorporated by any charter, or by or under the provisions of any act of parliament.'[55]

Special jurors were not called at felony trials until the Prevention of Crime (Ireland) Act 1882, which was passed after the Phoenix Park murders, allowed either the attorney general or the prisoner to ask for a special jury, which was special in the sense that it was selected by ballot from among the special jurors in the jurors book. The Crown retained its power to order jurors to stand by and the prisoner kept his twenty peremptory challenges.[56] At Timothy Kelly's second trial, for example, 200 special jurors were summoned; 120 answered, and 65 names were taken from the ballot box; as the 65 were called, Kelly challenged in the ordinary way, using his last peremptory challenge when 10 had been sworn.[57] Kelly's second trial, like his first, ended when the jury disagreed. Earnan P. De Blaghd, who examined Kelly's three trials, gave a qualified approval to their results. 'If I had been a wholly unbiased juror at the first or second trials, I should have held firmly out for a verdict of "not guilty",' he wrote. The third trial was a different matter: 'After Joe Hanlon's clear evidence, my own doubts of Tim Kelly's guilt – which had been very strong before reading the report of the third trial – finally evaporated.'[58]

There were references to 'special' jurors at felony trials before 1882 but these seem to have been 'special' only in the sense that they were empanelled at special commissions. Serjeant Armstrong described such 'special' juries. 'Men who were upon the grand jury panel of a county were summoned, and constituted a jury at a special commission,' he told the Hartington committee. 'At present, with a special commission, you have nothing but an ordinary jury in a case of treason or felony.'[59] Most of the jurors at the special commissions in Clare and Limerick in 1848, for example, were JPs. All of William ('Puck') Ryan's jurors, for example, were either JPs or could plausibly be connected with JPs.[60] These 'special' juries

55 39 & 40 Vict., c. 21, s. 2(4) (30 June 1876).

56 45 & 46 Vict., c. 25, s. 4(1) (12 July 1882). Section 4(2) provided that the procedure should be the same as that laid down in 39 & 40 Vict., c. 78, s. 19 (15 Aug. 1876). The use of special jurors was carried on by 50 & 51 Vict., c. 20, s. 3 (19 July 1887). In relying on special jurors, parliament obviously agreed with George Battersby, who believed that where jurors were of a higher class 'they act with perfect honesty and independence against their own prejudices' (*First, second, and special reports from the select committee on juries (Ireland)* ..., p. 91, HC 1873 (283), xv, 495).

57 *Report of the trials at the Dublin Commission Court, April and May, 1883, of the prisoners charged with the Phoenix Park murder, the attempt to murder Mr Field, and the conspiracy to murder; before the Hon. Mr Justice O'Brien; reported by W.C. Johnston* (Dublin, 1883), pp 221–5.

58 Earnan P. De Blaghd, 'Tim Kelly guilty or not guilty?' in *Dublin Historical Record*, 25:1 (Dec. 1971), 23–4.

59 *First, second, and special reports from the select committee on juries (Ireland)* ..., p. 49, HC 1873 (283), xv, 453.

60 John Simpson Armstrong, *A report of trials held under a special commission for the county of Limerick, held at Limerick, January 1848* (Dublin, n.d. [1849]), p. 12. See also Larcom Papers (NLI, MS 7618, item 72).

came to an end with O'Hagan's act. George Battersby QC explained to the Hartington committee how a misunderstanding between the sub-sheriff of Meath and the crown solicitor, which occurred at a special commission in Trim in 1871, marked the end of juries, where 'the panel returned always included every man who was not actually sworn upon the grand jury, and the panel to try cases then consisted of the highest men in the county.'[61] The crown solicitor, Stephen Seed, had expected a long panel where the gentry were well represented. The sub-sheriff, Harcourt Lightburne, and the high sheriff (the Hon. Jenico Preston, 'who is as honourable a man as any in the world') constructed the long panel anticipating the alphabetical nostrum of O'Hagan's act, and 'to prevent any local prejudice, they took jurors from every part of the county at random, and neither the one nor the other knew the men that they were choosing.' The fact that neither Preston nor the sub-sheriff knew what they were doing was hailed as a virtue. Preston 'never associated with the petty jurors, nor did he know them'; the sub-sheriff had been only recently appointed, and 'he never knew anything of the county; he was a practising attorney in a very limited practice in Trim, and he did not know the jurors.' Seed set aside a large number of jurors because the long panel did not produce 'such a jury as Mr Seed had a right to expect, or that he had ever seen in the box before, and that led him to make those observations, I suppose, which do appear to be rather rash.' The sub-sheriff of Meath threatened to sue Seed for libel.

O'Hagan's act was more innovative in its provisions than Perrin's, even considering the lapse of time between the two. It was not, however, very innovative. It did not, for example, establish majority verdicts, although a private member's bill had been introduced into the commons in 1871, proposing to have majority verdicts returned by juries of fifteen.[62] The new qualifications were not all that low, in spite of what was said and done at the time. They were much higher than the parliamentary franchise, for example, and the requirement to have property of a net annual value of £20 allowed in only the top quarter of the country's agricultural tenants. There was not even a huge increase in the number of existing jurors. Table 4.1, based on returns from the clerks of the peace of the number of jurors in jurors books shows that the numbers qualified just about doubled, which is not remarkable considering how few there had been under the old arrangements.[63]

Many lawyers professed to be shocked by the new jurors. James Hamilton QC told the Hartington committee they 'were grossly ignorant, and very badly dressed ... they could not understand us as a general rule, and in cases where there was no disturbing element they simply did what the judge told them.'[64] Hamilton expatiated on the deterioration of juries on the north-west circuit: in

61   *First, second, and special reports from the select committee on juries (Ireland)* ..., p. 94, HC 1873 (283), xv, 498.
62   *A bill to assimilate the law of trial by jury in Ireland to that of Scotland*, HC 1871 (bill 47), vi, 473.
63   *First, second, and special reports from the select committee on juries (Ireland)* ..., p. 287, HC 1873 (283), xv, 691.
64   Ibid., pp 1, 46, 64, 103.

TABLE 4.1

NUMBERS IN JURORS BOOKS IN THE THREE YEARS 1870–2 AND IN 1873

county	average of 1870, 1871, 1872	1873
Armagh	868	2966
Carlow	1171	1218
Cork	4228	8425
Donegal	895	1663
Galway	911	1855
King's	365	1527
Leitrim	745	1193
total	9183	18,847

Cavan, 'they were very inferior to what they were'; in Fermanagh, they had not deteriorated so much, because Fermanagh 'has always supplied rather an inferior jury'; Tyrone had suffered an 'immense' change, although he recalled that 'there were no better juries in Ireland than in Tyrone formerly, in my opinion, but now they are very much inferior indeed'; in Donegal, 'they were a very wretchedly poor class, and they complained bitterly of the distances that they were obliged to walk to attend the assizes.'[65] Constantine Molloy, who had drafted the act, was not so critical: the jurors in Kildare and the Queen's County 'appeared to me to consist of the class that I usually saw attending', but in four other counties of the home circuit (Carlow, King's County, Meath, Westmeath) they were 'of an inferior class'. Even Molloy thought that the property qualification should be raised. Charles Hare Hemphill (chairman of Kerry quarter sessions) was more cheerful: in Kerry, in Leinster, and in Dublin, the new juries acted 'in a very reasonable manner'. Serjeant Armstrong, who at least had the experience of having been convicted by an Irish jury, was more resigned to change than most when he said that under O'Hagan's act occurrences that had the 'aspect of novelties, were to my mind but the recurrence of difficulties that I had observed under the old system.' For all the complaints about the new juries, however, the conviction rate remained stable: in 1868–72 58.6% of trials on indictment ended in a conviction, compared with 57.5% in 1873–7.[66]

65 When convictions in counties (as a percentage of those returned for trial) are compared in the two five-year periods, 1866–70 and 1871–5, Cavan fell from 52% to 42; Fermanagh stayed steady at 57%; Tyrone increased from 53% to 58; Donegal fell from 51% to 41. There was a lot, therefore, in what Hamilton said, although he was wrong about Tyrone. (*Judicial Statistics (Ireland), 1870*, pp 158–9 [C 443], HC 1871, lxiv, 388–9 and *Judicial Statistics (Ireland), 1875*, pp 158–9 [C 1563], HC 1876, lxxix, 430–1).

66 D.S. Johnson, 'Trial by jury in Ireland 1860–1914' in *Journal of Legal History*, 17:3 (Dec. 1996), 272. For convictions as percentages of homicides in individual counties, see Carolyn A. Conley,

After the torrent of criticism at the Hartington committee, however, Molloy's opinion that the qualification should be raised carried the day. A new act in 1873 raised the qualification to a net annual valuation of £30.[67] A second act in 1876 raised it to £40 for most counties.[68] These two acts removed a large percentage of those who had been admitted by O'Hagan's act. The registrar general in his introduction to the *Judicial Statistics 1878* noted that the total number of jurors in the corrected jurors books in the whole country was 59,953, which was 'a general increase of only 4,493, or about 8 per cent, on the number (55,460) on the general jurors lists in 1871, the last under the old law.'[69]

CHALLENGING THE ARRAY

When a prisoner pleaded not guilty, the names of the long panel were called out, and the clerk of the crown warned the prisoner of his right 'to challenge twenty peremptorily, and as many more as you can shew cause for.'[70] Before the prisoner challenged individual jurors, or the *polls*, as they were called, he could challenge the long panel *in toto*, which was known as challenging the array. He could skip that and go on to challenge the *polls*, but once he challenged an individual juror, he could not retrace his steps and challenge the array.[71] When prisoners challenged the array, they had to do it for 'cause', which was subdivided into challenges for 'principal' or 'favour'. A 'principal' fact revealed 'such a manifest presumption of partiality or of default, on the part of the officer arraying or returning the panel, as to make it unnecessary to refer the question to triers.' An example of a 'principal' fact was the sheriff's selecting the long panel 'at the nomination, or under the direction, of either party'.

A challenge to the array for 'principal' was resolved by the judge, but a challenge for 'favour' required the appointment of triers.[72] At the special

Melancholy accidents: the meaning of violence in post-Famine Ireland (Lanham, MD, 1999), pp 142–3.

67   36 & 37 Vict., c. 27, first schedule (16 June 1873).

68   39 & 40 Vict., c. 21, first schedule (30 June 1876).

69   *Judicial Statistics (Ireland), 1878*, p. 73 [C 2389], HC 1878–9, lxxvi, 351.

70   Purcell, op. cit., pp 173–4. The quotation has omitted the alternative form of words used in non-capital trials. In Scotland the prisoner had only five peremptory challenges (James Paterson, *A compendium of English and Scotch law stating their differences: with a dictionary of parallel terms and phrases* (Edinburgh, 1860), p. 331).

71   Purcell, op. cit., pp 175–80. For a discussion of challenges to the array in England and Ireland see R. Blake Brown, '"A delusion, a mockery, and a snare": array challenges and jury selection in England and Ireland, 1800–1850' in *Canadian Journal of History*, 39:1 (Apr. 2004), 1–26 (from http://www.findarticles.com (10 Aug. 2006)).

72   Purcell, op. cit., p. 175. For the appointment of triers and their functions see Joseph Chitty, *A practical treatise on the criminal law, comprising the practice, pleadings, and evidence, which occur in the course of criminal prosecutions whether by indictment or information: with a copious collection of precedents of indictments, informations …*, 4 vols (2nd ed., London, 1826), i, 547–8.

commission in Maryborough in 1832, Francis Adams and Thomas Langton, who were about to be tried for administering unlawful oaths, challenged the array, alleging that Thomas Kemmis, the high sheriff, had allowed the sub-sheriff to summon a long panel that excluded those likely to acquit and included those likely to convict. Two triers were appointed, the prisoners' counsel having suggested two members of the grand jury, and the attorney general having agreed. The triers had to resolve two issues: 'Whether the panel was arrayed by the sheriff or not ... Whether the array was an impartial one or not.'[73] The prisoners' counsel examined the high sheriff and the sub-sheriff, and the attorney general cross-examined them. Lord Chief Justice Bushe then 'charged' them on the first issue, and they found that the panel had been arrayed by the sheriff. The whole procedure was gone through again on the second issue. The triers, who on this occasion were addressed by both judges, found 'that the panel has been impartially arrayed.' Sir William Cusack Smith, who was sitting with Bushe, expressed opinions that would have graced the columns of *The Nation* a decade later. The last sentence in the following extract from his speech would have been hailed as the effusion of a brilliant young man had it been made in 1843:

> I protest against this doctrine ... that a Catholic prisoner is not safe in the hands of a Protestant jury ... By a parity of reasoning we should have to hold, that a Protestant prisoner would not be safe in the hands of a Catholic jury. If a Roman Catholic cannot safely trust his case to a Protestant juror, can he securely trust it to the decision of a Protestant judge? Or when Roman Catholics are appointed judges, can the rights of Protestants be safely committed to their protection? I have now been for many years upon the bench ... I have never bestowed a thought upon the question of what was the religion of the prisoner whom I was trying, or the suitor upon whose rights it became my duty to decide. In Church I am a Protestant – everywhere else I am but an Irishman and a judge.[74]

The report of this trial-within-a-trial filled thirty-five pages of print! The same great principle, that sauce for the goose was sauce for the gander, was laid down at John Mitchel's trial at the Dublin Commission in 1848, when Thomas Lefroy slightly extended it. 'Suppose there were a great many rich men on the panel, and a poor man was to be tried, or that there were a great many very poor men on the panel, and a rich man was to be tried,' he asked, 'would it be an impartial panel?'[75]

'A successful challenge to the array would make a man's fortune almost at the bar as a junior,' James Hamilton QC told the Hartington committee in 1873.

---

73   James Mongan, *A report of trials before the Rt Hon. the Lord Chief Justice, and the Hon. Baron Sir Wm. C. Smith, Bart at the special commission, at Maryborough, commencing on the 23rd May, and ending on the 6th June* [1832] (Dublin, 1832), pp 205–40.

74   Ibid., p. 240.

75   *Mitchel* (1848) 3 Cox CC 1, at p. 30. For the challenge to the array at O'Connell's trial in 1844,

'Young barristers are very anxious to distinguish themselves by a thing of that sort.'[76] Hamilton had challenged the array at the Tyrone assizes in 1862 when Joseph Donnelly was charged with the murder of Patrick Hillon. The case was, according to Hamilton, one 'in which an Orangeman was tried for the homicide of a Catholic'. Charles McCrossan was the sub-sheriff and his brother John McCrossan ('a man of very great ability and a strong politician') was 'attorney for next of kin of the deceased, and actively assisting in the prosecution.'[77] The McCrossan brothers were Catholics and Liberals. The challenge to the array claimed that the sheriff had summoned jurors whose names were not in the jurors book, that he had summoned others because they were 'more likely to convict than to acquit the said prisoner', and that he had excluded others because he 'deemed them more likely to acquit than to convict.'[78] No great knowledge of denominational nomenclature or topography was necessary to guess the religious denomination of those whose names were not in the jurors book: Gilbert McHugh, of Castlederg; Francis O'Neill of Mount Pleasant; Hugh Quinn of Creggan; Francis McCrossan, of Tullymuck. As the list went on, however, its bias became less pronounced, and the following appeared: James Graham, James Buchanan, James Armstrong, John Graham, and William Hamilton.

The Crown demurred, the judge overruled the demurrer, and the panel was quashed. The reply to a challenge was by demurrer, counterplea, or traverse. Demurrer admitted the facts but questioned the legal validity of the challenge; counterplea replied by 'setting up some new matter consistent with the matter of challenge to vacate and annul it'; traverse denied the facts alleged.[79] Reply by demurrer could be long-winded. At the Queen's County spring assizes in 1839, when two prisoners, who were charged with murder, challenged the array, the crown counsel 'put in a demurrer *ore tenus*, and there was a joinder in demurrer', which meant in practice three speeches, one by the crown counsel and two by the prisoner's counsel.[80]

In 1869 the sub-sheriff of Monaghan showed that an Orangeman could do as well as a Liberal Catholic when it came to concocting a long panel.[81] At the spring

see John Simpson Armstrong & Edward Shirley Trevor, *A report of the proceedings on an indictment for a conspiracy in the case of the Queen v. Daniel O'Connell, John O'Connell, Thomas Steele, Charles Gavan Duffy, Rev. Thomas Tierney, Rev. Peter James Tyrrell, Richard Barrett, John Gray, and Thomas Matthew Ray in Michaelmas term, 1843, and Hilary term* (Dublin 1844), pp 117–47.

76   *First, second, and special reports from the select committee on juries (Ireland)* ..., pp 67, 77, 83, HC 1873 (283), xv, 471, 481, 487.

77   For John McCrossan's murder in Omagh two years later see below, pp 323–4.

78   Copy *'of the challenge to the array of the jury panel at the late Tyrone assizes, and of Mr Justice Christian's ruling when quashing the said panel, as returned by the sheriff'*, pp 1–3, HC 1862 (232), xliv, 651–3.

79   William G. Huband, *A practical treatise on the law relating to the grand jury in criminal cases the coroner's jury and the petty jury in Ireland* (Dublin, 1896), p. 686 (citing *Edmonds* (1821) 4 B & Ald 471, 106 Eng Rep 1009).

80   *Conrahy and Lalor* (1839) 1 Cr & D 56, at pp 56, 59, 61, 63.

81   For an account of the affair see John F. McEldowney, 'The case of *The Queen v. McKenna*

assizes when a number of prisoners, both Protestant and Catholic, were put on trial for two murders arising out of an Orange affray in Monaghan town in July 1868, the sub-sheriff, William Mitchell, drew up a long panel, of which the first 48 names were all Protestants, except 2, who were Catholics. John McKenna's counsel, Isaac Butt and Denis Caulfeild Heron, challenged the array. They did so on the grounds that the high sheriff and the sub-sheriff had excluded Catholics and summoned Protestants and that the high sheriff, Captain Thomas Coote, and the sub-sheriff were both Orangemen, which was a weighty accusation coming from Butt, who probably believed that it took one to know one.[82] The first 2 jurors on the long panel were appointed as triers. As it happened they were the only 2 Catholics among the first 50 names on the long panel, and they found that the panel had been selected on grounds of religion. The panel was quashed.

After this struggle, the sub-sheriff's copy of the jurors book for 1869 fell into the hands of John Reilly, who was the prisoners' attorney. According to Reilly every Roman Catholic in the jurors book was marked with a cross: 422 of the 1269 in the whole book were marked, but only 7 of those appeared among the first 70 on the long panel, which did not suggest random selection.[83] Reilly was no firebrand: he had served as sub-sheriff in 1846–7 and as election agent for Colonel Charles Powell Leslie, tory MP for Co. Monaghan from 1843 to 1871. Mitchell was ready with an answer. 'After the quashing of the panel at the spring assizes in that year [1869],' he told the Hartington committee, 'I went over the jury book for the purpose of ascertaining the proportions of Protestants and Roman Catholics on that book, and I placed opposite the name of every Roman Catholic a cross.'[84] When pressed on the strange distribution of names, he replied that he had 'never formed a panel according to religion.' As Serjeant Armstrong told the same committee on the same subject, 'there are a good many engaged in such matters that are hardly aware that they are doing it, they are so much in the habit of it.'[85]

Challenges to the array were rare, in spite of the prominent rascality of the sub-sheriffs of Tyrone and Monaghan. In a return to the Hartington committee, 28 sub-sheriffs, with a combined service of over 360 years, were able to recollect only 10 challenges to the array, which considering that the sub-sheriffs between them must have produced well over 700 long panels was not an impressive

(1869) and jury packing in Ireland' in *Ir Jur*, n.s., 12 (winter 1977), 339–53. See also R. Blake Brown, op. cit., p. 20, where it is argued that the effect of cases in 1848, involving William Smith O'Brien, Charles Gavan Duffy, John Mitchel, and Kevin Izod O'Doherty, 'was to make it nearly impossible to successfully challenge an array on the ground that the religious composition of the jury panel was unrepresentative of the broader community.' The cases at Omagh and Monaghan suggest, however, that there were limits, albeit generous ones, to the bias that was permitted.

82 McEldowney, '*The Queen v. McKenna*', 342–3.

83 *First, second, and special reports from the select committee on juries (Ireland)* …, pp 258–9, HC 1873 (283), xv, 662–3.

84 Ibid., pp 271–2.   85 Ibid., p. 53.

number.[86] The panels were quashed in only four cases. O'Hagan's act[87] and its successor in 1876[88] made challenges to the array almost impossible. The latter provided that 'no challenge to the array shall be allowed for cause except partiality, fraud, or wilful misconduct of the sheriff or other officer returning the panel.' Challenges to the array, however, still occurred. In Limerick in 1874 when Mary M'Mahon was indicted for the murder of Ellen Sexton, she challenged the array three times at one of her trials; the first two were successful, but triers found against the third.[89]

The infrequency of successful challenges might be a sign of the sheriffs' probity. It might also be a sign of the judges' attitudes to juries, which can be described as one of tolerant resignation. It is hard to resist the conclusion that as far as the judges were concerned any twelve men present in court could form a jury, which in certain circumstances, of course, was still the law.[90] Two examples will show how tolerant of apparent irregularities judges were. At Carlow summer assizes in 1838 a prisoner indicted for perjury challenged the array for two reasons, both of which seemed important: first, 355 names returned by the barony constables as qualified had been struck off by the justices without being given a chance to show they were qualified; secondly, the sheriff had not taken the long panel from the jurors book for 1838.[91] The challenge was held to be bad 'because it did not state any valid objection to the persons whose names appeared on the panel, nor did it aver, that the jurors book contained an insufficient number of names.' At the spring assizes in Tipperary in 1846 William Fogarty and Patrick Rice challenged the array because

> the jurors on the panel were not duly or at all summoned as by law they ought; that the entire of the jurors on the panel were not summoned six days before the commission, or six days before the day on which they were to attend; that the names of the jurors were not specified in a warrant signed by the sheriff, and directed to any bailiff or other officer appointed by the sheriff to summon juries; that the sheriff had returned on the panel the names of persons not contained in the jurors book; that there were not thirty-six jurors on the panel summoned, as by law they ought.[92]

In spite of these irregularities, the judge, Nicholas Ball, did not quash the panel. A writ of error took the case to the Queen's Bench where the judges decided that section 18 of the Juries (Ireland) Act 1833 did not apply to 'jurors in attendance in criminal cases', that sections 18 and 34 were 'directory, not mandatory', and

---

86   Ibid., p. 323.
88   39 & 40 Vict., c. 78, s. 17.
87   34 & 35 Vict., c. 65, s. 23.
89   *R. v. M'Mahon* (1875) IR 9 CL 309, at p. 341.
90   For the appointment of jurors from the by-standers in court (known as *talesmen*) to make up a jury if there were not enough properly summoned jurors present, see Purcell, op. cit., pp 167–9.
91   *Fitzpatrick* (1838) Cr & Dix Abr 513, at pp 513, 514, 515.
92   *Fogarty* (1846) 10 Ir LR 53, at p. 53.

that the presence of jurors whose names were not in the jurors book was not a ground of challenge.[93]

A challenge to the array was one means of impugning the long panel; an application for a change of venue was another. The attorney general's application to the Queen's Bench in June 1872, to change the venue of Hugh Fay's trial from Co. Cavan to Co. Tyrone, showed that not even the fenians could shake the judges' faith in juries. Fay had been in custody since 2 March 1870 charged with murdering his pregnant fiancée Mary Lynch.[94] At the request of the Crown, his trial had been postponed at the summer assizes of 1870 and the spring assizes 1871; then there were three abortive trials – at the summer assizes of 1871, at the spring assizes 1872, and at an adjourned spring assizes in 1872. After these postponements and aborted trials, the attorney general applied for a writ of *certiorari* to change the venue. The Crown's affidavits described remarkable circumstances: the prisoner and his brothers were fenians; their father had collected money, not only to bribe jurors but to bribe the sub-inspector of constabulary; the family had attempted to intimidate jurors ('the jurors generally, throughout the county, were afraid of injury to their farms or trade, if they should find a verdict of guilty').[95] An affidavit on behalf of the prisoner's father denied that he had collected a large sum of money ('the prisoner's father said he had collected no money except a sum of about £10 which had been contributed by some friends in Drogheda, and that he had been obliged to sell off all his stock, and was, besides, in debt to the extent of £80, owing to the expense of the defence of his son, which had utterly ruined him').[96] He tried to explain his sending money to the sub-inspector 'by stating that the sub-inspector was very harsh and relentless towards the prisoner, and was manufacturing evidence against him; and that he, deponent, had been driven half mad by the sub-inspector's conduct, and had sent the money in order to put an end to the persecution of the prisoner.'

The Queen's Bench refused to change the venue. The judges had two reasons for their belief that Fay could have a fair trial in Cavan. First, the fact that the Crown had put the prisoner on trial three times without complaining of the quality of Cavan juries showed that their loss of confidence in them had come late in the day, and until the third trial, 'there is not the slightest hint of any bad state of feeling among the jurors of the county of Cavan'. Judge Fitzgerald, who made this remark, also pointed out that an adjourned assizes was never granted in criminal cases 'except at the motion of the attorney general or someone acting for him'.[97] Secondly, at the third aborted trial the sub-sheriff had summoned 300 extra jurors ('it is stated that the attendance of jurors in Cavan that day was the largest ever known'), but the Crown had not made use of them, and their failure to ask the judge to enlarge the panel from these extra jurors, in order to 'give them what they had a right to – an impartial and thoroughly independent jury', showed

93   3 & 4 Will. IV, c. 91.

94   *Fay* (1872) IR 6 CL 436.

95   Ibid., pp 438–9.

96   Ibid., p. 440.

97   Ibid., p. 447.

that they did not believe there was intimidation on a large scale.[98] Fay was released in July 1872, went to the United States, and was shot in November 1872 'by a female cousin of the unfortunate woman who had been defiled and murdered.'[99]

Given the number of complaints about juries, it is remarkable how rare applications for changes of venue were. When the attorney general applied to have Peter Barrett tried in Co. Dublin instead of Co. Galway, one of the questions to be decided was whether the Queen's Bench had the power to change the venue in cases of felony. Lord Chief Justice Whiteside was quite sure that it had, and he devoted four pages to the subject, citing *Conway and Lynch,* and *Gray,* as well as English cases, which suggests he was labouring to make a point.[100] Yet in 1849 Purcell in *Pleading and evidence* was quite clear that the court could 'change the place of trial in all felonies and misdemeanours whenever it is necessary, for the purpose of receiving, as far as possible, a fair and impartial trial.'[101] Purcell cited only one authority, an English one, but he could have referred to *Gray.* When the jury disagreed at Sam Gray's third trial, at the 1842 spring assizes in Monaghan, the Crown moved the indictment into the Queen's Bench by *certiorari* and applied for a change of venue; the court refused, and sent the case back to Monaghan to be tried on the civil side of the court.[102] Whiteside's long justification of the court's jurisdiction in *Barrett,* therefore, suggests that before 1870 applications were so infrequent that the memory of them had receded into partial oblivion. Another case that suggested that changes of venue were rare was *M'Eneany* in 1878, when it was a prisoner and not the Crown that applied for a change of venue. Judge Fitzgerald noted that 'it was urged in argument that there was no instance of such a change in a capital felony at the instance of the prisoner', which suggests, but does not prove, that there had not been such a change of venue within living memory.[103] Why crown counsel did not apply more frequently for changes of venue is puzzling; perhaps they did not believe that the Queen's Bench had the power to change the venue (Purcell had cited only one authority); perhaps juries were not as perverse as was made out.

Were there any conceivable circumstances in which the judges would accept that a jury was irremediably biased? Obviously blatant chicanery such as that at Omagh and Monaghan was enough, although Lord Chief Justice Lefroy in *Hardy*

---

98 Ibid., p. 444.   99 Conley, *Melancholy accidents,* p. 113.
100 *Barrett* (1870) IR 4 CL 285, at pp 288–93. The Peace Preservation Act 1870 allowed the attorney general to change the venue of cases from proclaimed districts. The argument that the Queen's Bench could not change the venue might have been strengthened by reference to 3 & 4 Will. IV, c. 79 (28 Aug. 1833), which was passed to allow the King's Bench to change the venue of crimes arising out of 'illegal combinations'. The act was a temporary one, and expired on 1 Aug. 1834.
101 Purcell, op. cit., p. 102, citing *Holden* (1833) 5 B & Ad 347, at p. 354; 110 Eng Rep 819, at p. 821 where Denman stated that the King's Bench's power to change the venue 'may be exercised, where it is absolutely necessary, in cases of felony.'
102 *Conway* (1858) 7 ICLR 507, at p. 514.   103 2 LR Ir 236, at p. 240.

v. Sullivan in 1862 was quite clear that the sheriff's summoning a dispropor-
tionate number of Catholics or Protestants did not disclose 'a corrupt design', nor
was it 'a substantial ground on which to challenge his array'.[104] In 1870 in the case
of Peter Barrett, the Queen's Bench did allow a change of venue, although there
was not much difference between *Barrett* and *Fay* in terms of local disorder. The
pressure on Galway jurors when Barrett was put on trial was described in
affidavits: 'several of the jurors were threatened, and thereby intimidated and
prevented from attending the assize.'[105] One of the jurors, known to be in favour
of convicting Barrett, was 'hunted, stoned, and ill-treated by the mob, and was
with much difficulty rescued by a Roman Catholic clergyman and a number of the
constabulary', but worst of all, during the trial 'when the judges were proceeding
from the court-house to their lodgings, a large stone was thrown at and struck the
window of the carriage in which they were riding.'

In the case of Bryan M'Eneany, referred to above, the need for a change of
venue seemed almost as strong as in the Barrett case. The prisoner had been put
on trial at Belfast winter assizes for the murder of his brother in Co. Monaghan in
August 1877; the jury had disagreed, and the prisoner applied to the Queen's
Bench to be tried in Louth because of ill-feeling against him in Monaghan.[106]
The prisoner's solicitor's affidavit gave an example of the feeling against his client:
30 or 40 jurors living near Monaghan town had said 'they would have found the
prisoner guilty at once, and would have no hesitation at all in hanging every
member of his family.' The two judges who heard the case at first disagreed on
whether the venue should be changed or not: O'Brien thought it should be
changed, Fitzgerald thought 'there is no well-founded reason to suppose that the
prisoner would not receive an impartial trial in the county of Monaghan.'
Fitzgerald, however, yielded and the venue was changed.

CHALLENGING THE POLLS

Prisoners could challenge twenty individual jurors *peremptorily*, which meant that
they did not have to give a reason; they could also make an unlimited number of
challenges *for cause*, which meant they had to give a reason.[107] The prisoner had

---

104 I am indebted to Professor Desmond Greer for drawing my attention to this case, which was a
    libel case brought by the sub-sheriff of Armagh, and for giving me his notes on it.
105 *Barrett* (1870) IR 4 CL 285, at p. 286. See below, p. 265, for the deliberations of the Dublin jury
    that tried the case against Barrett.
106 (1878) 2 LR Ir 236, at pp 236, 237, 238, 242.
107 In 1848 the Queen's Bench and the house of lords decided, in William Smith O'Brien's case,
    that in Ireland a person on trial for high treason had the right to only 20 peremptory challenges,
    not 35, as in England (*W.S. O'Brien and others v. The Queen* (1849) 3 Cox CC 360, at p. 361;
    Huband, op. cit., pp 648–9 (citing *O'Brien* (1849) 1 Ir Jur OS 169). 9 Geo. IV, c. 54 s. 9 had
    enacted that 'no person arraigned for treason or murder, or for other felony, shall be admitted
    to any peremptory challenge above the number of twenty.'

to make his challenge before the juror began to take the oath.[108] Challenges for cause, as in challenges to the array, could be for principal or favour. On the subject of principal, Purcell was technical and Latinized;[109] on favour, he was vague, stating that 'the causes of favour are infinite'.[110] Challenges to the polls for cause were resolved in the same way as challenges to the array: the judge decided on principal, triers were appointed to decide on favour. If 2 members of the petty jury had been sworn they acted as triers; when the next 2 jurors were sworn, they replaced the first two, and so on; if no jurors had been sworn, the judge chose the triers.[111] At the Kilkenny assizes in 1832 when John Kennedy was tried for the murder of Edmond Butler at the Carrickshock affray, the prisoner's counsel, Daniel O'Connell, challenged the first juror, William Neville, 'as not standing indifferent between the Crown and the subject'.[112] The clerk of the crown and the clerk of the peace were sworn as triers. Neville, who was a magistrate, was sworn and examined:

> Mr O'CONNELL.– Mr Neville, will you state upon your oath, whether you were not challenged by a prisoner yesterday on a trial, in which the Crown prosecuted?
> Mr NEVILLE.– I was.
> Mr O'CONNELL.– After that, is it true, that you attended to give assistance to the crown solicitor in the prosecution of prisoners?

108 Purcell, op. cit., p. 181. 'In England', according to Purcell, 'the oath is considered to be commenced when the juror takes the book in his hands; in Ireland it has been generally held that the oath has not been commenced until after the clerk of the crown has said "Juror look upon the prisoner; prisoner look upon the juror".'

109 There were four *principal* causes (1) *propter honoris respectum* ('by reason of the rank and dignity of the juror'), which meant that a peer, for example, could be challenged; (2) *propter defectum* ('personal incapacity or disqualification'), which excluded those who were aliens, or too young, or too old, or who did not have enough property; (3) *propter affectum* ('bias or partiality alleged to exist in the juryman'), which existed 'if the juror be of blood or kindred to either party within the ninth degree, or allied by marriage ... or stand to him in the relation of master, servant, steward, counsellor or attorney, or be godfather to the child of the plaintiff or defendant'; (4) *propter delictum* ('where the person is convicted of treason, felony or an infamous crime, or is an outlaw under criminal process') (Purcell, op. cit., p. 178). Chitty gave a nice example of partiality: 'if it be proved that the juror has, in contempt, called his dogs by the names of the king's witnesses' (Chitty, op. cit., i, 541).

110 Purcell, op. cit., p. 180.

111 Chitty, op. cit., i, 549. The triers could examine the juror 'upon his *voire-dire, veritatem dicere*, as to the leaning of his own affections, or the sufficiency of his own estate; but he cannot be interrogated as to the circumstances which may tend to his own disgrace, discredit, or the injury of his character.'

112 James Mongan, *A report of the trials of John Kennedy, John Ryan, and William Voss, for the murder of Edmond Butler, at Carrickshock on the 14th December, 1831, tried before the Hon. Baron Foster, at the spring and summer assizes of Kilkenny, 1832* (Dublin, 1832), pp 2–6. For a description of the Carrickshock affray, which resulted in the deaths of 13 policemen, see Stanley H. Palmer, *Police and protest in England and Ireland 1780–1850* (Cambridge, 1988), pp 335–8.

Mr NEVILLE.– I did make some remarks to him.

Mr O'CONNELL.– Were those remarks to give him information whom to set aside on the part of the Crown?

Mr NEVILLE.– I do not believe that he set any one aside at my suggestion?

Mr O'CONNELL.– I have not asked you what the crown solicitor did, but what you yourself did. Upon your oath did you make those remarks by way of giving assistance and advice to the crown solicitor?

Mr NEVILLE.– I believe I did.

O'Connell did most of the questioning, although the attorney general sporadically intervened to assert that Neville's 'unindifference' had not been established. Baron Foster's short address to the triers gave them a strong hint: 'I shall leave it entirely to the triors [*sic*], at the same time I wish it to be understood that I do not by any means admit it as a general rule, that because a magistrate gives his opinion to the crown solicitor, with respect to persons whom he may not think to be proper jurors, he is therefore disqualified to serve as a juror.' The triers 'found for the challenge.'

Jurors enjoyed latitude in the matter of 'unindifference'. At Francis Hughes' trial at Armagh assizes in 1842, Crampton agreed with Sir Thomas Staples QC that 'it was not sufficient to set aside a juror to show that he has expressed an opinion on the prisoner's guilt; it must be shown that he did so from malice or ill will towards the prisoner.'[113] Eccentric conduct, even after a juror was sworn, might be tolerated. At the trial of Elizabeth O'Neill and Marianne Henderson at the Dublin Commission in 1843 'for feloniously stealing certain articles', a juror left Green Street during an interval in the trial and made his way to Westland Row; he was brought back, joined his fellows, and they found the prisoners guilty.[114] Chief Baron Brady did not think there had been a mistrial because there was no evidence 'either of misconduct of a party, or of prejudice to the prisoner'. Nor was service on a jury that had just brought in a verdict in a similar case a reason for allowing a challenge. At the Phoenix Park murder trials Daniel Curley was put on trial after Joseph Brady. The attorney general allowed six jurors to be excused because they had been on the jury that had just convicted Brady. The attorney, however, made it clear he was being generous in allowing them to be excused. 'We shall not ask any gentleman to serve upon this trial who served upon the last,' he said, 'That is, of course, an exception only for this trial.'[115] The judge, William O'Brien, agreed, and even Thomas Webb, Curley's fiery counsel, agreed that 'it is a matter of favour on the part of the Crown.' When Timothy Kelly was put on trial after Curley, his counsel, Denis B. Sullivan, argued that 'it would be

113   *Hughes* (1842) 2 Cr & Dix 396, at pp 399, 400.
114   *O'Neill and Henderson* (1843) 3 Cr & Dix 146, at p. 149.
115   *Report of the trials at the Dublin Commission Court, April and May, 1883, of the prisoners charged with the Phoenix Park murder, the attempt to murder Mr Field, and the conspiracy to murder; before the Hon. Mr Justice O'Brien; reported by W.C. Johnston* (Dublin, 1883), pp 118–9, 221.

reasonable that none of the gentlemen who served on the former juries should be empanelled on this', but the attorney general insisted 'it will not be possible in the course of these trials to excuse every gentleman who has served upon a jury.' The judge admitted that jurors could be called to serve again because 'there is no legal objection to it.'

Prisoners did not have to use up their peremptory challenges before challenging for cause – if the latter failed against a particular juror they could resort to the former.[116] Prisoners who were tried together could 'sever' or 'join' their challenges. By 'severing' their challenges, and insisting on twenty challenges each, they could threaten to exhaust the long panel, which was an indirect way of enabling them to secure separate trials.[117] John Ahearne, Maurice Ahearne, and Patrick Power were indicted at Waterford spring assizes in 1852 for conspiracy to murder James Troy. They pleaded not guilty, 'but having refused to join in their challenges, the counsel for the Crown put the prisoner John Ahearne on his trial.'[118] At the special commission at Ennis in 1848, when James Hayes and Patrick Ryan pleaded not guilty to the murder of James Watson, their counsel 'stated that he did not wish to put the Crown to inconvenience; and if they allowed the prisoners the power of challenging 30, they would join in their challenges; and if a sufficient number of jurors did not appear, he would not object to a jury being sworn.'[119] Thirty challenges shared by two prisoners from the same locality and charged with the same murder were probably as good as two twenties employed separately, but the Crown haggled, and eventually the prisoners accepted 23. In the event it did not matter: Hayes and Ryan made only 10 challenges. There was a nice discrimination employed in this kind of bargaining. A few days earlier at the special commission in Limerick, the Crown had agreed to allow three prisoners 30 challenges.[120] The Crown or the judge could decide to 'sever' the prisoners and to try them separately even if they were prepared to join in their challenges.[121] When John Twiss and Eugene O'Keeffe were indicted for the murder of James Donovan in April 1894, their counsel, Alexander Sullivan, assumed that they would be allowed 40 peremptory challenges, if tried together. The Crown, however, 'elected to proceed against each of the accused separately.'[122] O'Keeffe did well by being tried on his own: he was acquitted. Twiss was hanged on 9 February 1895.

116 Edmund Hayes, *Crimes and punishments, or a digest of the criminal statute law of Ireland, alphabetically arranged, with ample notes, in which are discussed the powers and authorities of the several courts of criminal jurisdiction in Ireland; the duties, responsibilities, and privileges of magistrates, coroners, constables, and other officers, in bringing criminals to justice, and also the practice of the courts in punishing offences upon indictment*, 2 vols (2nd ed., Dublin, 1842), ii, 446.
117 Purcell, op. cit., pp 173–4. See also Chitty, op. cit., i, 535.   118 2 ICLR 381, at p. 381.
119 John Simpson Armstrong, *A report of trials under a special commission for the county of Clare, held at Ennis, January 1848* (Dublin, n.d. [1849]), p. 1. See also Armstrong, *A report of trials held under a special commission for the county of Limerick, January 1848*, p. 154 for an example of nine prisoners refusing to join in their challenges.
120 Ibid., p. 112.   121 Hayes, op. cit., ii, 440.   122 A.M. Sullivan, *The last serjeant*, p. 89.

The prisoner was allowed to inspect the long panel seven days before the assizes 'without any fee or reward',[123] which allowed his solicitor 'to inform himself of the personal character and outlook of as many members as possible, and to mark his list with emblems of a descending scale, discriminating the most dangerous from the merely dangerous, the doubtful, the possibly favourable, the good friend, and the ferocious partisan.'[124] Emblems, when used by Cork solicitors, were innocuous. When used by crown counsel, they were opprobrious, as Peter O'Brien recalled:

> During the trial of Myles Joyce, my brief in the case was abstracted from my brief-bag, and was missing for three years. To the brief were attached some names from the jury panel, and in the marginal note was the letter C, which indicated that the Crown would exercise its prerogative to challenge. In 1885, during the debate in the House known as the Maamtrasna debate, my brief, the letter C on which was represented as meaning *Catholic*, was produced by one of the Nationalist members of parliament, in order to support the statement that I had endeavoured to prevent Catholics from serving on juries.[125]

The seven days allowed by Perrin's act for inspecting the long panel did not leave the prisoner or his solicitor much time to find witnesses to testify against jurors who were to be challenged for cause. Challenging sounded easy, but it was only easy while the prisoner could use his peremptory challenges.

Thomas Dunn discovered the importance of witnesses when he was tried at a special commission in Cavan in 1856 for the murder of Charlotte Hinds.[126] Dunn challenged twenty jurors peremptorily, and 'after having done so he made an objection for cause to a juror who was called, namely William Nixon.' The Crown, however, objected 'to memorialist's attorney asking the said William Nixon any questions and memorialist not being prepared at the time with witnesses to prove the cause of challenge he was obliged to submit to the said William Nixon being sworn on the jury who was to try him.'[127] (It is worth noting here the apparent

---

123 3 & 4 Will. IV, c. 91, s. 14 (28 Aug. 1833). In England as late as 1848 a judge refused to give the prisoner a copy of the long panel (*Dowling* (1848) 3 Cox CC 509, at p. 510). In Scotland the jury list was given to prisoners fifteen days before their trials (Paterson, op. cit., p. 331). Stephen did not think that seeing the list mattered ('if the sheriff wishes to pack a jury, he must be very clumsy if he does not provide a sufficient number of partial jurors, free from any legal objection'), (*A history of the criminal law of England,* 3 vols (London, 1883), i, 399).

124 Healy, *The old Munster circuit*, p. 223.

125 Georgina O'Brien, *The reminiscences of the Right Hon. Lord O'Brien (of Kilfenora) lord chief justice of Ireland*, p. 49.

126 NAI, CRF/1856/Dunn/26. For the Hinds case see Frank Sweeney, '"Those in whom you trust will always be the first to betray you"' in Frank Sweeney (ed.), *Hanging crimes* (Dublin, 2005), pp 230–62.

127 On the need for 'extrinsic evidence' to show that jurors had 'expressed opinions hostile to the defendants and their cause' see Purcell, op. cit., p. 182.

inconsistency between the fact that O'Connell had been able to question Neville at Kilkenny in 1832, but Dunn could not question Nixon at Cavan in 1856.) Dunn objected to Nixon because he was 'a man who memorialist had good reason to believe was deeply prejudiced against him being as memorialist has been informed & believes the personal friend and companion of Mr Moses Netterfield who was the agent of the late Miss Hinds and was one of the most active persons in getting up the prosecution ag[ain]st memorialist.'[128] Just after the Crown had opened its case, one of the jurors 'complained of being unwell'. He was excused, the jury was discharged, and a new jury was sworn. The new jury consisted of the eleven from the first jury, including William Nixon, and a new juror, John Edgar. The prisoner was asked if he wanted to challenge Edgar, 'to which he replied that he did not know him and had therefore no objection to make to him.' Dunn later contended that he 'was not informed that he had a right to challenge any of the eleven men who were on the first jury.' There was no doubt that Dunn had the right to challenge peremptorily the original eleven as well as the new juror,[129] so he applied to the attorney general to issue a writ of error, but the attorney refused, and Dunn was hanged. The fact that Dunn did not have his witnesses ready suggests that his right to see the long panel did not help him much. Nor was his attorney, Samuel Nixon Knipe, much help, since he did not know that the eleven jurors could be challenged *de novo*. Neither the judges, nor the attorney general, nor the clerk of the court, nor the prisoner's counsel intervened to remind the prisoner of his right to challenge.

The apparently unhelpful passivity of the judges at Dunn's trial seems to have been correct. At Francis Hughes' trial at Armagh spring assizes in 1842 'when the second person called as juror came to the book, counsel for the prisoner asked him whether he had expressed any opinion as to the prisoner's guilt or innocence on the charge for which he was then to be tried. The juror replied that he had formed and expressed an opinion of his guilt. The prisoner's counsel then challenged the juror *propter affectum*, and the Crown making no objection, the juror was ordered to stand aside.'[130] When the next juror was called, the prisoner's counsel asked him the same question, but the crown counsel objected, although he had not objected to the same question only a few minutes before. The judge, Philip Crampton, laid down the law, which showed that the crown counsel's silence when the first witness was questioned was assumed to be acquiescence:

> A juror coming to the book may be asked any question not tending to disgrace him; but he cannot be asked if he has formed or expressed an opinion against the prisoner at the bar. Such, if it be the fact, must be

---

128 Moses Netterfield was a substantial landholder in the town of Ballyconnell and in the surrounding parish of Tomregan (*General valuation of rateable property in Ireland. County of Cavan. Valuation of the several tenements comprising that portion of the union of Bawnboy, situate in the county above named* (Dublin, 1857), pp 69–80).

129 Purcell, op. cit., pp 206–7.   130 *Hughes* (1842) 2 Cr & Dix 396, at p. 396.

proved by extrinsic evidence. The juror must first be challenged, then the fact, the ground of the challenge, is proved by extrinsic evidence ... If the counsel for the Crown make no objection to the question put by the prisoner's counsel, the Court is not called upon to interfere, as in the case of the second gentleman called on the jury to whom the question was put, and the gentleman having answered in the affirmative that he had formed an opinion unfavourable to the prisoner, the fact thus brought before me that he did not stand in an indifferent position towards the prisoner, I must order him to stand aside.[131]

Crampton's statement explains the apparent contradiction in practice between O'Connell's questioning of Neville above and Dunn's inability to question Nixon, which was based on the assumption that it was up to the Crown and the prisoner to exercise or not to exercise their rights, without any help or comments from the court. After Crampton's refusal to allow the juror to be questioned, Hughes' counsel challenged him *propter affectum*, triers were sworn, and a witness 'deposed that at the last trial of the prisoner the person challenged was asked whether he had expressed any opinion of the prisoner's guilt, and had answered, as witness recollected, in the affirmative, and that he was thereupon set aside.' The triers found against the challenge. During this exchange there was a discussion about the actual words that counsel should use when they questioned a juror. Hughes' counsel, Whiteside, had asked him, 'Whether he had formed any opinion on the case beforehand?' Crampton said that the proper words should have been, 'Have you expressed any opinion beforehand with regard to the guilt or innocence of the prisoner?'[132]

Peremptory challenge was peculiar to trials for treason and felony, being regarded as a humane benefit allowed to prisoners who were on trial for their lives. As more and more felonies became non-capital, the question arose whether prisoners on trial for non-capital felonies had the right to make peremptory challenges. In 1832 the Irish judges decided that such prisoners had no such right. At the trial of Francis Adams and Thomas Langton, the clerk of the crown had stopped the prisoners' counsel making a peremptory challenge, Lord Chief Justice Bushe reserved the point, and the twelve judges decided that prisoners had no right of peremptory challenge in non-capital felonies.[133] The English judges did not follow their Irish brethren, and continued to allow twenty peremptory challenges in non-capital felonies. The legal practice of Ireland and England, which seldom diverged, was reunited by the Orangeman, Sam Gray, whose trials formed a legal saga that was probably unique in the history of the British empire.

131 Ibid., p. 398.
132 *Francis Hughes' case* (1841) Ir Cir Rep 274, at p. 274.
133 *R. v. Francis Adams and Thomas Langton* (1832) Jebb Rep 135; James Mongan, *A report of trials before the Rt Hon. the Lord Chief Justice, and the Hon. Baron Sir Wm. C. Smith, Bart at the special commission, at Maryborough, commencing on the 23rd May, and ending on the 6th June* [1832]

Gray was put on trial five times for what was arguably the same crime: he was acquitted at the Monaghan 1841 spring assizes of the murder of Owen Murphy; he was indicted at the 1842 spring assizes for shooting at James Cunningham, who had been standing close to Murphy when he was shot, 'but owing to the illness of a juror, the jury were discharged without arriving at a verdict'; at the 1842 summer assizes another jury disagreed, and yet another one disagreed at the spring assizes in 1843; at the fifth trial, on 13 July 1843, Gray was convicted.[134] The case had been punctuated by removals into the Queen's Bench: after the summer assizes in 1842 the Crown applied for a change of venue, and the court sent it back to be tried on the civil side of the assizes at Monaghan. In May 1843 the case came before the Queen's Bench again when it dismissed Gray's plea of *autrefois acquit*.[135] After his conviction, Gray once again appeared in the Queen's Bench when he moved in arrest of judgment in November 1843, arguing that he had been denied the right of peremptory challenge when his challenge of William Charles Waddell was refused by the trial judge, Perrin. The court, with the exception of Perrin, decided against him. Chief Justice Pennefather's statement showed how deeply committed the Irish judges were to their practice of not allowing peremptory challenges:

> I should feel that I was acting against my own conviction, against reason, and against what I have always considered to be the common law of the country, if I was to say that the right of peremptory challenge, which is granted in *favorem vitæ*, should be extended to cases in which life is not in jeopardy. I think it would be introducing a new principle in to the common law. This may be done by the court of dernier resort, or it may be introduced by an act of parliament.[136]

Gray took his case to the court of *dernier resort* by means of a writ of error, and the lords decided that he should have been allowed his twenty peremptory challenges, and issued a writ of *venire de novo*, which in theory allowed the Crown to put him on trial again. The Crown dropped the case.[137] It is worth noting that Sam Gray's 'persecution' and eventual escape took place under a tory government.

(Dublin, 1832), pp 241–2, 257; Henry H. Joy, *On peremptory challenge of jurors, with the judgment of the Queen's Bench in the Queen v. Gray* (Dublin and London, 1844), p. 5.

134 For a fascinating account of the case and its background, see D.S. Johnson, 'The trials of Sam Gray: Monaghan politics and nineteenth century Irish criminal procedure' in *Ir Jur*, n.s., 20 (1985), 109–34. *Conway* (1858) 7 ICLR 507, at p. 514 gives a useful summary of the proceedings.

135 5 Ir LR 524.   136 *Gray* (1843) 6 Ir LR 259, at p. 290.

137 *Gray v. The Queen* (1844) 6 Ir LR 482; 11 Cl & Fin 427, 8 Eng Rep 1164.

SETTING ASIDE

The Crown did not have the right of peremptory challenge, but the crown solicitor could order an indefinite number of the long panel to 'stand by' without his having to give a reason.[138] If the whole of the long panel failed to yield twelve 'unexceptional' men, those ordered to stand by were called again.[139] When they were regurgitated, the crown solicitor had to give reasons for rejecting them. At Peter Barrett's trial at Galway, for example, the panel was exhausted, the Crown had to challenge for cause, and 'the jury was made up from "stand-bies"', most of whom no doubt had been offended because they were challenged.[140] When the actual moment came to object, the crown solicitor did not have to take the initiative because 'the prisoner must declare whether he intends to challenge or not before the crown counsel can be asked to state their intention.'[141]

The Crown's right to set aside was shared by private prosecutors. In 1839 Perrin told a select committee of the house of lords of how, not very many years before, 'it was the custom at one time to attend very much to the suggestions of the private prosecutor or the agent for the private prosecutor, and to commit the exercise of the power to him; and on several occasions I thought it had been very injuriously exercised.'[142] Perrin was speaking of a time when there was 'scarcely a prosecution in Ireland, or at least there was not when I practised on the north-east circuit, where there was not a private prosecutor and an agent, and very often counsel, employed with the counsel for the crown, and those acting under the attorney general.'[143] Even when crown counsel were not employed, private prosecutors could exercise the power. Constantine Molloy referred to two cases, one in 1857 and the other in 1862, when private prosecutors had ordered jurors to stand by.[144] Molloy deplored the exercise of this right by private individuals

> As there is hardly, if ever, a case in this country which is properly the subject of a criminal prosecution that is not taken up by the Crown, and as private prosecutions in the majority of cases are instituted either for the

138 For Constantine Molloy's history of the subject see *First, second, and special reports from the select committee on juries (Ireland)* ..., pp 298–300, HC 1873 (283), xv, 702–4.

139 For a discussion of the Crown's right to set aside see John F. McEldowney, '"Stand by for the Crown": an historical analysis' in *Criminal Law Review 1979*, 272–83.

140 *R. v. M'Mahon* (1875) IR 9 CL 309, at p. 333. See also *Barrett* (1870) IR 4 CL 285. When the panel was exhausted by challenges and orders to stand by, it was said to have been 'perused' (*M'Mahon*, p. 316).

141 Huband, op. cit. p. 644 (citing *Brandreth* (1817) 32 How St Tr 755).

142 *Minutes of evidence taken before the select committee of the house of lords appointed to enquire into the state of Ireland, since the year 1835, in respect of crime and outrage, which have rendered life and property insecure in that part of the empire*, pt III, *evidence 12 June to 19 July*, p. 1055, HC 1839 (486-III), xii, 191.

143 Ibid., p. 1056.

144 *First, second, and special reports from the select committee on juries (Ireland)* ..., p. 300, HC 1873 (283), xv, 704.

purpose of establishing a civil right by means of a criminal prosecution, or of obtaining for the private prosecutor some advantage which he would not have if he adopted a civil proceeding to obtain redress for the injury of which he complains, I think that a privilege of such great magnitude as the right to order jurors to stand by, and one which is liable to be abused, ought not to be entrusted to an irresponsible private prosecutor, and should, by express legislation, be confined to cases where the prosecution is conducted by the attorney general in person, or by his direction.

O'Hagan's act abolished the privilege for private prosecutors,[145] but five years later a new jury act, amending O'Hagan's act, gave them the right to make six peremptory challenges.[146]

Even when the practice of asking jurors to stand by was exercised by the crown solicitor on his own behalf, it was regarded as objectionable. Perrin told the house of lords select committee in 1839:

> As to jurors it must be a disagreeable thing to a man to be set aside; he may feel it as a kind of stigma; that is a trivial matter compared with the general impression as to the administration of justice, where it is injurious as tending to create a feeling that the verdict is not the result of a cool, deliberate, and impartial trial, but may have been affected by the opinions of particular individuals designedly put upon the jury.[147]

The Crown's power was particularly objectionable in misdemeanour cases where traversers had no right of peremptory challenge to balance the Crown's power to set aside. This imbalance was politically important because most criminal cases arising out of political agitation were misdemeanours. The act of 1876 only slightly redressed the balance when it gave traversers six peremptory challenges in misdemeanour cases, including cases initiated by criminal informations.[148]

To prevent the abuse of the Crown's power Perrin, during his short period as attorney general (April to August 1835), instructed the crown solicitors 'that no person should be set aside unless there was a substantive objection to him; that the crown solicitors should not delegate or commit their power to others, but should exercise it themselves; that if a private prosecutor suggested an objection, he should be called upon to furnish the ground of it.'[149] Perrin's instruction seems to have been the beginning of formal and elaborate instructions that reached a

145 34 & 35 Vict., c. 65, s. 24.
146 39 & 40 Vict., c. 78, s. 16 (15 Aug. 1876).
147 *Minutes of evidence taken before the select committee of the house of lords appointed to enquire into the state of Ireland, ... pt III, evidence 12 June to 19 July,* p. 1057, HC 1839 (486-III), xii, 193.
148 39 & 40 Vict., c. 78, s. 10.
149 *Minutes of evidence taken before the select committee of the house of lords appointed to enquire into the state of Ireland, ... pt III, evidence 12 June to 19 July,* p. 1055, HC 1839 (486-III), xii, 191.

temporarily definitive form in Maziere Brady's 1839 version.[150] The instructions allowed the crown solicitors to use their personal knowledge of jurors, that of their assistants, and that emanating from 'parties who may be personally interested or engaged in the prosecution or defence.'[151] They had to act without much help from the crown counsel because the latter was likely to be 'a perfect stranger to the county',[152] but they could turn to magistrates, police officers, and other 'public' officers. They were warned, however, to check their sources: 'You should make a note of the name of the person giving it, and in order that if found to be inaccurate, inquiry may be made into the conduct of the individual making the communication; and should any instance occur in which it may come to your knowledge that a public officer has knowingly misled you, or sought to do so by false information respecting a juror, I need scarcely remind you that it will be your duty, without delay, to report such conduct to government.' In practice the crown solicitors did not have much time to consult anyone. McEldowney, for example, refers to a circular in 1868 that required the sheriffs to provide the crown solicitors with jurors lists 'at least four days before the assizes began'.[153]

The instructions put two major restrictions on the crown solicitor's freedom to set aside: 'first, that no person should be set aside by the Crown on account of his religious or political opinions; secondly, that the crown solicitor should be able, in every case in which the privilege is exercised, to state the grounds on which he thought proper so to exercise it.' The instructions did at least enumerate the circumstances where the crown solicitor could set aside jurors without falling foul of the attorney general: he could set aside those connected with the prisoners, those who were biased, those who were members of secret societies (irrespective

---

150 *A copy of the instructions given to the respective crown solicitors on each circuit, respecting the challenging of jurors in crown cases, by each of the following gentlemen when filling the office of attorney general in Ireland: Mr Richards, now Baron Richards; Mr O'Loghlen, now Sir Michael O'Loghlen, baronet; Mr Brady, now Chief Baron Brady; Mr Pigott, late attorney general for Ireland; Mr Blackburne, now attorney general for Ireland; specifying the particulars in which they differ*, HC 1842 (171), xxxviii, 339. For Robert Warren's instructions, which were issued in 1868, see *First, second, and special reports from the select committee on juries (Ireland) ...*, pp 105–6, HC 1873 (283), xv, 509–10. For those that replaced Warren's see *Return of copy of rule for guidance of crown solicitors in Ireland in relation to the impanelling of jurors*, p. 2, HC 1894 (33), lxxii, 31.

151 *A copy of the instructions given to the respective crown solicitors ...*, p. 3, HC 1842 (171), xxxviii, 341. For an example of the constabulary being reminded of their duty to get jurors' lists from the clerks of the union and to send them to the sessional crown solicitor see TNA (UK), HO 184/115, circular dated 20 Aug. 1878. See also ibid., 18 June 1877, which suggested that the crown solicitor should confer with the sessional crown solicitor and the constabulary 'as to the proper persons to be ordered to stand aside when the jury is being sworn'.

152 *First, second, and special reports from the select committee on juries (Ireland) ...*, p. 66, HC 1873 (283), xv, 470.

153 John F. McEldowney, 'Crown prosecutions in nineteenth-century Ireland' in Douglas Hay & Francis Snyder (eds), *Policing and prosecution in Britain 1750–1850* (Oxford, 1989), p. 437. See also Ian Bridgeman, 'The constabulary and the criminal justice system in nineteenth-century Ireland' in *Criminal Justice History*, 15 (1994), 107.

of 'whatsoever sect or party they may belong'), those who were publicans ('especially those residing in the country in remote or unfrequented situations'), those who could not speak English, those who might be biased if the subject of the trial was a trade dispute, and those who came from the locality where the crime had been committed, if the crime had been 'attended with such peculiar local excitement in a particular town or district, as to render it very desirable that the jury should not comprise any persons from that locality.'[154] The pre-1839 versions of the instructions required that crown solicitors who had set aside jurors 'should be able, in every case in which the privilege is exercised, to state the grounds on which he thought proper to exercise it.' In 1839 Brady repeated this: 'you must consider yourself responsible for the propriety of the act in each case, and accordingly be prepared to show that it was founded on information, either within your personal knowledge or that of some of your assistants, or derived from authentic and trustworthy sources, on the accuracy of which you can reasonably rely.'

Perrin's instructions did not put an end to the Crown's power to set aside. He gave three examples of the power being used in cases where he had been the judge, including a murder case at the Sligo summer assizes in 1838 when 'somewhere about thirty-nine, or perhaps more' were set aside. On this occasion he had 'felt intensely anxious, in the case of a capital charge where so many persons were set aside',[155] and suggested to the house of lords select committee that 'the principle upon which special juries are struck might be beneficially extended to criminal cases.' The cases of Francis Hughes and Patrick Woods, who were tried at Armagh summer assizes in 1841 for the murder of Thomas Powell, showed what could happen when the Crown's power to set aside became entangled with political conflict. The two cases also showed how searching the attorney general's scrutiny of a crown solicitor could be. The 1841 summer assizes coincided with a general election, and the correspondence between the crown solicitor, Maxwell Hamilton, and the whig attorney general, David Pigot, took place just as Lord Melbourne was giving way to Sir Robert Peel.[156] Even if there had not been a general election, the affair had enough sectarian associations to be contentious. Thomas Powell had been murdered in his house, between

154 In 1871 79% of publicans and hotel-keepers were catholics (Vaughan, 'Ireland *c*.1870' in Vaughan (ed.), *A new history of Ireland*, v, *Ireland under the union, I, 1801–70* (Oxford, 1989), p. 741). Eventually publicans became respectable enough to serve on juries; there were *three* on John Toole's jury at Dublin in 1901. They were assisted by a tobacconist, a plumber, a house owner, a decorator, a dairy keeper, a draper, a provision dealer, and two timber merchants, one of whom was a JP (NAI, CRF/1901/Toole/6). For Toole's hanging see Tim Carey, *Mountjoy*, pp 159–60.

155 *Minutes of evidence taken before the select committee of the house of lords appointed to enquire into the state of Ireland,* ... pt III, *evidence 12 June to 19 July*, p. 1059, HC 1839 (486–III), xii, 193.

156 NAI, CRF/1841/Woods/26. See especially the file entitled 'Correspondence in reference to the juries which tried these prisoners for the murder of Mr Powell, at Armagh summer assizes 1841'.

Newtownhamilton and Crossmaglen. Powell had been a Protestant, the prisoners
were Catholics, and the dispute that caused the murder seems to have been
agrarian. At the summer assizes Hughes' jury disagreed, 8 were for conviction
and 4 for acquittal (the minority were 'a highly respectable Presbyterian
gentleman and three respectable Roman Catholics'). The Crown had more success
with Woods, who was convicted and sentenced to death. The sharpness of the
political debate that ensued was demonstrated by a letter from the Roman
Catholic chaplain of Armagh gaol to Dawson Rawdon (whig MP for Armagh city,
1840–52), arguing that Woods was innocent and deploring the setting aside of
Catholic jurors, who were 'all respectable men, men of the most conscientious
feelings and sterling honesty. Never did the Catholicks of the North of Ireland
feel more insulted.' The Crown's tactics were all the more galling because the
Catholics 'thought the time of packing juries had passed away not to return, at
least under the present administration.'

After the assizes the crown solicitor reported to Pigot on the jurors he had set
aside. At Hughes' trial he had set aside 11, 4 because they were publicans, 6
because they had served on Hughes' jury at the spring assizes, and 'one who I was
informed has expressed his opinion as to Hughes' innocence.' (Hughes had
challenged 20 peremptorily and 14 for cause.) At Woods' trial he had set aside 12,
8 because they were publicans, 2 who were supposed to be prejudiced in favour of
the prisoner, one who had been on Hughes' jury, and one who was unwell. (Woods
had challenged 18 peremptorily and 12 for cause.) The crown solicitor's report,
however, was too vague for Pigot, who summoned him to a meeting and ordered
him to give 'a specification of the grounds of objection to each person'.

The crown solicitor produced his list the day after Pigot asked for it. He gave
the names of the 23 he had set aside at both trials and his reasons for setting them
aside. The 12 whom he had set aside because they were publicans had a mixture
of Protestant and Catholic names, for example, John Simpson, William Adams,
William Boyd, jr, James Donnelly, Philip Keenan, and Owen McAnespil. The 7
whom he had set aside because they had served on Hughes' first jury had
Protestant-sounding names (John Corry, Crozier Christy, Thomas Bell, Thomas
Craig, John McClure, William Boyd, jr). The one whom he had set aside as
unwell was William Boyd, sr, who sounded Protestant. It is worth noting that
William Boyd, jr, managed to appear twice on the list and to get on to Hughes'
first jury in spite of being a publican. The publicans, the former jurors, and the
stricken William Boyd, sr, were straightforward, their exclusion was plausible, and
they were nicely balanced between Protestants and Catholics. What mattered were
the remaining three who were set aside for 'prejudice'. All three were Catholics:
Charles Connolly (set aside at Hughes' trial), John Vallely and John Gribben (set
aside at Woods' trial). Two of the three were almost as plausibly straightforward
as the publicans and former jurors. Connolly, according to the crown solicitor,
'had been heard to say since the last trial of Hughes at [the] spring assizes "that
he considered him innocent".' Vallely 'was heard to say after counsel for the

defence had concluded his address to the jury "that no man would find Hughes guilty, and that he had always been of opinion that the prisoners now in gaol for this murder were innocent".' John Gribben was less straightforward. The crown solicitor had set him aside because he 'is joined with his brother who keeps a public lime kiln near Newtownhamilton, this local connection raising a fair presumption of the juror's mind being likely to be prejudiced as also being under apprehension of the consequences which would result to his trade if a conviction took place.'

These exclusions seemed straightforward under Brady's rules. Even Gribben came clearly under the rule about disturbed localities. The attorney was determined not to be satisfied, however. He admitted the crown solicitor had been right to set aside the first two, Connolly and Vallely, but he had done it badly because he should have stated the reasons for setting them aside when they came to be sworn. This was slightly unfair to the crown solicitor because Brady's instructions were contradictory on giving reasons for setting aside: on the one hand, the instructions said objections should not be put forward 'in the first instance'; on the other hand, they said that 'where the cause of objection is apparent, it may generally be convenient, and prevent misconstruction, that it should be openly stated at the time of your asking that the juror should be ordered to stand aside.'[157]

It was Gribben's setting aside that vexed the attorney most. 'The only fact stated as a ground for setting him aside is', he complained, ' "that he was joined with his brother who keeps a public lime kiln near Newtownhamilton".' Although Powell's murder had taken place near Newtownhamilton, the attorney noted that 'it is not stated that any peculiar excitement prevailed at Newtownhamilton on the subject of this trial which would render it proper according to the instruction given in 1839.' As he went on, he warmed to his subject: 'I find nothing in any former instructions to warrant, on such a ground as this, the setting aside of a person by the Crown, and of such a course I feel it my duty to express my decided disapprobation. To adopt it as a rule of exclusion, would be, in effect, to prohibit all local traders from serving as jurors, lest their verdict might be influenced by apprehension of mischief to their trade.'

These were strong words, especially 'decided disapprobation', but Pigot's reference to the tranquillity of Newtownhamilton suggested Carthusian remoteness. Hamilton made the inevitable reply:

> I should have hardly thought it necessary for me to have informed you by my report of the 23rd inst that excitement prevailed at Newtownhamilton upon the subject of Mr Powell's murder … I am quite sure that I should be confirmed in my opinion that excitement does prevail at Newtownhamilton

---

157 *A copy of the instructions given to the respective crown solicitors …*, p. 5, HC 1842 (171), xxxviii, 345.

by a reference to the lieutenant of the county of Armagh, and all the local magistrates who on that score applied for and obtained a large additional police force for the southern district of the county and a stipendiary magistrate to be resident at Newtownhamilton ... These and various other circumstances I had supposed were known to you from perusal of the police reports which are forwarded from time to time to the Castle.

This riposte, which was stronger than 'decided disapprobation', seems to have taken most of the wind out of Pigot's sails. He admitted that the 1839 instructions 'appear upon your last statement to have warranted the exclusion of Gribben', and he excused his ignorance of events in Armagh ('the reports to the Castle, and other matters to which your letter refers, did not come before me. I was absent from Ireland (with the exception of a very few days) from the middle of January to the end of June.') His capitulation, however, was not complete. He came back to Gribben and declared that his being merely a *partner* in the lime kiln at Newtownhamilton was not a strong enough connection ('to act on such a ground alone as a rule for the exclusion of persons called upon the jury panel would be wholly unwarranted by any instructions now prevailing for the guidance of crown solicitors upon this subject.') The correspondence ended, however, on a civil note, but it was Robert Granville Wallace, the prisoner's attorney, who struck it. When thanking the attorney general for his efforts he remarked that 'for Mr Hamilton the crown solicitor I entertain sentiments of sincere respect to which he is justly entitled by the admirable performance of his public duties.'[158]

The attorney general's instructions and the fact that Perrin's act set a limit on the size of long panels seem to have mitigated the problem of setting aside from the 1830s until O'Hagan's act removed the restriction on the size of long panels in the 1870s.[159] From 1873 the sheriffs began to summon very long panels, and crown solicitors began to set aside large numbers of jurors: over a hundred at one of Montgomery's trials, 36 at Patrick Joyce's, and 54 at one of the Phoenix Park trials.[160]

158 In the following year 1842, at the Armagh spring assizes, Francis Hughes was tried for the third time and convicted. Charles Gavan Duffy in the *Belfast Vindicator* accused the new tory attorney general, Francis Blackburne, of judicial murder. Duffy was prosecuted in the Queen's Bench, charged with 'wickedly and maliciously contriving and intending to bring the administration of justice into contempt'. Thomas O'Hagan, who had been one of Woods' counsel, was Duffy's counsel. Duffy was acquitted. If he had been convicted it is highly unlikely that he would have been editor of the first issue of *The Nation* when it appeared on 15 October 1842 (John F. McEldowney, 'Lord O'Hagan (1812–1885): a study of his life and period as lord chancellor of Ireland (1868–1874)' in *Ir Jur*, n.s., 14 (1979), 360). See also *A full report of the trial in the cause of The Queen at the prosecution of the attorney-general, versus Charles Gavan Duffy, Esq., proprietor of the* Belfast Vindicator, *on Monday, the 20th day of June, 1842, in the Court of Queen's Bench, with the speeches of the counsel for the prosecution and for the traverser, the charge of Chief Justice Pennefather at length. Compiled by a Law Student* (Dublin, [1842]).

159 3 & 4 Will. IV, c. 91, s. 12 (28 Aug. 1833); 34 & 35 Vict., c. 65, s. 18 (14 Aug. 1871).

160 D.S. Johnson, 'Trial by jury in Ireland 1860–1914' in *Journal of Legal History*, 17:3 (Dec. 1996), 284.

The increase in setting aside began almost as soon as O'Hagan's act came into effect. 'I have seen more jurors made to stand aside in the last circuit than I used to see before,' Lawson told the Hartington committee. 'In truth, summoning men of that kind is summoning them there almost for the purpose of telling them to stand aside.'[161] If large numbers could be set aside, O'Hagan's act would have changed the balance between Crown and prisoner. Or did it? 'It is manifest that from the increase in the number of jurors returned by the sheriff,' Constantine Molloy wrote, 'this right of the Crown has been materially altered, so that the Crown has again, for all practical purposes, virtually the right of peremptory challenge.'[162] The memorandum in which Molloy wrote this was dated 2 March 1871, which was before the act became law. In the same memorandum he noted that 'at the present day … and in practice on circuit the sheriffs rarely, if ever, return less than 100; the usual number is from 150 to 200; and where important cases are to be tried, the number generally exceeds 200; and in the case of state prosecutions it is still larger.' This statement makes one wonder why there were so many complaints about setting aside after O'Hagan's act came into operation, or why there was talk of a shortage of jurors before the act became law?

The abolition of the sheriff's power to nominate the long panel meant that there was now no means of weeding out unsatisfactory jurors until the clerk of the crown called out their names in court. The crown solicitor now had to do publicly what the sheriff had formerly done discreetly. 'I think that that power, largely exercised by the crown solicitor, throws a much greater suspicion on the administration of justice than the power exercised by the sub-sheriff in preparing the panel in the old way,' James Hamilton QC told the Hartington committee. 'I say, as a matter of experience, that where that power is largely exercised, for instance in fenian or agrarian cases, we have the whole national press coming out with the outcry that men were excluded from the jury on account of their religion.'[163] The problem of replacing the sheriff's *sub rosa* power seemed insoluble. The suggestion that the chairman of the quarter sessions should do it *in camera*, advised by the constabulary, was denounced by Hamilton as 'one of the most unconstitutional propositions that I ever heard made.'[164] O'Hagan and Molloy might have argued that something had been gained: the sheriff had operated in semi-darkness, the crown solicitor had to operate in daylight.

There were a number of attempts to abolish the crown's right to ask jurors to stand by. In 1872, before the problems of very long panels created under O'Hagan's act, Sir Colman O'Loghlen QC (MP for Co. Clare, 1863–79) introduced a bill to abolish the Crown's power to set aside 'without cause assigned'.[165] O'Loghlen saw his bill 'as a supplement to Lord O'Hagan's act, and he only regretted that the noble lord had not had the courage to go a step further

161 *First, second, and special reports from the select committee on juries (Ireland)* …, p. 155, HC 1873 (283), xv, 559.

162 Ibid., p. 300.   163 Ibid., p. 65.   164 Ibid., p. 74.

165 *ILT & SJ*, 7 (15 June 1872), 322, 323.

than he had done, and to have rendered his measure complete by embodying in it the proposals which were put forward in the present bill.' The two most important provisions of the bill were that juries in criminal cases should be chosen by ballot from the long panel as in civil cases, and that 'the Queen shall have the same right of challenge, peremptory or otherwise, as the subject, and no other; and henceforth no judge or court in Ireland … shall order a juror to stand by until the pannel shall be gone through at the prayer of them that prosecute for the Queen.'[166]

During the debate on the second reading of O'Loghlen's bill, little was said to demonstrate that the Crown had abused its power. O'Loghlen was not able to point to a recent or even a venerable example of abuse. He lamely referred to Perrin's evidence given to the house of lords select committee in 1839, which was mentioned above, but that was all. Jonathan Pim (MP for Dublin City, 1865–74) said he wished 'to secure a fair jury, and what he wanted was not only a jury which should be fairly chosen, but which would have all appearance of being so chosen, so that no Irishman could say that anything unfair had been done.'[167] Pim did not give any examples of jury-packing, nor did Patrick McMahon, nor did John Francis Maguire. Indeed, Maguire praised the Irish judges, who 'laid aside the advocate the moment they assumed the ermine', and he singled out Whiteside, 'whom he had seen conducting himself upon the bench with great dignity, moderation, and impartiality.' His praise of the judges had little relevance to the chicanery of crown solicitors, but it allowed him to note that 'there were exceptions, or, he might say, there was an exception, which proved the rule, though the rule made that exception more scandalous.' The debate took place on 15 June 1872. Judge Keogh, who was the scandalous exception referred to, had delivered his diatribe on the bishop and clergy of Galway on 27 May. At the end of the debate, Richard Dowse (attorney general from January to November 1872) made a predictable point when he told the house that O'Loghlen, who was second serjeant, had prosecuted for the Crown on the Munster circuit, 'where he carried out principles very different from those which he had that day advocated in the house.'[168] Dowse also pointed out that when O'Hagan's bill was going through the commons 'not one of the Irish members made the slightest suggestion with reference to an alteration' in the Crown's power to set aside.

From the prosecution's point of view, setting aside was as necessary to them as peremptory challenge to the prisoner. Even from the prisoner's point of view the Crown's power was occasionally beneficial. At the special commission in Limerick in 1848 when Andrew Dea was put on trial for the murder of Edmond Murphy, 'four jurors were set aside by the Crown as having been members of the grand

---

166 *Bill to provide that jurors in criminal trials in Ireland should henceforth be chosen as in civil trials by ballot, and to abolish the power of crown in such trials to set aside jurors without cause*, pp 1–3, HC 1872 (bill 47), i, 407–9.
167 'Criminal trials bill' in *ILT & SJ*, 6, 325.
168 Ibid., p. 324.

jury at the last assizes, that grand jury having found the bills against the prisoner.'[169] At Stephen McKeown's trial at Armagh summer assizes in 1876, the prisoner asked for a postponement of his trial because of the ill-feeling that had been aroused against him, especially in the south of the county. Judge Fitzgerald refused the application, but 'alluded to the course adopted by the Crown in the Montgomery trial, of excluding from the jury all persons from the locality of the murder, to remove even a suspicion of an unfair trial, and recommended its adoption in the present instance.'[170] The crown solicitor seems to have taken the hint. He ordered 57 of the long panel of 200 names to stand by. Even this beneficial power came to be regarded with suspicion. Thomas Broughton was indicted for murder at Kildare assizes March 1894. He was gamekeeper on an estate in Co. Kildare that had fallen foul of the Plan of Campaign, and massive setting aside was obviously called for. The Queen's Bench Division, however, preferred to change the venue because 'the court, in the exercise of its discretion, should not allow the fair and impartial trial of a prisoner to depend upon the power of the officials representing the Crown to order jurors to stand aside, but should remove the proceedings by writ of *certiorari*.'[171]

The Crown's right to ask jurors to stand by was the subject of one of the most revealing cases of the period. Mary M'Mahon was indicted at the city of Limerick spring assizes in 1874 for the murder of Ellen Sexton. After three challenges to the array, she was put on trial. The jury disagreed. At her next trial, the long panel consisted of 69 jurors. M'Mahon challenged 7 peremptorily and 24 successfully for cause, the Crown ordered 12 to stand by, 18 were exempted, 30 did not appear, and 8 were sworn.[172] At this point, with only 8 jurors sworn and 12 standing by, the panel was exhausted. The crown counsel applied for a postponement to the next assizes. The prisoner's counsel did not object or ask for the jury to be completed from the twelve standing by. Judge Fitzgerald agreed to the postponement 'for default of jurors'. Before the next assizes, however, the venue was changed to the city of Cork, where she was put on trial at the summer assizes of 1874. The jury disagreed. She was put on trial again, at the Cork spring assizes, where she was found guilty on 23 March 1875.

M'Mahon's case was removed to the Court of Queen's Bench by a writ of *certiorari*, and in May her counsel applied for either a *venire de novo* or an arrest of judgment. There were two grounds for the application. First, because 'the postponement of the trial at Limerick, under the circumstances and for the reasons stated on the record, was a violation of the provisions of the stat. 9 Geo. 4, c. 54, s. 9, and a deprivation of the right conferred upon the prisoner by that statute.' Secondly, because Fitzgerald's decision to postpone the trial amounted to 'the adoption by the judge at the trial of an illegal and unconstitutional course

169 Armstrong, *A report of trials held under a special commission for the county of Limerick, January 1848*, p. 100.
170 *Belfast Newsletter*, 19 July 1876.   171 [1895] 2 IR 386, at p. 386.
172 *M'Mahon* (1875) IR 9 CL 309, at pp 311, 313–14.

to the prejudice of the prisoner.'[173] The Criminal Law (Ireland) Act 1828, which was the act referred to, had attempted to stop the Crown from arbitrarily postponing trials by factitiously exhausting long panels with numerous orders to stand by. The words of section 9 of the act were:

> that in all inquests to be taken before any of the courts in Ireland, wherein the King is a party, howsoever it be, notwithstanding it be alleged by them that sue for the King that the jurors of those inquests, or some of them, be not indifferent for the King, yet such inquests shall not remain untaken for that cause; but if they that sue for the King will challenge any of those jurors, they shall assign of their challenge a cause certain.[174]

Since 1828, therefore, 'the Crown has no power whatever ... to force the postponement of a trial by peremptory challenges; and if, on the panel being exhausted by such challenges, the Crown refuse to have the jurors who have been set aside called again and sworn, unless successfully challenged for cause, it is in the power of the judge, and *prima facie* his duty, to discharge the prisoner.'[175] The argument on behalf of the prisoner was that Fitzgerald should have insisted on the Crown's calling the twelve jurors who had been ordered to stand by, and if the Crown had refused to call them, he should have discharged the prisoner.

Although the case covered 75 pages of print and many points were discussed, the important question was whether the indictment at Limerick and the conviction at Cork 'were destroyed by the erroneous postponement'? According to Barry, 'in the series of cases commencing with *The Queen v. Conway* and ending with *The Queen v. Winsor*, the question whether an abortive trial, which the proceeding at Limerick at the most amounted to, rendered invalid a subsequent trial on the same indictment, was always treated as depending upon the question, whether it was bar to a subsequent indictment.'[176] He denied that an aborted trial was a bar because

> these cases lay down in express and unqualified terms three propositions. First, that the defence to an indictment founded upon a former trial, are a former conviction or a former acquittal, for the same offence. Secondly, that a trial abortive without a verdict, being neither conviction nor acquittal, constitutes no such defence. And, thirdly, that such abortive trial not being a bar to a fresh indictment, is no ground of error on a subsequent trial on the same indictment.[177]

173 Ibid., pp 314–15.
174 9 Geo. IV, c. 54, s. 9 (15 July 1828).
175 *M'Mahon* (1875) IR 9 CL 309, at p. 317.
176 Ibid., p. 319. See *Conway and Lynch* (1845) 7 Ir LR 149; *Winsor* (1865) 10 Cox CC 276.
177 *M'Mahon* (1875) IR 9 CL 309, at pp 323–4.

Fitzgerald, who was the second judge to give his opinion, had no doubt he had done the right thing at Limerick: 'there was at the trial no mistake, as there could be no doubt on the law and practice applicable to the state of facts that arose.' He justified his decision by pointing to two facts. First, he had offered to complete the jury from the jurors who were standing by 'if either party required it'. Secondly, he had the power to discharge the jury – the cases of *Winsor* and *Charlesworth* allowed the judge to discharge the jury even after the trial had begun, and if he had the power to discharge the jury after the trial had begun 'it seems to me to admit of no doubt that he at least equally possesses it before the jury has been sworn or the prisoner given in charge.'[178]

At this point there might appear to be nothing left to say. The two senior judges of the court, O'Brien and Whiteside, nevertheless, had a lot to say. O'Brien argued that there had been an error: 'the clear inference from this part of the record is, that the trial was postponed only on the supposition that there was a default of jurors; no other ground for the postponement is suggested on the record, or can be properly inferred from it.'[179] The statement that there had been a default of jurors was 'clearly erroneous' because 'it cannot be said, having regard to the foregoing statutes, and the decisions on them, that there was any default of jurors till the names of the twelve jurors who had been ordered "to stand by" had been again called over, and the Crown required to assign cause for challenging any of those twelve jurors.'

Whiteside took a higher line, declaring *en passant* that this was 'the most important question of criminal law which has been raised by the Crown during my experience.'[180] He concentrated on the attorney general's arbitrary power to say 'I do not like the jury, I will stop the case':

> A prisoner some time in prison receives notice of trial from the Crown, and being asked whether he or she is ready for their trial, answers yes, having probably exhausted all his or her means to prepare for the trial, and got to the assizes all the witnesses to establish whatever case he or she may have. The counsel for the Crown makes no application to postpone the trial; on the contrary, the trial is pressed on, the prisoner arraigned, the jury panel called over, many nice questions decided on challenges, the attorney general or crown counsel bids a score of jurors to stand by, and they do so; and, then, more than half the jury being sworn, not liking the jurors he has directed to stand by, but who are all present, qualified and bound and ready to serve, can he, the attorney general, in a case of murder or treason, suddenly stop the case, assigning for his reason that the jury-panel is exhausted – a fallacy and contrary to the fact, as is attested by the entry and expanded on the record, by which it appears that abundant jurors are present and legally qualified to serve?

178 Ibid., pp 332–4. *Winsor* (1865) 10 Cox CC 276; *Charlesworth* (1861) 9 Cox CC 44.
179 *M'Mahon* (1875) IR 9 CL 309, at p. 342.   180 Ibid., p. 358.

He went on to reflect on fundamentals: 'two great objects were aimed at by those who founded our legal constitution and framed such laws as Magna Charta and this statute of Edward [which had restricted the crown power to order jurors to stand by] – a prompt trial expressed by the words that the inquest shall not remain untaken, prolonged imprisonments without just cause or arbitrary postponements of trial are here forbidden.'[181] The court was evenly divided. Barry, as the junior judge, withdrew, the majority decided that judgment should be arrested, and the crown counsel 'subsequently intimated to the court that the attorney general did not intend to bring a writ of error', which meant that Mary M'Mahon would not be put on trial again.[182]

The Crown's right to ask jurors to stand by became prominent just on the eve of a period of intense political agitation. It inevitably became the staple of political controversy, especially in view of the fact that some of the most contentious trials of the 1880s were cases of misdemeanour, where traversers had only six peremptory challenges to match the Crown's unlimited power to set aside.[183] An anonymous pamphleteer in 1887, for example, described trials at Sligo winter assizes in 1886–7 when 'peasants from a neighbouring county were tried in batches of from 4 to 9 on a charge of opposing their own eviction.' The long panel had 250 names, each batch of prisoners could challenge only 6, but

> the Conservative prosecutor *ordered thirty jurors to stand by, many of these being after the accused's six challenges had been exhausted* ... So strong was the *animus* of the government, so determined was it on conviction, not justice, that Catholics were altogether excluded from two of the juries selected to try these Catholic peasants.[184]

The pamphlet included resolutions from Catholic bishops and clergy, from the Catholic jurors of Sligo, and from 'Sligo non-Catholic jurors', all of whom condemned the crown solicitor's actions.[185] The author also described the melancholy plight of five MPs (Daniel Crilly, John Dillon, William O'Brien, W.H.K. Redmond, David Sheehy) who were awaiting trial in Dublin 'on a charge of showing tenants how legally to resist the extortion of impossible rents by certain rapacious landlords.'[186] The five traversers applied to the Queen's Bench Division to be tried at bar with a special jury 'under what is called the old system', which would have produced a panel of 24 jurors and given the Crown and the traversers 6 challenges each. Their application was refused.

The actual trial of Dillon, O'Brien, and the others, might act as a parable of jury-packing in Ireland.[187] The Crown practised chicanery at every point of the

---

181 Ibid., p. 359.   182 Ibid., p. 383.   183 Above, p. 148.
184 E.P.S. Counsel, LL.D, TCD, *Jury packing* (2nd ed., Dublin, 1887), pp 9–10.
185 Ibid., pp 14–19.   186 Ibid., pp 11–12.
187 The story was told by Crilly in *Jury packing in Ireland* (Dublin, 1887); for the details see pp 8, 27, 32, 46, 47.

proceedings. The trial was moved from the city of Dublin, where the sheriffs tended to be nationalists, to the county of Dublin where the sheriffs were unionists (the sub-sheriff of Co. Dublin was actually secretary of the Property Defence Association). An exorbitant number of jurors was called, 250 instead of the usual 100. When the names were called those present noted the 'remarkable fact that the names high up on the dictionary order, even in the unexhausted letters, are in Dublin mainly Protestant names.' The long panel had 106 Catholics and 144 non-Catholics – if it had been randomly chosen it should have had 162 Catholics and 88 non-Catholics. The Crown ordered 29 jurors to stand by, of whom 26 were Catholics. The 5 traversers had only 6 peremptory challenges between them. The result of this manoeuvring, however, was far more interesting than any of its statistical details: the petty jury had 9 Protestants and 3 Catholics, 2 of whom were prominent nationalists; the trial lasted ten days, but in the end the jury was could not agree because they were *equally* divided!

THE PROBLEM OF THE JURY

Forming the petty jury could be a difficult affair. Challenges to jurors, from the Crown and the prisoner, eliminated a large proportion of even a copious long panel. At the trial of Daniel Curley, one of the Phoenix Park murderers, for example, 79 jurors had to be called before the jury was formed. The crown solicitor, Samuel Lee Anderson, had ordered 38 to stand by, the prisoner had challenged 20 peremptorily, 6 were excused because they had served on Brady's jury, and 3 were excused for other reasons.[188] Absenteeism increased sub-sheriffs' difficulties. At the Mayo assizes in 1851, for example, the twelfth juror sworn in the case of *The Queen v. Thadeus Derrig and others* was no. 103 on the long panel. The Crown had set 9 aside. Assuming that the prisoners challenged 40 peremptorily, 42 names were unaccounted for. It was highly unlikely that the prisoners' challenges for cause accounted for more than half a dozen of the 42 unaccounted for. At least 36, therefore, were absent, which was over a third of the long panel.[189]

Prisoners' complaints in the Convict Reference Files put juries third after complaints about the Crown's conduct of the case and the conduct of the prisoner's defence, which might be considered a compliment to Irish juries.[190] Only 5 of the 15 complaints about juries implied finesse or carelessness on the part of the crown solicitor or the sheriff: Patrick Woods at Armagh in 1841 complained that the crown solicitor had excluded Roman Catholics from his

188 *Report of the trials at the Dublin Commission Court, April and May, 1883, of the prisoners charged with the Phoenix Park murder, the attempt to murder Mr Field, and the conspiracy to murder; before the Hon. Mr Justice O'Brien; reported by W.C. Johnston* (Dublin, 1883), pp 118–20.
189 *A return 'of the jury panel in the criminal court at the last assizes for the county of Mayo ...*, HC 1850 (235), l, 655.
190 Below, pp 360–1.

jury;[191] Thomas Dowling at Tullamore in 1844 complained his jury was 'exclusively' Protestant;[192] Thomas Dunn complained that he had been deprived of his right of challenge;[193] Daniel Ward complained that his jury was from Belfast and prejudiced against him;[194] Thomas Cuneen complained that his jury 'between the rising of the court on the evening of the second day of the trial and sitting of the court on the morning of the third day of the trial had been … supplied with newspapers some of which were the Cork daily newspapers, containing accounts of the second day's proceedings which were in the main accurate but omitted some particulars favourable to your memorialist.'[195]

Carelessness rather than design caused 2 of these 5 complaints: Dunn's predicament was created by his attorney's inattention; Cuneen's complaint, which received little sympathy from the judge, probably owed more to an over attentive hotel-keeper than to the machinations of the crown solicitor. In only 3 of the 5 cases was jury-packing implied. In Ward's case, the implication was that the sheriff or the crown solicitor should have excluded jurors from Belfast, a form of jury-packing of a different order from that usually ascribed to the Crown. Of the remaining 2 complaints, only Woods mentioned the Crown's right to order jurors to stand by. Whether Dowling's jury was exclusively Protestant because the crown solicitor excluded Catholics, or refused to exclude Protestants, or because the sheriff returned a Protestant long panel was not clear. Neither the crown solicitor nor the sheriff was mentioned in the memorial. The memorial's authors described the method of selection that should have been used: they did not believe 'that Protestants as such would feel indisposed to do justice to the Catholic tenantry of Ireland; but because they feel that Catholic jurors are from their situation and opportunities in life generally well acquainted with the habits and feelings of the peasantry, and from association are likely to be often divested of an amount of prejudice which must inevitably prevail, more or less, among those whose lives are spent exclusively in other circles.' This nostrum sounded like a new form of jury-packing. If knowledge of the peasantry's habits was the *sine qua non* for jury service, a long panel of the county's constabulary might have been a better solution.

The remaining 10 complaints about juries arose intrinsically from trial by jury. Patrick Kenna and Patrick Nangle believed that a majority of their jury was in favour of their acquittal 'and would have done so were it not for the tenacity of some members of the jury who refused to yield their opinions and that those persons finding this to be the case and dreading to be locked up for the night in the event of their disagreeing, the entire jury then agreed to find your petitioners guilty.'[196] Thomas Warnock, one of Stephen McKeown's jury, complained that he was bullied by the other 11 jurors ('He was asked whilst deliberating in the jury

191 NAI, CRF/1841/Woods/12.

192 Ibid., CRF/1844/Dowling/11.

193 Ibid., CRF/1856/Dunn/26.

194 Ibid., CRF/1863/Ward/5.

195 Ibid., CRF/1879/Cuneen/2.

196 Ibid., CRF/1841/Kenna/12.

room, "Would he take part with a murderer?" ').[197] Bernard Cangley complained that 'the men who composed his jury, however well disposed to dispense justice, were from their position in society, their imperfect education and their limited opportunity for acquiring knowledge totally unfitted and unqualified to form an opinion, and pronounce judgment on the defence set up for him by his counsel.' This was probably true, but it was in the nature of things. Cangley, nevertheless, 'exonerates his jury from all imputations of partiality.'[198]

These complaints do not suggest that jury-packing was common. It would be hard to argue, however, that the complaints in the Convict Reference Files reflected fully the difficulties of the jury, if only because they occurred only when juries had returned verdicts of guilty, and not when they acquitted or could not reach a verdict. There was a stream of criticism in the newspapers, expatiating on hung juries, on juries that acquitted the guilty, and on juries that could not agree. There were recurring signs of parliamentary concern, as shown by the number of parliamentary papers relating to Irish juries.[199] Even John Pentland Mahaffy, who delineated the institutions of Greece in the imperative manner of Mount Sinai, believed that 'Ireland would now benefit beyond conception by the abolition of the jury system.'[200] As the century progressed more cases were disposed of summarily at the petty sessions, which evaded trial by jury.[201] Eventually the fallibility of juries was recognized when full courts of criminal appeal were established, in England in 1907, in the Free State in 1924, and in Northern Ireland in 1930.[202]

The problems that afflicted Irish juries were not peculiar to Ireland.[203] Serjeant John Parry in his evidence to the Richmond commission and Charles Sprengal

197 Ibid., CRF/1876/McKeown/22.   198 Ibid., CRF/1864/Cangley/13.
199 Parliamentary unease about Irish juries in the 1870s did not end with the Hartington select committee, which was followed by two more: *Report from the select committee on jury system (Ireland); together with the proceedings of the committee, minutes of evidence, and appendix*, HC 1874 (244), ix, 557; *Report from the select committee of the house of lords on Irish jury laws; together with the proceedings of the committee, minutes of evidence, and appendix*, HC 1881 (430), xi, 1.
200 J.P. Mahaffy, *Social life in Greece from Homer to Menander* (London, 1874), p. 363. See ibid., pp 369–70 for his comparison of Greek and Irish juries: 'I cannot but hazard the conjecture that the Athenian juries, with their native shrewdness, and intelligence, their great impulsiveness, their tendency to override strict law, and their facility of being gained over by clever speaking, though beside the point, were more like the Irish juries of the present day than any other parallel which can be found.'
201 In 1994 in the Republic of Ireland and Northern Ireland only 240 people were tried by jury. In England and Wales (with almost ten times the population of Ireland) 18,000 were tried by jury (D.S. Johnson, 'Trial by jury in Ireland 1860–1914' in *Journal of Legal History*, 17:3 (Dec. 1996), 270). The fact that juries decide who shall win the Eurovision Song Contest does not alter the picture of the jury's decline.
202 Claire Jackson, 'Irish political opposition to the passage of criminal evidence reform at Westminster, 1883–98' in McEldowney & O'Higgins (eds), *The common law tradition* (1990), p. 190. 7 Edw. VII, c. 23, s. 3(b) (28 Aug. 1907) allowed appeals 'on any ground of appeal which involves a question of fact alone, or a question of mixed law and fact, or any other ground which appears to the court to be a sufficient ground of appeal'.
203 For problems with juries that would have been familiar to Irish lawyers, see Richard W. Ireland,

Greaves in his report on criminal law procedure in 1856 said things about English juries that could have been said about Irish ones. It was difficult to get guilty verdicts in murder cases where the evidence was circumstantial.[204] Juries were reluctant to convict in cases of infanticide.[205] Many jurors disapproved, on conscientious grounds, of hanging.[206] Juries did not like prosecutions carried on by public prosecutors. It is easy to get the impression that vigorous challenging was more common in Ireland than in England. Alexander Sullivan, for example, when describing Sir Roger Casement's trial noted that 'no one who had practised in an English court had ever seen a jury challenged. No one in an Irish court had ever seen a jury sworn without challenge.'[207] David Bentley, who is a powerful illuminator of the dark places of nineteenth-century criminal law, devotes only a page and a bit to challenging, which suggests it did not loom large.[208] Serjeant Parry, however, described challenges in England in terms that suggested there was little practical difference between England and Ireland: 'in one or two cases in which I have defended for murder, I have pursued that course where persons have been got upon the jury who are conscientiously opposed to capital punishment, who would never find a verdict according to their oaths, but who take hold of any opportunity, that is plausible, in order that they should not be parties to the punishment of death; I am certain of that.'[209]

The problems of the jury trial in Ireland have not gone unnoticed by historians. John F. McEldowney alluded to the contemporary belief that jury trial in Ireland 'was nothing more than a "delusion, mockery, and snare".'[210] R.W.

'Putting oneself on whose country? Carmarthenshire juries in the mid-nineteenth century' in T.G. Watkin (ed.), *Legal Wales: its past, its future* (Welsh Legal History Society, vol. i, Cardiff, 2001), pp 63–87. See also J.S. Cockburn & Thomas A. Green (eds), *Twelve good men and true: the criminal trial jury in England, 1200–1800* (Princeton, NJ, 1988), passim.

204 *Report of the capital punishment commission, together with the minutes of evidence, and appendix*, p. 335 [3590], HC 1866, xxi, 387.

205 Ibid., p. 344. Parry also believed that juries were reluctant to hang women. ('Whether that has sprung from the fact of our being governed by a Queen, or not, I do not know. It is more prevalent in recent times than it used to be.')

206 Ibid., p. 354.

207 *The last serjeant. The memoirs of Serjeant A.M. Sullivan, QC* (London, 1952), p. 272.

208 David Bentley, *English criminal justice in the nineteenth century* (London and Rio Grande, 1998), pp 95–6.

209 *Report of the capital punishment commission, together with the minutes of evidence, and appendix*, p. 354 [3590], HC 1866, xxi, 406.

210 John F. McEldowney, 'Some aspects of law and policy in the administration of criminal justice in nineteenth-century Ireland' in McEldowney & O'Higgins (eds), *The common law tradition* (1990), p. 154. The parish priest of Cloughjordan, when denouncing the Cormack brothers' trial, agreed: 'the foremost and available jurors, therefore, empanelled to try the unfortunate Catholic accused must be, almost to a man, taken from the ranks of a party who have ever manifested the most open and avowed hostility to his class, his religion, and his rights, thereby converting the right of challenge of the accused into a mockery, and his trial by jury of his fellow-countrymen into a mere delusion and a snare' (Larcom Papers (NLI, MS 7636 [*Freeman's Journal*, 31 Aug. 1858]). See also R. Blake Brown, '"A delusion, a mockery, and a

Kostal, in a study of the trials of Thomas Clarke Luby, John O'Leary, and Jeremiah O'Donovan Rossa, was more impressed by the difficulty of jury-packing than by its prevalence, concluding that 'the weight of numbers alone made jury-packing, at least in its most blatant forms, difficult for the Crown to achieve.'[211] McEldowney was not sure that packing was common. Jury-packing 'had frequently been alleged but seldom proved to exist in Irish juries', he wrote in 1977. 'McKenna's case was one of the few cases to prove its existence.'[212] If a successful challenge to the array, which had occurred in McKenna's case, was the only way of proving that jury-packing existed, then it has to be admitted that there were very few cases in nineteenth-century Ireland.

A number of things have to be remembered about accusations of jury-packing. First, the actions that caused complaint were likely to be used in different ways at different times. Chicanery by the sheriffs was possible before 1873, but difficult afterwards. Setting aside on a generous scale was possible before and after 1873, but seems to have caused many more complaints after 1873. Chicanery by prisoners was hardly ever described in detail. Secondly, the methods of 'packing' were more or less public. The sheriff might concoct his long panel in private, but he had to make it available to the prisoner before the assizes, and it had to be read out before the trial itself. The crown solicitor had to set aside jurors in open court. Thirdly, the government had very little control over the sheriffs before 1873. After 1873 the attorney had apparently more control over the selection of juries through the crown solicitors. Fourthly, the relative rarity of applications for changes of venue suggests that the Crown was not as embarrassed by recalcitrant juries as was sometimes alleged. Fifthly, cases such as *Fay* and *M'Mahon* do not suggest a judiciary worried about the weaknesses of jury trial, nor do they suggest a nervous judiciary, easily led by the attorney general. In the light of these considerations, it is difficult not to dismiss a great deal of the criticism of the formation of Irish juries as exaggerated. In the light of the complaints made above, it is difficult not to dismiss many of them as feeble.

There is also the fact that neither Perrin's act nor O'Hagan's act went in for root-and-branch reform. Both tidied up, both defined qualifications and procedures more clearly, and both were innovative, especially the latter, but neither contemplated majority verdicts or putting the Crown and the prisoner on equal terms in the matter of challenges. Reform should have been easy because the history of juries provided numerous venerable precedents for reform. The special jury, for example, which was used mainly for the trial of complicated civil

snare": array challenges and jury selection in England and Ireland, 1800–1850' in *Canadian Journal of History*, 39:1 (Apr. 2004), 1–26 (from http://www.findarticles.com (10 Aug. 2006)).

211 R.W. Kostal, 'Rebels in the dock: the prosecution of the Dublin fenians, 1865–6' in *Éire-Ireland*, 34:2 (summer 1999), 80; at p. 93 Dr Kostal also points out that 'if juries were packed, they were packed from an extremely large pool of "reliable" men.'

212 John. F. McEldowney, 'The case of *The Queen v. McKenna* (1869) and jury packing in Ireland' in *Ir Jur*, n.s., 12 (winter 1977), 352.

cases and for the trial of misdemeanours, was a model of random selection. The sheriff gave a number to every name on the special jurors' list, 'beginning the numbers from the first name, and continuing them, in a regular arithmetical series, down to the last name'. He wrote the numbers on cards, 'being all as nearly as may be of equal size', put the cards in a box, shook them, and drew out '48 of the said numbers'.[213] The parties were allowed 12 challenges each, and the jury was chosen by ballot from the remaining 24. The striking of the special jury, according to George Battersby, 'appears to be, and I have always observed it to be, as far as I could judge, the fairest way of striking a jury that can be thought of.'[214] Charles Coffey, the chairman of Londonderry quarter sessions, thought that there should be special juries in capital cases.[215]

The obvious reform of the Irish jury system was to establish majority verdicts. In 1852 the inspector general of constabulary urged the Napier committee to consider majority verdicts. The committee evaded the question and suggested that there should be only one jury panel for both civil and criminal cases, and that the Queen's Bench should be able to change the venue when a murder had been committed by an 'unlawful confederacy'.[216] Nine years later Arthur Houston advocated majority verdicts, pointing out that jury unanimity was peculiar because 'in the whole of our legislative and judicial system this is the only department in which it is thought essential that such universal agreement should exist.'[217] A bill was introduced in 1871, but got nowhere.[218] There were three occasions when majority verdicts were used that might have served as examples for Ireland: at trials in Scotland,[219] at trials of peers

---

213 Purcell, op. cit., pp 163–4.

214 *First, second, and special reports from the select committee on juries (Ireland)* ..., p. 91, HC 1873 (283), xv, 495. See above, p. 128, for the different system of balloting introduced by 39 & 40 Vict., c. 78, s. 19 (15 Aug. 1876). In ancient Rome, the judge chose the jury by taking names from an urn (Thomas MacKenzie, *Studies in Roman law with comparative views of the laws of France, England, and Scotland* (Edinburgh and London, 1862), p. 337). In the colony of Natal a system of selection like that described by Battersby prevailed; it produced exclusively White juries to try Blacks, Coloureds, and Indians (P.R. Spiller, 'The jury system in early Natal (1846–1874)' in *Journal of Legal History*, 8:2 (Sept. 1987), 127–47).

215 *First, second, and special reports from the select committee on juries (Ireland)* ..., p. 45, HC 1873 (283), xv, 449.

216 *Report from the select committee on outrages (Ireland); together with the proceedings of the committee, minutes of evidence, and appendix and index*, pp iv, 211–12, HC 1852 (438), xiv, 4, 229–30. Lord Eglinton (lord lieutenant, 1852, 1858–9) agreed with the inspector general (Virginia Crossman, *Politics, law and order in nineteenth-century Ireland* (Dublin, 1996), p. 93). The subject was taken up in 1871 when agrarian murders were again a problem (Larcom Papers (NLI, MS 7719 [*Spectator*, 6 May 1871]). Majority verdicts were occasionally proposed as a desirable change in England (see, for example, Sheldon Amos, *The science of law* (London, 1874), p. 267).

217 'Observations on trial by jury, with suggestions for the amendment of our present system' in *Journal of the Statistical and Social Inquiry Society of Ireland*, 3 (May 1861), 105.

218 Above, p. 130.

219 The jury consisted of 15; 8 could return a verdict; the prisoner was allowed only 5 peremptory challenges (Paterson, op. cit., p. 331).

by the house of lords,[220] and in courts martial, where a simple majority was enough, 'except to pass sentence of death, where two-thirds of the members present must concur'. [221]

If a majority was good enough to hang a Scot, to decapitate a duke, or to shoot an admiral, it should have been good enough for Ireland. Yet Irish lawyers, for all their experience of inconclusive juries, were attached to unanimity. Serjeant Armstrong could 'see no sufficient reason ... for departing from the present rule of unanimity ... It is one of those ancient landmarks of the law which is as old as the jury system itself.'[222] Charles Coffey thought 'that the abuses have not been so great as to render it advisable to alter the constitutional practice which has existed thereto.' James Hamilton did not want to abandon unanimity 'because I do not want to frighten the people too much with the law.' Charles Hare Hemphill, chairman of Kerry, thought that, if there were two or three men on a jury who are known to be in the minority, I think that such a verdict would not be accepted by the portion of the public who may have sympathized with the accused.'

There were two models that might have been exemplars for forming juries to deal with sectarian cases or political cases. First, there was the jury chosen to try felonies before the high steward of the University of Oxford, when 6 graduates and 6 freeholders sat together.[223] Secondly, there was the jury *de medietate linguæ*, which was a crude but noble attempt to give foreigners a chance to transcend their origins.[224] Six foreigners, chosen regardless of nationality, trying a foreigner, who

---

220 Edward Fischel, *The English constitution*; translated from the second German edition by Richard Jenery Shee (London, 1863), p. 285.

221 Thomas Frederick Simmons (continued by Thomas Frederick Simmons), *The constitution and practice of courts martial with a summary of the law of evidence as connected therewith; also some notice of the criminal law of England with reference to the trial of civil offences* (7th ed., London, 1875), p. 10.

222 *First, second, and special reports from the select committee on juries (Ireland)* ..., p. 52, HC 1873 (283), xv, 456.

223 Fischel, op. cit., p. 282.

224 Before 1870 an alien had the right to be tried by a jury 'consisting one half of alien foreigners generally, and not exclusively, of the prisoner's countrymen' (Purcell, op. cit., p. 166). See also *The key to the examination questions, containing the examiners' questions from 1835 to 1851, with full answers, by the editors of the* Law Student's Magazine. *Division V: criminal law* (2nd ed., London, 1851), pp 110–11). 3 & 4 Will. IV, c. 91, s. 37 (28 Aug. 1833) tried to provide aliens with jurors of their own nationality: the sheriff was to 'return for one half of the jury a competent number of aliens, if so many there be in the town or place where the trial is had, and if not, then so many aliens as shall be found in the same town or place, if any.' When Serafino Pelizzioni was tried for murder at the Old Bailey in 1866 he was offered a choice between a mixed English-Italian jury or an ordinary jury; he opted for the latter; he was convicted (Richard S. Lambert, *When justice faltered. A study of nine peculiar murder trials* (London, 1935), p. 246). There was no jury *de medietate linguæ* in Scotland, but 'a landed man has a privilege to have the majority of the jury landed men like himself' (Paterson, op. cit., p. 332). Timothy Brecknock, who was tried for murder at the Castlebar assizes in 1786, claimed a jury *de medietate linguæ* because he was an Englishman, an argument that the lord chief baron dismissed with a fine Magna Carta flourish: 'the people of Ireland and England speak one tongue, have one common language, and are

might not be a countryman of even one of the 6, was not perfect, but it was better than 12 Protestants trying a Catholic, 12 farmers trying a labourer, 12 men trying a woman, or 12 tenants trying a landlord. John Reilly, the sub-sheriff of Monaghan, told the Hartington committee how he produced Co. Cavan's equivalent of the jury *de medietate linguæ*: he made up his long panel 'according to the numbers of the different religious denominations on the jurors book returned to me ... I took first two Protestants, then one Catholic, then two Protestants, then one Catholic, and so on.'[225] He approved of the alphabetical system introduced by O'Hagan's act ('I would have the alphabetical system, no matter what the consequence, because nobody could say that there was any unfairness used'). What was sauce for the goose was sauce for the gander: 'I would as soon myself be tried by 12 Protestants as by 12 Catholics but the lower orders who are those that are mostly tried, would not like that.'[226]

THE PRISONER IS GIVEN IN CHARGE

Each juror took the oath when he passed the scrutiny of the Crown and the prisoner. When twelve had been assembled, the clerk of the crown ordered the crier to count them, using the Norman-French word *contez*.[227] The crier called out their names and asked them if they were 'all sworn'. Having been reassured on this point, he shouted: 'Twelve good men and true, stand together and hear the

governed by one common sovereign; and let it not go abroad, that Englishmen are considered as aliens in this kingdom. Englishmen inherit in Ireland, and, *vice versa*, Irishmen in England. Both countries have the same laws, the same constitution, and the same happy government' (*The trials of George Robert Fitzgerald, Esq; and Timothy Brecknock, for the procurement of James Fulton and others, for the murder of Pat. Ran. M'Donnell and Charles Hipson. Also the trial of John Gallagher and others, for an assault on Geo. Rob. Fitzgerald, in the gaol of Castlebar* ... (2nd ed., Dublin 1786), p. 155). The jury *de medietate linguæ* was abolished by the Naturalization Act (33 & 34 Vict., c. 14, s. 5 (12 May 1870)).

225 *First, second, and special reports from the select committee on juries (Ireland)* ..., pp 256, 262, HC 1873 (283), xv, 660, 666. Henchy, J. would have approved of John Reilly, because in *de Burca v. The attorney general* in 1976 he asserted that 'the jury must be drawn from a pool broadly representative of the community so that its verdict will be stamped with the fairness and acceptability of a genuinely diffused community decision' (Paul Anthony McDermott, 'Criminal procedure and evidence' in Paul O'Mahony (ed. with seven introductory essays), *Criminal justice in Ireland* (Dublin, 2002), p. 44). For the criminal code of the province of Quebec, which provided for mixed juries of French- and English-speakers, see Graham Parker, 'Jury trial in Canada' in *Journal of Legal History*, 8:2 (Sept. 1987), 184.

226 For a highly contentious murder trial, arising out of a rebellion in Lower Canada, where the prisoners used their challenges to secure an exclusively Canadien jury, see F. Murray Greenwood, 'The Chartrand murder trial: rebellion and repression in Lower Canada, 1837–1839' in *Criminal Justice History*, 5 (1984), 129–59.

227 Purcell, op. cit., pp 188–9.

evidence.'[228] The clerk of the crown then charged the jury, a procedure that took place only at trials for treason and felony: he told the prisoner to hold up his hand and said: 'Gentlemen of the jury, look on the prisoner and hearken to his charge.' Then he read out the indictment, and continued, 'Upon this indictment, he hath been arraigned, and thereunto hath pleaded not guilty: and for his trial hath put himself upon God and his country, which country you are. Your charge therefore is to inquire whether he be guilty of this felony ... in manner and form he stand indicted, or not guilty. Hear your evidence.'

228 O'Hagan's act explicitly excluded women (the term juror, according to s. 3, 'shall mean male persons only'). Women were admitted to juries by the Sex Disqualification (Removal) Act 1919 (9 & 10 Geo. V, c. 71 (23 Dec. 1919)), which envisaged, in certain circumstances, juries 'composed of men only or women only as the case may require'.

CHAPTER FIVE

The Crown's case

THE CROWN OPENS THE CASE

ACCORDING TO JUDGE FITZGERALD, 'until the jury had been selected and sworn, and the solemn form gone through of giving the prisoner in charge, the trial cannot be said to have commenced.'[1] The senior crown counsel usually, but not always, made the Crown's opening speech. If the prisoner had no counsel, which was unlikely in capital cases, the crown counsel did not make an opening speech, 'unless there be some peculiarity in the facts of the case to require it.'[2] Counsel were 'to be assistant to the court in the furtherance of justice and not to act as counsel for any particular person or party.' Joseph Napier told the select committee on public prosecutors in 1853 that 'it is considered to be the duty of those who represent the attorney general to administer justice in a becoming way, and never unduly to press a case, and never to exercise any severity which the purposes of justice do not require.'[3] David J.A. Cairns, writing of England, enumerated other things that prosecuting were not supposed to do: they were not to state doubtful facts; they were not to repeat confessions and conversations; they were not to use invective, to reason on facts, to anticipate the defence, or to appeal to the jury's passions and prejudices.[4] They could, however, take the offensive on certain matters: they could anticipate, in murder cases, 'an attack upon the character of any particular witness for the Crown'; they could also anticipate the argument that the Crown's case was based only on circumstantial evidence by reading out 'the general observations of a learned judge, made in a case tried some years before, on the nature and effect of circumstantial evidence.'[5]

---

1 *M'Mahon* (1875) IR 9 CL 309, at p. 333. For the emergence of criminal trials dominated by counsel see John H. Langbein, *The origins of adversary criminal trial* (Oxford, 2003).

2 Theobald A. Purcell, *A summary of the general principles of pleading and evidence, in criminal cases in Ireland: with the rules of practice incident thereto* (Dublin, 1849), p. 190.

3 *Report from the select committee on public prosecutors; together with the proceedings of the committee, minutes of evidence, appendix and index*, p. 146, HC 1854–5 (481), xii, 154. See also *Impartial Reporter*, 19 July 1849 where the judge, Robert Torrens, told an attorney at the Enniskillen assizes that counsel 'never unduly press matters' on the north-west circuit.

4 David J.A. Cairns, *Advocacy and the making of the adversarial criminal trial 1800–1865* (Oxford, 1998), p. 39.

5 Purcell, op. cit., p. 191. The case Purcell referred to was *Courvoisier* (1839) 9 Car & P 362, 173 Eng Rep 869 where there is a reference to the observations of Lord Chief Baron Macdonald on circumstantial evidence. See Cairns, op. cit., pp 129–35.

Nowhere was candour more discreetly deployed than in the crown counsel's warning to the jury of the danger of believing approvers' evidence. At Patrick Woods' trial at Armagh assizes in 1841, the first crown witness was an approver. 'I am bound to tell you,' Sir Thomas Staples QC told the jury, 'that except so far as his evidence is corroborated by other respectable and unimpeachable witnesses, you are not bound to give credit to him.'[6] Having admitted what could not be denied, Sir Thomas added hopefully, 'but so far as it is, so far you are entitled to rely and act on it if you believe it in other respects.' Sir Thomas, who had been called in 1802, was not giving much away: the prisoner's counsel was going to attack the approver anyway; the judge would warn the jury in his summing up, and even if not warned, the jury were not likely to miss the fact that the approver had betrayed his confederates in return for his life.

Even experienced counsel broke the rules. One might say experienced counsel were more likely to break them. One of the clearest rules was that 'the counsel for the prosecution ought not to state any particular expressions supposed to have been used by the prisoner, nor the precise words of any confession, but he may state the general effect of what the prisoner said.'[7] At Westmeath summer assizes in 1863 when George Battersby QC 'was about to state to the jury the particulars of certain statements which the prisoner had made to police constables and a magistrate after his arrest', the prisoner's counsel objected. The judge, Pigot, declared that 'in the course of his experience as crown prosecutor he had never known such statements to be introduced into the addresses of counsel opening the case for the Crown; and that even if it were necessary now to create a precedent, he would make one, and rule that they should not be stated.'[8] It is highly unlikely that Battersby was ignorant of Pigot's aversion to police questioning.

Practically any opening speech reveals prosecuting counsel's range of rhetorical devices. Hugh Law QC made the opening speech at John Gregory's trial at the Downpatrick spring assizes in 1871.[9] Law was not the senior crown counsel, being junior to Thomas McDonnell QC, who also appeared for the Crown. Law was not even one of the regular crown counsel for Co. Down, but he had the advantage of youth: he was 54 while McDonnell was 78. He was, moreover, well on the way to the top, and would be lord chancellor, 1881–3. Law's rhetoric began at the very beginning when he promised the jury that he would give 'a brief outline of the facts which would be proved before them in evidence.' This promise, 'to prove in evidence', was potentially misleading. To the jury it implied that the witnesses would convince them of the truth of the Crown's case. Lawyers, however, defined the words idiosyncratically: 'evidence' was the information that the law of evidence allowed witnesses to repeat in court; 'to prove' meant to utter that information under oath in court. William Wills, who wrote a perceptive book on evidence, had protested in vain against using the word proof as a synonym for

6 NAI, CRF/1841/Woods/26.   7 Purcell, op. cit., p. 190.
8 *Bodkin* (1863) 9 Cox CC 404, at p. 404.   9 NAI, CRF/1871/Gregory/9.

evidence. 'The term PROOF is often confounded with that of evidence, and applied to denote the *medium* of proof,' he complained, 'whereas in strictness it marks merely the *effect* of evidence.'[10]

Some counsel liked to begin by expatiating on their invidious duty. Law did not expatiate at length, but he did not let his melancholy duty pass unnoticed ('the duty devolved on him – a duty which he regretted very much'). Nor did he start with the finding of the body, which was a good place to start; instead he described in a few words the aristocratic milieu in which the murder had taken place. The dead man, John Gallagher, and the prisoner, John Gregory, had worked for William Brownlowe Forde JP, DL, of Seaforde (owner of 20,000 acres in Co. Down, MP for Co. Down, 1857–74, and lieutenant-colonel of the South Down Militia). The dead man and the prisoner lived within a mile of each other near the village of Seaforde. The prisoner had been a gatekeeper; the dead man had been a foreman, one of whose duties was to pay 'the labourers on the estate their wages from week to week, and their payment took place on Fridays.' The mere mention of money allowed the jury to flatter themselves by silently concocting a motive for the murder.

Having set the scene and hinted at a motive, Law turned to the finding of Gallagher's body on Saturday 30 July 1870. His description was not blood-curdling. He did it in fifty-two words: 'The body was lying on the right side. There was a mark of violence on the head, which at that time was not discernible as a gunshot wound. It was a curious wound at the back of the head, and blood flowed from it over his left ear and down his breast.' As he introduced the body, Law casually linked Gregory twice in a tendentious way with Gallagher's disappearance: (1) Gallagher's body had been found 'midway between the commencement of the wood, as they came from the village, and going towards Gregory's gate'; (2) Gallagher was last seen alive 'between the village of Seaforde and Gregory's house'. Law's use of Gregory's house as a reference point for locating Gallagher's body was unnecessary because a map had been made, but it nicely demonstrated Sydney Smith's argument that in counsel's speech 'meaning is given to insignificant facts.'[11]

Apart from rhetorical devices such as these, and one instance where he managed to work in a conversation about the prisoner's bloody hands, Law's speech was mainly a blow-by-blow account of the prisoner's movements before and after the sound of the shot that was supposed to have killed Gallagher, which

---

10 William Wills, *An essay on the rationale of circumstantial evidence; illustrated by numerous cases* (London, 1838), p. 2.

11 Counsel, according to Smith, 'does not describe scattered brains, ghastly wounds, pale features, and hair clotted with gore' because these things 'are not to English taste' (*The works of the Revd Sydney Smith*, 4 vols (London, 1839–40), ii, 367). Cain and Abel were also unmentionable, according to Smith. It is not difficult to find them in Ireland. The crown counsel, Thomas O'Shaughnessy KC, at the trial of James Doherty for the murder of his son, alluded to Cain and Abel – and to Mount Sinai (NAI, CRF/1902/Doherty/69).

was supposed to show that Gregory had an opportunity to kill Gallagher. The other definers of guilt, motive, means, and suspicious conduct, were inserted incidentally into the description of Gregory's movements. Motive was revealed in dribs and drabs as the story progressed: there were two references to the dead man's money at the beginning of the speech; there was a statement that Gregory was in debt, and that he had been dismissed from his job as gate-keeper; there was a puzzling reference to a linen bag in which the dead man kept his money.

Means were more coherently presented. About a fortnight before Gallagher's death, the prisoner 'was endeavouring to get the loan of a pistol, and succeeded in getting one from a man named Hugh Morrison, the prisoner stating that he wanted it to shoot rabbits.' When Law added the statement that 'Rabbits, he might tell the jury, were not generally shot with a pistol', he was merely confirming what they were already thinking. As well as borrowing a pistol, Gregory 'commissioned a person to purchase for him, at Downpatrick, some ounces of gunpowder and a halfpenny worth of percussion caps.' After the discovery of Gallagher's body, Gregory's house was searched, 'but no powder, percussion caps, or pistol were found.' The pistol had not been returned to its owner, nor had it been found, 'although every inquiry and search had been made.' These facts were, on their own, weighty, but Law was not finished: 'On Colonel Forde's estate there was a carpenter's shop, and in that shop there were, among other articles, a number of small bolts lying about.' A week or so before the murder, Gregory had been in the carpenter's shop and, 'strange to say, the bolt found deep-seated in the brain of the murdered man was similar to the bolts in the carpenter's shop.' Law finished with a fine flourish that combined means and motive: the missing percussion caps and Gallagher's blue linen bag, 'containing part of the money', were found in a deserted house opposite Gregory's house.

Apart from one small effort to anticipate the argument that the Crown's case was based on circumstantial evidence ('The jury might ask what evidence was there that John Gregory committed this murder? No eye saw him fire the fatal shot.'), Law did not anticipate the prisoner's arguments, which were easily predictable. Gregory's counsel, John Monroe, would argue that the Crown's timetable was improbable ('the prosecution rested on minutes'); that only a fool would have done what the prisoner was supposed to have done ('Did the jury think that the prisoner was a fool or idiot – that, having killed and robbed his victim, he would secrete his plunder in a spot the most likely of all others to be searched?'); that Gregory's motive was shared by others ('How many men were in dependent circumstances, and were they to suppose, that being so, they would commit murder?'); that the pistol and the percussion caps were common possessions ('How many hundred people had pistols in their possession?'); that the bolt from the carpenter's shop meant little ('Many people had opportunities of going in there and taking bolts.').

It is worth noting what Law did not do in his speech. He did not use it as a mnemonic device to prepare the jury for the Crown's thirty witnesses. Only a few witnesses were alluded to – Gallagher's daughter, Mr and Mrs Morrison, two men cutting the hedge, and a man called O'Connell, ethnically transmogrified to M'Connell. Nor did Law present the case analytically, delineating the case under the headings of motive, means, opportunity, and suspicious conduct: Gallagher had money and Gregory needed money; Gregory had procured the means of committing the crime (the pistol, the percussion caps, and the projectiles); Gregory had created an opportunity to attack Gallagher (he had arranged to meet him); Gregory had begun to exploit that opportunity (he had been seen going along the road, and he had been near the scene of the crime just after the shot was heard); Gregory had behaved suspiciously after the shot was heard (there was blood on his hand, and he had been seen at the house where the linen bag was found). If there had been no jury, no public, no reporters, but only a professional tribunal, such an exposition would have been the way to put the case. Law's blow-by-blow approach, however, had advantages: the fact that the jury were told what happened probably helped to convince them that it had happened; the story could not be countered by the prisoner, except by producing witnesses, but a case presented analytically could have been countered by disparagement.

Law's speech took up about 1,500 words in the *Belfast Newsletter*. How long did it take to deliver? Edward Gibbon at the impeachment of Warren Hastings 'had the curiosity to enquire of the short-hand writer, how many words a ready and rapid orator might pronounce in an hour. From 7,000 to 7,500 was his answer.'[12] At this rate Law's 1,500 words would have taken only twelve minutes, which suggests that newspaper reports were not verbatim, a conclusion that is reinforced by the fact that on the second day of Gregory's trial, three speeches (Monroe's second speech for the prisoner, Law's concluding speech, and the judge's summing up) filled the period from 10 a.m. to 4 p.m., but their reported length was only 5,000 words. At this rate Law's speech would have taken about an hour and a half.[13] Yet if Law's 1,500 words actually took one-and-a-half hours, it is not easy to see where that amount of time could have come from on the first day of trial. On that day the court sat from 10 a.m. to 4 p.m., and the following business was transacted: Judge Fitzgerald sentenced a house-breaker, Patrick McKeown, to ten years' penal servitude, 'after commenting on the prisoner's career of crime which commenced in 1850', Gregory was arraigned, the jury was

12 Edward Gibbon, *Memoirs of my life*, ed. with an intro. by Betty Radice (Harmondsworth, 1984), p. 185.
13 George Smyly's opening speech at William Burke Kirwan's trial filled 10 pages of print, or 4,000 words, or 33 minutes according to Gibbon. The trial's two days filled 83 pages, which implied that Smyly's speech must have taken about one–eighth of 2 days' sitting, which would be much closer to 2 hours than to 33 minutes (John Simpson Armstrong, *Report of the trial of William Burke Kirwan, for the murder of Maria Louisa Kirwan, his wife, at the island of Ireland's Eye, in the county of Dublin on the 6th September, 1852, before the Hon. Judge Crampton and the Rt Hon. Baron Greene, at the Commission Court, Green Street, on the 8th and 9th December, 1852* (Dublin, 1853), pp 2–12).

empanelled, Law made his opening speech, and 30 crown witnesses were examined and cross-examined. If the Crown's 30 witnesses took only 10 minutes each, taking up 5 hours, there was not enough time between 10 a.m. and 4 p.m. for a long speech from Law, even assuming that the sentencing of the house-breaker had taken only a few minutes, that the jury's empanelling had been quick, and that there had been no adjournment for lunch. Either the speech was short, or the examination of the witnesses was done very quickly indeed. Sir Thomas Staples' speech at Daniel Ward's trial took only 20 minutes, a fact noted by the judge, Rickard Deasy, who also noted that McMechan's speech for the prisoner took 4 hours, that Serjeant Sullivan's reply took an hour, and that his own speech to the jury and the jury's deliberations took two and half hours.[14] The fact that Sir Thomas was nearly 90 may have explained his relative taciturnity.

EXAMINATION-IN-CHIEF

After the opening speech the Crown called its witnesses. 'The advocate should, in nearly every case, put his most intelligent and most honest witness in the box first,' Frederic Wrottesley advised.[15] Crown counsel in a murder case could not pick and choose. They might get the proceedings started with something uncontentious, such as introducing a map of the locality, but they usually had to put the finding of the body near the beginning. Counsel elicited witness' evidence by questions, a procedure known as examination-in-chief or as 'direct' examination, as opposed to cross-examination, which was done by the other side.[16] In examination-in-chief 'leading' questions were not usually allowed: the witness' story had to be elicited by means of questions that did not 'plainly suggest to him the answer he is expected to make.'[17] Leading questions could be used in examination-in-chief to set the scene and to elicit the witness' name and occupation, or as Purcell wrote, counsel could ask a question 'which, if answered by *Yes* or *No*, would not be conclusive on any of the points of the issue'. Leading questions could also be used to stimulate the memory of a forgetful witness and to interrogate a witness who was 'hostile to the party who has called him, or reluctant to state the truth.' The last two required the judge's permission. There was another exception that was more likely to occur during the examination-in-

---

14   NAI, CRF/1863/Ward/5.

15   Frederic John Wrottesley, *The examination of witnesses in court including examination in chief, cross-examination, and re-examination* (2nd ed., London, 1926), pp 12–13.

16   A synonym for examining a witness, which was also used as a taunt, was the expression 'to put him on the table'. In some courthouses witnesses actually sat on a chair on a table where they were well above the level of counsel, who stood on the floor. See for example pl. 1 in Éanna Hickey, *Irish law and lawyers in modern folk tradition* (Dublin, 1999). Purcell mentions a witness 'box' (Purcell, op. cit., p. 195).

17   Ibid., p. 196.

chief of the prisoner's witnesses: where a witness was called to contradict what a previous witness had said, 'it is the usual practice to ask whether those particular expressions were used, or those things said, without putting the question in general form by inquiring what was said.'

Counsel's questions guided the witnesses to the important points. The application of the law of evidence kept them from digressing. When the two were combined they produced short, tight statements, whose important points could be easily grasped. The examination-in-chief of the witnesses at the trial of George Jubee, a private in the 5th Fusiliers, showed the capacity of examination-in-chief to elicit the few facts that mattered and to separate facts from inferences. Jubee had shot the battalion's adjutant, Robertson Mackay, on the parade ground at Birr in August 1843. Sergeant George Raymond told the whole story in a few words. The judge, Richard Greene, noted the gist of what he said:

> Heard a shot. Saw the deceased in the act of falling and the prisoner with his firelock between his legs holding it by the muzzle and trembling exceedingly. The prisoner was within a few yards of the deceased. Saw the deceased on the ground ... Heard a corporal say to prisoner, 'Jubee was it you did this?' Prisoner said 'Yes. I may as well be hanged as killed with drill.' Witness examined the gun. It had recently been discharged. It belonged to the prisoner. After the prisoner was taken to the guard room witness examined his pouch. There was one round deficient.'[18]

The questions that produced these statements can be easily imagined. Jubee was hanged at Tullamore on 10 April 1844.

Examination-in-chief was done quickly. At Daniel Ward's trial the judge, Deasy, noted that on the first day of the trial, the examination-in-chief, cross-examination, and in some cases, the re-examination, of thirteen witnesses filled 6 hours and 45 minutes.[19] Assuming that there were no breaks, each witness took about half an hour, which is rather longer than seems to have been taken at Gregory's trial. Ward's four witnesses, who gave him a good character, took only 35 minutes. Witnesses were nudged towards divulging prosaic but important details; they were kept away from the gossip, malice, and conjecture that they probably wanted to divulge. At Ward's trial, as well as at most other trials, the typical witness contributed only one useful piece of information. If the Crown's opening speech was a connected story, the examination-in-chief was a string of details, divulged by different people, and connected only by the sequence in which they were divulged. If the opening speech resembled Dr Watson's narratives in the *Strand Magazine*, examination-in-chief resembled Handel's *Messiah*.

The law excluded 'incompetent' witnesses even though their evidence was important. The most important exclusion was the prisoner, who could not be

18   NAI, CRF/1844/Jubee/1.   19   Ibid., CRF/1863/Ward/5.

examined or cross-examined. Also excluded were those who were mad,[20] infamous,[21] privileged,[22] too young, or 'interested'.[23] The last were generally prisoners' spouses, whose exclusion was 'founded on the acknowledged infirmity of human nature', which produced some strange results: what a wife said in the presence of her husband could be repeated by a witness who heard it, but the wife could not give evidence to contradict it. At John Gregory's trial, for example, Margaret Morrison was able to say that 'Gregory came in and sat down by the side of the door, and his wife said, "But John, what put the blood on you?"', but Gregory could not call his wife to contradict this.[24] Wives were not completely excluded: they could give evidence against their husbands in cases where they alleged their husbands had abducted, raped, assaulted, poisoned, or shot them.[25] The rule that a wife could not give evidence against her husband applied only to what she could say in court. In June 1857 Mrs Spollen told the DMP that her husband James had murdered George Little, the cashier of the Midland Great Western Railway, and that she knew where the money was hidden (the murder had taken place in November 1856). The hiding place was searched, the money found, and Spollen arrested and committed, but the magistrates refused to admit his wife's evidence.[26] The law, moreover, appeared to be biased. Prisoners' spouses were excluded, but a technical argument allowed the spouses of those who had been murdered to give evidence because a criminal prosecution 'is always at the suit, not of the prosecutor, but of the Queen', which meant that the deceased's relations were not 'interested' parties.[27]

The requirement that evidence had to be given on oath excluded witnesses who had scruples about taking oaths, who did not know what an oath was, or who

20 For idiots, monomaniacs, and lunatics, and for the difference between *non compos mentis* and in *lucidis intervallis*, see Henry Roscoe, *A digest of the law of evidence in criminal cases* (2nd ed. by T.C. Granger, London, 1840), pp 116–17. For the legal presumption that the deaf and dumb were idiots see Purcell, op. cit., p. 334.

21 Infamy was a precise quality otherwise the courts would have been empty. The infamous were those who had been convicted of treason, felony, or *crimen falsi*, which was a portmanteau term for perjury, subornation of perjury, suppression of testimony by bribery, and 'conspiracy to procure the absence of a witness' (Purcell, op. cit., pp 337–8). The infamous were made competent in 1843 (6 & 7 Vict., c. 85 (1843)). For infamy and interest see C.J.W. Allen, *The law of evidence in Victorian England* (Cambridge, 1997), pp 95–100.

22 Barristers and attorneys when acting professionally could not give evidence against their clients. Clergymen were not privileged, although in practice they were not obliged to reveal 'communications made in confidence, and under the seal of religious duty.' Certain kinds of information were also privileged, such as state secrets, the names of those employed in the discovery of crime, and the names of those who employed them (Purcell, op. cit., pp 319–24).

23 Ibid., pp 325–6, 339.   24 NAI, CRF/1871/Gregory/9.

25 Purcell, op. cit., pp 343–4. See for example *Wasson* (1796) 1 Cr & Dix 197, at p. 197 where the prisoner, who was on trial at Green Street for administering poison to his wife, objected to the reception of his wife's evidence. The judge allowed her to be examined, and the twelve judges decided that her evidence was admissible.

26 Frank Thorpe Porter, *Gleanings and reminiscences* (Dublin, 1875), p. 174.

27 Purcell, op. cit., p. 341.

could not be bound by an oath because they were atheists.[28] From 1833 Quakers and Moravians could affirm,[29] from 1833 Separatists,[30] and from 1861 those who had scruples, but atheists had to wait until 1869.[31] Those who were not Christians could be sworn by any ceremony that bound them. Jews swore on the Pentateuch, Muslims on the Koran, and the Chinese broke a saucer. It was one thing to have a strange God, or even a colourless, secular God, but to have no God at all was not quickly tolerated.

The testing of a witness' 'competence', which was called examination on the *voire-dire*, was done by the judge and could be quite elaborate, requiring the examination of witnesses. According to Purcell, 'an examination on the *voire-dire* is allowed to be conducted without strict regard to the general rule of evidence, which requires the best possible proof of a fact and admits no other.'[32] At Matthew Bryan's trial at the Maryborough summer assizes in 1840, for example, the first witness was Bridget Brennan, 'a girl of very small stature who appeared at first to be too young to understand the nature of an oath.' Her mother, however, was able to say that Bridget was 13 years old and 'had been educated with a knowledge of religious obligation & duties, which further appeared by putting some preliminary questions to her.'[33] The lord chief justice, Bushe, allowed her to give evidence.

The array of witnesses at any well prepared trial demonstrated the Crown's formidable capacity to marshal a case, especially one based on circumstantial evidence. Matthew Phibbs was charged with the murder of William Callaghan, who had a shop on the main street of Ballymote, where he lived with his wife and servant. The bodies of all three had been found mutilated, Callaghan was reputed to be well-off, and there were signs that money had been taken from his house. At Phibbs' first trial the jury disagreed. At his second trial, at the Sligo summer

28 For oaths see Purcell, op. cit., pp 335–7. The Oaths Act 1909 (9 Edw. VII, c. 39 (25 Nov. 1909)) changed the oath-taking ceremony. From 1909 a Christian held a copy of the New Testament in his 'uplifted hand' and repeated the words after the officer who administered the oath ('I swear by Almighty God that my evidence will be the truth, the whole truth, and nothing but the truth'). Before 1909 the officer did the speaking: 'the witness holds the book, the New Testament or the Old Testament, in his hands; the officer says, "The evidence you shall give shall be the truth, the whole truth, and nothing but the truth, so Help You God,", and the witness then kisses the Testament' (James O'Connor, *The Irish justice of the peace: a treatise on the powers and duties of justices of the peace in Ireland, and certain matters connected therewith* (Dublin, 1911), pp 258–9).

29 3 & 4 Will. IV, c. 49, s. 1 (28 Aug. 1833). For a history of nineteenth-century changes in the rules about incompetency 'from defect of religious principle', see Allen, op. cit., pp 50–94. See also 3 & 4 Will. IV, c. 49 (28 Aug. 1833), 1 & 2 Vict., cc 77, 105 (10, 14 Aug. 1838). For the Seceders, who insisted on raising their hand while taking the oath, but who refused either to hold the book, or to kiss it, see *Woods* (1841) Ir Cir Rep 276.

30 3 & 4 Will. IV, c. 82 (28 Aug. 1833).

31 24 & 25 Vict., c. 66 (1 Aug. 1861) extended to criminal trials the conscientious scruples against swearing accepted in civil cases. For atheists, see Allen, op. cit., pp 51, 58, 60–1.

32 Purcell, op. cit., pp 195–6 (the phrase was Norman-French: *voir*, true; *dire*, to say).

33 NAI, CRF/1840/Bryan/50.

assizes in 1861, the Crown called 44 witnesses. The Crown's opening speech and the examination of 24 of the 44 witnesses filled the first day of the trial.[34] The first 7 witnesses established the time of the murders. From the Crown's point of view these 7 did well, giving 5 almost consecutive descriptions of the mutilated corpses, which was all to the good because 4 of them were not necessary. The surgeon, Joseph Lougheed, used few words and was the least gruesome of the 5: William Callaghan had 'an incised wound from below & behind the left ear to about the same place on the right side but rather further back. It passed through all the soft parts & cut down to the bones of the neck through the larynx. It was done by a sharp cutting instrument & was sufficient to cause death.'

When these 7 witnesses had established that the murders had taken place between Monday evening and Wednesday morning, the next 4 connected Phibbs with Callaghan's house between those times. Two of these were the Crown's most important witnesses: they saw Phibbs 'jump down the wall at the gap' at the back of Callaghan's house between 10 and 11 on the Tuesday morning. The next 4 witnesses observed Phibbs' movements as he left Ballymote and headed for Collooney. He called at Mary Flaherty's public house 4 miles from Ballymote ('He asked for a glass of spirits & an ounce of tobacco. He paid me 1s. in all for debt & goods.') A customer in the public house was able to confirm that Phibbs paid Mary Flaherty '3d. he owed her', which contributed to the picture of Phibbs as a man who had been impecunious, but was now flush. When Phibbs left the public house, John Kearns, the customer who had noted the payment of the 3d., followed him and saw something that greatly added to the Crown's case: 'I saw him pull out papers from his pocket & tear & throw them on the road.' When Kearns heard of the murders, he described what he did next: 'I went to see what he had thrown on the hedge. I picked up the papers. They were lodged among the bushes. I put them in my pocket where they remained for 2 or 3 hours & I then gave them to Peter Durham. There was blood on the papers that I had kicked on the road.'

At this point the Crown broke away from Phibbs' journey from Ballymote to Collooney and called 9 witnesses to establish the provenance and ownership of the blood-stained papers: 5 recounted how the papers had passed from Kearns, through Peter Durham, 'until they were at length produced in court'; 3 (the postmaster in Ballymote, his wife, and the postman) showed that one of the papers was a letter that had been delivered to William Callaghan's house (the postmaster also identified Callaghan's signature); the ninth and last witness in this group (and the Crown's twenty-fourth witness) was Joseph Cogan MD, who also identified Callaghan's signature. After Cogan's examination, the court adjourned until the next morning.

34 This description of the examination-in-chief of the witnesses is taken from the judge's notes in NAI, CRF/1861/Phibbs/5. The judge was Edmund Hayes, who had been appointed to the Queen's Bench in 1859. For more on the Phibbs case, see Edward Wylie-Warren, '"The eagerness of the lower orders to press the case against the prisoner", Ballymote, Co. Sligo, 1861' in Frank Sweeney (ed.), *Hanging crimes* (Dublin, 2005), pp 48–71.

The Crown resumed the story of Phibbs' movements by calling 13 witnesses to describe his journey from Collooney to Sligo, his doings in Sligo, and his arrest at Riverstown, most of which showed how he spent the money he was supposed to have taken from Callaghan's house. Phibbs' career of extravagance in Sligo included a visit to Alexander Sleator's in Castle Street where he bought a pair of 'short Wellington boots', for which he paid 10s. 6d. in silver ('the silver was very dirty. A dark waxy substance was on several pieces of it'). Phibbs put his right hand into one of the boots: 'when he took his hand out, it was bleeding a good deal. He said there had been glass inside the boot, which cut his hand. I said it could not be & I felt the boot. There was no such thing or any thing to cut his hand like that. I examined his hand. Blood came from one of the fingers. I asked to tie it up & I did so. There was a deep cut across the finger.' How Phibbs had cut his finger was hinted at by a cutler, William Smith, to whose shop Phibbs took a razor to be sharpened. Smith described the state of the razor: 'I always examine every razor given to me to see its condition; & I did examine this one by the gas. I found it all gapped from heel to point. Very heavy gaps. He said he wanted it to be ground. I asked him how it happened to be so gapped. He said he borrowed it from a neighbour; and after laying it down, a little boy took it up & was cutting sticks with it.'

The last 2 of these 13 witnesses were policemen, who described Phibbs' arrest at 2.15 p.m. at the door of Pat Conway's public house in Riverstown, to where the news of the murder had spread from Ballymote in a couple of hours. When the policemen searched him they found £17. 17s. 3¼d. They also found 3 razors and a watch-key, and they took possession of 'a blue frock coat' that he was wearing. The second Riverstown policeman was the Crown's thirty-seventh witness. Walter Bourke QC, the senior crown counsel for Co. Sligo, was not finished, however. The next 3 witnesses were able to say that the blue frock-coat was William Callaghan's; one of the 3 was also able to identify the watch-key as Callaghan's. Of the 3, the most impressive was the tailor, William Morrison, who had made the coat. He was reassuringly cautious ('I won't swear that the coat was made by me'), but he produced his book of measurements, which showed the 9 measurements that he had taken in March 1859 when he made the coat for Callaghan: 4 of the 9 measurements fitted exactly the coat taken from Phibbs and 5 were close.

As the witnesses succeeded each other, there had been hints that Phibbs had been in reduced circumstances before the murders. He had paid back a loan of 3d., for example, to the publican Mary Flaherty. The car-driver who had driven him from Collooney had noticed his 'very indifferent shoes' (this came out in cross-examination). The Crown now brought their case to an end with three witnesses who gave more information about Phibbs' impecuniosity: John Reid said that Phibbs had borrowed half-a-crown from him in December 1860; an auctioneer told how Phibbs, who had had a shop in Ballymote, had had to sell the remnants of his stock. The third witness corroborated John Reid.

When the forty-third witness was finished (a forty-fourth was 'tendered by the Crown for cross-examination' but seems to have contributed nothing), the

Crown's case seemed strong. Phibbs' presence at Callaghan's house on the Tuesday morning ('jumping down the wall at the gap') had been established; the papers found on the road, the frock coat, and the watch-key suggested he had been inside Callaghan's house; Phibbs' affluence in Sligo and his poverty a few weeks before suggested robbery as a motive; Callaghan's throat, cut from ear to ear, Phibbs' cut finger, and the damaged razor suggested means. The way that clusters of witnesses verified different parts of the case was impressive: 2 witnesses saw Phibbs near Callaghan's on Tuesday morning; 2 saw him at the public house; 10 witnesses found, traced, and verified the blood-stained papers. The Crown's weakness was the long time that had elapsed between the last sighting of the Callaghans and the discovery of their bodies. It is hard, nevertheless, to see how a jury could have escaped a verdict of guilty. It was difficult, for example, to see Phibbs as the victim of an accidental concatenation of circumstances, or of conspiracy. It would not have been easy to have organized 43 witnesses, including shopkeepers in Sligo, a medical doctor in Ballymote, and a postmaster, into a conspiratorial clique. Phibbs had accumulated about his person so many guilty attributes that they excluded the possibility that somebody else had murdered the Callaghans. That possibility, however, had caused the jury at the spring assizes in Sligo to disagree, but the jury at the summer assizes found him guilty.

Phibbs was probably the first, and certainly the last, Primitive Methodist to be publicly hanged in Sligo. He is also memorable because he shared his name with one of the partners of the famous firm of Sligo solicitors, Argue & Phibbs. A week before his execution he confessed to a warder 'that it was his hand that had deprived Mr and Mrs Callaghan and their servant of life.'[35] He revealed that 'he had hidden some of the property he had taken in a field.' The warder hurried to Ballymote, found a watch, a watch-chain, a watch-key, a seal, a case of pistols, two large silver table spoons, six silver tea spoons, and two pewter spoons, but he could not find the £14 that Phibbs thought he had hidden under a rock. Robert Forde, who lived in Ballymote, told the warder that 'he and twenty others had searched the same ground, but only found a muslim handkerchief.' The warder 'acquainted Phibbs with his fruitless search, and questioned him about the handkerchief, and Phibbs described the handkerchief, a cross-barred muslim, so as to leave no doubt that it was the one referred to by Mr Forde. Phibbs' recollection was, that this handkerchief was put by him in the same spot, as the £14.'

THE NATURE OF THE EVIDENCE PRESENTED BY THE CROWN

The evidence elicited by examination-in-chief was only a fraction of the information collected by the police. To the layman evidence meant information that incriminated or exculpated; to the lawyer evidence meant only that fraction

---

35   Larcom Papers (NLI, MS 7620 [*Packet*, 12 Aug. 1861]).

of information that the law of evidence allowed witnesses to give in court. Martin, a baron of the English Court of Exchequer, made the distinction between information and evidence in *Rowton*, which had arisen from a charge of indecent assault:

> If I were investigating for my own private satisfaction whether or not the prisoner did commit this offence my first inquiry would be what was the prisoner's character, and, if the answer was, that he was notoriously addicted to acts of this sort that answer would influence me as much as anything else. But, if a man were indicted in a court of law, no one could give such evidence to a jury. The jury was sworn to try whether an assault was actually committed or not: and the witnesses are sworn to give evidence upon that issue; and their evidence must be confined to matters bearing upon it.[36]

The law of evidence in the nineteenth century generally excluded hearsay, opinions, the prisoner's character, 'similar facts', and facts that were 'irrelevant', a word whose meaning had to be learnt from 'crooked and narrow illustrations'.[37] Irish lawyers did not regularly produce the great treatises on evidence that were produced in England. In practice they tended to cite the English treatises. In *Gillis*,[38] for example, the prisoner's counsel, George Waters QC, referred to *Starkie*[39] and Denis Caulfeild Heron QC referred to *Russell*.[40]

Irish writers were not entirely silent on the law of evidence. Henry Joy, *On the evidence of accomplices* (Dublin 1836), and Henry H. Joy, *On the admissibility of confessions and challenge of jurors in criminal cases in England and Ireland* (Dublin and London, 1842) were useful discussions of two aspects of the law of evidence where the judges were divided. *The admissibility of confessions* was particularly useful because it gave full reports of the cases discussed, Joy having complained that the textbooks reported them 'in a form so condensed, and the facts upon which they are founded are so sparingly detailed, that it seems often unfair to the judges who pronounced them, to press them on the courts as authorities.'[41] The excellent work of Purcell, which was published in 1849, had no subsequent editions. Purcell is a comprehensive guide to the law of evidence in 1849 and a source for the history of its development in the previous decades, but after 1849

36 *Rowton* (1865) Le & C 520, at p. 537; 169 Eng Rep 1497, at p. 1505.
37 Stephen, *The Indian evidence act (I. of 1872), with an introduction on the principles of judicial evidence* (Calcutta, Bombay, and London, 1872), p. 4.
38 (1866) 17 ICLR 512, at pp 520, 523.
39 Thomas Starkie, *A practical treatise of the law of evidence and digest of proofs, in civil and criminal proceedings*, 4th ed. by G.M. Dowdeswell and J.G. Malcolm (London, 1857).
40 Sir William Oldnall Russell, *A treatise on crimes and misdemeanours*, 3 vols (4th ed. by Charles Sprengel Greaves, London, 1865).
41 Joy, *Admissibility*, p. 2.

new statutes and cases, both in England and Ireland, made some of his detail no longer accurate.

The Irish courts did not have to deal with the varied and numerous issues that have been so well described by C.J.W. Allen in his book on the law of evidence in England.[42] Irish cases were not numerous. Between 1867 and 1893, for example, there were only 7 cases relating to evidence in criminal trials in the Irish law reports.[43] On the other hand, the number of English cases cited in Irish cases was substantial. In *Johnston*, Baron Deasy referred to 20 cases, of which only 5 were Irish.[44] English cases proliferated. Stephen estimated that John Pitt Taylor had referred to 5,000 cases in the first edition of his book.[45] Taylor's second edition in 1855 referred to 'at least 1,300 more decisions than had been noticed in the first.'[46] Lawyers complained that 'the frightful rapidity with which cases and precedents increase tends to displace all law, and to render useless the investigation of fundamentals ... In fact if some system be not adopted, law must be ephemeral, and learning of ten years' standing will become obsolete.'[47] Gibbon's remark about learning the law that 'few men without the spur of necessity have resolution to force their way through the thorns and thickets of that gloomy labyrinth' seems particularly apposite when applied to the law of evidence.[48] William Guppy was more emphatic when he said he had been admitted as an attorney only 'after undergoing an examination that was enough to badger a man blue, touching a pack of nonsense that he don't want to know.'

Since Purcell is an indigenous source, his description of the law of evidence is perhaps the most appropriate one to use to here, although it must be emphasized that it related only to 1849. His enumeration of what was necessary and what was

42   *The law of evidence in Victorian England* (Cambridge, 1997).

43   R.D. Murray & G.Y. Dixon, *Digest of cases decided by superior courts of common law and equity, landed estates court, courts of admiralty, bankruptcy, probate and matrimonial causes, for crown cases reserved, and for land cases reserved; and by the Court of Appeal, and the several divisions of the High Court of Justice in Ireland. From the commencement of Hilary term, 1867, to the end of the Michaelmas sittings, 1893* (Dublin, 1899), pp 335–9. For a richer harvest see Thomas Brunker, *A digest of all the reported cases decided in the superior and other courts of common law in Ireland, and in the Court of Admiralty; from Sir John Davies reports to the present time, with references to the statutes and general orders of court* (Dublin, 1865), pp 618–37. See also T. Henry Maxwell, *A digest of cases decided by the superior and other courts in Ireland from the commencement of Hilary sittings, 1894, to the end of Michaelmas sittings, 1918 (including also the cases reported in volumes 16 & 17 Irish Common Law Reports)*, (Dublin, 1921), pp 390–6.

44   (1864) 15 ICLR 60, at pp 70–80.

45   *Treatise on the law of evidence as administered in England and Ireland with illustrations from the American and other foreign laws*, 2 vols (London, 1848).

46   Allen, op. cit., p. 25.

47   *A manual for articled clerks; or, guide to their examination & admission: containing courses of study in conveyancing, equity, bankruptcy, common law, special pleading, criminal law, etc. ... to which is prefixed, A lecture on the study of the law by J.J.S. Wharton, Esq., S.C.L* (5th ed., London, 1847), pp 38–9.

48   Edward Gibbon, *Memoirs of my life*, ed. with an intro. by Betty Radice (Harmondsworth, 1984), p. 108.

excluded was relatively simple. First, the burden of proof was on the prosecutor, but the law 'presumes every act, in itself unlawful, to have been criminally intended, until the contrary be proved ... Thus, on every charge of murder, malice is presumed from the fact of killing, unaccompanied with circumstances of extenuation; the burden of disproving the malice is thrown upon the accused.'[49] Secondly, the information admitted had to be relevant:

> the facts laid before the jury should consist exclusively of the transaction which forms the subject of the indictment, which alone [the prisoner] can be expected to have come prepared to answer ... This rule excludes all evidence of unconnected *collateral facts*, or those which are incapable of affording any reasonable presumption or inference as to the principal fact or matter in dispute; and the reason is, that such evidence tends to draw away the minds of the jurors from the points in issue, and to excite prejudice and mislead them; while the adverse party, as already observed, having had no notice of such a course of evidence, is not prepared to rebut it.[50]

Thirdly, the prisoner's other crimes could not be brought up: the prosecutor cannot 'give evidence of facts tending to prove another distinct and unconnected offence, for the purpose of raising an inference that the prisoner has committed the offence in question. Thus, in a prosecution for an infamous crime, an admission by the prisoner that he had committed such an offence at another time, and with another person, and that he has a tendency to such practices, ought not be received in evidence.'[51] Fourthly, the evidence was to be 'the best possible evidence', a rule that excluded 'evidence which itself indicates the existence of more original sources of information, and requires that no evidence shall be received which is merely substitutionary in its nature, so long as the original evidence can be had.' This rule 'is illustrated by the case of a written document, the instrument itself being always regarded as the primary or best possible evidence of its existence and contents.'[52] Fifthly, hearsay was excluded by the rule that 'oral testimony should be delivered in the presence of the court or a magistrate, under the moral and legal sanctions of an oath, and where the moral and intellectual character, the motives and deportment of the witness can be examined, and his capacity and opportunities for observation, and his memory can be tested by cross-examination.'[53]

49 Purcell, op. cit., p. 235.
50 Ibid., pp 244, 245.
51 Ibid., p. 245. It is worth noting that Purcell did not use the word 'similar fact'. Stephen referred to 'facts similar to, but not specially connected with, each other' and used the term *res inter alios acta* (Stephen, *A digest of the law of evidence*, 12th ed., revised by Sir Harry Lushington Stephen Bt., & Lewis Frederick Sturge (London, 1948), p. xiv).
52 Purcell, op. cit., pp 266, 267.
53 Ibid., p. 285.

To all of these rules and principles there were many and detailed qualifications and exceptions – to the extent that Purcell devotes over a hundred pages of his *Pleading and evidence* to their elucidation. Stephen produced a simplified version of the law of evidence for Indian lawyers. While his work does apply to Ireland, his three-tiered hierarchy of facts, which tried to simplify the definition of relevance, is useful as a mnemonic for anyone trying to grasp the law of evidence. First, there were 'facts in issue', which were the fundamental facts that had to be established to convict the prisoner ('A's beating B with a club. A's causing B's death by such a beating. A's intention to cause B's death.').[54] Secondly there were 'relevant' facts, which were those that 'may affect the probability of the existence of facts in issue, and be used as the foundation of inferences respecting them.' Thirdly, there were 'introductory' facts, which were 'necessary to explain or introduce a fact in issue or a relevant fact.' Stephen's definition of relevance was capacious: he admitted facts that were the occasion, cause, or effect of relevant facts or of facts in issue; he admitted facts that showed motive, preparation, and opportunity; he admitted facts that showed guilty knowledge and the prisoner's suspicious conduct.

Although the law of evidence excluded character, similar fact, opinion, hearsay, and 'irrelevant' facts, it allowed exceptions to these exclusions. The prosecution could not give evidence showing that the prisoner had a bad character, but in 1865 the English Court for Crown Cases Reserved made an exception when it decided in *Rowton* that if a prisoner called witnesses to give him a good character, when in fact he had a bad one, the prosecution could call witnesses to contradict them because 'nothing could be more unjust than that he should have the advantage of a character which in point of fact, may be the very reverse of that which he really deserves.'[55]

The arguments of the judges in this case revealed a number of interesting points about the exclusion of such evidence. Willes, for example, pointed out that

> if the prosecution were allowed to go into such evidence, we should have the whole life of the prisoner ripped up, and, as has been witnessed elsewhere, upon a trial for murder you might begin by shewing that when a boy at school the prisoner had robbed an orchard, and so on through the whole of his life; and the result would be that the man on his trial might be overwhelmed by prejudice, instead of being convicted on that affirmative evidence which the law of this country requires. The evidence is relevant to the issue, but is excluded for reasons of policy and humanity, because, although by admitting it you might arrive at justice in one case out of a hundred, you would probably do injustice in the other ninety-nine.[56]

---

54 Stephen, *Indian evidence act,* pp 150, 9–10, 154, 151. According to K.J.M. Smith, 'Stephen's concern was not simply to achieve a concise and evaluative exposition of law and principle, but also to expose and reformulate the subject's elusive and disputed theoretical basis' (*James Fitzjames Stephen: portrait of a Victorian rationalist* (Cambridge, 1988), pp 84–5).

55 *Rowton* (1865) Le & C 520, at p. 529; 169 Eng Rep 1497, at p. 1502.

56 Ibid., p. 1506.

According to Martin the law had made an exception to the rule in favour of the prisoner:

> a practice has sprung up, when a man is accused of an offence of any kind, to admit evidence of his good character with respect to the species of crime charged against him, with the view of shewing the unlikelihood of his committing that crime. It seems to me that this is an anomaly, but it has been allowed as I learn from the textbooks, not as bearing upon the issue, but *in favorem vitæ*, as a matter permitted by the benignity of the law. This practice has prevailed for the last 200 years, and in no single recorded instance during the whole of that period has evidence of general bad character been given in reply to evidence of the prisoner's good character.[57]

Similar fact was excluded, but another crime perpetrated by the prisoner could be admitted if it provided a motive. When Purcell discussed this point he referred to *R. v. Clewes*. When Clewes was tried at Worcester assizes in 1830 for the murder of Richard Hemmings, the fact that Hemmings had shot the rector of Oddingley in 1806 at the instigation of Clewes and others was admitted as evidence against Clewes, because it showed that he and others had murdered Hemmings 'to prevent a discovery of their own guilt'.[58] Purcell described three other situations where hostile acts could be introduced to show the prisoner's malice: (1) where there had been 'former grudges and antecedent menaces'; (2) 'upon an indictment for maliciously shooting, if it be questionable whether the shooting was by accident or design, proof may be given that the prisoner at another time intentionally shot at the same person'; (3) in poisoning cases, 'other acts of administering may be given in evidence to show that it was done with the intent charged in the indictment.'[59]

Hearsay's exclusion was remarkable.[60] No historian, no policeman, no gossip columnist would exclude information purveyed through intermediaries.[61] On the other hand, laymen probably take the legal exclusion of hearsay too seriously. Dickens caused most of the trouble when he made Mr Justice Stareleigh tell Sam Weller that he must not say what the soldier said, which created the impression

---

57 Ibid., p. 1505.
58 *Clewes* (1830) 4 Car & P 221, at p. 222; 172 Eng Rep 678, at p. 679; Purcell, op. cit., p. 247.
59 Ibid., pp 251–2.
60 Kenny gave an example of multiple hearsay: 'in a recent famous Belgian trial the following fifth-hand evidence was received, "He told me that Mme Lagasse had heard from a lady that Van Steen told her he knew the prisoners were guilty"' (Courtney Stanhope Kenny, *Outlines of criminal law; based on lectures delivered in the University of Cambridge* (Cambridge, 1902), p. 364).
61 Historians and lawyers share a commendable ambition to get at original sources. Even the greatest may be found wanting, however. 'Since Froude had not personally examined the [1641] depositions in Trinity College,' Donal McCartney has written, 'Lecky too considered it unnecessary to examine these manuscripts, and confined himself instead to the published works' (*W.E.H. Lecky, Historian and politician 1838–1903* (Dublin, 1994), p. 74).

that all reported speech was excluded.[62] There were in practice many occasions when a witness had to say what the soldier had said. The exceptions to the rule, therefore, were great and included confessions, dying declarations, and any words that were part of the *res gestæ*.[63] The *res gestæ* can be translated as 'things done', but that does not take the argument very far. In the following passage from Purcell there can be discerned the definition of what nineteenth-century lawyers meant when they used the words *res gestæ*:

> All *other declarations* which are introduced, not as a medium of proof in order to establish a distinct fact, but as being in themselves a part of the transaction in question, are admitted as original evidence, being distinguished from hearsay by their *connexion with the principal fact under investigation* … The principal tests to be applied in such cases are, whether the circumstances and declarations offered in proof were *contemporaneous with the main fact under consideration*, and whether they were so connected with it as to *illustrate its character and object*.

Purcell produced a wide definition of the exceptions admitted by the *res gestæ* rule:

> these, although all involved in the principle of *res gestæ*, may, for the sake of greater distinctness, be arranged into four classes:– the *first* class consisting of those cases where the fact that the declaration was made, and not its truth or falsity, is the point in question; the *second*, including expressions of bodily or mental feelings, where the existence or nature of such feelings is the subject of inquiry; the *third*, consisting of cases of pedigree, and including the declarations of those nearly related to the party whose pedigree is in question; and the *fourth*, embracing all other cases, where the declarations offered in evidence may be regarded as part of the *res gestæ*.

Purcell gave the following examples to illustrate these exceptions: what a man said after he was knocked down by a cabriolet; what a sick person said to his medical attendant ('what a man has said of himself to his surgeon is admissible as original evidence of what he has suffered by the assault'); what a woman said after she was raped ('the fact of a woman having made a complaint soon after the assault took place, is original evidence; but the statement of the particulars and details of her complaint cannot be given in evidence, its being no legal proof of their truth').

There were exceptions to the exceptions, especially to the exceptions that allowed confessions and dying declarations. The latter were confined, for example, to cases 'where the death of the deceased is the subject of the charge.'[64] Those who made them had to be competent witnesses. Atheists, children, lunatics, and

---

62   Dickens, *The posthumous papers of the Pickwick Club* (Oxford, 1959), p. 483

convicts, therefore, were at a disadvantage when they were murdered. The witness who relayed the dying declaration to the court, whether magistrate, policeman, or by-stander, had to be able to say that it had been 'made under a sense of impending death.' The standards of impending death were high. In a trial at the Dublin Commission in 1851, the case for admitting the dying declaration of a woman killed by her husband seemed strong: she had been told by a doctor that she was dangerously ill; she had been warned by a clergyman to prepare for death; she had been heard commending her soul to God.[65] On the other hand nobody had told her 'expressly' that she was dying, nor had she actually said that she knew she was dying. Chief Baron Pigot decided that her declaration 'would not be evidence, unless she was under a clear impression that she was in a dying state. It must be proved, to the satisfaction of the court, that she was dying, and that she was aware of the fact.' If she had received extreme unction her declaration would have been admissible.

Two aspects of the law of evidence were of particular interest in Ireland: confessions and statements by approvers. There were a number of reasons for this. First, the popular view of Irish trials was frequently preoccupied with the latter, and occasionally with the former. Secondly, both subjects give interesting insights into the attitudes of the judges. Thirdly, both subjects are prominent in the case law of the period.

CONFESSIONS

The judges excluded confessions that were 'forced from the mind by the flattery of hope, or by the torture of fear.'[66] Such confessions were rejected not 'from a regard to public faith' but because 'confessions are received in evidence, or rejected as inadmissible, under a consideration whether they are or are not intitled to credit.'[67] Extorted confessions were not rejected from a sense of fairness to the prisoner because the law admitted information obtained from such confessions if it led to discoveries that corroborated it. As the judge in *Warickshall* declared, 'this principle respecting confessions has no application whatever as to the admission or rejection of facts, whether the knowledge of them be obtained in consequence of an extorted confession, or whether it arises from any other source,

63 Purcell, op. cit., pp 286–90; Roscoe, op. cit., pp 22–34; Russell, op. cit., iii, 246–9.

64 Purcell, op. cit., pp 294–9. There was an exception to this restriction: 'the dying declaration of a *particeps criminis* in an act which has resulted in his own death, is admissible against one indicted for the same murder' (ibid., p. 295).

65 *Mooney* (1851) 5 Cox CC 318. Bentley described Pigot's decision in this case as being an instance of 'excessive judicial scrupulosity' (David Bentley, *English criminal justice in the nineteenth century* (London and Rio Grande, 1998), p. 216). See also Purcell, op. cit., pp 296–7.

66 *Warickshall* (1783) 1 Leach 263, at pp 263–4; 168 Eng Rep 234, at p. 235.

67 Ibid., p. 234.

for a fact, if it exist at all, must exist invariably in the same manner, whether the confession from which it is derived be in other respects true or false.'[68] If an improperly obtained confession was corroborated, the corroborating information was admissible. If the confession for example, led to the discovery of the murder weapon or blood-stained clothes 'it is competent to shew that such discovery was made conformably with the information given by the prisoner.'[69] The list of nefarious means other than threats and promises that could be used to elicit admissible confessions was considerable; Purcell, for example, mentioned as possible means artifice, deception, making the prisoner drunk, playing on his feelings, eavesdropping, and making false promises to keep the matter secret. Confessions obtained by religious exhortation were also admitted.

In *Gibney* in 1822, the twelve Irish judges took the line, which they described as 'well established', that 'a voluntary confession shall be received in evidence, but if hope has been excited, or threat, or intimidation held out, it shall not.'[70] Gibney had been arrested for the murder of his child. As the police were taking him to gaol they passed the field where the child's body was lying. A crowd that had gathered insisted that the prisoner be made to touch the child's body, a form of trial by ordeal based on the belief that when the murderer touched the corpse of the person he had murdered, the corpse bled. According to one of the policemen who had arrested Gibney:

> when they came into the field, the cry of the people was greater; this was calculated to affect the mind of the prisoner. He cried bitterly from the time witness got him into custody. When witness asked him did he kill his child, he did not tell him he would give what he said in evidence, and he did not suppose the prisoner thought he would. He said he was willing to die, and hoped God would have mercy on him. Dr Fitzpatrick, who was present, was anxious that the prisoner should touch the body; witness had heard an opinion that if the murderer touches the body of the person he has killed, the nose of the deceased person will bleed.[71]

The policeman went on to describe how Gibney actually confessed:

> The prisoner said nothing to the witness while he was in the field; he was brought to the body and touched it; the people were about him, and talking on the subject of the murder. After he had brought away the prisoner, and had proceeded about a quarter of a mile towards the gaol, witness said to

68   Ibid., p. 235.   69   Purcell, op. cit., p. 313.

70   Jebb Rep 15, at p. 19. For a comprehensive account of the law relating to confessions in Ireland, which has been an invaluable guide in what follows, see J.D. Jackson, 'In defence of a voluntariness doctrine for confessions: *The Queen v. Johnston* revisited' in *Ir Jur*, n.s., 21 (1986), 208–46.

71   Jebb Rep 15, at pp 16–19.

him, 'You must be a very unhappy boy to have murdered your own child, if it be the case.' The prisoner was crying very severely. Witness then said, 'Did you kill the child?' The prisoner then said he had done so, about a fortnight before May–day ... that he had tied up the child and put it in a hole in the bog.

The policeman insisted that no hope had been held out to the prisoner or any threat made – he had to actually say under oath, in other words to 'prove', that the no hope had been held out to the prisoner or threat made. The judges unanimously decided that the confession had been properly received because 'they held the rule to be well established, that a voluntary confession shall be received in evidence, but if hope has been excited, or threats, or intimidation held out, it shall not. The fear, however, to be produced, must be of a temporal nature, and in this case there was no such threat or intimidation, nor any fear of a temporal nature produced; any terror that might have been excited was to what might happen in the next world.'

A minority of the judges were uneasy about the admission of Gibney's confession, presumably because they thought the pressure exerted on him, even if it fell short of actual threats and inducements, made his confession an involuntary one. A sign of judicial unease was the fact that 'on account of the extraordinary circumstances of the case, the prisoner was recommended to mercy; and he was not executed.'[72] As J.D. Jackson noted, the judges' uneasiness persisted and 'there followed throughout the next forty years a number of Irish decisions by individual trial judges which excluded confessions on a much wider basis than the narrow voluntariness rule applied in *Gibney*.'[73] It is worth emphasizing, however, the role of individual judges and noting that the judges were not all of one mind on the subject. The judges who disapproved of police questioning seem to have feared that if the courts readily accepted confessions elicited by policemen, they would create a situation where 'the whole energy of the police is diverted into adroitly bringing pressure to bear upon the minds of those they suspect. The next result is a silent and widespread terrorism, and the birth of a corrupt brood of spies and informers. The final result is the immolation of public liberty, while its names and forms may still be scrupulously cherished.'[74]

72 Ibid., p. 19.
73 Jackson, op. cit., p. 210.
74 Sheldon Amos, *The science of law* (London, 1874), p. 277. Lawyers did not have to look further than India where confessions 'were instrumental in securing the conviction of those found guilty, yet simultaneously ensured that most crimes went unpunished. This contradiction, which lay at the heart of many claims of torture, did not pass unnoticed. "The smallest discrepancies in the evidence are held to invalidate truth, but when witnesses agree in any particular point, this agreement is also looked to be the surest form of their falsehood"' (Douglas M. Peers, 'Torture, the police, and the colonial state in the Madras presidency, 1816–55' in *Criminal Justice History*, 12 (1991), 48). The house of lords discussed torture in India in 1856. An example of Indian torture was placing prisoners in nests of red ants. See

From the late 1830s Irish judges regularly expressed their disapproval of police questioning. In 1839, in *Hughes*, Doherty deplored 'the impropriety of a police officer's interrogating his prisoner upon the subject of his guilt or innocence.'[75] In 1840, in *Doyle*, Bushe rejected a confession made by a woman to a policeman after her committal on a charge of poisoning her child, even though the policeman had been careful in 'cautioning her against saying any thing which might criminate herself, or be used for the purpose of convicting her.'[76] In 1847 Perrin disapproved of policemen 'holding conversations with prisoners on the subject of the charge against them & recommend juries to receive and consider such evidence jealously & with great caution.'[77] In 1855 Lefroy refused to admit 'answers given to a constable upon questions put by him, though he had given the prisoner a previous caution.'[78] At the Dublin Commission in 1856, Pigot seemed to exclude almost any statement made to a policeman when he refused to admit what a woman said to an inspector of the DMP, because 'it is difficult to place reliance upon a person who, however truthful and well-disposed he may be, is naturally anxious to get evidence.'[79] Richards, who was sitting with Pigot, appeared to go further, pointing out that 'from the mere circumstance of being in custody, the prisoner was not on equal terms with her interrogator.' At the trial of John Hassett at Kilkenny assizes in 1861, the prisoner's counsel objected to the admission of a conversation that had taken place between the prisoner and the prosecutor in the presence of the policeman who had arrested the prisoner. When the policeman was called he said that before he brought the prisoner into the prosecutor's presence he had taken him before a magistrate where he had been cautioned. The prisoner's counsel objected that this caution was not 'sufficient', and referred to *Hughes* and the Petty Sessions (Ireland) Act 1851, section 14.[80] The trial judge, Christian, 'observed that there was a difference in the value of testimony voluntarily given, and that elicited in answer to questions. He objected to the police questioning persons while in their custody on a criminal charge, and he thought the counsel for the Crown ought not to press this particular evidence.' At the Westmeath summer assizes in 1863 Pigot declared that even when a policeman had given a prisoner 'the usual and proper caution, ... he ought to abstain from asking questions; he ought to leave that duty to the magistrate, who alone has the power to reduce to writing, what is said by the prisoner.'[81]

Speech of the earl of Albemarle, on torture in the Madras presidency, delivered in the house of lords, 14th April, 1856 (London, 1856) and Malcolm Lewin, *Torture in Madras* (London, 1857).

75   1 Cr & Dix 13, at p. 15.   76   Ibid., 396, at p. 396.   77   NAI, CRF/1847/Ryan/24.

78   *Grey* (1855), a case at Trim summer assizes, referred to in a note in *Eliza Toole* (1856) 7 Cox CC 244, at p. 246, and in Edward Parkyns Levinge, *The justice of the peace for Ireland; comprising the practice in indictable offences, and the proceedings preliminary and subsequent to convictions; with an appendix of the most useful statutes, and an alphabetical catalogue of offences* (2nd ed., Dublin, 1862), p. 54.

79   *Toole* (1856) 7 Cox CC 244, at p. 245.

80   *Hassett* (1861) 8 Cox CC 511, at pp 511–12; 14 & 15 Vict., c. 93.

81   *Bodkin* (1863) 9 Cox CC 403. Russell believed that this case 'seems to deserve reconsideration' (Russell, op. cit., iii, 407).

The regular occurrence of these cases suggested that the judges were struggling with a problem that persisted in spite of their condemnations. Doherty, for example, condemned police questioning in *Hughes* in 1839. In the following year he condemned it again *R. v. Glennon, Toole, and Magrath*,[82] which suggests neither the police nor the crown counsel had taken much notice of Doherty's statement in *Hughes* that 'in future, I never will permit admissions obtained from prisoners in the manner this has been, to be given in evidence in cases before me.'[83] It may have been that Doherty had apparently nullified the effect of *Hughes* by his decision in *Nolan*, made on the same circuit shortly after *Hughes*, to admit John Nolan's confession made to the police in Myshall police barracks.[84] Doherty's decision in *Nolan* did not modify his decision in *Hughes* because the police in Myshall had elicited his confession, not by questioning him, but by making him drunk and playing on his wish to exonerate his father. In the English case, *Spilsbury* in 1835, the judge had decided that a prisoner's statement made when he was drunk was admissible even 'if a constable gave him liquor to make him so, in the hope of his saying something.'[85]

Apparent impropriety on the part of the police and crown counsel persisted in spite of *Glennon*. In *Devlin* in 1841, just a year after *Glennon*, when the prisoner's counsel objected to words elicited by police questioning being given in evidence against his client, the crown counsel, John Brooke QC, argued that 'the dictum of Chief Justice Doherty, in the case of *R. v. Hughes*, was extra-judicial, as the admission in that case was quite immaterial. ... Evidence, such as is now objected to, has been frequently received both in this country, and in England.'[86] The trial judge, Burton, having consulted Chief Baron Brady, 'stated that his lordship concurred with him in thinking that the prisoner's answer, which had been objected to, ought not to be received in evidence.'

There are remarks in some of these cases about the superior scrupulosity of magistrates, which inevitably implied that policemen were not as scrupulous as their betters. Doherty in *Hughes*, observed that

> magistrates, who are persons of education and intelligence, in receiving the statements of prisoners, always take the precaution of warning them not to say any thing that may criminate themselves, and of informing them that what they do say will be taken down, and may used against them afterwards; but this is seldom done by persons of an inferior class.[87]

Pigot in *Toole* argued that the

---

82 (1840) 1 Cr & Dix 359, at pp 362–3.   83 (1839) 1 Cr & Dix 13, at p. 15.
84 (1839) 1 Cr & Dix 74. See above, pp 67–8.
85 7 Car & P 187, at p. 187; 173 Eng Rep 82, at p. 82.
86 *Devlin* (1841) 2 Cr & Dix 151, at p. 152.
87 1 Cr & Dix 13, at p. 15. See also *R. v. Bryan* (1834) Jebb Rep 157.

new act, 14 & 15 Vict. c. 93, s. 14 [Petty Sessions Act 1851], points out the authority before whom the prisoner is to be taken, namely, a justice or justices of the peace; and provides that after a solemn inquiry, and after the prisoner has heard the evidence for the prosecution, has learned the nature of the offence with which he is charged, and received the caution prescribed, that then his statement shall be taken down in writing, and may be given in evidence against him. When the legislature thinks a prisoner should be protected from improper or unfair influence by such precautions, I never can be satisfied that the proper caution has been given, depending on the fleeting memory of an individual.[88]

The constabulary authorities tried to avoid judicial condemnation. On 27 May 1847, for example, the inspector general instructed the constabulary not to interrogate suspects or those under arrest, reminding them that it was 'the province of the magistrates to interrogate persons so suspected or under arrest.'[89] The judges' hostility to police questioning was not a particular response to the zeal of the Irish constabulary, but to all over-zealous policemen. Doherty, for example, was careful to point out in *Hughes* that his dislike of police questioning was shared by English judges, recollecting that on a recent occasion 'being an auditor in a court of justice in England he had heard the same sentiments expressed, and the same view taken upon the same subject, by the very eminent judge who presided in that court.'[90] According to Bentley, the English judges had set their faces against police questioning since the late 1830s, which coincided roughly with *Hughes*, *Glennon*, and *Doyle*, and by the 1850s 'the new doctrine had carried the day.'[91] On the other hand, Pigot in *Johnston* hinted that Ireland was peculiar, saying that although there was 'diversity of practice among judges' on the subject of police questioning, 'the great preponderance of authority, in this country, has been against its reception.'[92]

A change came in 1864 when a majority of the Irish Court for Crown Cases Reserved decided to admit evidence of police questioning when they considered the case of Mary Johnston, who had been convicted at the Dublin Commission of stealing boots from a shop in Kingstown. As she was leaving the station at Westland Row, two policemen in plain clothes stopped her, and one of them

> told her we belonged to the police, and that she was described to us as having stolen boots from shops in the city. I also said to her that she was charged as committing felony. I asked her what she had in the parcel. I

88   (1856) 7 Cox CC 244, at p. 245.

89   TNA (UK), HO/184/112.

90   *Hughes* (1839) 1 Cr & Dix 13, at p. 15.

91   Bentley, op. cit., p. 230.

92   *Mary Johnston* (1864) 15 ICLR 60, at p. 118. See also Jackson, op. cit., p. 215 where it is stated that *Johnston* 'finally settled Irish law along the lines adopted in England that the true test of exclusion was whether a confession had been obtained by a threat or promises held out or excited by a person in authority.'

would not have let her go; but I did not tell her that I would not do so ... I did not, before I asked her that question, or before the prisoner answered it, give her any caution, or hold out any inducement.[93]

In reply, Johnston said 'she was made a present of them in Kingstown.' When the policeman accused her of taking them from a particular shop in Kingstown, she admitted that she had. A majority of eleven Irish judges decided the policeman's questions did not of themselves necessarily exclude her confession. Deasy, having discussed twenty reported cases, including *Gibney*, decided that Pigot's decision in *Toole* did not exclude police questioning:

> That case therefore is not an authority for the general proposition submitted to us, that any statement made by an accused person, in answer to questions put by a constable, is, upon that ground alone, to be rejected. The fact that the statement was elicited by questions so put, may be an element in leading to the conclusion that it was made under the influence of fear or hope, excited by a person in authority, but we could not decide that it was *per se* sufficient to cause the rejection of the statement, without overruling the numerous cases in which such statements have been received in evidence against prisoners both in England and Ireland.[94]

Deasy based himself not on Pigot's exclusion of evidence elicited by police questioning in *Toole*, but on his statement that

> it is essential that the judge should be satisfied that the statement of the prisoner has not been the result of some influence acting upon the mind, either of hope or fear. I am not satisfied upon that point, and therefore I reject the evidence.

This statement implied that the judge was to decide in each case whether evidence elicited by police questioning had actually aroused hope or fear in the prisoner's mind. Hughes, the two Fitzgeralds, and Keogh made no speeches and concurred with Deasy in affirming the conviction. Monahan and Ball added their voices to this compact group. The dissenting judges, who were Hayes, Lefroy, O'Brien, and Pigot, stood for a wider exclusion than that based merely on threats and inducements. According to Lefroy, who was one of the dissenters:

> The great inquiry in all such cases must be, whether the confession was made under circumstances which show that it was made freely and voluntarily; and the great mistake that has been made is that the inquiry has been, not whether the confession was made freely and voluntarily, but

---

93 *Johnston* (1864) 15 ICLR 60, at pp 61–2.   94 Ibid., p. 80.

whether it was made in the absence of any threat or inducement. It may have been made under circumstances showing that it was not made under the influence of any threat or inducement, and yet may not have been made freely and voluntarily. And what I lay my finger on in the present case, as showing the violation of this great principle of the law, is that the party was entrapped into making the confession by the course taken by the sergeant of police, in following up his examination of the prisoner.[95]

Pigot was more outspoken. He argued that *Gibney* had not admitted police questioning because Gibney's disclosures were not made 'in reply to the questions which were put to him, but were, according to his own statement, the result of the impulse of his own conscience.'[96] He also argued that neither Bushe nor Burton, who later excluded evidence elicited by police questioning in *Doyle* and *Devlin*, could have been in favour of police questioning in *Gibney*. 'It has been suggested that Lord Chief Justice Bushe and Mr Justice Burton must have forgotten the decision in *Rex v. Gibney*, where they ruled as they did in *Regina v. Doyle* and *Regina v. Develin*,' he said. 'In my opinion, it is to be presumed that they so ruled because they knew that the contrary had *not* been decided in *Rex v. Gibney*.'[97] He admitted that there had been diversity of practice among the judges, but appealed to the weight of those who had excluded police questioning – Bushe, Doherty, Brady, Burton, and Christian. To these he added Perrin, who had resigned from the Queen's Bench four years before, pointing out 'that that most learned and able judge – and a higher authority I could not cite on criminal and constitutional law – invariably rejected this species of evidence. His view was … that, to obtain admissions by interrogatories put to a prisoner *in vinculis*, was a species of torture – that it savoured of the Inquisition, as it once prevailed in some Continental countries, and was abhorrent to the principles and spirit of the English law.'[98]

Pigot was prepared to admit that the Irish judges were not unanimous, but 'against this weight of judicial authority in Ireland,' he stated, 'there is but one reported decision in favour of the admissibility of such evidence, that of Mr Justice Crampton, in *Regina v. Francis Hughes*.'[99] Pigot's objection to admitting answers to police questions is worth quoting at length:

> In considering whether statements made by a prisoner, in answer to questions put by the officer of the law in whose custody he is when questioned, are voluntary statements, we must have regard not only to the relative position in which they stood towards each other, but also to the ordinary infirmities of mankind, especially those which are likely to exist among the ignorant and uneducated in the lower classes of society …

95   Ibid., pp 130–1.   96   Ibid., p. 115.   97   Ibid., p. 116.   98   Ibid., p. 119.
99   Ibid. *Francis Hughes* is reported in Henry H. Joy, *On the admissibility of confessions and challenge of jurors in criminal cases in England and Ireland* (Dublin and London, 1842), p. 39.

A prisoner so circumstanced may not hear, in terms, one word of hope held out or of mischief threatened; and he may, and in many cases must, be actuated by hope that his answers will lead to his liberation, or fear that his answers may cause his detention in custody. He is placed in immediate contact with one who for the time is his gaoler, for the most part with no third person present to witness what passes, and almost always without the presence of any person to whom he can appeal for protection, or who may control the examination within fair or reasonable bounds. Manner may menace and cause fear as much as words. Manner may insinuate hope as well as verbal assurances. The very act of questioning is in itself an indication that the questioner will or may liberate the answerer if the answers are satisfactory, and detain him if they are not. ...

If the constable puts a series of searching interrogatories, he virtually, and, I think actually and in effect, abandons the caution, and announces, by the very course of interrogation which he applies, that it is better for the prisoner to answer than to be silent. The process of question [*sic*] impresses, on the greater part of mankind, the belief that silence will taken as an assent to what the questions imply. The very necessity which that impression suggests, of answering the question in *some* way, deprives the prisoner of his free agency; and impels him to answer, from the fear of the consequences of declining to do so.[100]

Why did the majority of Irish judges go back on what appears to have been the practice of many of them for so long? An obvious explanation was that they were influenced by *Cheverton*[101] and *Mick*,[102] two recent cases in England. Deasy, for example, referred to *Cheverton*, and Pigot referred to *Mick*.[103] Yet these cases gave little comfort to those who wanted to admit evidence elicited by policemen. In *Cheverton*, Erle rejected what a prisoner had said to a policeman who had told her 'You had better tell all about; it will save trouble', but he admitted as evidence what she had said to a police superintendent, who had questioned her 'without cautioning her, or explaining the object of his inquiries.' Erle told the superintendent, however, that 'to put such questions without any caution was most improper, especially since the prisoner does not seem to have been aware of their drift or object.[104] In *Mick*, Mellor admitted the prisoner's answers but told the policeman who had asked them, 'I entirely disapprove of the system of police officers examining prisoners. The law has surrounded prisoners with great precautions to prevent confessions being extorted from them, and the magistrates are not allowed to question prisoners, or to ask them what they have to say; and it is not for policemen to do these things.'[105]

100 *Johnston* (1864) 15 ICLR 60, at pp 121–2.   101   (1862) 2 F & F 833, 175 Eng Rep 1308.
102 (1863) 3 F & F 822, 176 Eng Rep 376.
103 *Johnston* (1864) 15 ICLR 60, at pp 75, 119.
104 *Cheverton* (1862) 2 F & F 833, at p. 835; 175 Eng Rep 1308, at p. 1309.
105 *Mick* (1863) 3 F & F 822 at p. 823; 176 Eng Rep 376 at p. 376.

It is tempting to seek an explanation in contemporary events in Ireland. The murder of three landlords in 1862, for example, had released a torrent of criticism of the constabulary, as the judges knew only too well from the addresses presented to them by grand juries. *Johnston* may well have been their way of tilting the balance against those who seemed to be able to kill landlords with impunity. The judges' decisions, however, in *Fay*, *Gillis*, and *M'Mahon* suggest they were too Olympian to be swayed by the braying of country gentlemen or the nervousness of politicians. Another possible explanation is that the judges may have come to the conclusion that the Irish constabulary and the DMP had established themselves as well-conducted forces that could be relied on not to abuse their prisoners. In 1862 the *Irish Times* had made that very point, although they had not meant to pay a compliment to the constabulary:

> The native quickness and inventive faculties of Irishmen seem never to have been successfully used in the detection of crime. We do not recollect a single instance where sharp and clever strategy has been brought to bear upon the detection or capture of criminals. We fear that the system of the constabulary in Ireland is calculated to make them look down upon such expedients as beneath their dignity, to induce them to regard themselves as fine stalwart, chivalrous soldiers, rather than vulgar, practical thief-takers.[106]

There is a third possible explanation of the judges' change: they had to recognize that there had been a difference of opinion among themselves for years, as Pigot admitted. The array of cases alluded to in the seventy-five pages of *Johnston* was impressive but contradictory, to put it mildly. The fact that Deasy, who was in favour of police questioning, cited *Cheverton*, and Pigot, who was against it, cited *Mick*, showed how refined the argument had become. One way of reconciling the contradiction was to reaffirm the principle that confessions must be voluntary and to accept that police questioning did not necessarily render them involuntary. Anyone who reads *Johnston* will understand why Wigmore gave it the accolade of being a 'great' case and why J.D. Jackson could write that 'it gave the seal of approval, albeit by a majority ruling, to the rule of voluntariness which with certain modifications still represents the law of confession in Ireland today.'[107] In practice, in the decades after 1864, *Johnston* made some difference, but not much. It may have encouraged the 'conversational' approach adopted by some policemen,[108] but the difference after 1864 was not great: out of 1029 pieces of evidence presented in murder cases between 1836 and 1914, only 44 pieces were based on the police relaying what prisoners had said; 16 of these occurred before 1864 and 28 after.[109] Considering that more evidence of all kinds was presented in the period after 1864 than in the period before, the difference

106 *Irish Times*, 5 Sept. 1862.   107 Jackson, op. cit., p. 209.
108 Above, pp 63–5.   109 Below, p. 207.

between 16 and 28 is not as great as it seems. In any case the figure 28 hardly suggests an opening of the flood-gates after 1864.

Irish cases on confessions after *Johnston* did not all deal with police questioning. *Unkles*,[110] *Sullivan*,[111] and *McNicholl*[112] were about the sufficiency of confessions on their own to convict. Only in *Doherty*,[113] *Mayorisk*,[114] and *Devine*[115] was the problem of police questioning dealt with. In *Doherty*, Whiteside refused to admit what the prisoner said to a policeman who cautioned, but did not question: 'I interrogated him in no way. He asked me could he see his father. I told him he could not, and for him not to say anything to criminate himself, for that anything he would say would hereafter come in evidence against him.' In *Mayorisk*, Madden refused to admit what a woman had said after a policeman had told her 'she had better tell the truth.' In *Devine*, Palles, taking his great predecessor, Pigot, as his exemplar, rejected what the prisoner had said to a policeman, and declared that:

> the relative position of the accused with regard to the person to whom the statement is made is of the greatest importance. With regard to the statements made to police officers the English cases afford little help. The position of a constable of the Royal Irish Constabulary to an Irish peasant is not similar to the position of an English constable. There is always a suspicion that the accused felt bound to make some statement, true or false, to the constable as a representative of the government. The education and social position of the accused is of importance in determining the question.

Johnston, for all its 'greatness', seems to have left the role of police questioning flexible but obscure, which may not have been an accident. James O'Connor in his handbook for magistrates, which was published in 1911, wrestled with *Johnston*, but in the end had to solve the problem of police questioning by quoting what an English judge had said decades before. The passage suggests that policemen had to practice a nice balancing of propriety and impropriety, of prudence and initiative

> It is quite right for a police constable or any other police officer when he takes a person into custody to charge him and let him know what it is he is taken up for; but the prisoner should be previously cautioned, because the very fact of charging induces a prisoner to make a statement, and he should have been informed that such statement may be used against him. The law does not allow the judge or a jury to put questions in open court to prisoners, and it would be monstrous if the law permitted a police officer to go, without anyone being present to see how the matter was conducted, and

110 *Unkles* (1874) IR 8 CL 50, at pp 57–8.
111 *Sullivan* (1887) 16 Cox CC 347.
112 *McNicholl* [1917] 2 IR 557.
113 *Doherty* (1874) 13 Cox CC 23.
114 *Mayorisk* (1898) 32 ILTR 56.
115 *Devine* (1904) 38 ILTR 227.

put a prisoner through an examination, and then produce the effects of the examination against him. Under these circumstances, a policeman should keep his mouth shut and his ears open. He is not bound to stop a prisoner in making a statement; his duty is to listen and report, but it is quite another thing that he should put questions to prisoners. A policeman is not to discourage a statement, and certainly not to encourage one. It is no business of a policeman to put questions which may lead a prisoner to give answers on the spur of the moment, thinking perhaps he may get out of a difficulty by telling lies.[116]

APPROVERS

The judges were strict about receiving approvers' evidence, although perhaps not as strict as they were about confessions. The fact that an accomplice had been accepted as an approver by a magistrate did not mean that he would be accepted at the assizes: an application had to be made to the judge, 'stating the insufficiency of the evidence otherwise to obtain a conviction.'[117] The approver's examination preceded that of the witnesses who were likely to corroborate him. In *Glennon, Toole, and Magrath*, Doherty pointed out that 'the usual course is to produce the approver in the first instance, and then the witnesses to corroborate him'; to examine the corroborating witnesses before the approver 'deprives the prisoner's counsel of a great advantage, namely, that of cross-examining the corroborating witness after the examination of the approver has concluded on both sides.'[118]

There were three questions posed by approvers' evidence. Did they need corroboration? Must their statement about the prisoner's participation be corroborated, or was it enough to corroborate other parts of their evidence? Should the judge direct the jury to acquit the prisoner if the corroboration was not enough, or should he leave it to them to decide? According to Bentley the Irish judges took a prominent part in calling for a stricter definition of corroboration.[119] As early as 1826 they had considered the question of corroboration in *Sheehan*, when they had decided 'that in point of law, the testimony of an accomplice, though altogether uncorroborated, was evidence to be submitted to a jury, and that a conviction upon it would be legal.'[120] This did not take the question very

---

116 O'Connor, op. cit., p. 275, n1.
117 Edmund Hayes, *Crimes and punishments, or a digest of the criminal statute law of Ireland, alphabetically arranged, with ample notes, in which are discussed the powers and authorities of the several courts of criminal jurisdiction in Ireland; the duties, responsibilities, and privileges of magistrates, coroners, constables, and other officers, in bringing criminals to justice, and also the practice of the courts in punishing offences upon indictment*, 2 vols (2nd ed., Dublin, 1842), i, 5.
118 (1840) 1 Cr & Dix 359, at pp 360–1.
119 Bentley, op. cit., pp 255–6.
120 Jebb Rep 54, at pp 56, 57, 58. See Declan McGrath, 'The accomplice corroboration warning' in *Ir Jur*, n.s., 34 (1999), 171, 181–2.

far because it was impossible to exclude the possibility of a conviction obtained on the sole evidence of an approver of palpable honesty, disinterest, and integrity. The judges' unanimity did not extend to the degree of corroboration that might be desirable in practice. Five of them thought that the corroboration of details that did not necessarily implicate the prisoner was enough ('generally speaking, a corroboration in the circumstances of the crime charged, though entirely unaccompanied by any circumstance applicable to the prisoner on trial, or to any other person charged by the accomplice, was a substantial corroboration, fit to be examined and weighed'). The other six were for a more pointed corroboration that implicated the prisoner in the perpetration of the crime (juries ought 'to be told, that a mere confirmation of the circumstances of the transaction, not brought down in any respect either to the prisoner on trial, or to any other person charged by the accomplice, generally speaking, scarcely, if at all, distinguishes the case from one of no confirmation').[121] The judges were also divided on the subject of judges warning juries. The restrictive six thought juries should be warned, and the capacious five thought 'that there ought not to be any rule of practice, by which juries ought be advised to disregard, or to pay slight attention to, such circumstances.'

In 1836, ten years after *Sheehan*, Henry Joy, speaking of an approver's evidence, wrote that 'judges, considering the light in which he appears, have in modern times been in the habit of recommending it to the jury not to found a verdict upon his testimony, unless that testimony has received some corroboration.'[122] At the same time he insisted that 'that is a mere matter of practice, voluntarily adopted by the judges, affecting the exercise of their discretion on a subject upon which it is not their province to decide.' Hayes writing in the early 1840s noted that 'there is great diversity of opinion as to the extent of corroboration requisite.'[123] On corroboration that confirmed the approver's story on some details, but was 'silent to the persons engaged', the best he could do was to display the authorities on both sides: the 12 judges of England in 1788 and in 1813 and 6 of the Irish judges, including the 5 in *Sheehan*, thought confirmation of details was enough; 6 of the Irish judges in *Sheehan*, and 7 English judges in a variety of cases, thought that 'the testimony of the unimpeached witness must affect the person on trial.'

Judges continued to exercise their discretion. In *Aylmer* in 1839, Bushe set his face against one approver corroborating another, although he was apparently prepared to contemplate two approvers corroborating each other, if they had been confined separately before the trial.[124] Three years later in *Magill*, where 4 out of

---

121 In the previous year, 1825, Jebb in *Green* had told a jury 'that corroboration of the approver in all the general facts of the case is not enough, unless he is also corroborated in some particular attaching guilt to the prisoner' (1 Cr & Dix, 158, at p. 160).

122 Rt Hon. Henry Joy, *On the evidence of accomplices* (Dublin 1836), p. 2.

123 Hayes, op. cit., i, 7–8.

124 1 Cr & Dix 116. See McGrath, op. cit., p. 184.

5 Crown witnesses were accomplices, Perrin decided that 'if the case rested with them I should direct the jury to acquit the prisoners. But I do not think it clearly appears that the fifth witness was an accomplice, and the case must go to the jury.'[125] In *Casey and M'Cue* in 1837, the twelve judges considered the soundness of a conviction based only on the evidence of an approver and his wife. There was corroboration in the case, but only of the approver's wife's involvement in disposing of stolen goods, not of the prisoners' involvement.[126] At the trial of Casey and M'Cue at the Dublin Commission their counsel, Francis Macdonogh, had argued that uncorroborated evidence of an approver should not be acted on, that such corroboration 'must have a specific application to the prisoner on trial', that the evidence of another accomplice or the wife of an accomplice was not corroboration, and that in the absence of 'unobjectionable' corroboration, 'the jury should be told by the judge that they ought to acquit the prisoners.' The judge, Burton, had been one of the minority in *Sheehan*. In his summing up he warned the jury of the 'general objections' to the accomplices' credit, advised them to resist the plausibility of the 'many circumstances collateral to the alleged actual guilt of the prisoners', and not to convict 'if they entertained a reasonable doubt', but he 'did not direct the jury to acquit … but he left the objections to the witness' credit (explaining to them the grounds of those objections) to their consideration.' He reserved the case and the twelve judges decided that the conviction was right.

In 1839, in *Curtis*, several prisoners were indicted for theft.[127] An approver's evidence was corroborated by the confession of one of the prisoners, but the confession did not mention the other prisoners. Doherty decided that 'notwithstanding the conflicting decisions upon the subject of the admissibility of the unsupported testimony of accomplices, I am of opinion, that the testimony of an approver is evidence to go to the jury, although no judge will permit such testimony to go up without observing strongly upon the questionable nature of evidence derived from a source so polluted.' A note to the case tried to make sense of the current attitude to approvers' evidence: 'inasmuch as judges have considered it to be their duty to send up such uncorroborated evidence accompanied by observations, which, in point of fact, amount to a direction to acquit, recent writers upon this branch of the law of evidence, and, amongst others, the lord chief justice of the Queen's Bench in Ireland, have chiefly directed their attention to the degree of weight to be attached to the testimony of approvers.'

Judges went on agonizing about the 'weight to be attached to the testimony of approvers.' Purcell described what had become by the late 1840s an elaborate procedure for dealing with approvers. First, 'the usual course is to leave out of the indictment those who are to be called as witnesses.' Secondly, the admission of an accomplice already indicted 'to testify as a witness *for the government*, is by no

---

125 (1842) Ir Cir Rep 418.   126 Jebb Rep 203, at pp 206, 207–8.
127 *Curtis, Reilly, and others* (1838) Cr & Dix Abr 274, at pp 275, 278–9.

means a matter of course, but will be determined by the judges, in their discretion, as may best suit the purposes of justice.' Thirdly, an accomplice who appeared to be 'the principal offender' was not accepted. Fourthly, 'the court will not usually admit more than one accomplice ... but under peculiar circumstances, three have been admitted.'[128] The judge's discretion extended to evaluating the importance of the approver's evidence before the trial: 'the court usually considers not only whether the prisoners can be convicted without the evidence of the accomplice, but also whether they can be convicted with his evidence. If, therefore, there be sufficient evidence to convict without his testimony, the court will refuse to allow him to be admitted as a witness. And in like manner the court will refuse to admit him if there be no reasonable probability of a conviction, even with his evidence.'

When it came to corroboration, however, Purcell was able to speak with certainty on only some points: one accomplice could not corroborate another; the wife of an accomplice could not corroborate her husband.[129] Corroboration was now required by 'settled practice', but '*yet the manner and extent of the corroboration* are not so clearly defined': 'some judges have deemed it sufficient if the witness be confirmed in any material part of the case; others have required confirmatory evidence as to the *corpus delicti* only; and others have thought it essential that there should be corroboratory proof that the *prisoner* actually participated in the offence; and that when several prisoners are to be tried, confirmation is required as to all of them before all of them can be safely convicted.' At this point Purcell tried to move on to firmer ground by saying that the view that the corroboration must extend to the prisoner and not just to the crime and its circumstances 'now seems to be the prevailing opinion, the confirmation of the witness as to the commission of the crime being regarded as no confirmation at all as it respects the prisoner. For in describing the circumstances of the offence, he may have no inducement to speak falsely, but, on the contrary, may have every motive to declare the truth, if he intends to be believed when afterwards he fixes the crime upon the prisoner.' In other words 'the prevailing opinion' in Ireland seems to have been moving in a line parallel with that of England where the Court for Crown Cases Reserved in *Stubbs* in 1855 would decide 'that a judge should advise the jury to acquit, unless the testimony of the accomplice be corroborated, not only as to the circumstances of the offence, but also as to the participation in it by the accused, and that where there are several prisoners, and the accomplice is not confirmed as to all, the jury should be directed to acquit the prisoners as to whom he is not confirmed.'[130]

Judicial caution about approvers' evidence did not dissipate. In *Gillis*, in 1866, which came only two years after *Johnston*, a majority of the Court for Crown Cases Reserved decided that an approver's statement could not be used against

128 Purcell, op. cit., pp 354–5.   129 Ibid., p. 356.
130 (1855) Dears 555, at p. 555; 169 Eng Rep 843, at p. 843.

him.[131] George Gillis had been sentenced to five years' penal servitude at a special commission in Dublin in 1866. The evidence against him was an information he had sworn on 27 September 1865, describing his part in the fenian movement. Gillis, who lived at 83 Francis Street, Dublin, was a cart and dray maker. On 26 September 1865 a member of the G Division of the DMP went to his premises in which there was a forge. Gillis was helpful, almost effusive in his exchanges with the policeman, especially about his forge: 'of his own accord and voluntarily, he stated that he had let it to Michael Moore, a blacksmith, and that pikes were made in it; that he had attended a fenian meeting at which there were seventy-five officers; and that he was "a serjeant in the society". All this he said, without any inducement whatever, and the statement was given in evidence without objection, and might have been sufficient of itself to secure a verdict against him.'[132] When the head of the G Division, Superintendent Ryan, 'asked him, if he had any objection to give information before the magistrate, and be a witness; he said he had none.' (It is worth noting how the detective used words such as *of his own accord*, *voluntarily*, and *without any inducement*.) On 27 September Ryan took him before John Calvert Stronge, a divisional magistrate, where 'he detailed his own complicity with the conspiracy, and that of others, was interrogated and pressed for further evidence, without any caution, and disclosed fully the entire case against himself.' When he refused to give evidence at the trials of his fellow-conspirators, he was put on trial, and this information and others he had made later were produced against him. His counsel, Isaac Butt, objected to their admission, 'as being made under an expectation that [the] prisoner would be taken as an approver or witness; and secondly, that being on oath, he was bound to answer all the questions put to him, unless he said it would incriminate himself to do so.' The two judges at the special commission, Keogh and Baron Fitzgerald, reserved the case.

Six of the nine judges who were present at the Court for Crown Cases Reserved decided that the informations should not have been used against Gillis. The arguments against accepting them were reminiscent of those used by the minority in *Johnston*. Lefroy, for example, quoted Sir William Hawkins and objected to making Gillis 'the deluded instrument of his own conviction'.[133] Considering the political state of the country in 1866 some of the opinions expressed by the judges were magnificent. O'Hagan proclaimed that

> our judicial system is distinguished from those of many other countries, in which, though physical torture be abolished, it is thought fit and proper to extract, from an accused man, proof of his own guilt through judicial cross-examination. They may do these things better on the continent of Europe; and I am quite aware there are plausible arguments for preferring their practices to ours; but, at all events, we have never adopted, in modern times,

131 (1866) 17 ICLR 512, at pp 532, 515.   132 Ibid., p. 532.   133 Ibid., p. 563.

and, for my own part, I trust we never shall adopt, the plan of extorting confessions by putting people, morally, to the question.[134]

The majority of the judges did not have much doubt about the involuntariness of Gillis' information. According to O'Hagan

> in the first place, when all this occurred, he was virtually in custody; he had avowed his guilt; he was in the power of the police; it was their duty to arrest him; and, if he had refused to give evidence, they would, undoubtedly, have done so. In the next place he was solicited so to give evidence, by a person having authority instantly to arrest him, and give him up to justice, if he hesitated to swear against his confederates.[135]

On the subject of how to treat approvers who broke their bargain with the Crown, O'Hagan believed they could be put on trial, but their informations could not be used against them:

> if the approver breaks his bargain with the Crown, he shall not be allowed the benefit of it. The witness and the prosecutor are thereupon relegated to their original relation; and, if the prosecutor can make out his case by legal evidence, whether that be evidence of a confession or any other, the prisoner must take the consequences. But, the evidence for his conviction must be legal evidence; and the confession accepted against him must have been voluntarily made, and without the inducement of hope or fear. That is common sense and common justice.[136]

Gillis was not the only case where the judges dealt with the admission of informations and depositions. In 1858 in *Lydane* the Court for Crown Cases Reserved dealt with the admission of an information sworn in connection with a crime that was distinct from that for which the prisoner was on trial.[137] Patrick Lydane was found guilty at the Galway spring assizes in 1858 of the murder of his wife Mary in August 1856. Part of the case against him was that his future wife had sworn an information against him for rape, committed when she was a servant in his father's house, but

> at the approach of the assizes, however, he married the prosecutrix and in consequence the prosecution was not proceeded with. Evidence was given of statements made by Patrick, some before and some after the marriage, the purport of which was that he married to prevent the prosecution; that the marriage would not make her much good; that she and her mother swore

---

134 Ibid., pp 535–6. 135 Ibid., p. 533. 136 Ibid., p. 536.
137 8 Cox CC 38, at pp 38, 39, 40. See also NAI, CRF/1858/Lydane/15.

falsely against him; that he would give her a short life; that he would have her soul.

Clewes was a precedent for admitting evidence of one crime to prove a motive for a second one, but the correspondence between the two cases was not complete: the murders of the rector of Oddingley and of Hemmings were facts that were sworn to in court, but Mary Lydane's information was a mere accusation, unsubstantiated and easy to make. It was a form of hearsay, a premature dying declaration by a witness who was nowhere near dying. Christian admitted the information and Lydane's recognizance,

> but told the jury that they were not to regard them as evidence of anything, save simply of the facts, that before the parties married such a charge had been made, and the accused placed under recognizance to stand his trial for it; that they had nothing whatever to do with the question whether that charge was true or false, but that the acts evinced by the mere existence of these documents might be taken into their consideration, along with the other circumstances, specially, as bearing upon the question of the existence of a motive which might have prompted the prisoner to the commission of the act with which he stood charged.

Christian reserved the case and the Court for Crown Cases Reserved decided that the information and recognizance had been properly admitted. *Lydane* found its way into *Russell on crime*.[138]

Three other complicated cases involved the admission of informations and depositions. *Mullen* and *Galvin* arose from the Petty Sessions (Ireland) Act 1851, section 14, which regulated the taking of depositions at committal proceedings, and provided for their admission as evidence if the deponent died before the trial.[139] *Coll* dealt with an information sworn by a policeman.[140] Two of them were very long. *Galvin* and *Coll* between them covered nearly a hundred pages of print. All three were technical in the sense that they were about rules rather than principles. The speeches of the judges who dealt with them were occasionally illuminated by flashes of principle, but there was nothing in them to compare with Pigot in *Johnston*. Lefroy in *Mullen* probably summed up the process of argument in all three cases when he said 'we have come to this conclusion by different views on the several points, but not in such a preponderance on any point as to render it of importance to the public that we should give any further grounds of judgment.'[141]

Mullen was a manslaughter case in Sligo. A man stabbed in the street had sworn a deposition in the presence of the prisoner. The dying man signed with a

138 Russell, op. cit., iii, 484.
139 (1862) 9 Cox CC 339; (1863) 16 ICLR 452; 14 & 15 Victoria, c. 93 (7 Aug. 1851).
140 (1889) 24 LR Ir 522.   141 (1862) 9 Cox CC 339, at p. 341.

cross, but 'by mistake the clerk wrote the prisoner's name to the mark, so that it *prima facie* appeared to be the deposition of the prisoner, accusing himself.'[142] The problem here was the rule that oral evidence should not be substituted for written evidence where the law required the evidence to be in writing. Depositions were supposed to taken down in writing, but for this one to make sense it 'would require oral testimony to explain a patent ambiguity.' The judges decided the deposition had been properly admitted, agreeing with Lefroy that the document was complete before the signature was added because 'this document was signed by a mark, and that signature cannot be vitiated by what another person wrote'.

Galvin, which was a manslaughter case in Limerick, covered forty-three pages of the law reports. It was concerned with several issues, the most important of which was the fact that a deposition sworn in the prisoner's presence by John Hickie, who had died of his injuries, had 'nothing to show on its face that the prisoner had been made aware of the charge on which he was in custody.'[143] *Galvin* divided the nine judges who heard it in the Court for Crown Cases Reserved into two groups of four who were able to arrive at two decisions only because Lord Chief Justin Monahan distributed himself impartially between them. Monahan and four judges (Deasy, Baron Fitzgerald, O'Brien, and Pigot) were against receiving the information, while Monahan and four judges (Christian, Hayes, Hughes, and O'Hagan) decided that all that Petty Sessions (Ireland) Act 1851, section 14 required 'is that the charge should be made to the magistrate before he proceeds to take the deposition.' The judges who were against admitting the deposition argued that parliament had conferred on the prisoner the right of cross-examining witnesses at his committal and that 'a person accused might be utterly unable to cross-examine a witness produced against him with effect, or at all, unless he was apprised, at least in general terms, of what was the nature of the charge against him, which that witness' testimony was intended to establish.' Those who were in favour of admitting the deposition argued that it should have been admitted because the prisoner had had 'full facility of hearing the examination and making the cross-examination.'

Coll, which arose out of the trial of William Coll at the Queen's County assizes for the manslaughter of District Inspector W.L Martin, was about the admissibility of an information that Constable Varilly had sworn on 14 February 1889. At Coll's trial Varilly swore that he had seen Coll strike Martin ('he was one of the men who struck Martin with stones when lying near the window').[144] During his cross-examination by The MacDermot QC, Varilly 'said that he believed that he stated on an information before a magistrate, made upon the 29 March, 1889, the names of all the persons present at the attack whom he knew, but added that he made a mistake. The deposition of 29 March, 1889, was then entered for the defence, and it appeared that C[oll] was not referred to in it.'[145]

142   Ibid., pp 339, 340. See also Purcell, op. cit., pp 268–9.
143   16 ICLR 452, at pp 452, 468, 465.   144   (1889) 24 LR Ir 522, at pp 524.
145   Ibid., p. 522.

The effect of this exchange was to imply that Varilly's identification of Coll was an afterthought, what the trial judge, Gibson, called 'inventive meditation afterwards'.[146] The attorney general replied to this by offering to give as evidence another information sworn by Varilly, this one on 14 February 1889, naming Coll as one of those who had attacked Martin. The information of 14 February presented problems as admissible evidence. It was not made in the prisoner's presence, the informant had not been cross-examined, it was a species of hearsay, and 'as a general rule, neither upon direct examination nor re-examination, is evidence of previous statements made by a witness admissible to confirm or set up the credit of such witness.'[147] The trial judge, moreover, was 'impressed by the mischief that might be caused to a prisoner if the statement relied upon was combined with matter which might not be evidence at all.'[148] Eventually Gibson decided not to allow the statement to be read out, but allowed the attorney general to ask the following question: 'Did witness, on 14 February, 1889, state on oath that he saw the prisoner, William Coll, on 3 February, throw stones at William Martin whilst lying on the ground near the door of the dwelling-house of the Rev. Father M'Fadden, and did he mention the prisoner by name?' The MacDermot objected to the question, the judge said he would consider reserving the case, the question was asked, and Varilly answered, 'I did.' A majority of the Court for Crown Cases Reserved decided that the information was admissible. Sir Michael Morris and Palles were in the minority of four. The important point seems to have been the lengths to which The MacDermot took the cross-examination of Varilly. Not content with showing the inconsistency of what Varilly had sworn in court with what he had *not* sworn before the magistrate on 29 March, he went on 'to show that the charge against Coll was a subsequent concoction' and that 'Varilly had, subsequently to the month of March, fabricated the story about Coll.'[149]

THE EFFECTS OF THE LAW OF EVIDENCE

Was the law of evidence merely a way of avoiding a dreary narrative of 'not only the whole life of the suspected person, but the whole order of the universe'?[150] According to Sheldon Amos, 'the only recognized objects of a law of evidence in modern times are (1) to shorten and simplify legal proceedings by excluding evidence on the ground of its invariable unreliableness or its useless prolixity; (2) to determine the mode of taking evidence both in court and out of court, and to devize such securities as may seem most expedient for imparting to it the greatest possible value.'[151] At least one Irish lawyer did not take the law of evidence

146 Ibid., p. 531.
147 Ibid., pp 529–30. See Purcell, op. cit., pp 285–6.
148 24 LR Ir 522, at pp 532, 526–7.
149 Ibid., p. 542.
150 James Fitzjames Stephen, *A general view of the criminal law of England* (London and Cambridge, 1863), p. 306.
151 *The science of law* (London, 1874), p. 300.

seriously. George French QC, assistant barrister of Longford, was 'well grounded in the principles of the law, but ... the English law of evidence he looked upon (as a French lawyer would) as so much trash, and his only aim was to make out the truth, caring not a jot whether it was hearsay evidence or not.'[152] When he retired in 1851 'he had gone 109 circuits, and his temper was becoming daily more and more irascible.'

Ramifying exceptions to every exclusionary rule seemed to exclude little in the end. The prisoner's silence, whether in court or before the magistrates, for example, was not absolute. Prisoners' words played a considerable part in the cases against them. A selection of 54 cases, taken mainly from the judges notes in the Convict Reference Files, and covering the period from the 1830s to the early 1900s, yielded a total of 1029 pieces of evidence admitted at trials; 142 pieces out of this total were prisoners' words relayed to the court, which shows that the law did not keep prisoners quiet.[153] It is worth noting, however, that only 44 of these 142 pieces were relayed by policemen. Prisoners, moreover, seemed to act as transmitting media for hearsay because the very act that they had perpetrated allowed reported words to be admitted if they were part of the *res gestæ*.[154] It must be admitted, however, that this exception to the hearsay rule admitted only a handful of the 1029 items mentioned above. There was too the contrast between the prisoner's silence and the loquacity enjoyed by approvers, who became a sort of proxy who could virtually confess on the prisoner's behalf.

Prisoners' lips were sealed, but their clothes, face, and hands could be made to speak. At the Carlow spring assizes in 1838, Patrick Cain was found guilty of the murder of his sister-in-law, Bridget. His face, trousers, and shirt were made to speak against him. His face was scratched when he was arrested, and the chief constable reported that: 'deceased was in a monthly disorder, that women are subject to. It struck me that if he took liberties with her, his shirt had the marks of blood, on my return to the barracks, I had his breeches taken down and I examined his shirt, and the flap of his trowsers, were bloody.'[155] Searches by policemen of prisoners' clothes and houses yielded 46 pieces of evidence, out of the total of 1,029 – a small but rich harvest in terms of incrimination.

Important information, nevertheless, was excluded by the law of evidence. Hearsay, in the ordinary common meaning of the word, was excluded – one policeman could not say what another policeman said the prisoner had said. Of the total 1,029 pieces of evidence, only 16 pieces were words that witnesses heard other witnesses saying. Confessions could not be beaten out of prisoners; the selection of cases from which these pieces of evidence were taken included only one confession. The ban on induced confessions stopped shameless plea bargaining; the selection of cases included only two guilty pleas. The dying

152 Oliver J. Burke, *Anecdotes of the Connaught circuit: from its foundation to close upon the present time* (Dublin, 1885), pp 275–6, 278–9.

153 Above, p. 2.   154 Purcell, op. cit., p. 289.

155 NAI, Outrage Papers/Carlow/1838.

declarations of all but the murdered person were excluded; even if the actual perpetrator of the crime made a death-bed confession, his dying declaration could not be repeated.

The effects of the law of evidence on the police's preparation of cases can be demonstrated by analysing the evidence presented in court. The 54 cases already referred to showed a strong bias to the palpable in evidence. Of the 1,029 pieces of evidence yielded, opportunity accounted for 46%, means for 20%, motive for 12%, suspicious conduct for 11%, malicious words for 4%, and similar fact for 2%. Dying declarations, confessions, admissions, and guilty pleas, when combined, accounted for only 29 pieces of evidence, which was just under 3%, and the biggest item among these was the 18 admissions.[156] (Confessions in this selection of cases were taken to mean the full, formal confession made to a magistrate or a policeman; admissions were words that more or less admitted having done the deed; malicious words showed intention.) There was in effect only one confession out of the total of the 54 cases. A further measure of how the law of evidence influenced the police's collection of evidence is the fact that the evidence police themselves gave as witnesses (181 pieces out of the 1,029) was predominantly elicited in certain circumstances: 50 pieces at the scene of the crime, 45 at the prisoner's arrest, and 46 from a search of the prisoner. Hardly anything came from prisoners when they were in custody or examined before the magistrates. Hardly anything came from the police's own knowledge of the prisoner's behaviour before or after the crime.

The paucity of confessions, admissions, and guilty pleas was remarkable. If the police had been allowed to conduct their investigations without restraint, it is unlikely that this category would have been so small. One indication, albeit not a perfect one, of what characteristic police evidence might have been like, is suggested by the evidence that policeman actually did give at trials. Their evidence was remarkably skewed in certain directions: means accounted for 27% of their evidence (compared with 20% for witnesses as a whole), suspicious conduct accounted for 24% (compared with 11% for witnesses as a whole), and admissions for 6% (compared with 2%). There was a tendency, therefore, for policemen, as policemen, to generate evidence about weapons, suspicious conduct, and incriminating words. The Dublin police magistrate, Frank Thorpe Porter, described how a system thoroughly dominated by the police might have worked, especially in the matter of suspicious conduct:

> The essential difference between our police and that which I have observed in France, Belgium, and Rhenish Prussia, is exhibited in the speedy arrests of suspected persons here, compared with the tardiness of apprehension in

156 This is a modest harvest. According to Peers, 'one contemporary source estimated that only 4 in every 100 convictions in Britain arose from confession as compared to 70 out of 100 in India' (Peers, 'Torture, the police, and the colonial state in the Madras presidency, 1816–55', p. 48).

the latter countries, unless the prisoner is actually caught in *flagrante delicto*. The moment that a suspicion is entertained in Ireland, the supposed delinquent is seized, and thereby all chance of obtaining evidence by his subsequent acts is completely lost. The foreign system is to watch him night and day. This frequently eventuates in detecting him concealing property, weapons, or blood-stained clothes, or suddenly quitting his abode without any previous intimation, and perhaps under an assumed name. If we are to have an efficient police, we will find it indispensably necessary to keep well-informed, shrewd, patient, watchful detectives. I have known many who contended that a constable should adopt no disguise, but that, in the uniform of the force to which he belongs, he should perambulate the streets, suppress disorders. apprehend offenders, and when directed to execute warrants, he should go in search of the culprit openly and avowedly.[157]

The power of the police in the law-enforcement system became greater as the century progressed. The fact that trials became longer, for example, suggested their growing power – there were 9 crown witnesses at each murder trial before 1850 compared with 20 after 1850. A law-enforcement system dominated by policemen would not only have produced a different pattern of evidence, with confessions and systematic observation of the prisoner's behaviour playing a larger part, but it would also have produced more approvers. The Crown used approvers in only 8 of the 54 cases that formed the selection of cases referred to above, and they were corroborated by 54 pieces of evidence, which suggests that the crown solicitors took corroboration seriously. One of the most controversial Irish cases involving an approver showed the practical problems of corroboration. William and Daniel Cormack were tried at Nenagh spring assizes in 1858 for the murder of John Ellis. An approver, Timothy Spillane, told a clear, damning story, which was corroborated by two witnesses. (1) Tom Bourke, the driver of Ellis' car, saw Daniel, William, and the approver hiding in the hedge where Ellis was ambushed; William was holding a gun; a shot was fired. (2) John Sadleir, the keeper of Thurles bridewell, overheard an incriminatory conversation between William and Daniel while they were in the bridewell.[158] There was other evidence but the approver and these two witnesses were the Crown's indispensable triumvirate. The problem was that Tom Bourke was either an accomplice, or could be plausibly stigmatized as one, and the judges had decided that one accomplice could not corroborate another. The bridewell keeper's evidence smacked of the Bastille and the Holy Office.

---

157 Frank Thorpe Porter, *Gleanings and reminiscences* (Dublin, 1875), pp 176–7. On magistrates' fears of police officers acting as spies and *agents provocateurs*, see Elizabeth Malcolm, 'Investigating the "Machinery of Murder": Irish detectives and agrarian outrages, 1847–79' in *New Hibernia Review*, 6:3 (autumn 2002), 80.

158 Judge Keogh's crown book (MS in possession of St Patrick's College, Thurles, Co. Tipperary), pp 123–37. (I am indebted to the Revd Christy Dwyer, formerly president and archivist of St

COMPLAINTS ABOUT THE CROWN'S CASE

The behaviour of crown counsel and crown solicitors produced more complaints than any other aspect of murder trials. Of 63 complaints produced by the selection of 85 cases taken from the Convict Reference Files, 19 were about the Crown's conduct of the case: 5 were about approvers, 5 about crown counsel, 3 about producing surprise witnesses, 2 about postponing trials, 2 about not postponing trials, and 2 about plea bargaining.[159] Some of these can be seen as routine, almost inevitable. Approvers, for example, were intrinsically obnoxious; of the 5 complaints about them, however, only 2 were about corroboration, and in both cases the trial judges believed there was enough corroboration.[160] The 2 complaints about plea-bargaining were again almost inevitable, if only because plea-bargaining allowed the prisoners to live to regret their bargains.

Some complaints were not weighty. Michael Mullin and James Downie complained about the solicitor general's 'consummate addresses', which meant only that that high official had been earning his keep.[161] Patrick Woods complained that counsel retained by the murdered man's family had assisted the crown counsel, but next of kin had a right to retain their own counsel.[162] Thomas Dowling complained that a 'high law officer' had been sent down to prosecute him, but the solicitor general was at liberty to appear if he believed the case was important.[163] Daniel Ward complained that Serjeant Edward Sullivan had invited the jury to view the case with 'the feelings of fathers'. (Charles Wilgar, the murdered man, had a father.) More damaging than Sullivan's appeal to paternal feelings was his calling two policemen, at the very end of the Crown's case, to give evidence about the speed at which Ward was supposed to have walked. It was not so much that they appeared without warning, it was the fact that they were the last of the Crown's witnesses and the last of that day's witnesses. 'This cannot have been accidental,' wrote Ward's counsel, William McMechan, 'The obvious purpose was that it might stand prominent in the memory of the jury, who had the night to contemplate it, and every other part of the case before observations on behalf of the prisoner could be made.'[164] The fact that there were only 3

Patrick's College, Thurles, for providing me with a copy of this MS and for allowing me to quote from it.)

159   Above, pp 95–6.
160   NAI, CRF/1840/Glennon and Toole/4; ibid., 1841/Woods/26.
161   Ibid., CRF/1843/Mullin/50.
162   Ibid., CRF/1841/Woods/26. For an attorney general's opinion that the aggrieved party could employ counsel to assist the crown counsel, see above, p. 94.
163   NAI, CRF/1844/Dowling/11.
164   Ibid., CRF/1863/Ward/5. After Ward's trial, McMechan wrote a letter of *sixty-nine* pages, complaining of the trial's postponement, of the change of venue from Downpatrick to Belfast, of the fact that Ward had no legal representation when the venue was changed, of the arrangements for Ward's identification, of the influence of the 'penny' press, of the selection of the jury, of Serjeant Edward Sullivan's tendentious speech, and of the way the Crown introduced evidence about the speed at which a man could walk.

complaints about surprise witnesses in the whole selection of 85 cases is striking, considering the advantages their use conferred on the Crown: either they were rare, or they were not resented.

There were 2 complaints about the Crown's postponement of trials, which suggest that that insidious problem remained only a potential one. Patrick Lydane complained that the Crown postponed his trial 'at the two following assizes for further evidence'. Not only did this enable the crown solicitor to gather more evidence, but it also meant that Lydane was in prison for almost two years, from August 1856 until March 1858, before he was convicted.[165] Daniel Ward complained that his trial had been postponed from the summer assizes in 1862 to the spring assizes in 1863, which was not surprising since the murder of Charles Wilgar had occurred just before the summer assizes. Lydane's case was obviously one where the Crown was hoping for something to turn up. Ward's postponement was more justifiable. Ward's counsel, nevertheless, complained bitterly: 'Under ordinary circumstances the postponement of a trial by the Crown, as crown counsel are allowed to do in this country, but not in England without cause alleged by affidavit, is an admission that then available evidence is not sufficient to convict & it also involves an intimation that the discovery of further witnesses is probable', but the mere expectation 'that existing witnesses would thereafter make new disclosures would be no ground for postponement at all but the strongest reason for at once proceeding with the trial.'[166]

Postponement, however, was not done at the whim of the crown counsel. The judge had to give permission publicly and formally in court. Some judges did not like postponements. According to McMechan, Perrin was a stickler for explanations ('How Irish judges can reconcile it with their oaths & the terms of their commission of jail-delivery to postpone trials after indictment found, without cause shewn, Judge Perrin could never understand.') The 2 prisoners who complained that their trials had been postponed were balanced by the 3 who complained that theirs had not been postponed. John and James Power complained 'that in consequence of its having been represented to the friends of your memorialists the day before their trial occurred, that their trial would not be proceeded with at that assizes your memorialists were not prepared at their trial with all their witnesses.'[167] They named 5 witnesses; the witnesses produced five declarations. Their petition did not say who had told their friends the trial would be postponed. Christos Bombos also complained of the Crown's precipitancy: 'if time had permitted additional evidence might have been adduced which would have tended to mitigate his punishment.'[168] There were no complaints about judges who discharged juries 'where the prosecution case broke down, in order to give the Crown the chance to plug the gap in its case', a practice described by Bentley as 'obnoxious'.[169]

165 Ibid., CRF/1858/Lydane/5.
166 Ibid., CRF/1863/Ward/5.
167 Ibid., CRF/1841/Power/13.
168 Ibid., CRF/1876/Bombos/26.
169 Bentley, op. cit., p. 79.

In addition to these 19 complaints about the Crown's conduct, there were 6 statements that mentioned that the prisoner had been tried before. These were not mentioned as a complaint, but to cast doubt on the second or third jury's verdict. Possibly these 6 cases should be added to the 19 complaints made against the Crown, but whether multiple trials are to be seen as an illiberal 'stratagem' or as the Crown's stern dedication to duty is not easy to decide. The Crown brought the prisoner to trial. A jury failed to reach a verdict; another trial, therefore, became necessary, unless it was to be accepted that one or two jurors could acquit a prisoner. James Lawson stated the law in the Queen's Bench Division in December 1883 in *Poole* in terms that suggested a nice balancing of interests: 'the duty of a judge under the commission is to proceed to try the prisoner until he is convicted or acquitted and so long as there is not a verdict, the judge has no power to decline performing that duty if the Crown put the prisoner on trial a second time.'[170]

---

170 14 LR Ir 14, at pp 21–2. See above, p. 116.

CHAPTER SIX

The prisoner's defence

COUNSEL

PRISONERS COULD HAVE as many counsel as they could afford, but generally they had only one, usually a junior. William McMechan, for example, who was counsel for Daniel Ward and John Logue, who were hanged in 1863 and 1866, never took silk; he did, however, become a crown counsel for Co. Monaghan. Usually the prisoner's solitary counsel confronted a numerous array of crown counsel. At Stephen McKeown's trial at the Armagh summer assizes in 1876, for example, Walter Boyd, who was a 'doctor', but not yet a QC, confronted a QC and two juniors (Andrew Porter QC, Dr J. Favière Elrington, and Dr William Kaye).[1] When prisoners were tried together, they could be represented by one counsel, or they could have separate counsel. When they had separate counsel, 'the senior counsel, employed on that side should cross-examine, and address the jury first on the part of whichever traverser he may be employed by; and, as soon as he has concluded his address to the jury then the counsel for the other defendants should address the jury in succession.'[2] If the prisoners could not agree on the order in which their counsel were to address the jury 'the court will call upon them, not in the order of their seniority, but in the order in which the names of the prisoners stand in the indictment.'[3]

Being a crown counsel in one county of a circuit did not prevent a barrister being a prisoner's counsel in another. The attorney general's appointment of crown counsel encouraged barristers to defend prisoners, if only because their successes as prisoners' counsel might persuade him to transmute poachers into gamekeepers. Prisoners' counsel were not distinguished from the crown counsel by any special dress, or by where they sat in the court-room. The visible distinctions were not between crown counsel and prisoners' counsel but between QCs and 'outer' barristers. The former wore full bottomed wigs and silk gowns, and sat in front of the latter, separated from them by a 'bar', which might in practice be nothing more than the back of a bench. The appearance of advocates in Irish courts, therefore, was strikingly different from their appearance in Continental courts. When James Whiteside attended a trial in Rome, for example,

---

1 NAI, CRF/1876/McKeown/22.
2 Theobald A. Purcell, *A summary of the general principles of pleading and evidence, in criminal cases in Ireland: with the rules of practice incident thereto* (Dublin, 1849), p. 193.
3 Ibid., p. 194.

he noted that the public prosecutor wore a black silk gown and sat close enough to the judges to be able to whisper to them; the prisoners' advocates wore coarse black gowns and sat at a table on their own.[4] Irish barristers did not appear in their wigs and gowns at the assizes until well into the nineteenth century. James Whiteside, for example, proposed the wearing of wigs and gowns to the north-east bar in 1850, but his proposal was rejected by 47 to 25. It was rejected again in 1851, 1852, and 1862, and not adopted until 1867.[5]

The best prospect for the not guilty was a rising barrister. When Sam Gray was tried for murder, he knew what he was doing when he secured the services of George Tombe and James Whiteside, both of whom were about to take silk. Thanks to their skill Gray's career did not end in 1841. Prisoners' counsel often had distinguished careers ahead of them. At the Armagh summer assizes in 1841, Patrick Woods' counsel were James Whiteside (lord chief justice, 1866–76), Joseph Napier (lord chancellor, 1858–9), and Thomas O'Hagan (lord chancellor, 1868–74, 1880–1).[6] For young barristers who took on capital cases, there were advantages such as publicity, the gratification of doing a good job in desperate circumstances, and compliments from the judge, which were usually profuse, especially when counsel had failed to get a guilty prisoner acquitted. Judge Fitzgerald told William Gregory's jury at Downpatrick in 1871 that 'the prisoner has been defended with an ability that I have rarely seen equalled. Every observation on the evidence that I could possibly make has been anticipated.'[7] Gregory's counsel were Andrew Porter and John Monroe, who were rising men at the bar: Porter was appointed QC in 1872 and Monroe in 1877; Porter was attorney general in 1883, and Monroe was solicitor general in Lord Salisbury's government in 1885.[8] In spite of the prestige of appearing in capital cases, barristers found them horrifying. 'In my time I defended as many as a score of prisoners for their lives,' wrote Mathias Bodkin, 'but I had the same feverish anxiety in the last case as in the first.'[9] Alexander Sullivan almost fainted when

4 James Whiteside, *Italy in the nineteenth century, contrasted with its past condition,* 3 vols (London, 1848), iii, 294. For more, see below, pp 367–9.

5 Daire Hogan, *The legal profession in Ireland 1789–1922* (Dublin, 1986), p. 48.

6 NAI, CRF/Woods/1841/26. The importance of each step in legal promotion was nicely gauged by the 'fines' levied by the Munster bar on rising members. The fines were measured in bottles of champagne: 'for appointments as King's Counsels, two dozen; crown prosecutor, two dozen; county court judges, three dozen; king's serjeants, four dozen; solicitor general, attorney general, judge of the high court, six dozen; lord chief justice, ten dozen; lord chancellor or lord of appeal, twelve dozen' (A.M. Sullivan, *Last serjeant,* p. 222).

7 NAI, CRF/1871/Gregory/9 [*Belfast Newsletter,* 6 Mar. 1871].

8 The fact that the careers of both Thomas O'Hagan and Peter O'Brien started auspiciously with criminal cases was noted by contemporaries (Oliver J. Burke, *The history of the lord chancellors of Ireland* (Dublin, 1879), pp 317–20 and *The reminiscences of the Right Hon. Lord O'Brien (of Kilfenora) lord chief justice of Ireland,* pp 18–19).

9 Mathias M'D. Bodkin, *Recollections of an Irish judge: press, bar and parliament* (London, 1914), p. 140.

John Twiss was found guilty at the Cork winter assizes in 1895.[10] Twiss sent him a message telling him 'not to take it too hard'.

Judges could assign counsel to defend prisoners who could not pay for their defence, a practice that existed in Ireland as early as the 1830s.[11] In 1883 William O'Brien assigned Thomas Webb QC and Richard Adams to defend Joseph Brady, the first of the Phoenix Park murderers to be tried. Webb was not pleased, complaining that he would have 'to set aside all other business, however momentous, for a space of a month or six weeks.' The judge was firm, saying that it was 'not open to counsel assigned to decline a case', and that the bar's honour was at stake. Webb and Adams, he opined, 'cannot decline to act without inflicting upon their profession a wound that would be difficult to heal'. O'Brien conceded that it was unusual to assign a QC, but he 'was determined to overcome every technical objection for the purpose of securing the proper defence of the accused.'[12] O'Brien's hand may have been strengthened by the Prevention of Crime (Ireland) Act 1882, which provided 'for the payment of counsel required for the defence of a person brought for trial before a special commission court,' although this was not a special commission as defined by the act.[13] O'Brien's remarks suggested that only a QC could provide a 'proper' defence, which might suggest there had been growing elaboration of prisoners' representation in recent years,[14] but it is possible to find the Crown actually paying a QC to defend prisoners as early as the 1830s. Perrin, for example, told the house of lords select committee in 1839 of a special commission in Co. Tipperary where John Hatchell QC was sent down to represent the prisoners 'at the public expense'.[15] The sending of Hatchell was perhaps remarkable, but the Crown assisting prisoners was not unusual. In the 1830s 'there was a general authority' given to the crown solicitor, in 'cases of importance', to pay for counsel and attorney if the prisoner could not afford to do so.[16]

10   Sullivan, *Last serjeant*, p. 91; see also id., *Old Ireland: reminiscences of an Irish KC* (London, 1927), p. 114.
11   *Minutes of evidence taken before the select committee of the house of lords appointed to enquire into the state of Ireland, since the year 1835, in respect of crime and outrage, which have rendered life and property insecure in that part of the empire*, pt III, *evidence 12 June to 19 July*, p. 878, HC 1839 (486–III), xii, 14. On the history of assignment in England see David Bentley, *English criminal justice in the nineteenth century* (London and Rio Grande, 1998), pp 110–15.
12   *Report of the trials at the Dublin Commission Court, April and May, 1883, of the prisoners charged with the Phoenix Park murder, the attempt to murder Mr Field, and the conspiracy to murder; before the Hon. Mr Justice O'Brien; reported by W.C. Johnston* (Dublin, 1883), pp 2, 4, 6.
13   45 & 46 Vict., c. 25, s. 1(6), (12 July 1882).
14   When Alexander Sullivan went to London to defend Sir Roger Casement, the English attorney general wanted the lord chancellor to make Sullivan an English KC because 'he wished that the leader for the defence should lead within the bar' (Sullivan, *Last serjeant*, p. 274).
15   *Minutes of evidence taken before the select committee of the house of lords appointed to enquire into the state of Ireland*, … pt III, *evidence 12 June to 19 July*, p. 1060, HC 1839 (486–III), xii, 196.
16   Ibid., p. 1060.

Discussions about paying counsel's fees occasionally occurred in open court. Francis Macdonogh QC, 'who had been very generously paid on each occasion' when he acted as Thomas Hartley Montgomery's counsel at his first two trials, refused to perform at Montgomery's third trial 'unless his fees were secured to him.' The attorney general, Christopher Palles, who had come to Omagh to prosecute, 'was so indignant that he insisted that the Crown should guarantee the fees, rather than a man should be deprived of the service of the advocate he had chosen.'[17] At his second trial at Cavan assizes, Laurence Smith, who was charged with the murder of Patrick Lynch, complained that *'he was not prepared for his trial as he had no one to defend him* and had no means to fee counsel.'[18] William Mahaffy, his attorney at his previous trial, stated 'that two months ago he was only offered 2 guineas and 3 guineas for counsel, an offer which he at once repudiated, and thereen [*sic*] and then withdrew from the case. In reply to Baron Dowse, Mr Mahaffy stated that he would *not undertake the responsibility* of so serious a case on such short notice.' Dowse replied to this tale of hardship by stating 'that in the exercise of his authority he would be obliged to assign the prisoner counsel, and he hoped Mr Irvine, who had defended him before, would undertake the task of seeing justice done to the prisoner.' William Irvine, however, had better things to do. As he told Dowse, 'his engagements in the record court would deprive him of defending the prisoner.' After a wrangle, 'which went hard against the legal gentlemen present', Dowse got his way, and Irvine agreed to act, but tried to put a good face on it, stating 'that the assignment of an advocate was very short notice in a case where a man *was on trial for his life,* but that he would undertake it in accordance with his lordship's directions.' Smith was found guilty and hanged on 16 August 1873.

The judge's power to assign an attorney was not so well established. At the Downpatrick assizes in 1851 Andrew Fogarty was put on trial for poisoning his wife. The chief baron, David Pigot, 'after conferring with the crown solicitor, addressed Mr Macmeehan[*sic*], and requested that he would undertake the defence of the prisoner, who was unable to employ attorney or counsel.'[19] ('Macmeehan' was the barrister William McMechan, whose name was rarely spelt correctly in reports of trials.) McMechan refused because 'there was a feeling and opinion existing on the subject among the bar which compelled him to beg that his lordship would excuse him for declining.' The father of the north-east bar,[20]

---

17   Healy, *The old Munster circuit,* p. 269.
18   NAI, CRF/1873/Smith/18. There does not seem to have been an Irish equivalent of Sir William Follett, who died 'in sight of the lord chancellorship', but whose approach to the woolsack was marked by 'taking briefs that he could never read, and for pocketing retainers in causes he could never plead' (*Fraser's Magazine,* quoted by David J.A. Cairns, in *Advocacy and the making of the adversarial criminal trial 1800–1865* (Oxford, 1998), p. 128).
19   5 Cox CC 161, at pp 161, 162. See also Bentley, op. cit., pp 114–5.
20   The father of the circuit was its longest-serving member. Sir Thomas Staples JP, DL, of Lissan, Co. Tyrone, was born in 1775, called in 1802, and made a KC in 1822.

Sir Thomas Staples, supported McMechan, saying that 'no counsel could, with propriety, undertake the defence of a prisoner without receiving instructions from an attorney. He also had to say, not on the part of Mr Macmeehan, but on the part of the bar, that in every case in which counsel was assigned, the Crown should pay him a fee; up to a very recent period it was a rule to do so.' Pigot agreed that McMechan should be paid, but could do nothing about the attorney because 'a judge might with propriety call on a barrister to give his honorary services to a prisoner who was unable to employ one, but he thought the case different as regarded an attorney.' Pigot pointed out that at the special commission at Clonmel, Charles Rolleston had been assigned, and 'he consented to do so without the assistance of an attorney.' (Rolleston, called in 1833, was the crown counsel for the county and city of Kilkenny.) McMechan expressed his 'great respect' for Rolleston, but insisted that 'Perrin, J, had expressed a decided opinion that counsel ought not to act without an attorney.' Pigot then fired his biggest gun: 'he could not compel counsel to act; he could do no more than appeal to the sense of feeling of the bar.' McMechan agreed to act but only when an attorney, Edward Murphy, agreed to act as well.

In England 'dock briefs' got over the need to employ a solicitor. A prisoner could choose, without the mediation of a solicitor, '"any counsel robed in court, other than the counsel for the prosecution", and he is entitled to such services for the sum of one guinea.'[21] Maurice Healy could 'not remember a single dock brief during my time at the Irish bar.' There was a reference to a dock brief at Joseph Brady's trial when Denis B. Sullivan, was 'named from the dock', but this was an incident in the assignment of Thomas Webb QC and Richard Adams.[22] The Scottish practice of providing legal aid had much to commend it

> every prisoner, however poor, is entitled by statute 1587, c. 91, to have counsel to defend him. If the prisoner has not previously applied for counsel, the court will, as a matter of course, assign them to him as soon as the diet is called. If no other counsel are present, the sheriff of the county, who is a counsel generally in actual practice, and who must give his attendance at circuit, is named by the court to defend.[23]

There were also 'certain advocates, generally junior counsel, [who] are assigned annually by the Faculty of Advocates to be advocates for the poor.'

Assignment left counsel no time to prepare the case or to find witnesses. At the trial of Matthew Bryan, who was charged with murdering his mother, Bushe

21 Healy, op. cit., p. 101. For dock briefs in England see Bentley, op. cit., pp 116–22.
22 *Report of the trials at the Dublin Commission Court, April and May, 1883, of the prisoners charged with the Phoenix Park murder, the attempt to murder Mr Field, and the conspiracy to murder; before the Hon. Mr Justice O'Brien; reported by W.C. Johnston* (Dublin, 1883), p. 2.
23 James Paterson, *A compendium of English and Scotch law stating their differences: with a dictionary of parallel terms and phrases* (Edinburgh, 1860), pp 331, 426.

assigned him 'able' counsel, who was Edmund Hayes, later solicitor general and a judge of the Queen's Bench. Hayes complained that 'it was not until after the trial was called on, & the unfortunate man actually given in charge to the jury that I was assigned by the lord chief justice as his counsel. The trial immediately proceeded during which I had not even the assistance of a professional man as attorney to communicate with the prisoner and prepare his defence. Under such untoward circumstances then, my duty was confined almost exclusively to cross-examination of the witnesses for the prosecution and addressing the jury on his behalf.'[24] Bryan was found guilty, and sentenced to death, but his sentence was commuted to transportation for life, partly due to Hayes' vigorous activity after the trial. Whether prisoners to whom counsel were assigned were much worse off than others in the matter of preparation is debatable. Professional etiquette in Ireland discouraged, in the interests of fair trade, premature contacts between barristers and attorneys, which did not imply weeks of preparation before the assizes.[25] In England 'well into the nineteenth century it was usual for a criminal brief not to be delivered to counsel until the day of the trial.'[26] Some barristers, however, were involved well before their clients' trials. William McMechan was present at the identification parade in Belfast gaol when his client Daniel Ward was identified; Charles O'Malley was present at the inquest on Mrs Walsh, whose husband he defended at the assizes.[27]

Some judges thought preparation was a luxury. Torrens at Enniskillen summer assizes in 1849 asked an attorney to act for a prisoner charged with murder. The attorney protested that he was 'ignorant of the case' and that he had not even got a copy of the informations. 'You will hear the substance of the informations in the opening of the case,' was Torrens' reassuring reply.[28] Other judges were more demanding than Torrens. At the Dublin Commission in 1848 when it was suggested that counsel should be appointed to take over a case from the clerk of the crown, who had too much on his plate, Richard Pennefather refused: 'I disapprove of employing counsel *on the moment*, as I do not think a prosecution can be properly carried on in that way.'[29] 'Any one who has ever acted as an advocate knows what it is to be called upon to defend a man at a moment's notice,' complained James Fitzjames Stephen.[30]

Communication between prisoners and counsel in court was not easy. The dock was usually behind the table where counsel sat. The prisoner could not, therefore, catch counsel's eye. John Logue had a clear grasp of his disadvantageous position when he was tried for murder at Downpatrick assizes:

24   NAI, CRF/1840/Bryan/50.
25   Daire Hogan, *The legal profession in Ireland 1789–1922* (Dublin, 1986), p. 47.
26   Cairns, op. cit., p. 34.
27   NAI, CRF/1863/Ward/5; ibid., CRF/1873/Walsh/11.
28   *Impartial Reporter*, 19 July 1849.
29   *Farrell and Moore* (1848) 3 Cox CC 139, at p. 140.
30   James Fitzjames Stephen, *A history of the criminal law of England*, 3 vols (London, 1883), i, 398.

And for interrup [*sic*] the councellor [*sic*], while pleading would not be allowed, and then as soon as he would have done he would order then [*sic*] down, so that I could not suggest anything to him and it was against the rules of the court to allowe [*sic*] the prisoner to speak whilst he had a lawyer employed. And the councellor not knowing the nature of some of the perjury which was sworing [*sic*], and the point that they could be refuted it, and that owning to me not getting communicating to him in due season. They were ordered down, and what ever they said, was taking As [*sic*] truth.[31]

Logue was hanged. Most barristers probably did not want to be interrupted, except possibly in a stage-managed way to make a point. Thomas Hartley Montgomery, who had a high opinion of his own powers as a lawyer, 'kept passing notes to Macdonogh, suggesting questions to him'.[32] The notes annoyed Macdonogh, who in any case had just had a humiliating row with the attorney general over his fees. Montgomery became 'very pertinacious; and the moment came when he passed a note, suggesting a particular question. Macdonogh took the note in full view of the jury, asked the question, and received a deadly answer. Immediately he turned towards Montgomery and threw his hands up in horror! Many people thought that this episode caused the conviction of his client.'

The simultaneous sitting of the two judges in two courts at the assizes meant that attorneys and barristers had to scurry about from one part of the courthouse to another. William McMechan, for example, Daniel Ward's counsel, was not present when Serjeant Edward Sullivan made the Crown's closing speech at Ward's trial.[33] Attorneys were often not present when their clients were being tried. Patrick Lydane was not able to communicate with his counsel because 'unfortunately the attorney to whom the defence was confided happened to be previously engaged on a case of his own in the civil court before and during the trial in the crown court.'[34]

---

31   NAI, CRF/1866/Logue/6.
32   Healy, op. cit., pp 269–70. Macdonogh dressed like an eighteenth-century dandy, wearing white gloves and a stock, and carrying a tasselled cane. He attracted attention: 'when he was strutting along the front at Brighton, with his man trailing a few yards behind him, he asked: "Who do these people say that I am, Rooney?". Rooney's answer – unmercifully blunt – is said to have been: "They say you're a lunatic, sir, and that I'm your keeper"' (From the Hon. Mr Johnston's review of Denis Johnston's radio play on the Newtownstewart murder, in *Radio Times*, 1 Oct. 1937. I am indebted to William F. Cooper for this reference). When Macdonogh asked Rooney this question, he broke one of the rules of cross-examination, which laid down that counsel should never ask a question whose answer he did not know. For more on the Montgomery case see Austin Stewart, '"Every word spoken by the prisoner may be taken *cum grano salis*", Newtownstewart, Co. Tyrone, 1871' in Frank Sweeney (ed.), *Hanging crimes* (Dublin, 2005), pp 134–67.
33   NAI, CRF/1863/Ward/5. The serjeants had the right to appear for the Crown in every criminal prosecution on their circuits (A.R. Hart, *A history of the king's serjeants at law in Ireland: honour rather than advantage?* (Dublin, 2000), p. 119).
34   NAI, CRF/1858/Lydane/15.

What was a barrister paid for representing a prisoner in a capital case? John Holden's father-in-law was reported to have sold the tenant-right of his farm to pay his son-in-law's counsel, Isaac Butt.[35] After the trial of James Kirk and Patrick McCooey in Dundalk in 1852, where the attorney general, Napier, appeared for the Crown, the prisoners' counsel, William McMechan, and their attorney, Joseph Dickie, were paid 9 guineas each by the government.[36] In a murder case at Kilkenny summer assizes in 1852 an attorney was paid a much smaller amount ('Mr Kemmis the crown solicitor has been instructed to pay you the sum of £3. 6s. 1d. for your fee &c for defending W[illia]m Brophy charged with murder at last Kilkenny assizes')[37]. McMechan and the two attorneys did better than an attorney and barrister in the west riding of Yorkshire, where two items in an account were 'to attorney, for examining witnesses, taking instructions for brief, drawing same, and copy for counsel, and for attending the court £1. 6s. 8d.', and 'to counsel and clerk in each case £1. 3s. 6d.'[38] McMechan would have needed a large number of capital cases to have made him a high-flyer at the bar.[39]

Attorneys did most of their work before the assizes. They appeared before the coroners and the magistrates, they prepared the brief, and they chose the prisoner's counsel. Counsel and prisoners did not usually meet face-to-face. After the Cormack brothers were hanged at Nenagh in 1858, it was said that they had confessed to their attorney and counsel. Their attorney denied that they had confessed, and stated that their counsel, Charles Rolleston, 'had not any personal communication with them, and therefore, could not well have received any such confession.'[40] They ordered things differently in France. Emile Chédieu told the royal commission on capital punishment that French advocates saw their clients

35   *Tyrone Constitution*, 31 Aug. 1860.
36   NAI, CSO LB 41, the earl of Clarendon's country letters no. 5 (2 Jan. 52 to 23 Dec. 53), p. 87. McMechan's fee was generous compared with fees received thirty years before. According to Sir Anthony Hart, who has studied Thomas Lefroy's fee books, 'even at the height of his success in 1829, almost all the fees are for amounts of less than 5 guineas, and are rarely more than 10 guineas. As his income in that year, from the beginning of Hilary term to the end of the year, was £2,928, it is evident that he dealt with an enormous volume of work' (Hart, op. cit., p. 192).
37   NAI, CSO LB 41, the earl of Clarendon's country letters no. 5 (2 Jan. 1852 to 23 Dec. 1853), p. 97.
38   *A 'return of the rates of allowance for prosecutors' and witnesses' expenses, and for attorney and counsel, as settled in each county, under the act 7 Geo. 4, c. 64 …'; … 'return from each clerk of assize, and clerk of the peace, of the whole number of prosecutions for felonies, and misdemeanors specified in the act 7 Geo. 4, c. 64, s. 23, in each county in England and Wales …'*, p. 25, HC 1845 (390), xli, 435.
39   In the early 1870s that there were 'not three men' earning £3000 a year at the bar, but there were 'a fair number earning from £1000 to £2000 a year' (*Report of the commissioners appointed by the lords commissioners of Her Majesty's Treasury to enquire into the condition of the civil service in Ireland on the Local Government Board, General Register Office, and general report: together with the minutes of evidence and appendices*, p. 40 [C 789], HC 1873, xxii, 40).
40   Larcom Papers (NLI, MS 7636 [*Post*, 9 Sept. 1858]).

'with the greatest liberty', which he thought was a good thing 'because if we see a man several times we know all his life and feelings, he is no more an indifferent being to us, and in fact we become devoted to that poor man, thinking that he may be innocent, or if not that he may be repentant.'[41] There is, however, an anecdote of a meeting between an Irish prisoner and his counsel that suggests that sympathy did not always develop. A barrister who was assigned to defend a prisoner charged with murder visited his client to read out the speech he proposed to deliver to the jury. The meeting was not a happy one; 'the declamation of the first few pages was somewhat mournfully listened to, but the orator was cheered by some semblance of interest on the part of the person concerned who eventually interrupted by asking, "Could you tell me, Mister Mac, is hanging a painful death?"'[42]

Barristers' insulation from prisoners probably enabled them to expatiate more disinterestedly on their clients' innocence. The division of the legal profession into barristers and attorneys also meant that those who played the public part in either prosecuting or defending were, to some extent, sheltered from local animosity because most of them lived in Dublin. Not all barristers, however, lived in Dublin or the bigger towns. Samuel Yates Johnstone, who was junior crown counsel at the Enniskillen assizes in 1860, for example, lived at Snowhill, about five miles from Enniskillen.[43] Charles O'Malley, who was Edward Walsh's counsel at Castlebar assizes in 1873, lived at Kilboyne, near Castlebar.[44] The separation of attorneys and barristers also protected the latter from embarrassment. Alexander Sullivan described an embarrassing moment. A prisoner, who was certain to be hanged if found guilty, asked his solicitor, Daniel Comyn, 'a very unpleasant question. "Do you think, Dr Comyn," he had said, "that if I am convicted of this I'd get a very long term?" "I don't think so," replied Dan; "no, I don't think so."'[45] Comyn's answer was not only diplomatic but true: about three weeks would have elapsed between his client's sentence and execution.

In the 1830s and 1840s attorneys examined and cross-examined witnesses even at the assizes. Thomas Lefroy reported a case that showed their right to do so was being challenged:

> At the spring assizes for the county of Cork, in the year 1844, a prisoner was indicted for felony, and tried before Chief Baron Brady. The prisoner had no counsel, but was defended by an attorney, who cross-examined the witnesses produced for the prosecution, and at the close of the case for the Crown, claimed the right of addressing the jury on behalf of the prisoner

41 *Report of the capital punishment commission, together with the minutes of evidence, and appendix*, p. 408 [3590], HC 1866, xxi, 460.
42 Sullivan, *Old Ireland*, p. 100.
43 Larcom Papers (NLI, MS 7620 [*Express*, 14 Mar. 1860]).
44 NAI, CRF/1873/Walsh/11 (see Brief on behalf of the Crown, p. 15).
45 Sullivan, *Last serjeant*, p. 101.

... The prisoner's counsel referred to the terms of the 6 & 7 Will. 4, c. 114, s. 1 [the Prisoners' Counsel Act 1836] and contended that as by the practice of the assize courts at the time of the statute being passed, attorneys acted as fully in the defence of prisoners in cases of felony as counsel could do, viz. by the examination and cross-examination of witnesses; and as the statute was passed for the benefit of persons accused, if attorneys were allowed to conduct a prisoner's defence at all, their power should not be abridged, nor the prisoner deprived of the benefit intended to be conferred by that statute.[46]

The chief baron decided 'he would not in that case deprive the prisoner of the benefit thus claimed for him, but reserved the question for the consideration of the twelve judges. And the judges having met in the following Easter term, were unanimously of opinion that the attorney for the prisoner might properly be permitted to examine and cross-examine the witnesses produced on the trial, but ought not be permitted to address the jury.' The attorney at Cork assizes had had ostensibly a good case because the title of the prisoners' counsel act referred to 'defence by counsel or attorney', but section 1 of the act limited attorneys 'to courts where attornies practise as counsel.'[47] The judges' decision did not end the practice of solicitors representing prisoners at the assizes, as the incident referred to above at Enniskillen assizes in 1849 shows.[48] If the practice survived into the 1850s and 1860s, it survived without attracting much attention. There were no references, for example, to solicitors acting as advocates in the Convict Reference Files.[49]

Prisoners' counsel were supposed to do 'every thing professional' for their clients, even if they thought they were guilty.[50] Perrin, for example, said that even if the prisoner's attorney told him his client was guilty, he would use his 'best exertions', which included taking advantage of all technical objections to the Crown's case. Perrin also said he would do all of this, even if he 'had been a crown counsel retained for the prisoner.'[51] Prisoners' counsel had three weapons to defend their clients: they could make a speech (two speeches after the Criminal Procedure Act 1865),[52] they could cross-examine the Crown's witnesses, and they could call witnesses to contradict the Crown's case. They could also object to the

46   Thomas Lefroy, *An analysis of the criminal law of Ireland, giving in alphabetical order all indictable offences, with their respective punishments and the statutes relating thereto, together with explanatory observations and notes; also an appendix of forms for the use of magistrates* (Dublin 1849), pp xli–xlii. The solicitors' limited right to participate was noticed by Trollope (*The MacDermots of Ballycloran*, ed. Robert Tracy (Oxford, 1989), p. 510).

47   6 & 7 Will., c. 114 (20 Aug. 1836).

48   Above, p. 218.

49   Below, pp 248–9.

50   *Minutes of evidence taken before the select committee of the house of lords appointed to enquire into the state of Ireland, ... pt III, evidence 12 June to 19 July*, p. 1061, HC 1839 (486–III), xii, 197.

51   Ibid., p. 1063.

52   28 & 29 Vict., c. 18, s. 2 (9 May 1865).

reception of inadmissible evidence, and raise points of law. The speech, the cross-examination, and the calling of witnesses, however, were the most common and the most important weapons. If counsel could cast doubts on the sufficiency of the Crown's case or weaken it by calling witnesses to contradict it, they might secure an acquittal. Another possibility was to attempt to show that the crime committed did not amount to murder but to manslaughter, or to justifiable or excusable homicide. If they tried to do this, however, the onus of proof was on them because the law presumed any killing to be murder 'until the contrary appears', and the Crown was not 'bound to prove malice, or facts or circumstances, besides the homicide, from which the jury may presume it; and it is for the defendant to give in evidence such facts and circumstances as may prove the homicide to be justifiable, or excusable, or that at most it amounted to but manslaughter.'[53]

The onus of proof was also on the prisoner if the defence were provocation or insanity. The former could reduce murder to manslaughter, although 'no provocation whatever can render homicide justifiable, or even excusable.'[54] Insanity when proved led to an acquittal but in that event the court ordered the prisoner to be detained at the discretion of the lord lieutenant. In infanticide cases the prisoner was in a slightly stronger position. First, the jury could find women guilty of concealing the birth, which was not a capital offence. Secondly, the prosecution had to prove that the child had been born alive, which was not easy.[55] The results of the strategies that could be adopted by prisoners and their counsel are to some extent revealed by the figures on verdicts discussed below.[56]

The rule that the onus of proof was on a prisoner charged with manslaughter was challenged in 1872 in *Cavendish*, a case where the driver of a cab 'went over the deceased as she was crossing the street, and inflicted such injuries on her that she died in three days.'[57] When Baron Fitzgerald charged the jury, he told them

> in order to convict the defendant they should be satisfied that the death of the deceased was caused by the act of the defendant; and that, if they were satisfied of that, it lay upon the defendant to show, either by independent evidence, or from the facts as proved on the part of the prosecution, that he was excused; that the act of driving a cab in the street was a lawful one, and that he would be excused if that act was done with due care and caution on his part; that they need not trouble themselves with any particular consideration of the party on whom the burden of proof lay; that the real question was, whether, on all the facts, due and proper caution was exercised by the defendant or not.

53   Above, p. 12.   54   Above, pp 14, 20–1.
55   Above, pp 15–16.   56   Below, pp 279–82.
57   *Cavendish* (1873) IR 8 CL 178, at p. 179 (I am indebted to Desmond Greer for drawing my attention to this case).

The prisoner's counsel, John Adye Curran, in a requisition, 'objected to the latter part of the direction, and called on the judge to tell the jury that unless they were satisfied beyond reasonable doubt that there was a want of due and proper caution on the part of the prisoner, they ought to acquit him.' Fitzgerald refused Curran's application, but reserved the case.

The Court for Crown Cases Reserved, with the exception of James O'Brien, affirmed the conviction. O'Brien's dissent was long and detailed, but among other things he argued that 'in the present case, from the directions given to the jury upon the question of the prisoner having exercised due care and caution, it was to be implied that they need not consider upon what party the burden of proof lay.'[58] The opinion of the majority was expressed by Dowse who said that 'if the prisoner had been indicted for murder, to reduce the offence to homicide by misadventure, the prisoner would be bound to prove, either by his own witnesses, or from the case of the Crown, that he was engaged in a lawful act when the homicide took place, and that there was no want of due and proper care to be attributed to him, the burden of proof would rest on him, and his counsel would not be entitled to make such a requisition as he has made in this case.'[59] Dowse was emphatic in his assertion of the similarity of murder and manslaughter: 'it would certainly be an anomalous state of the law that if a man is indicted only for the less offence – manslaughter – the burden of proof should be shifted, and the whole course of the trial altered, and what is of more importance, the cause of justice defeated; for any one who has experience of criminal courts knows what a weapon this doctrine of the doubt is in the hands of an experienced counsel.'

COUNSEL'S SPEECH

The prisoners' counsel act, which came into force on 1 October 1836, allowed the prisoner's counsel to make a speech after the last prosecution witness had been examined.[60] The act was short, with only five sections, three of which were to have a great effect on the conduct of criminal trials: (1) 'that from and after the first day of October next all persons tried for felonies shall be admitted, after the close of the case for the prosecution, to make full answer and defence thereto, by counsel learned in the law, or by attorney in courts where attornies practice as counsel'; (2) 'that all persons who after the passing of this act shall be held to bail or committed to prison for any offences against the law shall be entitled to require and have, on demand, (from the person who shall have the lawful custody thereof, and who is hereby required to deliver the same,) copies of the examinations of the witnesses respectively upon whose depositions they have been so held to bail or

58   Ibid., p. 189.   59   Ibid., pp 180–1.
60   6 & 7 Will. IV, c. 114 (20 Aug. 1836). For a history of the question see Cairns, op. cit., pp 67–87.
     For the Scottish practice, see Paterson, op. cit., p. 335. Richard Martin, MP for Co. Galway, was
     one of the champions of the right of prisoners' counsel to make a speech.

committed to prison, on payment of a reasonable sum for the same, not exceeding three halfpence for each folio of ninety words'; (3) 'that all persons under trial shall be entitled, at the time of their trial to inspect without fee or reward, all depositions (or copies thereof) which have been taken against them, and returned into the court before such trial shall be had.'

The proposal to allow those charged with felony to have counsel and to be on the same footing as those charged with treason or misdemeanour, or those who were parties in civil cases, had been fiercely opposed on previous occasions when it had been made.[61] When the 1836 bill was debated in the house of lords some of the judges were hostile. Lord Wharncliffe thought it 'would have the effect of increasing that uncertainty upon which professed rogues were accustomed to calculate.'[62] Lord Abinger thought it would have the opposite effect: 'when it was considered that the counsel who defended the prisoners were generally young men not of much experience, the tendency of the bill would, in all probability, be to facilitate convictions.' The bill had, however, eloquent supporters. In the house of commons in 1836, for example, Daniel O'Connell stigmatized the existing law as 'abominable'. 'Nothing,' he said, 'could be more frightfully unjust. In a criminal prosecution the prosecutor's counsel might make two speeches, while the prisoner's counsel was not allowed to say one word.'[63] Outside parliament the arguments in favour of allowing a speech seemed weighty. Sydney Smith expatiated on the prisoner's plight. 'It is a most affecting moment in a court of justice, when the evidence has all been heard, and the judge asks the prisoner what he has to say in his defence,' he wrote. 'The prisoner, who has (by great exertions, perhaps of his friends,) saved up money enough to procure counsel, says to the judge, "that he leaves his defence to his counsel." We have often blushed for English humanity to hear the reply. "Your counsel cannot speak for you, you must speak for yourself."'[64]

Before the act the prisoner's counsel had been able to cross-examine witnesses. At William Kilfoyle's trial in 1832, for example, the crown counsel made the opening speech, the Crown's witnesses gave their evidence, the prisoner's witnesses gave their evidence, and the judge charged the jury.[65] Prisoners could make speeches before 1836, but they were not made on oath, and the judge could comment on them, favourably or unfavourably. Under the Prisoners' Counsel Act, 'the question immediately arose as to whether the prisoner's right to address the jury had survived.'[66] The English judges decided that a prisoner who had counsel

---

61 John Hostettler, *The politics of criminal law reform in the nineteenth century* (Chichester, 1992), pp 45–6.
62 *Hansard 3*, xxxv, 172, 182 (14 July 1836).
63 Ibid., xxx, 497 (17 Feb. 1836).
64 Sydney Smyth, *The works of the Rev. Sydney Smith*, 4 vols (London, 1839–40), ii, 369.
65 James Mongan, *Report of the trial of William Kilfoyle, upon the charge of killing Mary Mulrooney at Newtownbarry, on the 18th of June, 1831 ...* (Dublin, 1832), passim.
66 Bentley, op. cit., pp 156–7.

could not make a speech. The Irish judges followed, and decided that 'a prisoner charged with felony who is defended by counsel, ought not to be allowed to make a statement in addition to the defence of counsel, unless under very peculiar circumstances.'[67] Hayes described such a circumstance, although it was not one likely to occur at a murder trial: 'where the only persons present at the transaction were the prosecutor and prisoner, the latter was allowed to make a statement before his counsel addressed the jury.'[68] If prisoners conducted their own defence, they could not only address the jury and examine witnesses, they could also have counsel to argue points of law and to suggest questions for cross-examination.[69]

The English judges in *Beard* in 1837 decided the prisoner's counsel could not tell the prisoner's story.[70] The Irish judges again followed them, and Hayes was able to write in 1842 that 'counsel for the prisoner, in addressing the jury, ought not to make a statement of facts which he is not in a position to prove.'[71] In 1879 Lord Chief Justice Cockburn in *R. v. Weston*[72] ruled that the 'the prisoner's counsel were in place of the prisoner, and entitled to say anything which he might say', a decision, which, according to Bentley, 'represented a repudiation of *Beard*, which had, for nearly forty years, been regarded as settling the point.'[73] On 26 November 1881 the English judges passed a resolution that tried to resolve the growing differences among themselves that Cockburn's decision had caused:

> that in the opinion of the judges it is contrary to the administration and practice of the criminal law as hitherto allowed, that counsel for prisoners should state to the jury as alleged existing facts matters which they have been told in their instructions, on the authority of the prisoner, but which they do not propose to prove in evidence.[74]

67 Purcell, op. cit., p. 192. The author has not come across an Irish case where the prisoner addressed the jury. See Bentley, op. cit., pp 178–82 for cases after 1880 where English judges allowed prisoners to make speeches.

68 Edmund Hayes, *Crimes and punishments, or a digest of the criminal statute law of Ireland, alphabetically arranged, with ample notes, in which are discussed the powers and authorities of the several courts of criminal jurisdiction in Ireland; the duties, responsibilities, and privileges of magistrates, coroners, constables, and other officers, in bringing criminals to justice, and also the practice of the courts in punishing offences upon indictment*, 2 vols (2nd ed., Dublin, 1842), ii, 878.

69 Ibid. and John G. Thompson, *The law of criminal procedure in Ireland* (Dublin, 1899), p. 88.

70 *R. v. Beard* (1837) 8 C & P 142, 173 Eng Rep 434. In *Beard* Coleridge said he could 'not permit a prisoner's counsel to tell the jury anything which he is not in a situation to prove. If the prisoner does not employ counsel, he is at liberty to make a statement for himself and tell his own story; which is to have such weight with the jury, as all circumstances considered it is entitled to; but if he employs counsel, he must submit to the rules which have been established with respect to the conducting of cases by counsel' (ibid., p. 434). See also Bentley, op. cit., pp 157–8 and Cairns, op. cit., p. 118.

71 Hayes, op. cit., ii, 877.   72 *R. v. Weston* (1879) 14 Cox 346, at p. 350.

73 Bentley, op. cit., p. 176.

74 *Archbold's pleading and evidence in criminal cases; with statutes, precedents of indictments, &c., and the evidence necessary to support them by John Jervis* (20th ed. by William Bruce, London, 1886), p. 180.

This did not settle the question in England,[75] nor did it settle it in Ireland. J.G. Thompson, writing about Ireland at the end of the 1890s, for example, noted that 'there have been conflicting decisions as to whether the prisoner's counsel may state to the jury alleged facts which he has learned from the prisoner, but which he is not in a position to prove.'[76] He noted that the English judges had passed the resolution quoted above 'in consequence of the unsettled state of practice on the subject'.

There were ways, however, in which counsel could tell the prisoner's story: they could insinuate it into their cross-examination of the Crown's witnesses, and they could state it as a hypothesis in their speech. If the prisoner had told his story to the magistrate or to the police it could be repeated in court. At Laurence Smith's trial at the Cavan assizes in 1873 for the murder of a neighbour, Patrick Lynch, Sub-Inspector Ware, who arrested Smith, repeated what Smith had said after he was cautioned: 'I do not consider myself an assassin. What I did, I did in my own defence. I look upon myself as a soldier defending myself.'[77] Smith's counsel, William Irvine, in his speech to the jury relied on self-defence.

After a long campaign parliament passed the Criminal Evidence Act 1898, which allowed those charged with criminal offences and their husbands and wives to give evidence.[78] The act did not apply to Ireland, having been staunchly opposed by Irish MPs.[79] The 1898 act tried to strike a balance between allowing defendants to give evidence and forcing them to incriminate themselves. Those on trial could not be compelled to give evidence, and 'the failure of any person charged with an offence, or of the wife or husband, as the case may be, of the person so charged, to give evidence, shall not be made the subject of any comment by the prosecution.'[80] If a prisoner did give evidence, he could be cross-examined, although he could 'not be required to answer, any question tending to show that he has committed or been convicted of or been charged with any offence other than that wherewith he is then charged, or is of bad character.'[81] There were three exceptions to this prohibition: (1) 'the proof that he has committed or been convicted of such other offence is admissible evidence to show that he is guilty of the offence wherewith he is then charged'; (2) 'he has personally or by his advocate asked questions of the witnesses for the prosecution with a view to establish his own good character, or has given evidence of his good character, or

75 Bentley, op. cit., p. 177.
76 Thompson, op. cit., p. 88.
77 NAI, CRF/1873/Smith/18.
78 61 & 62 Vict., c. 36, s. 1 (12 Aug. 1898). For an editorial that condemned allowing prisoners to give evidence on their own behalf as 'a most illusory choice offered to the accused', see *ILT & SJ*, 31 (17 July 1897), pp 327–8. (I am indebted to Desmond Greer for this reference). For a history of the subject see C.J.W. Allen, *The law of evidence in Victorian England* (Cambridge, 1997), pp 123–7.
79 Claire Jackson, 'Irish political opposition to the passage of criminal evidence reform at Westminster, 1883–98' in McEldowney & O'Higgins (eds), *The common law tradition* (1990), pp 185–201.
80 61 & 62 Vict., c. 36, s. 1(b) (12 Aug. 1898).
81 Ibid., s. 1(f).

the nature or conduct of the defence is such as to involve imputations on the character of the prosecutor or the witnesses for the prosecution'; (3) 'he has given evidence against any other person charged with the offence.' Similar legislation was not introduced into Ireland until 1923 and 1924.[82] The Northern Ireland act and the Free State act followed the 1898 act closely, making the same arrangements to protect the prisoner's character and allowing the three exceptions mentioned above.

In the debate on the prisoners' counsel bill Lord Abinger had predicted that 'where the prisoner's guilt is clearly proved, no counsel of the least discretion would think of addressing the jury to assert his innocence.'[83] Abinger was wrong. Counsel evinced an enthusiasm for making long speeches even in the most hopeless cases. William McMechan, for example, at Daniel Ward's trial, began his speech just before ten o'clock and ended just before two o'clock.[84] At Matthew Phibbs' first trial Frederick Sidney 'concluded an able and eloquent address of three and a half hours' duration by calling for an immediate acquittal.'[85] In 1856 Charles Sprengal Greaves proposed a change that suggested Abinger's distaste for oratory still persisted: the prisoner's counsel should be given 'the option of waiving his right to address the jury on the close of the case for the prosecution, and of making one general address at the close of the evidence he adduced.'[86] This seemed to favour the prisoner, for a speech at that point would have made more of an impression than one delivered earlier. Greaves' intention, however, was to get rid of the speech altogether. 'It sometimes happens,' he wrote, 'that the witnesses for the defence so completely break down, that no counsel would endeavour to support the case they came to prove.'

'The counsel for the prisoner may use arguments which he does not believe to be just,' Stephen wrote.[87] Counsel's freedom was considerable. In 1855 the Court of Queen's Bench heard that in *Kiernan v. Aylmer* at Kilkenny, Serjeant Armstrong, who represented Aylmer, imputed to Francis Kiernan, the plaintiff, 'deliberate and infamous perjury', and 'unscrupulous, corrupt, shabby and sharp practice'.[88] Kiernan, who was a solicitor, called Armstrong 'a mercenary coward' and a 'hireling bully', and challenged him to a duel.[89] Armstrong applied to the Queen's Bench for leave to file a criminal information. The judges were sure there

82 Criminal Evidence Act (NI) 1923 (13 & 14 Geo. 5, c. 9 (10 May 1923)); Criminal Justice (Evidence) Act 1924 (No. 37 of 1924).
83 *Hansard 3*, xxxv, 183 (14 July 1836).
84 NAI, CRF/1863/Ward/5.
85 Larcom Papers (NLI, MS 7620 [*Packet*, 11 Mar. 1861]).
86 *A report on criminal procedure to the lord chancellor; by Charles Sprengal Greaves, Esq., one of her majesty's counsel*, p. 35 [456], HC 1856, l, 113.
87 James Fitzjames Stephen, *A general view of the criminal law of England* (London and Cambridge, 1863), p. 168.
88 *Armstrong v. Kiernan* (1855) 7 Cox CC 6, at p. 8. See Cairns, op. cit., pp 126–62 for a discussion of counsel's 'latitude'.
89 7 Cox CC 6, at pp 7, 10.

was a rhetorical line that should not have been crossed, but were not sure where it was. Crampton became lyrical: 'Human nature is frail; there are securities, however, against abuse. Self-respect, considerations of duty, feelings as a gentleman, a barrister, and a Christian, the interference of the presiding judge, even the personal interest of the advocate, are better safeguards than statutes or the interference of criminal courts.'

So well established was the tradition that the prisoner's counsel could resort to any stratagem, that their self-restraint was noted. C.P. Crane, for example, noted the reticence of the prisoner's counsel when they examined Mary Murphy, the daughter of a murdered tenant: 'I at length got this girl into a convent in England. She was sent off at night, under an assumed name known only to the Reverend Mother and a few, and in that convent she remained during the preliminary stages of the inquiry, emerging to give her evidence at the assizes in Cork. The counsel for the defence, to their honour, refrained from asking the name of the convent in court.'[90]

Prisoner's counsel used certain well-worn rhetorical devices. They were there 'to assist' (they had, as it were, dropped in casually, and in a friendly move were offering their services to all concerned). They praised the jury, they impugned circumstantial evidence, and they expatiated on the prisoner's enforced silence. At James Doherty's trial at the Connacht winter assizes in 1902, for example, his counsel pointed to the prisoner's silence: 'they had an old man behind the prison bars, dumb, his lips sealed by the law, and only able to speak through him, his counsel.'[91] Counsel did not scruple to invoke the hangman and to warn the jury that theirs was an awesome responsibility. After Joseph Kelly's trial at Wexford assizes in 1863, the judge, Henry Hughes, noted that: 'The prisoner's counsel appeared to think (according to the fact as I was afterwards informed) that two of the jury had expressed strong opinions against the propriety of capital punishments, & Mr Hemphill pressed this topic, to the utmost limit, upon the feelings of the jury. I was obliged to counteract this; and I made observations to the jury on their duties, and their obligation to find their verdict on the evidence, irrespective of the consequences.'[92] It is tempting to dismiss defence speeches as so hackneyed that they could have been reduced to a system of semaphore, but at the very least they raised doubts in the jury's minds that might not have been raised by a mere recital of the evidence. They also counteracted the Crown's opening speech, where a blow-by-blow account of what had happened may have created the impression that the Crown's case was irrefutable.[93]

90   C.P. Crane, *Memories of a resident magistrate 1880–1920* (Edinburgh, 1938), pp 107–8.
91   NAI, CRF/1902/Doherty/69.
92   Ibid., CRF/1863/Kelly/15.
93   Prisoners' counsel rarely matched Charles Phillips' eloquence at Galway Lent assizes 1817 in *Blake v. Wilkins*. Mrs Wilkins was sued for breach of promise by a man much younger than herself. Phillips, who was one of her counsel, tried to show that it was unlikely that a promise of marriage had ever been made by Mrs Wilkins, or if made, had been accepted. Was it likely,

When Sam Gray was tried at Monaghan spring assizes in 1841 for the murder of Owen Murphy, the case against him was strong: he had been seen at the scene by two witnesses; he had a motive, he had been seen 'with the butt-end of a pistol peering out of his pocket', and he had taken to his bed at an odd time of the day. His counsel, George Tombe, drew sparingly on the armoury of rhetorical devices, which was probably a sign of his skill: 'he would endeavour to assist them', and 'he would address himself to their reason and dispassionate understandings', but he did not point to the prisoner's silence, he did not invoke the hangman, and he did not impugn circumstantial evidence – the case was strongly based on direct evidence, which was probably, but not necessarily, an obstacle to that argument.[94] He allowed himself a small deviation, however: he denied that Gray was likely to commit such a murder. 'Had his worst enemy ever heard of his being charged with a crime like that until the present transaction?' he asked. 'Was he the man likely to commit a murder such as had been perpetrated on the unfortunate Owen Murphy?' In 1824 Sam and Henry Gray had been tried for the murder of Bernard McMahon. The jury had acquitted them after two minutes' deliberation.[95]

Tombe had three reasons for his self-restraint: first, three witnesses saw Gray in his house at the time when they heard the shots; secondly, there was a plausible alternative culprit because two witnesses saw another man, Charley Wylie, coming along the road after the shots were fired; thirdly, Tombe was determined to do something that he should not have done. 'He would produce,' he said, 'the testimony of a Presbyterian clergyman to whom a man, who died since the murder was committed, confessed that it was he who shot Owen Murphy.' The repentant sinner was Charley Wylie, which was not surprising. One of the easier rules of evidence to understand was the one that admitted the dying declarations only of those who had actually been attacked.[96] The judge, Robert Torrens, mildly interrupted Tombe (he 'begged leave to interrupt him, but such a declaration could not be received in evidence, either for or against the prisoner, or that of any man who had not been himself wounded, and was dying of such wounds').

The Torrens' interruption was mild, given that Tombe had just done something that would have embarrassed a tyro.[97] Whatever Tombe was, he was

---

Phillips asked the jury, that the plaintiff, 'for the gratification of his avarice … was contented to embrace age, disease, infirmity, and widowhood, to bend his youthful passions to the carcass for which the grave was opening, to feed, by anticipation, on the uncold corpse, and cheat the worm of its reversionary corruption.' The jury found for Mrs Wilkins, but she was not grateful to Phillips: 'hardly had he emerged in the street when Mrs Wilkins rushed at him, and struck him violently with a horse-whip on the face and shoulders' (Oliver J. Bourke, *Anecdotes of the Connaught circuit: from its foundation to close upon the present time* (Dublin, 1885), pp 201–2).

94　*Impartial Reporter*, 25 Mar. 1841.
95　D.S. Johnson, 'The trials of Sam Gray: Monaghan politics and nineteenth century Irish criminal procedure' in *Ir Jur*, n.s., 20 (1985), 110.
96　Above, pp 186–7.
97　The first English case 'in which a new strict rule was applied' (that dying declarations were admissible only in homicide cases) had been in 1820 (Bentley, op. cit., p. 215). In Scotland the

not a tyro: he had been called to the bar in 1822. Tombe took his rebuke with equanimity ('he would not press the court') and brought his speech, which had lasted for almost two hours, to a conclusion. When the prisoner's witnesses had been examined, Tombe again dragged in the minister: 'The evidence of the Rev. Mr McDowell, the Presbyterian minister alluded to by Mr Tombe, was then tendered to prove the dying declaration of Charles Wylie, but the court held it to be inadmissible, and the case for the defence closed.' (The minister seems to have been the Revd Martin McDowell, the minister of Crieve.) Tombe risked a scalding reprimand when he dragged in Wylie's dying declaration for the second time, but he had succeeded in twice drawing the jury's attention to it. The Revd Martin McDowell's evidence was probably more powerful when hinted at than it would have been if it had actually been given in court. Tombe was successful, Gray was acquitted, and 'this announcement was received with cheering by the friends of the accused'. If Gray had been found guilty, he would have been hanged on 1 May 1841 with Mary Ann McConkey, who was sentenced to death at the same assizes for poisoning her husband. His acquittal spared the whig lord lieutenant, Viscount Ebrington, the duty of consigning a well-known Orangeman to the gallows.[98]

After the 1836 act the English judges decided that the speech of the prisoner's counsel would be the last word, but only if he did not call witnesses, or if he did not cross-examine on discrepancies between what a prosecution witness said in court and what he had said in his deposition. If prisoner's counsel did either of these things, the prosecutor's counsel had the right to make a second speech after the prisoner's witnesses had been examined, which gave the prosecution the last word.[99] If the attorney general conducted the case, however, he always had the last word, regardless of whether the prisoner had called witnesses or cross-examined on the depositions.[100] Since murder cases in Ireland were conducted by counsel representing the attorney general, the prosecution always had the right to make a second speech, which would be the final speech, even if the prisoner did not call witnesses or cross-examine on the depositions. The Criminal Procedure Act 1865 gave the prisoner's counsel the right to make a second speech after he had

---

dying declaration of any witness, even if he were not the person injured and even if his declaration had not been made in the prisoner's absence, was admissible, but it had to be made on oath before a magistrate or the procurator fiscal. It was not necessary that the witness should 'believe himself to be dying' (William Gillespie Dickson, *A treatise of the law of evidence in Scotland*, 2 vols (2nd ed. by John Skelton, Edinburgh, 1864), ii, 1138–9). Dickson admitted that magisterial questioning 'must often be a poor substitute for a cross-examination on behalf of the prisoner, by which the accuracy of the witness may be tested, and exculpatory circumstances brought to light.' Dickson also noted that 'the prisoner may, by the same means, provide against loss of exculpatory evidence'.

98 For the tory government's efforts to convict him after this remarkable acquittal see above, p. 146.

99 See Cairns, op. cit., pp 117, 182–3. For the Scottish practice, which allowed the prisoner's counsel the last word, see Paterson, op. cit., p. 335.

100 Hayes, op. cit., ii, 879.

examined his witnesses, but before the Crown's concluding speech, which still left the Crown the last word.[101] At Stephen McKeown's trial at Armagh summer assizes 1876, for example, J. Favière Elrington made the opening speech for the Crown; when the Crown's witnesses had been examined and cross-examined, Walter Boyd made a speech for the prisoner; when the prisoner's witnesses had been examined and cross-examined, Boyd made a second speech, and Andrew Porter QC replied on behalf of the Crown.[102]

CROSS-EXAMINATION

Although cross-examination of the Crown's witnesses was probably the most important part of the prisoner's defence, the very first thing that counsel usually did for the prisoner was to object to portions of the Crown's evidence. At the first of the Phoenix Park murder trials the solicitor general got no further with his first witness, Robert Farrell, than eliciting the fact that he was a labouring man, when he was interrupted by Thomas Webb, Joseph Brady's counsel, and during the next page and a half of Farrell's examination-in-chief, Webb made no fewer than eight objections to Farrell's evidence.[103] The practice of eliciting evidence by questions enabled the prisoners' counsel, if they were on the *qui vive*, to object to inadmissible evidence before the witness could answer, which created the pleasing impression that the Crown was not going to be allowed to throw dust into the jury's eyes. The reasons for objecting, however, were often too technical to be obvious to the jury. Courtney Stanhope Kenny warned that 'every objection is apt to prejudice the jury, who are always inclined to resent any technicality which "closes the avenues to truth".'[104] What Kenny said applied to England. It is arguable if it applied to Ireland. It is highly unlikely that an experienced barrister such as Thomas Webb would have pursued a course of action that was likely to antagonize a jury. This quotation from Kenny, however, points to a fact that is easily forgotten: in nineteenth-century courts arguments about the admissibility of evidence, including confessions, were made in the jury's presence. The admissibility of particular witnesses or pieces of evidence depended on the judge. According to Huband, 'the acquiescence of a prisoner upon his trial for felony, even when he is defended by counsel, will not excuse irregularity in taking the evidence of the Crown witnesses.'[105] If the judge admitted evidence that should

101   28 & 29 Vict., c. 18, s. 2 (9 May 1865).

102   NAI, CRF/1876/McKeown/22.

103   *Report of the trials at the Dublin Commission Court, April and May, 1883, of the prisoners charged with the Phoenix Park murder, the attempt to murder Mr Field, and the conspiracy to murder; before the Hon. Mr Justice O'Brien; reported by W.C. Johnston* (Dublin, 1883), pp 18–19.

104   Courtney Stanhope Kenny, *Outlines of criminal law, based on lectures delivered in the University of Cambridge* (Cambridge, 1902), p. 342.

105   William G. Huband, *A practical treatise on the law relating to the grand jury in criminal cases the coroner's jury and the petty jury in Ireland* (Dublin, 1896), p. 697 (citing *Bertrand* (1867) 10 Cox CC 618).

not have been admitted, the prisoner's counsel could ask for the question to be sent to the Court for Crown Cases Reserved.

Effective cross-examination ideally began with the Crown's first witness. 'If the witnesses for the prosecution are not challenged the verdict is almost irrevocably arrived at within a few minutes of the opening of the case,' Alexander Sullivan wrote.[106] If counsel did not cross-examine on a certain point, his omission 'admits the accuracy of the evidence.'[107] The cross-examining counsel's peculiar weapon was the leading question, which either suggested the answer the cross-examiner wanted or which could be answered only 'yes' or 'no'.[108] It was difficult for counsel to cross-examine without creating an atmosphere of disparagement, and even raillery.[109] Thomas Webb lost no time when he began to cross-examine James Carey at the first of the Phoenix Park murder trials.

> Carey, are you a man that makes any profession of religion? – No, not a profession of it.
>
> What is the point you make by emphasizing profession. – I leave that to you.
>
> Pray, sir, don't attempt to bandy words or chop logic with me. I ask you that question, do you make any profession of religion? – I am a professed Roman Catholic.[110]

106 Sullivan, *Last serjeant*, p. 124. For a fictional example of cross-examination, see Trollope, *The MacDermots of Ballycloran*, pp 517–20. For Sir Robert Morton's cross-examination of Ronnie Winslow and his revelation of how his cross-examination elicited the truth, see Terence Rattigan, *The Winslow boy* (London, 1946), pp 55–63, 73. Two cross-examinations by Irish barristers became famous: Charles Russell's cross-examination of Richard Pigott before *The Times* special commission in February 1889, and Sir Edward Carson's of the postmistress in the Archer-Shee case in 1910. According to the *DNB*, Carson devoted ten days to George Archer-Shee's case for a nominal fee. His conduct of the case 'vindicated the honour of a young Osborne cadet against all the forces of the Crown and its law officers.'

107 Stephen, *General view*, p. 281. Stephen had less confidence in cross-examination than Sullivan: 'A cool, steady liar who happens not to be open to contradiction will baffle the most skilful cross-examiner in the absence of accidents, which are not so common in practice as persons who take their notions on the subject from anecdotes or fiction would suppose' (Stephen, *The Indian evidence act (I. of 1872), with an introduction on the principles of judicial evidence* (Calcutta, Bombay, and London, 1872), p. 41).

108 Purcell, op. cit., pp 196–7; Sir William Oldnall Russell, *A treatise on crimes and misdemeanors*, 3 vols (4th ed. by Charles Sprengel Greaves, London, 1865), iii, 522; Bentley, op. cit., p. 140.

109 Alexander Sullivan recalled that in his youth 'there were three counsel who attained great eminence and held high office who used to hold themselves out in competition of readiness to make any suggestion their client would like to the disparagement of his opponent in cross-examination, and they did a large trade in purchased defamation' (Sullivan, *Last serjeant*, p. 121). It takes only a superficial knowledge of the nineteenth-century bar to suspect that Serjeant Armstrong was one of the three. For a specimen of what Armstrong's clients could buy see above, p. 228.

110 *Report of the trials at the Dublin Commission Court, April and May, 1883, of the prisoners charged with the Phoenix Park murder, the attempt to murder Mr Field, and the conspiracy to murder; before the Hon. Mr Justice O'Brien; reported by W.C. Johnston* (Dublin, 1883), p. 37.

Cross-examination was more discursive than examination-in-chief. The cross-examiner could test witness' memory, he could ask how they acquired their knowledge, why they had formed their opinions; he could ask them to describe their relations with the prisoner, to describe what they had heard, read, or written about the case; he could ask them about their character, motives, and prejudices; he could make them explain why they had said different things on different occasions and why they had not mentioned important facts at an earlier stage of the investigation.[111] There was a limit to the range of cross-examination. A witness could not be asked about matter 'irrelevant to the matter in issue, unless calculated to elicit his title to credit', nor could he be asked about 'a distinct collateral fact, irrelevant to the matter in issue, for the purpose of afterwards impeaching his testimony by calling other witnesses to contradict him.'[112]

The power to ask questions that impugned a witness' 'title to credit', a procedure known as 'examining as to credit', gave the cross-examiner many opportunities.[113] The questions were supposed to be confined to witness' 'credit' ('questions which, although they may disgrace the witness, yet do not at all affect his credit, ought not be asked, inasmuch as such questions are clearly impertinent, since they do not lead to this end').[114] Purcell also noted that it was not clear 'whether the inquiry into the general character of a witness shall be restricted to his reputation for veracity, or may be made in general terms, involving his entire moral character and estimation in society, is a point not yet definitely settled.'[115] Sixty years later the subject was no clearer: James O'Connor noted that 'it seems unsettled whether, in such a case, evidence as to the witness' entire moral character can be given.'[116]

The simplest way to discredit witnesses was to ask them about their criminal record. At the trial of three soldiers at Naas assizes in 1859 for the murder of a prostitute, for example, one of the Crown's witnesses, Bridget Kenny, under cross-examination 'admitted having been several times in gaol for stealing.'[117] The right to ask witnesses degrading questions, which was an exception to the collateral evidence rule, mentioned above, went through vicissitudes from the early nineteenth century until 1865 when 'any lingering doubt as to the right to question witnesses as to previous convictions was removed' by the Criminal Procedure Act 1865, section 6, which provided a cheap procedure for proving previous convictions.[118]

---

111 According to Éanna Hickey, 'time and time again in folk narratives, lawyers win cases by establishing confusion in the mind of a witness over small details' (*Irish law and lawyers in modern folk tradition*, p. 80).

112 Purcell, op. cit., p. 199.

113 Ibid.   114 Ibid., p. 348.

115 Ibid., p. 352.

116 *The Irish justice of the peace: a treatise on the powers and duties of justices of the peace in Ireland, and certain matters connected therewith* (Dublin, 1911), p. 269.

117 Larcom Papers (NLI, MS 7620 [*Packet*, 1 Aug. 1859]).

118 28 & 29 Vict., c. 18 (9 May 1865); Bentley, op. cit., p. 143.

Witnesses might be asked about something less definite than a conviction or term in gaol. At Patrick McDermott's trial at Roscommon assizes in 1841, for the murder of James McCormick, one of the Crown's witnesses said that the prisoner asked him to beat up McCormick.[119] When cross-examined the witness admitted that he had been dismissed by his mistress, Mrs Gorman, of Castle Plunket, but denied he had been accused of stealing sheep, and insisted that 'the prisoner's brother never accused me of taking away turkeys.' The case was a mysterious one. The dead man's wife described McDermott's attack on her husband, but she revealed nothing about the cause of the attack: 'I was with him coming from Castlebar from the market; he was driving a pig by a rope and had a piece of frieze under his arm. I was before him and I heard the sound of feet and turned round and saw Pat McDermott striking him with a shaft.' Mrs Gorman, the sheep, and the turkeys apparently had nothing to do with the attack. McDermott was convicted, and sentenced to death, but the sentence was commuted to transportation for life. The fact that witnesses could be questioned about their character, peccadilloes, and crimes was in marked contrast to the protection enjoyed by the prisoner.

Cross-examiners could compare what witnesses said in court with what they had said before the magistrate, which would either expose them as liars or create the impression they were unreliable. John McLoughlin had reached down from a first storey window in Castle Street, Omagh, and caught John McCrossan with a long hook with a demi-barb. At the assizes in 1865, John's brother, Charles, mentioned the prisoner's malevolent smile. The prisoner's counsel asked why had he not mentioned the smile in his deposition? 'I am not certain whether in the deposition I did or did not say anything of the prisoner's smiling,' McCrossan replied. 'I can not say whether it is or is not in the deposition. I have not seen a copy of my deposition since I signed it. I think I did so state at the inquest. I was sworn to tell the whole truth but I had suffered a great deal in the days before.' McCrossan's deposition was read out and the judge noted that 'it contained no statement that he had seen the prisoner smile' The judge underlined this sentence. McCrossan, nevertheless, had got in the smile, had alluded to his grief, and even made his confusion seem genuine.[120]

The prisoners' counsel act allowed prisoners to have copies of depositions made at their committal.[121] The English judges decided in 1837 that when a

---

119 NAI, CRF/1841/McDermott/44. There was a distinction between degrading and incriminating questions. A witness could not be forced to answer the latter, although the judge had the last word on whether he had to answer or not; if he answered, his answer was regarded as 'conclusive' and could not be 'contradicted' (see below, p. 245 for the technical meaning of these words), (Stephen, *General view*, p. 297; Russell, op. cit., iii, 541; Bentley, op. cit., pp 140–3).

120 NAI, CRF/1885/McLoughlin/18. If a witness introduced a fact that was not in his deposition, 'the magistrate's clerk ought to be called to prove the silence of the witness on the subject' (Purcell, op. cit., p. 192).

121 6 & 7 Will., c. 114, s. 3 (20 Aug. 1836).

witness was cross-examined on his deposition, the deposition had to be read out.[122] The Irish judges followed the English judges.[123] Reading out the deposition had disadvantages for the prisoner.[124] It allowed the Crown to present for a third time a piece of evidence that had already been alluded to in the opening speech and in examination-in-chief. It took the edge off cross-examination: the tension was broken, the element of surprise was lost, the witness was given a chance to concoct an explanation. Pigot tried to protect prisoners by allowing only excerpts to be read.[125] The rule was changed by the Criminal Procedure Act 1865, section 5, which provided that 'a witness may be cross-examined as to previous statements made by him in writing or reduced into writing relative to the subject matter of the indictment or proceeding, without such writing being shown to him; but if it is intended to contradict such witness by the writing, his attention must, before such contradictory proof can be given, be called to those parts of the writing which are to be used for the purpose of so contradicting him.'[126]

An even greater disadvantage was that the deposition might contain information that would not have been admitted as evidence in examination-in-chief. Alexander Sullivan remembered the disastrous cross-examination of a witness at the trial of John Twiss, who was tried at the Cork winter assizes in 1895 for the murder of James Donovan, the caretaker of an evicted farm. (The lawyers involved added a touch of distinction to Twiss' trial: the judge was the chief baron, Christopher Palles; the attorney general was The MacDermot (Hugh Hyacinth O'Rorke MacDermot, attorney general, 1892–5, and prince of Coolavin)). According to Sullivan, Mary Lyons' deposition when read out contained two pieces of information that damned Twiss, neither of which would have been admissible in examination-in-chief. (1) She had deposed that Twiss 'came into me twelve years ago for a bit of blackening to put on his face when he went to beat Pat Carver. On one Sunday, I was in from Mass, he came behind me. He had a revolver as big as half a gun. I never saw so big a one before or since. He asked had I seen Pat Carver here today. He is the game-keeper. He is dead.' (2) She had also deposed, 'I remember Twiss coming with another man to my house

122 Bentley, op. cit., p. 144.   123 Purcell, op. cit., p. 200.

124 Who actually did the reading seems to have varied. At Kirwan's trial the clerk of the crown read out some of the depositions, and the prisoner's counsel read out others (John Simpson Armstrong, *Report of the trial of William Burke Kirwan, for the murder of Maria Louisa Kirwan, his wife, at the island of Ireland's Eye, in the county of Dublin on the 6th September, 1852, before the Hon. Judge Crampton and the Rt Hon. Baron Greene, at the Commission Court, Green Street, on the 8th and 9th December, 1852* (Dublin, 1853), pp 16, 26–7, 37, 41).

125 John Adye Curran, *Reminiscences of John Adye Curran, KC, late county court judge and chairman of quarter sessions* (London, 1915), p. 16. Stephen thought reading out the deposition was not a grievance: it saved time and prevented quibbling (Stephen, *General view*, p. 316).

126 28 & 29 Vict., c. 18 (9 May 1865). See also Bentley, op. cit., p. 146 and *A report on criminal procedure to the lord chancellor; by Charles Sprengal Greaves, Esq., one of her majesty's counsel*, pp 36–7 [456], HC 1856, l, 114–15. 'The Queen's case', so frequently referred to in discussions of this matter, was George IV's attempt to divorce Queen Caroline in 1820.

one night. They had guns. After some time, they put their hands up the chimney and pulled down soot and blackened their faces. They left the house and went in the direction of the cross-roads. I heard shots that night, and next morning I saw the dead body of Culloty lying at the cross-roads.'[127] Sullivan concluded, fifty years later, 'that the murder for which Twiss was indicted was committed in the early hours of the morning of 21st April 1894, but the murder that caused his conviction had been committed many years before – the shooting of Culloty.'

This is a puzzling story, which would be hardly credible, if it had come from a source less scrupulous than Sullivan. The *Cork Examiner*'s account of the trial, for example, does not mention these statements.[128] Mary Lyons' deposition, which has been preserved in Twiss' Convict Reference File, does not make these statements in the detailed and dramatic form given by Sullivan. She is reported there as having said 'I saw him beating Pat Carver who is now dead about 12 years ago' and 'Twiss pulled out a revolver, pointed it at me and seemed as if about to fire at me.'[129] Lord Chief Baron Palles, however, in his summing up, showed that evidence that required explanation had been admitted:

> we are not trying whether other crimes took place in this district upon other occasions, and this was the reason why I endeavoured to check my friend Mr Burke in reading the statement of this woman, as to acts she alleged John Twiss had committed on other occasions. We are not trying him for these acts. I would not have received the evidence but that it had been given to Mr Burke to show that he had not been guilty of these acts. I am trying him only for this murder and this statement has been given in evidence only for the purpose of affecting the credit of Mrs Lyons.

The 'Mr Burke' to whom Palles referred was Matthew Burke QC, who was one of the crown counsel. What Palles meant when he said 'that it had been given to Mr Burke to show that he had not been guilty of these acts' is not clear, except that it probably meant that the subject had been introduced by the prisoner's counsel when the deposition was referred to. It is a pity that Palles did not explain why he had not done more than 'endeavour' to stop Burke. The interesting thing about this transaction, which showed the existence of a loophole in the laws of evidence that could be used by the Crown, is that the Crown did not use it more often. There were no complaints, for example, of the practice in the selection of cases described above.[130]

---

127 Sullivan, *Last serjeant*, pp 76, 82, 83. Mary Lyons' evidence impressed the jury because she was pregnant. According to Sullivan, 'by the moral code of the people to whom she belonged, a pregnant woman may not give false testimony. It brings a curse upon the unborn child' (ibid., p. 93).

128 *Cork Examiner*, 8 Jan. 1895 (press cutting in NAI, CRF/1895/Twiss/3).

129 Ibid. See also Pat Lynch, *They hanged John Twiss* (Tralee, 1982), pp 84, 153–4.

130 Above, pp 210–12.

Translation from Irish into English also weakened cross-examination. In a rape case at Castlebar assizes in 1858, the prisoner's witness had been examined in Irish, having 'professed an inability to speak English'.[131] The Crown had not objected to his examination-in-chief in Irish, but 'on cross-examination he was asked whether, on a recent occasion, he had not spoken in English to two persons who were present in court, and shown to witness'. He denied speaking English to the two witnesses, and they were called to swear they had heard him singing 'The Heights of Alma' in a lodging-house. The case raised two questions: (1) the right of witnesses to give evidence in Irish, even if they knew English; (2) the right to call witnesses to establish a fact that was not directly connected with the case.[132] James O'Brien reserved the case, and in the Court for Crown Cases Reserved he argued against allowing witnesses to choose their language:

> the question involved in the case is one of considerable importance as affects the administration of justice in those parts of this country where many persons profess not to speak or understand the English language, and are examined in Irish; and it is especially important with reference to cross-examination, the great value of which arises from the demeanour of the witness, and the hesitation or fairness with which he answers questions unexpected by him, and put suddenly to him, and his demeanour while being so cross-examined is powerful with the jury to judge of the credit which they ought to give to his testimony, and it is plain that the value of this test is very much lessened in the case of a witness having a sufficient knowledge of the English language to understand the questions put by counsel, pretending ignorance of it, and gaining time to consider his answers while the interpreter is going through the useless task of interpreting the question which the witness already perfectly understands.[133]

The majority of the court decided the witness had a right to give his evidence in Irish, even if he knew English. Christian spoke for the majority:

> I apprehend it is perfectly possible that the witness was actuated by an honest motive in wishing to be examined in Irish. He may have wished to express himself in the language which he knew best, in which he could most clearly express his thoughts; and is it not easy to imagine that one of us, a person of a rank of life above that of this witness, if giving evidence in an Italian or a French court of justice, would prefer to do so in the English language.[134]

131 *R. v. Burke* 8 Cox CC 44, at p. 44. According to Hickey, 'a … popular ruse was to deny a knowledge of English sufficient to give an accurate testimony' (Hickey, op. cit., p. 95).
132 Above, p. 234, and below, pp 246–7.
133 8 Cox CC 44, at pp 46–7.
134 Ibid., pp 54–5.

Christian even displayed a knowledge of fashionable life. 'If every lady who sings an Italian song is to be taken on that account to have a perfect knowledge of the Italian language,' he said, 'I can only say that a great number of ladies may very easily find themselves placed in a very unpleasant position indeed.' The majority of the judges also decided that the witness' ability to speak English was a collateral question: his statement on oath had to be accepted as 'conclusive', which meant that no witnesses should have been called to contradict him.[135]

John Adye Curran, who had watched his father's 'peculiarly effective mode of cross-examination', listed the rules of cross-examination. First, do not shout at a witness 'unless you have caught him in a contradiction which you wish to emphasize'. Secondly, avoid the 'cardinal' points of the case, and 'keep as much as you can to what I may call its fringe'; if a witness is telling the truth, rely 'on some discrepancy between the deposition and the evidence given in court, for such can nearly always be found'. Thirdly, avoid asking a question whose answer you do not know ('You may by asking such questions recall to a truth-telling witness some matter which he has inadvertently forgotten, or let in evidence that could not have been given by the Crown on the direct'). Fourthly, before examining a medical witnesses, 'read up the matter the night before', because medical witnesses 'frequently find themselves upset by questions as to the latest theories and practice found in the most recent textbooks.'[136]

The tactics of cross-examination can be discerned in any well reported trial. Stephen McKeown was tried at Armagh summer assizes in 1876 for the murder of Mary McShane near Forkill on Sunday 23 April 1876. McKeown lived with his family, was aged 27, and had come back from America two or three years before. Mary McShane, who lived with her widowed mother in the townland of Longfield, had been 'in the pride of life and youth'.[137] She was the second member of her family to be murdered. Her father, Laurence, had been 'found dead on the 3rd May, 1875, lying dead in one of his own fields with his head in a ghastly condition, with wounds and bruises, and evidently he was the victim of violence. No person was made amenable for that crime.'

Walter Boyd who was McKeown's counsel demonstrated the application of Curran's advice to keep away from the 'cardinal' facts and to concentrate on the 'fringe'.[138] (1) He showed that witnesses had contradicted themselves. Felix Deegan denied that he had told the coroner that he had seen McKeown opening a gate. Boyd read out his deposition stating that he had seen McKeown opening the gate. (2) He tried to discredit witnesses by showing that they had not come forward promptly to give evidence. Patrick Waters had seen Mary McShane on

135 Ibid., p. 65.
136 Curran, op. cit., pp 11–17.
137 NAI, CRF/1876/McKeown/22.
138 Boyd had been called to the bar in 1856, and in 1877 he took silk, became senior crown counsel for Co. Armagh, and Queen's Advocate. In 1885 he was appointed a judge of the Court of Bankruptcy, and in 1897 a judge of the Queen's Bench Division.

her way home from Forkill. 'Three weeks afterwards you recollected all about this?' Boyd asked. 'Yes,' Waters replied. Boyd was not satisfied with this simple admission. 'Although there was a magistrate's inquiry and coroner's inquest, you did not recollect it?' Waters lamely protested that 'there were some as late as me.' (3) He implied that the constabulary had been overzealous in getting up the case against McKeown. Boyd's question to Felix Deegan ('Have you been talking to the police about this matter?') implied gossip, rumour, and speculation. Deegan had to answer, 'Yes', which did not enable him to explain himself. Boyd's next question implied he had been coached: 'Did they read over to you what you swore before the coroner?'

It was Boyd's little touches of disparagement that probably mattered most. Thomas Fagan had been the first to reach the dying Mary McShane. Boyd's first question to him was: 'You were examined twice about this?', which implied that he had told his story reluctantly, or that he had embroidered it. In practice, witnesses were often examined twice, once by the coroner and once by a magistrate. Fagan replied simply 'Yes', which was about the best he could do, if only because it was short and true. Boyd, however, did not let him escape. His next question was: 'And you enlarged a little on the second occasion?' The word 'enlarged' presented Fagan as a raconteur. Fagan replied defensively, as he was meant to, 'I told the truth.' Boyd repeated the question, 'Did you enlarge?', and Fagan lamely answered, 'I might.' Three questions had turned the witness into a prevaricator from whom the truth had to be dragged. The triumph of Boyd's cross-examination, however, was what he concealed. In cross-examining 27 witnesses, he did not allow any of them to blurt out the fact that the prisoner had been in Armagh gaol in 1875 'on suspicion of the murder of the father of Mary McShane, the girl he murdered in April last'!

RE-EXAMINATION

After a witness had been cross-examined the other side could re-examine 'upon all the topics on which he has been cross-examined, to give him an opportunity of explaining any new facts which may have come out on cross-examination.'[139] At the trial of Timothy Keeffe, who had killed his uncle at Kingwilliamstown, part of the case against him was the fact that his boots matched footprints at the scene of the attack. Constable McArdle mentioned the similarity between Keeffe's boots and the footprints only at the end of his examination-in-chief. He did not make much of it: 'I brought the prisoner's boots next morning to the scene of the murder. There were tracks in a ploughed field facing away from the murder. I compared them with the boots, and believe they corresponded.'[140] Keeffe had

139 Purcell, op. cit., p. 201.
140 NAI, CRF/1883/Keeffe/13.

experienced counsel, Denis B. Sullivan and Richard Adams. Under cross-examination McArdle admitted that he had not actually fitted the boots into the footprints. In re-examination the crown counsel retaliated, and elicited from McArdle additional, damning details about the footprints: 'There were six rows of nails in the boots, and six in the tracks. There was a peculiar bevel in the heels and it was in the tracks. Also a peculiarity in the points of the boots, and in the tracks.' Keeffe was hanged at Cork on 30 April 1883.

PRISONERS' WITNESSES

The prisoners on average called only two witnesses each while the Crown called fifteen.[141] The prisoner's exiguous average concealed an even more exiguous statistic: over half of them called no witnesses at all. Judges appeared to be punctilious in enabling prisoners to call witnesses. At the Dublin Commission in 1851, for example, Pigot and Moore allowed an adjournment when a prisoner stated in an affidavit 'that, in consequence of the harshness of the governor of the gaol in which he is confined in refusing to allow him pens, ink, or paper whereby to communicate with his friends and prepare for his trial, he cannot procure witnesses whose names are given in the affidavit, and who are also stated to be necessary for his defence.'[142] The Crown occasionally paid the expenses of prisoners' witnesses,[143] although the attorney general, Joseph Napier, thought that such expenses were 'rarely allowed, because, generally speaking, I think you find that they manage somehow or other to be pretty well defended.'[144] The Crown did not know in advance what witnesses the prisoner would call or what they were going to say. At the trial itself crown counsel could cross-examine them in the same way the prisoner's counsel had cross-examined the Crown's witnesses, and the Crown could call witnesses to contradict them, but rarely did. The one thing the Crown could not apparently do was to comment on the prisoner's lack of witnesses. At Clonmel in 1847 the crown counsel pointed out that Thomas and Michael Ryan had called no witnesses, even though their trial had been postponed from the last assizes to allow them to call a material witness.[145] 'I was surprised indeed shocked thereby,' Perrin, wrote, '& expressed my disappointment & regret that such an observation should have been made & matter prejudicial to the

141 These figures, and those that follow in this section, are based on the selection of cases referred to above, p. 207.
142 *Walker* (1851) 5 Cox CC 320, at p. 320.
143 For an example of the Crown paying the expenses of prisoners' witnesses, see NAI, OP/107 and ibid., CRF/1839/Kelly/12. The Prevention of Crime (Ireland) Act, 1882 (45 & 46 Vict., c. 25, s. 1(6) (12 July 1882)) provided for the payment of witness' expenses.
144 *Report from the select committee on public prosecutors; together with the proceedings of the committee, minutes of evidence, appendix and index*, p. 147, HC 1854–5 (481), xii, 155.
145 NAI, CRF/1847/Ryan/24.

prisoners on trial stated in the hearing of the jury which was not in evidence.' The two prisoners, nevertheless, were convicted, sentenced to death, and hanged.

Prisoners' witnesses fell into three categories. In the selection of cases referred to above, they produced 18 character witnesses, 31 alibi witnesses, and 39 who either impugned the character of crown witnesses or contradicted their evidence in some particular other than the whereabouts of the prisoner, which was done by the alibi witnesses. Often the only witnesses were character witnesses. Such witnesses were supposed to speak generally of the prisoner's reputation, to 'give general evidence of the disposition of the man', and consequently 'evidence of particular facts is excluded because a robber may do acts of generosity, and the proof of such acts is therefore irrelevant to the question whether he was likely to have committed a particular act of robbery.'[146] John McLoughlin, who was convicted in March 1865 of the murder of the solicitor John McCrossan, called as character witnesses a magistrate, a parish priest, and two Presbyterian ministers. McLoughlin was a Catholic, and John McCrossan whom he had murdered had been a Catholic and a prominent Liberal. McLoughlin's witnesses, therefore, represented a nice balancing of political parties. They spoke warmly about him. His parish priest said he was 'a quiet, inoffensive, hard-working man', the Revd John Davison, the Presbyterian minister of Drumquin, found him 'a peaceable obliging workman', and the Revd Josias Mitchell, minister of 2nd Omagh, said 'his general character is excellent. He is a most peaceable man.'[147] Best of all from the prisoner's point of view was the magistrate, Alexander Buchanan (of Riverdale, Omagh), who said he 'could not point out a more peaceable and well disposed man amongst all the tradesmen of Omagh.'

Although crown counsel could cross-examine character witnesses, it was not usual to do so, 'unless there is some definite charge upon which to cross-examine them.'[148] At Patrick Woods' trial at Armagh in 1841, his character witnesses were cross-examined. Dr McFarland, who had known Woods for twenty years, was cross-examined by Sir Thomas Staples QC, but said nothing more compromising about Woods than that his 'first acquaintance with him was when I was a little boy he used to assist us fishing at the lake.' Samuel Bell, who had two possible claims to respectability (his father had been a magistrate and his first cousin was a landlord near Crossmaglen), revealed that 'he was occasionally a witness as to character in this court, not more than three times I recollect.'[149] Although the Crown could counter the prisoner's character witnesses by calling witnesses to show that he had a bad character, no example of this occurred in the selection of cases mentioned above.[150]

146 *Rowton* (1865) Le & C 520, at p. 541; 169 Eng Rep 1497, at p. 1507. See also James O'Connor, *The Irish justice of the peace: a treatise on the powers and duties of justices of the peace in Ireland, and certain matters connected therewith* (Dublin, 1911), p. 269.

147 NAI, CRF/1885/McLoughlin/18.   148 Purcell, op. cit., p. 353.

149 NAI, CRF/1841/Woods/26.

150 Above, p. 207.

It is difficult to say how useful character witnesses were. Baron Fitzgerald carefully noted what McLoughlin's character witnesses had said. At John Brewer's trial, Crampton let a character witness give evidence at the last moment: 'after my charge and *before* the jury retired to consider of their verdict a witness was produced who gave a good character to the prisoner.'[151] 'I have never heard an accused person receive a higher character than that given to Denis Dillane,' Judge Fitzgerald noted, when he heard the testimony of Morgan O'Connell MD, Head Constable White, and the rector of Kilmallock.[152] Dillane was hanged on 13 April 1863. After Mary Ann McConkey's trial the judge, Robert Torrens, noted that she had not called any character witnesses.[153] Character witness' social standing mattered. Mr Wickerby, Phineas Finn's attorney, had high hopes of those who would appear for his client, who was charged with murdering the president of the board of trade: 'We shall have half the cabinet. There will be two dukes ... There will be three secretaries of state. The secretary of state for the home department himself will be examined. I am not quite sure that we mayn't get the lord chancellor.'[154] Character witnesses may also have persuaded juries to accompany their guilty verdicts with recommendations to mercy.

Alibis were not as common as contemporaries' comments implied. The figure of 31 mentioned above concealed the fact that alibis tended to cluster together in particular cases (Patrick Woods alone accounted for 11 of the 31, and John and James Power accounted for 4). Although alibis were viewed with scepticism, judges did not dismiss them with contempt. When Patrick Beary was sentenced to death at Clonmel assizes in 1843, the judge, who was the second serjeant, Richard Warren, noted 'that a witness named Beary was produced by the prisoner, & he swore that the prisoner took his supper at his house on the night in question, at the hour at which the murder was stated to have been committed, & that his house was four miles from Mackim's.'[155] Warren took the alibi seriously enough to argue against its credibility. In his report for the lord lieutenant he wrote that he

> entertained no doubt that the prisoner was truly identified by Neill & Slattery. Neill appeared to me a very fair witness. He was reluctant to prosecute, and in the morning after he was robbed, he went into the Co. Cork, a distance of fifty miles from Mackim's, & he remained there for a fortnight when he was brought back by the police, and as he had previously known the prisoner, I saw no reason to suspect he might be mistaken. The witness Slattery was a very young lad, & had not any previous knowledge of the prisoner, but he gave his evidence with apparent candour & I believe he spoke the truth.

151 NAI, CRF/1837/Brewer/165.
152 Ibid., CRF/1863/Dillane/15.   153 Ibid., CRF/1841/McConkey/17.
154 Anthony Trollope, *Phineas Redux* (first published 1874; St Albans, 1973), p. 459.
155 NAI, CRF/1843/Beary/32.

The alibi witnesses were usually too close to the prisoner to be impartial. They were often nothing more than highly specialised character witnesses who were willing to commit perjury to show their loyalty to the prisoner. If prisoners had been obliged to reveal their alibis in advance they might have carried more weight. At any rate there would have been fewer of them.[156] Character witnesses and alibis were almost mutually exclusive: where the prisoner relied on the one, he disdained to use the other. A judge might have made a crude *triage* of his capital cases, based on their hopelessness: those without character or bi-location, those with bi-location but no character, those with character but no bi-location.

The 39 witnesses who impugned the Crown's witness' credit or contradicted the Crown's witnesses, other than as alibi witnesses, were more varied than the character and alibi witnesses: 14 directly contradicted what crown witnesses had said, 11 offered an exculpatory explanation of what crown witnesses had said, 4 were medical witnesses, and the remainder were a miscellaneous group that indirectly contested the truth of what the crown witnesses had said. Of the latter, 3 claimed that witnesses had not been where they said they were, 2 questioned the accuracy of witness' knowledge, one claimed a witness had said something different on another occasion, one questioned a witness' identification of the prisoner, and 2 impugned a witness' credit. At his trial at the special commission in Cavan, Thomas Dunn called as his fifth witness, Mary Martin, who said: 'I know Patrick Heavy the witness for the Crown in this case. I also know his general character. From his general character I do not consider him to be deserving of credit on his oath in a court of justice.'[157] She was followed by William Martin, who swore he knew Heavy and that 'his general character which is such that I do not consider him worthy of credit on oath in a court of justice.'

When such witnesses were asked about a witness' reputation, 'the examination must be confined to his general reputation, and will not be permitted as to particular facts.'[158] Mary Martin's cross-examination, however, elicited a very particular fact: 'He and I had a dispute about 1*s*. He voluntarily took an oath that he had paid it to me, which he had not, and that is my reason for thinking that he should not be believed on his oath. This transaction was in 1847.' The impugning witness 'ought himself to come from the neighbourhood of the person whose character is in question', and 'he must be able to state what is *generally* said of the person by those among whom he dwells.'[159] The Crown had a remedy against such witnesses. They could not only cross-examine them 'as to their means of

156 In Scotland 'a pannel is bound twenty-four hours before the trial, to give to the prosecutor a list of the witnesses he is to call; but this rule is not always enforced' (Paterson, op. cit., p. 330).

157 NAI, CRF/1856/Dunn/26.

158 Purcell, op. cit., p. 352. 'Such persons may not upon their examination in chief give reasons for their belief, but they may be asked their reasons in cross-examination, and their answers cannot be contradicted' (Sir James Fitzjames Stephen Bt., KCSI, DCL, *A digest of the law of evidence*. Twelfth edition, revised by Sir Harry Lushington Stephen Bt., & Lewis Frederick Sturge (London, 1948), p. 169).

159 Purcell, op. cit., p. 352.

knowledge, and the grounds of their opinion, or as to their own character and conduct', but they could produce 'fresh evidence either to support the character of the first witness, or to attack in turn the general reputation of the impeaching witnesses ... but no further witnesses can be called to impeach the characters of these last.'[160] By the early 1860s, according to Stephen, 'this mode of attacking a witness' credit has become practically obsolete.'[161] The practice was not obsolete in Ireland in the late 1850s, as the Dunn case showed.[162] Nor was it obsolete more than twenty years later when the two Peter Conways, father and son, were tried at Omagh assizes for the murder of James Miller, and the judge noted that the character of one of the crown witnesses, Sarah Murphy, 'was severely attacked by counsel for the prisoner & one or two witnesses were examined who swore that in their opinion and from general reputation she was not entitled to credit upon her oath.'[163]

When lawyers used the word 'contradict', they used it to mean the calling of a witness to counter what was said by another witness. It did not mean a mere assertion by counsel. Counsel could suggest in cross-examination that witnesses were cheats, rascals, or cowards, but they could not call witnesses to establish these facts, unless they were 'relevant' in the legal sense. The difference between those facts counsel could 'contradict' and those they could not was one of the most puzzling things in trials. Lawyers used the adjective 'collateral' to describe facts that were not 'relevant', or directly connected with the facts in issue. When a witness answered a 'collateral' question, his answer had to be accepted as 'conclusive', which did not mean that it settled the question but only that it had to be accepted as final in that particular trial and that no witness could be called to 'contradict' it. If there was another trial, a collateral fact, such as the witness' perjury, might become 'relevant'.

The law of evidence, however, allowed contradiction to go beyond relevant facts. Witnesses who were called to impugn the credit of other witnesses, for example, were an exception to the rule. In *Hitchcock* the judges of the English Court of Exchequer tried to define the circumstances in which such contradiction could take place.[164] Chief Baron Pollock said that 'a distinction should be observed between those matters which may be given in evidence by way of contradiction, as directly affecting the story of the witness touching the issue before the jury, and those matters which affect the motives, temper, and character of the witness, not with respect to his credit, but with reference to his feelings towards one party or the other.'[165] Pollock went on to say

160 Ibid., p. 353.
161 Stephen, *General view*, p. 296. According to Stephen the decline of such witnesses led to an increase in cross-examination as to credit.
162 For an example at Lifford assizes in 1859, see Larcom Papers (NLI, MS 7620 [*Packet*, 26 July 59]).
163 NAI, CRF 1880/Conway/19.
164 *Attorney General v. Hitchcock* (1847) 1 Exch 91, 154 Eng Rep 38.
165 Ibid., p. 42.

it is certainly allowable to ask a witness in what manner he stands affected towards the opposite party in the cause, and whether he does not stand in such a relation to that person as is likely to affect him, and prevent him from having an unprejudiced state of mind, and whether he has not used expressions importing that he would be revenged on some one, or that he would give such evidence as might dispose of the cause in one way or the other. If he denies that you may give evidence as to what he has said, not with a view of having a direct effect on the issue, but to shew what is the state of mind of that witness in order that the jury may exercise their opinion as to show how far he is to be believed.

Alderson offered another example of a fact that might have 'a bearing on the general status of the witness': if he offered a bribe to another witness or accepted a bribe, 'the circumstance of the witness having offered or accepted a bribe shews that he is not equal and impartial.'[166] Baron Rolfe, however, tried to set a limit to how far contradiction should go:

The laws of evidence on this subject, as to what ought and what ought not to be received, must be considered as founded on a sort comparative consideration of the time to be occupied in examinations of this nature, and the time which it is practicable to bestow upon them. If we lived for a thousand years instead of about sixty or seventy, and every case were of sufficient importance, it might be possible, and perhaps proper, to throw a light on matters in which every possible question might be suggested, for the purpose of seeing by such means whether the whole was unfounded, or what portion of it was not, and to raise every possible inquiry as to the truth of the statements made. But I do not see how that could be, in fact, mankind find it to be impossible. Therefore some line must be drawn, and I take it the established rule is, that you may contradict any portion of the testimony that is given in support or contradiction of the issue between the parties. That is clear. Then, undoubtedly, mankind have felt that, as facts are frequently to be proved by the testimony of men of suspicious character, you may inquire into the genuineness and truthfulness of the party who gives such testimony.[167]

In *R. v. Burke*, the Irish Court for Crown Cases Reserved followed *Hitchcock* in deciding whether the Crown was right to call two witnesses to prove that an Irish-speaking witness in a rape case had sung 'The Heights of Alma'.[168] The court decided that the witnesses should not have been called because the witness' language was a collateral fact and his answer should have been accepted as conclusive. The court rehearsed the circumstances in which witnesses might be

166 Ibid., p. 43.   167 Ibid., p. 44.
168 *Burke* (1858) 8 Cox CC 38, at pp 49, 50, 53. See above, pp 238–9.

called in matters that were partly relevant, partly collateral. (1) If witnesses denied committing a crime, their denial had to be accepted as conclusive 'except in the case of a former conviction'. (2) If they denied their connection with either party. (3) If they denied taking bribes or having 'tampered with other persons'. The essential principle that allowed contradiction of apparently irrelevant facts was 'that the matter which is to be inquired into, must be of a kind to bring the witness into a special connection with the subject matter of the particular issue, or with one of the parties to that issue.' Stephen put it more succinctly: 'if a witness is asked any question tending to show that he is not impartial, and answers it by denying the facts suggested, he may be contradicted.'[169]

Baron Rolfe's fear that a lifetime of a thousand years would be necessary for the consideration of proliferating questions led to some remarkable decisions. In 1828 the Irish judges in *Moran, Macken, and others*, which was a murder case at Westmeath assizes, tried to limit the use of depositions. Counsel for the crown, having examined two witnesses, did not examine a third witness who had been called and sworn, 'upon which the counsel for the prisoners insisted upon their right to cross-examine him, which was assented to:

> Upon his cross-examination, he stated some circumstances differently from what had been sworn by the first two witnesses, and favourably for the prisoners; after which the counsel for the crown examined him as to some of the matters which he had sworn, and then asked if he had given a different account of the matter when examined upon the coroner's inquest, and when he swore informations before a magistrate? and upon his saying that he had not, they put into his hand his depositions on the inquest, and his informations before the magistrate; upon which the counsel for the prisoners objected, and contended that the counsel for the crown had not a right to examine him to that effect, or read his depositions or informations to the jury.[170]

Lord Chief Justice Bushe allowed the depositions to be read and reserved the case. Ten of the twelve judges decided that the conviction was wrong because the depositions should not have been admitted.

An incident described by Mathias Bodkin demonstrated the niceness of contradiction. A publican called Clarke was tried for the murder of a policeman in Loughrea. The Crown's most important witness, who had been Clarke's servant girl, 'swore that she heard her master relate to his wife in circumstantial detail how he committed the murder.' Her story was a plausible one, because Clarke 'had had many quarrels with the constable with regard to licensing prosecutions, and the impossibility of believing that a young girl could or would

169 Stephen, *A digest of the law of evidence*, p. 167.
170 Jebb Rep 91, at p. 91.

invent such a story told powerfully against the prisoner.' The publican's solicitor found out that the witness had had an illegitimate child in Portumna workhouse. He brought the workhouse's master, matron, and midwife to the assizes to prove it. Bodkin, who was Clarke's counsel, told the solicitor he had wasted his time. '"Not one of them will be allowed to open their lips in the case," I explained. "Her denial on cross-examination as to character must be accepted as conclusive."' At the trial the witness 'denied point-blank the incident at the Portumna workhouse.' Bodkin used a stratagem, which would have been the subject of a complaint if it had been used by the Crown:

> This time I succeeded in getting the truth in by a side door. I told the witness to look at the master of the workhouse, where he sat fronting the jury. 'Did you ever see that man before?' 'Never!'. The expression on his face was more valuable than any evidence he could have given on his oath. The matron's face when her turn came was a still more emphatic contradiction. But the midwife lost all control of herself when the witness denied having seen her, she threw up her hands and her eyes in eloquent protest. 'Oh, you huzzy, you lying huzzy,' she cried, 'how dare you swear the like of that!' There was a sharp order of silence in the court, but the truth had got to the jury in spite of the law.[171]

PRISONERS' COMPLAINTS ABOUT THEIR DEFENCE

Of the 63 complaints produced by the selection of 85 cases taken from the Convict Reference Files, 17 were about the prisoners' defence. Of these 17 complaints, 12 were about the conduct of prisoners' counsel and attorneys, which made them second only to complaints about the Crown's conduct of the case. Of the remaining 5 complaints, 4 were about prisoners' witnesses not attending and one was about prisoners being tried together. Only one prisoner complained that he did not have counsel. James McKeever, a soldier convicted of bestiality in 1857, complained that he 'was undefended at his trial and was totally incapable of defending himself so that it was impossible for him to expose the false testimony on which he was convicted.'[172] The fact that all of the prisoners in the selection of cases, except McKeever, had counsel suggests that there was some foundation for the boast of the *Irish Law Times* that Ireland 'was the only country in the world where the system of assigning counsel in capital cases exists.'[173]

---

171 Bodkin, op. cit., pp 142–3.
172 NAI, CRF/1871/McKeever/34. See Bentley, op. cit., pp 111–13 for examples of prisoners in England being tried on capital charges without counsel being assigned to them; Bentley found nine cases in the years 1860–9.
173 *ILT & SJ*, 31 (1 May 1897), 199 (I am indebted to Desmond Greer for this reference).

The most predictable complaint was about the shortness of time that counsel had to prepare the case. When Patrick Cain was arrested on 3 March 1837 and put on trial on 20 March, his attorney was justified in complaining that he 'had but very few days to prepare his defence'[174] Mary Ann McConkey was assigned counsel but 'at so late a period and having had little or no previous communication with the condemned (an uneducated female who was at the time labouring under great mental excitement) it was impossible for her allotted legal defenders to collect information and make such arrangement as would afford her the full advantage of his lordship's kind consideration.'[175] Thomas Fahy had no money to employ attorney or counsel. Lefroy assigned him counsel, 'which was done a short time before the trial took place and [he] was therefore unable to instruct him as to the nature of his defence, and in consequence thereof some facts favourable to petitioner were not elicited upon trial.'[176]

Other complaints about defence counsel varied in their seriousness. Patrick Woods' life 'was left in the hands of young and inexperienced advocates', which was nonsense because his counsel were Napier, O'Hagan, and Whiteside.[177] John Logue's counsel was not up to the rascality of the Crown's witnesses, 'not knowing the nature of some of the perjury which was sworing [*sic*].'[178] Attorneys were blamed as well as barristers. John Brewer's character witnesses were not called 'from some unaccountable omission on the part of his attorney'.[179] Patrick Lydane's attorney 'happened to be previously engaged on a case of his own in the civil court before and during the trial in the crown court and was not able to attend at all whilst the trial was going on which was the cause of the jury taking a hasty view of the case.'[180] Lydane's predicament was made worse because 'the prisoner not understanding the English language did not know what was alleged against him at the trial and did not interfere whilst the trial was going on having left it to his attorney.' John Logue complained that 'the solicitor which I choosed [*sic*] never came to me while in the court, so that I could not get communicating with my councellor.'[181]

174 NAI, CRF/1837/Cain/199.
175 Ibid., CRF/1841/McConkey/17.
176 Ibid., CRF/1844/Fahy/7.
177 Ibid., CRF/1841/Woods/26.
178 Ibid., CRF/1866/Logue/6.
179 Ibid., CRF/1837/Brewer/165.
180 Ibid., CRF/1858/Lydane/5.
181 Ibid., CRF/1866/Logue/6.

CHAPTER SEVEN

Summing up

THE JUDGE'S NOTES

ALTHOUGH COUNSEL FOR THE Crown and for the prisoner dominated the proceedings from the moment the jury was empanelled, neither the judge nor the jury were passive spectators. Jurors could ask questions. The foreman of the jury at Stephen McKeown's trial questioned a crown witness just after he had been cross-examined.[1] The judge was obliged to intervene more frequently than the jury, whose interventions were voluntary and sporadic: he had to decide on the competency of witnesses when they were examined on the *voire-dire*, he had to rule on the admission of evidence, and he might remonstrate with counsel when they were carried away by exuberance. He might also question witnesses. When the foreman of the jury questioned the witness at the McKeown trial, the judge immediately tried to clear up the point by asking a question.

Whether judges intervened or not, the one thing they did at all trials was to keep notes. The judge's notes of the trial must be distinguished from the clerk of the crown's 'record', which included the prisoner's name, the indictment, the prisoner's plea, the jurors' names, the verdict, and the sentence, but not the witness' names or a summary of their evidence. The 'record' became important if the case were referred to the Court of Queen's Bench, either by *certiorari* or by a writ of error.[2] The judge's notes included a summary of witness' evidence, as well as some of the things that the 'record' included, and they were usually forwarded to the lord lieutenant when the prisoner appealed for mercy, or they might be referred to if the judge decided to 'reserve' the case for the twelve judges or for the Court for Crown Cases Reserved. The notes' main characteristic was

---

1   *Belfast Newsletter*, 19 July 1876.
2   For an example of a 'record' see *O'Neill* (1854) 6 Cox 495; *O'Brien v. The Queen* (1890) 26 LR Ir 451, at pp 453–6. See also Courtney Stanhope Kenny, *Outlines of criminal law, based on lectures delivered in the University of Cambridge* (Cambridge, 1902), p. 415, n2. The 'record' was produced by courts of 'record', which were courts regulated by the common law and which had the power to protect witnesses from arrest in civil suits and to punish for contempt (Edmund Hayes, *Crimes and punishments, or a digest of the criminal statute law of Ireland, alphabetically arranged, with ample notes, in which are discussed the powers and authorities of the several courts of criminal jurisdiction in Ireland; the duties, responsibilities, and privileges of magistrates, coroners, constables, and other officers, in bringing criminals to justice, and also the practice of the courts in punishing offences upon indictment*, 2 vols (2nd ed., Dublin, 1842), ii, 752–6).

terseness, which probably owed something to the fact that they were made in longhand.[3] Keogh's notebook had 64 pages for the Nenagh spring assizes in 1858, which sounds substantial; the trials of the Cormack brothers, however, accounted for 41 of the 64 pages, and 18 trials, including 4 murders, 3 manslaughters, and a rape filled the remaining 23 pages.[4] Even a long trial produced no more than a couple of dozen pieces of information, each of which could easily be summarized in a sentence or two. Judges were given the depositions before the trial, which meant they knew in advance the gist of the Crown's case, a fact that probably allowed them to summarize the evidence effectively.[5]

Some judges took pains with their notes. Pigot 'was a very accurate note-taker, and as a rule took down both question and answer, and the raising of his pen with the words, "I am writing," was always a signal to counsel to pause in his questioning. As a rule he adopted the same practice in taking down cross-examination, destroying altogether in most cases its effect, especially in the case of an untruthful witness.'[6] Some judges made light of their notes. Hayes told the royal commission on capital punishment that he had 'preserved no record of matters occurring in my experience, either as a judge presiding in a criminal court, or as a barrister.'[7] Some judges sent in newspaper reports to the lord lieutenant instead of their longhand notes. The former were easy to read, but were not as concise as the latter.[8]

The judges' handwriting varied. Bushe, even in his late sixties, wrote an easily read hand.[9] Torrens wrote illegibly.[10] Baron Fitzgerald wrote a minute, neatly

---

3   There are references to 'sworn shorthand writers' (for an example, see NAI, CRF/1880/ Conway/19), but actual shorthand notes do not appear in the Convict Reference Files. The legible, long-hand transcripts of trials, which occasionally appear, were probably made by the crown solicitors' clerks. For an example, see CRF/1841/Woods/26.

4   Judge Keogh's crown book (MS in possession of St Patrick's College, Thurles, Co. Tipperary), pp 80–143. William Keogh had been made a judge of the Common Pleas in 1856. English judges seem to have made more copious notes, ranging, according to Roger Chadwick, 'from less than 20 to over 200 pages'; James Fitzjames Stephen's notes in the case of Isaac Lipski in 1887 were 181 pages long (Roger Chadwick, *Bureaucratic mercy: the Home Office and the treatment of capital cases in Victorian Britain* (New York and London, 1992), pp 86, 202).

5   For Judge Fitzgerald referring to the 'informations' in his charge to a grand jury, see above, p. 105. Lord Abinger, speaking in the house of lords on the prisoners' counsel bill, admitted that 'the opening of counsel helped the judge to a right understanding of the case, and enabled him to know beforehand what were the facts in it essential to be proved', which suggests that some judges did not read the depositions (*Hansard 3*, xxxv, 183 (14 July 1836)).

6   John Adye Curran, *Reminiscences of John Adye Curran, KC, late county court judge and chairman of quarter sessions* (London, 1915), p. 45.

7   *Report of the capital punishment commission, together with the minutes of evidence, and appendix*, p. 616 [3590], HC 1866, xxi, 668.

8   See, for example, NAI, CRF/1876 McKeown/22.   9   Ibid., CRF/1839/Sheeran/45.

10   Ibid., CRF/1836/Agnew/3. In the 1830s, 'the opinion existed that it was beneath a gentleman to write legibly, or with a hand in the least suitable to a clerk' (George Eliot, *Middlemarch. A study of provincial life*, with an introduction by R.M. Hewitt (London, 1961), p. 604).

formed hand.[11] Doherty suggested a cumbersome method of deciphering his notes: 'should any part of this note (taken during the trial) be illegible if Mr Drummond takes the trouble of sending for Mr [John J.] Stanford (Chief Justice Doherty's registrar) to No. 18 Warrington Place, he will probably be able to read it.'[12] Successive lords lieutenant put up with execrable handwriting, but it is surprising that Thomas Larcom put up with it. Given that the judges' notes 'frequently become of very great importance in subsequent proceedings', and given their large incomes, the cost of transcription would not have beggared them.[13] Eventually the typewriter improved matters. In 1902, for example, George Wright, newly appointed as a judge of the King's Bench Division, sent the lord lieutenant a typed version of his notes of James Doherty's trial; he also enclosed the *Sligo Champion*'s report.[14]

SUMMING UP

When the crown counsel's second speech ended, the judge addressed the jury. At Matthew Phibbs' first trial, Judge Fitzgerald spoke for one-and-half hours, which was short compared with 'the able and eloquent address of three and a half hours' duration' made by Phibbs' counsel.[15] Some judges spoke very briefly. At Thomas Hinchy's trial at the Limerick special commission in 1848 'for appearing in arms at night', Pigot's address consisted of one sentence: 'Gentlemen of the jury, if you believe the evidence you can have no difficulty.'[16] Purcell offered a guide for judges that implied more elaboration than was used by Pigot at Limerick:

> When the evidence on both sides is closed, and the speeches of counsel are ended, it then becomes the duty of the judge to sum up the evidence to the jury, at greater or less length, according to the extent of the evidence, or the difficulty or importance of the case. In the exercise of this duty he usually states shortly the substance of the offence with which the defendant is charged, divesting it of all technical phraseology which may encumber it, in order to direct the attention of the jury to the precise issue which they have to try; he then marshals the evidence, so that they may be enabled the more easily to apply it to such issue; observing, if he thinks it necessary to do so, upon the credit due to the several witnesses from the nature of their testimony, and their mode of delivering it; and where the evidence affects

11 NAI, CRF/1864/Cangley/13.   12 Ibid., CRF/1839/Murphy/93.

13 Theobald A. Purcell, *A summary of the general principles of pleading and evidence, in criminal cases in Ireland: with the rules of practice incident thereto* (Dublin, 1849), p. 204.

14 NAI, CRF/1902/Doherty/69.

15 Larcom Papers (NLI, MS 7620 [*Packet*, 11 Mar. 1861; *Irish Times*, 11 Mar. 1861]).

16 John Simpson Armstrong, *A report of trials held under a special commission for the county of Limerick, held at Limerick, January 1848* (Dublin, n.d. [1849]), pp 121, 123.

differently several defendants, he may select the evidence applicable to each, and leave their cases separately to the jury. It is, of course, also his duty to expound the law to the jury, where the case involves any point which requires explanation; and he usually concludes by telling them, that if upon the whole of the evidence they should entertain a fair and reasonable doubt of the guilt of the prisoner, they should give him the benefit of that doubt and acquit him.[17]

This is one of the few long passages in Purcell's book that is not frequently intersected with references to reported cases, which suggests that judges were not in the habit of lecturing each other on how to sum up. When Bushe described how he summed up, he used fewer words than Purcell: 'I never charge in such a way as to intimate my own opinion upon the facts of the case. I always explain the law, and I assist the jury in comparing the evidence; but I never intimate the inclination of my mind as to the conclusion to be drawn from controverted facts.'[18] A rare incidence of judges saying how summing up should be done occurred when the house of lords considered *M'Naghten's* case, and Lord Chief Justice Tindal prescribed in detail what should be said to the jury if the prisoner's insanity were an issue.[19]

Judges warned juries of the problems associated with the evidence of approvers. At the trial of Hartnett and Casey, an approver, Patrick Roche, told a damning story. The judge, Richard Moore, noted that 'in charging the jury I called their attention to all those discrepancies and told them that very little reliance ought to be placed on anything that Roche had stated, except where he was corroborated by other trustworthy evidence.'[20] At Thomas Dowling's trial for murder at the Tullamore spring assizes in 1844, when the case depended on an approver, Burton noted that the prisoner's counsel, Macdonogh, 'proceeded to reason upon what he considered the imperfection of that supposed corroboration, with very great force and ability' and to suggest 'that it would be for the judge to consider, whether he ought not to inform the jury that the evidence of such corroboration was insufficient, in which case they, the jury, would feel themselves bound to find a verdict of acquittal; or whether he would think it right to leave that question (namely the effect and extent of that corroboration) to the jury.'[21] Burton chose the latter course: 'I, having thought it right to leave the evidence upon this subject to the jury, recommended to them a very close attention to the grounds upon which he objected to the sufficiency of the corroboration.'

17   Purcell, op. cit., pp 203–4.
18   *Minutes of evidence taken before the select committee of the house of lords appointed to enquire into the state of Ireland, since the year 1835, in respect of crime and outrage, which have rendered life and property insecure in that part of the empire*, pt III, *evidence 12 June to 19 July*, p. 877, HC 1839 (486–III), xii, 13.
19   Above, p. 21.   20   NAI, CRF/1840/Casey/43.
21   Ibid., CRF/1844/Dowling/11.

Although the jury found Dowling guilty, Burton decided to reserve the case for the consideration of the twelve judges, the question being 'whether I ought to have advised the jury to acquit the prisoner on the ground of an insufficient corroboration of the approver's evidence under the authority of the late cases upon the subject, in which it is held that under certain circumstances, the jury ought (although not be directed) to be advised to find a verdict of acquittal.' The judges, with the exception of Perrin, thought that the corroboration was sufficient.

When Judge Fitzgerald tried Edward Walsh at Castlebar assizes for the murder of his wife, he knew that there was bad feeling in the town against Walsh. Sub-Inspector Louis Molloy, for example, had stated, in an affidavit, that a mob 'followed hooting and groaning the prisoner and charging him with the murder of his wife who was then lying dead in his house.'[22] In his summing up, Fitzgerald did not denounce the prisoner, he did not dwell on Mrs Walsh's horrible wounds, he did not warn jurors of imminent social chaos.[23] There was no sarcasm in his speech unless it was his dismissal of the argument put forward by the prisoner's counsel, Charles O'Malley, that Mrs Walsh's injuries were caused by a fall 'as the merest piece of imagination'. There was no attempt to imply that the jurors were men of the world who could reach only one verdict. His summing up, nevertheless, was relentless, and economical, amounting to just under 3,000 words in the *Mayo Examiner*.

Fitzgerald divided the case into three 'phases'. Did Mrs Walsh 'meet her death by violence'? Was the prisoner guilty of that violence?' Was there 'any circumstance of palliation which can reduce this crime from the character of murder'? He answered the first by reciting the medical evidence in a way that was terse and damning: 'several wounds upon her head and chest, and lacerated wounds on her scalp, on her forehead, on her temples, and on her legs – even on the back of her hands – and her two arms broken – the right arm broken just before the wrist, and the left before the wrist and again close to the elbow.' He answered the second question by describing the Crown's strongest witness in terms that left the jury in no doubt about her reliability. 'I will read the evidence of the intelligent little girl, Jane McKeon, who gave her evidence certainly in the clearest and most intelligent manner,' he told the jury. 'There is nothing in the case which would induce me, if I were a juror, to doubt anything which she has said. She may be inaccurate. She may not correctly recollect what took place; but certainly nothing in her manner, history, or conduct would lead me to the conclusion that she would wilfully tell you a lie.'

---

22   Ibid., CRF/1873/Walsh/11.
23   Judges could draw attention to unpleasant facts by telling juries to ignore them. Monahan at Trim in 1871 told a jury 'they were not, in consequence of the miserable state of the county, the prevalence of crime, and the number of murders and outrages that had been committed, to find

These statements were not hints, or nice balancings of probabilities, but hammer-blows. Fitzgerald's problem was not to make the jury answer his first two questions in the affirmative, but to prevent them from evading a decisive answer to the third, which involved 'any circumstance of palliation'. He blocked the predictable escape routes by considering three questions, which had been dwelt on by Walsh's counsel. Did drunkenness mitigate Walsh's offence? Was Walsh insane because of a head injury received thirteen years before? Was the crime premeditated? He disposed of these decisively: drunkenness did not palliate the crime; Walsh's injury of thirteen years before was too remote in time to make him mad ('there should be some intermediate medical evidence'); Walsh did not have to plan the murder of his wife to be guilty ('if any of you go to beat any person without lawful excuse or authority, and in the course of that beating kill him, it is murder'). Any juror who was worried about Walsh's drunkenness, possible insanity, and absence of premeditation would have had his mind set at rest. Fitzgerald even went so far as to use the expression 'If I were a juror.' He did not attempt to purge his address of value-words, or to avoid giving the jury a lead. He made up his mind, and told the jury what to do.[24]

At Cork ten years later Charles Barry dealt with a case of wife murder in similar terms. The defence had been absence of premeditation. Barry told the lord lieutenant why Thomas Haynes should hang:

> that he was in the habit of using violence to her is plain from the evidence of her sister (Hannah O'Brien) and of the servant boy (Denis Murphy) who slept in a loft over their bedroom – and swore that he 'frequently heard the blows' and the woman 'crying & calling out for the priest'. Nor can I regard the threat which the sister says he 'repeated several times' – '*Mind you, my lady, I will stiffen you one of these days to come*' – as nothing more than a

a verdict against the accused unless they were satisfied beyond all doubt of his guilt' (Larcom Papers (NLI, MS 7719 [*Express*, 4 Mar. 1871]).

24 According to Bentley, in England 'the judge would often have no scruples about advising the jury to convict. Such conduct was viewed far less critically than it is today. It was the right of the judge, declared Brougham, to tell the jury what his opinion of the case was. This was not a minority view' (David Bentley, *English criminal justice in the nineteenth century* (London and Rio Grande, 1998), p. 275). Stephen, who became a high court judge, was reticent about the art of judging: 'the observations of which the matter admits are either generalities too vague to be of much practical use, or they are so narrow and special that they can be learnt only by personal observations and practical experience.' The practical experience he referred to was not generally applicable: a barrister in Ceylon watched witness' toes because 'as soon as they began to lie they always fidgeted with them' (James Fitzjames Stephen, *The Indian evidence act (I. of 1872), with an introduction on the principles of judicial evidence* (Calcutta, Bombay, and London), pp 43–4). Mr Justice Stareleigh almost exhausted judicial resources in his summing up in *Bardell v. Pickwick*: 'If Mrs Bardell were right, it was perfectly clear that Mr Pickwick was wrong, and if they thought the evidence of Mrs Cluppins worthy of credence they would believe it, and, if they didn't why they wouldn't' (Charles Dickens, *The posthumous papers of the Pickwick Club*, intro. by Bernard Darwin (Oxford University Press, 1959), pp 486–7).

'mere brutal expression'. It seems to me to show at all events that he contemplated beating her savagely, without regard to the consequences ... Finally the nature of the injuries done to the woman – the bruises on her arms & legs – (which as Dr Alcock deposed 'were a mass of bruises') – and the use of a knife inflicting 5 severe wounds on the head & face leaving bloodmarks at 5 different places along the road – coupled with the number of places at which the woman was seen prostrate ... all seem to me to indicate a series of attacks, rather than one made in a sudden fit of (supposed) passion ... Even at this time too, he was able to consider the injury his mare might sustain from a quick ride – she being then in foal – and refused more than once to let Ryan's son ride her home to get a cart to bring the wife, then dying, to her house.[25]

How much did judges know about the background of the cases they tried? When Bushe sentenced Thomas McCowley to death at the King's County summer assizes in 1839, he was 'not acquainted with any particulars of the prisoner's case', except 'what appears upon the report of the trial and the copy of the prisoner's confession.'[26] Some judges discussed cases with local grandees. When Torrens tried John and James Power at Clonmel in August 1841 the high sheriff of Tipperary, Thomas Lalor (of Cregg, Carrick-on-Suir), remembered that Torrens 'charged the jury more in favour of the prisoners than against them, and on their retiring to consider their verdict, his lordship turned and asked me what my opinion was.' To which Lalor had replied, 'if I was on the jury I would feel great difficulty and doubt as to the verdict I should bring in.' It is perhaps worth noting that Torrens did not consult the sheriff until the jury had retired. The sheriff's doubts were not shared by the jury: they found the two prisoners guilty, and Torrens did not consider them 'proper objects for a mitigation of punishment.' They were hanged on 4 September 1841.[27]

John Adye Curran remembered a case where Whiteside knew the prisoner's background: 'I defended a man for the abduction of a young widow. I had a very good defence, as in my cross-examination of the prosecutrix I made it appear that she was to a certain extent a consenting party. Unfortunately, it was known to the judge, Chief Justice Whiteside, and to the jury, that my client was a leader of the Whiteboys in the county. The prisoner was convicted and sentenced to ten years' penal servitude.'[28] After the conviction of William and Daniel Cormack at the Nenagh spring assizes in 1858, a juror told Keogh that the murdered man, John Ellis, had seduced the Cormacks' sister.[29]

Judges were criticised for the way in which they addressed juries. Burton's charge at Thomas Dowling's trial was, according to a printed memorial drawn up on

25   NAI, CRF/1882/Haynes/35.   26   Ibid., CRF/1839/McCowley/71.
27   Ibid., CRF/1841/Power/13.   28   Curran, op. cit., p. 44.
29   Judge Keogh's crown book (MS in possession of St Patrick's College, Thurles, Co. Tipperary),
      p. 137.

Dowling's behalf, 'grossly defective, and highly calculated to have misled the jury.'[30] As we have seen, Burton reserved the case for the consideration of the twelve judges, which suggests scrupulosity rather than gross defectiveness. Keogh was accused of bias in his summing up at Cormacks' trial. In a debate in the commons The O'Donoghue complained that Keogh, 'setting aside the calm and impartial bearing which ought to distinguish the judicial bench, addressed the jury in the excited tones and language of an impassioned advocate.'[31] The attorney general, Whiteside, defended Keogh in terms that suggested that judicial heat was not rare.

> One judge might speak more decidedly than another, and if he stated the law and the facts fairly to the jury, it would be unjust to censure him for what might be no more than his ordinary manner. The trial took place according to law, the judgment was submitted to Lord Eglinton, six weeks elapsed between the passing of the sentence and its execution, the learned judge furnished his report upon the case; from first to last the proceedings were conducted according to law and ought to be satisfactory to that House.

Judges had distinctive styles. Richard Dowse, for example, 'does not take any pains to put on a show of impartiality in charging the jury in a criminal case.'[32] William O'Brien, on the other hand, 'dispels all mists, shows every fact in its true light and its true bearing on every other fact ... He knows well what so many judges appear not to know, that simply to read aloud the contents of the judicial note-book, with, perhaps, a running commentary thrown in, is of no real use to the jury.' Thomas Lefroy 'had a wonderful ascendancy over juries.'[33] Christopher Palles had 'the gift of firmness of purpose, and of the sense of right in a degree possessed by very few men.' Baron Fitzgerald, however, 'had too much simplicity for common jurors.' There were 'prisoners' judges'. Pigot and James O'Brien 'did their best to help prisoners during their trial, but were very severe in their sentences in the case of conviction.'[34] Pigot pronounced only two death sentences between 1852 and 1873. O'Brien pronounced none.

---

30 NAI, CRF/1844/Dowling/11. When Burton died in 1847 the *Freeman's Journal* paid him a handsome tribute, acknowledging that 'none ever accused Judge Burton of tampering with his high trust. No man's reason was less swayed by party feeling' (quoted in *The Times*, 13 Dec. 1847; I am indebted to Desmond Greer for this reference).

31 *Hansard 3*, cli, 18, 25 (18 June 1858). See also Larcom Papers (NLI, MS 7636). Nancy Murphy described Keogh's address as: (1) 'an impeccable account of the common law's prescription as regards the jury's attitude to the innocence or guilt of the accused'; (2) 'a meticulous trawl through the evidence recorded in his notebook' (Nancy Murphy, *Guilty or innocent? The Cormack brothers: trial, execution and exhumation* (Nenagh, Co. Tipperary, 1998), pp 66–7).

32 Rhadamanthus, *Our judges* (Dublin, 1890), pp 64, 74–5.

33 William O'Connor Morris, *Memories and thoughts of a life* (London, 1895), pp 148, 151, 154.

34 Curran, op. cit., p. 45.

'HANGING' JUDGES

'I have observed judges who are perfectly firm in every case lose their firmness and vigour in trying capital cases,' James Lawson told the capital punishment commission.[35] Lawson spoke with authority: he had been crown counsel, solicitor general, 1861–5, attorney general, 1865–6, and would be a judge of the Court of Common Pleas, 1868–82, and a judge of the Queen's Bench Division, 1882–7. Of the senior Irish lawyers who gave evidence to the capital punishment commission only Lawson and O'Hagan were abolitionists. Lefroy, Baron Fitzgerald, Deasy, Hayes, and Hughes, who also gave evidence, were retentionists. When Lawson became a judge his abolitionism did not protect him from the necessity of conducting capital trials. In a judicial career that lasted almost 20 years, he sentenced 14 prisoners to death, 8 of whom were hanged.

Since hanging was the mandatory punishment for murder, the term 'hanging judge', if it meant anything, meant a judge who had the nerve to nudge the jury towards a guilty verdict, and to advise the lord lieutenant, without fussing, whether to commute or execute the sentence. It was not easy for the judges themselves or even for the government to arrange for a particular judge to try a particular case, because the alternation of the two assize judges from county to county according to their seniority made arranging difficult. The government's power to assign a particular judge to a case was, of course, greater when a special commission was appointed. Certain names crop up again and again in capital cases. At the top of the league was Richard Moore (judge of the Queen's Bench 1847–57) who in his last five years on the bench pronounced sentence of death on 9 prisoners, of whom 3 were hanged, which implied a rate of 18 death sentences and 6 executions in a ten-year period.[36] Taking ten years on the bench as the standard of measurement, only 2 judges came close to Moore: William O'Brien, who pronounced 16 sentences of death in a ten-year period, and Barry, who pronounced 11. According to *Vanity Fair*, Barry 'has never hesitated to hang a man for whom hanging has appeared to be the correct remedy.'[37] In terms of actual numbers as opposed to ten-year rates, O'Brien and Barry were impressive: O'Brien sentenced 19, of whom 14 were hanged, Barry sentenced 18, of whom 10 were hanged. William O'Brien, therefore, can be singled out as the judge who passed most sentences of death. His high score was partly caused by the Phoenix Park murder trials, which accounted for 5 of those whom he sentenced. O'Brien had competitors among his contemporaries, apart from Barry. Lawson, for example, sentenced 14, of whom 8 were hanged.

35   *Report of the capital punishment commission, together with the minutes of evidence, and appendix*, pp 383, 388 [3590], HC 1866, xxi, 435, 441.

36   All death sentences passed from 1852 were noted in the Death Book, which continued in use until 1932 (NAI, GPB/CN/5). The amount of information gathered was not great: the prisoner's name, the judge's name, the county where sentence was passed, and the date of the execution, reprieve, or commutation.

37   Quoted in Rhadamanthus, op. cit., p. 43.

The median rate for judges was quite low: just under 4 death sentences per ten-year period. It is worth noting that the two Fitzgeralds, who seemed to be bloody and ubiquitous in the 1860s, had a combined rate that just exceeded the median, just over 4 in a ten-year period, which was low.[38] Keogh, who was probably the most execrated judge in the whole period, had a rate of just under 3 sentences of death per ten-year period, which was well below average. There were judges who did not pronounce sentence of death even once. O'Hagan, Barton, and Cherry never pronounced sentence of death.[39] Whiteside sentenced the fenians in 1867, but that was the only occasion when he pronounced sentence of death, and none of the fenians whom he sentenced was hanged. James O'Brien did not pronounce sentence of death while a judge of the Queen's Bench (1858–82), although he had pronounced sentence of death 3 times when he was second serjeant (1851–8). The low median rate for judges as a whole and the fact that some judges seemed to avoid capital trials enhance the scores of William O'Brien, Barry, and Lawson. About a quarter of all those hanged in Ireland in the period 1852–1914 were sentenced by these three; 63% of the prisoners they sentenced were hanged, which was high considering that less than half of all those sentenced to death in the decade 1881–90 were hanged.[40]

William O'Brien certainly attracted criticism. Before he had finished passing sentence on Daniel Curley for his part in the Phoenix Park murder, Curley interrupted him, making a predictable remark that 'it is a most unfortunate thing, my lord, that the Irish Bench has never been without either a Norbury or a Keogh.'[41] Alexander Sullivan was scathing about O'Brien: 'William O'Brien was a disgrace to the bench. He was a dishonest partisan who brought the administration of justice into contempt. He hated the people whose political favours he had unsuccessfully sought, and he used his position on the bench to wage war upon those whom he disliked … By way of counterpoise, he went to Mass every morning, he starved himself and fed the poor, and he shivered in threadbare garments while he clothed the naked.'[42] Yet, in spite of William O'Brien and

38 The Fitzgeralds were the Castor and Pollux of the assizes in the 1860s and 1870s. Francis Alexander Fitzgerald, who had been one of William Smith O'Brien's counsel, was made a baron of the Exchequer in 1859 by Lord Derby; John David Fitzgerald was made a judge of the Queen's Bench in 1860 by Lord Palmerston; the baron was a Protestant and the judge a Catholic (F. Elrington Ball, *The judges in Ireland, 1221–1921*, 2 vols (London, 1926), ii, 262–3).

39 Cherry was a member of the Anti-Vivisection Society and its president three times, which might imply a dislike of hanging. He was lord chief justice of Ireland at a time when hanging was not the favoured method of inflicting judicial death (Daire Hogan, 'R.R. Cherry (1859–1923), lord chief justice of Ireland, 1914–1916' in Greer & Dawson (eds), *Mysteries and solutions in Irish legal history*, p. 172).

40 Below, p. 379.

41 *Report of the trials at the Dublin Commission Court, April and May, 1883, of the prisoners charged with the Phoenix Park murder, the attempt to murder Mr Field, and the conspiracy to murder; before the Hon. Mr Justice O'Brien; reported by WC Johnson* (Dublin, 1883), p. 219.

42 *Old Ireland. Reminiscences of an Irish KC* (London, 1927), pp 72–3.

Keogh there were very few complaints about judges' bias; there were only five complaints, arising from three cases, for example, in the selection of cases discussed below.[43]

THE JUDGES' GRANDEUR

The judges had risen to the bench by a mixture of forensic ability and political pull.[44] They were usually the oldest and most experienced lawyers in court.[45] As outsiders in most of the counties where they sat, they were independent of local influence. As very rich men, at the top of their profession, they should have been beyond the blandishments of politicians,[46] and independent of the government, which could not remove them without the consent of both houses of parliament.[47] There was not much left in the way of public office for the judges, even the junior ones, to aspire to. The three senior judges, who were the two chief justices and the chief baron of the exchequer, rarely rose higher, although promotion was not impossible. Francis Blackburne, who became chief justice of the Queen's Bench in 1846, was lord chancellor in 1852 and again in 1866–7.

A few of the nine junior or 'puisne' judges, of which there were three in each of the courts of Queen's Bench, Common Pleas, and Exchequer, were promoted.

43 Below, p. 361.
44 Over half of the judges appointed to the four courts between 1801 and 1877 and to the high court and court of appeal after 1877 had been MPs, and 'nearly three quarters had been law officers' (R.B. McDowell, 'The Irish courts of law, 1801–1914' in *IHS*, 10:40 (Sept. 1957), 366). In England 53% of judges appointed between 1850 and 1875 had been MPs (Daniel Duman, *The judicial bench in England 1727–1875* (London, 1982), p. 78). The Irish attorney general had a 'traditional prerogative' to be appointed to any judicial vacancy that occurred while he was in office. For an exception see Daire Hogan, '"Vacancies for their friends": judicial appointments in Ireland, 1866–1867' in Hogan & Osborough (eds), *Brehons, serjeants and attorneys* (1990), p. 223.
45 Even the most experienced nineteenth-century judge would probably not have been as experienced as Sir Michael Davies, who tried 200 murder cases during his twenty-four years as a high court judge. He was a high court judge, 1973–91, and an acting high court judge, 1991–7. (BBC Radio 4, 27 Feb. 2000).
46 Judicial salaries were princely. The lord chief justice of the Queen's Bench had a salary of £5,074. 9s. 4d., which was rather more than the £3,688. 12s. 4d. received by the puisne judges of the same court (*Thom's Directory 1870*, p. 796). The English judges were better paid, with the lord chief justice getting £8,000 a year in 1850 and puisne judges £5,000 (Duman, op. cit., pp 22, 111–16, 122–4).
47 21 & 22 Geo. III, c. 50 (27 July 1782) laid down 'that from and after the passing of this act, the present, and all future commissions of judges for the time being, shall continue and remain in full force during their good behaviour.' If they misbehaved, 'it shall be lawful for his Majesty, his heirs and successors, to remove any judge or judges upon the address of both houses of parliament.' For the history of commissions quamdiu se bene gesserint see Henry Hallam, *The constitutional history of England from the accession of Henry VII to the death of George II*, 3 vols (7th ed., London, 1854), iii, 192–3.

O'Hagan, who had been made a judge of the Commons Pleas in 1865, became lord chancellor in 1868. John David Fitzgerald, who had been appointed a judge of the Queen's Bench in 1860 and a lord of appeal in 1882, refused the chancellorship in 1885. Michael Morris, a Catholic and a tory, was appointed a judge of the Common Pleas in 1867, chief justice of the Common Pleas in 1876, lord chief justice of Ireland in 1887, and a lord of appeal in 1889 (he was also made a baronet and raised to the peerage as Lord Killanin). Puisne judges might also aspire to the mastership of the rolls. In 1866 Lord Derby, for example, thought of promoting Francis Fitzgerald to be master of the rolls.[48] If Fitzgerald had been promoted his salary would have gone up from £3,688. 12s. 4d. to £3,969. 4s. 8d.; he would have done better as a lord of appeal in ordinary with £4,000. There were a few other things that puisne judges might aspire to. Lawson, who was appointed a judge of the Common Pleas in 1868, was made a commissioner of the church temporalities in 1869, which was not a trifle.[49] Most of the puisne judges, however, spent their careers as puisne judges.

The judges may have been superior to the temptations of wealth and blind to the frowns of politicians, but it was not easy to put them beyond the blandishments of snobbery. When Napier, who had been lord chancellor (salary £8,000), resigned in 1866 as lord justice of appeal (salary £4,000) because of his deafness, he expected a baronetcy. When Lord Derby offered him 'in lieu of a baronetcy the immediate honour of an English privy councillorship', he refused. The advantage of the baronetcy, presumably, was not only the title, but the *post-mortem* status it would confer on his wife, Charity, and on his son, William John. The privy councillorship would have been grander, but only in Napier's lifetime. He got his baronetcy in 1867, which was the year in which Benjamin Lee Guinness, who had just spent an enormous sum on the restoration of St Patrick's cathedral, got his.[50]

Judges could put on the grand manner in court. In 1865 Deasy dealt abruptly with Sub-Inspector Fawcett, who interrupted him while he was addressing a jury at Armagh spring assizes.

> His lordship – Stop, sir. Who is that person?
> Sub-Inspector Fawcett – My name, my lord, is Fawcett.
> His lordship – Well, sir! Who are you, sir? For this unseemly interference, sir, you should be committed for a contempt of court. (A pause) You stand committed, sir, for having made an observation to the jury of what you could or might have proved. You stand committed for that, sir. (Sensation)[51]

48   Hogan, '"Vacancies for their friends"', p. 223.
49   For judges' biographical details see Ball, op. cit.
50   Hogan, '"Vacancies for their friends"', p. 225.
51   Larcom Papers (NLI, MS 7620 [*Mail*, 11 Mar. 65]).

Thomas Larcom noted that 'the conduct and demeanour of the judges towards policemen, police magistrates, and officials, is systematically repulsive, and ... calculated to damp their ardour, to throw impediments in their way, and to make them feel that, in coming before a judge of assize, they were coming before a tribunal where their humility and forbearance were to be tested to the highest degree.'[52] Policemen were not the only recipients of the judge's reproofs. At the Wexford summer assizes in 1861, Judge Fitzgerald told the grand jury that 'if a suitable place were not provided in Wexford for the administration of justice, it was not improbable that one would be provided elsewhere. I may tell you Enniscorthy will be made the capital of the county, rather than that the administration of justice shall continue to take place in a structure like this.'[53] On the other hand, judges behaved with conspicuous forbearance towards prisoners. Judge Fitzgerald rebuked the Wexford grand jury, but he also ordered the governor of Castlebar gaol to provide a seat for Edward Walsh, who was about to be tried for the murder of his wife. The grandeur of the judicial office went well with humility, whether assumed or genuine.[54]

It was remarkable that these judicial leviathans were despatched twice a year to small country towns to try cases that that could have been tried by a county court judge.[55] Yet the practical effect of bringing so much prestige to bear on simple cases in provincial courthouses was more important than its apparent anachronism. The very use of such senior judges generated the power to maintain the highly artificial law of evidence and to restrain the police. Only royal splendour combined with high professional competence could have maintained a system whose main characteristics were the anomalous silence of the prisoner and the exclusion of much useful evidence. Judicial grandeur probably reached its peak in 1882 when Baron Fitzgerald became one of the few judges ever to resign on a matter of principle. When the government introduced the prevention of crimes bill after the Phoenix Park murders, the Irish judges unanimously

52 Ibid. (NLI, MS 7618 [*Express*, 26 Mar. 1862]).

53 Ibid. (NLI, MS 7620 [*Freeman's Journal*, 15 July 1861]).

54 Irish judges were not so grand outside their courts. They were not lords like the Scottish judges (twelve of whom had the title 'lord'); they were not knights like the English judges, all of whom were knights in 1870. On the other hand, they were more likely than English judges to be privy councillors (of the 12 Irish judges in 1870 only 3 were not privy councillors). See Kenneth Ferguson, *King's Inns barristers 1868–2004* (Dublin, 2005), p. 438 for an interesting note on judicial knighthoods and membership of the privy council. In the order of precedence the judges came very far down, coming after the lord mayor of Dublin, the peers, sons of peers, bishops (including Catholic bishops), and, surprisingly, after the attorney general. It was probably some consolation to them that they took precedence of knights, baronets, the provost of Trinity College, and the inspector general of constabulary (*Thom's Directory 1870*, pp 210–11, 902, 985).

55 Pronouncing sentence of death was not the exclusive prerogative of common law judges or judges of assize. For an assistant barrister sentencing a man to death in 1842 for killing a goat, see NAI, CRF/1842/Collings/5.

condemned the clause that provided for the trial of certain crimes, including murder, by three high court judges sitting without a jury. The government persisted, and the obnoxious clause became section 1(2) of the act.[56] Fitzgerald resigned 'because in his opinion the duties cast upon the judges by the act were unconstitutional.'[57] The three-judge court never actually sat.

An obvious reform of the legal system in the nineteenth-century would have been the use of less weighty judicial figures than the common law judges. The Treasury, one suspects, would have approved of less expensive judges. In the 1830s and 1840s it was common for the serjeants to be among the going judges of assize.[58] The serjeants, nevertheless, were employed less frequently rather than more frequently in the second half of the nineteenth century, although the practice of sending them on circuit persisted. Alexander Sullivan, for example, narrowly escaped assassination at Tralee assizes in 1921.[59] The last sentence of death pronounced by a serjeant seems to have been that pronounced by the second serjeant, John Howley, at Mayo assizes in 1860. Occasionally the government appointed as judges barristers who were not serjeants; O'Hagan, for example, while solicitor general was a judge at the spring assizes on the north-west circuit in 1860. On other occasions QCs were appointed. The last sentence of death, pronounced by a judge who was neither a common law judge nor a serjeant, was that pronounced by John Thomas Ball QC on Patrick Power at Wexford spring assizes in 1866.[60] These cases, however, were exceptions, and the practice of sending only the common law judges on assize persisted.

56 45 & 46 Vict., c. 25 (12 July 1882).

57 Curran, op. cit., pp 148–9.

58 A.R. Hart, *A history of the king's serjeants at law in Ireland: honour rather than advantage?* (Dublin, 2000), pp 113–22. For Richard Moore (first serjeant) on assize see NAI, CRF/1840/Byrne/40, ibid., CRF/1840/Casey and Hartnett/43.

59 Hart, op. cit., pp 121–2.

60 Death Book, 1852–1932 (NAI, GPB/CN/5). Ball was, however, of sound judicial timber: he served as judge of the consistorial court, Armagh, and as solicitor general, attorney general, and lord chancellor.

CHAPTER EIGHT

The verdict

WHEN THE JUDGE FINISHED his summing up, the clerk of the crown gave the jury the 'issue' paper, and the initiative passed to the jury.[1] The jury could give their verdict without leaving the jury-box. At the special commission at Ennis in January 1848, 'the jury, without leaving the box, found a verdict of guilty' against Thomas McInerney for the murder of Martin McMahon. Their promptness impressed the other three prisoners who were about to be tried for the same murder: their attorney 'applied to withdraw their plea of not guilty, and to plead guilty.'[2] At the special commission in Limerick in the same year, jury after jury returned verdicts without leaving the jury-box. The Limerick juries' promptness pleased the lord chief justice, Edward Pennefather: 'I never knew jurors to discharge their duties with more firmness or patience, or with more manifest conscientiousness … no doubt the country owes them a debt of gratitude.'[3] Their promptness resembled the Roman practice: 'the judge distributed among the jury small tablets, upon which they wrote secretly an A. (*absolvo*) or a C. (*condemno*), or N.L. (*non liquet*). After examining these tablets, the judge pronounced sentence, according to the opinion of the majority.'[4]

---

1 Edmund Hayes, *Crimes and punishments, or a digest of the criminal statute law of Ireland, alphabetically arranged, with ample notes, in which are discussed the powers and authorities of the several courts of criminal jurisdiction in Ireland; the duties, responsibilities, and privileges of magistrates, coroners, constables, and other officers, in bringing criminals to justice, and also the practice of the courts in punishing offences upon indictment*, 2 vols (2nd ed., Dublin, 1842), ii, 449. An exchange between Charles Hare Hemphill and Lord Hartington in 1873 suggested that the issue paper was peculiarly Irish (*First, second, and special reports from the select committee on juries (Ireland); together with the proceedings of the committee, minutes of evidence, and appendix*, p. 19, HC 1873 (283), xv, 423). Cf. Landseer's 'Laying down the law', where the dog nearest the judge is holding a piece of paper in his mouth.
2 John Simpson Armstrong, *A report of trials under a special commission for the county of Clare, held at Ennis, January 1848* (Dublin, n.d. [1849]), p. 150.
3 Armstrong, *A report of trials held under a special commission for the county of Limerick, held at Limerick, January 1848* (Dublin, n.d. [1849]), pp 45, 58, 79, 109, 138, 142, 145, 184, 208, 305. Pennefather's speech is at p. 314.
4 Thomas MacKenzie, *Studies in Roman law with comparative views of the laws of France, England, and Scotland* (Edinburgh and London, 1862), p. 338.

When the jury retired to consider their verdict, what went on in the jury room does not seem to have been a secret. In *R. v. M'Eneany,* for example, Judge Fitzgerald deplored the fact that the prisoner's solicitor had gone around asking jurors for their opinions of his client's guilt, which he thought 'was fraught with danger to the administration of justice and nearly approaches and may lead to the canvassing of jurors', but he did not say that what went on in the jury-room was supposed to be a secret.[5] Occasionally there are clues to how the jurors struggled towards their verdict. Peter Barrett, a postman in London and a member of the Middlesex Volunteers, fired five shots at Captain Thomas Eyre Lambert, a Galway landlord, who had evicted his father. Captain Lambert lived to give evidence against Barrett at Galway assizes, but the jury failed to agree. The Crown moved the trial to Dublin. In the chief crown solicitor's papers there is a letter, written by the foreman of the Dublin jury, which revealed 'the inner life and sentiments of the jury'.[6] The foreman, James Barrett, was one of the majority in favour of convicting the prisoner, but he acknowledged the two jurors who had held out for an acquittal as 'the two most intelligent and independent-minded men on the jury'.[7] The foreman also believed that the jury would have been unanimous for conviction, if the prisoner had been charged with aiding and abetting. The foreman was not impressed by Captain Lambert. 'No honest intelligent jury could convict on the evidence as to the identification by Captain Lambert,' he wrote. 'It was given just as a schoolboy would repeat a story he had got by heart, but when put out by cross-examination, his sole effort seemed to be to fence, and shuffle, and hesitate respecting details that he must have known and should have stated, if he meant to tell the plain truth; in fact, Captain Lambert appeared too anxious to get a conviction, and with that view exercised a cunning in avoiding to give answers to the plainest questions.'[8]

The jury's difficulties might be discussed in court. After Kilkenny summer assizes in 1841, the judge, Richard Pennefather, described how a jury inched its way to convicting Patrick Donovan of murder:

---

5   (1878) 2 LR Ir 236, at p. 242.
6   NAI, CCS/1870/197. I am indebted to Ruth Thorpe for providing me with a copy of this letter, which is at p. 10 of the Crown's brief.
7   There were two 'J. Barretts' and two 'James Barretts' at *Thom's Directory 1870*, p. 1687. One of the 'James Barretts' was a solicitor and the other a barrister, which excluded both from jury service. Of the two 'J. Barretts', one was J.T. Cresswell Barrett, of 121 Leinster Street, Rathmines, and the other an umbrella manufacturer at 45 Wicklow Street. Daniel F. Brady, to whom the letter was sent, was described in CCS/1870/197 as 'a gentleman of the highest position' (which was probably true because he was MD, FRCSI, JP, MRIA, and lived at The Hut, Howth).
8   For a description of an American jury's deliberations see Michael Traub, 'Judgment day' in *New York Review of Books*, 4 Oct. 2001, pp 17–18, which is a review of D. Graham Burnett, *A trial by jury* (New York, 2001). Burnett, who served as foreman of a jury at a homicide trial in Manhattan Criminal Court, observed that he and his fellow jurors were more attracted to wildly elaborate hypothetical possibilities than to straightforward explanations. He also observed that the sharply divided jury began to think of a compromise, 'as if the goal was consensus rather

The jury retired and after some time sent to inform me that they were not likely to agree. I had them brought into court and asked them if I could assist them, by explaining further, or going over again any portion of the evidence. They replied that they did not want any further assistance from me, that eleven were satisfied, but one juror declined to agree with them. I told them that they must retire again to their jury room and consult together on the case; they again retired, and in about two hours returned into court with a verdict of guilty, the foreman saying that if I could discover any mitigating circumstances one or two or two or three of the jury were desirous of recommending the prisoner to mercy. I then asked them to point out what circumstances of mitigation occurred to any of them, and, upon my pausing and not receiving any answer, the foreman said that the desire of recommendation did not proceed from the jury at large, but from one or two members of it.[9]

Part of the problem of getting a verdict was the fact that the jury should be unanimous, a requirement that led to some strange practices. If the whigs had invented the jury in the 1830s, they would probably have established majority verdicts, as in Scotland and France. In Scotland 8 of the 15 jurors could give a verdict.[10] In France, where juries had 12 members, the law of 28 February 1832 declared that 'no decision can be given against the accused except by a majority of more than 7 votes.'[11] Majority verdicts might have prevented the practice of starving juries into returning verdicts. From the moment the clerk gave the foreman the issue paper, the jurors were condemned to be starved into unanimity. The bailiff who guarded them swore to keep them 'from all manner of easement, meat, drink, or fire; candlelight only excepted.'[12] In *Conway and Lynch*, a murder case in 1845, the Queen's Bench heard how a jury had been locked up for 24 hours, and they also heard of a case in Limerick where Serjeant Greene had kept a jury locked up for 36 hours.[13] By the late 1840s, however, the rule about food and drink 'has been occasionally relaxed; and on special application the court may allow refreshment to be supplied to the jury.'[14] Jurors' discomfort was formally mitigated by the Juries Procedure (Ireland) Act, 1876, section 12, which provided that 'jurors, after having been sworn, may, in the discretion of the judge, be

than justice', and that 'the frustrated feelings of the jury – the impatience, the rising irritation, the dread of spending another night in the hotel – began to warp its deliberations.'

9 NAI, CRF/1841/Donovan/53. Donovan was hanged on 28 August 1841.
10 James Paterson, *A compendium of English and Scotch law stating their differences: with a dictionary of parallel terms and phrases* (Edinburgh, 1860), p. 331.
11 MacKenzie, op. cit., pp 357–8.
12 Hayes, op. cit., ii, 454.
13 *Conway and Lynch* (1845) 7 Ir LR 149, at pp 194, 156.
14 Theobald A. Purcell, *A summary of the general principles of pleading and evidence, in criminal cases in Ireland: with the rules of practice incident thereto* (Dublin, 1849), pp 204–5. See for example *Locke and M'Garry* (1845) 3 Cr & Dix 393, at p. 394.

allowed, at any time before giving their verdict, the use of a fire when out of court, and be allowed also to obtain reasonable refreshment.'[15] Even before the 1876 act, some judges tried to avoid locking up juries for the night. At the end of the Crown's second speech at Stephen McKeown's trial, Judge Fitzgerald announced that he would keep his summing up until the next morning, 'as it was a case requiring the greatest consideration by the jury. If he proceeded now it was likely the jury would require to be locked up all night.'[16]

In capital cases jurors could not be discharged 'until they have given in a verdict, unless in a case of *evident necessity*.'[17] Evident necessity included the danger that a juror might die 'if longer confined'. Even when there was medical evidence that the jurors had had enough, discharge was not a foregone conclusion. At John Ryan's trial at Kilkenny assizes in 1832, for aiding and assisting at the murder of Edmond Butler, 'the jury retired to their chamber, where they remained until the following morning, without agreeing as to their verdict. It having been then announced to the court, that Mr J. Burchell, (a juror) was dangerously ill, his lordship directed that two medical gentlemen should attend him. Doctor Alcock and Surgeon Peele having accordingly examined the nature of the juror's indisposition, reported to the court that it would be unsafe to keep him locked up any longer.' Baron Foster had no doubt of his 'complete' discretion to discharge the jury. Crown counsel, however, objected, and asserted that the Crown 'cannot be a party to any thing like an assent to the discharge of the jury.'[18]

The established remedy for jurors who could not agree was 'carting': they were kept until the end of the assizes, loaded into a cart and taken to the boundary of the county. In a larceny case at Roscommon assizes in 1793, 8 jurors were for a verdict of guilty, and 4 for acquittal; the judge ordered the carts to be prepared; 'the foreman, accordingly, insisted that those differing from him, 4 in number, should give way, and find the prisoner guilty. They, with equal determination, resisted all persuasion. A hand-to-hand fight ensued.'[19] In *Conway and Lynch* it was claimed that carting had been practised in Ireland within the last ten years by Bushe, who had a jury carted for 20 miles from Trim; it was also claimed that Torrens had had a jury carted for 23 miles.[20] This practice, according to Purcell, 'is now exploded ... and the proper course for the judge to adopt in such cases

15 39 & 40 Vict., c. 78 (15 Aug. 1876). According to Bentley (*English criminal justice in the nineteenth century* (London and Rio Grande, 1998), p. 277) the rule about fire, food, and drink had in practice been abolished in Ireland by the 1860s.

16 NAI, CRF/1876/McKeown/22.

17 Purcell, op. cit., p. 205. See also Bentley, op. cit., pp 275–7.

18 James Mongan, *A report of the trials of John Kennedy, John Ryan, and William Voss, for the murder of Edmond Butler, at Carrickshock on the 14th December, 1831, tried before the Hon. Baron Foster, at the spring and summer assizes of Kilkenny, 1832* (Dublin, 1832), pp 110, 184–6.

19 Oliver J. Burke, *Anecdotes of the Connaught circuit: from its foundation to close upon the present time* (Dublin, 1885), pp 163–4. Neal Garnham mentions the use of donkeys and panniers to carry recalcitrant jurors (*The courts, crime and the criminal law in Ireland 1692–1760* (Dublin, 1996), p. 115).

20 (1845) 7 Ir LR, 149, at p. 156.

appears to be to discharge the jury, and to cause the reasons which have induced him to consider it necessary to do so to be set out upon the record, in order to their being reviewed, if necessary, by a higher court.'[21]

Purcell was reflecting the decision of the Queen's Bench in *Conway and Lynch*. Patrick Lynch and Edward Conway were tried at Limerick summer assizes in 1843 for the murder of Charles Dawson; the jury disagreed and were discharged.[22] The prisoners were put on trial again at the adjourned summer assizes when two juries failed to reach a verdict, in one case because a juror was taken ill, and in the other because they could not agree; eventually the jury that could not agree was 'discharged at a late hour on Saturday night.' The decision to discharge the jury was so momentous that it was done 'with the concurrence of the *two* judges before whom the assizes were held.'[23] The prisoners were put on trial for the fourth time in March 1844, when their counsel 'tendered a plea, setting out the facts of the prisoners having been tried before, and the jury being discharged without the occurrence of any fatality or accident, they not having agreed to a verdict.'[24] This was a plea of *puis darrein continuance*, which was of rare occurrence; it implied that something had happened since the last sitting of the court to affect the proceedings. The judge, Joseph Devonsher Jackson, who had presided at the earlier trials, had tried to anticipate the problem:

> The point having been raised before, as it was a new one, I took every pains to have the matter investigated, and I wrote to Mr Justice Cresswell on the subject, who informed me that a similar case was not known to have occurred except once before Lord Denman, and that on that occasion the feeling in Westminster Hall on the subject was in favour of the point that a jury might be discharged under such circumstances, and the prisoner legally tried again. I endeavoured to obtain the opinion of the twelve judges upon the point, but unfortunately some of them were ill; however, the majority of them attended, but they had an objection to go into any case *à priori*, and declined coming to any resolution on the subject.[25]

The point may have been a new one, as Jackson stated, but the problem was not. Four years before, in 1839, Bushe had told the house of lords select committee on the state of Ireland that 'there has been the occurrence of late years of one failure of justice much more frequently than formerly, from ... the jury not agreeing, and the judge being therefore obliged to discharge them.'[26] Jackson,

---

21   Purcell, op. cit., p. 206.
23   7 Ir LR 149, at p. 188.
25   Ibid., p. 82.

22   (1844) 1 Cox 81, at p. 81.
24   1 Cox 81, at p. 82.

26   *Minutes of evidence taken before the select committee of the house of lords appointed to enquire into the state of Ireland, since the year 1835, in respect of crime and outrage, which have rendered life and property insecure in that part of the empire*, pt III, *evidence 12 June to 19 July*, p. 875, HC 1839 (486–III), xii, 11.

perhaps to resolve a point that was becoming contentious, decided to let the fourth trial continue, and to reserve the case. The prisoners were found guilty of murder, and their case was brought to the Queen's Bench by a writ of error in January 1845. Why a writ of error was used when the judge had decided to reserve the case for the twelve judges is not clear. It is possible that the prisoners' counsel felt they had a better chance of success before the Queen's Bench because one of its judges, Philip Crampton, had discharged two juries at the Tipperary spring assizes in 1839.[27]

The prisoners' counsel stated their case succinctly: 'We say it is contrary to the law of the land to discharge a jury charged in a capital case with prisoners, on the supposition that reasonable time had elapsed for their finding a verdict.'[28] The report of the case filled forty-six pages of the *Irish Law Reports*. Three of the four judges decided that the convictions should be reversed, which meant that the Irish Court of Queen's Bench had gone against the opinion of Westminster Hall, as conveyed by Cresswell to Jackson, that 'a jury might be discharged under such circumstances, and the prisoner legally tried again.'[29] The prisoners were discharged and released. The issues were momentous. Was such a discharge the same as an acquittal? According to Burton the prisoners were asking that they 'might be discharged without a day from the premises in the indictment and that the same might not be further prosecuted against them'.[30] If such a discharge was not an acquittal, and if the prisoners were put on trial again for the same offence, was that not contrary to 'the humane principle of our criminal law … that the life of a prisoner shall not be twice put in jeopardy, as it is contended by the prisoners' counsel has been done in the present case'?[31] Did such an exercise of judicial power go too far? Perrin thought it did, for he would 'not acknowledge the existence of any discretionary power in a judge to act upon his own opinion, without grounds shown, which may be considered by a superior court. I know of no authority for such a position.'[32]

None of those involved, counsel or judges, denied that jurors could be discharged in certain circumstances. Christopher Copinger, counsel for the prisoners, for example, argued that the Crown's replication did not mention the circumstances that would have justified the discharge of the jury, an enumeration of which showed that discharge was possible:

> it does not appear from it whether the assizes had terminated with the trial of these prisoners, nor that there was no other business to be disposed of, nor that the jury were discharged at the bounds of the county, nor that they were carried from county to county during the continuance of the

27 Ibid., p. 877.   28 7 Ir LR 149, at p. 154.
29 For English judges' references to *Conway and Lynch*, see *R. v. Newton* (1849) 3 Cox CC 489, at pp 495, 496, 498.
30 7 Ir LR 149, at p. 187.   31 Ibid., p. 178.
32 Ibid., p. 164.

commission, nor that they were discharged at the request of the prisoners, nor for the benefit of the jury themselves; nor does it appear that they were discharged by any misconduct of the prisoners, or any fatality happening, or any sudden interruption to the due course of justice, or any violation of their duty as jurors, or any disqualification of them by attainder or otherwise from serving.[33]

The gravamen of the case was stated by Perrin:

Whether after the lapse of more than what the presiding judge considers a sufficient and reasonable time to enable the jury to consider and fully deliberate upon their verdict, and agree to it, and when they, in open court, declare before the judge, that they had not agreed, and that they would not agree together upon a verdict, nor find or say whether the prisoner was guilty or not; whether upon that lapse of time, sufficient in the estimation of the judge, he may, of his own authority and in the exercise of a discretionary power in him vested, and without the consent either of the prisoner or of the prosecutor, discharge the jury from giving a verdict?[34]

Perrin not only stated the issue clearly, he also produced powerful arguments against discharging recalcitrant juries. First, he believed that if juries could be discharged because they disagreed, 'there would be a number of instances in which the case of no verdicts being given would be considerably increased.'[35] Secondly, he denied that judges had the power to act on their own opinion 'without grounds shown':

I know of no authority for such a position; none such is alluded to in the argument of counsel, or in the very deliberate judgments and reasoning of the Judges Foster and Wright, in *Kinloch's case*; nor do I find the existence of a power and authority of such extent in any of the books. I recollect even in civil cases, when juries remained in a considerable time, it was considered a juror could not be withdrawn without consent.[36]

Thirdly, he referred to his own notes of a case that had occurred at Carrickfergus in 1809: William Kell was indicted for rape, pleaded not guilty, but the jury was discharged when the prosecutrix 'appeared so much agitated and in so infirm a state' that she could not be examined.[37] At the following summer assizes when Kell was about to be given in charge to the jury

---

33   Ibid., p. 154.   34   Ibid., p. 160.
35   Ibid., p. 164.
36   *Alexander and Charles Kinloch* (1746) Fost 16, 168 Eng Rep 9. In this case the judges (who were Willes CJ, Foster J, and Clive B) refused to allow the twelfth juror sworn to be withdrawn in order allow the prisoners to withdraw their pleas of not guilty.
37   7 Ir LR 149, at p. 162. See also *Kell* (1809) 1 Cr & Dix 151.

Fox, J., stated that Daly, J., had laid the circumstances of this case before the judges in Dublin, who were of opinion, that the prisoner could not be again tried for the same offence; that the consent of his counsel made no difference; that they had considered all the cases; that a discretionary power had been before the Revolution exercised by the judges, of interrupting and then postponing trials; that they considered such conduct highly dangerous, and likely to be oppressive.

Perrin and the two judges who were in favour of reversing the judgment seem to have represented the opinion of most of the Irish judges. In two other cases in 1844, before the Queen's Bench had made its decision in *Conway and Lynch*, other judges had followed the same line anticipating the Queen's Bench's decision. In *Lecken*, which was a murder trial at the Meath spring assizes, Doherty discharged a jury that had been locked up from the evening of one day to 5 p.m. on the following day, but he did so only because of the illness of one of the jurors: he was at pains to say that he would not have done so, 'were I not convinced that confinement would be attended with danger to one of the jurors, I would feel bound to adhere to the English practice, and keep the jury together until the termination of the assizes.'[38] At the trial of Jeremiah Leary and John Cooke at the Tipperary spring assizes, Ball refused to discharge the jury even though the foreman said they were not likely to agree and asked to be discharged.[39] His decision apparently reflected the thinking of the judges:

It is quite true that on former occasions the course now suggested was adopted: but, at a meeting held shortly before the circuits, the judges came to the conclusion that, whatever the practice may have been in particular instances hitherto, they were not warranted in discharging a jury for mere disagreement. Upon looking more accurately into the law, they have arrived at the conclusion, that it is not within the power of the judges to discharge a jury, merely because they have remained for a considerable time without any prospect of an agreement.

This is a remarkable statement, when read in the light of Jackson's statement in *Conway and Lynch* at the Limerick summer assizes where he contended, almost simultaneously, that the judges had not made a decision on the matter.

Crampton, who was the only one of the four judges who thought that hung juries could be discharged, stressed the evolutionary nature of law and pointed to the future:

There may be (and no doubt often are) cases in which different men will honestly draw different conclusions from the same evidence, and to attempt

---

38 (1844) 3 Cr & Dix 174, at p. 175.   39 (1844) 3 Cr & Dix, 212, at p. 213.

by punishment to force men to agree to verdicts contrary to their conviction, is the height of injustice, and pregnant with the most mischievous consequences. The principle then of punishing juries into agreement is exploded; but some of the rules flowing mainly from that principle still continue to operate; these, however, have been greatly modified in modern practice.[40]

The modifications that showed the rule was 'exploded' were: jurors were now allowed to have candle-light at night; criminal courts could adjourn from day to day and did not have to sit in continuous session until the trial ended; carting had fallen into disuse; 'the rule as to discharging juries, who after a reasonable time cannot agree, has been also greatly relaxed.'

Crampton might also have referred to the trial of four prisoners at a special commission in Cork in 1829, when Richard Pennefather and Torrens had appeared to fix a confinement of 37 hours as the *ne plus ultra* of jury misery.[41] The trial began at 9 a.m. on Monday, 26 October. The jury retired at about 11 p.m.; at 2 a.m. they acquitted Barrett, but could not agree on the others. At 10 a.m. on the Tuesday, 'the judges returned to court, and they were called out. They said they had not agreed, and that although they had canvassed the case over and over again, it was impossible they could agree; they were then sent back to their room, and kept as strictly as before.'[42] At 6 p.m. the judges returned, and the jury still had not agreed, but some of them now complained of sickness, which was not surprising since the trial had now been going on for 33 hours. Physicians examined them, and declared that one of them 'could not be confined another night without danger to his life, in a room without fire or food. They said, however, that there would not be much risk in his remaining until ten o'clock.' At 10 p.m. the jurors were still divided, and the judges decided to discharge them, but 'counsel for the prisoners objected to the discharge of the jury, but said they would consent to their getting nourishment.'[43] The Crown struck a neutral attitude: 'the solicitor general replied, that they would not interfere or give any consent, but that the course about to be adopted met with their full concurrence.' On the following day the solicitor general proposed to put the three prisoners on trial again, but their counsel objected, insisting that the jury had been improperly discharged and that the prisoners could not be tried again! The judges decided to reserve the case. The twelve judges 'were unanimously of opinion, that the jury were properly discharged, and that the prisoners were triable again at the same commission, if the judge had thought proper to try them.'[44]

It was not finally established until 1865 that the judge could discharge a hung jury and put the prisoner on trial a second time. In that year in *R v. Winsor* Lord Chief Justice Cockburn brought the middle ages to an end:

40 7 Ir LR 149, at p. 170.
41 *R. v. Barrett, Connors, and two others* (1829) Jebb Rep 103.
42 Ibid., p. 104.   43 Ibid., p. 105.   44 Ibid., p. 106.

Our ancestors insisted on unanimity as the very essence of the verdict, but they were unscrupulous as to the means by which they obtained it; whether the minority gave way to the majority, or the reverse, appears to have been a matter of indifference. It was a struggle between the strong and the weak, the able-bodied and the infirm; which could best sustain hunger and thirst, and all the misery incidental to it … We now look upon the trial by jury, as regards the principles on which juries are to act, in a different light. We do not desire that the unanimity of a jury should be the result of anything but the unanimity of conviction … I hold it to be of the essence of a juryman's duty, if he has a firm and deeply seated and rooted conviction, either in the affirmative or in the negative of the issue he has to try, that he is not to give up that conviction although the majority may be against him, from any desire to purchase his freedom from confinement or constraint, or the various other inconveniences that jurors are subject to. That being so, when a reasonable time has elapsed, and the judge is perfectly convinced that the unanimity of the jury can only be obtained through the sacrifice of honest conscientious convictions, why is he to subject them to torture and to the misery of being shut up without food, drink, or fire, in order that the minority may give way, or the majority, possibly (who can tell?), and so purchase ease to themselves by a sacrifice of their conscience?[45]

It was only when the jury retired to consider their verdict that their misery began. They could be treated hospitably during the trial if it lasted for more than one day.[46] The accommodation provided for jurors varied from county to county. In 1852 Kirwan's jury was sent to the Northumberland Hotel on Eden Quay; in 1863 Ward's jury was put up in special accommodation provided in Belfast courthouse.[47] During Francis Hynes' trial in Dublin in 1882, the sub-sheriff lodged the jury in The Imperial Hotel in Sackville Street, which was an indiscreet choice, because The Imperial, which had been for years the resort of parish priests, was where the Irish National Land League had been founded on 21 October 1879,

45 (1865) 10 Cox CC 276, at p. 310.
46 The right of courts to adjourn during criminal trials was established in England in 1794 during the treason trials (James Fitzjames Stephen, *A history of the criminal law of England*, 3 vols (London, 1883), i, 403). There is a history of adjournment in Ireland in *Copies "of any documents (except official documents of a confidential and privileged character) in the nature of evidence or memorials, submitted for the consideration of the Irish executive, with reference to the alleged misconduct of members of the jury, the verdict, and the sentence, in the case of Francis Hynes, convicted of murder in the Dublin Commission Court on the 12th of August 1882, and executed in Limerick; and, of any letters written by the lord lieutenant with reference to such documents"*, pp 28–9, HC 1882 (408), lv, 194–5. See William Roughead, *Twelve Scots trials* (Edinburgh and London, 1913) for the long sittings of Scottish eighteenth-century courts, which sat continuously until both sides were heard. At Katherine Nairn's trial, for example, the jury repeatedly '"dispersed into different corners of the house," eating and drinking as they pleased, and talking to the crown witnesses and the counsel for the prosecution' (p. 127).
47 NAI, CRF/1863/Ward/5.

and since then land league MPs had made a 'special affectation' of staying there.[48] What the jurors drank at dinner in The Imperial became a matter of public curiosity when William O'Brien denounced their conviviality in a letter to the *Freeman's Journal*. O'Brien was within months of being elected home rule MP for Mallow, but he had already established himself as a power in the land. A parliamentary inquiry elicited the details of what the jurors had drunk on the evening of the first day of the trial.[49] Three had not drunk anything alcoholic, either before or during dinner, which might suggest that the temperance movement had won over one-quarter of the Dublin middle class. Ephraim Phillips, draper, 37 Grafton Street, for example, said he was 'a pledged total abstainer', but he was one of six jurors who went to play billiards after dinner, which does not suggest unbending self-righteousness. The foreman noted what he had ordered for the nine jurymen who were not abstainers: before dinner half a pint of sherry and a half pint of gin; at dinner three bottles of claret, one pint of sherry, one bottle of champagne, and one pint of whiskey. After dinner 'while in the billiard room, the only drink taken by the jurors was: Mr Reis 2 half glasses of brandy and soda, Mr Gibson 2 glasses of beer, Mr Wardrop 2 half-glasses of whiskey and water, and myself 2 glasses of sherry and soda-water, which, with the wine which I before mentioned as being drunk by me, was the entire stimulants of which I partook while at the hotel; the other 2 jurors in the billiard room, *videlicet*, Mr Phillips and Mr Maconchy, did not take anything.' The foreman seems to have been the paymaster. 'These were the only things brought to us,' he said, 'and I believe nothing was ordered except by me.'

The wine, beer, and spirits took their toll. When Margaret Walsh closed The Imperial's bar at 12.20 a.m., the jurors 'were jumping across each other.' The night porter described their return to the third floor where their bedrooms were: 'They were playing tricks with one another; one of them wanted to steal the boots of the other.' The juror who had been the heart and soul of the party, Charles Lionel Reis, became embroiled with a hip-bath that had been left in the corridor. He complained later that the corridor was badly lighted, that he had no candle-

---

48 Frederick Moir Bussy, *Irish conspiracies: recollections of John Mallon (The Great Detective) and other reminiscences* (London, 1910), p. 217.

49 *Copies 'of any documents'*, pp 13–15, HC 1882 (408), lv, 179–81. The jurors in Hynes' case were well-behaved compared with those in a civil case in 1869, which was tried by Michael Morris, then a newly appointed judge of the Common Pleas. As Morris was about to charge the jury, 'one of the jurors asked to have one of the witnesses recalled. On re-examination the witness admitted that he treated two of the jury, and told them he knew more about a certain point in dispute. The judge said that in his opinion the conduct of two of the jury going into a public house with the witness, and being treated by him and discussing the case, was very improper; but it did not strike him as amounting to misconduct affecting the trial. And he came to the conclusion that the meeting with the witness was accidental and the conversation one not affecting the result. He was not dissatisfied with the verdict' (William G. Huband, *A practical treatise on the law relating to the grand jury in criminal cases the coroner's jury and the petty jury in Ireland* (Dublin, 1896), p. 715 (citing *Harris v. Harris* (1868) IR 3 CL 294, at pp 298, 302–3).

stick, and that he was short-sighted. 'I did not notice a bath which was lying against the wall,' he said. 'My foot came against it and it fell; on replacing it it fell again, and then somewhat noisily I put it up against the wall.' (Reis was the proprietor of a firm of jewellers and goldsmiths at 5 Grafton Street.) The jurors believed that they had the third floor to themselves, which should have been the case. Two of the hotel's permanent lodgers, however, had been left in their rooms when the floor was 'cleared' for the jury. One, Elizabeth Josephine Carberry, complained that 'they came to my door several times and turned the handle. They kicked at the door again and again. I thought they would smash the fanlight over the door by knocking at it with their knuckles; only that my door was locked I believe that they would have forced it in.' Unfortunately for the jury, the other permanent lodger was William O'Brien, who made the affair public in a letter to the *Freeman's Journal* of 14 August. 'The disturbance lasted for a considerable time before my door was burst open,' he wrote. 'The man who entered my room was under the influence of drink. He was a low-sized dark-complexioned black-haired man, and wore glasses. After he left the room I rang and complained to the night porter of the intolerable misconduct that was going on.' The *Freeman*'s publication of O'Brien's letter led to its editor, Edmund Dwyer Gray, being imprisoned for contempt by the trial judge, James Lawson, which in turn led to a debate in the house of commons. The fact that Gray was also high sheriff of the city of Dublin and responsible for the custody of the jury added a certain piquancy to the affair. The jury found Hynes guilty, and in spite of the controversy associated with their deliberations, he was hanged on 11 September 1882.[50]

THE VERDICT

The jury had to give their verdict in open court and in the prisoner's presence. When they had reached their verdict, their foreman gave the clerk of the crown the issue paper, 'upon which he has previously entered the verdict.'[51] The clerk called out the names of the jurors, 'who must be all within hearing, and must respectively answer to their names', and asked them: 'Gentlemen have you agreed upon your verdict? Who shall say for you?' To this they were supposed to answer 'Our foreman.' The clerk asked the foreman for the verdict. When the foreman answered, the clerk entered the verdict in his book, which made it a part of the

---

50 Sir Robert Ponsonby Staples Bt. (1853–1943) exhibited 'Guilty or Not Guilty' at the Royal Academy in 1883 and at the Royal Hibernian Academy in 1886. It shows twelve men gathered round a table; there is a revolver on the table; the juror in the foreground is standing and addressing the others. For a reproduction see Christie's *The Irish Sale, Thursday 20 May 1999*, p. 147. Even if Staples did not take his subject from the Hynes case, his painting would have reminded the public of it.

51 Purcell, op. cit., p 207.

'record' of the trial. The clerk again asked the jury if 'this is your verdict, and so say you all?'[52]

The judge could ask the jury to reconsider their verdict, but in the end they could insist on having their verdict recorded,[53] which left the judge only a cumbersome solution

> if a jury give a verdict against all reason, and convict a man without, or against all evidence, and against the direction of the court, the court may reprieve him before judgment, and acquaint the sovereign, and certify for his pardon; or, on the other hand, if the jury acquit him in like manner, the court may send them back again (and so in the former case) to consider better of it before they record the verdict; but if they are peremptory to it, and stand to their verdict, the court must take their verdict, and record it.[54]

The judge's intervention could come even earlier in the trial when he could direct the jury to acquit the prisoner. James O'Brien recalled that at the city of Limerick spring assizes in 1865 'at the close of the case for the Crown, it was contended that there was not sufficient evidence to go to the jury to sustain the charge against Thomas Galvin sen. I was of that opinion; and crown counsel did not press the case against him. I therefore directed the jury to acquit him, which accordingly they did.'[55] The judge could insist that the trial go on, even if the case were a clear one. At the special commission in Clare in 1848, for example, Patrick Cusack offered to plead guilty after the jury were empanelled, but the lord chief justice insisted that the trial go on.[56]

'Guilty' or 'not guilty' were known as general verdicts. The jury could also return a special verdict when it found 'the particular facts proved in evidence, and leaves it to the court to draw the inference, whether or not those facts amount to the crime charged'; in a special verdict for murder, 'the jury need not find malice, that being a conclusion of law from the facts.'[57] When a special verdict was returned, 'it should be removed by *certiorari* into the Queen's Bench for argument.'[58] According to Stephen, writing of England, special verdicts 'have now gone almost entirely out of use, having been superseded by the establishment of a court called the Court for Crown Cases Reserved',[59] but a year after this

---

52 Newspapers did not always report the different stages of the verdict in detail; see, for example, NAI, CRF/1873 Walsh/11.

53 Purcell, op. cit., pp 206–7; John G. Thompson, *The law of criminal procedure in Ireland* (Dublin, 1899), p. 91. Cf. *Conway and Lynch* (1845) 7 Ir LR 149, at p. 178 where Crampton stated that 'no verdict can be recorded without the sanction of the court'.

54 Purcell, op. cit., p. 172.   55 *Galvin* (1865) 16 ICLR 452, at p. 456.

56 Armstrong, *A report of trials held under a special commission for the county of Limerick ... January 1848*, p. 26.

57 Hayes, op. cit., ii, 919, 920; Thompson, op. cit., p. 91.

58 Hayes, op. cit., ii, 921.

59 *A history of the criminal law of England*, 3 vols (London, 1883), i, 311.

TABLE 8.1
VERDICTS IN MURDER AND MANSLAUGHTER CASES, 1866–75

results	manslaughter	murder
guilty	356	32
not guilty	226	91
acquitted as insane	0	19
other	175	102
total returned for trial	757	244

statement was made, the jury returned a special verdict in *R. v. Dudley and Stephens*, the nautical cannibalism case. According to Brian Simpson, who has studied *R. v. Dudley and Stephens*, the last special verdict in England had been in 1785, which vindicates Stephen's grasp of history, but not his capacity to foretell the future.[60] There were special verdicts in Ireland long after 1785. In 1826, at Clonmel, for example, John Larkin was indicted on two counts; the first was for firing a shot at James Jones with intent to murder him, and the second for firing a shot at John Cantrell with intent to murder him. Jones and Cantrell had been trying to execute a special warrant on a civil bill ejectment against Larkin. The jury found Larkin guilty on both counts, 'but stated to the judge, that they believed he fired at both Jones and Cantrell with intent to kill whichever of the two the shot should strike; but they did not believe he intended to kill both.'[61]Bushe reserved the case for the 12 judges, 9 of whom 'held it to be fully established by the authorities that if there be malice against one, and the shot be fired with a malicious intent against him, and it should strike another against whom there was no malice, yet the offence under the act is complete.'[62]

It may be argued that this was not a true special verdict: it did not go before the King's Bench but to the twelve judges, and the jury had found Larkin guilty. A true special verdict, however, occurred in *R. v. Milles*, a bigamy case in 1842, when the statement of the jury ran to two pages of print, ending with the words 'and the jurors pray the advice of the court.'[63] The case was before the Queen's Bench for 'several' days; two of the judges were of the opinion that the first marriage was valid, two were of the opinion that it was invalid. Perrin, who thought the first marriage was valid withdrew his judgment 'in order to allow the question to be brought before the house of lords'.

The jury could also bring in a general verdict 'accompanied by a special case, in which the facts are set out, for the purpose of obtaining the opinion of the

60 A.W. Brian Simpson, *Cannibalism and the common law* (Chicago, 1984), p. 209.
61 Jebb Rep 60, at p. 60.   62 Ibid., p. 61.
63 4 Ir LR 495, at p. 496.

judges.'[64] At the 1840 spring assizes in Cork, for example, Patrick Murphy was indicted for soliciting James Barrett to poison his wife. Perrin

> requested the jury, if they believed the evidence, and found a verdict of guilty, to inform him whether they were of opinion that the solicitation had been to murder generally, or to administer salt petre with intent to murder; and that the salt petre had been administered, or only attempted to be administered. The jury found the prisoner guilty, and in compliance with the request of the learned judge, informed him that they were of opinion that the solicitation had been to administer salt petre with intent to poison, and that the salt petre had been attempted to be administered.[65]

A general verdict accompanied by a special case might be a better description of *Larkin* referred to above, although there is a distinction between the two: in *Larkin* the initiative came from the jury, but in *Murphy* the initiative came from the judge.

The jury could return a guilty verdict that was less than murder. According to Purcell, 'if A. be charged with the murder of B., i.e. with feloniously killing B. of malice prepense, and all but the fact of malice be proved, A. may be clearly convicted of manslaughter, for the indictment contains all the allegations essential to that charge. A. is fully apprized of the nature of it, the verdict enables the court to pronounce the proper judgment, and A. may plead his acquittal or conviction in bar of any subsequent indictment founded on the same facts.'[66] Purcell also noted a limitation on how far the jury could go, for while 'it is sufficient to prove so much of the charge as constitutes a substantive offence punishable by law', the offence proved must 'be of the *same class* with that charged in the indictment … This distinction runs through the whole criminal law.' What this meant was that a prisoner charged with a felony could not be found guilty of a misdemeanour, and vice versa, 'except under an express statutory provision'.[67] An example of an act that allowed juries to find prisoners guilty of a misdemeanour, even if they had been put on trial for a felony, was the act of 1837 that abolished capital punishment for certain offences against the person: it allowed juries in cases where prisoners were charged with 'any felony whatever, where the crime charged shall include an assault against the person' to acquit the prisoner of felony and to find a verdict of guilty of assault.[68] In 1841, at Tullamore assizes, Doherty left it

---

64 Hayes, op. cit., ii, 919.
65 *Patrick Murphy* (1840) Jebb Rep 315, at p. 318. Above, p. 113.
66 Purcell, op. cit., p. 261.
67 Thompson, op. cit., p. 93; Hayes, op. cit., ii, 918.
68 7 Will. & 1 Vict., c. 85, s. 11 (17 July 1837). Section 11 was repealed by 24 & 25 Vict., c. 95 (6 Aug. 1861) but was maintained in a slightly different form by 24 & 25 Vict., c. 100, ss 23–5. Section 60 of that act also provided that a prisoner charged with child murder could be convicted of endeavouring to conceal birth.

to a jury to find the prisoner guilty of assault in a case where the Crown had proved that the prisoner had attacked the deceased, but had 'failed to prove the death of the party.'[69]

Manslaughter was by far the most common verdict returned by juries in homicide cases, as is shown by Table 8.1, which gives the results of murder and manslaughter trials during the years 1866–75. The figures are taken from the *Judicial Statistics*, to which full references are given in the Bibliography.

It is also worth noting that the proportion convicted was much higher for manslaughter than for murder, which suggests that juries were far more likely to convict when hanging was not the punishment to be meted out. The 'other' category, which included cases where there was 'no prosecution', where bills had been 'nilled', and where prisoners had been bailed or declared insane on arraignment, was also much higher for murder than for manslaughter, which suggests more doubt and equivocation in murder than in manslaughter. Taking murder and manslaughter together the conviction rate was substantial: 39% of those returned for trial were convicted. In one respect this table gives a misleading impression: of the 244 returned for trial for murder, none is returned as being found guilty of manslaughter. Yet it was quite common at assizes for those put on trial for murder to be found guilty of manslaughter. In Judge Keogh's notebook, for example, in 6 murder cases, one jury disagreed, 3 acquitted, one convicted, and 2 returned verdicts of manslaughter.[70]

It seems, therefore, that the *Judicial Statistics* excluded from murder trials those returned for trial for murder but found guilty of manslaughter or some lesser offence. Two pieces of evidence support this conclusion. First, in the years 1866–75, the number returned for trial for manslaughter (757) exceeded those committed (429) or bailed to stand trial for manslaughter (229). The missing 99 must have come from those committed to stand trial for murder but put on trial for manslaughter, or from those actually put on trial for murder but found guilty of manslaughter. Not all of those committed for manslaughter were put on trial for manslaughter, which increases the discrepancy between committals for manslaughter and those put on trial for manslaughter. Patrick McGrath, for example, killed his stepfather, was returned for trial for manslaughter 'but was indicted for a minor offence only, and found guilty of a common assault.'[71] Secondly, a statement by the registrar general confirms the fact that many committed for murder were not put on trial for murder. In a selection of over 250 cases of murder that he had assembled, he found that 310 persons were committed for trial for murder; of these 31 were convicted of murder, 63 were acquitted or discharged, 15 were acquitted as insane, in 8 cases the jury disagreed,

69   *Wilson* (1841) Ir Cir Rep 17.
70   Judge Keogh's crown book (MS in possession of St Patrick's College, Thurles, Co. Tipperary), passim.
71   NAI, Irish Crime Records, 1870, *homicide* no. 16.

and 103 were convicted of 'lesser offences'.[72] Although the 103 convictions for 'lesser offences' greatly changes the picture of what happened to those committed for murder, the fact remains that nearly one-third of those committed for murder (90 out of the registrar general's 310 committed for trial) seem never to have came before a petty jury. The 90 consisted of 23 cases where the grand jury did not find a bill, of 14 cases where prisoners were found insane before trial, of 3 cases where the prisoners died before trial. When these are added up, there were still 50 cases where prisoners were committed for murder but were not even brought before a grand jury. It is possible, however, that they were indicted for manslaughter, put on trial, and acquitted – the registrar general seems to have included only those *convicted* of manslaughter and lesser offences in his selection.

Maurice Healy described how a murder charge could diminish as the trial approached. A woman was committed for trial for murder at Limerick assizes in 1911. Healy, who was her counsel, contemplated a defence based on provocation and found witnesses to testify 'to various acts of eccentricity on the part of the prisoner'. The crown prosecutor, Wood G. Jefferson KC, decided to send a bill of manslaughter to the grand jury, but Healy refused to advise his client to plead guilty to manslaughter, and apparently Healy and Jefferson haggled. Eventually Jefferson, who had 'a very important political engagement in Dublin', approached Lord Chief Baron Palles who 'was most sympathetic' and promised Jefferson 'that the largest sentence … would be about six months hard labour' – if she pleaded guilty. Palles in fact did not impose even six months' hard labour, but merely bound her over. As Healy noted, a woman who had entered the courthouse charged with murder pleaded guilty to manslaughter, and left a free woman.[73]

The road to a verdict could be even longer than the one described by Healy. At Carrickfergus summer assizes in 1847 James Boyle was indicted for the murder of his wife. The jury disagreed, 'although locked up all night', and Boyle was 'admitted to bail for his appearance at [the] following assizes to take his trial for said murder.'[74] At the next assizes the Crown entered a *nolle prosequi* on the indictment for murder and indicted Boyle for manslaughter. Boyle was acquitted of manslaughter, but convicted of assault. John Walsh went through a slightly simpler procedure at Galway assizes in 1853: at the spring assizes the jury disagreed, at the summer assizes he withdrew his plea of not guilty to the indictment for murder and pleaded guilty of manslaughter.[75] He was sentenced to twelve months' imprisonment.

72 *Judicial Statistics (Ireland), 1871*, p. 26 [C 674], HC 1872, lxv, 260.
73 Healy, *The old Munster circuit*, pp 103–7.
74 Return 'of the number of cases in Ireland, during the last twenty years, wherein persons accused of capital offences have been remanded to prison for re-trial, or have been set at large, in consequence of the inability of juries to agree to a verdict; specifying the name of the accused, the crime charged, the year in which the trial or re-trial took place, and the assize town in which it had been held; the return being made up to the 31st March 1865', p. 5, HC 1865 (352), xlv, 327.
75 Ibid., p. 7.

The jury could find the prisoner not guilty but insane. James Murphy, the Mohill publican, who had discharged a blunderbuss at Lord Leitrim was found not guilty but insane, and was ordered to be confined in a lunatic asylum during her majesty's pleasure. The evidence of his madness came from a medical practitioner, Robert Gwydir, and from John McCluskey, who had known Murphy for twenty-five years. Murphy had told the doctor that he was prime minister of England; he had told McCluskey he was king of Ireland, which was strange office to combine with the premiership.[76] In 1883 the verdict in such cases was changed to guilty but insane by the Trial of Lunatics Act 1883.[77] At Galway assizes in 1886, Benjamin Terence Brodie, for example, was found 'guilty but was insane at the time he committed the action.'[78] Insanity was a sort of special verdict that obliged the judge to 'order such person to be kept in strict custody ... until the pleasure of the lord lieutenant, &c., shall be known.'[79]

Insanity could intervene at an earlier point in the trial. Prisoners committed for trial, even if they were not prosecuted, could be confined: 'if any person charged with any offence shall be brought before any court to be discharged for want of prosecution, and such person shall appear to be insane, it shall be lawful for such court to order such person to be kept in strict custody.'[80] When a prisoner was arraigned, a jury 'lawfully impanelled for that purpose' could decide that the prisoner was not fit to be tried', which did not prevent him from being put on trial when he recovered. If the prisoner became insane after the verdict but before sentence, 'he cannot be hanged until his recovery, for he may have some plea which, if sane, he could urge in stay of execution.'[81] The only point in the trial where the prisoner's insanity could not be considered was before the grand jury.[82]

In Table 8.1 above 19 of those returned for trial for murder were 'acquitted' as insane at the time when they had committed the offence, which was not much less

---

76 Larcom Papers (NLI, MS 7634 [unidentified press cutting between ff 69 & 70]).
77 46 & 47 Vict., c. 38, s. 2 (25 Aug. 1883).
78 NAI, Crown Book at Assize, Co. Galway, 1886.
79 Joseph Gabbett, *A treatise of the criminal law; comprehending all crimes and misdemeanors punishable by indictment; and offences cognizable summarily by magistrates; and the modes of proceeding upon each*, 2 vols (Dublin, 1843), ii, 516–17. For the M'Naghten case, see above, pp 20–1. See also Simon N. Verdun-Jones & Russell Smandych, 'Catch 22 in the nineteenth century: the evolution of therapeutic confinement for the criminally insane in Canada, 1840–1900' in *Criminal Justice History*, 2 (1981), 89, and Pauline M. Prior, 'Dangerous lunacy: the misuse of mental health law in nineteenth-century Ireland' in *Journal of Forensic Psychiatry & Psychology* (2003), 1–17, 'Mad, not bad: crime, mental disorder and gender in nineteenth-century Ireland' in *History of Psychiatry*, 8 (1997), 501–16, 'Prisoner or patient? The official debate on the criminal lunatic in nineteenth-century Ireland' in *History of Psychiatry*, 15:2 (2004), 177–92, and 'Murder and madness: gender and insanity defense in nineteenth-century Ireland' in *New Hibernia Review* (winter 2005), 19–36.
80 Gabbett, op. cit., ii, 516.
81 Courtney Stanhope Kenny, *Outlines of criminal law, based on lectures delivered in the University of Cambridge* (Cambridge, 1902), p. 59.
82 Huband, op. cit. p. 188 (citing *Hodges* (1838) 8 Car & P 195, 173 Eng Rep 457).

than the 32 who were convicted. The registrar general believed that juries used insanity as a means of evading a verdict in capital cases; in his comments quoted above he also ascribed the large number of convictions for 'lesser offences' in murder cases 'to the very strong feeling against capital punishment'.[83] There seems to have been a similar feeling in England. The role of 'lesser offences' seems to have been the same there; 8% of those returned for trial for murder in England and Wales were acquitted for insanity – the figure for Ireland was also 8%. The number of manslaughter trials in England was inflated by transfers from those who were committed for murder – only 1495 had been committed and 536 bailed, but 2527 were returned for trial for manslaughter. Individual cases in Ireland showed juries not taking advantage of insanity when they could plausibly have done so. Edward Walsh, for example, tried at Castlebar in 1873 for the murder of his wife, called two medical witnesses to show that he had suffered an injury to his head, but he was found guilty.[84]

Nearly one-third of the juries in a selection of 85 cases, recommended prisoners to mercy, which was the nearest the jury could come to making a distinction between capital and non-capital murder. Such a recommendation may have been jurors' way of nerving themselves to bring in a guilty verdict, or it may have been a way of conciliating the prisoner's friends, or it may just have been the propensity of twelve reasonable men to put in a good word for Barabbas.[85] When James and Henry Agnew were found guilty at the Londonderry summer assizes in 1836, the jury recommended them to mercy. The judge, Robert Torrens, 'asked them whether that recommendation proceeded from any doubts of the prisoners' guilt, & if so, to go back & give the prisoners the benefit of that doubt against them. The jury then informed me, that they had no doubt of the prisoners' guilt, but that their recommendation proceeded from the prisoners' good character.'[86] At Carlow spring assizes in 1839 Torrens asked the same question when Patrick Cain was found guilty of murdering his sister-in-law. The jury replied that 'they did not think the prisoner intended to commit murder & that as he had received an excellent character they were desirous to commend him.'[87] In the Agnew case, Torrens told the jury that he 'would not forward a recommendation on that ground to the government or act on it.' In Cain's case he was less dismissive, telling the jury 'that altho' I should transmit it to the government I could not support it.'

---

83 *Judicial Statistics (Ireland), 1871*, p. 26 [C 674], HC 1872, lxv, 260.

84 NAI, CRF/1873 Walsh/11.

85 'Indeed, from one perspective the capital sanction was instrumental not only because it induced terror but also because it allowed the higher orders to conceive of themselves as merciful even as they sent thousands into long and often cruel exile' (Thomas A. Green, 'A retrospective on the criminal trial jury, 1200–1800' in J.S. Cockburn & Thomas A. Green (eds), *Twelve good men and true: the criminal trial jury in England, 1200–1800* (Princeton, NJ, 1988), p. 387).

86 NAI, CRF/1836/Agnew/3.

87 Ibid., 1839/Cain/45.

As it happened neither Cain nor the Agnews were hanged. Torrens had second thoughts about Cain: 'I have very attentively reflected on this case & consulted my learned colleague on the circuit with me & the result of my reflection has been that I ought not to withhold from the prisoner the benefit of my mature consideration of the facts of his case or deny him even my feeble concurrence in the recommendation given by the jury.' The Agnews also escaped. The citizens of Derry begged the lord lieutenant not to 'inflict on your memorialists as citizens and inhabitants of Derry, the dreadful punishment of having two human beings in health and strength launched into eternity at their very door, your memorialists not being accustomed to such tragedies.' They reminded the lord lieutenant that mercy 'is not strained, it droppeth as the gentle dew upon the place beneath.'[88] The decisive voice was neither the jury's nor the citizens', but that of George Robert Dawson, of Castledawson, who was one of the largest landowners in the county, a former minister in Lord Liverpool's government, and Sir Robert Peel's brother-in-law. It took two letters from Dawson, however, to make the lord lieutenant, Lord Mulgrave, stand up to Torrens, who at first refused to budge.

The one thing that a jury was not supposed to do was to avoid a verdict. There was no equivalent of the Scots verdict of 'not proven', which Sir Walter Scott called 'that bastard verdict ... that Caledonian *medium quid*'.[89] If a jury could not agree all that remained for the judge, certainly until 1865, was to find some grounds of 'evident necessity' for discharging it. In the cases of the 310 persons committed for murder, analysed by the registrar general and discussed above, there were 8 cases where juries disagreed.[90] This was a small enough number compared with the 31 convictions for murder in the same return, and the 63 acquittals, 15 acquittals as insane, and 103 convictions for 'lesser offences'. In the *Judicial Statistics* there was no category for cases where the jury disagreed, although the registrar general's figures showed that such cases were noted. A parliamentary return on the subject in 1865, which was a sign of concern among MPs, attempted to clothe the generally held opinion in details.[91] The return, however, did not furnish much that was impressive: in the twenty years 1845–65 there were only 72 cases of hung juries in capital cases, which was less than four a year; in 20 counties and counties of towns and cities there were no hung juries at all in that twenty-year period; even in a large county such as Cork there were none, and in the county of Limerick and in the county of the city of Limerick there were none. In the years 1846–65 there were 240 sentences of death

88 The original is better: 'it droppeth as the gentle rain from heaven upon the place beneath.' The memorial is in NAI, CRF/1836/Agnew/3.

89 William Roughead, *Twelve Scots trials* (Edinburgh and London, 1913), p. 189. See also Paterson, op. cit., p. 337.

90 Above, pp 279–80.

91 Return *'of the number of cases in Ireland, during the last twenty years, wherein persons accused of capital offences have been remanded to prison for re-trial, or have been set at large, in consequence of the inability of juries to agree to a verdict ...*, HC 1865 (352), xlv, 323.

pronounced,[92] which suggests that hung juries in that twenty-year period were about 30% of convictions. A second parliamentary return of juries' deliberations in the early 1870s also showed that disagreeing juries were rare. At the spring assizes in 1871, for example, juries disagreed over the fate of 18 prisoners while finding 282 guilty and acquitting 225.[93]

Irish juries' reluctance to convict was a commonplace of nineteenth-century debate. James Lawson told the select committee on Irish juries in 1881 that 'they will not find a man guilty of assault in Limerick, no matter how clearly the offence may have been proved.'[94] Richard Adams when he was county court judge of Limerick dismissed a prisoner with the words: 'You have been acquitted by a Limerick jury, and you may now leave the dock without any other stain upon your character.'[95] Yet even Limerick juries convicted for murder. There were four hangings in Limerick between 1862 and 1879; three of them, however, were in two years, 1862–3, which suggests spasmodic rather than sustained effort.[96] If Limerick was picked out for animadversion, other parts of the country were chosen to receive praise. When Lawson condemned Limerick, he praised the north-east circuit, and pointed to a case on the Munster circuit where an agrarian assassin was found guilty of murder (the case was that of Thomas Crowe, sentenced to death by Lawson at Cork in 1876). Judge Fitzgerald praised the north-west circuit, although he mentioned a case where he had fault to find, but 'it was a case in which a row arose between the Orangemen and Roman Catholics', and that 'you will have to the end of time.'[97]

Between 1866 and 1875 about 42% of those tried for all indictable crimes were acquitted. This might appear high, but it had been higher in the past.[98] The

92 See Appendix 1, below, pp 377–8.

93 *Returns 'from the clerks of the crown in each county in Ireland, of the number of criminal cases in each county tried before a jury at the spring assizes of the years 1871, 1872, and 1873, with a description of the crime charged, and the result of the trial, specifying in each case whether the prisoner was found guilty (and, if so, of what offence) or acquitted, or the jury disagreed'; 'of the number of cases postponed on the application of counsel for the Crown, or in which nolle prosequi was entered'; 'and, from the secretaries of the grand juries of Ireland respectively, of any resolutions adopted by any of the grand juries referring to the Juries Act (Ireland) of 1871'*, p. 2, HC 1873 (220), liv, 360.

94 *Report from the select committee of the house of lords on Irish jury laws; together with the proceedings of the committee, minutes of evidence, and appendix*, p. 436, HC 1881 (430), xi, 1. John Ryan noted James Lawson's anger at Limerick: 'in a manslaughter case today, a tolerably clear one, the jury acquitted the prisoner, which so incensed Judge Lawson that he exclaimed he had never in all his experience seen a jury so deliberately violate their oath' (Diary of John Ryan (TCD, MS 10350 (no. 4), p. 42)).

95 Healy, *The old Munster circuit*, pp 228–9.

96 Death Book, 1852–1932 (NAI, GPB/CN/5).

97 *Report from the select committee of the house of lords on Irish jury laws ...*, pp 433, 437, 451, 453, HC 1881 (430), xi, 1.

98 Neal Garnham found an acquittal rate of 77% at the assizes in pre–1780 Ireland (*The courts, crime and the criminal law in Ireland 1692–1760* (Dublin, 1996), p. 243). For a discussion of the perversity of Welsh juries (which might have surprised even Irish crown solicitors) see Richard

acquittal rate in murder cases was also high: of the 244 returned for trial for murder in the ten years 1866–75, 91 were acquitted (37%) and only 32 (13%) were convicted. (The figures are taken from the *Judicial Statistics*, to which full references are given in the Bibliography.) In England and Wales in the same period 42% of those returned for trial for murder were acquitted, which is higher than Ireland's 37%, but 35% were convicted, which is much higher than Ireland's 13%. The difference between Ireland and England, however, may have been caused not by Irish jurors' reluctance to convict, but by the Crown's success in bringing cases to trial. If murders in the two countries are compared with convictions and executions, the comparison suggests Irish juries were slightly more likely to convict. In Ireland in the decade 1866–75 there were 11 sentences of death and 4 hangings for every 100 murders returned by the coroners; in England there were 9 sentences of death and 5 hangings for every 100 murders returned by the coroners.[99] The real difference between Ireland and England was in the number of cases brought to trial: for every 100 murders (including infanticides) in England, 17 persons were returned for trial for murder; in Ireland 42 were returned, which is a striking difference.

In misdemeanour cases, a new trial was a possibility, but in felony cases the jury's verdict case was almost as irreformable as a papal pronouncement *ex cathedra*. 'A verdict is conclusive,' wrote James Fitzjames Stephen, 'the law providing no method of opening the question which it decides.'[100] In the mid-1860s the judicial committee of the privy council could not discover 'any valid authority for holding a verdict of conviction or acquittal in a case of felony delivered by a competent jury before a competent tribunal in due form of law to be a nullity by reason of some conduct on the part of the jury which the court considers unsatisfactory.'[101] The Queen's Bench or the house of lords might decide that there had been an 'error' in the proceedings, and order a new trial, but even in that case the infallibility of the jury was preserved by the fiction that no

W. Ireland, 'Putting oneself on whose country? Carmarthenshire juries in the mid–nineteenth century' in T.G. Watkin (ed.), *Legal Wales: its past, its future* (Welsh Legal History Society, vol. i, Cardiff, 2001), pp 63–87. Ireland gives the example of Thomas Davies, a farmer, tried in Carmarthenshire in 1866, for an unnatural offence with a heifer. He was acquitted. 'Perhaps the strongest evidence in favour of the prisoner was given by his sister who stated that on the day in question (a Sunday) she saw her brother read the Pilgrim's Progress.' Miss Davies might have spared the court Bunyan's complicity, because 'Davies would not be convicted of this offence. None of those charged with it before a jury ever were in the evidence assembled for this paper' (p. 73). For acquittals in Essex in the period 1740–1805 see P.J.R. King, '"Illiterate plebeians, easily misled": jury composition, experience, and behaviour in Essex, 1735–1815' in J.S. Cockburn & Thomas A. Green (eds), *Twelve good men and true: the criminal trial jury in England, 1200–1800* (Princeton, NJ, 1988), pp 254–5.

99 For a study of indictments, inconclusive trials, and verdicts, which suggests that Ireland was not peculiar, see David J. Bodenhamer, 'The efficiency of criminal justice in the antebellum South' in *Criminal Justice History*, 3 (1982), 81–95.

100 Stephen, *A general view of the criminal law of England* (London and Cambridge, 1863), p. 223.

101 Huband, op. cit., p. 720 (citing *Murphy* (1869) LR 2 PC 535, 16 Eng Rep 693).

trial had actually taken place and that the verdict was not a real verdict but a defective one. This led to nice distinctions between different kinds of defective verdicts: those that were 'a mere nullity' and those that were 'not void *ab initio*, but are voidable only at the discretion of the court.'[102] An example of former was where one of the jurors had been challenged 'but the challenge has been improperly disallowed'; an example of the latter, 'is one which is against the weight of evidence.' Where the verdict was a nullity the Queen's Bench could issue a writ of *venire de novo* to empanel a new jury. The contention that this was not a *new* trial was logical: a *venire de novo* 'must be granted upon matter appearing on the record, but a new trial may be granted upon things out of it.'[103] The reference to a 'new' trial here seems to refer to its possibility in misdemeanour cases, where a new trial was possible.

The Prevention of Crime (Ireland) Act 1882 paid a remarkable compliment to Irish juries, although it seemed to supplant them in the trial of certain cases.[104] Section 1(2) provided for three judges, without a jury, to try murder and other serious crimes in certain circumstances, which implied that juries were not capable of acting properly in those cases. At the same time section 2 provided an appeal court to review the judges' verdicts 'on any ground, whether of law or of fact', but it did not provide an appeal from the verdicts of the special juries it provided for trials where the judges did not act as the tribunal. Judges could be judged by their peers, but juries could not be judged even by their betters until 1907 in England and Wales, and until 1924 and 1930 in Ireland. There were no trials under section 2(1).

When judges were doubtful, they used the jury's infallibility as a crutch. At Nenagh spring assizes in 1844 John Hickey, Martin Casey, and Martin Ryan were tried for conspiring to murder Michael Hanley. Casey and Ryan were acquitted, but Hickey was found guilty. The judge, Nicholas Ball, admitted that the acquittal of Casey and Ryan 'would appear to have discredited the witnesses whose evidence went to implicate them in the conspiracy with Hickey.'[105] The only evidence that differentiated Hickey from his co-accused was that of the murdered man's widow. According to Ball's notes,

> It appeared that some time after the murder Hickey proposed to marry the widow of Hanley. He proposed also to take from her some land which had been farmed by her husband in his lifetime & that he had an interview with her for the purpose of coming to an agreement about the land. On this occasion he stated to her that if he had known she was the person who was married to Hanley, he would have prevented the latter from being murdered, that it would have been as easy for him to have done so as to have turned his hand.

102 Ibid., p. 1000.
103 Ibid., p. 1002 (citing *Witham v. Lewis* (1744) 1 Wilson 48).
104 45 & 46 Vict., c. 25 (12 July 1882).   105   NAI, CRF/1844/Hickey/17.

Hickey jilted Mrs Hanley, married another, 'and on the third night after his marriage Hanley's widow processed him to be arrested by the police on the charge for which he was brought to tryal [*sic*] and found guilty.' The judge had warned the jury of the 'improbabillity' [*sic*] of the prisoner telling the murdered man's widow that he was implicated in her husband's murder, but they found him guilty. 'I cannot say I was dissatisfied with the conclusion at which they arrived,' Ball wrote. 'Perhaps they may have been aware that in that district of the country where the murder was committed men are to be found fearless in the open avowal of crime.'[106] Hickey's widowed mother petitioned the lord lieutenant for mercy: she 'mourns over the ignominy of his death that to use her expression he is to [be] hanged like a dog.'[107] Three other prisoners had been sentenced to death at the assizes. Mercy might have been expected, especially in a case where the judge was struck by the 'improbabillity' of a witness' story. Ball was remorseless: all four were left to hang, two on 18 May 1844 (Hickey and John Cooke), and two on 25 May (John and Thomas Wade).[108]

---

106 The idea that the jury could itself be a source of fact lingered into the nineteenth century. 'The jury may give a verdict without testimony,' wrote Purcell, 'when they themselves have a conusance of the fact' (Purcell, op. cit., p. 209).

107 On the hanging of dogs see V.A.C. Gatrell, *The hanging tree: execution and the English people 1770–1868* (Oxford, 1994), p. 283. See also E.P. Evans, *The criminal prosecution and capital punishment of animals* (London, 1906), pp 175–7.

108 For John Cooke, and John and Thomas Wade, see NAI, CRF/1844/Cooke/32.

CHAPTER NINE

Judgment

JUDGMENT

IN CRIMINAL TRIALS, 'judgment' was not the jury's verdict, but 'the conclusion and sentence of the law, pronounced by the court against the party, after his trial and conviction.'[1] Between 1830 and 1836 judges pronounced sentence of death immediately after the verdict.[2] From 1836 the practice varied, and some judges sentenced prisoners immediately, while others postponed it.[3] From 1861 the Offences Against the Person Act 1861 provided that sentence of death should be pronounced 'in the same manner in all respects as sentence of death might have been pronounced ... before the passing of this act, upon a conviction for any other felony for which the prisoner might have been sentenced to suffer death as a felon', which in practice seems to have meant that the judge could either pronounce sentence immediately, or postpone it.[4] Judge Fitzgerald sentenced John Gregory immediately after conviction at Downpatrick assizes in 1871, but at Castlebar assizes in 1873 he sentenced Edward Walsh the morning after the jury had found him guilty.[5] Occasionally there was confusion. At the Limerick special commission in 1848 the jury without leaving the box found William 'Puck' Ryan guilty of murder. The two judges put on their black caps, and the chief baron was about to pronounce sentence when he was stopped by the attorney general, who 'observed that, under the act under which the judges were bound to pass sentence, Baron Pennefather had expressed an opinion that, in consequence of the peculiar wording of that statute, the prisoner ought to be remanded to prison after conviction, before the final sentence should be passed upon him.'[6] The chief

1 Theobald A. Purcell, *A summary of the general principles of pleading and evidence, in criminal cases in Ireland: with the rules of practice incident thereto* (Dublin, 1849), p. 215.
2 10 Geo. IV, c. 34, s. 5 (4 June 1829) extended to Ireland the provisions of 9 Geo. IV, c. 31 (27 June 1828), which had provided that murderers should be sentenced immediately after conviction.
3 6 & 7 Will. IV, c. 30, s. 2 (14 July 1836) allowed the judge to postpone passing sentence until the end of the assizes.
4 24 & 25 Vict., c. 100, s. 2 (6 Aug. 1861).
5 NAI, CRF/1871/Gregory/9; ibid., 1873/Walsh/11.
6 John Simpson Armstrong, *A report of trials held under a special commission for the county of Limerick, held at Limerick, January 1848* (Dublin, n.d. [1849]), p. 45. The act referred to by the attorney was 4 & 5 Will. IV, c. 26, s. 2 (25 July 1834), which provided 'that in every case of conviction in Ireland of any prisoner for murder the court ... shall direct each prisoner to be

justice remanded the prisoner until nine o'clock the next morning. Pennefather's doubts did not apparently affect Purcell, who laid down in 1849 that 'in capital cases the sentence is usually pronounced immediately after the conviction, but the court may adjourn to another day, and then give judgment.'[7]

Before the sentence was pronounced, the court crier commanded 'all manner of persons to keep silence whilst judgment is given against the prisoner at the bar, upon pain of imprisonment.'[8] The threat of imprisonment was not an empty one. John Adye Curran remembered the lord chief justice, Michael Morris, sentencing a man to six months' imprisonment because he applauded an acquittal.[9] Then the clerk of the crown asked the prisoner if he had anything to say why sentence of death should not be pronounced against him, a question that was known as the allocutus. The question had to be asked in all cases of conviction for felony. The clerk had to get the words right. Robert Henry O'Neill, sentenced to death at the spring assizes at Belfast in 1854, successfully applied for a writ of error because the words 'against him' were omitted from the allocutus.[10] The Queen's Bench decided that 'there could not be any imaginable doubt but that this was addressed to him.'

Prisoners usually did not have much to say. Matthew Bryan, convicted of murdering his mother, asked Bushe to 'remember what his mother said to Sergeant Jessop of the police, as to his being a good son when sober.'[11] At Sligo in 1902 James Doherty said he was 'as innocent as the child unborn', which was almost the same as what Michael Kenny had said in 1838 at Longford assizes when he compared his innocence to that 'of the child born last night'.[12] At

buried within the precincts of the prison *within which such prisoner shall have been confined after conviction*, and the sentence to be pronounced by the court shall express that the body of such prisoner shall be buried within the precincts of the such prison.' The attorney was worried by the passage in italics.

7 Purcell, op. cit., pp 217–18.
8 Ibid., p. 219. For the more elaborate eighteenth-century procedure, which included asking the prisoner to raise his right hand, see George Joseph Browne, *A report of the whole of the proceedings previous to, with a note of the evidence on, the trial of Robert Keon, Gent. for the murder of George Nugent Reynolds, Esq. and also of the charges of the judges thereon, together with the arguments and replies of counsel on the motion in arrest of judgment and the decision of the court thereon* (Dublin, 1788), pp 158–9. See also Neal Garnham, *The courts, crime and the criminal law in Ireland 1692–1760* (Dublin, 1996), p. 115.
9 *Reminiscences of John Adye Curran, KC, late county court judge and chairman of quarter sessions* (London, 1915), p. 37.
10 *O'Neill in error v. R* (1854) 6 Cox CC 495, at p. 504. See also Purcell, op. cit., p. 218.
11 NAI, CRF/1840/Bryan/50. Éanna Hickey tells of a prisoner who was convicted of murdering his wife and who 'proceeded to read out a poem he had written, praising the beauty of his young wife, and lamenting her death. The judge, greatly affected by this display of remorseful, tortured love, ordered the man to be set free' (*Irish law and lawyers in modern folk tradition* (Dublin 1999), p. 64). It is difficult to imagine such a scene occurring before Bushe or Torrens.
12 NAI, CRF/1902/Doherty/69. For Michael Kenny see Desmond McCabe, '"The part that laws or kings can cause or cure": crown prosecution and jury trial at Longford assizes, 1830–45' in Raymond Gillespie & Gerard Moran (eds), *Longford: essays in county history*, p. 154. For Myles

Tyrone assizes in 1853, Robert Torrens noted that Alexander Mullan could not speak for himself: 'I was informed by the Protestant chaplain of the jail, that the convict at the time of his committal had little or no knowledge of the fundamental principles of our common faith. I was therefore induced to extend the time for execution, for a month, a longer period than is usual in cases of atrocious homicide, in order that he might profit by clerical instruction in the interval.'[13]

At Belfast summer assizes in 1918 when the prisoner Joseph Charles Fitt was asked if he had anything to say, his counsel asked the judge 'to abstain from passing sentence of death until he had an opportunity of considering the effect of the provisions of the Children's Act 1908.'[14] Fitt was sixteen when he was convicted but had been under sixteen when he had committed the murder.[15] The judge, Chief Justice Molony, reserved the case to the Court for Crown Cases Reserved, which decided that 'the words of s. 103 appear to us to be applicable to the time when the judge comes to pronounce sentence. He is then to ask himself whether the prisoner, as he stands in the dock is a child or young person within the definitions contained in s. 131 and if he is not a child or a young person at that time, he is not entitled to the benefit of the act.'[16] The court decided that Fitt should be sentenced to death. The sentence was commuted to penal servitude for life.

What was said on Fitt's behalf was important, but usually what prisoners said was not of much legal significance. Judges usually noted what they said, however. Lawson noted that Christos Bombos had admitted 'he held the man while Big George was stabbing him.'[17] Judges may also have noted what the prisoner said because it was part of the 'record'; Michael O'Brien's silence at the Limerick assizes in 1890 was noted in the record of the case when it came before the Queen's Bench ('and he is asked has he anything to say why sentence of death and execution should not be awarded against him according to law, and does not allege anything').[18]

The prisoner could make a formal attempt at this point to stop the judge from passing sentence by moving 'in arrest of judgment', but only if he could show that there was a defect in the indictment or in some other part of the 'record', but not because there was a weakness in the evidence or because the trial had not been

Joyce making the same claim, see Jarlath Waldron, *Maamtrasna: the murders and the mystery* (Dublin, 1992), p. 122. The unborn child was much invoked as a paradigm of innocence. Sir James Galbraith, the clerk of errors, when accused of taking illegal fees, 'took the opportunity to repeatedly declare in the most solemn manner that he was as ignorant and as innocent as the child unborn' (R.B. McDowell, 'The Irish courts of law, 1801–1914' in *IHS*, 10:40 (Sept. 1957), 384).

13   NAI, CRF/1853/Mullan/32.   14   *Fitt* [1919] 2 IR 35, at pp 35–6.
15   8 Edw. VII, c. 67, s. 103 (21 Dec. 1908) provided that 'sentence of death shall not be pronounced on or recorded against a child or young person'; s. 131 defined a 'young person' as a person 'who is 14 years of age or upwards, and under the age of 16 years'.
16   2 IR 35, at pp 41–2.   17   NAI, CRF/1876/Bombos/26.
18   *O'Brien v. The Queen* (1890) 26 LR Ir 451, at p. 455.

properly conducted.[19] The judge himself could arrest judgment without any motion from the prisoner.[20] If he thought there was a good reason for arresting judgment, he respited the sentence to give time 'to take the opinion of the Twelve Judges'; if he thought there was no good reason for arresting judgment, he could pass sentence, but even then he might still decide to reserve the case.[21] The prisoner could also make 'a plea in stay of judgment', which might be based on the fact that he had been pardoned or that he was not the person named in the indictment.[22] These facts might be relied on after sentence had been pronounced, when they were known as pleas in bar of execution.[23] If the Crown opposed either the plea in stay of judgment or the plea in bar of execution, 'the court will order a jury to be returned forthwith, or at such convenient time as may be appointed, for the purpose of trying the issue so joined; and according to the result, the prisoner is discharged, or sentence is passed against him.[24] The most remarkable plea in bar of execution was that allowed to women who were pregnant. When this was made:

> the judge orders the doors of the courthouse to be closed, that the females may not be permitted to leave it; and that the sheriff shall forthwith impannel a jury of married women, from the bystanders, or those who can otherwise be procured. When sworn and charged by the court, the jury and the prisoner are conducted to a private apartment, and a bailiff is sworn to keep them.[25]

If this jury of matrons, as it was called, found that the prisoner was 'quick with child', her execution was respited until the next assizes.[26]

---

19 Purcell, op. cit., pp 210–13; John G. Thompson, *The law of criminal procedure in Ireland* (Dublin, 1899), pp 93–4.

20 Ibid., p. 94.

21 Edmund Hayes, *Crimes and punishments, or a digest of the criminal statute law of Ireland, alphabetically arranged, with ample notes, in which are discussed the powers and authorities of the several courts of criminal jurisdiction in Ireland; the duties, responsibilities, and privileges of magistrates, coroners, constables, and other officers, in bringing criminals to justice, and also the practice of the courts in punishing offences upon indictment*, 2 vols (2nd ed., Dublin, 1842), i, 418.

22 Ibid., p. 410.   23 Ibid., p. 420.

24 Ibid., p. 410.   25 Ibid., pp 420–1.

26 The jury of matrons was abolished in Ireland by the Juries Procedure (Ireland) Act, 1876 (39 & 40 Vict., c. 78, s. 13 (15 Aug. 1876)). Serjeant Parry had seen the matrons in action at the Old Bailey: 'The old ladies had, according to custom, a glass of gin each and some bread and cheese, and examined the woman in gaol, and they declared her not to be pregnant. Medical men examined her, and found that she was pregnant' (*Report of the capital punishment commission, together with the minutes of evidence, and appendix*, p. 344 [3590], HC 1866, xxi, 397). Taylor noted the matrons being summoned as late as 1862 (Alfred Swaine Taylor, *The principles and practice of medical jurisprudence* (London, 1865), pp 756–8). Taylor deplored the fact 'that the question of pregnancy is allowed to be determined by a jury of ignorant women, accidentally present in court.' For an example of mercy being extended to a woman who just given birth see NAI

When the prisoner had spoken, the judge made a short speech, which was addressed to the prisoner. Judge Fitzgerald's speech to Walsh at Castlebar in 1873 was about 800 words. In the course of it, 'his lordship was affected to tears'. He did not, he told Walsh, 'intend in anything I say to hurt your feelings.'[27] George Wright was laconic at Sligo in 1902 when he sentenced James Doherty for the murder of his son. His speech took up about fifty words in the *Sligo Champion*, but short as it was, Wright said all that needed to be said: he thought the jury could have come to no other conclusion; he would forward their recommendation to mercy to the lord lieutenant; he would not hold out hope of mercy to the prisoner, whom he advised to make his peace with God, 'and assuming the black cap, he pronounced sentence of death, the last penalty of the law, to be carried out in Sligo Jail on Tuesday, 30th December.'[28]

Hughes' speech to John Holden at Omagh in 1860 was interrupted by the prisoner:

> Prisoner (interrupting) – My Lord, before you speak, I wish to say that, as it has been stated that M'Clelland was shot, and as it is the opinion of the jury that I shot him, I should be shot also. I wish to be shot also as that was the case.
>
> Baron Hughes – Have you anything more to say?
>
> Prisoner – Nothing, unless to ask that you will be so kind as to grant this request. I will be very happy to be shot.
>
> Baron Hughes – I cannot.
>
> Prisoner – I would be very happy, and I have a few personal friends among the police whom I would select. I would rather be shot by my friend than by my enemy.
>
> Baron Hughes – Prisoner, I would beg of you to dismiss from your mind all such notions; and I assure you that I shall not dwell on anything, or say a single word, which could increase those feelings of distress under which you must be at present labouring.[29]

CRF/1839/Feeney/24. For a comprehensive account of the subject see James C. Oldham, 'On pleading the belly: a history of the jury of matrons' in *Criminal Justice History*, 6 (1985), 1–64.

27 NAI, CRF/1873/Walsh/11.

28 Ibid., CRF/1902/Doherty/69.

29 *Tyrone Constitution*, 3 Aug. 1860. Holden's request would probably have required an act of parliament. According to Chitty, 'it has been even laid down by great authority [Coke], that the king himself cannot totally change the sentence, so as to order him to be beheaded, who was sentenced to die by hanging' (Joseph Chitty, *A practical treatise on the criminal law, comprising the practice, pleadings, and evidence, which occur in the course of criminal prosecutions whether by indictment or information: with a copious collection of precedents of indictments, informations*, 4 vols (2nd ed., London, 1826), i, 785). Whether death by shooting was a mitigation of hanging is a nice point, often debated. In Shaw's *The devil's disciple* (London, 1984), Richard Dudgeon asks to be shot instead of hanged ('Shoot me like a man instead of hanging me like a dog'); General Burgoyne remonstrated with him: 'Now there, Mr Anderson, you talk like a civilian, if you will excuse my saying so. Have you any idea of the average marksmanship of the army of His Majesty

The most important part of the judge's speech was a warning to the prisoner not to expect mercy. Perrin was bleak, when sentencing two murderers, James Kelly and Matthew Hourigan, at the special commission in Clonmel in January 1839. 'The punishment of murder is death,' he told them. 'You must therefore prepare for that death, the dreadful punishment of your dreadful offence. I cannot extend any hope of mercy to you.'[30] The two prisoners did indeed seem to be irrevocably doomed when the under-secretary, Thomas Drummond, wrote to the keeper of Clonmel gaol saying that the lord lieutenant had decided that 'the law shall take its course.' At that point six of the jurors who had convicted Kelly and Hourigan presented a petition in their favour. Burton, who had been on the bench with Perrin, wrote to Drummond on 5 February:

> to observe that, as he has already stated, neither Judge Perrin or himself would have been dissatisfied if the verdict had been manslaughter and can now further state that if the verdict that was found had been accompanied by a recommendation like the present from the whole jury, he would have immediately promised to transmit it to his excellency with an assurance that it would meet with very great attention. Under the circumstances, the purposes of justice may be sufficiently served by the commutation of the sentence to that of transportation for life.

Before the judge passed sentence, he put on the black cap. John Ryan described Lawson donning the black cap after he had spoken 'a few words as to the circumstances of the case' to William Tobin, who had just been found guilty at Cork assizes in March 1875:

> Then there was a pause, followed by a groan from the large body of people in the court, and looking up I saw the judge had covered his wig with a big square black cloth, which could not be said to add to his dignity. He then sentenced Tobin to hang that day month.[31]

King George the Third? If we make you up a firing party, what will happen? Half of them will miss you: the rest will make a mess of the business and leave you to the provo-marshall's pistol. Whereas we can hang you in a perfectly workmanlike and agreeable way' (pp 79–80).
30 NAI, CRF/1839/Kelly/12.
31 Diary of John Ryan (TCD, MS 10350 (no. 4), p. 47). Sentence of death attainted the prisoner: his lands were forfeit, and his blood corrupted (Chitty, op. cit., i, 726, 739). The effects of attainder were gradually mitigated in the course of the nineteenth century: 3 & 4 Will. 4, c. 106, s. 10 (29 Aug. 1833) allowed land to be inherited through the attainted prisoner, and 13 & 14 Vict., c. 60, s. 46 (5 Aug. 1850) provided that 'no land, chattels, or chose in action, vested in any person upon trust, or by way of mortgage, or any profits thereof, shall escheat or be forfeited to Her Majesty ... by reason of the attainder or conviction for any offence of such trustee or mortgagee.' 33 & 34 Vict., c. 23, s. 4 (4 July 1870), however, empowered the judge in a felony case 'to order a convicted prisoner to pay a sum not exceeding one hundred pounds, by way of compensation for any loss of property suffered by any person through the felony'.

The sentence stunned some prisoners. When John Russell was sentenced at Clonmel in 1875, the medical superintendent of the district lunatic asylum noted 'the vacant simper spreading over his countenance, almost breaking into a laugh, after the impressive delivery of the judge, and his general stolidity afterwards'. At Cork in 1886 William Sheehan smiled, and 'humble persons who happened to be in court and saw Sheehan smile in the dock after the judge pronounced sentence on him remarked that there must be a screw loose in his mental faculties.'[32] Judges added to the drama. Barry wept when he sentenced Patrick Joyce for his part in the Maamtrasna murders. Joyce was unmoved.[33] The prisoner was not supposed to speak after he was sentenced, because he was legally dead.[34] William O'Brien after he had sentenced Daniel Curley refused to let him speak, but Curley, who had earlier likened O'Brien to Norbury and Keogh, thanked his counsel and shouted 'God save Ireland.'[35]

From 1823 to 1836 judges could 'record' sentence of death for all felonies except murder; from 1836 to 1861 they could record sentence of death even for murder.[36] Sentence was recorded when the judge 'shall be of opinion that, under the particular circumstances of the case, the offender is deserving of the royal mercy.'[37] Anne Madden was convicted of murder at Tullamore summer assizes in 1860. According to Lefroy, who recorded sentence of death,

> it is not possible in this case to cast a shade of doubt on the verdict which has found the prisoner guilty of the murder of her infant child. It was an

---

32 NAI, CRF/1875/Russell/1; ibid., CRF/1886/Sheehan/2.

33 Georgina O'Brien, *The reminiscences of the Right Hon. Lord O'Brien (of Kilfenora) lord chief justice of Ireland*, p. 48; Waldron, op. cit., pp 87–8.

34 NAI, CRF/1902/Doherty/69. Charles I tried to speak after he was sentenced but John Bradshaw refused to let him, because 'a prisoner condemned to death was already dead in law and could not speak.' The king's ignorance astounded Bradshaw; this fact was 'so familiar to him that it had not occurred to him that the prisoner did not know it' (C.V. Wedgwood, *The trial of Charles I* (London, 1964), pp 163–4).

35 *Report of the trials at the Dublin Commission Court, April and May, 1883, of the prisoners charged with the Phoenix Park murder, the attempt to murder Mr Field, and the conspiracy to murder; before the Hon. Mr Justice O'Brien; reported by W.C. Johnston* (Dublin, 1883), p. 219.

36 4 Geo. IV, c. 48, s. 1 (4 July 1823) provided that 'whenever any person shall be convicted of any felony, except murder, and shall by law be excluded the benefit of clergy in respect thereof, and the court before which such offender shall be convicted shall be of opinion that, under the particular circumstances of the case, such offender is a fit and proper subject to be recommended for the royal mercy, ... the court shall and may and is hereby authorized to abstain from pronouncing judgment of death upon such offender; and instead of pronouncing such judgment to order the same to be entered of record.' 6 & 7 Will. IV, c. 30, s. 2 provided that 'sentence of death may be pronounced after conviction for murder in the same manner and the judge shall have the same power in all respects as after convictions for other capital offences.' 24 & 25 Vict., c. 100, ss 1, 2 (6 Aug. 1861) did not mention recorded sentences, but s. 1 provided that 'upon every conviction for murder the court shall pronounce sentence of death', which in effect abolished recorded sentences.

37 Purcell, op. cit., p. 218.

illegitimate child about two months old which she had suckled with all the tenderness & care of a fond mother for that time but it appeared from some expressions dropt by her as if stung by a sudden & overwhelming sense of her disgrace she committed the crime to hide her shame from her family. I recorded the sentence of death & it remains for his excellency to deal with as to his clemency & judgment seems fit.[38]

Madden's death sentence was commuted to ten years' penal servitude. When the judge decided to record sentence of death, he simply stated the fact that he was recording sentence of death and refrained from actually pronouncing sentence.[39] At the special commission for Co. Clare in 1848, for example, Pigot told four prisoners who had pleaded guilty to charges of murder that he was recording sentence of death 'but if that mercy be extended, it can only be by a substitution for the punishment which the law awards for this homicide ... it will lead to your transfer for the remainder of your lives to wretchedness and slavery in another land!'[40] The last recorded sentence was in 1861 when Judge Fitzgerald recorded sentence of death against Ellen Ryan, who had been convicted of arson.[41]

Interesting details of stage-management were revealed when judges made mistakes. When Hughes sentenced Joseph Kelly at Wexford summer assizes in 1863, he used 'a small pocket almanack' to fix 11 August for the execution. 'I thought I saw the 11th of August fell on a Monday,' he wrote. 'I asked some of the officials if there was any fair or market, or festival, or public meeting in or about Wexford on that day, and having been answered in the negative I passed sentence on the prisoner in the usual form, naming the day for the execution, Monday, the 11th of August.'[42] Kelly was taken back to the gaol. 'Immediately afterwards (within half an hour on the same day) the clerk of the crown & crown solicitor informed me that the 11th of August was a Tuesday,' Hughes continued. 'I had the prisoner recalled, and sentence pronounced for Tuesday the 11th of August. I had full authority to do this. It was done during the assizes, and while the courts were sitting in the assize town.' Kelly did not take his second sentence with equanimity. He complained to the lord lieutenant:

38 NAI, CRF/1867/Madden/22.
39 Hayes, op. cit., i, 415.
40 John Simpson Armstrong, *A report of trials under a special commission for the county of Clare, held at Ennis, January 1848* (Dublin, n.d. [1849]), pp 182–3.
41 Death Book, 1852–1932 (NAI, GPB/CN/5); ibid., CRF/1861/Ryan/15.
42 Ibid., CRF/1863/Kelly/15. Kelly was in distinguished company when he used 'president' instead of 'precedent'. See Oliver Lawson Dick (ed.), *Aubrey's brief lives* (London, 1949), p. 12: 'The Earle of Manchester being removed his Place of Lord chiefe Justice of the Common-Pleas to be Lord President of the Councell, told my Lord [Bacon] (upon his Fall) that he was sorry to see Him made such an Example. Lord Bacon replied *it did not trouble him, since he was made a President.*'

What wonder then if I complain of having been brought back from jail to receive a second sentence on pretence of an oversight? I underwent two sentences of death which were far from being the same, a novelty unheard of in criminal jurisprudence. This is my plea. On this I rest my cause. The pains and penalties decreed in both cases are the same but the times are wide of each other. I abide the first sentence with resignation and with reverence because it has the sanction of the jury and the authority of God. The second sentence is a stranger unknown to the laws which may hereafter be pleaded as president [*sic*] to give strength to oppression's rage.

The lord lieutenant refused to intervene, being unmoved by Kelly's concern that 'the wondering multitude' would be troubled when they saw 'the divine face of the law deformed and changed into a monkey.'

REVERSING THE JUDGMENT

If the prisoner's motion to arrest judgment or his plea in stay of judgment did not succeed, he had remedies even after he was sentenced: he could petition the lord lieutenant for a pardon, a reprieve, or a commutation of his sentence; the attorney general might issue a writ of error to enable him to take his case before the Court of Queen's Bench; the judge might reserve his case for the twelve common law judges before 1848 and for the Court for Crown Cases Reserved after 1848.[43]

A new trial, which was a substantial remedy, was not available to those convicted of felony. The list of grounds on which a misdemeanant might get a new trial described succinctly what was denied to those convicted of felony: a misdemeanant could move for a new trial 'on any ground on which a new trial might be moved for in a civil case, such as the improper reception or rejection of evidence, misdirection by the judge, that the verdict was against the weight of evidence, gross misbehaviour of the jury among themselves, surprise, or the like.'[44] Between 1844 and 1899 thirty bills were introduced in parliament proposing to set up a full court of criminal appeal that would have allowed prisoners to appeal on matters of fact as well as of law. Eventually in 1907 a court of criminal appeal was established in England, but not in Ireland, where prisoners had to wait until 1924 in the Irish Free State, and until 1930 in Northern Ireland. The time-lag between England and Ireland was caused by the opposition of Irish MPs.[45]

43 Desmond Greer, 'A security against illegality? The reservation of crown cases in nineteenth-century Ireland' in Dawson (ed.), *Reflections on law* (2006), pp 164–6.
44 Thompson, op. cit., p. 100.
45 Claire Jackson, 'Irish political opposition to the passage of criminal evidence reform at Westminster, 1883–98' in McEldowney & O'Higgins (eds), *The common law tradition* (1990), pp 185–201. For the case of Adolph Beck, whose wrongful convictions influenced English public opinion, see David Bentley, *English criminal justice in the nineteenth century* (London and Rio Grande, 1998), p. 296.

Although Irish MPs opposed the establishment of a full court of criminal appeal in the 1890s and early 1900s, Irish MPs had played a part in the campaign for setting up such a court in the 1850s and 1860s. After William Burke Kirwan's conviction in December 1852 for the murder of his wife on Ireland's Eye, his counsel, Isaac Butt, took up the parliamentary campaign for the establishment of a full court of criminal appeal. The Kirwan case demonstrated, probably better than any other case in nineteenth-century Ireland, the need for a full court of criminal appeal. The judge, Philip Crampton, refused to reserve the case, in spite of the points raised by Butt at the trial. When new evidence appeared after the trial, he prevaricated. 'I was not at the time dissatisfied with the verdict nor was my learned colleague nor should I have been dissatisfied with the verdict had it been the other way,' he wrote to the under-secretary on 24 December 1852. 'The question was a fair jury question & entirely for a jury. But I own after reading the documents which came in your enclosure & <u>numerous</u> letters which I have had from medical and non-medical persons both of England & of Ireland, that my satisfaction with the verdict is not as strong as it was.'[46] He recommended that the sentence be commuted, which was a timid compromise. 'My recommendation to commute the sentence to transportation for life was not founded upon my own doubts as to the propriety of the verdict or of the prisoner's guilt,' he explained, *'but upon my doubts as to what the verdict would have been had the matters put forward since the trial been in the [first] instance laid before the jury & credited by them'*[47] (Author's italics).

In 1848 two new courts were established in England and Ireland to which judges could reserve 'any question of law' that had arisen at trials where they had presided.[48] The new Irish Court for Crown Cases Reserved could 'reverse, affirm, or amend any judgment, which shall have been given on the indictment or inquisition on the trial whereof such question or questions have arisen, or to avoid such judgment.'[49] The court was to consist of at least five of the common law judges or barons, one of whom at least had to be either the chief justice of the Queen's Bench, or the chief justice of the Court of Common Pleas, or the chief baron of the Exchequer.[50] The new court was a continuation of the practice of referring points of law to the twelve judges.

---

46 NAI, CRF/1853/Kirwan/1. For Butt's points see John Simpson Armstrong, *Report of the trial of William Burke Kirwan, for the murder of Maria Louisa Kirwan, his wife, at the island of Ireland's Eye, in the county of Dublin on the 6th September, 1852, before the Hon. Judge Crampton and the Rt Hon. Baron Greene, at the Commission Court, Green Street, on the 8th and 9th December, 1852* (Dublin, 1853), pp 84–5. See also Greer, 'A security against illegality', pp 188–96, and Richard S. Lambert, *When justice faltered: a study of nine peculiar murder trials* (London, 1935).

47 Some legislative proposals to set up appeal courts limited the right of appeal to capital cases; see, for example, *Bill to provide a court of appeal for persons convicted of capital offences in certain cases*, HC 1870 (85), i, 193.

48 The Irish Court for Crown Cases Reserved was set up by 11 & 12 Vict., c. 78 (31 Aug. 1848). See also 40 & 41 Vict., c. 57, s. 50 (14 Aug. 1877).

49 11 & 12 Vict., c. 78, s. 2.   50 Ibid., s. 3.

Desmond Greer has elucidated the history of the twelve judges: their meetings 'from an early date', their dealing with criminal cases from the assizes and commissions, with cases arising from civil bills, with jury presentments, and with parliamentary registry cases, but not with cases from the quarter sessions; the role of counsel and judges in initiating the reservation of cases, and the unfettered discretion of the trial judge in deciding which cases to reserve; the fewness of the cases reserved – about two or three crown cases a year before 1848; the growing rigour of the judges' proceedings, as exemplified by their decision in 1826 to allow counsel to argue cases and their adoption in 1838 of rules of procedure drawn up by Bushe.[51]

Hayes described what happened when a judge decided to reserve a case for the twelve judges:

> when a difficulty arises in the mind of the presiding judge, as to the details of proceeding, or as to the admission, weight, or effect of evidence, it is usual for him to decide against the prisoner, and so let the trial proceed to verdict, and sometimes (in case of conviction) even to judgment. In such event, the question is reserved for the consideration of the assembled judges of the three law courts; and if they should be of opinion that the decision of the judge below was erroneous, the prisoner is of course recommended to the executive for a free pardon on that indictment.[52]

Hayes' description is the same as Thompson's fifty years' later.[53] The judges met in Queen's Bench chamber, where 'the questions reserved are discussed and decided in solemn consultation'. If the judge who had reserved the point 'considers it of sufficient difficulty or importance to require the aid of counsel, he intimates his wish to that effect: and a day is appointed, when the matter is argued in the Exchequer Chamber in open court, before the assembled judges, by one counsel at each side.' The judges' decision was not pronounced in open court, but in private, and the judge who had reserved the case announced the decision at the next assizes. 'Such decision of the majority of judges, is understood to be binding on all judges, until subsequently overruled by equal or superior authority.'

The cases dealt with by the twelve judges before 1848 and by the new court afterwards were similar: they were mainly about the interpretation of the law and about the admissibility of evidence – but not about its reliability. After Patrick Woods' conviction at Armagh assizes in 1841, for example, several points had been referred to the judges, including the right of a Seceder to take the oath in a particular way.[54] The solicitor general appeared for the Crown and Joseph Napier appeared for Woods. The case was heard on 8 November, which was a long time after the trial. The judges rejected Napier's arguments, the conviction was

51   Greer, 'A security against illegality?', pp 165–73.
52   Hayes, op. cit., i, 237–8.   53   Thompson, op. cit., pp 100–1.
54   (1841) 2 Cr & Dix 268.

confirmed, and Woods was hanged. The case of Thomas Dowling in 1844 raised the question of the corroboration of an approver as well as doubts about the words used in the sentence of death.[55] The cases dealt with by the new court were not very different from these: in *Redmond* the problem was whether the evidence was sufficient to sustain the verdict;[56] in *Burke*, the problem was the admission of two witness' evidence on a collateral matter;[57] in *Lydane* the admission of evidence of another crime;[58] in *Johnston* the admission of evidence elicited by police questioning;[59] in *King* the description of the venue.[60]

There were limits to what the twelve judges and the new court could do. First, they were both confined to points of law and did not consider the quality of the evidence, but only its admissibility. Secondly, they could consider only cases that the trial judge decided to reserve. It is not difficult to find examples of judges refusing to reserve cases: Deasy refused to reserve the question of the admissibility of two policemen's evidence in Daniel Ward's case;[61] Hayes refused to reserve the question of the admissibility of some letters in Matthew Phibbs' case.[62]

Prisoners could also challenge the judgment by means of a writ of error. According to Purcell, 'the course of proceeding in order to obtain the attorney general's *fiat*, is to send a copy of the record, or at least of the indictment, when the error is in that, together with counsel's opinion and certificate as to the errors, (containing a statement of the grounds of that opinion,) to the attorney general, who thereupon signifies his determination to grant or refuse his *fiat*.'[63] The attorney general himself could proceed by writ of error. In *M'Keever* in 1871, for example, the Crown used a writ of error 'for the purpose of having an erroneous sentence reversed' and in the subsequent arguments in the Queen's Bench the difference between a 'cock' of hay and a 'stack' played an important part.[64] The writ of error, which could be applied for only after judgment,[65] took the case to the Queen's Bench, and from the Queen's Bench immediately to the house of lords in cases initiated by indictments; in cases initiated by informations 'where the Crown is represented by the attorney general as plaintiff' cases could be taken from the Queen's Bench to the Court of Exchequer Chamber, and then to the house of lords.[66] After the passage of the Supreme Court of Judicature (Ireland) Act 1877 all cases involving writs of error went from the Queen's Bench Division

55 NAI, CRF/1844/Dowling/11.
57 (1858) 8 Cox CC 44.
59 (1864) 15 ICLR 60.
61 NAI, CRF/1863/Ward/5.
63 Purcell, op. cit., p. 225.
65 Hayes, op. cit., i, 232–3.
56 (1853) 3 ICLR 494.
58 (1858) 8 Cox CC 38.
60 (1865) 16 ICRL 50.
62 Ibid., CRF/1861/Phibbs/5.
64 IR 5 CL, 86, p. 86.
66 Ibid., p. 233. For a return of cases taken to the house of lords by writs of error, see *Lists of writs of error and appeals from courts of common law and equity in the United Kingdom of Great Britain and Ireland, distinguishing English, Scotch and Irish cases, which have been heard by this house, from the 1st January 1846 to the present time; distinguishing the cases affirmed, reversed, varied, and remitted, and showing the date of the sentence appealed from, and the date of the final judgment in each case*, HC 1856 (272), l, 9.

to the new Court of Appeal and then to the house of lords.[67] The writ directed the judge of the court where the prisoner had been sentenced 'to send the record and proceedings of the indictment, etc., on which judgment has been pronounced and in which error is alleged.'[68] The prisoner was removed to the Queen's Bench by a writ of habeas corpus.[69]

The writ applied only to errors in the *record*, a limited term which included the indictment, the empanelling of the jury, the verdict, and the sentence, but not the evidence at the trial or the judge's summing up. If the prisoner were successful, in either the Queen's Bench or the house of lords, his victory was a limited one: 'if a judgment by confession, or on verdict, be reversed on error, all former proceedings will be set aside, and the party shall stand as if he had never been accused. But he still remains liable to another prosecution for the same offence, for the first being erroneous, he was never in jeopardy thereby.'[70] This last sentence draws attention to how lawyers coped with the legal maxim that a prisoner should not be put in jeopardy twice for the same crime: since there was an error in the first trial, the prisoner had not in fact been tried. The new trial brought about by the issue of a writ of *venire de novo* was not a new trial but an attempt to have a proper one.

'Error' consisted of two categories, 'errors in fact' and 'errors in law'; the former applied to actual mistakes in the *record* itself and the latter to the application of the law as revealed by the *record*.[71] When Sam Gray was found guilty at Monaghan in 1843, he moved in arrest of judgment in the Queen's Bench, arguing that he should have been allowed to challenge jurors peremptorily. When three of the four judges decided that judgment should not be arrested, Gray obtained a writ of error, which brought his case to the house of lords, where it was decided to issue a writ of *de venire novo*, which was in effect a first step towards a new trial. It is worth noting that Gray moved in arrest of judgment in the Queen's Bench and not at the Monaghan assizes where he had been found guilty. The reason for this was that his case had been earlier moved into the Queen's Bench by a writ of *certiorari*, the court had returned it to be tried at nisi prius at Monaghan, and it was usual in such cases for the prisoner to be returned to the Queen's Bench for sentence.[72]

The writ of error had two major limitations. First, it was confined to the record, which did not include the evidence presented at the trial or the judge's summing up, although it did provide opportunities for challenging the indictment and the selection of the jury. Secondly, the attorney general was not obliged to issue his *fiat*. Thomas Dunn, who believed that he had been deprived of his right to challenge a juror, was refused a writ of error. Dunn's protest was impressive but

---

67   40 & 41 Vict., c. 57, ss 24, 86 (14 Aug. 1877).

68   Thompson, op. cit., p. 98.   69   Hayes, op. cit., i, 234–5.

70   Ibid., i, 237.   71   Ibid., p. 236.

72   Above, p. 88; Hayes, op. cit., i, 411.

unavailing: 'memorialist sheweth that he has been advised and believes that hitherto the granting of a *fiat* by the attorney general to a certificate of error signed by counsel has been considered a matter more of form than of favour and that in a case in which the life of one of Her Majesty's subjects however insignificant was at issue it has seldom if ever been withheld. Memorialist has already in the face of his country solemnly declared his innocence of the crime of which he was so convicted. He has been advised and verily believes he has not been legally convicted and he is now deprived by the attorney general of an opportunity of proving the illegality of that conviction.'[73]

The third method of proceeding was by using the writ of *certiorari*, although this was not technically a means of challenging the judgment because it was supposed to be used before judgment, in those cases 'where a writ of error does not lie.'[74] Prosecutors, prisoners, or the attorney general when he was involved, could apply to the Court of Queen's Bench, or after 1877 to the Queen's Bench Division, for a writ of *certiorari*, which would move the case from the court where it was being tried to the Queen's Bench. This was not an appeal procedure as generally understood, but an intervention that could subject an ordinary trial's procedure to scrutiny by the Queen's Bench, even before a verdict was returned. Cases could also be removed from coroners' inquests. The attorney general, for example, removed by *certiorari* the inquisitions arising out of the Sixmilebridge massacre, and applied to the Queen's Bench in November 1852 to have them quashed 'on the ground that the finding of the coroner's jury was against law and evidence.'[75] The attorney general had the right to remove a case as a matter of course, but others had to apply to the court for a conditional order, which might or might not be followed by an absolute order. No case could be removed into the Queen's Bench, except at the instance of the attorney general, 'unless it be made to appear to the court or a judge by the party applying that a fair and impartial trial of the case cannot be had in the court below, or that some question of law, of more than usual difficulty and importance, is likely to arise upon the trial.'[76] According to Hayes 'the Queen's Bench will not remove proceedings from the higher jurisdictions, where some of the judges preside, as at the assizes or Green-street commission, without strong grounds being produced as a reason for the application.'[77] The Queen's Bench removed cases 'to bring under its consideration their validity and legality, to prevent a partial or insufficient trial, to enable the defendant to plead a pardon ... Convictions and orders are removed by *certiorari*, not to try the merits of the question, but to see whether the limited jurisdiction has exceeded its bounds.'[78]

When an indictment was removed into the Queen's Bench the court could decide to deal with it in three different ways: first, it could send it back to its

---

73 NAI, CRF/1856/Dunn/26.   74 Hayes, op. cit., i, 119; Thompson, op. cit., p. 4.
75 See for example *Casey* (1852) 3 ICLR 22, at p. 23.
76 Thompson, op. cit., pp 4–5.   77 Hayes, op. cit., i, 123.
78 Ibid., pp 119–20.

county of origin to be tried by the civil side of the court; secondly, it could send it 'to an indifferent county, if it appears that a fair and impartial trial cannot be had in the county in which the indictment was found.'[79] The third method was rarely used, even in England: the case could be tried in the Queen's Bench itself, 'at bar', as the expression was, but before a jury brought up from the county where the indictment had been found, or before a jury from an 'indifferent' county. The attorney general, prosecuting on behalf of the Crown, had a right to demand a trial 'at bar'.

Joseph Poole was indicted for the murder of John Kenny at Seville Place in July 1882. He was tried at the Dublin Commission by a special jury in November 1883 under section 4 of the Prevention of Crime (Ireland) Act 1882. The jury disagreed.[80] The Crown put Poole on trial for the second time, but 'on which occasion the clerk of the crown was proceeding to call out the names of the special jurors, when counsel for the prisoner objected to have him tried by a special jury as no new notice of intention on the part of the Crown to have the case tried by a special jury had been served.'[81] The judge, James Murphy, overruled the objection, refused to reserve the case, but 'directed that it should be stated on the record that no new notice of intention to have the case tried by a special jury was served on the prisoner or his solicitor.' The second jury found Poole guilty and Murphy sentenced him to death. Poole's counsel moved in the Queen's Bench Division for a conditional order of *certiorari*

> to bring up the record in his case, in order that the verdict therein had might be set aside, and that the judgment there might be avoided, and that a *venire de novo* might be awarded; for that the alleged trial of said Joseph Poole was a mis-trial, inasmuch as he was tried before a jury which was not competent to try him, the notice prescribed by the Prevention of Crime (Ireland) Act not having been served on the prisoner, and the number of special jurors prescribed by the said act not having been summoned, returned and empanelled, and the said trial, verdict and judgment being contrary to law.[82]

The Queen's Bench Division refused Poole's application.

The fact that Poole's counsel applied for *certiorari* in the first place, and not for a writ of error, is worth noting because both Hayes and Thompson were quite clear that writs of *certiorari* were the remedy *before* judgment and writs of error *after* judgment.[83] In the case of William Nally, for example, who was convicted and sentenced at Cork spring assizes in 1884 for conspiracy to murder, *certiorari* was refused by Lawson, who declared that 'there was not tyro at the bar, or even a law student attending lectures who, if asked the question, would not answer, that

---

79   Thompson, op. cit., p. 5.   80   (1883) 14 LR Ir 14, at pp 14, 15.
81   Ibid., p. 16.   82   Ibid., p. 15.
83   Thompson, op. cit., p. 4; Hayes, op. cit., ii, 733. See above, p. 301, however, where Hayes refers
      to 'convictions' being removed by writs of *certiorari*.

after conviction and judgment no *certiorari* would lie. It does not need much authority to prove that after judgment the only mode of proceeding is by writ of error.'[84] When *Poole* was brought by *certiorari* into the Queen's Bench Division, the trial judge's direction that an entry should be made to the record was referred to in terms that suggested that they regarded the *certiorari* and writ of error as interchangeable, although not usually so: 'the learned judge ... allowed some entry to be made on the record, which counsel for the motion states shows error in law on the record. If that be so, the usual and ordinary course would have been to proceed by writ of error, which might have been taken to the court of ultimate resort: but it is stated that the present course is adopted because it leaves writ of error still to be resorted to.'[85] The alternation in certain circumstances of the two writs was partly explained by the quotation from Hayes above that 'convictions and orders are removed by *certiorari*, not to try the merits of the question, but to see whether the limited jurisdiction has exceeded its bounds.' This plethora of remedies made no difference to Poole: he was hanged on 18 December 1883.

84 *Nally and others v. R* (1884) 16 LR Ir 1, at p. 9.
85 (1883) 14 Ir 14, at p. 23.

CHAPTER TEN

The prerogative of mercy

CONVICT REFERENCE FILES

FEW PRISONERS' CASES went to the Queen's Bench or the Court for Crown Cases Reserved, but most of those convicted of murder or other capital offences presented memorials to the lord lieutenant begging him to exercise the royal prerogative of mercy to commute their sentences. Prerogative meant what it said, 'a peculiar privilege shared by no other'.[1] The lord lieutenant did not sign death warrants, as was commonly believed; he did not even confirm the sentence of death pronounced by the judge; the actual death warrant was issued by the clerk of the crown on behalf of the judge. The lord lieutenant issued a warrant only for a commutation of sentence, a reprieve, or a pardon; his warrant merely stopped the ineluctable progress of the law as pronounced by the judge.

The lord lieutenant dealt with the memorials himself. There was no established tribunal to assist him, there was no committee of the privy council, and no regular meetings of the judges and law officers.[2] In the early part of the period, viceregal decisions were made with a certain practised insouciance. Between May 1835 and April 1837, for instance, Lord Mulgrave dealt with 2,318 memorials; he dealt with a quarter of them (588) without consulting anyone; before disposing of the rest, he consulted judges, assistant barristers, magistrates, medical officers, and governors of gaols.[3] If it is assumed that the viceregal working-year consisted of 250 days, Mulgrave dealt with about five memorials a day, which does not imply

---

1 *The Shorter Oxford English Dictionary*, ii, 1658, defines prerogative as 'a sovereign right (in theory) subject to no restriction or interference'.

2 In Scotland memorials in capital cases were referred 'not to the judge who tried the case, but to the lord justice clerk, who is the head of the criminal court. He communicates with the judge who tried the case, and the lord justice clerk reports upon the case' (*Report of the capital punishment commission, together with the minutes of evidence, and appendix*, p. 214 [3590], HC 1866, xxi, 266). For the elaborate procedure that evolved in the Home Office see Roger Chadwick, *Bureaucratic mercy: the Home Office and the treatment of capital cases in Victorian Britain* (New York and London, 1992), pp 144–50.

3 *A return of all the criminal cases submitted for the decision of the lord lieutenant, on memorial and recommendation, from 12 May 1835; distinguishing those decided unfavourably, without reference to judge or assistant barrister; those decided favourably without such reference, those decided unfavourably after, and favourably after similar reference; of those decided favourably without reference to judge or assistant barrister; distinguishing how many were referred to magistrates or others for local information, how many to gaol authorities for report of conduct, how many were discharged on medical report, and how many on recommendation of character*, HC 1837 (195), xlvi, 7.

long hours of deliberation.[4] The procedures were informal, but thorough, which was not surprising in an administration controlled by under-secretaries such as Thomas Drummond and Thomas Larcom. Letters were answered punctiliously; judges were informed of decisions; prison governors were notified of reprieves; prisoners were told the law would take its course; promoters of petitions were told whether their protegés would be hanged or spared.

Lords justices exercised the prerogative of mercy when they temporarily replaced lords lieutenant. In the Shepherd case in 1839, the archbishop of Dublin, Richard Whately, who was one of the lords justices, behaved much more officiously than most lords lieutenant. The trial judge, Philip Crampton, had recommended the commutation of Shepherd's death sentence to transportation for life. Whately refused to sign the warrant 'till further reasons are laid before me, for which there is ample time, between this & 13th April.' (Shepherd was to be hanged on 13 April.) Crampton's reason for commutation was clearly implied in his first letter: Shepherd's four accomplices had been convicted two years before in 1837, and one had been hanged. Eventually Crampton sent his notes to Whately and spelt out his reason for commuting Shepherd's sentence: the hanging of the 'principal offender' in 1837, was 'sufficient in the way of example to satisfy the purposes of justice.' Whately was not mollified. 'I must observe that none of these circumstances were laid before *me* when the case was first sent up to me,' he wrote. 'I c[oul]d not know what the circumstances were that had weighed with a *former* govt without seeing or even hearing of the documents.'[5] The former government seems to have been that of the marquis of Normanby, formerly Lord Mulgrave, who was replaced by Viscount Ebrington on 1 March 1839, a change that explains why there were lords justices in office.

The lord lieutenant usually followed the trial judge's advice. There were no judge's notes in one-third of the 'death' cases in the Convict Reference Files, which suggests that lords lieutenant did not want to review the evidence against the prisoners in those cases. In the late 1830s, however, there were a few cases where lords lieutenant did not follow the judges' advice. Bushe, for example, told the house of lords select committee on the state of Ireland of a case in 1835 when he had sentenced four prisoners to death for wounding with intent to kill. Bushe recommended that one be hanged and the others transported for life; the former was hanged, but the lord lieutenant commuted the sentences of the others to two years' imprisonment.[6] Doherty told the same select committee of a case in 1838

---

4 Twentieth-century politicians were more laborious. R.A. Butler (home secretary, 1957–62) always had on the mantelpiece in his office a list of those lying under sentence of death. Before he made up his mind, 'he locked himself away for forty-eight hours and read all the relevant papers.' Brian Faulkner (Northern Ireland minister of home affairs, 1959–63) 'adopted a similar approach' on the four occasions when he had to review death sentences. 'Two were reprieved and two were not,' he recalled. 'They were the four most difficult decisions I have ever taken, but I am convinced they were right' (Brian Faulkner, *Memoirs of a statesman*, ed. John Houston (London, 1978), p. 25).

5 NAI, CRF/1839/Shepherd/13.

when he had recommended the commutation of a rapist's death sentence to transportation for life; the lord lieutenant commuted the sentence to twelve months' imprisonment.[7]

Occasionally the lord lieutenant consulted the law officers and the lord chancellor. The attorney general, for example, advised Lord Ebrington to ask the twelve judges to consider the case of James Casey and Michael Hartnett.[8] In the case of Thomas Dunn, sentenced to death in 1856 for the murder of Charlotte Hinds, Richard Moore, one of the judges at the special commission that had tried Dunn, suggested a meeting of the attorney general, the solicitor general, the chief justice, the lord chancellor, and himself to consider Dunn's petition.[9] This arrangement for dealing with Dunn may have been adopted because the attorney general had refused to issue a writ of error to enable Dunn to take his case to the Queen's Bench.[10] After Daniel and William Cormack were sentenced to death at Nenagh spring assizes in 1858 the lord lieutenant, Lord Eglinton, asked the attorney general, James Whiteside, for advice. Whiteside refused to give it. 'Upon reflection I feel I ought not as prosecuting counsel offer any opinion upon the propriety of yielding to the communication of the jury in Cormacks [*sic*] case,' he wrote. 'The zeal of counsel induces him, as his duty requires him in such a case to press for a conviction. He is not therefore the proper person to consult upon the propriety of extending or refusing mercy.'[11] Eglinton took nearly two months to make up his mind. The Cormacks, who were sentenced to death on 16 March 1858, were not hanged until 11 May.

The lord lieutenant rarely consulted legal authorities in England. In the case of Bryan Kilmartin, convicted in December 1882, 'all the papers in that case were referred by the then lord lieutenant, Lord Spencer, to Lord Selbourne, then lord chancellor of England.' The question came up again in 1893 when William Kenny QC (MP for Dublin Stephens Green, 1892-8), asked the chief secretary: '1. Whether the exercise in Ireland on the advice of the lord chancellor of England of the royal prerogative of mercy is a departure from precedent. 2. And whether he can refer to any case in which the prerogative was so exercised.'[12]

---

6   *Minutes of evidence taken before the select committee of the house of lords appointed to enquire into the state of Ireland, since the year 1835, in respect of crime and outrage, which have rendered life and property insecure in that part of the empire*, pt III, *evidence 12 June to 19 July*, p. 872, HC 1839 (486–III), xii, 8.

7   Ibid., p. 881. See also below, p. 385.

8   NAI, CRF/1840/Casey/43; *Hartnett and Casey* (1840) Jebb Rep 302; *Casey and Hartnett* 2 Cr & Dix 65.

9   NAI, CRF/1856/Dunn/26.   10   Above, pp 143-4.

11   Larcom Papers (NLI, MS 7636, f. 4). See also Nancy Murphy, *Guilty or innocent? The Cormack brothers: trial, execution and exhumation* (Nenagh, Co. Tipperary, 1998), pp 70, 89.

12   The references to Kilmartin's case and William Kenny's questions are taken from NAI, CRF/1867/Burke/21, where they were retrospectively placed. Cf. *Hansard* 4, viii, 997–9 (9 Feb. 1893) where Kenny does not mention the royal prerogative. After Kenny became a judge of the Queen's Bench Division in 1897, he had his share of the royal prerogative: five of those he sentenced to death were hanged, including Mary Daly, the first woman to be hanged in Ireland for thirty years (Death Book, 1852–1932 (NAI, GPB/CN/5)).

From the 1840s onwards when death sentences became much less frequent than they had been, only a handful of those sentenced to death did not present a memorial. The Convict Reference File for the three Stackpooles (two sisters and a brother hanged at Ennis in 1853) contained no memorial, but this was so remarkable that a clerk inserted a note in the file to the effect that 'no application was made on behalf of the convicts.'[13] In the file relating to two prisoners sentenced to death in 1847 there was no memorial and no judge's notes, only a letter from the governor of Kilkenny gaol, stating 'that James Larkin and James Daniel prisoners in this gaol who were tried at summer assizes 1847 convicted of murder, and sentenced to be hanged on the 25th August and their bodies to be buried within the precincts of the prison were executed on this day.'[14] Such reticence was rare, and the large number of surviving memorials suggests that the lord lieutenant was regarded not so much as the fountain of mercy but as a generously constructed aqueduct.[15] Prisoners' optimism was not misplaced. In the ninety years between 1831 and 1920, the lord lieutenant commuted the sentences of more than half of those sentenced to death.

The memorials in the Convict Reference Files contain some remarkable life-stories. John Carroll was sentenced at Clonmel to transportation for life for manslaughter in 1832. He told his story in a memorial in 1838:

> he was sent to New South Wales, and spent three or four years in the country, when petitioner was one of a party who was sent with Major Brew to explore the country, and on the discovery of Port Philip in the back part of the island, they were so set upon by the savages, they were obliged to seperate [*sic*]. When petitioner was on his way to the north west of the island, and after undergoing numerous hardships he arrived on the coast, where I espied a vessel at sea, and committing myself to the boisterous ocean, swam to it, proved to be William the fourth commanded by Captain Chamberlain, and proceed to Vandeamansland.[16]

Sentence of death was recorded against him at Tipperary spring assizes in 1838 for returning from transportation. After sentence 'he contrived to suspend himself in the prison by the neck and was not discovered until life was nearly extinct.' Even when the memorials do not tell life-stories they are often a treasure house of fragments of eloquence, cliché, esoteric knowledge, and humbug. The

---

13 NAI, CRF/1853/Stackpoole/6.   14 Ibid., CRF/1847/Larkin/30.
15 James Berry, who had a pecuniary interest in the prerogative, believed that 'there is an idea that the home secretary is "a very kind gentleman," who will "let 'em off"', if he possibly can' (James Berry, *My experiences as an executioner*, ed. by H. Snowden Ward; with a new introduction and additional appendices by Jonathan Goodman (Newton Abbot, 1972), p. 109). According to Roger Chadwick, the number of petitions presented to the home office declined during the second half of the nineteenth century (Chadwick, op. cit., p. 392).
16 NAI, CRF/1838/Carroll/50.

Revd Lawrence J. Browne, parish priest of Kilseedy, Co. Clare, for example, who wrote to Lord Spencer in August 1882 on behalf of Francis Hynes, expatiated on confession and contrition. Fr Browne was troubled by the murdered man's dying declaration; phrases such as *per signa* and *copia confessioni*, tumbled out.[17] Finally, Fr Brown thought he could move Lord Spencer by a more personal allusion. 'Would that today were alive your illustrious uncle, the great and saintly Father Ignatius Spencer, whose name, as an ornament and a credit to the Catholic church, is embalmed with undying recollection in every Irish Catholic heart,' he wrote. 'He, I verily believe, would give the weight of his name and the expression of his theological opinion in favour of the contention that consciousness could not exist when the Sacraments of Penance and Extreme Unction were administered *sub conditione*.'

The memorials, which were nearly always written in the third person, recounted the prisoner's grievances, mentioned mitigating circumstances, and flattered the lord lieutenant. Occasionally something more than conventional phrases appeared. John Logue, who was sentenced to death at Downpatrick in 1866 for the murder of Thomas Graham, wrote his own memorials. His spelling was not perfect, but generally accurate:

> Now I beseech you my most gracious governor[,] the ruler of this land which I am now condemned to die in[,] that for the love of that most just and holy God[,] who has his eyes ficksed[*sic*] on all us human creatures on earth[,] who at one day will judge us all, I implore of you that it will please your excellency to look after my trial.[18]

Lord Wodehouse decided to let the law take its course. Logue presented a second memorial, which elicited the same bleak answer as the first. Logue did not give up. He wrote a third memorial, which was written on a religious tract, entitled *Come to Jesus to be Reconciled with God*, published by The Religious Tract Society. By any standards the third memorial came close to 'authenticity'.

---

17 Copies 'of any documents (except official documents of a confidential and privileged character) in the nature of evidence or memorials, submitted for the consideration of the Irish executive, with reference to the alleged misconduct of members of the jury, the verdict, and the sentence, in the case of Francis Hynes, convicted of murder in the Dublin Commission Court on the 12th of August 1882, and executed in Limerick; and, of any letters written by the lord lieutenant with reference to such documents', pp 26–7, HC 1882 (408), lv, 192–3. Fr Ignatius started life as the Honourable George Spencer. When H.V. Morton visited SS Giovanni e Paolo, the Passionist monastery on the Caelian, he was shown Father Spencer's portrait: 'A long corridor is lined with the portraits of distinguished Passionists. Father Alfred paused in front of one. "Does he remind you of anyone?" he asked. "Yes," I replied. "Father Winston Churchill!" "Absolutely correct," said Father Alfred. "He is Father Ignatius Spencer, a Passionist, and a great-uncle of Winston Churchill"' (*A traveller in Rome* (New York, 1957), pp 178–9).

18 NAI, CRF/1866/Logue/6. See also Tim Carey, *Mountjoy: the story of a prison* (Cork, 2000), pp 156–7.

In a few days I'll either go to heaven or hell and my last prayer on earth will be that you shall be taken & hired [*sic*] up by the two big toes in hell. So now you whore's get that you are you can stick your pardon in old Judge Fitzgeralds arc [*sic*] for I'll ascend the scaffold like a hero. You bloody bugger I have to loss my good track [*sic*] by sending my prayer to you. May the devil take you before the 19th.

Logue, who was hanged on 19 April 1866, was the last prisoner to be hanged in public in Ireland.

The Convict Reference Files often provide information that had not been revealed in court. This was particularly true in cases of sodomy and bestiality, where the Crown and the judges were anxious to avoid publicity. The depositions in James Kelly's case showed why crown counsel and judges were anxious to be discreet. Henry Dunne, a labourer from Athy, described what he saw at Coneysborough in February 1848: 'he saw a man named James Kelly, having one of his master's (Jas Byrne's) Kerry heifers in the grip of a ditch and he Kelly with his trousers down, and he Kelly taking the tail of the said heifer aside and there having carnal beastial [*sic*] knowledge with said heifer.' As Kelly was buttoning his trousers, Dunne 'asked the said Kelly how he could be guilty of such an act and could he not get a woman for himself.' Kelly replied that 'he had no money and to say nothing about the matter.' Dunne, at the end of his information, admitted that 'he was so vexed [with] the said Kelly for committing such an act that he gave him ... a blow of his fist.'[19] Bestiality as a capital offence had a sporadic history in Ireland. There had been no death sentences pronounced between 1822 and 1840, and then there had been a handful of cases in the 1840s and 1850s.[20] It is tempting but probably erroneous to assume that the efflorescence in the early 1850s was caused by the conversion from tillage to pasture that Professor J.J. Lee described so many years ago. None of those convicted was hanged. In 1861 penal servitude

19 NAI, CRF/1860/Kelly/16. For other cases see ibid., CRF/1858/Wiggins/17, CRF/1861/ Lowry/16, CRF/1869/Leary/13, CRF/1871/McKeever/34. If Kelly had committed his crime in an Australian colony he might have been hanged. In 1865–7 in New South Wales and Victoria, whose combined populations were about a quarter of Ireland's, there were 27 hangings, including one for sodomy. There were only 8 hangings in Ireland in the same period and all were for murder (Vaughan, *Sin, sheep and Scotsmen: John George Adair and the Derryveagh evictions, 1861* (Belfast, 1983), p. 30). For definitions of buggery, sodomy, and bestiality see Terry L. Chapman, '"An Oscar Wilde type": "the abominable crime of buggery" in Western Canada, 1890–1920' in *Criminal Justice History*, 4 (1983), 98, 104; see also A.D. Hervey, 'Bestiality in late-Victorian England' in *Journal of Legal History*, 21:3 (Dec. 2000), 85.

20 The figures for 1840s and 1850s are taken from *Thom's Directory*. Sodomy had a slightly different history: no death sentences were passed on sodomites in the 1820s and apparently only two in the 1830s and none thereafter (*Summary statements of the number of persons charged with criminal offences, who were committed to the different gaols in Ireland for trial at the assizes and sessions held in the several counties, cities, towns, and liberties therein, during the last seven years ... 1822–1828*, p. 8, HC 1829 (256), xxii, 434; *Thirteenth report of the inspectors general on the general state of the prisons of Ireland, 1835*, p. 61, HC 1835 (114), xxxvi, 441).

for life replaced hanging as the punishment for 'the abominable crime of buggery, committed either with mankind or with any animal.'[21]

There is an eye-witness account of a lord lieutenant disposing of a prisoner's memorial. Lord Frederic Hamilton pestered his father, the duke of Abercorn (lord lieutenant, 1866–8, 1874–6), to allow him to watch the signing of a 'death warrant'.[22] The case was not a difficult one: a man at Cork had kicked his wife to death.[23] Lord Frederic went into his father's study 'on the tip-toe of expectation'. The Hon. Luke Gerald Dillon, Abercorn's private secretary, came in 'just as usual, carrying an ordinary official paper, precisely similar to dozens of other official papers lying about the room.' The ensuing exchange between Dillon and Abercorn did not suggest soul-searching:

> 'It is the Cork murder case, sir,' he said in his everyday voice. 'The sentence has to be confirmed by you.'
>
> 'A bad business, Dillon,' said my father. 'I have seen the Chief Justice about it twice, and I have consulted the judge who tried the case, and the solicitor and the attorney general. I am afraid there are no mitigating circumstances whatever. I shall certainly confirm it,' and he wrote across the official paper, 'Let the law take its course,' and appended his signature, and that was all!

Lord Frederic was disappointed. 'Could anything be more prosaic?' he lamented. 'What a waste of an unrivalled dramatic situation!' His reading of Harrison Ainsworth had led him to expect more: the secretary would enter dressed in black; the duke would recoil slightly; the duchess 'would burst into the room, and falling on her knees, with streaming eyes and outstretched arms, she would plead passionately for the condemned man's life.' The reprieve, granted by the duke, after he had brushed away 'a furtive and not unmanly tear', would arrive just as the condemned man was being taken to the scaffold. All would be pleased, except the hangman, 'who would grind his teeth at being baulked of his prey at the last minute.'

THE *VOX POPULI*

The typical signers and concocters of memorials were local worthies, such as JPs, parish priests, Protestant clergymen, medical practitioners, shopkeepers, and farmers. Occasionally they enhanced themselves by roping in grandees, such as

21   24 & 25 Vict., c. 100, s. 61 (6 Aug. 1861).
22   Lord Frederic Hamilton, *The days before yesterday* (London, n.d. [1920]), pp 73–5.
23   The case seems to have been that of William Tobin, hanged at Cork on 19 April 1875 for the murder of Johanna Cotter, who was not in fact his wife, but a woman whom he had robbed and murdered. See NAI, CRF/1875/Tobin/3.

MPs, peers, grand jurors, and even bishops. Having caught their grandees, they brandished them in the lord lieutenant's face. The petitioners on behalf of James and Henry Agnew, sentenced to death at Londonderry summer assizes in 1836, for example, 'humbly take the liberty of calling your excellency's attention to the recommendation of the Right Revd. the Lord Bishop of Derry who has signed above.'[24] This petition, which had 300 signatures, was an impressive one, even without the bishop. Signers used abbreviations that indicated rank or status, which suggests that the memorials are an excellent source for finding out a locality's important and self-important inhabitants. The petitions in favour of Francis Hynes contained names whose weight was increased by abbreviations: W.H. O'Shea JP, MP; The O'Gorman Mahon JP, DL, MP; George Unthank Macnamara LRCSI; John Hayes PP, VF; Edward Power PP, VG; Michael Hogan PLG, VC; John Gallagher VC; M. Dinan OFAG. Two signers spurned the use of abbreviations and spelt out their offices: R.W. Nesbitt, rector, Newmarket-on-Fergus, and James Molony, president, Irish Medical Association.[25]

The number of signatories varied. The memorial presented on behalf of Mary Ann McConkey, sentenced to be hanged on 1 May 1841 at Monaghan, had well over a hundred signatories.[26] John Logue, who was hanged at Downpatrick on 16 April 1866, wrote powerfully on his own behalf, as we have seen, but he was supported by a memorial, whose signatories included the dean of Down and about 40 of the inhabitants of Downpatrick.[27] Patrick Donovan, who was sentenced to death at Kilkenny assizes on 28 August 1841, succeeded in adding to his memorial not only the signature of Edward W. Briscoe, who may have been related to a JP called Henry Harrisson Briscoe, but the signatures of all twelve members of the jury that had convicted him, as well the signatures of four priests and a rector.[28] The fact that clergy of different denominations cooperated publicly in a good cause showed that they welcomed a chance to do what they rarely dared to do in other circumstances.

The tendency for the merciful to be numbered in scores and hundreds rather than in thousands persisted throughout the second half of the century in spite of the spread of literacy, the extension of the franchise, and easier means of communication. The memorial on behalf of Peter Conway, who was hanged at Omagh on 14 April 1880, had over 300 signatories, who were spread over a considerable area of Tyrone, but it was not very different from Mary Ann

---

24 NAI, CRF/1836/Agnew/3.
25 Copies 'of any documents ... in the case of Francis Hynes, convicted of murder in the Dublin Commission Court on the 12th of August 1882, and executed in Limerick ...', pp 31–2, HC 1882 (408), lv, 197–8. For more on Hynes see NAI, CRF/1882/Hynes/40. The abbreviations are easily identified for the most part: VC is not Victoria Cross but vice chairman of a poor law board; the two PPs who were also VF and VG are almost certainly priests who were a vicar general and a vicar forane. OFAG is not easy to identify.
26 Ibid., CRF/1841/McConkey/17.   27 Ibid., CRF/1866/Logue/6.
28 Ibid., CRF/1841/Donovan/53.

McConkey's in 1841, except possibly in its topographical reach.[29] The memorial on behalf of James Doherty, who was hanged at Sligo on 30 December 1902, had about 50 signatories, including priests, Protestant clergymen, and local officials – just the sort of people who would have signed sixty years before.[30] What was different about Doherty's memorial, however, was its presentation: the actual prayer was written in a legible, well-trained hand, which was different from the spidery hand of many of the earlier memorials; the pages for the signatures were neatly ruled into three columns, each column with its own heading, 'name & signature', 'residence', and 'occupation', which were repeated on each page.

The petitions on behalf of John Holden, the policeman hanged in Omagh in 1860, were probably the most elaborate in mid-nineteenth-century Ireland. There was a predictable effort in Omagh, including 10 of the jurors who had convicted him, as well as the parish priest, the rector, and the Presbyterian minister.[31] There was also a petition from Dungannon where Holden had served, which was slightly surprising because he was probably not the most accommodating of policemen. According to the *Tyrone Constitution*, 'the eleven years of his service in the constabulary were every day marked by the silly pride shown in his dress and his stern demeanour towards his comrades.'[32] Even more remarkable were the efforts from beyond Co. Tyrone: a petition from Dubliners that included David McBirney, whose address was not surprisingly Aston's Quay; a petition from the 'Roman Catholic bishops of Ulster', who were led by the primate, Joseph Dixon; a petition from the 'Ladies of Ireland', a deputation of whom presented their petition to Lady Caroline Lascelles, who received it on behalf of the lord lieutenant. The ladies' petition, which claimed 'that within one clear day 2000 ladies, whose names are beneath attached, signed this petition', consisted of hundreds of sheets of paper stuck together, which are now too brittle to be examined, but a rough estimate of the size of the bundle suggests the promoters were not exaggerating. Whether the women went out themselves to collect the signatures is not clear. The petition states that 'the above signatures were obtained by Patrick Roe secretary to the Catholic Dormitory Society of our Blessed Lady of Charity and Refuge of Sinners, 80 Townsend Street', but that may mean only that he collated the signed sheets.[33] The cause of Holden's murdering Sergeant McClelland was his marrying without the inspector general's permission, and the subsequent disciplinary proceedings taken against him, for which he blamed McClelland. The women maintained that 'the marrying of a woman whom he had wronged, was, in itself the proof of an honest and upright mind.'[34] Holden was hanged at Omagh on 26 August 1860.

29 Ibid., CRF/1880/Conway/19.				30 Ibid., CRF/1902/Doherty/69.
31 Ibid., CRF/1860/Holden/26.				32 31 Aug. 1860.
33 Women rarely signed petitions. For other examples of women signers see NAI, CRF/1876/
    Bombos/26 and 1876/McKeown /22. Bombos' file contained a petition from about 70 women
    in Cork led by Kathleen Bryan.
34 Ibid., CRF/1860/Holden/26. For a description of how Richard Robert Madden concocted a

What arguments did the signers of petitions use? The reasons given for commuting the death sentence are given in Table 10.1, which is based on a selection of 85 petitions taken from the Convict Reference Files between the 1830s and the early twentieth century.[35] Previous good character, which was the

TABLE 10.1

REASONS FOR COMMUTING DEATH SENTENCES

reason given	no. of references	% of total
previous good character	39	26
not responsible for actions	35	23
jurors recommended mercy	28	18
dependent families	19	12
circumstantial evidence	13	8
innocence	11	7
disapproval of capital punishment	10	6
total	155	100

most frequently used argument, accounted for 26% of the arguments used. (About 20% of the witnesses called by prisoners at their trials had been character witnesses; the increase to 26%, therefore, might hint at a slight notional amelioration of their characters after conviction.) In her petitions to Queen Victoria and the prince of Wales, Bridget Dillane, whose husband Denis Dillane had procured two men to murder the landlord Francis Fitzgerald, mentioned her husband's 'irreproachable character'.[36] Mrs Dillane's admiration for her husband was shared by four priests, a Catholic curate, a Church of Ireland clergyman, a solicitor, a captain in the army, and Morgan O'Connell MD, FRCSI, who referred to Dillane's 'truly unimpeachable life, to his habits of untiring industry, steadiness, sobriety and honesty.' Dillane was hanged at Limerick on 13 April 1863. The two actual perpetrators of the murder, Thomas Beckham and James Walsh, had been hanged on 16 July and 1 September 1862.[37] Previous good character was an effective argument to use. In nearly two-thirds of the cases where it was used, the prisoner was not hanged. Partiality, however, occasionally outstripped credibility. Michael Moylan, who was hanged at Nenagh in 1843 for the murder of John Nolan, was described, admittedly by himself, as having

petition on behalf of a condemned man, see Thomas More Madden (ed.), *The memoirs (chiefly autobiographical) from 1798 to 1866 of Richard Robert Madden, MD, FRCS* (London, 1891), pp 6–7. (I am grateful to John McHugh for this reference.)

35 Above, p. 2.   36 NAI, CRF/1863/Dillane/15.

37 Death Book, 1852–1932 (NAI, GPB/CN/5); ibid., CRF/1862/Beckham/21; ibid., Walsh/16.

'hitherto borne an excellent character'.[38] Serjeant Warren, who tried Moylan, made his own inquiries. 'Although the prisoner did not examine any witness to his character,' he wrote, 'I thought it right to make inquiry on the subject, after his conviction, and before I pronounced the awful sentence of the law and I regret to say it appears from my notes which I made at the time, that I could hear nothing good respecting him.' Murder ran in Moylan's family: his grandfather had been hanged for murder.

Good character was mentioned so frequently that it takes an effort to remember that more than half the petitions did not mention it at all. There was an outpouring of eloquence on behalf of one of the few women hanged in this period, Mary Ann McConkey, but her good character was not mentioned.[39] She had dosed her husband with leaves of blue rocket, preparatory to eloping with her lover. Good character was not evoked in the case of Bernard Cangley, who had been released from Smithfield prison a couple of weeks before he murdered Peter Reilly. Nor was it invoked on behalf of John Logue, who had been released from Spike Island a few weeks before he murdered Thomas Graham.[40] Local worthies were generous but not indiscriminate.

Good character was closely followed by the argument that the prisoner was not fully responsible for what he had done. The grounds for irresponsibility varied. When George Jubee shot the adjutant of his battalion he was 'totally incapable of being master of his own actions or conduct',[41] and when Edward Walsh murdered his wife, his signers alluded to his propensity to drink, to the effects of a head injury, and to an 'absence of premeditation'.[42] About half of those whom the petitioners commended on grounds of irresponsibility were hanged, which suggests that the judges and the petitioners did not see eye to eye. In some of the cases where the petitioners urged the prisoner's irresponsibility, the exercise of mercy would not have seemed unreasonable. Bernard Cangley, who murdered Peter Reilly, did not apparently have a motive; he had only one arm, which did not exclude violent behaviour, but made it unlikely. Before he was sentenced at the spring assizes in Cavan in 1864, all he said was 'I was unconscious at the time.'[43] What condemned Cangley was that after attacking Reilly, he went to Virginia and gave himself up to the constabulary, which showed that he was not 'labouring under such a defect of reason, from disease of the mind, as not to know the nature and quality of the act he was doing; or, if he did know it, that he did not know he was doing what was wrong.'[44] John Russell, found guilty at Clonmel in 1875, was, according William Hastings Garnet, who was the resident medical superintendent of the district lunatic asylum, 'weak-minded to a degree and incapable of

38 Ibid., CRF/1843/Moylan/54.   39 Ibid., CRF/1841/McConkey/17.

40 Ibid., CRF/1864/Cangley/13; ibid., CRF/1866/Logue/6.

41 Ibid., CRF/1844/Jubee/1.   42 Ibid., CRF/1873/Walsh/11.

43 Ibid., CRF/1864/Cangley/13.

44 *M'Naghten* (1843) 10 Cl & F 200, at p. 210; 8 Eng Rep HL 718, at p. 722.

estimating at its true value the seriousness of the deed he committed and its consequences.' The lord lieutenant, the duke of Abercorn, was sympathetic to Russell's plea for mercy; his private secretary, the Hon. Luke Gerald Dillon referred the case to the lord chancellor, saying pointedly that 'if he thinks there are sufficient grounds for respiting the man, H[is] G[race] wishes it done.' The lord chancellor did not agree, and Russell was hanged on 9 April 1875.[45] The duke was closer to the *vox populi* than the lord chancellor.

There were 28 references to the fact that jurors had recommended prisoners to mercy, 21 when they returned their verdicts and 7 after the trial.[46] The reason for the jury's recommendation was usually easily discernible: Mary Ann McConkey was a woman, John Corderry was a soldier, who had shot a sergeant in his own regiment,[47] and Laurence Smith was blind.[48] Two-thirds of the prisoners whom juries recommended to mercy were not hanged, which was an impressive success rate. Irish juries were not prodigal with recommendations to mercy; only about a quarter brought recommendations to mercy with their verdicts, which was not excessive given the number of sentences that were regularly commuted. Certainly the frequency of juries' recommendations to mercy were not a subject of complaint in Ireland, as they were in France, where juries were allowed to consider 'extenuating' circumstances and where, as a result, 'moral considerations (including all the false moral notions prevalent in a partially educated and, perhaps, highly inflamed section of the community) are likely to have an overwhelming weight. What is an offence in one court is not one in another; and what is punished with death today is held to be an act attributable to the most generous and worthy motives tomorrow.'[49]

Jurors who merely added their names to petitions after the trial were less successful than those who made their recommendation when they returned their verdict: of the seven prisoners recommended by jurors after their trials, six were hanged.[50] There were suggestions in the files that jurors who signed memorials after trials did so under duress. After James Downie was sentenced to death at the Kilkenny summer assizes in 1843, Sub-Inspector Thomas Trant, of Callan, described how Downie's wife collected signatures: 'the wife of Downey called on Mr Mark Belcher, who was the foreman of the jury, and whose residence is in the midst of the relatives and friends of Downey, to sign a petition for a mitigation of punishment, and said to him "If you sign it you will have my blessing, – if you don't." Here she paused and left him to guess the rest. He considered it as a threat. He did not sign it. As every exertion is being made to have a petition

45 NAI, CRF/1875/Russell/1.
46 The jury in the Holden case did both; it is included with the 21 (NAI, CRF/1860/Holden/26). On juries in England recommending mercy see Chadwick, op. cit., pp 116–23.
47 NAI, CRF/1844/Corderry/22.   48 Ibid., CRF/1873/Smith/18.
49 Sheldon Amos, *The science of law* (London, 1874), p. 271.
50 For a case where the judges would almost certainly have hanged the prisoner, if the jury had not belatedly intervened, see above, p. 293.

signed, I submit this fact as to the means resorted to.'[51] Neal Browne, the RM in Tullamore, described a slightly less reprehensible effort on behalf of Thomas Dowling: a priest approached Samuel Ridgeway, one of the jurors, to sign a memorial because 'he had reason to know that the government were inclined to pardon Dowling ... and that all that the government required to make them to do so was a memorial from the jury who tried the case.' According to Browne, Ridgeway signed the memorial, but other jurors did not. In fact eight of the jury, including Samuel Ridgeway, had signed the memorial by the time it was forwarded by the parish priest of Tullamore.[52]

Good character, irresponsibility, and the jurors' recommendation to mercy accounted for two-thirds of all the arguments used to obtain mercy. They were followed at a distance by references to prisoners' dependent families and to the unreliability of circumstantial evidence. The former was referred to 19 times. Patrick Donovan, for example, was 'incumbered with a wife and two young children'.[53] Circumstantial evidence was referred to 13 times. Alexander Mullan's memorial stated 'that convictions obtained on such evidence alone should be visited with a mitigated punishment and only on strict ocular testimony that a penalty involving life should be enforced.'[54] Patrick Cain's memorial hinted that a prisoner 'must be seen committing the murder before he can be found guilty.' Cain had raped and murdered his sister-in-law near Ballinkillew in Co. Carlow.

There were only eleven references to innocence. John Brewer 'unavailingly but earnestly asserts his innocence' because the Crown's medical witness had been 'a young practitioner of only eighteen months standing'.[55] Patrick Woods vigorously asserted his innocence after his conviction at Armagh in 1841.[56] John and James Power, who were convicted of murdering John Peters near Bansha, were 'conscious' of their innocence. Their consciousness was shared by others, for 'the innocence of your memorialists is well known and perfectly notorious in the neighbourhood of the murder'. They had supporters even among the gentry; the high sheriff of Tipperary, Thomas Lalor, thought the case against them was one of 'great difficulty and doubt'.[57] Patrick Beary asserted that his innocence 'is now generally felt and believed throughout the country', and two magistrates supported him, saying 'there may be some mistake in the identification of Beary.'[58] Denis Healey's innocence rested on the alleged bad character of the Crown's witnesses.[59] Stephen McKeown 'persists in asserting his innocence', although it was not easy to see his reasons for doing so.[60] Timothy Carew had good grounds for his assertion of innocence. Having pleaded guilty to the murder of John Keeshan, he felt he should not be hanged because his two confederates,

51 NAI, CRF/1843/Mullins & Downie/50.   52 Ibid., CRF/1844/Dowling/11.
53 Ibid., CRF/1841/Donovan/53.   54 Ibid., CRF/1853/Mullan/32.
55 Ibid., CRF/1837/Brewer/165.   56 Ibid., CRF/1841/Woods/26.
57 Ibid., CRF/1841/Power/13.   58 Ibid., CRF/1843/Beary/32.
59 Ibid., CRF/1851/Healey/10.   60 Ibid., CRF/1876/McKeown/22.

including the principal, had been acquitted.[61] Peter Conway, who also relied on the justice of fairly applying sauce to geese of both genders, was sentenced to death at the same assizes where his father had been acquitted, 'although the evidence against him was in almost every respect the same.'[62] John Logue, hanged at Downpatrick on 19 April 1866, was modest, merely claiming to be 'not guilty'. He did not want a pardon or a reprieve, but a new trial.[63] The last 2 cases of the 11 were those of rapists, whose innocence was based on the loose characters of the women they raped.[64] All of these, except Timothy Carew, Patrick Beary, and the two rapists were hanged.

There were only ten references in the petitions to the abolition of capital punishment, which suggests that abolition was not an important item on the Irish political agenda. When abolitionists did appear they were not only small in numbers, but diffident. In 1841 a memorial from the Hibernian Anti-Punishment By Death Society made it clear that they did not expect much notice to be taken of their efforts: 'your memorialists were not on former occasions successful in inducing the lord lieutenant to listen with favorable ear to similar applications, yet they feel it to be their solemn duty again to appeal to him.'[65] Irish abolitionists were not prominent among the witnesses who gave evidence to the 1866 royal commission.[66] One of the fullest expressions of Irish abolitionism occurred in 1843 in the memorial on behalf of Michael Mullins and James Downie, which had 22 signatories including James Haughton, Thomas Davis, Daniel O'Connell, Richard Webb, and Samuel Haughton.[67] The memorial, moreover, was unusual in that it had women signers: Susan Eliza Grubb, Elizabeth Haughton, Sarah Cambridge Haughton, Mary Ann Haughton, Susan Grubb, Anne Morris, and Anne Duffy. The abolition they proposed was not to be total: it would apply only in time of peace and be limited to 'offences of the class for which the said prisoners are now under sentence.' The prisoners had been convicted of conspiracy to murder Laurence Hoynes, who had tried to raise his rents.

'There are,' the memorial said, 'peculiar reasons to induce a statesman to avoid capital punishment in this country, as tending to more harm than good.' The 'peculiar' reasons were historical: the civil wars of the seventeenth century had established 'a class of landholders differing in blood, language, creed and feelings

61 Ibid., CRF/1840/Carew/52.   62 Ibid., CRF/1880/Conway/19.
63 Ibid., CRF/1866/Logue/6.
64 Ibid., CRF/1841/Nangle/12; ibid., 1842/Flynn/5.
65 Ibid., CRF/1841/Power/13.
66 *Report of the capital punishment commission, together with the minutes of evidence, and appendix*, [3590], HC 1866, xxi, 1, passim.
67 NAI, CRF/1843/Mullins & Downie/50. For Samuel Haughton's involvement with hanging in later decades see below, pp 351–2. Samuel was James' step-nephew. Not all of those associated with *The Nation* were abolitionists. 'Jails ought to be places of discomfort,' John Mitchel wrote. 'The "sanitary condition" of miscreants ought not to be better cared for than the honest industrious people – and for "ventilation", I would ventilate the rascals in front of the county jails at the end of a rope' (Joseph McArdle, *Irish literary anecdotes* (Dublin, 1995), pp 71–2).

from the mass of the people'; the penal laws and 'an unjust system of government' had handed over the administration of justice 'to that favoured class'; the people had come to believe 'that there was one law for the rich and another for the poor nor were they wrong in the belief and therefore they resorted to modes of justice and redress beyond, and opposed to the law.' The signers admitted that much had changed: 'happily many of the causes of this feeling have been removed, the penal laws repealed, the landholders have grown to be regarded as natives, and the central administration of justice has aimed, and frequently practised, impartiality.' The improvements in the administration of justice that the petitioners approved of included 'great tenderness' in procuring evidence, 'peculiar mercy' in punishments, improvements in the selection of juries, and giving prisoners the benefit of counsel. Best of all was 'the limitation of capital punishments [that] has done more to reconcile men to law and therefore tend to procure peace and order than the bloody system which, till lately, prevailed.' The list was a compliment to the whig government's reforms. Whether Thomas Drummond, who was by this time in Mount Jerome, would have been satisfied by the remark that the whig government 'frequently' practised impartiality, is another matter. Drummond and his successor Edward Lucas might have been pleased by the remark about juries, especially when it is remembered that the bitter controversy over the cases of Patrick Woods and Francis Hughes had occurred less than two years before.

There was nothing as elaborate as this on abolition after the Famine. Matthew Phibbs' mother did not go into detail when she told Queen Victoria that 'the strongest objection exists among your majesty's loyal subjects in Sligo to capital punishment in any shape.'[68] The royal commission on capital punishment in 1865 may have inspired Downpatrick's display of abolitionist sentiment on behalf of John Logue in 1866: 'your petitioners have learned with much satisfaction that the question of capital punishment for murder is to be brought under the consideration of parliament at an early day, and your petitioners would therefore most earnestly urge upon the executive that in the present uncertain state of what the law may soon be criminals now under sentence of death should at least be respited until the wisdom of parliament has decided upon the subject.'[69] Five years later, a petition from Downpatrick, on behalf of John Gregory, admitted that opinion in the town was divided: 'the great majority' believed in penal servitude as a substitute for capital punishment, but 'some of your memorialists still believe in the necessity of capital punishment.'[70] The memorial had sixteen signatures.

As a guide to the *vox populi* the petitions had shortcomings. They were not local referenda, and there was no opportunity to vote against mercy for the prisoner. As a constituency, the signers were self-selecting and thin on the ground.

68 NAI, CRF/1861/Phibbs/5. For other short references see ibid., CRF/1875/Russell/1 and CRF/1880/Conway/19. For the decline of abolitionist sentiment in England after the 1860s, see Chadwick, op. cit., p. 357.

69 NAI, CRF/1866/Logue/6.   70 Ibid., CRF/1871/Gregory/9.

Yet as a measure of the *vox populi* the petitions have some value: those who signed were magistrates, jurors, clergymen, shopkeepers, and farmers; they were men of influence, or at any rate men to whom influence was ascribed.[71] The fact that there were petitions for mercy in nearly every capital case suggests that the popular voice was more lenient, more generous, and more inconsistent than the judges, especially in the matter of premeditation, mental state, and drunkenness. Opposition to petitions for mercy was rarely expressed. John McLoughlin's supporters presented 9 petitions between the commutation of his sentence in March 1865 and his release in June 1885. The McCrossan family protested against his release on 5 occasions, in 1868, 1870, 1872, 1878, and 1883.[72] The case became a conflict between liberalism and toryism in Tyrone. (John McCrossan, according to his widow, 'fell a victim of his persistent efforts in the cause of liberality.') When McLoughlin was released in 1885 Timothy Michael Healy asked the chief secretary 'on what grounds did Lord Spencer order the release of an Orangeman who murdered a Catholic solicitor in Omagh twenty-one years ago under the most horrible circumstances?'[73] McLoughlin was a Catholic.

The petitioners were not indiscriminate: they ascribed good character to only a minority of prisoners; they alluded to the irresponsibility of the condemned, but in only a minority of cases; juries recommended mercy in only a minority of cases; hanging was objected to, but usually only in the case in question, and abolition was infrequently advocated. In one case at least the popular view was *less* lenient than the judge's. James Casey and Michael Hartnett were sentenced to death for murdering a policeman. There did not seem to be much hope for them: they had gone out armed to commit a robbery, one had a sword, the other a gun; the expedition had been planned; the policeman they shot was wearing his uniform. The jury did not recommend them to mercy, but the judge, Richard Moore, took a merciful view: 'Tho' one of the police was killed, it was not the intention of the prisoners to do anything beyond what was necessary to effect their escape from arrest, and had my view of the law permitted it, I should have been glad that this had been only a conviction for manslaughter … It may be deserving consideration of his excellency, whether in this case the ends of justice may not be satisfied by the transportation for life of the prisoners.' The lord lieutenant, however, decided that the law should take its course, which made this one of the very few cases where the lord lieutenant and the jury took a harsher view than the judge.[74]

As a guide to the feelings of the prisoners themselves the memorials are handicapped by the fact that most were written by intermediaries. Flashes of feeling occasionally appear, but feeling was not as important as one might expect.

---

71 For an interesting exploration of the world below the respectable *vox populi*, see Frank Sweeney, *The murder of Conell Boyle, County Donegal, 1898*. Maynooth Studies in Local History, no. 46 (Dublin, 2002).

72 NAI, CRF/1885/McLoughlin/18.   73 *Hansard 3*, ccxcix, 909 (16 July 1885).

74 NAI, CRF/1840/Casey/43.

Repentance, remorse, and reparation came a long way behind good character, moral irresponsibility, and family ties. Only five petitions mentioned repentance, and only five mentioned shame, but it was the shame associated with hanging rather than the shame of committing murder. John Hickey's mother, through an intermediary, told the lord lieutenant that she 'mourns over the ignominy of his death that to use her expression he is to [be] hanged like a dog.'[75] James McKeever, whose death sentence for bestiality was commuted to penal servitude for life in 1857, complained, after ten years, of 'his unutterable woe', of 'the hardships and incessant sufferings of a convict prison', and of his 'daily torture'.[76]

COMMUTATION

Since the definition of murder was so capacious, the lord lieutenant and the judges had in effect to differentiate between capital and non-capital murder, a distinction that had no legal standing in the nineteenth century. As a result many of those sentenced to death had their sentences commuted and received the mercy for which they had petitioned. 'It is impossible not to recognize a difference in guilt between the man who deliberately poisons another in order to rob him and a man who shoots another in a duel in which he risks his own life upon equal terms,' James Fitzjames Stephen wrote. 'Each, however, kills intentionally and unlawfully.'[77] It is easy enough to see why some were hanged. Those who murdered for gain,[78] and those who murdered while they were robbing were hanged.[79] Men who poisoned their wives, and women who poisoned their husbands, were hanged.[80] Men who murdered their wives by means that implied less deliberation than the use of poison were hanged,[81] and men who murdered women with whom

---

75 Ibid., CRF/1844/Hickey/17.
76 Ibid., CRF/1871/McKeever/34.
77 Stephen, *A history of the criminal law of England*, 3 vols, (London, 1883), iii, 84. To show that 'murder, however, accurately defined, must always admit of degrees of guilt', Stephen mentioned seven circumstances that reduced guilt: (1) the absence of a 'positive' intention to kill; (2) provocation 'not falling within the line laid down by the existing law'; (3) mental disease that fell short of legal insanity; (4) where 'the deceased person consented to his own death'; (5) where 'the motives of the offender are compassion, despair, or the like'; (6) where 'a woman kills her new-born child under the distress of mind and fear of shame caused by child-birth'; (7) where 'the offender is extremely young' (Stephen, op. cit., iii, 85–6). For a discussion of Stephen's attempts to restrict the contemporary definition of murder, see K.J.M. Smith, *James Fitzjames Stephen: portrait of a Victorian rationalist* (Cambridge, 1988), pp 60–72.
78 NAI, CRF/1860/Hederman/23; ibid., 1861/Phibbs/5; 1863/Ward/5; ibid., 1875/ McDaid/5; 1898/Kenny/6.
79 Ibid., CRF/1847/Ryan/24; ibid., 1862/Moore/8; Larcom Papers (NLI, MS 7620 (the case of Laurence King)); NAI, CRF/1871/Gregory/9.
80 Ibid., CRF/1888/Cross/1; ibid., 1862/Burke/29; ibid., 1841/McConkey/17.
81 Ibid., CRF/1865/Hayes/21; ibid., 1882/Haynes/35; 1892/Heaney/1; 1893/Boyle/1; 1901/Toole/6.

they lived in sin were hanged.[82] Men who murdered children for whom they were responsible were hanged.[83] Sons who murdered their fathers,[84] and fathers who murdered their sons,[85] were hanged. Tenants who murdered landlords, agents or bailiffs were hanged.[86] Soldiers who murdered their officers,[87] sailors who murdered their captains,[88] and policemen who murdered their senior officers were hanged.[89] Men who murdered their neighbours or relations in internecine quarrels, especially quarrels about land, were hanged.[90] In all of these categories, however, the qualification 'but not in every case' might be added.

The use of firearms, knives, and poison, which suggested deliberation, were almost certain to lead to hanging, even if the motive for the murder was not clear. John Logue, for example, who shot Thomas Graham, when apparently he intended to shoot George Graham, was hanged.[91] Two cases nicely demonstrate the effect of the weapons used on the lord lieutenant's decision: Alexander Mullan who cut his aunt's throat with a razor was hanged; Matthew Bryan who beat his mother to death was not.[92] Yet deliberation was not an infallible characteristic of the crimes of those who were hanged. Alcohol, for example, which might suggest absence of deliberation, seemed to make things worse for the prisoner. Edward Walsh who was drunk when he beat his wife to death was hanged.[93] The brutality of an attack, even if it implied little deliberation, might tip the balance: John Daly beat his wife's aunt to death with a piece of wood, which did not suggest careful preparation, but the effects were shocking. According to the surgeon who examined the body: 'there was a lacerated wound of the genital organs externally and internally the passage to the artery was torn the gut was lacerated the bladder was lacerated the parts between were torn & in the bladder I found a boiled potatoe I could hardly reach it with my fingers ... there was no appearance of the use of any sharp instrument in making the wounds.'[94]

Some of those whose sentences were commuted were obvious candidates for mercy, such as those sentenced to death for crimes that were no longer regarded as hanging matters. Patrick Murphy who was convicted of rape in 1841,[95] for example, was not hanged, nor was Thomas Wiggins who was convicted of bestiality in 1849.[96] The largest category in this group were women, such as Mary

82 Ibid., CRF/1870/Carr/16; ibid., 1889/McKeown/2.
83 Ibid., CRF/1909/Justin/7. 84 Ibid., CRF/1865/Lynch/11.
85 Ibid., CRF/1902/Doherty/69. 86 Above, pp 57–8.
87 NAI, CRF/1841/Jubee/1. 88 Ibid., CRF/1876/Bombos/26.
89 Ibid., CRF/1860/Holden/26.
90 Ibid., CRF/1873/Smith/18; 1876/McKeown/22; 1883/Keeffe/13; 1889/Stafford/9; but see ibid., 1840/Ryan/37 for the reprieve of John and Edmond Ryan, who murdered a man in an affray about the enclosure of land.
91 Ibid., CRF/1866/Logue/6; see also ibid., 1864/Cangley/13.
92 Ibid., CRF/1840/Bryan/13; ibid., 1853/Mullan/32.
93 Ibid., CRF/1873/Walsh/11. 94 Ibid., CRF/1876/Daly/9.
95 Ibid., CRF/1841/Murphy/54. 96 Ibid., CRF/1858/Wiggins/17.

Ann Craig, who had murdered her illegitimate child, a crime that was capital, but whose non-capital quality was shown by the fact it was usually referred to as infanticide, especially in statistical returns.[97] More culpable were those who were convicted of attempted murder, which was capital until 1861. Their fate, to some extent, depended on the state of the country. John Macnamara, for example, who was convicted of attempted murder, was not hanged, because the judge, Nicholas Ball, was impressed by 'the present tranquil state of the country, & considering the disposition of the public mind that capital punishment should be reserved for crimes of greater atrocity.'[98] Others were not hanged because they were not really to blame. Patrick McDermott, who murdered James McCormick, was not hanged because the judge thought that McCormick would have 'recovered from the blow had he received any prompt medical attention.'[99] Some escaped because they were involved with others who were regarded as more culpable. Timothy Carew, who did *not* fire the fatal shot and helpfully pleaded guilty,[100] and Patrick Beary, who helped one of the actual perpetrators to escape,[101] were members of gangs that set out to commit murder, but neither Carew nor Beary were hanged because they were not the actual perpetrators. James and Daniel Handley murdered Mary Ann Lyons in 1892; Daniel was hanged on 19 April, but James was spared because the judge, Hugh Holmes, agreed with the jury who recommended him to mercy 'on the ground of his youth and that in their opinion he had acted under the influence of his brother.'[102]

On rare occasions the judges and lords lieutenant were so baffled that they had to admit that mercy was better than death. Lefroy described such a case in 1844 when a peaceful family gathering round a fire came to a violent end:

> The house was dark, no candle – the shutter shut & the fire smoking, so that one of the witnesses said he could only identify the prisoner by his voice – but immediately after this conversation a blow was heard & the deceased was observed to fall – Thady Hopkins immediately got up & addressed the prisoner – 'if it was you did that it was a great shame for you' & put him out of the house – the other brother lit a candle & they found the deceased stretched on the floor with a cut on the side of his head of which he died that night ... I told the jury that in my opinion there was no evidence to warrant their finding any other verdict than that of murder ... all the circumstances which distinguish it from cases where the murderous design could not be doubted, can only operate as an inducement to mercy & as such I submit them along with the strong recommendation of the jury to his excellency's consideration.[103]

---

97   Ibid., CRF/1837/Craig/171.   98   Ibid., CRF/1840/Macnamara/78.
99   Ibid., CRF/1841/McDermott/44.   100 Ibid., CRF/1840/Carew/52.
101 Ibid., CRF/1843/Beary/32.   102 Ibid., CRF/1901/Handley/2.
103 Ibid., CRF/1844/Fahy/7; for a similar case see ibid., 1866/Rourke/25.

There were cases that were not obscure, but where the commutation of sentence was surprising. James and Henry Agnew should have been hanged, if principle, precedent, and expediency had been any guides: they planned the murder of Henry McWilliams, they brought in assassins to beat him to death, but they were not hanged.[104] Patrick Cain raped and murdered his sister-in-law, Bridget Cain. If there was anything that guaranteed hanging it was committing murder in the course of committing another felony – and in 1839 rape was still a capital offence, although there had not been a hanging since 1835. The judge, Torrens, was at first for carrying out the sentence, but changed his mind, and Cain did not hang.[105] James Kelly and Matthew Hourigan would certainly have hanged after the special commission in Clonmel in 1839 if six of the jurors had not signed a petition on their behalf after their trial.[106]

Two cases showed how fine the judges' distinctions could be. Charles McCormick was convicted at Longford summer assizes in 1863 of the murder of Michael Beglan; John McLoughlin was convicted at Omagh spring assizes in 1865 of the murder of John McCrossan. Judge Fitzgerald tried McCormick; Baron Fitzgerald tried McLoughlin. The murder weapons in both cases were memorable: in the former a bull's pizzle and in the latter a long hook called a 'cleak'. In both cases the judges admitted that murder had not been intended. 'The impression conveyed *strongly* to my mind by the whole of the case was that the assailants of the deceased man, Michael Beglan, *did not intend to take his life,*' Judge Fitzgerald wrote. 'They did desire to give him a severe beating but probably never contemplated killing him.'[107] 'The prisoner did not intend to take the life of the deceased,' Baron Fitzgerald wrote. 'I believe that I laid down the law correctly, but I confess that if not bound so to do, the general character of the case would have struck me rather as that of aggravated manslaughter than murder.'[108]

The merits of the two cases could be discussed at length. McCormick's offence was the more deliberate because he was a member of a gang that attacked Beglan on a fair day; McLoughlin attacked McCrossan while his brother the sub-sheriff was trying to execute a writ of *fieri facias*. McCormick's killing of a small farmer's son in an obscure dispute needed to be discountenanced; a skilled workman murdering a successful, Liberal, Catholic solicitor in a respectable Ulster town was not the prelude of a murderous pandemic. The bull's pizzle was an offensive weapon but not necessarily a lethal one; the 'cleak' at its most offensive was used for catching salmon, but it was a dangerous implement when poked into the neck of a respectable solicitor. There is no doubt that McLoughlin was the more deserving of the two, even if it is admitted that neither intended to commit murder. McCormick was hanged, and McLoughlin's sentence was commuted to penal servitude for life. Baron Fitzgerald added to his report on McLoughlin,

104 Ibid., CRF/1836/Agnew/3.
106 Above, p. 293.
108 Ibid., CRF/1885/McLoughlin/18.

105 Ibid., CRF/1839/Cain/45.
107 NAI, CRF/1863/McCormick/30.

TABLE 10.2

MURDERERS SENTENCED TO DEATH, HANGED, OR REPRIEVED, 1822–1919

years	sentenced	hanged	% commuted
1822–30	280	190	32
1831–40	260	158	39
1841–50	159	68	57
1851–60	69	23	67
1861–70	41	19	54
1871–80	30	16	47
1881–90	71	30	58
1891–1900	33	16	51
1901–10	28	15	46
1911–19	13	1	92
total	984	536	46

without comment, an interesting detail that may explain everything or nothing: there had been a dispute between McLoughlin and his neighbour about a party wall; John McCrossan was the neighbour's solicitor; the neighbour was awarded damages of £8; 'judgment was marked on the verdict for damages & costs to the amount of £56. 4s. 4d.' Baron Fitzgerald did not add, indeed he did not need to add, that the costs amounted to £48. 4s. 4d., which was *six* times the amount of the damages.

Table 10.2 shows that commutations were less frequent in the 1820s and 1830s when many offences were capital and many prisoners were hanged for offences other than murder. The figures are taken from Appendix 1.

From the 1840s commutations were more frequent than executions in every decade except the 1870s and early 1900s. Although sentences and executions declined dramatically from the 1830s there was a break in the steady decline in the 1880s when hangings were more frequent than in any decade since the 1840s, but it is worth noting that commutation did not decline as a percentage of sentences even in that troubled decade. The results for the decade 1911–19 were even more remarkable: the number of sentences was very low compared with any previous decade and all but one was commuted. Capital punishment had practically ceased to exist in Ireland by 1914.

What did commutation mean in practice? John McLoughlin was in gaol for twenty years. Matthew Leary, a trooper in the 4th (Royal Irish) Dragoon Guards, who pleaded guilty to bestiality, was in gaol for fifteen years and seven months.[109]

---

109 NAI, CRF/1869 Leary/13. Bestiality was erratically punished. At Fermanagh spring assizes in 1854, which was two years before O'Leary was convicted, Pigot sentenced Patrick Cowan, aged

Catherine Hennessy, who was sentenced to transportation for life for infanticide in 1851, died in Mountjoy on 3 March 1877, having served a longer term of imprisonment than either McLoughlin or Leary.[110] A few death sentences were commuted to short terms of imprisonment, but most were commuted to transportation for life until 1857 when transportation was replaced by penal servitude.[111] In 1862 Walter Crofton tried to define what had been, what were, and what should be, the rules governing death sentences that had been commuted to transportation for life or to the new punishment of penal servitude for life.[112] 'The home office regulations governing the time to be served by convicts under the sentence of transportation for life,' Crofton wrote, 'direct that they should be considered eligible for liberation on licence at 10 years from the date of their conviction.'[113] The Irish government, however, 'detained *very grave offenders* under sentence of transportation for life, two years longer than the period named in the home office regulations.' When penal servitude replaced transportation, the home office decided that prisoners sentenced to penal servitude for life should be eligible for release on licence after twelve years. Crofton hoped that the home office might go further, 'as in sanctioning 12 years for those under sentence of penal servitude for life, the home office appear to have adopted the term practised in Ireland, it is probable that the Irish practice may be still further extended in what I consider the right direction.' Sir Robert Peel, the chief secretary (1861–5), for whom Crofton had drawn up this short report, believed that 'Captain Crofton justly interprets public opinion in his wish to see this class of offender subjected to a further term of imprisonment.' Crofton's reason for wanting a term longer than twelve years was not his fear of recidivism: 'I am bound to add that the

18, of Maguiresbridge, to 2 years' imprisonment for bestiality with a cow. Pigot noted that 'at the previous, (summer) assizes, I happened to be the judge of assize in the crown court and at my instance, (to prevent the exposure, in court, of the evidence and circumstances connected with the commission of an offence which very rarely occurs) the trial was postponed.' Cowan may have been dealt with more leniently than his contemporary, Leary, because the case against him implied only intention to commit the crime. According to Pigot 'it was proved, by a woman who attended cows in a bire, or cow house, that the prisoner was seen in a situation unquestionably shewing his intention to commit the crime, and leading to the inference ... that it had been perpetrated' (ibid., CRF/1854/Cowan/42).

110 Tim Carey, *Mountjoy*, pp 147–9.
111 Transportation, which was formally abolished by 20 & 21 Vict., c. 3 (26 June 1857), stopped in 1856. It was replaced by penal servitude, which had been established by 16 & 17 Vict., c. 99 (20 Aug. 1853). The first use of the term 'penal servitude' occurred in the Death Book in 1857 (Death Book, 1852–1932 (NAI, GPB/CN/5)). See also Patrick Carroll-Burke, *Colonial discipline: the making of the Irish convict system* (Dublin, 2000), pp 60, 103, 195 and R.B. McDowell, *The Irish administration 1801–1914* (London and Toronto, 1964), p. 155.
112 For the 'stages' of the penal servitude regime and for prisoners' progress through the penal 'classes' and the use of badges, uniforms, and gratuities, see Carroll-Burke, op. cit., pp 103–6, 116–21. For Michael Davitt's endurance of penal servitude in England, see T.W. Moody, *Davitt and Irish revolution 1846–82* (Oxford, 1981), pp 145–64.
113 NAI, OP (MA)/145/4 [1862].

conduct of this class of offender has been after liberation exceedingly satisfactory', but 'for the sake of example, I should wish to see the term of their
detention still further extended.'

In 1865 the attorney general, James Lawson, was asked, in the case of Agnes
Burns, 'whether death commuted to penal servitude for life is ... to be regarded
as precisely the same as an original sentence of penal servitude for life?' Lawson,
who was an abolitionist, took a harsh view: 'I have a very strong opinion, that in
the cases where sentence of death is commuted to penal servitude for life, and the
offence is deliberate murder, the convict should not under any circumstances be
set at liberty.'[114] At about the same time as the Burns case, Lawson suggested to
the commission on capital punishment that murderers should be treated as 'civilly
dead': 'As soon as a man in convicted of murder, I think that he should be
immediately, without seeing any friends or relatives, removed from the dock to
this prison, and there kept ... I think that he should be completely excluded from
all communication with the outer world, and that he should be immured there for
the rest of his life.'[115] In spite of Lawson, however, the routine was established
that a commuted sentence might be reviewed after 10 or 12 years; in 1868, the
attorney general, Robert Warren, when consulted about the release of John
McLoughlin, thought the case 'may properly be brought under the consideration
of the gov[ernmen]t after an interval of 10 or 12 years from conviction.' When
another petition was presented in favour of McLoughlin in 1882, however, the
attorney general, William Johnson, alluded to a new rule: 'the rule usually
observed is that the cases of convicts whose death sentences have been commuted
to penal servitude for life, are not considered for licence until they have served 20
years. At the expiration of 20 years these cases are brought forward for
consideration and the granting of a licence depends upon the conduct of the
convict during his imprisonment & upon the character & circumstances of the
crime of which he was convicted.'[116] McLoughlin was discharged in June 1885.

---

114 Ibid., OP/149 [1865].
115 *Report of the capital punishment commission, together with minutes of evidence, and appendix*, p. 382
       [3590], HC 1866, xxi, 434.
116 NAI, CRF/1885/McLoughlin/18.

CHAPTER ELEVEN

Death by hanging

EXECUTION OF THE SENTENCE

THE WARRANT THAT AUTHORIZED the sheriff to carry out the sentence was signed by the clerk of the crown on behalf of the judge who had passed sentence. The warrant in the case of Christos Bombos, for example, which was signed by Rickard Donovan, the clerk of the crown for Co. Cork, did not name James Lawson, the judge who had sentenced Bombos to death, but it did mention Queen Victoria, who tactfully reminded the sheriff that execution 'yet remaineth to be done'.[1] According to Purcell, 'the usage is for the judge in the case of all trials at the assizes, to sign the calendar or list of all the prisoners' names, with the separate judgments in the margin, which is left with the sheriff as his warrant or authority; and if the sheriff receives afterwards no special order to the contrary, he executes the judgment of the law accordingly.'[2]

The sheriff could not change the means of execution 'without being guilty of felony himself'.[3] When Thomas F. Bourke was sentenced to death for treason in 1867, the warrant to the high sheriff of Dublin ordered him 'to repair' to Kilmainham gaol, and 'thereout take the body of the said Thomas Bourke, otherwise called Thomas F. Bourke, and that you cause execution of the judgment in manner and form as above set forth.' The use of the word 'repair' gave the sheriff's trip to Kilmainham a festive air, reminiscent of John Gilpin's expedition to The Bell at Edmonton. The 'manner and form' of the judgment was that Bourke 'be drawn on a hurdle to the place of execution on Wednesday the 29th day of May in the year aforesaid, and that he be there hanged by the neck until he be dead, and that afterwards his head should be severed from his body, and the body divided into four quarters.' The marquis of Abercorn used the royal prerogative to omit 'that part of the sentence which directs that the head be severed from the body and that the body be divided into four quarters and disposed of as Her Majesty directs.'[4]

The sheriff was also obliged to see that the sentence was 'completely executed': if the prisoner 'be not thoroughly killed, but revives, the sheriff must hang him

---

1 NAI, CRF/1876/Bombos/26.
2 Theobald A. Purcell, *A summary of the general principles of pleading and evidence, in criminal cases in Ireland: with the rules of practice incident thereto* (Dublin, 1849), p. 223.
3 Ibid.   4 NAI, CRF/1867/Burke/21.

again; for the former hanging was not an execution of the sentence, which implies a completion of it; and if a false tenderness were to be indulged in such cases, it would lead to a multitude of collusions.' The law did not allow divine intervention, although one such intervention did apparently occur in 1885 in Exeter gaol when John Lee had a miraculous deliverance. The hangman Berry described what happened when he pulled the lever: 'the noise of the bolts sliding could be plainly heard, but the doors did not fall. I stamped on the drop, to shake it loose, and so did some of the warders, but none of our efforts could stir it.'[5] Lee was taken away. The doors were tested, and fell easily. Lee was brought back, but again the doors refused to fall. The *deus ex machina* seems to have been the prison carpenter, who inserted a wedge in the doors. Lee's sentence was commuted.

Hangings were in public until the Capital Punishment Amendment Act 1868 provided for them to be inside gaols.[6] Before 1868 it was usually the sub-sheriff who executed the warrant, although some high sheriffs refused to leave the dirty work to be done by their sub-sheriffs. The high sheriff of Wexford, Major John Harvey, of Bargy Castle, for example, was present at Joseph Kelly's execution in 1863; a deputy lieutenant, George Robinson, and a JP, Thomas Kidd, were present at Armagh in 1852 at the hanging of Francis Berry, who had been convicted of the attempted murder of a landlord, Merideth Chambré.[7] After 1868 high sheriffs began to attend executions more frequently: Charles Howe Knox, high sheriff of Mayo, was present at Edward Walsh's hanging in Castlebar in 1873; Mark Seton Synnot JP, DL, high sheriff of Armagh, was present at Stephen McKeown's hanging in 1876.[8] Not all high sheriffs after 1868 attended. When John Russell was hanged in Clonmel, for example, the sub-sheriff appeared without his superior.[9] The high sheriffs' more frequent appearance after 1868 had a number of causes: their presence lent the weight of landed respectability to a new-fangled procedure; they now attended, as a matter of official privilege, an exclusive and esoteric transaction, which had lost some of its vulgarity.[10] It is ironic that at a time when the gentry were losing touch with the enforcement of the criminal law, they should have started to appear at its consummation.

5   James Berry, *My experiences as an executioner*, ed. by H. Snowden Ward; with a new introduction and additional appendices by Jonathan Goodman (Newton Abbot, 1972), p. 60. T. Crofton Croker told the story of Patrick Redmond, a robber, who 'after hanging a short time', was cut down and revived by his friends (*Researches in the south of Ireland, illustrative of the scenery, architectural remains, and the manners and superstitions of the peasantry, with an appendix, containing a private narrative of the rebellion of 1798* (London, 1824), p. 191).

6   31 Vict., c. 24 (29 May 1868). The last prisoner to be hanged in public in Ireland was John Logue, who was hanged on 19 April 1866.

7   *Banner of Ulster*, 10 Aug. 1852.

8   NAI, CRF/1873/Walsh/11; ibid., CRF/1876/McKeown/22. 31 Vict., c. 24, s. 3 (29 May 1868) did not specifically require the high sheriff, as opposed to the sub-sheriff, to be present; it merely mentioned the 'sheriff charged with the execution'.

9   NAI, CRF/1875/Russell/1.

10 'From now on street theatre – a mediaeval mystery play – before an untutored and dissolute audience was replaced by a private performance before invited and appreciative guests' (Harry

The sentence was carried out at the gaol where the prisoner was confined at the time of his conviction, which in practice meant the gaol in the assize town.[11] When winter assizes were established in 1877, prisoners might be tried in the assize town of a neighbouring county, but they would be brought back to their own county town to be hanged.[12] Thomas Cuneen, for example, murdered a woman in Limerick, was tried in Cork, and hanged in Limerick on 10 January 1879.[13] As county prisons were closed, however, prisoners were hanged in the surviving gaols in the larger towns such as Belfast, Cork, and Sligo. James Doherty, for example, who had murdered his son in Co. Leitrim, was hanged, not in Carrick-on-Shannon, but in Sligo on 30 December 1902.[14]

Until an act of 1836 provided for a longer interval between sentence and execution, prisoners were hanged 'on the day next but one after that on which the sentence should be passed.'[15] The aim of the 1836 act, which did not prescribe any particular time for the execution of the sentence, was 'to afford time for

Potter, *Hanging in judgment: religion and the death penalty in England from the bloody code to abolition* (London, 1993), p. 87).

11 There was an exception to this, however; prisoners sentenced after a trial 'at bar' in the Queen's Bench in Dublin were sent back to be hanged in the county where the offence had been committed, unless the crime had been committed in Dublin.

12 Winter assizes were held in November, December, and January. The larger towns, such as Cork, Belfast, and Sligo, were the assize towns for the surrounding counties. (See above, pp 86–7.) The rule that a prisoner should be hanged in the county where he committed the crime was maintained even in the Prevention of Crime (Ireland) Act 1882, s. 6(1) (45 & 46 Vict., c. 25 (12 July 1882)).

13 NAI, CRF/1879/Cuneen/2.

14 Ibid., CRF/1902/Doherty/69. The old custom of hanging prisoners near the spot where they committed their crimes had died out by the 1830s. The memory, however, lingered. In 1841 the grand jury of Kilkenny suggested to Richard Pennefather, who had tried Patrick Donovan at the summer assizes, that Donovan be hanged 'on the spot where the murder was committed'. Pennefather told them that he 'did not consider that it was for the judge to fix on any other than the ordinary place of execution, that their application for this purpose ... should be made to the lord lieutenant' (ibid., CRF/1841/Donovan/43).

15 6 & 7 Will. IV, c. 30, s. 1 (14 July 1836) repealed ss 5 and 7 of 10 Geo. IV, c. 34 (4 June 1829) that had extended the provisions of 9 Geo. IV, c. 31 to Ireland. The provisions that were repealed in 1836 were: (1) that those who were sentenced to death for murder 'should be executed according to law on the day next but one after that on which the sentence should be passed, unless the same should happen to be Sunday, and in that case on the Monday following, and that sentence should be pronounced immediately after the conviction of every murderer, unless the court should see reasonable cause for postponing the same'; (2) that 'every person convicted of murder should after judgment be fed with bread and water only, and with no other food or liquor, except in case of receiving the sacrament, or in case of any sickness or wound'; (3) that 'no person but the gaoler and his servants, and the chaplain and surgeon of the prison, should have access to any such convict without the permission in writing of the court or judge before whom such convict should have been tried, or of the sheriff or his deputy.' The Executions for Murder Act 1836, s. 2 also provided that 'after the passing of this act sentence of death may be pronounced after convictions for murder in the same manner and the judge shall have the same power in all respects as after convictions for other capital offences'.

further inquiry before the full powers of the law were carried into effect.'[16] After 1836 'the sheriff on the receipt of his warrant is to do execution within a convenient time, which is generally left at large, as the time and place of the execution are by law no part of the judgment.'[17] But judges seem to have preferred to fix the date themselves instead of leaving it to the sheriffs. Crampton, for example, at the Tyrone assizes in 1849 fixed Wednesday, 15 August, for the hanging of the child-murderer Charles Monaghan, which left an interval of almost four weeks.[18] Perrin made a point of leaving an even longer period, explaining that in the case of Thomas and Michael Ryan, whom he sentenced at Clonmel in 1847, 'in fixing the day for their execution at the end of two months from the conviction I merely conformed to my usual course since the statute requiring execution in case of murder to be done on the day after conviction has been repealed.'[19]

Hangings were ad hoc affairs. Hangings were rare in most counties, which meant that no routine was established in gaols. Between 1852 and 1914 there were none in Carlow, Donegal, Fermanagh, and Roscommon.[20] Even in the largest counties there were not many. In Cork, for example, which had more executions than any other county, there were only 14 between 1852 and 1914; in Dublin there were 13, in Galway 12, in Antrim 8, in Tipperary 6, in Kilkenny 4, and in Down 2. Because hangings were so few, the sub-sheriff, the governor of the gaol, and the chaplain probably had not been present at a hanging before. Even the hangman might be inexperienced. James Berry, for example, had not been at a hanging before his first engagement at Edinburgh in 1884.[21] The only person present who usually had experience of inflicting violent death was the prisoner. The duke of Richmond in 1866 summed up the local authorities' predicament: 'the government provides everything up to the sentence and then retires from the scene and leaves it to an annual officer who performs the duty without any peculiar law to guide him.'[22] The government's lack of interest in executions, certainly before 1868, was revealed by the fact that there is little information in the Convict Reference Files about hangings, apart from some scraps of information about prisoners' behaviour.[23] Charles McCormick 'was very quiet

---

16 *Hansard 3*, xxxiii, 467 (29 Apr. 1836). Some judges were slow to implement the new act. The house of commons heard on 1 August 1836 that two men had been hanged on 21 July in Clonmel within forty-eight hours of being sentenced, in spite of the fact that the act had become law on 14 July (ibid., xxxv, 745 (1 Aug. 1836)).

17 Purcell, op. cit., p. 223.

18 *Tyrone Constitution*, 20 July 1849.

19 NAI, CRF/1847/Ryan/24.

20 Death Book, 1852–1932 (NAI, GPB/CN/5).

21 Berry, op. cit., p. 19.

22 *Report of the capital punishment commission, together with the minutes of evidence, and appendix*, p. 429 [3590], HC 1866, xxi, 481.

23 17 & 18 Vict., c. 76, s. 27 (7 Aug. 1854) obliged the prison governors to write to the directors of prisons after the assizes 'whether the said several sentences have been executed, respectively, or

during the past week.'[24] That was written by the governor of Longford gaol on 23 July 1863. (McCormick had been convicted on 2 July, and was to be hanged on 4 August.) Edward Walsh, according to the governor of Castlebar gaol, 'tries to keep up, but evidently feels his awful position daily more.' 'I notice his beard going grey,' the governor added.[25]

The scaffold was often not a permanent fixture, although some gaols had permanent contraptions that were pressed into service at irregular intervals. At Waterford in 1864 Thomas Walsh, 'an old man with venerable grey hairs', was hanged on a portable gallows, which moved on wheels on the roof of the gate-house and which, 'owing to the long time that had elapsed since it was used for the revolting purpose for which it was constructed, was quite rusty.'[26] (The last hanging in Waterford had taken place eleven years before.) Walsh and the hangman were perched on this contraption, which was then rolled along the roof to the front of the gaol, where 'the culprit was placed before the thousands that had assembled to see the penalty paid for one of the foulest and most barbarous murders ever committed in Ireland' (Walsh had murdered Thomas Connolly, cut up his body with a blunt hatchet, and buried the pieces in a bog.) When the hangman had completed his arrangements, he 'descended from the gallows, and the murderer was left alone; the bolt was drawn, but the drop did not fall.' The hangman got a sledge-hammer and 'struck the drop a heavy blow, and it fell, launching the murderer into eternity, apparently without a struggle.' While the hangman was getting the sledge-hammer, 'the culprit evinced not the slightest emotion.'

Few of those hanged were socially distinguished. Richard Bourke, hanged at Clonmel in 1862 for poisoning his wife, had been clerk of Waterford poor law union; Matthew Phibbs had been a shopkeeper in Ballymote; Lt. Col. Philip Cross, hanged at Cork in 1888 for poisoning his wife, had been an army surgeon; Thomas Hartley Montgomery had been a sub-inspector of constabulary.[27] Below these there was a sprinkling of working men. A Belfast riveter, John McDaid, for example, was hanged in Sligo in 1875. The biggest group, as one might expect, consisted of farmers and agricultural labourers. The affairs of James Heany, who was hanged in Sligo gaol on 12 January 1892 for the murder of his wife, showed

whether the whole or any and what part or parts of them have been remitted, and to transmit the same to the said directors of prisons within ten days after the termination of the said assizes.' The establishment of the General Prisons Board, which took over the control of all prisons on 1 April 1878, gave the government more opportunities to interfere (40 & 41 Vict., c. 49, s. 17 (14 Aug. 1877)). See also Beverley A. Smith, 'The Irish General Prisons Board, 1877–1885: efficient deterrence or bureaucratic ineptitude?' in *Ir Jur*, n.s., 15 (1980), 122–36; R.B. McDowell, *The Irish administration 1801–1914* (London, 1964), pp 159–60.

24 NAI, CRF/1863/McCormick/30.
25 Ibid., CRF/1873/Walsh/11.
26 *Impartial Reporter*, 21 Apr. 1864 [from *Evening Freeman*].
27 For details of Montgomery's career, see Stephen Ball (ed.), *A policeman's Ireland: recollections of Samuel Waters, RIC* (Cork, 1999), p. 26.

that a revolution in the ownership of landed property had taken place. Heany had been threatened with ejectment from his farm, not by his landlord, but by his wife, referred to as 'the deceased':

> it appears from the records of the case that by a supplemental deed of settlement dated 8th March 1889 the farms were conveyed to two trustees for the joint use of the deceased and the prisoner during their lives. After some litigation two brothers of the deceased namely Michael and Peter Murphy were appointed the two trustees, and these two persons in whom the legal estate was vested obtained an order at the spring assizes 1890 in an ejectment on the title ousting the prisoner from possession of the farm.[28]

Protestants were under-represented on the gallows, accounting for less than a quarter of those hanged, which was their proportion of the population, but they were prominent: Philip Cross, Phibbs, and Montgomery were Protestants. Joseph Taylor, who was hanged on 7 January 1903, was not only a Protestant but one of the few men hanged for what might be described as a *crime passionel*. His paramour, Mary Daly, the wife of John Daly whom Taylor had murdered, was hanged two days later. Recidivists were well represented. James Kirk, hanged at Dundalk in August 1852, for attempting to murder a landlord, James Eastwood JP, had been tried and acquitted in 1826 of murdering his wife.[29] Thomas Beckham, hanged at Limerick in 1863 for the murder of a landlord, had been arrested for murder in 1847, and released, 'the evidence against him not being deemed conclusive'; in 1853 he had been sentenced to seven years' transportation for robbery.[30]

Between 1852 and 1921 out of 47 women sentenced to death, only 4 were hanged: Bridget and Honora Stackpoole in 1853, Margaret Shiels in 1871, and Mary Daly in 1903. It is worth noting that none of the women hanged were hanged for murdering children. The Stackpooles and Shiels were hanged for a murder committed as a result of disputes about land, and Mary Daly was hanged for her part in a *crime passionel*. In England far more women were hanged; between 1843 and 1862, 23 women were hanged; between 1862 and 1882, 17 were hanged.[31] Why women should be so poorly represented is not clear, but Judith Knelman's *Twisting in the wind* suggests that Ireland exported some of its most formidable female murderers.[32] Ellen Cook, for example,

> 'a tall, powerful Irishwoman,' to quote *The Times*, kept a coffee house in London's east end with her husband James. One morning, tired of his habit

28 NAI, CRF/1892/Heany/1.   29 *Belfast Newsletter*, 2 Aug. 1852.
30 *Irish Times*, 17 July 1862.
31 Judith Knelman, *Twisting in the wind: the murderess and the English press* (Toronto, Buffalo, and London, 1998), p. 17.
32 Ibid., p. 107.

of taking prostitutes to not only her house, but her bed, she invited him upstairs to bed herself. She then told him he must do penance, tied him by the arms and legs to the bedstead, and began sharpening a knife ... *The Times* reported ... 'she stooped over him and he felt himself cut about in a frightful manner'.

It is clear, moreover, that women were more likely to be killed than to kill: Carolyn Conley has calculated that between 1866 and 1892, out of a total of 1,926 homicides, women were the assailants in only 71 cases but were attacked in 338 cases.[33]

Those who were hanged had ordinary, common, even rational, motives for the murders they perpetrated: they had murdered their wives, either because they wanted to be rid of them (Patrick Lydane, hanged 11 May 1858), or out of vexation of spirit (Edward Walsh, hanged 19 August 1873); they murdered for gain (Laurence King, hanged 6 September 1865, and John Gregory, hanged 12 April 1871); they murdered for love (Patrick Kilkenny, hanged 20 July 1865). As noted above a high proportion of those hanged in the 1850s and 1860s were hanged for agrarian murders.[34] The large number of hangings in the years 1882 and 1883 was caused by the political upheaval that had begun in 1879. The 6 hangings in Dublin in 1883 included 5 of the Phoenix Park murderers. The dreary casual quarrels that characterized the homicide reports were transmuted on the gallows into something a bit more noteworthy.

PUBLIC HANGING

The crowds at Irish executions seem to have been smaller than at English ones, which is not surprising given the smallness of Irish county towns. At the hanging of James Kirk and Patrick McCooey in 1852, the *Belfast Newsletter* pointed to the contrast with England:

> The number of persons present was inconsiderable, consisting chiefly of the inhabitants of Dundalk, the peasantry having been forbidden by their priests to attend. Throughout the solemn scene the crowd conducted themselves quietly, and altogether the place of execution presented a laudable contrast to the exhibitions of which the public have read and heard so much, as occurring in England on similar occasions, when every species of vice and immorality prevail, as if to bid defiance to the law in its sternest aspect, and convert what ought to be a scene of fearful warning and example into an impious *saturnalia* of sin.[35]

33 Carolyn Conley, 'No pedestals: women and violence in late nineteenth-century Ireland' in *Journal of Social History*, 28:4 (summer 1995), 802.
34 Above, pp 57–8. 35 *Belfast Newsletter*, 2 Aug. 1852.

The railway companies seem to have followed where the clergy led. When John Holden was to be hanged at Omagh, special trains 'were applied for at Londonderry and Enniskillen to convey excursionists', but the Irish North-Western Railway Co. refused to put them on.[36] The public were not to be so easily thwarted, however, because 'the ordinary forenoon train from Londonderry brought a considerable number of third class passengers, who were, of course, too late to witness the revolting sight. A telegraphic despatch to Enniskillen prevented any ingress of visitors from that direction.'

The clergy's efforts to keep their parishioners away were not always successful. At Phibbs' hanging in Sligo on 19 August 1861 there was a 'vast concourse', but their conduct was 'exemplary'.[37] At Richard Bourke's hanging in Clonmel on 25 August 1862 'all the approaches to the gaol were crowded, gas lamps, pumps, &c. from which a view of the fatal trap could be obtained, being filled with occupants. The windows immediately in front of the gaol were crowded with spectators, amongst whom were several respectably dressed females.'[38] Bourke's hanging was predictably an interesting one: he had had been a clerk of Waterford poor law union, he had murdered his wife, and it was generally expected that he would not carry himself bravely. There were some poor turn-outs. Only about 200 appeared in Wexford for the hanging of Patrick Power on 4 April 1866, which was in contrast to Joseph Kelly's well-attended hanging in 1863.[39]

The crowds did not always gather to mock or gloat. At Cavan in 1856 at the hanging of James Murphy and Thomas Dunn, the crowd, which had been gathering from an early hour, emitted 'a loud outburst of horror', when Murphy appeared. When he had been hanged, the crowd dispersed, 'so that when Dunne [*sic*] came forward the place was almost wholly in the possession of the police and military.'[40] At Monaghan in 1854 when Neal Quin and Bryan Grant appeared dressed in their shrouds and white caps, 'a fearful shout was raised by the male portion of the spectators, the women assembled shrieked bitterly, and the murmuring wail throughout the entire crowd was of the most agonizing description.'[41] When they were followed by Patrick Coomey, 'the screaming of the females, some of whom fainted, on the third white figure appearing on the gallows, was heartrending; and the lamentations of the masculine portion of the assemblage were, for the moment, more painful than any other incident in the terrible transaction.' At a later period, James Berry noted the difference between Irish and English crowds: 'In England, if there is any sort of demonstration, it is a cheer; in Ireland it is hooting and groaning.'[42]

---

36 *Tyrone Constitution*, 31 Aug. 1860.
37 Larcom Papers (NLI, MS 7620 [*Belfast Newsletter*, 22 Aug. 1861]).
38 *Irish Times*, 29 Aug. 1862.   39 Ibid., 5 Apr. 1866.
40 *Belfast Newsletter*, 19 May 1856.   41 *The Banner of Ulster*, 11 Apr. 1854.
42 Berry, op. cit., p. 128. For Irish crowds on other occasions of popular entertainment see Peter Jupp and Eoin Magenis (eds), *Crowds in Ireland, c. 1720–1820* (London, 2000).

Although crowds gathered to watch hangings, most people knew of them through the newspapers, whose reporters were much better informed about details than those who stood outside the prisons. Most information about hangings, even after 1868 when hangings took place inside prisons, came from newspapers, of which the best informed were those in the towns where the hangings took place: the *Tyrone Constitution* in Omagh, the *Impartial Reporter* in Enniskillen, the *Irish Times* in Dublin. Reporters were often close to what they described.[43] Mathias Bodkin watched John McDaid on the scaffold in Sligo in March 1875:

> In slow procession there came upon the platform the condemned man and the chaplain walking side by side, the sheriff and the governor of the jail followed close behind, and at a greater distance a shy and shamefaced hangman brought up the rear. My eyes went at once with horrible fascination to the face of the man about to die. He was pale all over, ghastly pale, cheeks, lips and forehead a uniform colour, not white, but ashen-grey and shiny with moisture when the light touched it. From the grey lips issued a hollow murmur of prayer. He seemed to move and speak mechanically as if stupefied by fear. Slowly they went past, and the doomed man, still moving like one in a dream, was led to the drop, three paces from where I stood. Then for the first time he seemed to wake to consciousness and, like an animal shying at danger, refused to step upon the drop. The hangman coaxed and pushed him on as one would coax a refractory child. For a moment the trembling figure stood black outlined against the glow of the morning, while the hangman busied himself with the nice adjustment of the rope, and drew over the stooped head the cap that shut out for ever the light of heaven and the beauty of earth.[44]

43 The 'press-room' was frequently alluded to (Dickens mentioned a 'press-yard', as well as a 'press-room' at Newgate), which suggests, but obviously does not prove, that while newspaper reporters had a vantage point inside the gaol, they did not freely wander about. (See Charles Dickens, *Sketches by Boz illustrative of every-day life and every-day people* (London, 1973), p. 209). When Thomas Kerr and Thomas Wilson were lying under sentence of death in Enniskillen gaol, the *Impartial Reporter*'s editor and proprietor, William Trimble, had regular access to them (*Impartial Reporter*, 16 Aug. 1849; see also below, pp 340–1). The gaols, certainly convict prisons, became 'private' when 17 & 18 Vict., c. 76, s. 14 (7 Aug. 1854) provided that 'no person, except the judges of her majesty's superior courts of law in Ireland, the judges of assize, the directors, officers, and servants of the prison, or such other persons as shall be authorized by the directors or by the rules to be made under this act, shall be allowed at any time to enter any part of any convict prison, or to converse or hold communication of any kind with any of the prisoners.'

44 Mathias M'D. Bodkin, *Recollections of an Irish judge: press, bar and parliament* (London, 1914), pp 43–4. For another eyewitness account of a hanging see Diary of John Ryan (TCD, MS 10350 (no. 4), pp 54, 60).

The interval between sentence and execution often provided better copy than the last moments on the scaffold. Joseph Kelly, hanged at Wexford on 11 August 1863, had been put in a kitchen at the back of the gaol after he was sentenced to death. (Many gaols did not have condemned cells. There was no condemned cell at Downpatrick in 1871, for example, when John Gregory was lying under sentence of death; the governor had to use prisoners to look after Gregory because he had only eight warders to look after forty prisoners.)[45] When Kelly's 'languid and emaciated appearance' alarmed the warders, the prison doctor was called in. Wine and 'other nourishment' were ordered:

> The improved scale of dietary had a most beneficial effect, and in a few days he regained his wonted health and spirits. During the first week of his confinement the demeanour of the culprit was ill-suited to the awful position in which he was placed, and all attempts made to engage his mind on religious subjects were unsuccessful. At this period he was visited by his father. The interview took place in the presence of the governor, and did not occupy many minutes. On entering the room the wretched man attempted to embrace his parent, but the latter pushed him away with his hands, and repulsed his advances. A conversation then ensued respecting the disposition of some trifling household articles, and an anxious inquiry by the father as to his obtaining possession of the son's clothes after he was hanged. Upon the father inquiring to whom he purposed leaving his Sunday clothes, he replied, 'To you, father, of course,' adding that although he had intended to be hanged in his best apparel, if his old clothes were brought to him, he would put them on. One of the prison officers casually remarked that he supposed the father would not like to wear the garments in which the wretched man would be hung, to which Michael Kelly, the culprit's sire, exclaimed, 'Try me.' Throughout the entire interview no allusion whatever was made to the murder, or the necessity that existed for the prisoner preparing to meet his awful doom, until the governor interposed to point out to the elder Kelly the impropriety of continuing in such a strain, whereupon the latter, addressing his son said, 'Well, Joey, at all events, don't die with a lie in your mouth.' The other replied that 'he was not the only man that was persecuted.' They thereupon shook hands, and separated, never again to meet on this side of the grave.[46]

This was good copy, as good as most prisoners provided; but Kelly was a man of resource, and he managed to get even more into his weeks of confinement:

> In consequence of a certain levity of manner manifested by the unhappy criminal, in declaring his ability to beat a dozen of men, placing his right foot on a given point on the ceiling of the room in which he was confined,

45 NAI, CRF/1871 Gregory/9.   46 *Irish Times*, 12 Aug. 1863.

and performing other similar agile feats of dexterity, which had the effect of creating a feeling of nervousness in the minds of the officials, it was deemed advisable to have leg-irons placed on him at night. On Thursday week he had an interview with his wife, who, with his father, were the only relatives or friends who visited him since he had been remitted to prison. This was the only occasion on which he saw his partner before his execution, and certainly the meeting was not characterized by that love and affection which ought to subsist between persons in the relation which they bore to each other. An angry altercation arose relative to some household matters, and neither of the parties appeared to be much affected when taking a final farewell of each other. Kelly attempted to kiss his wife when she was about leaving, but she recoiled from his touch, effecting her retreat as speedily as possible. A complete alteration was observable in the deportment of the wretched man for the last three weeks; instead of being frivolous in manner, he became serious and devout, and listened with apparent interest to the ministrations of the Roman Catholic clergymen who attended him. The Rev. Mr Roche, PP, the chaplain of the prison, and the Rev. Messrs Roice and Cloney, assistant chaplains, were in constant attendance on him each day, and through their counsel and advice he was induced to devote the few short remaining days he had to live to laying hold of the consolations of that Church of which he was a member. The prison officers were indefatigable in their attentions to the condemned, every privilege that could contribute to his comfort being generously accorded him. He partook heartily of his meals, was allowed a moderate supply of tobacco, which he appeared to highly appreciate, and slept soundly at night. At no period since his conviction, it must be admitted, did he appear to be imbued with a deep and heartfelt feeling of sorrow for the terrible crime he had committed. While solicitous in complying with the formularies of his Church, which he evidently got through in a mechanical manner, he freely chatted with the sub-sheriff and governor about the prospects of the harvest, the fineness of the weather, or inquiring how the wheat looked, and if the hay was being cut.

Kelly gave a slightly different account of his thoughts in his last days in his memorial to Lord Carlisle. 'All my thoughts during the day are occupied with contemplation & sorrow for my wickedness,' he wrote. 'In my dreams during short and disturbed repose I visit the fatal ground which opened its pores to receive the martyred blood. I take the dead man by the hand, press it to my bosom and shed a torrent of penitential tears on his lifeless body.'[47]

Although the weeks between conviction and sentence could produce good copy, newspapers' interest naturally quickened the day before the hanging. Quin, Grant, and Coomey, who were hanged at Monaghan on 10 April 1854 for the

47 NAI, CRF/1863/Kelly/15.

murder of Thomas Bateson JP were nonchalant on the evening before they were to be hanged. Coomey, 'whiffling his pipe', asked, '"What time the morrow will that be" in a tone and manner from which no one could have discovered to what he referred.'[48] Quin wanted to know if they would all 'go at once', but on being told that the scaffold could take only two at a time, he told the governor that 'he and Bryan would like "to go together".' The night before his execution on 9 June 1883, Timothy Kelly, sentenced to death for his part in the Phoenix Park murders, 'awaked the echoes of the prison singing in his strong resonant voice the favourite Catholic hymn, "Salve Regina". He varied this occasionally with Balfe's "The memory of the past".'[49]

Prisoners' devotions were described by the newspapers in varying degrees of detail. The clergy in attendance were carefully identified (more than one frequently turned up), but usually their liturgical practice was described only in general terms. The reasons for this are not clear. It may have been caused by a general reticence about religious practice dictated by denominational diplomacy; it may have been caused by reporters' ignorance, especially their ignorance of other denominations' practices, which was probably slightly greater than their ignorance of their own. Yet the chaplains who accompanied prisoners to the scaffold had liturgical resources that were clearly defined: Roman Catholic priests had the *Rituale Romanum*, Church of Ireland clergymen had the Book of Common Prayer, and others vigorously extemporized. According to the Revd James O'Kane, the senior dean of Maynooth in the late 1860s, the condemned were to be treated like other dying Christians; they were to receive the viaticum, which 'prepares them for the passage out of this world into the next' and which could be administered to prisoners 'on the very day on which they are executed.'[50] Prisoners were not given extreme unction, according to O'Kane, because 'the subject of extreme unction must be in danger of death'. There were exceptions to this rule, one of which showed that O'Kane represented a robust judicial tradition: 'if, being condemned to die by slow torture, he has already suffered enough to cause death, in any such case Extreme Unction may be administered if there be an opportunity, since there is then a dangerous ailment actually affecting the body.'

The Book of Common Prayer had 'a form of prayer for the visitation of prisoners', which had been adopted by a synod in Dublin in 1711.[51] After

---

48 *The Banner of Ulster*, 11 Apr. 1854. See also Vaughan, *Landlords and tenants in mid-Victorian Ireland* (Oxford, 1994), p. 188.

49 Frederick Moir Bussy, *Irish conspiracies: recollections of John Mallon (The Great Detective) and other reminiscences* (London, 1910), p. 139.

50 James O'Kane, *Notes on the rubrics of the Roman Ritual, regarding the sacraments in general, baptism, the eucharist, and extreme unction* (Dublin, 1867), pp 474–5, 484–5, 548, 614. The *Rituale Romanum*, according to O'Kane (p. 3) was 'published under this title by the authority of Pope Paul V.' The Gilbert Collection in the Library of Trinity College, Dublin, has a copy of the *Rituale Romanum Pauli V* (KK.k.54), which was published in Paris in 1665 *cum accentibus*. For a reference to *Rituale*'s use at an execution see *The Banner of Ulster*, 11 Apr. 1854.

51 I am indebted to the Ven. Canon Brian Snow for drawing my attention to this service and for

disestablishment the Church of Ireland retained this service in its 1878 prayer book, with only small changes that were concessions to the practical problem of conducting a service on the scaffold.[52] In spite of these amenities, however, the chaplain still had to leaf back through the prayer book to find the 'Commendatory prayer for a sick person at the point of departure', an operation that he might well have been spared at such a time.[53] There was nothing mealy-mouthed about the exhortation that began the service for the condemned: 'Dearly beloved, it hath pleased Almighty God, in his justice, to bring you under the sentence and condemnation of the law. You are shortly to suffer death in such a manner that others, warned by your example, may be the more afraid to offend.' The exhortation became even more pointed as it proceeded: 'You are soon to be removed from among men, by a violent death, and you shall fade away suddenly like the grass, which in the morning is green and groweth up, but in the evening is cut down, dried up and withered.' Just before the prisoner was actually hanged, the minister said the 'Commendatory prayer for a sick person at the point of departure', which commended the prisoner's soul to God, and besought Him to: 'wash it, we pray thee, in the blood of that immaculate Lamb, that was slain to take away the sins of the world; that whatsoever defilements it may have contracted in the midst of this miserable and naughty world, through the lusts of the flesh, or the wiles of Satan, being purged and done away, it may be presented pure and without spot before thee.'

The words of this service should have struck anyone with an ear for words, but they did not strike the ears of those who reported executions.[54] At the hanging of Mary Ann McConkey, who was a member of the Irish Church, there is no

providing me with a copy. The passages quoted here have been taken from a prayer book that seems to have been used between 1837 and 1862; the prayers for those under sentence of death are at pp 413–16 (Dept of Early Printed Books, Trinity College, Dublin (Gall. L. 16. 28)).

52 See *The book of common prayer, and administration of the sacraments, and other rites and ceremonies of the church, according to the use of the Church of Ireland; together with the psalter or psalms of David, pointed as they are to be sung or said in churches; and the form and manner of making, ordaining, and consecrating of bishops, priests, and deacons* (Dublin, 1878). The service for prisoners comes after 'The form of consecration of a churchyard or other burial ground' and before the Articles of Religion. The annotated copy of the prayer book used by Archdeacon Samuel Kyle, who was one of the General Synod's committee of revision, is in the Dept of Early Printed Books, TCD, at Press B. 3. 18.

53 Warder Regan in *The Quare Fellow* described a Protestant clergyman at an execution: 'The young clergyman was great; he read a bit of the Bible to the little Protestant lad while they waited and he came in with him, holding his hand and telling him, in their way, to lean on God's mercy that was stronger than the power of men. I walked beside them and guided the boy on to the trap and under the beam ... And still the young clergyman called out to him, in a grand steady voice, in through the hood: "I declare to you, my living Christ this night ..." and he stroked his head till he went down. Then he fainted' (Brendan Behan, *The complete plays: The Quare Fellow; The Hostage; Richard's Cork Leg* ..., introduced by Alan Simpson with a bibliography by E.H. Mikhail (London, 1991), p. 101).

54 For the 'Form of service to be used at an execution' used in England between 1897 and 1927, see Potter, op. cit., p. 118.

mention of such a service: in the chapel 'she partook of the Lord's Supper in an orderly and pious manner'; as she was led to the press-room, she 'continued in earnest prayer with the chaplain'; on her way to the scaffold, 'she called on all about her to join in prayer for her Saviour to receive her soul.'[55]

The *Rituale Romanum* and the Book of Common Prayer ensured a seemly economy. Occasionally something more protracted was provided. At the Fermanagh assizes on 12 July 1849 Thomas Wilson, Thomas Kerr, and Robert Cathcart were sentenced to hang on 9 August. Cathcart's sentence was later commuted to penal servitude for life.[56] For nearly four weeks Wilson and Kerr were looked after by four clergymen: the two prison chaplains, who were clergymen of the established church, and two Methodist ministers who told the story of their campaign in a 10,000-word letter to the memorably named *Impartial Reporter*.[57] The two clergymen of the established church concentrated on Kerr, and the two Methodists on Wilson, who had been a Methodist. At midnight on the day before the execution, the clergymen of the established church went home, but the two ministers and their supporters decided to spend the night with Wilson, engaged in 'exercises of prayer', which included hymns such as 'How happy every child of grace', 'And when to that bright world I rise', 'The worst of sinners here may find', and 'Vain world adieu.' Wilson's ear was good: 'At one time when there was some little discord, for we all sung more "lustily" than harmoniously, he significantly remarked, "There will be no mistuned voices in heaven!"' He was, the ministers noted, 'thoroughly evangelical now in his views.' At 4 a.m. the prisoners were taken to 'a little room adjoining the place of execution'. The two ministers 'were required to withdraw that the necessary preparations might be gone through', but not before they sang one more hymn ('Jesus the name that charms our fears'). They came back just before 9 a.m., having been asked by Wilson to 'give him the Sacrament of the Lord's supper.' There were more hymns, including, 'We feel the resurrection near.' When the blacksmith arrived to take off Wilson's chains and 'while thus engaged we gave out "Jesus the prisoner's fetters breaks".' Wilson wanted a hymn to be sung on the scaffold. The ministers decided that William Cowper's great hymn was appropriate, and as they stepped on to the scaffold, Wilson 'declined to take our arms, but offered us his, and then led us along with firm step and placid look, while he mingled his voice with ours in singing':

> There is a fountain filled with blood,
> Drawn from Emmanuel's veins,
> And sinners plunged beneath that flood,
> Lose all their guilty stains.

55 *Northern Standard*, 1 May 1841.
56 Cathcart was lucky. The leading citizens of Enniskillen secured his release from Spike Island in July 1859, which ended a relatively short incarceration. His uncle, a Methodist preacher, offered to pay his passage to America (NAI, CRF/1859/Cathcart/24).
57 *Impartial Reporter*, 16 Aug. 1849.

The ministers 'made a little alteration with his consent in the third line of the next verse.' As the hangman, 'who had just come out with his black mask', was pinioning Wilson's arms, they sang the amended version, in which 'have' replaced 'may':

> The dying thief rejoiced to see
> That fountain in his day;
> And there *have* I, as vile as he
> Wash'd all my sins away!

Having sung the last two lines three times, Wilson was led to the drop, where 'we now left him in the hands of the executioner, and he was thrown off as he was repeating audibly in the ears of some immediately under the drop, "Lord Jesus receive my spirit!"' There was less fuss with Kerr, probably because he was accompanied by the two clergymen of the established church, who represented a more reticent liturgical tradition: he made a speech deprecating bad company, card playing, etc., and 'in a moment he was in eternity.'

Protestants made a fuss about confessing, which, considering that auricular confession was not generally available to them, was not surprising. Matthew Phibbs, a Primitive Methodist, admitted 'that it was his hand that had deprived Mr and Mrs Callaghan and their servant of life.'[58] Probably fewer Catholics than Protestants confessed publicly, but some did. Charles McCormick asked all young men to be warned by his 'dark fate', and he acknowledged his guilt by 'implication'.[59] Patrick Power, who was the second last prisoner to be hanged in public in Ireland, confessed his guilt several times, and in the end his confession was written down and witnessed by two warders and the Catholic curate.[60] Power had murdered his father; his father and mother had been constantly quarrelling since the father took up with another farmer's wife. In one version of his confession Power stated he was 'happier to be here and to die, than to have my liberty, and go home again.'

What prisoners ate was more minutely described than their devotions. Francis Berry 'rose at six o'clock, and appeared quite strong in mind'. After mass had been celebrated, 'he partook of a little stirabout for breakfast, and afterwards part of a glass of wine sent him by the governor.'[61] Thomas Beckham had tea and toast; Thomas Kelly had sherry and biscuits.[62] The procession to the gallows, which might not take place until well after breakfast, was described with a nice regard for *placement*. Kirk and McCooey left their cells in Dundalk gaol at 11.50 a.m., and 'the melancholy procession was formed in the corridor, every one present being uncovered. First came Mr [Francis] Lamb, governor of the prison,

---

58 Larcom Papers (NLI, MS 7620 [*Packet*, 12 Aug. 1861]).

59 Ibid. [*Irish Times*, 5 Aug. 1863].   60 *Irish Times*, 5 Apr. 1866.

61 *Banner of Ulster*, 10 Aug. 1852.   62 *Impartial Reporter*, 24 July 1862, 12 Jan. 1899.

the next Mr [Burton] Brabazon, the under sheriff, immediately preceding the convicts. McCooey walked first, attended by the Very Rev. Dr Kieran, wearing his stole, and reciting, in a loud voice and solemn tone, the litany for a soul departing, according to the ritual of the Roman Catholic church.'[63] Kirk came next, attended by Revd Mr Weir, 'who was also reciting the service prescribed for the occasion.' (The Very Revd Michael Kieran was the prison chaplain and parish priest of Dundalk; Weir seems to have been Fr George Weir, who was from Forkill, but was not listed as a parish priest or curate in the *Catholic registry & directory 1852*.)[64] After Kirk and Fr Weir came the prison officers 'whose duty it was to see to the execution of the sentence of the law.' Next came the governor of Maryborough gaol and Francis Good, deputy governor and master of works at the prison at Smithfield. Irish prisoners' equanimity was admirable. Panic or fainting either did not occur or were not reported.[65]

Prisoners were dressed in shrouds, often with white gloves and white cap, which added to the drama of their sudden appearance from inside the gaol.[66] The dress was not uniform. Thomas Dunn at Cavan in 1856 was dressed 'in a brown tunic, with white cap and gloves', while his fellow prisoner, James Murphy, was more conventionally turned out 'in a complete white overdress'. When Bernard Cangley was hanged at Cavan on 4 April 1864, 'his face and body were covered with a shroud, so that no portion was visible but the feet.' In spite of this costume, 'he walked firmly on the trap.'[67] Fashion was changing, however. John Holden, hanged at Omagh in August 1860, was 'dressed in a black morning-coat and waistcoat, and drab pantaloons; and a tie was thrown loosely round his neck, leaving the greater part bare. At his special request, the usual white shroud was dispensed with.'[68] Gradually the shroud and gloves gave way to everyday clothes, with reticent tweed suits eventually replacing morning-coats. The white cap, which complemented the judge's black cap, was the part of the ensemble to survive longest.[69]

The hangman might be already on the scaffold when the procession started, or he might appear suddenly as the procession approached the scaffold, which added

---

63 Ibid., 5 Aug. 1852. The governor of Maryborough gaol in 1852 was 'A. Wilson'.
64 The government prisons provided rosary beads, which suggests a willingness to encourage the ministrations of Catholic priests (NAI, GPO LB 2 (1 Jan. 1849 to 31 Dec. 1852), no. 484).
65 Cf. V.A.C. Gatrell, *The hanging tree: execution and the English people 1770–1868* (Oxford, 1994), pp 38–9.
66 'Let a man do what he will to abstract from his imagination all idea of the whimsical, something of it will come across him when he contemplates the figure of a fellow-creature in the day-time (in however distressing a situation) in a night-cap' (Charles Lamb, quoted in Gatrell, op. cit., p. 275).
67 *Irish Times*, 5 Apr. 1864.
68 *Tyrone Constitution*, 31 Aug. 1860.
69 For a mention as late as 1909 see Johnston J. Fitzgerald, *From the inside out: an account of all prisoners hanged at HMP Belfast* (1995), p. 56. The black cap also survived; the black cap worn by the judge who sentenced Robert McGladdery at Newry in 1961 is on display in the police museum in the Ulster Folk Park at Cultra, Co. Down.

to the Punchinello quality of the proceedings. While Charles McCormick was praying in the press-room at Longford gaol, 'the hangman noiselessly emerged on tip-toe from an adjoining room, his face being draped with crape, and, stepping behind the prisoner, whose face was turned in an opposite direction, commenced to pinion him, which operation was submitted to without the slightest resistance.'[70] In spite of being 'pinioned', McCormick shook hands with the governor, forgave the hangman and 'those who had injured him.' As the hangman was about to put the rope round McCormick's neck, the chaplain 'pointed out to the functionary the propriety of first drawing the white cap over his head, but this arrangement was objected to by the finisher of the law, who, holding up the noose in one hand and significantly placing the fore-finger of the other under his right ear, conveyed more than language could have expressed.' After this exchange, the rope was put round McCormick's neck, his handcuffs were taken off, and 'he ascended the steps leading to the scaffold with unfaltering step.'

Hangmen were not easy to identify before the 1870s. The *Tyrone Constitution* described but did not name the hangman who hanged John Holden: he had 'his head covered with a workhouse cap, black crape as a mask over his face, and large brogues, smeared with mud, on his feet. His face, which we saw clearly, gave full assurance that he belonged to the lowest order of English society.'[71] Holden shared the social outlook of the *Tyrone Constitution*: he shook hands with the warders, but 'took no notice of the outstretched hand of the hangman.' John Ryan described William Tobin's hangman as 'an American sailor named Wagner, who is the son of a Pennsylvanian Methodist preacher, and who is serving a short sentence for insubordination.'[72] In the decades before 1870 if the hangman was named, it was by a sort of generic title such as Calcraft or Jack Ketch, which was no more revealing about his actual identity than the similar practice of referring to the emperor Franz Josef as Caesar Augustus.[73]

A few prisoners made noteworthy speeches. Thomas Beckham's at Limerick was so good that his words found their way into a ballad: he told the crowd he would not turn 'stag', that he forgave Francis Fitzgerald's widow, whose evidence had helped to convict him; that he was the first man from his locality to be hanged; that he was Tom Beckham of the Co. Limerick.[74] Michael Kenny hanged at Longford in 1838 was laconic; he said, 'in a most determined, emphatic and

---

70 *Irish Times*, 5 Aug. 1863. Cf. 'The hangman with his gardener's gloves/ Slips through the padded door/ And binds one with three leathern thongs,/ That the throat may thirst no more'.

71 *Tyrone Constitution*, 31 Aug. 1860.

72 Diary of John Ryan (TCD, MS 10350 (no. 4), p. 60).

73 Calcraft retired from the service of the sheriffs of London in 1874 (Berry, op. cit., p. 122). In the early nineteenth century Richard Robert Madden referred to Thomas Gavin as the 'Irish Calcraft' (Thomas More Madden (ed.), *The memoirs (chiefly autobiographical) from 1798 to 1866 of Richard Robert Madden, MD, FRCS* (London, 1891), p. 6).

74 *Irish Times*, 17 July 1862. The ballad had one good line: 'The rope and cap & fatal trap have stopped my wild career' (John Davis White Ballad Collection (Dept of Early Printed Books, Trinity College, Dublin), ii, 40).

vindictive tone', 'Beware of the breed of Breslan.'[75] Patrick Lydane at Galway spoke boldly, if not to the point. When the executioner, who was a convict from Mountjoy, put the rope round his neck, he 'proceeded to address the crowd in the Irish language, in a clear and firm voice, and without the least indication of nervousness, and apparently very little, if at all, affected by the awful position in which he stood.'[76] The Very Revd George Commins, the gaol's chaplain and parish priest of St Nicholas West, acted as interpreter. 'He was,' Fr Commins translated, 'as innocent as the child unborn', a statement that caused a sensation. 'Eleven witnesses had sworn, and they had sworn falsely,' Lydane went on, 'for they knew nothing whatever of what he had done ... he alone committed the murder, but that no human eye saw him do it, and that it was known only to God Almighty.' Finally, he 'forgave everyone on the earth, and he hoped to be forgiven by God; and he besought the prayers of the people for his soul, that he might receive mercy not alone for the crime for which he was about to suffer, but for all the sins of his past life.' The governor of Galway gaol, in his report to the under-secretary, wrote that 'the convict acknowledged his guilt, & I am happy to say died repentant.'[77] In spite of examples such as these, speeches on the scaffold were rare. The long period between sentence and execution after 1836 cooled the rhetorical ardour of all but the toughest.[78]

Protestations of innocence on the scaffold were also rare. When William and Daniel Cormack were hanged at Nenagh on 11 May 1858, they asserted that they were innocent of John Ellis's murder. Thomas Larcom noted the fact by preserving a press cutting from the *Waterford News*, which described the scene: 'on the very threshold of eternity, surrounded by all the influences of religion, with the priests of their church by their side, and the words of the litany just passed their lips, they, in the most solemn and impressive manner, declared that they had not hand, act, or part in the murder for which they were about to die!'[79] The fact that their hanging was followed by 'a fearful storm' added weight to their assertions, because 'storms could also act as omens of innocence.'[80]

When the speech ended, the prisoner was, to use the most common cliché, 'launched into eternity'. The prisoner's chances of being smoothly launched did not amount to a certainty. The *Irish Times* reported Charles McCormick's confused end at Longford gaol. The hangman, referred to as 'Calcraft' by the

---

75 Desmond McCabe, '"The part that laws or kings can cause or cure": crown prosecution and jury trial at Longford assizes, 1830–45' in Gillespie & Moran (eds), *Longford: essays in county history*, p. 155.

76 *Impartial Reporter*, 20 May 1858.

77 NAI, CRF/1858/Lydane/15.

78 For eighteenth-century speeches, see James Kelly, *Gallows speeches from eighteenth-century Ireland* (Dublin, 2001).

79 Larcom Papers (NLI, MS 7636 [*Evening Post*, 27 May 1858]).

80 For the storm, see Nancy Murphy, *Guilty or innocent? The Cormack brothers: trial, execution and exhumation* (Nenagh, Co. Tipperary, 1998), p. 90. For omens of innocence and guilt, see Éanna Hickey, *Irish law and lawyers in modern folk tradition* (Dublin, 1999), pp 118–23.

Irish Times and as 'a professional Jack Ketch' by the *Daily Express*, had arrived ten days before the execution, which did not suggest a busy summer schedule.[81] His preparations included 'oiling the springs of the traps, soaping the rope, and performing other similarly delicate duties in connexion with his profession.' When the trap was released, McCormick 'was precipitated on the pavement beneath without apparently his having sustained much injury.' The hangman, with the help of the warders, 'set about raising the body by means of a windlass placed inside the press-room.' This operation, which was 'painfully slow', excited 'universal disgust'. According to the *Irish Times*, McCormick's body when viewed from the ground was 'fearfully convulsed' and appeared 'rather to have been strangled than hanged.' The *Daily Express* contradicted the *Irish Times*, asserting that McCormick died instantly after a drop of 12 or 14 feet; the rope had slipped on the drum on which it was coiled, but only after he died. An unidentified press cutting between the two cited above gave more details: the hangman, having fixed the rope round McCormick's neck, shouted, 'with disgusting solicitude', 'Stand clear of the drop'; when the drop was released 'the wretched man fell on his knees on the steps in front of the entrance of the jail. Pinioned and half stunned he strove to rise to his feet, and he writhed about.' Two of the constabulary fainted 'at the soul-sickening sight'. The acting governor of Longford gaol, in his report to the chief secretary, did not mention that anything had gone wrong. The sentence, according to the acting governor, 'has been carried into effect in front of the gaol.'[82]

The newspapers noted the disposal of prisoners' bodies. Whether their bodies were buried within the gaol or given to their friends depended on their crime. Those who carried out a murder, as opposed to having attempted it, or planned it, were sentenced to be buried within the gaol. Kirk and McCooey had only attempted to murder the landlord James Eastwood JP. When their bodies had hung for three quarters of an hour, 'they were then cut down and brought into the prison yard.'[83] McCooey's friends had brought a 'miserable' coffin; Kirk's coffin was provided 'at the expense of the county'. The bodies were examined by the gaol's medical officer, placed in the coffins 'with their clothes on', and given to their friends, 'not more than three or four persons appearing there to claim them'. The constabulary superintended the progress of the cortege through the town, and 'no riot or tumult ensued.' At Cavan in 1856 James Murphy, after hanging for forty-five minutes, was cut down 'by three prisoners from the gaol'. He was

---

81 *Irish Times*, 5 Aug. 1863; Larcom Papers (NLI, MS 7620 [*Express*, 6 Aug. 1863]).
82 NAI, CRF/1863/McCormick/30. Botched executions were not peculiar to Ireland. On Guernsey in 1854, the hangman, who held the office for life, bungled what was only his third hanging in a career of twenty-three years (the prisoner had revived and attempted to climb back up through the trap). The hangman's stipend had cost the island £900 during his years in office; he offered to resign if he were given a pension of 12s. a week for the rest of his life (TNA (UK), HO 45/5194A).
83 *Impartial Reporter*, 5 Aug. 1852.

buried inside the gaol.[84] The body of Thomas Dunn, who was hanged after Murphy, was given to his friends, 'who carried it off upon a car, no hearse being procurable.'

The law obliged judges to make the distinction between actual murderers and the rest when they passed sentence. At the special commission at Ennis in 1848, when John Crowe was sentenced to death, he was removed from the dock, but 'not being guilty of the actual murder, the CHIEF BARON had him brought to the dock, and again pronounced sentence, omitting that portion in reference to his being buried within the walls of the prison.'[85] After Thomas Dowling's trial at Tullamore spring assizes in 1844, there was a dispute about whether the sentence should contain the direction that the prisoner's body should be buried within the precincts of the prison. Burton had included the direction because he claimed that section 2 of the Executions for Murder Act 1836 had not repealed section 2 of the Hanging in Chains Act 1834, which had provided that 'in every case of conviction in Ireland, of any prisoner for murder the court before which such prisoner shall have been tried shall direct such prisoner to be buried within the precincts of the prison within which such prisoner shall have been confined after conviction; and that the sentence to be pronounced by the court shall express that the body of such prisoner shall be buried within the precincts of such prison.'[86] The twelve judges decided that Burton's direction was correct. The distinction between the punishment of actual murderers and the rest persisted until the Offences Against the Person Act 1861 provided that 'the body of every person executed for murder shall be buried within the precincts of the prison in which he shall have been last confined after conviction and the sentence of the court shall so direct.'[87]

Prisoners petitioned the lord lieutenant to allow their bodies to be given to their friends. In 1840, James Casey and Michael Hartnett, sentenced to death for shooting Constable Patrick Lawlor, memorialized the lord lieutenant, Viscount Ebrington, 'to order our bodies to be given to our friends for interment after our execution.' Ebrington decided that there was 'no ground for deviating from the ordinary course of law in this case.'[88] In the same year Thomas Glennon and John Toole prayed that 'your excellency will be pleased to extend unto the disconsolate and afflicted relatives the liberty of taking with them the bodies of your memorialists after execution.' A note on the memorial stated 'we have no instance

---

84 *Belfast Newsletter*, 19 May 1856.

85 John Simpson Armstrong, *A report of trials under a special commission for the county of Clare, held at Ennis, January 1848* (Dublin, n.d. [1849]), p. 181.

86 6 & 7 Will., c. 30 (14 July 1836); 4 & 5 Will., c. 26 (25 July 1834). See p. 27 of Burton's notes on the trial in NAI, CRF/1844/Dowling/11. See also *Dowling* (1844) 3 Cr & Dix 178 where this aspect of the case was not mentioned.

87 24 & 25 Vict., c. 100, s. 3 (6 Aug. 1861). See NAI, CRF/1867/Burke/2 for a fenian prisoner's attempt to have his body given to his friends after his execution for treason.

88 Ibid., CRF/1840/Casey/43.

in the office of such a request (though not unfrequently made) having been acceded to.'[89] According to Deasy there was 'a strong anxiety to be buried by and with the family and friends, and the prevention of such burial adds to the horror of death by the hand of the public executioner. In one case before me the unhappy culprit, when asked by the officer of the court whether he had anything to say why sentence of death should not be passed, implored of me to allow his body to be given to his friends, and said he was quite satisfied to die if that request was complied with.'[90] Even after the passage of the Offences Against the Person Act 1861, such requests were made. Thomas F. Bourke, sentenced to death for treason in 1867, asked that his body should be given to his solicitor 'for the purpose of interment in consecrated ground'.[91] Occasionally a compromise might be arrived at. When Charles McCormick's body was cut down,

> the two brothers and the uncle of the deceased came forward and wept bitterly as they placed the lid on the remains of him who had just paid a terrible penalty for his crime. The coffin having been raised on the shoulders of these poor afflicted people, they bore it within the prison walls, and on to the grave which had been dug for its reception. The funeral service was recited by the clergy, and the two brothers and the uncle shovelled the shingle of a back prison yard on the body of their unfortunate relative, and left the jail, and were lost amongst the crowd.[92]

BUREAUCRATIC HANGING

The Capital Punishment Amendment Act 1868, which provided that executions were to 'be carried into effect within the walls of the prison in which the offender is confined at the time of execution', eventually changed the way sentences were executed. What had been a public spectacle, stage-managed, and often mismanaged, by local officials, became an affair of secrecy, regulated by civil servants, and carried out by trained executioners.[93] The change took place slowly,

89 Ibid., CRF/1840/Glennon & Toole/4. For the exhumation and reinterment of the Cormack brothers in 1910, see Murphy, op. cit.
90 *Report of the capital punishment commission, together with the minutes of evidence, and appendix,* p. 615 [3590], HC 1866, xxi, 667.
91 NAI, CRF/1867/Burke/2.
92 Larcom Papers (NLI, MS 7620 [unidentified presscutting between *Irish Times*, 5 Aug. 1863 and *Express,* 6 Aug. 1863]).
93 31 Vict., c. 24, s. 2 (29 May 1868). Three days before the act received the royal assent Michael Barrett was hanged outside Newgate, having been convicted of murder for his part in the Clerkenwell explosion. The first intra-mural hanging in Britain was at Maidstone on 13 August 1868. The last public hanging in Ireland was that of John Logue in Downpatrick, 19 April 1866; the first intra-mural hanging was at Tullamore on 27 May 1870 when Laurence and Margaret Shiels were hanged.

and for decades after 1868 hangings remained semi-public affairs. The act even made elaborate arrangements to maintain enough publicity to assure the public that the prisoner had actually been hanged: the sheriff, or the sub-sheriff, the governor of the prison, the chaplain, and the surgeon were obliged to be present; the sheriff and the board of superintendence could permit members of the public and the prisoner's relatives to be present; JPs for the county or borough in which the prison was situated could also be present. After the prisoner was hanged, three formal statements of the fact were made: the prison surgeon was obliged to examine the body, and sign a death certificate;[94] the coroner held an inquest, empanelling a jury in the usual way;[95] the sheriff, the governor, and the chaplain signed a declaration stating that the hanging had been carried out. The high sheriff of Longford (Alexander White), the Catholic chaplain (P.A. Flanagan), the governor, and the chief warder, for example, signed the declaration that James Heany had been hanged in their presence in Sligo gaol on 12 January 1892.[96] Arnold Power (the under sheriff of Tipperary), Patrick Nugent (the mayor of Clonmel), Thomas Stringer (governor of Clonmel gaol), and Archdeacon Latham C. Warren signed the declaration that Wilfred E. Kenny had been hanged in their presence on 5 April 1898.[97]

The coroner's jury maintained a vestige of public participation, if only because it gave jurors an opportunity to ask questions, to make comments, and to know more of the details of hangings than the public had known before 1868. The jury empanelled after Lt. Col. Philip Cross' hanging at Cork on 20 January 1888, for example, wanted to know the name of the hangman, but the governor of the prison refused to reveal it (it was in fact Berry).[98] Wrangling between the coroners' juries and prison officials about examining the hangman as a witness continued into the twentieth century. After John Berryman's hanging in Derry in 1908, for example, 'one juryman also asked the length of the drop & was informed that the drop given was in accordance with regulations; the coroner permitted no further questions on this subject.'[99] The medical officer's examination meant that

94 31 Vict., c. 24, ss 3, 4.
95 Ibid., s. 5. Even before 1868 coroners investigated the deaths of all who died in prison; prisoners hanged outside the prison did not, of course, die *in* prison. According to Gabbett 'the coroner may and ought to inquire of the death of all persons who die in prison, that the public may be satisfied that such persons came to their deaths by the course of nature, and not by duress of imprisonment, or default of the gaoler' (Joseph Gabbett, *A treatise of the criminal law; comprehending all crimes and misdemeanors punishable by indictment; and offences cognizable summarily by magistrates; and the modes of proceeding upon each*, 2 vols (Dublin, 1843), ii, 56).
96 NAI, CRF/1892/Heany/1.
97 Ibid., CRF/1898/Kenny/6.
98 For the squabbling after Cross' execution see NAI, CRF/1888/Cross/1. On the other hand, the jury empanelled after Carr's hanging heard, according to the coroner, 'the entire evidence' before bringing in their verdict (NAI, CRF/1870/Carr/16).
99 Ibid., CRF/1908/Berryman/42. The juror's curiosity was pertinent: the hangman, Henry Albert Pierrepoint, 'decided to give a longer drop than the one suggested on the scale of drops for a prisoner of his weight owing to the strength of his neck.'

hangings were more clearly described. William Woods' hanging was, according to the governor, 'carried out without the slightest hitch [*sic*].'[100] The medical officer, John Stewart, was more forthcoming: 'Death was instantaneous. I examined the body after it was taken down and found the face livid, the head, face and neck congested. Blood on lips and tongue. A deep circular indentation around the neck which was thoroughly dislocated ... There was expulsion of urine but no faeces.'

At first it seemed the 1868 act would remove the crowd from executions. At the hanging of Laurence and Margaret Shiels in Tullamore gaol on 27 May 1870, the first hangings in Ireland since the passing of the act, 'no assemblage of the public took place.'[101] Indifference did not persist, however. When Andrew Carr was hanged on 28 July 1870 in the Richmond Bridewell for the murder of Margaret Murphy, 'though a person outside the gates of the prison could neither see nor hear anything of the execution, yet there were knots of idlers to be found, as early as six o'clock, in front of the gloomy pile.' Words such as 'knots' and 'hitch' seemed to slip into descriptions of hangings. When Peter Wade was hanged in Kilmainham in 1884, the governor commended the hangman, Bartholomew Binns, and noted that 'everything passed off most satisfactorily, there not being a hitch of any kind.'[102] The 1868 act also affected what the readers of newspapers learnt of executions. The high sheriff had the last word on whether newspaper reporters should be admitted; some allowed them to be present, and some did not.[103] Even when reporters were excluded they were not without resources. They were excluded from Joseph Brady's hanging in Kilmainham in May 1883, for example, but they drew up a list of questions that could be answered 'yes' or 'no', found 'a willing official' who was to be present at the execution, and 'within five minutes of the black flag being hoisted outside the gaol that official came through the gates and handed us our sheaf of foolscap pages, with the great bulk of our questions marked "yes" or "no".'[104] Reporting became more detailed: the corpse was carefully described – the pallor of the face, and signs of bruising and bleeding; the statements of coroners, jurors, and governors, who expatiated on prisoners' demeanour, were noted; the length of the drop, which had been occasionally mentioned before 1868, became a regular preoccupation. A picture of the ideal execution developed: courageous but repentant prisoner; kindly governor and warders; adept hangman; broken neck; composed countenance. The hangman, who had been a vulgar bogeyman before 1868, became a modestly respectable *fonctionaire*.

Section 7 of the 1868 act obliged the chief secretary to make regulations for the execution of capital sentences.[105] Chichester Fortescue approved the first set of

---

100 Ibid., CRF/1900/Woods/37.   101 *Irish Times*, 28 May 1870.
102 See NAI, CRF/1883/Wade/45.
103 In 1880, for example, Thomas Henry Burke, the under-secretary, told the sub-sheriff of Tyrone that the admission of reporters was a 'matter entirely in the hands of the high sheriff whose direction the sub-sheriff should take' (NAI, CRF/1880/Conway/19).
104 Frederick Moir Bussy, *Irish conspiracies: recollections of John Mallon (The Great Detective) and other reminiscences* (London, 1910), p. 211.
105 Section 8 was another sign of the preoccupation with publicity that permeated the act: 'all such

new regulations on 4 June 1869: 'the mode of execution and the ceremonial attending it shall be the same as heretofore in use'; executions were to take place at 8 a.m.; a black flag was to be hoisted on the prison and 'shall remain so displayed for one hour'; the prison bell was to be tolled for fifteen minutes before and after the execution.[106] These regulations remained in force until George Wyndham approved new ones on 23 August 1902. The bell was still to ring, but the black flag was replaced by a notice 'under the hands of the sheriff and the governor of the prison, of the date and hour appointed for the execution, to be posted on the prison gate not less than 12 hours before the execution, and to remain until the inquest has been held'; the sentence was to be carried out 'in the week following the third Sunday after the day on which the sentence is passed, on any weekday but Monday, and at 8 a.m.'; the hangman and his assistant were 'to report themselves at the prison not later than 4 o'clock on the afternoon preceding the execution, and to remain in the prison from the time of their arrival until they have completed the execution, and until permission is given them to leave.'

Andrew Carr was hanged in the Richmond Bridewell in Dublin on 28 July 1870. Among those assembled at what was the second intra-mural hanging in Ireland were 13 newspaper reporters, 3 Catholic priests, and '3 medical gentlemen witnessing the execution'.[107] The scaffold had been erected at a window on the third storey of the prison building. Only the governor, the chaplain, and the hangman were on the scaffold with Carr. The spectators were in the yard below. According to the *Irish Times* when Carr stepped on to the drop, he stood 'just as he might once have stood on parade, without flinching in the least', which was not surprising given his twenty years' service in the army. The governor was uneasy about the hangman, whom he later described as 'inexperienced'. (Like Carr, the hangman was an ex-soldier, who had served in the Crimea.) Carr complained of the tightness of the rope. According to the chaplain, Carr asked, 'Will you strangle or choke me before the time.' The bridewell's surgeon had ordered that Carr be given a fourteen-foot drop. When the hangman released the drop, the *Irish Times* described what happened: 'immediately the rope "jerked" when its full extent had fallen, the convict's neck became severed, the head sprang off from the body against the wall, blood spouted and spattered all around, and the trunk fell in a pool of it on the ground. The body quivered slightly about three minutes after the execution.' The governor described what he saw: 'By a sudden recoil of the rope immediately when the drop fell, together with the noise of something falling on the flags below, I became aware that some accident had occurred. On

rules and regulations shall be laid upon the tables of both houses of parliament within six weeks after the making thereof.'
106 The 1869 and 1902 rules are to be found in Death Book, 1852–1932 (NAI, GPB/CN/5). See also Potter, op. cit., p. 104.
107 Most of what follows is taken from *Irish Times*, 29 July 1870 and from NAI, CRF/1870/Carr/16.

looking down through the open trap, I saw the body of the deceased, Andrew Carr, lying in the yard beneath, decapitated, the head lying several feet from the body, and blood pouring in torrents from the trunk and head.' Of the thirteen newspaper men who were admitted to witness the hanging, only two were present at the inquest, which suggests that while some rushed off to file their copy, others were overcome by their feelings.

A soldier's violent death in July 1870 should not have attracted much attention, but a hanging that turned into funicular decapitation did not please the public; it smacked of Continental despotism and the Reign of Terror. On 1 August 1870, which was the Monday after Carr's execution, Lord Spencer ordered John Lentaigne, the inspector general of prisons, and George W. Hatchell MD, inspector of lunatic asylums, to hold 'an enquiry on oath'. On 3 August, Lentaigne and Hatchell examined those responsible, with the exception of the hangman, who was condemned in his absence 'as ignorant of the duties of the office which he had undertaken to discharge.' The most interesting statement was made by the bridewell's surgeon, Humphrey Minchin, who told the inquiry that it was his 'duty to give directions to prevent unnecessary torture'; that he had not consulted anyone before the execution; that he had 'consulted the only work within reach on the subject, a work by Professor Haughton MD, fellow of Trinity College, which work I got out of [the] library of the College of Surgeons.'[108] According to Minchin, Samuel Haughton had demonstrated that 'a force of 2240 lbs acting at 1 foot distance is ... exactly sufficient to secure instant and painless death.' Minchin applied this rule by dividing 2240 'by the weight of the culprit, namely 158 lbs, and the quotient is more than 14, which represents the distance of fall necessary.'[109] When he examined Carr's body, he was 'forcibly struck with the extremely placid expression presented by the countenance of [the] deceased.'

Lentaigne and Hatchell did not examine Haughton because they believed 'that gentleman was then absent from Dublin', which was not surprising given that it was the long vacation.[110] Haughton was not abroad, however, because on 30 July

---

108 The article consulted was 'On hanging, considered from a mechanical and physiological point of view' in *The London, Edinburgh, and Dublin Philosophical Magazine and Journal of Science*, 4th ser., 32:213 (July 1866), 23–34. The article begins with a historical introduction that includes the hanging of 'the twelve faithless handmaids of Penelope'.

109 Minchin did not think that the long drop had caused Carr's decapitation; he cited Haughton's description of Patrick Kilkenny's hanging ('On hanging', p. 32).

110 For Haughton's versatile career, which included being registrar of the medical school in Trinity, starting the Indian Civil Service School there, and opposing the theory of evolution, see R.B. McDowell & D.A. Webb, *Trinity College Dublin 1592–1952: an academic history* (Cambridge, 1982), pp 294–6. See also W.J.E. Jessop, 'Samuel Haughton: a Victorian polymath' in *Hermathena*, 116 (winter 1973), 5–26. Sarah Purser's portrait of Haughton and his dog is probably the most memorable portrait in the Trinity common room (plate 20 in McDowell & Webb, op. cit., p. 297). When Provost Salmon saw the portrait for the first time, he said, 'Excellent! Excellent! You can just hear the lies trickling out of his mouth.' Stanford & McDowell have established a connection between Haughton's *Principles of animal mechanics* and 'The ballad of Reading gaol' (*Mahaffy: a biography of an Anglo-Irishman* (London, 1975), p. 156). If this is so, Andrew Carr

he wrote from Trinity denying the *Irish Times'* report that he had been present at Carr's hanging.[111] He also wrote a long letter to Lentaigne and Hatchell, describing his interest in hanging. 'Having been engaged for years in collecting materials for a work on animal mechanics, & never having an opportunity of examining the body of a man who had met with a sudden death, I asked & obtained leave from the authorities to make an examination of the body of Kilkenny, who was executed in 1865 at Kilmainham goal [*sic*],' he wrote. 'My object in doing so was to ascertain the exact weights of certain muscles in the living body, & thus to interpret the results I had obtained by weighing the muscles of whose who had died from natural causes.' It was from Patrick Kilkenny that he derived his formula of 2240 foot-pounds: 'the criminal weighed 160 lbs, and was allowed to fall through 14 feet 6 inches, which, allowing for some elasticity in the rope, would correspond with 2240 foot-pounds of shock; in this case the superior articulating surfaces of the second vertebra were fractured near their posterior border.'[112] Haughton asserted the superiority of the long drop, which 'has been used in Ireland from time immemorial with the humane object of shortening the sufferings of the criminal, & the records of Irish executions show that the drop has ranged from 9ft to 16ft.' In England, on the other hand, 'the drop ranges from 2ft to 3ft only, and I am informed by Mr Gibson, surgeon to Newgate, that during his long experience, he has known but one case, in which death was rapid.' Minchin, according to Haughton, was making practical the old Stoic maxim for the alleviation of pain, mentioned by Cicero: '*Si longus, levis; si gravis, brevis*'![113]

is almost certainly the original of the soldier 'who did not wear his scarlet coat.' Vincent Delany (in *Christopher Palles, lord chief baron of Her Majesty's Court of Exchequer in Ireland, 1874–1916: his life and times* (Dublin, 1960) p. 25) repeated a jingle that reflects Salmon's opinion: 'Sam Haughton is a wily man/ Of scientific scope/ And yet we know he'd *hang* himself/ If he but got the rope'.

111 *Irish Times*, 1 Aug. 1870. Haughton did not waste his long vacations. See, for example, his research on the effects of nicotine and strychnine on frogs, most of which died miserably. One, however, survived: it had been 'placed in a mixed bath of nicotine and strychnine ... and removed after an interval of 10 minutes. After removal, in 32 minutes, the first symptom of emprosthotonos appeared, and the convulsions continued for many hours; but the animal ultimately recovered completely, and is still in the enjoyment of health and life, after a lapse of many days' ('On some experiments on the poisonous properties of strychnine and nicotine' in *Proceedings of the Royal Irish Academy*, 6 (1853–7), 423). The nearly expiring frog was luckier than a large white dog that Haughton dosed with nicotine and strychnine: it fell into a 'tetanic convulsion' after 89 minutes and died after 101 minutes ('On nicotine considered as an antidote to strychnia' in *Proceedings of the Royal Irish Academy*, 7 (1857–61), 84–8 (paper read 28 June 1858), p. 87). I am indebted to Professor Gordon Herries Davies for drawing my attention to Haughton's work on frogs and dogs.

112 Haughton also describes in detail the hanging of two convicts at Galway (John Hurley and Patrick Lydane); he got his information on these from Charles Croker King, professor of anatomy at the Queen's College, Galway ('On hanging', pp 33–4).

113 The affair in the Richmond Bridewell could have been worse. Haughton described a procedure that would have given even greater scope for accidents: 'Efforts have been made in the United States to give to hanging all the rapidity of death by the guillotine without the painful spectacle

The Carr inquiry defined how hanging should be done: 'death should be instantaneous and for that purpose the cervical vertebrae should be dislocated or fractured, by the fall of the culprit from the drop.' The inquiry, however, did not solve the problem of botched hangings. On 15 December 1882 Marwood botched Myles Joyce's hanging in Galway. On this occasion it was not the length of rope, but the fact that it became entangled with Joyce's arm, that caused the trouble.[114] There was an obvious solution to the problem of botched hangings, apart from abolition: to carry them out in a central prison, where the staff could gain experience. The solution adopted, however, was to employ 'professional' hangmen. An apostolic succession of hangmen from England began in Ireland in the 1870s: Marwood, Berry, Binns, Billington, and the Pierrepoints, who were nearly always referred to by their surnames, as if they were butlers or gardeners. Scott's name was occasionally preceded by his initials, 'T.H.', which at least made him sound like an architect.[115] Professionalism did not triumph easily. In 1882, for example, the sub-sheriff of Cork asked for permission to employ a prisoner in Cork gaol to hang Thomas Haynes.[116] An incident in 1890 revealed that the

of bloodshed. This method, which is borrowed from the mode of execution practised on board ship, consists in suddenly lifting the criminal into the air by means of a great weight attached to the other end of the rope fastened round his neck; the rope passes over a pulley placed vertically over the patient, lifting him suddenly into the air. Sufficient attention, however, has not been paid, even in that enlightened country, to the conditions necessary to be fulfilled in this mode of suspension; for in many of their executions, the only care that seems to have been taken was to make the falling weight heavier than the criminal, so as to ensure his permanent suspension by the neck until death terminated his sufferings' ('On hanging', p. 30). Alexandre Dumas described a remarkable execution in the Piazza del Popolo (which was only a short walk from the Collegio di Propaganda Fidei, where the future cardinal, Paul Cullen, was a student and later rector). The executioner was 'a man of vast stature and proportions'; he was naked, 'with the exception of cloth drawers, at the left side of which hung a large knife in a sheaf, and he bore on his right shoulder a heavy mace.' His two assistants dragged the prisoner to the scaffold, where in 'spite of his struggles, his bites, and his cries', they forced him to his knees; 'during this time the executioner had raised his mace, and signed to them to get out of they way; the criminal strove to rise, but, ere he had time, the mace fell on his left temple. A dull and heavy sound was heard, and the man dropped like an ox on his face, and then turned over on his back.' If that had been the end of the prisoner, papal Rome might have claimed to have possessed a humane form of judicial killing. It was not, however, the end: 'The executioner let fall his mace, drew his knife, and with one stroke opened his throat; and, mounting on his stomach, stamped violently on it with his feet. At every stroke a jet of blood sprang from the wound' (Alexandre Dumas, *The count of Monte Cristo*, intro. by Richard Church (London and Glasgow, 1955), pp 352–3).

114 Jarlath Waldron, *Maamtrasna: the murders and the mystery* (Dublin, 1992), p. 151. For a picture of Marwood hanging Charles Peace, see Leonard Cottrell, *Madame Tussaud* (London, 1951), pl 18 (between pp 94 and 95).

115 The hangmen did, however, have Christian names: James Marwood, James Berry, Bartholomew Binns, John Billington, and Albert Pierrepoint. For a description of Henry Albert Pierrepoint (Albert's father) and Thomas William (Albert's uncle) hanging a prisoner in Kilmainham, impeded by two officious priests, see Albert Pierrepoint, *Executioner: Pierrepoint* (Litton, n.d. [1978]), pp 110–11. See also pp 139–40 for Henry Albert's receiving a condemned man's confession.

116 NAI, RP/1882/34,767.

arrangements that were made for paying executioners were hardly those that nurtured professional expertise. When Michael O'Brien was reprieved at the last minute, the sub-sheriff of Limerick was out of pocket £7. 7s., which included £5. 5s. for the hangman, James Berry, who had actually arrived in Limerick before the sentence was commuted.[117] The sub-sheriff complained but got nowhere. The Treasury, since the Prisons (Ireland) Act 1877,[118] paid for the gallows as part of prison maintenance, but the sheriff had to pay the hangman.[119] In the matter of late respites, the government was unsympathetic and did not regard them as a reason for making the Treasury pay: 'The precedent would be a bad one, because the respite or reprieve of a condemned person is generally issued at the last moment, probably after the executioner's arrival.'

Eventually the home office extended its scrutiny of hangings to Ireland, where specially printed forms had to be filled in and returned to the home office as well as to the chairman of the General Prisons Board.[120] When James Doherty was hanged at Sligo in 1902, the governor and the sheriff wrote to the chairman of the General Prisons Board confirming that they had written to the home secretary describing how the executioner had carried out his duty; they had also filled in Form 80E 02 A.D. 157, which noted Doherty's height, weight (201 lbs), build, and age, as well the length of the drop (5 ft 6 in.), 'as determined before the execution'. The form also noted that Doherty's death was caused by dislocation of the vertebrae, and not by asphyxia.[121] One of the questions on the form ('if there were any peculiarities in the build or condition of the prisoner, or in the structure of his neck, which necessitated a departure from the scale of drops, particulars should be stated') implied that a standard scale of drops had been devised. The drop in Doherty's case was just half of what Haughton would have allowed, but it was nearly twice what Berry would have allowed.[122] The form also provided for a short report on the hangman: in Doherty's case John Billington, of Bolton, had performed his duty 'quite satisfactorily, his 'general demeanour' had been satisfactory, and there was no 'ground for supposing that he will bring discredit upon his office by lecturing, or by granting interviews to persons who may seek to elicit information from him in regard to the execution.' A barbaric ritual had become a bureaucratic procedure.[123]

117 Ibid., RP/1890/3635.
118 40 & 41 Vict., c. 49, s. 19 (14 Aug. 1877). 6 & 7 Will. IV, c. 116, s. 80 (20 Aug. 1836) had made the grand jury pay for the gallows.
119 *Report from the select committee of the house of lords on high sheriffs; together with the proceedings of the committee, minutes of evidence, and appendix*, p. 78, HC 1888 (257), xii, 294.
120 For the changes initiated by the home office's departmental committee under Lord Aberdare, see Potter, op. cit., p. 102.
121 NAI, CRF/1902/Doherty/69.
122 For a table of drops dated April 1892, see Tim Carey, *Mountjoy: the story of a prison* (Cork, 2000), p. 129. For Pierrepoint's formula (the length of the drop was estimated by dividing 1260 foot-lbs by the prisoner's weight in lbs), see Pierrepoint, op. cit., p. 131.
123 In the 1950s the royal commission on hanging heard that 'Mr Pierrepoint said that the time

The era of hanging in a stress-fee environment, which was to be the great achievement of the twentieth century, was dawning. As the high sheriff of Belfast told newspaper reporters after Richard Justin's hanging: 'Since I first saw this man and came in contact with the governor and officers of this prison I have been greatly gratified at the kindliness of their manner towards him, the attention shown him, and the feeling manifested towards him. I could not have believed that in any public institution it would have been possible for men accustomed to deal with people in certain circumstances to have manifested such a spirit as the officers of this prison showed towards this man.'[124]

which elapses between the entry of the executioner into the cell and the pulling of the lever is normally between 9 and 12 seconds but may be 20 to 25 seconds in a few prisons where the condemned cell does not adjoin the execution chamber' (*Royal commission on capital punishment 1949–1953. Report*, p. 250 [Cmd 8932], HC 1952–3, vii, 936).

124 NAI, CRF/1909/Justin/7.

CHAPTER 12

A rough engine?

THE MOST OBVIOUS CHARACTERISTIC of the criminal justice system was the apparent simplicity of its proceedings, but that simplicity was a carefully contrived superstructure that rested on a foundation of complexity. Even the use of archaic language was formidable, but the complexity went beyond the occasional use of Norman-French and Latin tags, and the mysterious significance of words such as *contradict* and *conclusive*. There was the division of function between the different courts, the difference between felonies and misdemeanours, and the *collateral* rule, for example. Above all there were the partially hidden facts that impinged only slowly on the mind of the inquirer: the fact that there was no system of full appeal, but important remedies nevertheless; the fact that prisoners were silent at every point in the proceedings; the fact that magisterial inquiry could not begin until a particular person was accused – a rule that was eventually eroded by legislation.

There was also the separation of functions between those who investigated crime in its early stages. During the pre-trial stages the magistrates and the police were not a uniform, official hierarchy: those who wanted to make an arrest had to argue their case before, in most cases, a magistrate who was unpaid, lived locally, was legally untrained, and was probably a substantial landowner. At the trial itself there was a clear distinction between the judge and the prosecution, and between the crown counsel and the prisoner's counsel. Above all there was the distinction between the judge and the jury, with one saying what the law was and the other saying what the facts were. These things existed in any country where the common law prevailed, but the most remarkable aspect of the nineteenth-century Irish courts was the prisoner's silence. Given the disturbed state of the country, the elaborate methods of dealing with crime, and the constant complaints about the inability of the police to bring criminals to justice, the restrictions on police questioning and confessions, even after *Johnston*, were surprising, to put it mildly.

There were considerable changes between 1836 and 1914. The most obvious were those brought about by legislation: the prisoners' counsel act, Lord Campbell's act, the jury acts of the 1870s, and the drastic abolition of capital punishment in the 1830s and 1840s. Less obvious but just as important were the changes brought about by the judges, acting in the Court for Crown Cases Reserved or in the Queen's Bench. The most important of these were changes in the rules about the admission of confessions and of the evidence of approvers. The former apparently changed course with *Johnston* in 1864, but the latter became

356

and remained more precise in their requirements, culminating with *Gillis*. The position of the judges was interesting; they had to respond to peculiarly Irish problems, especially those created by a powerful police force and a system of public prosecution, but they had to do it in a context of case law that was made not only in England but in other common law countries, such as the United States. Within that world they occasionally asserted their independence in a remarkable way, as in *Gray* and *Conway and Lynch*. Between legislation and the decisions of the Irish judges there was the occasional intervention by the house of lords, which as far as the criminal law was concerned was at its most peremptory in the case of *Gray*. There were also the administrative changes made by the government, the law officers, and the police – the increasing numbers of crown solicitors, for example, and the growing elaboration of the Crown's case at trials. There were changes that were hardly noticed. The apparent disappearance of surprise witnesses seems to have occurred without any dramatic intervention by the Irish judges. There were the changes that did not occur. The question of whether the prisoner's witnesses should be examined by the magistrates, for example, does not seem to have been resolved. There was also a remarkable continuity that arguably began in the year 1836 and depended on the coincidence of the prisoners' counsel act, of a centralized police force, and of a system of public prosecution by crown solicitors and crown counsel. More important than any of these, perhaps, were the changes brought about by the public, fewer of whom committed serious crimes as the century passed.

'If a complete account of the crimes and conduct at the place of execution of those who had been convicted by the law in Ireland since the Articles of Limerick, could now be drawn up,' wrote T. Crofton Croker, 'I am persuaded it would afford a moral and political view of the country, the result of which would surprise even the best acquainted with these subjects.'[1] If would be pleasant to agree with Croker. There is no doubt, for example, that the disturbances created by the Famine and the land war had their effect on the number of hangings in the country, which confirms Croker. On the other hand, the sharp reduction in executions and capital sentences from the 1830s onwards suggest a revolution so profound that it has been hardly noticed by historians. The fact, too, that capital punishment had almost ceased to be used by 1914 might be taken to show that the country had never been so well conducted or so well governed as it was on the eve of the first world war. The gallows in Ireland, and the proceedings that led to it, certainly reveal something about the country, including the ordinariness of its capital criminals and the rareness of hangings arising from political struggles. The Phoenix Park murders were about the only ones that arose directly from a great political agitation, but if one stretches a point, and adds the Maamtrasna murders

---

1 *Researches in the south of Ireland, illustrative of the scenery, architectural remains, and the manners and superstitions of the peasantry, with an appendix, containing a private narrative of the rebellion of 1798* (London, 1824), p. 183.

and the Cormack brothers, the toll is still a light one compared to most other European countries. The conduct of trials, characterized by the silence of the prisoner, the laws of evidence, the dominance of juries, do not suggest a country that was plagued by disorder. The Olympian calm of the judges suggest almost an academic engagement in matters of law enforcement.

The late David Johnson implied that law enforcement in Ireland was rougher than in England because the Crown adopted a number of 'stratagems' to secure convictions.[2] Venues were changed, jurors were set aside 'with great vigour', plea bargaining replaced trials, 'multiple retrials were common', and 'crimes were tried by special jurors, composed of the richer men of the country, rather than by the more usual (in England) petit or common juries.'[3] These 'stratagems' can be easily exemplified by well known trials. In 1882 in Francis Hynes' case the venue was changed to Dublin,[4] in the same year the Maamtrasna trials demonstrated ruthless plea-bargaining,[5] and between 19 April and 7 May 1883 Timothy Kelly was put on trial three times for his part in the Phoenix Park murders, a fact that might also suggest to the impartial bystander that jury-packing was not a refined art in Ireland.[6]

One problem with Johnson's conclusions is that they rely on a small number of well-known cases. There is another problem, which is that they depend on conflating the Crown's stratagems by assuming that their employment was uniform, ubiquitous, and endemic throughout the whole period. Three examples suggest that some of Johnson's stratagems were more commonly used at certain times than at others. First, there were no special juries in felony trials until the Prevention of Crime (Ireland) Act 1882 allowed either the Crown or the prisoner to ask for them.[7] Secondly, changes of venue, which were made easier by that act, do not seem to have been common before 1882, as Lord Chief Justice Whiteside's remarks in *Barrett*'s case above showed.[8] Thirdly, the setting aside of jurors 'with great vigour' seems to have been a result of O'Hagan's act, which had been intended to put jury selection beyond suspicion. Vigorous setting aside did not start with O'Hagan's act, but the meagre catalogue of examples that Sir Colman O'Loghlen gave in his speech in 1872 did not suggest there were many examples. As for plea bargaining, there is some evidence of it, but not much. A fair number of murders turned into manslaughters before the assizes, but there is no evidence that the prisoners involved pleaded guilty to the lesser offences. Many cases that had not started as manslaughters or murders also turned into manslaughters, which suggests that the Crown promoted as well as demoted. Even the 'hung'

2   D.S. Johnson, 'Trial by jury in Ireland 1860–1914' in *Journal of Legal History*, 17:3 (Dec. 1996), 270–1.
3   For 'special' jurors in felony trials in nineteenth-century Ireland, see above, pp 129–30.
4   Above, pp 273–5.
5   Jarlath Waldron, *Maamtrasna: the murders and the mystery* (Dublin, 1992), pp 124–31.
6   Johnson, 'Trial by jury', p. 288.   7   Above, p. 19.
8   Above, p. 138.

juries, about which contemporaries complained, although they are not part of Johnson's catalogue, were not as common as one might have expected.

A possible way of arriving at more broadly based conclusions is to use prisoners' complaints in the memorials in the Convict Reference Files, which offer a wider range of cases than the *causes célèbres* studied by Johnson and others. The memorials include complaints about judges, juries, witnesses, and counsel, which have the virtue of being routine, ordinary, and usually, but not always, made independently of contemporary political controversies. A selection of 85 Convict Reference Files showed that prisoners complained in 34 cases.[9] The significance of the 51 prisoners who did not complain is not easy to evaluate. They may have been too ignorant or too poorly represented to have spotted improprieties in the conduct of their trials, or they may have been too frightened to complain, or they may even have been satisfied customers who accepted the justice of their condemnation, or they may have been confident of a commutation of sentence and preferred not to make a fuss. There are two arguments that suggest that the 51 who did not complain can plausibly be said to incline slightly towards the satisfied rather than to the aggrieved.[10] First, nearly all of the 85 prisoners presented memorials, which suggests a capacity to make a case in spite of poverty, fear, and poor legal representation. Secondly, the range of criticism in the 34 cases where complaints were made suggests that memorialists were not inhibited by fear, certainly not by fear of judges, crown counsel, or police.[11] Even the small number of complaints generated by a selection of cases is better than diagnosis by means of a single specimen, which has often been the means of diagnosing the ills of criminal justice in nineteenth-century Ireland.

The 34 cases where there were complaints generated 63 complaints, which is not impressive. Complaints about the Crown's conduct of the case, the prisoner's defence, and about juries have already been described above.[12] Table 12.1 shows these and other causes of complaint.

Complaints about the Crown's conduct of the case were predictably the biggest group. The conduct of prisoners' counsel and attorneys was the second largest, which made them almost as obnoxious to prisoners as the agents of the Crown. Juries were only the third largest group, with only 10 complaints, which was less

9 Above, p. 2.

10 It is not easy to measure the public's satisfaction with its courts. If recourse to the courts is an indication of satisfaction, the Irish courts gave satisfaction. Desmond McCabe found that 'a myriad of complaints' were heard at the petty sessions and that 'the majority of these prosecutions seem to have been taken by country-people against their neighbours' (Desmond McCabe, 'Magistrates, peasants and the petty sessions courts: Mayo, 1823–50' in *Cathair na Mart*, 5:1 (1985), 48–9). In 1840 there were 146,000 summary convictions at the petty sessions; in 1880 there were 194,371, which suggests an almost three-fold increase, allowing for the fall in population from the late 1840s (Vaughan, *Landlords and tenants in mid-Victorian Ireland* (Oxford, 1994), p. 165).

11 For John Logue's capacity to complain, see above, pp 218–19.

12 Above, pp 160–2, 210–12, 248–9.

TABLE 12.1

THE CAUSES OF PRISONERS' COMPLAINTS

cause of complaint	number
crown counsel	14
prisoner's defence	12
juries	10
approvers	5
judges	5
non-attendance of prisoners' witnesses	4
newspapers	4
identification	3
legal technicalities	2
language used in court	2
venue	1
prisoners tried together	1
total	63

than one might have expected. These 3 causes of complaint accounted for over half of the complaints.

The remaining complaints had a variety of causes such as approvers, judges, and newspaper reports. Some of these might be distributed among the three big ones. Complaints about approvers might be added to complaints about the Crown; prisoners' witnesses not attending and the complaint about prisoners being tried together might be added to complaints about prisoners' defence. Complaints about newspapers and venue might be added to complaints about juries. Table 12.2 shows the result when these smaller causes of complaint are redistributed under the three main headings.

The three major causes of complaint now accounted for all but 12 complaints. Of these 12, four were not all that important: in the two cases where language was complained about, the prisoner's ignorance of English did make much difference to the result (in one case the prisoner was an Irish-speaker, in the other a Greek);[13] the two complaints about technicalities were of little importance – one was a nice but useless point about the composition of the grand jury, and the other about the indictment.[14] The most substantial complaints of the group of 12 were the three about identification, and the five about judges. The latter was a modest total considering the judges' importance at trials. One of the complaints about identification was simple: a crown witness claimed she recognized her husband's

13   NAI, CRF/1858/Lydane/5; ibid., 1876/Bombos/26.
14   Ibid., CRF/1839/McCowley/71; ibid., 1853/Mullan/32.

TABLE 12.2

PRISONERS' COMPLAINTS

cause of complaint	number
crown counsel	19
prisoner's defence	17
juries	15
judges	5
identification	3
legal technicalities	2
language used in court	2
total	63

assailants, even though it was dark at the time.[15] This was a case that might have troubled a modern appeal court, but which did not seem to bother the judge or the jury in the case. The other two were more interesting because they were complaints about how the constabulary and the RMs organized identity parades.[16] These two cases might well be added to complaints about how the Crown conducted its case, or they might form a small, but interesting, sub-section on complaints about the constabulary.

The remainder of this group, the five complaints about judges, were in fact about three judges: James Casey and Michael Hartnett complained that Moore 'has been led to over-estimate the particular degree of guilt attributable to memorialists';[17] Thomas Dowling complained that Burton had told the jury he was the murdered man's tenant, when in fact the murdered man was only the agent of the estate; Dowling also complained that Burton told the jury to rely on the approver independently of corroboration;[18] Matthew Phibbs complained that Hayes admitted illegal evidence and took an erroneous view of the law.[19] Of the three cases, Hayes' admittance of evidence to show that Phibbs had been in debt was the least contentious, because it showed he had a motive to commit the crime.[20] The other two cases went to the twelve judges, which suggests that both Moore and Burton were scrupulous in recognizing that there had been difficulties at the trials. In *Hartnett and Casey*, Moore actually took a less serious view of the prisoners' guilt than might have been expected, and the point he reserved was about the words used in the sentence of death; 6 of the 10 judges decided that the

15 Ibid., CRF/1841/Power/13.
16 Ibid., CRF/1843/Mullins/50; ibid., 1863/Ward/5.
17 Ibid., CRF/1840/Casey/43.
18 Ibid., CRF/1844/Dowling/11. Cf. above, pp 253–4.
19 NAI, CRF/1861/Phibbs/5.   20 Above, p. 179.

sentence was illegal and the prisoners were pardoned and discharged.[21] In Dowling's case Burton reserved 2 points for the judges, one about the words used in the sentence of death and the other about the corroboration of an approver.[22] The judges decided that he had been correct in both instances, although Perrin expressed his doubts.

How serious were these 63 complaints? According to Alexander Sullivan, who had begun his career when the only courts of 'criminal appeal' were the Queen's Bench and the Court for Crown Cases Reserved, 'few trials can escape suggestion of error in some small matter that has transpired.'[23] Stephen was more trenchant about the system in England and Wales: the criminal law was 'by far the roughest engine which society can use for any purpose.'[24] Of the 63 complaints generated by these 85 cases, only about a dozen were serious: 3 where surprise evidence was admitted (Mullins, Power, and Ward); 3 where the selection of the jury was criticized (Dowling, Dunn, and Woods); one where the trial was postponed to allow the Crown to fish for evidence (Lydane); 2 where a trial was not postponed (Bombos and Power); 2 where there was debate about the corroboration of approvers (Glennon and Woods).[25] Even this select group did not consist of complaints of equal weight. In none of them did the twelve judges, or the Court for Crown Cases Reserved, or the Queen's Bench quash the verdicts.

The fewness of complaints and their limited range suggest that the system worked much better than suggested by the criticism of contemporaries, either in parliament or in the newspapers or in confidential memoranda. For any historian of nineteenth-century Ireland, steeped in contemporary controversy and inured to complaints about the courts and the police, Pigot's speech in *Johnston*, Lefroy's speech in *Gray*, Whiteside's speech in *M'Mahon*, and Christian's speech in *Burke*, all of which are quoted above,[26] will come as thought-provoking surprises, suggesting that a Castle Catholic, an old tory, a young tory, and a trimmer could rise to heights of liberality. Compared with the land system, law enforcement worked with relatively little friction. If a sample of one hundred landlords was taken and if they were pursued through royal commissions, newspapers, and folklore it is highly unlikely that only 60 complaints would be found. More remarkable, however, than the fewness of the complaints were the complaints that were not made. There were no complaints about crown solicitors suborning witnesses;[27] there were no complaints about the intimidation of the prisoner's

21 *Hartnett and Casey* (1840) Jebb Rep 302, at p. 305. See also *Casey and Hartnett* 2 Cr & Dix 65. For Moore's view of their guilt, see also above, p. 319.

22 NAI, CRF/1844/Dowling/11. *Dowling* found its way into the law reports because Dowling's first jury had been discharged and the original copy of the indictment had been lost (*Dowling* (1844) 3 Cr & Dix 178).

23 A.M. Sullivan, *The last serjeant. The memoirs of Serjeant A.M. Sullivan QC* (London, 1952), p. 210.

24 Stephen, *Liberty, equality, and fraternity* (London, 1873), p. 146.

25 Above, p. 198.   26 Above, pp 79, 158–9, 194–5, 238.

27 Cf. Waldron, op. cit., passim for the accusations made against George Bolton's management of

witnesses; there were no complaints about the suppression of evidence. Complaints about the prisoners' defence were frequent, but these did not include complaints that prisoners' counsel betrayed their clients, or were corrupt, or cowardly. There were no complaints about magistrates, especially in the matter of concocting depositions in such a way that they admitted illegal evidence, which is surprising.

The most conspicuous absentees among those complained of were the police. In the selection of 85 cases there were no complaints of confessions wrung from prisoners, no complaints of confessions spontaneously emitted in prison cells at the dead of the night, and no complaints about suborned witnesses, no stories of prisoners' witnesses afflicted by amnesia.[28] Even in the five cases where there were complaints about approvers, neither the police nor the RMs were accused of coaching them. The nearest that the petitions came to criticizing the police were in the three complaints about identification. This apparent immunity of the police from complaint is probably the most important aspect of these complaints about trials: either the police had the country bound hand and foot, and too afraid to complain, or they had a good record of propriety. The former seems unlikely, and would have been a more noteworthy achievement than the latter. The judges' discouragement of confessions can be given much of the credit for the police's record. It might be argued that the most important struggle that went on in the nineteenth-century courts was between the police and the judges: the former, who were numerous, well-organized, and zealous, were restrained by the latter, who enjoyed enormous prestige. It was an achievement to control the new constabulary and to maintain a system of court procedure whose main characteristics were the exclusion of important evidence and the silence of the prisoner. Only a professional caste, like the judges, endowed with almost sacerdotal power, could have maintained courts whose procedures were as artificial as grand opera or the *commedia dell' arte*.

Compared with twentieth-century procedure much of what happened in the nineteenth seemed hurried and rough. The most notable difference between the two periods was probably the establishment in the twentieth century of full courts of criminal appeal and the right of the prisoner to give evidence. The twentieth-century advances that aided prisoners, however, must be set against changes that have worked against them. In England, for example, the following changes have weakened the prisoner's position: the 1898 criminal evidence act exposed

the two approvers in the Maamtrasna case. See also Joe Clarke, "'It's not fit for you to be keeping company with that unfortunate fellow", Ballyforan Bridge, Co. Galway, 1879' in Frank Sweeney (ed.), *Hanging crimes* (Dublin, 2005), p. 190.

28 There were no complaints in Ireland, for example, of a police practice in England that Bentley describes as the 'common police practice of sending into a prisoner's cell a fellow prisoner, or a policeman disguised as a prisoner, to win his confidence and worm admissions out of him, a practice still in use in Cumberland as late as 1883' (David Bentley, *English criminal justice in the nineteenth century* (London and Rio Grande, 1998), p. 227).

prisoners to cross-examination;[29] the police have gradually established the right to question suspects, albeit under strict conditions; since 1967 the accused have had to make pre-trial disclosure of alibis, expert evidence, and the general nature of their defence; since April 1995 the accused's failure to answer police questions or to give evidence 'have been matters from which a jury can be invited to draw an adverse inference.'[30] In addition jury unanimity and the right of peremptory challenge have been abolished, and the hearsay rule has been relaxed.

These changes in prisoners' rights and the prosecution's powers, which have been made in England, and partially followed in Northern Ireland and in the Republic of Ireland, certainly justify Bentley in writing that 'if present trends continue we may yet come to look upon [the nineteenth century], at least as far as its rules of criminal evidence are concerned, as a golden age.'[31] What would Torrens and Pigot have made of *The People v. Breathnach* in 1981 when 'the accused had been almost constantly interrogated for forty hours following his arrest; he had been denied access to legal advisers and to friends and his confession was made after he had been awakened from a few hours of much needed sleep, and brought down at 4.00 a.m. for further investigation into the passageway of the Bridewell Garda Station in Dublin.'?[32] Torrens would have thundered; Pigot would have committed the garda commissioner.

It is anachronistic to judge nineteenth-century practices by twentieth-century standards, but it is not anachronistic to compare Irish courts in the nineteenth century with courts in other countries in the nineteenth century.[33] England and Ireland were alike in so many respects of procedure that it is difficult to see any difference between them, but they were so dissimilar in the matter of public prosecution and the presence of a centralized police that comparison is difficult. The crown solicitors and the police, for example, seem to have brought far more cases before the Irish courts than was common in England. A comparison between Irish and Scottish courts is perhaps more useful. The Irish and Scottish courts had much in common. Both had juries, laws of evidence, independent judges, and a separate caste of advocates, who could represent both the Crown and the prisoner; both were suspicious of confessions and both imposed silence on prisoners.[34] There were differences, however: in Scotland, Crown and prisoner

29 Above, pp 227–8.   30 Bentley, op. cit. p. 300.
31 Ibid., p. 301.
32 Paul Anthony McDermott, 'Criminal procedure and evidence' in Paul O'Mahony (ed. with seven introductory essays), *Criminal justice in Ireland* (Dublin, 2002), p. 64. See above, p. 190.
33 See David J.A. Cairns, *Advocacy and the making of the adversarial criminal trial 1800–1865* (Oxford, 1998), pp 35–6 for a discussion of 'the fallacy of presentism', which he describes, quoting D. Hay, as 'working from present concerns to past origins, [which] is anathema to historians, but necessarily half the lawyer's method. Whatever its merits in finding supporting arguments for a brief, it has the effect in historical work of writing out of the past any developments which did not survive in much the same form into the present.'
34 James Paterson, *A compendium of English and Scotch law stating their differences: with a dictionary of parallel terms and phrases* (Edinburgh, 1860), passim.

had to give each other a list of their witnesses before the trial, the prisoner's counsel had the last word, and 8 of the jury of 15 could convict or acquit; there was an established system of legal aid that provided advocates for poor prisoners; the prisoner had the right to be tried within a fixed time, or 'running his letters', as it was called. The Scots prisoner was worse off in certain respects than the Irish one: he could peremptorily challenge only 5 jurors (compared with 20 in Ireland); he could be convicted by 8 jurors not 12; dying declarations were more readily admitted; dead witness' statements were more easily admitted (they did not have to be made in the presence of the accused); the rules admitting confessions were clearer. If Scots criminal procedure had been applied to Ireland, only the proper provision of counsel for poor prisoners, the proviso that the prisoner had to be put on trial within a certain time, and the fact that both parties had to reveal their witnesses before the trial might have helped prisoners. The remainder would have strengthened the Crown.

It would be interesting to see the Irish courts through the eyes of a well-informed stranger, not a stranger who saw them as an anthropological ritual, but one who saw them as the institutions of a province of Erewhon. When James Whiteside described Italian criminal courts in his *Italy in the nineteenth century*, which was an account of his two-year stay in Italy in the mid-1840s, he came as close to being the Samuel Butler of the Irish courts as we are likely to get. In his own way he is describing Ireland, or at least he is intensely aware of Ireland as he writes of Italy. When Whiteside went to Italy, he was among the leaders of the Irish bar, having taken silk in 1842 and having just acted as one of O'Connell's counsel in the state trial of 1843. After his return from Italy he was counsel for William Smith O'Brien in 1848 and for Maria Theresa Longworth in the Yelverton case in 1861, and in 1866 he became lord chief justice of the Queen's Bench. His *Italy in the nineteenth century* is a wide-ranging survey of Italian affairs, dwelling especially on the liberalism of the newly elected Pope Pius IX, and glowing with affection for the city of Rome.[35] More to the point, however, were his descriptions of the courts and lawyers in the different Italian states, especially those in Florence, Rome, and Naples. His eye-witness account of a capital trial in Rome is a rare thing in the English language – rare not only because it was written at all, but rare because it was written by a distinguished practising lawyer in the common law tradition.

Whiteside took with him to Italy the ordinary prejudices of a lawyer trained in the common law tradition. In the Woods murder case in Co. Armagh in 1841, for example, when he was the prisoner's counsel, he told the jury that 'in other countries a man's life is at the caprice of an individual, but we enjoy laws which forbid such tyranny.'[36] He was, however, aware of his prejudices, certainly when

35 James Whiteside, *Italy in the nineteenth century, contrasted with its past condition*, 3 vols (London, 1848).
36 NAI, CRF/1841/Woods/26 (crown solicitor's transcript, p. 32).

he wrote his book. 'The English', he wrote, 'are apt to look down with haughty contempt upon the legal systems of continental countries, and more especially in reference to their codes of criminal law.'[37] Much of what he saw in the Italian courts did not impress him favourably. He did not like the inquisitorial function of the judges: 'the president has the right of interrogating the accused; this I consider a grand error, and, from what I have seen in Italy, a mischievous practice; it is either a temptation to falsehood or an instrument of torture.'[38] He did not like the secrecy of the courts. The Neapolitan criminal code, for example, allowed

> secret trials; suppression of names of witnesses and prosecutors; refusal of means of making defence against a charge alleged, it may be, by a private enemy; torture of the accused by personal interrogatories in his prison; special commissions; the code, barbarous as it is, giving no definition of sedition or treason, and leaving it to a court so constituted, to condemn (upon an extorted or perverted answer), the unfortunate accused to death.[39]

He came back to the secrecy of the courts again and again: 'The judges, the prisoner, his advocate, the *procuratore fiscale* prosecuting, and the guard were the only persons permitted to be present at the trial. No relative or friend of the accused dares to cross the threshold of the court; no part of the evidence, trial, or sentence, can be published; the proceedings of the criminal tribunals are wrapped in impenetrable mystery.'[40] In political cases the secrecy was even more oppressive. In Naples, for example, 'the political offender is taken to a private room, often in the palace, and tried before commissioners named by the king in each case, two of whom are generally household officers ... What becomes of the political prisoner is not known; his trial is secret, and no part of the procedure is published, nor do the ordinary forms apply to this class of offence.'[41]

He was struck by the low standing of Italian lawyers: 'The profession of the law is considered by the higher classes to be a base pursuit; no man of family would degrade himself by engaging in it. A younger son of the poorest noble would famish rather than earn his livelihood in an employment considered vile. The advocate is seldom, if ever, admitted into high society in Rome.'[42] The future lord chief justice of Ireland, whose salary between 1866 and 1876, would be £5,074. 9s. 4d., was told that Neapolitan judges' salaries 'were very small, and their expenses considerable; they often borrow money from successful advocates.'[43] From one hobby horse, Whiteside nimbly vaulted to another:

> The pure administration of justice it is that sustains the fabric of society. The conviction was now forced upon me that under the papacy, which

37 Whiteside, op. cit., i, 373.   38 Ibid., i, 390.
39 Ibid., ii, 294–6.   40 Ibid., ii, 272–3.
41 Ibid., iii, 100.   42 Ibid., ii, 277–8.
43 Ibid., iii, 102.

affects to direct the Christian world as to the maxims of eternal justice, the profession of the law, that is, the being concerned in the administration of justice, was made a thing despicable; and this not from any peculiar wickedness in the rulers of the kingdom, but from their unfitness for civil government, and their unhappy delusion, that the elevation of their Church was the chief good to be secured on earth.[44]

Whiteside wrote of Italy, one suspects, in a Palmerstonian sense, being a tory at home and a liberal abroad. He admired Pius IX, liked Paul Cullen, the rector of the Irish College, and enjoyed the spectacle of papal Rome, the Christmas *presepii*, and the Holy Crib in Santa Maria Maggiore; but he did not like *popery*, the Jesuits, or the Dominicans, who reminded him of the Inquisition.

He found much, however, that he liked in the Italian courts. He liked the criminal codes, 'scientifically prepared, methodically arranged, with correct definitions, and accurate divisions.'[45] He liked 'the pains taken to prepare the case for trial', which 'far exceed the system of crown prosecutions in England – certainly in Ireland.'[46] He liked the way witnesses were summoned: 'No witness can be called not named in the list; and those who have deposed in the preliminary inquiry to matters of skill or experiments, or to the mere discovery of facts, and who have been *already sworn* need not be called – their depositions suffice.'[47] He liked the fact that all preliminary investigations were made 'accessible to the accused, his friends, and advisers',[48] and he liked the way that the prosecutor and the prisoner exchanged lists of their witnesses ('this regulation seems rational, and calculated to attain the elucidation of truth; each party has the means of inquiry afforded as to the character and knowledge of the witnesses to be examined on the trial; and the trial does not resemble a game of chance, as it sometimes does with us.')[49] He even liked the fact that the prisoner's advocate had the last word ('this custom prevails in several Continental countries, and is not unreasonable.')[50] The things that he liked about Italian courts were those that legal reformers in the United Kingdom promoted spasmodically in the nineteenth century.

When Whiteside went to watch a capital trial in Rome in March 1847, he was no ignorant or hostile critic of the Roman legal system. He was indeed imbued with the common law tradition, a man who had made a reputation as prisoner's counsel, and he was an Irish Protestant; but he was also a Romanophile, and by March 1847 an experienced observer of Italian legal procedure. Every detail of his account reveals his deep sense of the difference between the Roman system and his own. He had to apply, through an advocate of his acquaintance, for permission to attend, which 'was courteously granted.'[51] In Ireland, he would have had to fight his way into a courthouse where an interesting trial was taking place, but he would have fought his way in as of right.

44 Ibid., ii, 279.   45 Ibid., i, 373.   46 Ibid., i, 387.
47 Ibid., iii, 94.   48 Ibid., iii, 92.   49 Ibid., iii, 93.
50 Ibid., iii, 95.   51 Ibid., iii, 291.

The room in the Palazzo Medici where the trial took place was 'clean and profoundly quiet'. In Ireland, it is unlikely that the courthouse at the opening of the assizes would have been either clean or quiet.[52] The four judges sat on a raised platform; three wore black caps, and the fourth a dark purple gown. The procurator fiscal and the prisoners' advocates were differentiated by their dress and by where they sat. The former, dressed in a silk black gown, sat at the corner of the judges' table, 'near enough to whisper to the judges; *he* was a gentlemanlike person.' The prisoners' advocates, who were less stylishly dressed ('arrayed in coarse black gowns'), sat at a table below the judges' raised platform. The four prisoners sat on a bench opposite the judges, 'one leg of each was firmly bound by a rope to a holdfast behind the bench, the other leg left free', and guards with fixed bayonets stood behind them. 'No relative or agent of the prisoners was there to take a suggestion from them, or assist or befriend them,' he wrote.

As the trial proceeded, Whiteside noted the importance of the pre-trial document that outlined the case:

> A criminal process in the Roman law is a curious document. It is not a dry technical indictment; but a narrative of facts, a statement of evidence, with a copious argument on its effect ... The whole case is gone into, in sections, and by proofs and probabilities, and concise reasonings on both, concert, malice, and deliberation are established ... The contradictions in the statements of the accused are next pointed out with great particularity. We have now arrived at page 34 of the process. The precise case against each prisoner is now separately stated, and the evidence in sections regularly numbered, pointed, and applied to each of the accused, and thus the criminal process closes. This document was clear, methodical, and full, and would afford an admirable model for a criminal brief in serious cases, even in England.[53]

The chief judge, who was 'a coarse, blustering man', began by reading parts of the process, and then went on to interrogate each prisoner, 'first as to birth, occupation etc.; then on the merits, telling the accused what had been proved against them, and how very wicked they were, demanding what they had to say to that.' The prisoners did not take this quietly, for 'then began a shocking scene of abuse and noisy recrimination between the accused and the speaking judge, who was certainly "no well-tuned cymbal". The prisoners spoke with boldness and insolence. Whatever they alleged, the chief judge invariably answered, it was a lie.'

52 Ibid., iii, 294.
53 Ibid., iii, 292–4. I am indebted to Professor Raffaella Santi, of the University of Urbino, for supplying me with a copy of the 'sentence' in this case from the Archivio di Stato di Roma. The document, which runs to 18 pages of MS, is more detailed than the 'record' of a trial in Ireland, and it is fuller than most judges' notes. It begins auspiciously by describing Pius IX as 'felicemente regnante'.

After this scolding match, the chief judge 'cooled down', called the first witness, and 'examined him entirely himself.' The witness was sworn by putting his hand on a crucifix. 'Sometimes the judge scolded the witness for not giving such evidence as was expected; frequently he recounted to the witness what a previous witness had proved, or what was stated in the process, and asked him what he could say to that.' When the judge had finished examining the witness, he asked each prisoner what he had to say. 'The prisoner, shaking his loose leg, generally answered it was a lie. This inflamed the mild temper of the judge, who angrily asked the accused how he dared to say that; how could he expect the judges would disbelieve so many witnesses and his own partial confession?'

The advocates played only a small part in the examination of the witnesses. The procurator fiscal apparently asked no questions; the prisoners' advocates 'rarely' suggested a question. Not only did the chief judge have it all his own way, but 'there seems to be no law of evidence whatever, as we understand it, in the Italian procedure. The judge desires the witness to tell all he saw, heard, thought, or believed about the matter, and the witness does as he is bid, counsel never interrupting or remonstrating; every statement is received in evidence, a system fatal to innocence.'

When the chief judge had finished with the witnesses, the procurator fiscal spoke, 'sitting in the position described'. He spoke for an hour; his style was 'very gentlemanlike and easy'; he praised the Roman law and 'talked of *filosophia e divina sapienza*, in a very amusing strain'; he cited 'a few articles, to prove the crime premeditated murder; but he did not review the evidence, preferring generalities, and submitting to the profound wisdom of the court.' Next it was the turn of one of the prisoners' advocates. He also spoke sitting, and 'he ranted the most arrant bombast, with theatrical gestures and in the wildest manner, about philosophy, wisdom, the Roman heart, and the over-ruling Providence. Not an allusion did he make to law or fact, and concluded in a storm.' Then came Signor Raggi, 'the official defender of accused men who are too poor to employ advocates.' He spoke 'composedly, and like a man of sense.' He argued that the act was unpremeditated, dwelt on the excitement of the prisoners, and pointed out that no evidence had been produced to show that the knives used in the attack had been brought to the prisoners surreptitiously or to contradict their statement that they had found them accidentally. When Raggi was finished, it was time for the judges to make a decision. 'We were now turned out of the chamber where the judges remained.' After half an hour the judges made up their minds: they sentenced the four men to be guillotined, and 'until executed, to be loaded with irons, and confined in separate cells.' In the event, one died in prison and the other three were sent to the galleys for twenty years. Whiteside concluded his account by reflecting 'that the accused were no doubt guilty, but there was a coarse cruelty, a heartlessness, and insulting violence exhibited towards them, inexpressibly shocking to one accustomed to the temperate and impartial administration of justice.'[54]

54 Whiteside, op. cit., iii, 298.

There were weaknesses in the Irish system that were probably common to all judicial investigation in the nineteenth-century in countries where the common law prevailed. There was a tendency to accept that statements made on oath were true until proved false, and that things were actually heard and seen as described by witnesses, without giving much thought to establishing, except through cross-examination, that such things could be heard and seen.[55] There was indeed a parade of apparently precise measurement: there were frequent references to maps, there was agonizing over times and distances, 'expert' evidence, especially medical evidence, was invoked, but there were few attempts to strengthen or to refute the Crown's case by experiment. In the last resort, the jury filled the vacuum by conferring the status of *fact* on statements made by witnesses.[56] In the Kirwan case six crown witnesses said that they had heard screams coming from Ireland's Eye on the evening of Mrs Kirwan's death. Hugh Campbell, for example, who was standing on the quay wall opposite the light-house, 'heard a cry which seemed to come from Ireland's Eye; the voice was very weak when I heard it; it came from the eastward of the light-house at Howth; I was right opposite of the light-house.'[57] The prisoner's counsel, Isaac Butt, pointed out that neither the constabulary, nor the railway officials, nor the coast guard had heard the cries, but he took the matter no further. Only after Kirwan's conviction was the obvious experiment made. On 22 December 1852 Captain J.A. O'Neill, John W. Foakes,

55 For an answer to Pilate's question and an interesting insight into the reasoning of a great lawyer, see Simon Greenleaf, *An examination of the testimony of the four evangelists, by the rules of evidence administered in courts of justice with an account of the trial of Jesus* (2nd ed., London, 1847), pp 25, 28–9, 39–40. Greenleaf's *Treatise on the law of evidence* (1842–53) became 'in its completed form the foremost American authority' (*Concise Dictionary of American Biography* (New York, 1964), p. 371).

56 Alexis de Tocqueville had a cautionary tale that showed how fiction could become fact. 'In the first scramble which followed the entry of the National Guard, I had a little adventure which I should like to relate as a warning to judges against the errors to which their profession is liable. Coming to the assembly that morning I had brought with me a sword-stick which I left standing inside the entrance door. A moment later I was swept by the crowd to the side of a young man who, brandishing a bare sword in one hand and my stick in the other, was shouting with all his might: "Long live the National Assembly." – "One moment," I said, "this stick is mine." – "No, it is mine," he answered. – "It is mine," I said, "so much that I know that it contains a sword." – "I know," he said, "I have had a sword put in two days ago. But who are you?" he added. I told him my name. He at once took off his hat respectfully and offered me the stick by its knob: "Sir," he said, "this stick is mine, but I shall be glad to lend it to you for you may need it today more than I. I shall have the honour of coming to fetch it from you." Next day I found my stick in a corner of the Assembly. It was so exactly like that of my suspected thief that I could not tell the two apart. I never knew if it was my stick or his that I returned to him when he came to see me as he had announced' (*The recollections of Alexis de Tocqueville*. Trans by Alexander Teixeira de Mattos; edited with many additions and introduced by J.P. Mayer (London, 1948), pp 146–7).

57 John Simpson Armstrong, *Report of the trial of William Burke Kirwan, for the murder of Maria Louisa Kirwan, his wife, at the island of Ireland's Eye, in the county of Dublin on the 6th September, 1852, before the Hon. Judge Crampton and the Rt Hon. Baron Greene, at the Commission Court, Green Street, on the 8th and 9th December, 1852* (Dublin, 1853), pp 6–7, 25, 42–4.

Alexander Boyd, Walter Boyd jr, and John M'Intosh went to Ireland's Eye: 'Captain O'Neill and Alexander Boyd stationed themselves near the Martello Tower, and Walter Boyd and John M'Intosh went down into the Long Hole, and Walter Boyd shouted, screamed, and whistled on his fingers. Captain O'Neill and Alexander Boyd listened attentively during the time the others were down in the Long Hole, and heard no noise or screams whatever.'[58]

Judicial inquiry, according to Stephen, was a cruder thing than scientific inquiry ('the patient suspension of judgment, and the high standard of certainty required by scientific inquirers, cannot be expected. Judicial decisions must proceed upon imperfect materials, and must be made at the risk of error.')[59] Stephen's definition of the five characteristics of scientific observation, however, suggests that its incursion into judicial inquiry was neither difficult nor undesirable: (1) 'the facts which a scientific observer has to report do not affect his passions'; (2) 'his evidence about them is not taken at all unless his powers of observation have been more or less trained and can be depended upon'; (3) 'he can hardly know what will be the inference from the facts which he observes until his observations have been combined with those of other persons, so that if he were otherwise disposed to misstate them, he would not know what misstatement would serve his purpose'; (4) 'he knows that his observations will be confronted with others, so that if he is careless or inaccurate, and, *à fortiori*, if he should be dishonest, he would be found out'; (5) 'the class of facts which he observes, are generally speaking, simple, and he is usually provided with means specially arranged for the purpose of securing accurate observation, and a careful record of its results.'

A number of unexpected things emerge, when one tries to see the Irish criminal justice system in its own right. First, the appeal system was very limited in its scope and erratic in its effects, yet the Queen's Bench and the Court for Crown Cases Reserved were remarkable institutions when they laid down the law or tried to control its application. The judges in *Galvin*, *Fay* and *M'Mahon* were not afraid of the government, or worried about revolution, or determined that the wicked should be punished, or nervous about public opinion, or even worried about the dictates of common sense, that most commonly invoked source of nonsense; instead, they tried to apply the precedents as if they were in a laboratory, except that their laboratory was a public lecture theatre, and each step of the experiment was observed by an informed audience. There is a surprising

58 [John Knight Boswell], *The Kirwan case: illustrating the danger of conviction on circumstantial evidence, and the necessity of granting new trials in criminal cases* (Dublin, 1853), p. 117. Samuel Haughton later took up the problem of the tides at Ireland's Eye in an article 'On the true height of the tide at Ireland's Eye on the evening of the 6th September, 1852, the day of the murder of Mrs Kirwan' in *Proceedings of the Royal Irish Academy*, 7 (1857–61), 511–13 (paper read 27 May 1861).

59 Stephen, *The Indian evidence act (I. of 1872), with an introduction on the principles of judicial evidence* (Calcutta, Bombay, and London, 1872), pp 26–9.

element in their decisions in these cases, especially when they are considered against a background where complaints about perverse acquittals and fenian conspiracy were common.

Secondly, many important decisions about how suspects in murder cases should be dealt with were made before the trial began. The figures produced by the registrar general in 1871 bear repeating: of the 310 persons committed for trial for murder, only 117 were actually put on trial for murder; the rest were found insane, or died, or were released or not prosecuted, or were prosecuted for lesser offences, such as manslaughter. It does not appear that these figures were untypical of the period as a whole.

Thirdly, the laws of evidence and the silence of the prisoner were so artificial that their combined existence now seems an almost eccentric interlude in the history of legal procedure. The former imposed a pattern on the evidence received at trials that emphasized the palpable and the physical. Means and opportunity were the most common facts produced at trials; hardly anything else mattered, even motive came a not very distinguished third. The law of evidence gave the judges a most remarkable means of controlling the flow of information. In practice there was not much likelihood that the courts would be overwhelmed by hearsay evidence, but there was every likelihood that they would be overwhelmed with confessions elicited from prisoners. Yet at every stage the prisoner was protected from police and magisterial questioning, and in court he was silent from his arraignment until the allocutus. The cases that restricted police questioning and culminated in *Johnston* constituted a self-denying ordinance that was rare in law enforcement, and most unexpected in a country that was supposed to be endemically crime-ridden and sporadically seditious. Yet the exclusion of confessions did not rest on any great universal principle of fair play. As *Gibney* and *Nolan* showed, the judges had no objection to confessions elicited by fear of divine retribution, or by copious provision of alcohol, or by a prisoner's wish to clear his father of a charge of murder. The exclusion seemed to be aimed mainly at police questioning as a practical evil that was to be discouraged.

Fourthly, the importance of juries in the system cannot be exaggerated. The petty jury was only one among a number of juries that included the coroner's jury, the grand jury, and juries empanelled at the arraignment to consider the prisoner's sanity or silence, or after his conviction to consider his plea in stay of judgment or in bar of execution. The triers who were appointed to resolve challenges for cause or challenges to the array were small juries, who were in their own way as important as any of the others. Unfortunately this study has not revealed any example of the jury of matrons, although technically they existed until 1876. At every point, therefore, matters of fact were resolved by non-lawyers and in theory there was no appeal from their decisions, although occasionally they were in practice set aside. The petty jury, on which so much depended, was entrusted with a wide discretion in its verdicts: it could find a prisoner charged with murder guilty of manslaughter; it could bring in a special verdict, which might involve an elaborate statement of fact; it could find the prisoner not guilty but insane. The one thing it could not do was to make a distinction between capital and non-capital murder, except by recommending the prisoner to mercy. Most remarkable of all, after much doubt and hesitation, the jury was allowed to disagree and to be discharged without returning any verdict. The cases described above relating to the formation of juries suggested, however, that while the jury was all important as a tribunal, its formation was not a matter of great nicety, in spite of legislation that tried to secure properly summoned jurors. In fact, the cases above leave the impression that the judges believed that any twelve men, regardless of the means by which they had been summoned, were a fit jury, if they had come through the ordeal of being challenged and if they had taken the oath.

Nineteenth-century jury reform was a curate's egg: parts of it were thorough, and parts were perfunctory. Jurors' qualifications were changed by the acts of 1833 and 1871; the sheriff's discretionary power to select the long panel was taken away by the 1871 act; the establishment of the winter assizes in 1877 led to changes in venue, which meant that many prisoners were no longer tried by their own 'country'. The peace preservation act of 1870, the prevention of crime act of 1882, and its successor in 1887 made changes of venue easier in certain cases. The most surprising fact about the conduct of criminal trials in Ireland was the survival until 1871 of the sheriff's power to select the long panel, and even after 1871, the survival of the crown solicitor's right to order jurors to stand by. Every jury was 'packed', or partially packed, if not by the sheriff and the crown solicitor, then by the prisoner's challenges and by the jurors' vagaries of residence, status, and property. It was difficult to find cases where jury-packing was obvious, but the charge was easily made – by both Crown and prisoner. Sir Colman O'Loghlen, when he introduced a bill into the house of commons to limit the Crown's right to order jurors to stand by, could impugn the system that had conferred high office on him without descending to the necessity of describing any case in his own experience! Further reforms that were necessary to remove the possibility of such glibly made accusations were, in retrospect, obvious: (1) a method of selection that reduced challenges to a minimum, whether from the Crown or the prisoner; (2) majority verdicts, to reduce the need for challenges and to prevent miscarriages of justice caused by one or two partial jurors; (3) specially constructed juries to deal with cases that aroused sectarian animosity.

Death sentences and hangings in Ireland

THERE ARE SEVERAL SOURCES OF statistics of death sentences and hangings in nineteenth-century Ireland. The annual returns of committals and annual reports of the inspectors general of prisons, for example, which were published as parliamentary papers from the 1820s, have figures for sentences and executions (for references see Bibliography). For the years 1822–34, however, the most convenient sources are two parliamentary papers: *Summary statements of the number of persons charged with criminal offences, who were committed to the different gaols in Ireland for trial at the assizes and sessions held in the several counties, cities, towns, and liberties therein, during the last seven years* ..., pp 8–9, HC 1829 (256), xxii, 434–5, and *Thirteenth report of the inspectors general on the general state of the prisons of Ireland, 1835*, p. 60, HC 1836 (114), xxxvi, 440. The succeeding reports of the inspectors general of prisons have figures for the years from 1835 to 1851. The Death Book 1852–1932 (NAI, GPB/CN/5), which was compiled by the Convict Department, has a list of hangings from 1852. *Thom's Directory* has figures for hangings for the years 1837–56. The *Judicial Statistics* of Ireland, have the names and short descriptions of those who were sentenced to death and hanged from the mid-1860s onwards (for references see Bibliography).

NAI, OP (MA) 146/6 [1864], which was printed in *Report of the capital punishment commission, with minutes of evidence, and appendix*, pp 612–13 [3590], HC 1866, xxi, 664–5, gave for each of the years 1823–63 the number sentenced to death and the number hanged, distinguishing those sentenced and hanged for murder from those sentenced to death and hanged for other offences. A note in NAI, RP/1888/7593 states that OP (MA) 146/6 [1864] was compiled from returns made by the clerks of the crown, but in fact it seems to have come from the reports of the inspectors general of prisons and the Death Book.

NAI, RP/1888/7593 was compiled at the request of the home office, which in turn had been asked by the Belgian government for information on 'the infliction of the penalty of death in Great Britain and Ireland during the last 25 years'. This paper gives the number of those charged with murder, committed, sentenced, and hanged during the years 1862–86. An early draft had been corrected because of discrepancies between it and a table called 'A'. (The compiler noted that 'it will be observed that the number of prisoners condemned to death in 1862, 1871, 1881, 1882, and 1884, as shown in this Return, does not agree with the numbers for those years as given in Return already on File marked A.'). The cause of the problem was that the first compilation was based on the returns of the clerks of the crown, while table 'A' was based on the records of the Convict Department, which meant in practice the Death Book, already referred to. The compiler noted that 'the records of the convict dept are no doubt more correct than the returns of the clerks of the crown & peace from which I took the no. of condemned persons.'

(A) Death sentences and hangings 1822– 62

The figures given here are taken from NAI, OP (MA) 146/6 [1864], except those for 1822, which are taken from *Summary statements of the number of persons charged with criminal offences* ..., HC 1829 (256), xxii, 427. 'Murder' means actual murder, not attempted murder, conspiracy to murder, etc.. The figures in the square brackets give executions as percentages of sentences pronounced.

	sentences of death pronounced			number of executions		
years	for murder	for other crimes	total	for murder	for other crimes	total
1822	54	287	341	42	59	101
1823	21	220	241	18	43	61
1824	49	246	295	41	19	60
1825	17	164	181	9	9	18
1826	28	253	281	17	17	34
1827	22	324	346	12	25	37
1828	33	178	211	16	5	21
1829	28	196	224	21	17	38
1830	28	234	262	14	25	39
total	280	2102	2382	190[68]	219[10]	409[17]
1831	27	280	307	25	12	37
1832	19[1]	300	319	17	22	39
1833	38	199	237	26	13	39
1834	49	148	197	31	12	43
1835	31	148	179	19	8	27
1836	22	153	175	12	2	14
1837	21	133	154	10	0	10
1838	8	31	39	3	0	3
1839	30	36	66	15	2	17
1840	15	28	43	0	0	0
total	260	1456	1716	158[61]	71[5]	229[13]

[1] The figure of 31 is given in *Thirteenth report of the inspectors general on the general state of the prisons of Ireland, 1835*, p. 60, HC 1835 (114), xxxvi, 440.

[2] According to *Twentieth report of the inspectors general on the general state of the prisons of Ireland, 1841; with appendices*, p. 86 [377], HC 1842, xxii, 332 there were 4 hangings in 1841; at p. 84, however, the figure of 5 was given.

	sentences of death pronounced			number of executions		
years	for murder	for other crimes	total	for murder	for other crimes	total
1841	17	23	40	5	0	5[2]
1842	11	14	25	4	0	4
1843	12	4	16	4	1	5
1844	19	1	20	8	1	9
1845	9	4	13	3	0	3
1846	9	5	14	4	3	7
1847	23	2	25	8	10	18[4]
1848	44	16	60	24	4	28
1849[3]	0	1	1	0	0	0
1850	15	2	17	8	0	8
total	159	72	231	68[43]	19[26]	87[38]
1851	11	6	17	2	0	2
1852	14	8	22	3	3	6
1853	13	2	15	7	2	9
1854	4	2	6	3	1	4
1855	4	1	5	0	0	0
1856	6	2	8	2	1	3
1857	5	3	8	0	0	0
1858	5	3	8	4	0	4
1859	2	0	2	0	0	0
1860	5	2	7	2	0	2
total	69	29	98	23[33]	7[24]	30[31]
1861	1	1	2	1	0	1
1862	6	0	6	4	0	4

3 In *Thom's Directory 1851*, p. 183 the figures for 1849 were: sentences for murder 28, total death sentences 38, total hanged 15 (13 for murder, 1 for solicitation to murder, and 1 for shooting with intent to kill). The returns in *Thom's* were checked and found to coincide with those in *Tables of the number of criminal offenders committed for trial or bailed for appearance at the assizes and sessions in each county in the year 1849, and the result of the proceedings*, p. 90 [1271], HC 1850, xlv, 618.

4 At *Thom's Directory 1850*, p. 107 only 8 hangings, all for murder, were recorded for 1847.

(B) Numbers arrested for murder, returned for trial, sentenced to death, and hanged 1862–1919

The figures for 1862–86 are taken from 'Table A' in NAI, RP/1888/7593. Where these are not the same as the figures in Death Book 1852–1932 (NAI, GPB/CN/5), the figures from the latter are inserted in square brackets. The corrections suggest that in spite of the efforts of Charlemont House and Dublin Castle, something went wrong in compiling Table A in NAI, RP/1888/7593. Part of the problem was the fact that the compilers of RP/1888/7593 used the summary in the Death Book, which does not include all of the sentences and executions returned from the different circuits. The latter have been used here.

The figures for those 'prosecuted' and those 'committed' in RP/1888/7593 were almost certainly taken from the *Judicial Statistics*; those 'prosecuted' were those *arrested* for all murders, including infanticides; those 'committed', however, were not those 'committed', but those who were *returned for trial*, which was a smaller group.

The figures for death sentences and hangings for the period 1887–1919 are taken from the Death Book.

The fact that 11 were sentenced to death in 1883 and 12 hanged reflects the effects of the winter assizes: Sylvester Poff was sentenced in December 1882 and hanged in January 1883.

year	arrested	returned for trial	sentenced	executed
1862	–	41	7[6]	3[4]
1863	65	22	4	4
1864	53	27	7[8]	0[1]
1865	55	29	5	4
1866	55	17	4[6]	0[2]
1867	70	15	0[7]5	0
1868	53	22	0	0
1869	125	23	0	0
1870	90	28	4	3
1871	63	28	3[5]	1[2]
1872	70	39	2	0
1873	75	20	4	3
1874	74	26	3	0
1875	97	26	3	3
1876	67	27	4	4
1877	67	37	0	0
1878	55	26	3[2]	0
1879	78	33	4	2
1880	67	45	3	2

5   These seven death sentences were passed at the special commission that tried fenians such as Patrick Doran.

year	arrested	returned for trial	sentenced	executed
1881	106	36	5[7]	0
1882	176	49	21[22]	6
1883	64	39	11	12
1884	48	26	5[7]	2
1885	52	25	4	2
1886	40	21	3[5]	2
1887			2	0
1888			8	3
1889			4	3
1890			1	0
1891			4	2
1892			7	3
1893			5	3
1894			1	1
1895			2	1
1896			1	0
1897			2	0
1898			3	2
1899			5	3
1900			3	1
1901			3	3
1902			2	2
1903			3	2
1904			7	4
1905			6	1
1906			1	0
1907			0	0
1908			2	1
1909			1	1
1910			3	1
1911			1	1
1912			1	0
1913			1	0
1914			0	0
1915			3	0
1916			1	0
1917			3	0
1918			2	0
1919			1	0

The abolition of capital punishment

THE IRISH PARLIAMENT DID NOT produce the equivalent of the English 'bloody code'. According to Neal Garnham between 1690 and 1760 the Irish parliament passed only 29 statutes creating capital offences, which was 'less than half the number created at Westminster'.[1] Of 30 Irish acts dealing with offences against property passed during the reigns of George II and George III, for example, only 7 imposed death without benefit of clergy.[2] Both of these estimates suggest a meagre record compared with that of the British parliament, which, according to V.A.C. Gatrell, created 200 capital offences in the early nineteenth century alone.[3] The difference between England and Ireland is shown by the use of capital punishment in the two countries in the 1820s. Assuming that in the 1820s Ireland's population was about half that of England's, there were relatively fewer sentences of death pronounced in Ireland in 1822–8 (271 annually compared with 1,161 in England), and there were fewer hangings in Ireland for offences other than murder (18 annually compared with 44 in England).[4] On the other hand, there were far more sentences of death for murder pronounced in Ireland (32 annually compared with 15 in England), and more hangings for all offences (47 annually compared with 57 in England).[5]

The curtailment of capital punishment had a protracted and complicated history in the United Kingdom. In the case of Ireland the history seems to have begun in 1821 when parliament substituted imprisonment for hanging as the punishment for stealing goods worth 5s.[6] Two acts in 1823, extending benefit of clergy to certain offences, seem to have had little effect on Ireland: they did not refer to acts of the Irish parliament or to acts of the United Kingdom parliament applying to Ireland, and they did not reduce the number

1 Neal Garnham, *The courts, crime and the criminal law in Ireland 1692–1760* (Dublin, 1996), p. 25.

2 *The statutes at large, passed in the parliaments held in Ireland: from the third year of Edward II, AD 1310, to the thirty-eighth year of George III, AD 1798, inclusive, with marginal notes, and a complete index to the whole,* 18 vols (Dublin, 1799); Andrew Newton Oulton, *The index to the statutes, at present in force in, or affecting Ireland, from the year 1310 to 1835 inclusive* (Dublin, 1836).

3 *The hanging tree: execution and the English people 1770–1868* (Oxford, 1994), p. 7. See also David Bentley, *English criminal justice in the nineteenth century* (London and Rio Grande, 1998), p. 11.

4 These figures were taken from *Summary statements of the number of persons charged with criminal offences, who were committed to the different gaols in Ireland for trial at the assizes and sessions held in the several counties, cities, towns, and liberties therein, during the last seven years ... 1822–1828,* pp 8–9, HC 1829 (256), xxii, 434–5 and *Report of the capital punishment commission, with minutes of evidence, and appendix,* pp 656–7 [3590], HC 1866, xxi, 708–9.

5 The number of convictions for murder implied by these 32 sentences of death seems low (about 0.4 per 100,000 population). In Berlin, in the 1880s, for example, there was just under 1 conviction for murder per 100,000; in 1909–12 there were 8 per 100,000 (Vincent E. McHale & Jeffrey Bergner, 'Collective and individual violence: Berlin and Vienna, 1875–1913' in *Criminal Justice History,* 2 (1981), 31–6).

6 1 & 2 Geo. IV, c. 34 (28 May 1821).

of death sentences passed in Ireland.[7] The first major legislative change came in 1828 and 1829 when parliament passed four acts relating to Ireland, which were analogous to acts that had just been applied to England by Sir Robert Peel.[8] The first act repealed acts of the Irish parliament and acts of the United Kingdom parliament that had imposed the death penalty as a punishment for offences against property; the second and third defined the offences against property that would in future be capital; the fourth repealed capital statutes relating to crimes against the person and defined the offences against the person that would in future be capital. The acts relating to Ireland that were repealed by the Criminal Statutes (Ireland) Repeal Act 1828 and the Offences Against the Person (Ireland) Act 1829 were numerous: there were about 40 dating from the beginning of the reign of George II to 1800, and probably as many more for the periods before George II and after 1800.[9]

Having repealed numerous acts of parliament, three of the four acts created a new scale of punishments that included death, transportation, imprisonment, and whipping for offences against the person,[10] malicious offences against property[11], and larceny.[12] Capital punishment was still reserved for numerous offences other than murder. The Offences Against the Person Act 1829, for example, retained capital punishment not only for murder, attempted murder, conspiring to murder, and soliciting to murder, but also for sodomy, rape, having carnal knowledge of a girl under ten and for the forcible abduction of women.[13]

The two acts relating to larceny and malicious offences against property were sparing, compared with their predecessors, in their use of the death penalty. The larceny act made the following offences capital: robbery, stealing from a church, burglary, house-breaking, plundering a wrecked ship, and stealing horses, cattle, and sheep. Burglary, which was house-breaking during the night, included 'entering the house of another with intent to commit felony, or being in such dwelling house, shall commit felony'. House-breaking, which was by definition done during daylight, was capital if property 'to the value in the whole of five pounds or more' was stolen; if property less than this was stolen, house-breaking was capital only if 'any person therein' had been 'put in fear.' The act relating to malicious injuries to property made the following capital: setting fire to a house, outbuilding, church or chapel, coalmine, or a stack of corn; setting fire to a ship or showing false signals to lead a ship to its destruction, damaging the ship, or impeding those who were trying to save the ship's company; killing or maiming cattle.

These four acts were in effect a new penal code for offences against the person, larceny, and malicious injuries to property, but they were not a complete code, affecting all capital offences that existed in 1828. They did not refer to subjects such as treason, piracy, or forgery, nor did they refer to smaller subjects, such as embezzlement by servants of the Bank of Ireland, which remained capital until 1842. Capital punishment for many forms of forgery was indeed abolished in 1830 in England, but the act did not apply to Ireland or Scotland.[14] Nor did the four acts sweep away all of the old, rather redundant capital

7   4 Geo. IV, cc 53, 54 (8 July 1823). For sentences of death passed in Ireland, see Appendix 1, above, p. 376.

8   9 Geo. IV, cc 53, 55, 56 (15 July 1828), and 10 Geo. IV, c. 34 (4 June 1829). The analogous English acts were 7 & 8 Geo. IV, cc 29, 30, and 9 Geo. IV, c. 31.

9   9 Geo. IV, c. 53; 10 Geo. IV, c. 34.

10 10 Geo. IV, c. 34 (4 June 1829).   11 9 Geo. IV, c. 53 (15 July 1828).

12 9 Geo. IV, c. 54 (15 July 1828).   13 Above, p. 8.

14 11 Geo. IV & 1 Will. IV, c. 66, s. 29 (23 July 1830). In spite of the explicit statement in s. 29, excluding Ireland, s. 2 made it high treason to forge either the great seal of Ireland or the privy seal.

offences that had accumulated since the early eighteenth century. It remained, for example, a capital offence until 1842 to return to Ireland after serving in the French army or navy.

As a penal code the new legislation did not survive intact for long. In 1832 when the whigs amended the Irish larceny act (and its English equivalent) to make two of its offences non-capital, they began what became an almost annual assault on the acts of 1828–9: they made stealing property worth five pounds from a dwelling house and stealing horses, cattle, and sheep non-capital,[15] they made counterfeiting non-capital,[16] and they made forgery, other than the forging of wills and powers of attorney to transfer stock, including stock transferable at the Bank of Ireland, non-capital.[17] In 1833 the whigs again amended the larceny act (and its English equivalent) to make housebreaking, entering, and stealing non-capital.[18] In 1835 they amended the English and Irish larceny acts to make two more offences non-capital: letter stealing by servants of the post office (which involved repealing several acts of the Irish parliament) and stealing from a church.[19] These changes were so radical that they enabled the abolitionist MP, William Ewart, to claim that 'the whole of [Peel's] edifice, erected with so much care and trouble, was tumbling to pieces.'[20]

From 1835 there was a pause until 1837, when six acts repealed not only parts of the acts of 1828–9 but parts of the more recent acts as well. The first of the six acts amended the Offences Against the Person Act 1829: it retained capital punishment for attempted murder, for conspiracy to murder, for soliciting to murder, and for sodomy, rape, having carnal knowledge of a girl under ten and for the forcible abduction of women.[21]

Three of the six acts abolished practically every remaining capital offence relating to property. The first abolished capital punishment for burglary as such, but retained it for those who shall 'burglariously break and enter into any dwelling house, and shall assault with intent to murder any person being therein, or shall stab, cut, wound, beat, or strike any such person.' (Burglary was defined in section 4 as house-breaking taking place between 9 p.m. and 6 a.m.)[22] The second of these three acts made robbery and the plundering of wrecks non-capital.[23] The only capital offence connected with robbery that remained capital was when a robber 'at the time of or immediately before or immediately after such robbery shall stab, cut, or wound any person.' The third act retained capital punishment for setting fire to a house, for setting fire to a ship with intent to murder, and for showing lights to cause a shipwreck, but abolished it for impeding those trying to save shipwrecked sailors, and for setting fire to churches, chapels, ships, stacks of corn, and coal mines, all of which had been made capital in 1828.[24] This act did not, however, mention killing or maiming cattle, which remained capital until 1842.

The remaining two of the six acts addressed themselves to subjects not dealt with by the four acts of 1828–9: the first made forging wills and powers of attorney to transfer stock non-capital,[25] and the second made piracy non-capital except when piracy was preceded or followed by 'assault with intent to murder, any person being on board of or

15   2 & 3 Will. IV, c. 62 (11 July 1832).   16   2 & 3 Will. IV, c. 34, s. 3 (23 May 1832).
17   2 & 3 Will. IV, c. 123 (16 Aug. 1832).   18   3 & 4 Will. IV, c. 44 (14 Aug. 1833).
19   5 & 6 Will. IV, c. 81 (10 Sept. 1835).
20   Quoted in V.A.C. Gatrell, *The hanging tree. Execution and the English people 1770–1868* (Oxford, 1994), p. 570.
21   7 Will. & 1 Vict., c. 85 (17 July 1837). Above, p. 9.
22   7 Will. & 1 Vict., c. 86 (17 July 1837).   23   7 Will. & 1 Vict., c. 87 (17 July 1837).
24   7 Will. & 1 Vict., c. 89 (17 July 1837).   25   7 Will. & 1 Vict., c. 84 (17 July 1837).

belonging to such ship or vessel, or shall stab, cut, or wound any such person, or unlawfully do any act by which the life of such person may be endangered.'[26] The sixth act repealed acts that had made the following offences capital: seducing members of the armed forces from their allegiance and inciting to mutiny (which involved repealing an act of the Irish parliament), slave-trading, smuggling, and shooting at preventive officers.[27] This act also repealed two acts of the Irish parliament that had imposed death without benefit of clergy for rescuing murderers from prison and for inciting members of the armed forces to mutiny.

The act of 1842, which followed an act of 1841 for England, combined an assault on what was left of the acts of 1828–9 with a vigorous antiquarian clearing up of older acts.[28] Sections 13–15 addressed themselves to the acts of 1828–9 and made the following offences non-capital: rape, having carnal knowledge of girls under ten, abduction, and killing and wounding cattle. The following old acts were either repealed or made non-capital: an act to prevent marriages by degraded clergymen and popish priests (12 Geo. I, c. 3), an act for inflicting punishment of death on owners, masters, and sailors, who burnt their ships (11 Geo. II, c. 5), an act to prohibit the return of subjects of the king who had entered the service of the French king (29 Geo. II, c. 5), an act for inflicting punishment of death on servants of the Bank of Ireland who were guilty of embezzlement, an act for inflicting death for obstructing the corn trade, an act for preventing tumultuous risings and assemblies, an act for preventing mobs demolishing churches or chapels, an act for inflicting death on those who seized arms or ammunition, an act for inflicting death on those who received escaped prisoners, and an act for inflicting death on those who returned from transportation.

It requires a certain effort of memory to recall when certain offences ceased to be capital. Murder, attempted murder, solicitation to murder, conspiracy to murder, sodomy, 'unnatural offences', burglary with violence, arson of dwelling houses, and robbery with violence remained capital until 1861. Rape, carnal knowledge of children under ten, and abduction remained capital until 1842. The royal commission on capital punishment in its attempt to summarize the history of abolition in Ireland noted that after the legislation of 1837 capital offences in Ireland included murder, attempted murder (which included shooting at the person), conspiracy to murder, solicitation to murder, rape, carnal abuse of children, sodomy, bestiality, burglary with violence to persons, robbery 'attended with cutting or wounding', and arson of dwelling houses, 'endangering the lives of inmates'.[29] This list was not exhaustive, however; the commissioners went on to mention 'treason; piracy, where murder was attempted or life was endangered; abduction of women; casting away ships, and showing false signals to cause shipwreck; maiming cattle; destruction of buildings under certain circumstances; certain kinds of tumultuous assemblies, and the forcible seizure of arms; prison breach, returning from transportation before the term of sentence had expired, and harbouring the principal offenders; celebration of certain illegal marriages; embezzlement by servants of the Bank of Ireland.'

The commission noted that the act of 1842 got rid of rape and abduction as capital offences 'and most of the other offences lastly enumerated.' Nearly all of these 'lastly

26   7 Will. & 1 Vict., c. 88 (17 July 1837).   27   7 Will. IV & 1 Vict., c. 91 (17 July 1837).
28   5 Vict., c. 28 (18 June 1842).
29   *Report of the capital punishment commission, with minutes of evidence, and appendix,* pp 611–12 [3590], HC 1866, xxi, 663–4. See also NAI, OP(MA), 146/6 for a slightly different account.

enumerated' offences, except treason and piracy, can be identified in the paragraph above on the 1842 act, but not all. The 1842 act, for example, did not mention the repeal of the Burning of Buildings, etc. Act 1837, section 5, which made showing false signals to cause shipwreck a capital offence.[30] In practice, the commission is not a bad guide; it noted, for example, that killing and maiming cattle persisted as a capital offence until 1842, a point that troubled Richard Moore at Wexford summer assizes in 1840 when he came to sentence a woman who had been found guilty of poisoning a cow. Moore's uncertainty is reassuring to historians stupefied by attempts to describe the history of abolition:

> The statute under which she was indicted is 9 Geo. IV, c. 56, section 17 [Malicious Injuries to Property Act 1828], and the punishment there recorded is that of death. I cannot find that the punishment of death is commuted by any subsequent statute. The statute of 2 & 3 Will. IV, c. 62 [Punishment of Death Act 1832] which in many cases commutes the punishment of death to transportation for life does not refer to the statute of 9 Geo IV. The statute of 1 Vict., c. 89 [Burning of Buildings, etc. Act 1837] does refer to the above statute, and makes an alteration in the punishment in some of the offences therein mentioned, but does not extend to the offence of maliciously killing cattle. 1 Vict., c. 90, section 2 [Solitary Confinement Act 1837] recites the 7 & 8 Geo. IV, c. 3, which is the English act as to malicious injuries done to cattle & it there alters the punishment, but there is no reference to the Irish act of 9 Geo. IV relating to the same offences. On consulting with Judge Perrin, and also with crown counsel, it appeared to us all that the punishment of death awarded by 9 Geo. IV has not been commuted, and I was therefore under the necessity of recording sentence of death against the prisoner.[31]

He asked the lord lieutenant to commute the recorded sentence of death to four months' imprisonment! Killing and maiming cattle was not the only capital offence that survived longer in Ireland than in England. Returning from transportation, for example, which had been made capital in Ireland only in 1828 remained capital until 1842, although it had been made non-capital in England in 1834.[32]

In practice the crimes for which prisoners were hanged were not as numerous or as varied as the abolishing acts suggested. Of the 332 hangings in Ireland in the years 1822–8, murder accounted for almost half (155). Other offences against the person accounted for 25 (abduction 5, cutting and wounding 7, and rape 13); offences against property accounted for 79 (burglary 56, highway robbery 23).[33] If arson (17) is added to offences

There is a useful, but not complete, list of offences that were capital in England after 1838 in *'Return of the number of persons capitally convicted in England and Wales from the year 1838 to 1852, both inclusive; specifying the offences and sentences, and whether and how carried into effect by execution or otherwise'*, HC 1852–3 (386), lxxxi, 277.

30   7 Will. and 1 Vict., c. 89.

31   NAI, CRF/1840/Byrne/40.

32   4 & 5 Will. IV, c. 67 (13 Aug. 1834) made returning from transportation non-capital in England; 9 Geo. IV, c. 54, s. 16 (15 July 1828), passed at a time when so many offences were being made non-capital, had made it capital it Ireland. For an example of a sentence of death being recorded in 1838 for returning from transportation see NAI, CRF/1838/Carroll/50.

33   *Summary statements of the number of persons charged with criminal offences, who were committed to the different gaols in Ireland for trial at the assizes and sessions held in the several counties, cities,*

against property they accounted for 96, which is almost one-third of the total. The remainder (56) was accounted for by riotous assembly (12, of which 11 were in 1822), appearing armed by night (1), attacking dwelling houses at night (15), and robbery of arms (8). Some capital offences were not capital in practice in the 1820s: 33 forgers were sentenced to death but none was hanged; 30 sheep-stealers were sentenced but none was hanged. None of the exotic offences, such as serving the French king, which would have given a touch of distinction to the dreary chronicle of killing, thieving, burning, and raping, provided the gallows with a victim.

The effect of the abolitionist legislation was demonstrated by the dates when the last hangings for particular offences occurred. The last hangings for burglary and larceny were in 1832 (3 for burglary and 3 for larceny); the last for robbery of arms were in 1833 (2); the last for arson (1), highway robbery (1), riotous assembly (1), and being an accessory and aiding in rape (3) were in 1834; the last for rape (4) and abduction (1) were in 1835.[34] It is worth noting here that in some of these cases the last hanging occurred years before the offence was made non-capital by law. The last hanging for arson in 1832 anticipated the removal of arson as a capital offence by nearly thirty years; the last hangings for rape and abduction in 1835 anticipated by seven years the act of 1842 that made them non-capital. Even though there was little chance that a sentence of death would be carried out judges were obliged to go on pronouncing sentence. The last death sentences for abduction were pronounced in 1841 (in 7 cases), although the last hanging had been in 1835; the last death sentences for rape were pronounced in 1842 (in 10 cases), although the last hanging had been in 1835. The fact that offences such as rape became non-capital in practice long before they ceased to be capital by law seems to have been due to the lord lieutenant's exercise of the prerogative of mercy. Lord Chief Justice Doherty, for example, told the house of lords select committee on the state of Ireland of a rape case he had tried at the Clonmel spring assizes in 1836. The lord lieutenant's commutation of the death sentence was not done with his consent:

> It appeared to me to be a peculiarly aggravated case, and the evidence clear. There was a reference to me in the usual way, to know whether there were any circumstances in the case which would render the prisoner a proper object of mercy. From the peculiar circumstances of that case, with the detail of which it is probably unnecessary to trouble your lordships, I felt bound to give it as my opinion that there were no circumstances in the case which rendered the prisoner a proper object of mercy. Mercy was extended to him subsequently; I am not aware upon what grounds.[35]

towns, and liberties therein, during the last seven years ... 1822–1828, pp 8–9, HC 1829 (256), xxii, 434–5.

34 This information in this paragraph on hangings and sentences of death was taken from the annual reports of inspectors of prisons; for full references to the reports published in the 1830s and 1840s, see Bibliography pp 400–1.

35 *Minutes of evidence taken before the select committee of the house of lords appointed to enquire into the state of Ireland, since the year 1835, in respect of crime and outrage, which have rendered life and property insecure in that part of the empire*, pt III, *evidence 12 June to 19 July*, p. 882, HC 1839 (486-III), xii, 18.

Weapons, motives, and people

The weapons that inflicted mortal wounds did not suggest sophistication. Table 1 shows the methods of inflicting death in 'homicides' returned by the police, which included murders and manslaughters but not infanticides.[1] The most common means of inflicting death were 'blunt instruments' and 'blows and kicks' which accounted for 63% of deaths

TABLE 1

DIFFERENT METHODS OF KILLING GIVEN AS PERCENTAGES

means	1830s/1840s	1860s/1870s
blunt instruments	36	19
blows and kicks	27	34
gunshot wounds	12	4
stabbings	6	12
fights and falls	5	8
poisoning	3	1
other	11	22

in the late 1830s and early 1840s. Stones, which were included with blunt instruments, were probably the most commonly used weapon, accounting for 16%, which was more than gunshot wounds and stabbings but behind blows and kicks. By the late 1860s and early 1870s, prosperity, literacy, and the removal of the cottiers produced killers who killed in slightly different ways, although it is difficult to discern a seismic increase in sophistication. Blunt instruments and blows and kicks accounted for 53%; stones accounted for 10%, which put them ahead of gunshot wounds, but just behind stabbings. The increase in stabbings to 12% (from 6%) may reflect more opportunities to use forks, which in turn depended on an increase in pastoral farming. The relative infrequency of gunshot wounds as a cause of death in both periods suggests that homicide was generally an intimate affair because most shooting incidents that did occur involved parties who were socially remote from each other. In July 1865 Edward Warren Gray, for example, was put on trial for shooting Peter Shevlin during an election riot. In the same month Laurence King shot James Henry Clutterbuck, a lieutenant in the 5th Fusiliers (the motive was robbery, which was a rare cause of murder in Ireland).[2] There were of course occasions

1 Table 1 and what follows on weapons, motives, location etc. is based on two samples of murder cases from collections in the National Archives: the first from the Outrage Papers (for years in the late 1830s and early 1840s) and the second from the Irish Crime Records (for years in the 1860s and 1870s).
2 NAI, Irish Crime Records, passim. For the negative relationship between firearms and social

when guns were used in what were obviously intimate rows. In 1888 a bridegroom was shot as he was about to be married in the parish church of Knocknamuckley near Portadown. The assailant was his brother-in-law, who had 'previously taken up a position in the church, drew a revolver, and shot him through the chest, from the effects of which he died after a few hours' suffering.'[3]

Before the Famine killings tended to be in public rather than in private, as Table 2 shows.

TABLE 2

DIFFERENT LOCATIONS OF HOMICIDES GIVEN AS PERCENTAGES

location	*1830s/1840s*
coming home from fairs and markets	25
in or near public houses	21
on roads	14
in fields	9
dances and weddings	3
faction fights and games	3
at home	18
other	7

The most dangerous activities were coming from fairs or drinking in public houses, which together accounted for 46% of homicides. If all the public and the quasi-public locations are combined, they account for 75% of locations, which is remarkable. By the 1860s and 1870s homicide had apparently become less public: only 56% were killed in public or quasi-public locations, such as coming home from fairs, or on the roads, or in public houses, or at weddings and games. Coming home from fairs fell to 15% (from 25%) and homicides in public houses fell to 9% (from 21%). Before concluding that homicide had become less public because the police were imposing order on roads and in public houses, two things must be remembered. First, the percentage killed in their own homes had hardly changed since the 1840s (17% compared with 18%). Secondly, in the 1860s and 1870s it was difficult to identify the place of attack in 26% of the cases. In December 1873, for example, James Connors, a publican aged 79, 'died from the effects of a bite in the thumb of the right hand, inflicted in a drunken quarrel by William Brown, who has absconded', but it is not clear where the attack took place.[4] If most of these 26%, whose location could not be identified, were distributed among the components of the 56% who were killed in public, they would bring the figure for the later period close to the figure of 75% that was obtained for the earlier period.

Those who were killed are easy enough to characterize. Before the Famine about a third were young children, but by the late 1860s and early 1870s young children were relatively more important (43% compared with 34% before the Famine). Table 3 shows the status or occupations of those who were not young children.

propinquity see Vaughan, *Landlords and tenants*, pp 144–5.
3   *Irish Ecclesiastical Gazette*, 10 Mar. 1888. (I am indebted to Dr Susan Hood, of the RCB Library, for this reference).
4   NAI, Irish Crime Records, passim.

TABLE 3

FARMERS, LABOURERS, AND WOMEN GIVEN AS PERCENTAGES OF THOSE KILLED

	1842–6	1860s/1870s
labourers	38	16
farmers	16	30
women	8	9
others	38	45

The second column, giving percentages for the years 1842–6, is based on a return of murders and attempted murders that was published as a parliamentary paper in 1846.[5] Farmers and labourers accounted for 54% in 1842–6, women for only 8%; the remaining 38% included a diversity of male occupations, such as bailiffs, soldiers, policemen, rent-warners, gardeners, stone masons, and an itinerant piper. By the 1860s and 1870s farmers and labourers had fallen to 46% (compared with 54% before the Famine), and women to 9% (compared with 8%), which suggests that women were neither better nor worse off.[6] The remainder now amounted to 45% and consisted of skilled craftsmen (18%), children who were not 'infants' (5%), servants (2%), and a miscellaneous category (10%), which contained a petty sessions clerk, a harbourmaster, a publican, a private in the Tyrone militia, and an army pensioner. The big change, however, between the two periods was not the decline in farmers and labourers, but the inversion of their position, with the former emerging as more numerous than the latter, which reflects the great changes that had taken place in the countryside after the Famine.

Why did people kill each other? Table 4 suggests that they killed for fairly common-place reasons.

In the late 1830s and early 1840s the most common causes of homicides were brawls, quarrels, and family disputes, which together accounted for 61%. These were followed by landlord and tenant disputes (8%), litigation and the enforcement of legal rights (5%), robbery (5%), 'immorality' (4%), disputes between tenants (3%), trade disputes (3%). ('Immorality' in practice meant men killing women whom they had raped or were trying to rape.) At the bottom, in the 'others' category was a miscellany of minor causes, such as faction fights, tithes, party feuds, rows about wills, criminal negligence, attacks by maniacs, and 'love' (whose paucity suggests that the *crime passionel* was not common in Ireland).

---

5   *A return 'of all murders that have been committed in Ireland since the 1st day of January 1842; specifying the county, and the barony of the county where such murder had been committed; the name and condition of the person so murdered; also, a return of the rewards offered in each such instance; where such rewards have been claimed; and where conviction has followed …'*, HC 1846 (220), xxxv, 293.

6   Cf. Carolyn Conley who has found that women were almost 18% of those killed between 1866 and 1892, which is higher than the figure given here for the late 1860s and early 1870s (Carolyn Conley, 'No pedestals: women and violence in late nineteenth-century Ireland' in *Journal of Social History*, 28:4 (summer 1995), 802). For one of nineteenth-century Ireland's most interesting homicides, the killing of Bridget Cleary, see Angela Bourke, *The burning of Bridget Cleary: a true story* (London, 1999).

TABLE 4

CAUSES OF HOMICIDAL ATTACKS GIVEN AS PERCENTAGES

causes	1830s/1840s	1860s/1870s
brawls	22	16
quarrels	20	26
family disputes	19	13
landlord and tenant disputes	8	2
disputes between tenants	3	5
litigation	5	4
party feuds	1	7
trade disputes	3	1
robbery	5	2
'immmorality'	4	5
others	10	19

By the late 1860s and early 1870s the casual still predominated: brawls accounted for 16% (compared with 22% before the Famine), quarrels accounted for 26% (compared with 20%), and family disputes for 13% (compared with 19%). When these were combined they amounted to 55% (compared with 61% before the Famine), which suggests a modest decline in the casual. Party feuds were now 7% (compared with 1%), disputes between tenants were 5% (compared with 3%), litigation and the enforcement of legal rights 4% (compared with 5%), landlord and tenant disputes 2% (compared with 8%), and trade disputes were 1% (compared with 3%). The remaining 19% were caused by criminal neglience (7%), insanity (3%), 'jealousy' (4%), and no explanation (5%). Stealing arms, faction fights, and tithes were not represented in the sample. The most remarkable increase was in homicides caused by party feuds, which increased from 1% in the 1840s to 7%, but party feuds were prominent in the sample for the later period only because it included homicides associated with a by-election in 1864, the riots in Belfast in 1864, and the general elections of 1865 and 1868.

The result of these two samples, which confirm the results of an earlier sample,[7] suggest in a tentative way certain characteristics of Irish society, if it can be assumed that homicides were relatively well documented episodes of social intercourse. Farmers and labourers and their activities (such as coming home from fairs) were prominent in both periods, although farmers were more prominent than labourers in the later period. The casual was dominant in both periods, suggesting irritability rather than deeply felt

7   Cf. Vaughan, 'Ireland *c.*1870' in Vaughan (ed.), *A new history of Ireland,* v, *Ireland under the union I, 1801–70* (Oxford, 1989), p. 771: 'An analysis of the causes of homicide, made by the police in 1876, for example, showed that out of 106 cases only 5 were caused by disputes between landlords and tenants, and that was more than was usual through the decades after the Famine. The most common causes of homicides were 'casual' quarrels (23) and drunken brawls (27), which together accounted for almost half; next in importance were family disputes (10) and occasions for the protection of property or the enforcement of legal rights (9). At the bottom were party fights (6), criminal neglience (6), disputes between tenants about land (4), 'immorality' (4), and poaching affrays (3).'

grievances. The relative immunity of women suggested that they were not frequently involved in matters that caused disputes. The smallness of some causes of dispute, such as faction fights in the 1840s and landlord-tenant disputes in the 1860s, is surprising given contemporary views on the importance of these. What is also surprising are the causes that are poorly represented. Robbery, for example, was unimportant both before and after the Famine; disputes about wills were negligible; poaching was not mentioned;[8] illicit distillation was not a lethal trade; the *crime passionel* was practically unknown; the occasional assassination of a landlord added a touch of distinction to an otherwise pedestrian chronicle.

Carolyn Conley's examination of 1,934 reports of homicides in the Irish Crime Records between 1866 and 1892 takes the history of homicide another three decades beyond the period of the 1860s and 1870s described above. The results of Dr Conley's work, although they refer to a later period, are remarkably like those above. She shows that brawls caused 42.3% of homicides, family disputes caused 22.7%, agrarian and political disputes 11.4%, robberies and rapes 3.7%, religious disputes 2.6%, and other disputes 17.3%.[9] Although the categories and the periods covered are different, the similarity between Dr Conley's brawls and the brawls and quarrels category used above is noteworthy because both yielded 42%. The resemblance between family disputes in both cases is not so great, Dr Conley having 22.7% while the figure of only 13% was given above, but there is no reason why they should closely resemble each other since they represent different periods. Dr Conley's study of the means of inflicting death used different categories from those used above and applied only to brawls, but her category of beatings, kickings, and bitings, which accounted for 55.1% of her sample, is bigger than the 42% ascribed above to 'the blows and kicks' and 'fights and falls', but is not all that much bigger.[10]

The problem with all of these figures is that they do not take one very far. It is clear that most homicides were casual, that most were not committed for money or gain, and that agrarian motives, or political ones, were not common. Dr Conley has tried to take the argument a bit further. Of the 1,934 homicides, she has written that 'the overwhelming majority of them were expressive, i.e., there was no goal or incentive beyond the violence itself.'[11] This is fair enough, although 'inexpressive' might have been a better word to describe the laconic reports in the Irish Crime Records. Dr Conley goes on, however, to argue that 'most violent acts in late nineteenth century Ireland were not only expressive but actually recreational in nature; that is they occurred in brawls in which the parties had agreed to fight and hostility was minimal', and concludes that 'the most remarkable thing about violence in late nineteenth century Ireland was not its political manifestation, but its recreational aspects. Rather than brutal assassins, the characters who emerge from the criminal records are more often people who enjoyed fighting as a sometimes lethal, but rarely malicious form of entertainment.'[12]

---

8   For poaching in England see *Returns of the number of persons convicted of any offences against the game laws at any petty sessions, quarter sessions, or assizes, in England and Wales ... and of all inquests held by the coroners of England and Wales on the bodies of gamekeepers and poachers, from the 1st day of November 1832 to the 1st day of August 1848* ..., HC 1849 (440), xliv, 337.

9   Carolyn A. Conley, *Melancholy accidents: the meaning of violence in post-Famine Ireland* (Lanham, MD, 1999), p. 4.

10 Ibid., p. 34.   11   Ibid., p. 3.   12   Ibid., p. 17.

Recreational is not a bad word here because Table 2 above showed that 46% of homicides before the Famine occurred when those concerned were in public houses or coming home from markets and fairs; but recreational is not, perhaps, the *mot juste*. The problem is not so much 'recreational' in its ordinary meaning, but it is the fact that a precise definition is imposed on it to make brawling a form of duelling, which implies a formality of proceeding that bears little relation to many of the incidents described in the Irish Crime Records. The one activity in the brawls that might be said to resemble duelling was faction fighting, but Dr Conley has found only 40 faction fights in the outrage returns, a figure that accounted for only a small percentage of the 800 and more cases she put into recreational violence.[13]

It is cheering to think that the catalogue of violence in the Irish Crime Records could be made to show that the people of nineteenth-century Ireland were still afflicted by the fact that God had made them mad, and that all their wars were merry and all their songs were sad, but in practice this hopeful interpretation is difficult to establish. The terse, printed reports of homicides in the Irish Crime Records, on which Dr Conley has based her study, convey a remarkable amount of information, considering their brevity. It is easy enough, in many cases, to discern the circumstances of the disputes; it is also easy to identify the weapons; but to establish that the reports describe encounters 'in which the parties had agreed to fight and hostility was minimal' is not easy. The following three examples are from the reports in the Irish Crime Records for the province of Leinster in 1870 (the italics are in the originals):

> JOHN QUINN, pensioner, died from the effect of a fall, occasioned by a push given him by Patrick M'Grath, his step-son, in *a casual drunken quarrel*. M'Grath was sent to be tried at the assizes on a charge of manslaughter; but was indicted for a minor offence only, and found guilty of a common assault. He was sentenced to three months' imprisonment.
> EDWARD QUINN, labourer, died from the effects of kicks on the abdomen, inflicted by Thomas Doyle *in a drunken row*. Doyle was convicted and sentenced to twelve months' imprisonment, with hard labour.
> PATRICK REILLY, poor farmer, accompanied by three of his companions, was returning home at night from Kenagh, where they had been drinking in a public house. On the road a dispute arose between the parties, who were all more or less intoxicated, and in the altercation which ensued the deceased was struck with a heavy bludgeon or stone which fractured his skull, causing his death on the following morning. Francis Coughlan was tried for this offence at the spring assizes, 1871, and acquitted. *Drunkenness is the only cause that can be assigned for this outrage*, as the parties were on good terms before the occurrence.

The parties in these incidents may have agreed to fight, and the hostility may have been minimal, but that does not emerge from the reports. The same reservation about the reports' terseness might be applied to 'expressive' violence. Just because the homicide reports are silent does not mean there was not a reason for the dispute that led to the homicide, strange though that reason might appear when discovered. The trouble with

13 Ibid., p. 20.

mute inglorious Miltons is that they did not get their thoughts into police reports, but their muteness did not mean they were inglorious. Dr Conley has herself suggested a less procrustean definition of recreational violence, which presents fewer problems: 'criminal violence was not a function of political violence so much as a manifestation of custom, alcohol and a keen belief in answering insult with injury.'[14]

14   Ibid., p. 7.

Select bibliography

1. MANUSCRIPT MATERIAL

National Archives
Chief Secretary's Office:
Convict Reference Files; Irish Crime Records; Registered Papers; Official Papers; Outrage Papers; Government Letter Books; Earl of Clarendon's Country Letters; Resident Magistrates' Letter Books; Sheriffs' Letter Books
Chief Crown Solicitor's Office 1842–1921

National Library of Ireland
Larcom Papers

The Library of Trinity College, Dublin
Diaries of John Ryan, 1873–84 (MSS 10348–52)

Suffolk County Record Office
R. v. Corder, prosecution briefs 568/ (Kelly) and 568/2 (Andrews)

Manuscripts in private possession
Judge Keogh's Crown Book, 1856–60 (St Patrick's College, Thurles, Co. Tipperary)

2. HOUSE OF COMMONS SESSIONAL PAPERS

Royal commissions, select committees, and special returns

A copy of any reprieve, or of any pardon, that may have been granted, by the lord lieutenant, to Walter
   Hall, convicted of murder at the commission held in Dublin in February last; and also, copies of any
   report of the trial of the said Walter Hall; or of any other papers or documents relative to the same,
   that may be in the possession of the Irish government ..., HC 1812 (309), v, 1015

Returns of convictions in the provinces of Munster and Connaught during the last ten years; distinguishing
   those at assizes and quarter sessions from those under the insurrection act and peace preservation act;
   and stating the places at which such convictions have taken place and the nature of the offence,
   1814–23, HC 1824 (280), xxii, 15

Report from the select committee on the Irish miscellaneous estimates, with minutes of evidence and
   appendix, HC 1829 (342), iv, 127

Copy of memorial of Francis McBryan and other prisoners, charged with murder at Macken, to the lord
   lieutenant of Ireland, dated Enniskillen gaol, 1st March 1830, complaining of the sub-sheriff of
   Fermanagh county, Ireland, HC 1830 (150), xxvi, 301

Copy of the entry in the clerk of the crown's book, relative to the postponement from the last Cork assizes,
   of the trials of Leary, Magrath and others, charged with a conspiracy to murder, HC 1830 (131),
   xxvi, 637

A return of the number and nature of offences reported to the government as having taken place in the
   county of Clare, in the years 1831 and 1832, HC 1833 (79), xxix, 405

Return of persons for trial at last spring assizes in the counties of Monaghan, Armagh, Antrim and Down,
   and how disposed of; also, of the times appointed for opening the commission in those several counties,
   and of the times when the criminal business was actually commenced and proceeded upon in each ...,
   HC 1833 (402), xxix, 407

Returns of the number of persons tried and found guilty, and tried and acquitted, within the last twelve
   months, in the counties of Kilkenny, Mayo, and Queen's, distinguishing the nature of each offence,
   HC 1833 (66), xxix, 431

Return of the prisoners committed to the gaol of Dundalk, in the county of Louth, from 1st December 1832
   to the date of this return [4 Apr. 1834], setting forth the offence charged in each committal, and how
   disposed of, HC 1834 (386), xlvii, 247

Copies of the several indictments and verdicts against, and the judgements on, David M'Beth, William Murphy,
   and Neal Rock, tried at spring assizes, 1833, for the county of Louth ..., HC 1834 (139), xlvii, 339

Papers relating to the state of Ireland [459], HC 1834, xlvii, 417

Copies or extracts of any correspondence between the foreign office and his majesty's minister at Madrid,
   and the British consul at Malaga, relative to the seizure and putting to death of Mr Boyd, a subject
   of his majesty, HC 1834 (453), xlvii, 521

A return, showing the comparative number of criminal offenders committed in Ireland; and the number
   convicted in each of the last seven years [1828–34], HC 1835 (303), xlv, 343

Second report from His Majesty's commissioners on criminal law [343], HC 1836, xxxvi, 183

A return of all the criminal cases submitted for the decision of the lord lieutenant, on memorial and
   recommendation, from 12 May 1835 [to 31 Mar. 1837]; distinguishing those decided unfavourably,
   without reference to judge or assistant barrister; those decided favourably without such reference, those
   decided unfavourably after, and favourably after similar reference; of those decided favourably without
   reference to judge or assistant barrister; distinguishing how many were referred to magistrates or others
   for local information, how many to gaol authorities for report of conduct, how many were discharged
   on medical report, and how many on recommendation of character, HC 1837 (195), xlvi, 7

Statements on criminal law, prepared by direction of the secretary of state for the home department [88], HC 1837, xlvi, 127

A return of the number of executions which took place for London and Middlesex, in three years ending 31st December 1830; and in three years ending 31 December 1836; together with the number of commitments in each of those periods respectively, for offences that were capital on the 1st of January 1830, HC 1837 (165), xlvi, 255

A return of all rewards offered by proclamation of the lord lieutenant or lords justices of Ireland, for the discovery of the perpetrators of murders and other outrages, from the 1st of January 1836 to the 12th December 1837, with the dates of the proclamations; and distinguishing which of such rewards (if any) have been claimed, and paid by the Irish government ..., HC 1837–8 (157), xlvi, 427

A copy of the correspondence which has recently taken place between Her Majesty's government and the magistrates of the county of Tipperary, relative to the disturbed state of that county, HC 1837–8 (735), xlvi, 571

Report from the select committee of the house of lords, appointed to enquire into the state of Ireland in respect of crime, and to report thereon to the house; with the minutes of evidence taken before the committee, and an appendix and index, pt I, *report, and evidence 22 Apr. to 16 May 1839,* HC 1839 (486–I), xi, 1; pt II, *evidence 27 May to 11 June,* ibid. (486–II), 423; pt III, *evidence 12 June to 19 July,* ibid. (486–III), xii, 1; pt IV, *appendix, and index,* ibid. (486–IV), 477

A return of the number of executions which took place in England and Wales, 1829–33 and 1834–8, together with the number of commitments in each of those periods respectively, for offences which were capital at the commencement of the former period, viz., on the 1st day of January 1829, HC 1839 (547), xxxviii, 15

An abstract of the aggregate number of persons committed for criminal offences in England, Scotland and Ireland, in each of the three past years [1838–40], HC 1841(345), xviii, 543

Returns of the number of names of the barristers appointed in the present year to be supernumerary prosecuting counsel on each circuit in Ireland ..., HC 1842 (170), xxxviii, 1

A return of the number of inquests held by the several coroners of the counties and counties of cities in Ireland, in each month, during the year 1841; specifying the date, place, name of coroner before whom held, and finding of each inquiry, HC 1842 (206), xxxviii, 185

Copies of minutes of the board of treasury, dated the 12th day of October 1841, the 4th day of January 1842, and the 3d day of June 1842, regulating the emoluments of the crown solicitors in Ireland, HC 1842 (508), xxxviii, 259

Copies of the verdict and depositions taken by the coroner at an inquest held on the 19th day of December 1841, on the death of James Flanagan, at Clonearl, in the King's County; of all communications which have taken place between the Irish government, or the inspector-general of constabulary, and the resident stipendiary magistrate, or the local inspector or sub-inspector of police, relative to the death of the said James Flanagan; and of the correspondence which has taken place between Durham Dunlop, Esq. and the Irish government, relative to the death of said James Flanagan, HC 1842 (196), xxxviii, 275

A copy of the instructions given to the respective crown solicitors on each circuit, respecting the challenging of jurors in crown cases, by each of the following gentlemen when filling the office of attorney general in Ireland: Mr Richards, now Baron Richards; Mr O'Loghlen, now Sir Michael O'Loghlen, baronet; Mr Brady, now Chief Baron Brady; Mr Pigott, late attorney general for Ireland; Mr Blackburne, now attorney general for Ireland; specifying the particulars in which they differ, HC 1842 (171), xxxviii, 339

Copies of the memorial of the Rev. Patrick Morgan, parish priest of Drumgooland, near Castlewellan, county of Down, to the lord lieutenant of Ireland, dates on or about the 7th day of January 1842, on the subject of outrages committed in the above locality ..., HC 1842 (190), xxxviii, 375

A return of outrages reported by the constabulary in Ireland during the years 1837, 1838, 1839, 1840, and 1841; a like return of outrages during each month of the year 1842 and for the months of January, February, and March, 1843 [460], HC 1843, li, 149

Abstract of returns from county and other gaols in Ireland, in which none of those sentenced to death for murder from 1836 to 1842 inclusive were executed; stating for each county and year, the number of persons sentenced to death for murder, whose sentences were commuted ..., HC 1844 (521), xxxix, 367

A list of the names of all persons qualified to serve as jurors in the northern division of the county of Tipperary, returned by the collectors of jury cess to the clerk of the peace, submitted by him to the magistrates at special sessions, agreeably to the Act 3 & 4 Will. 4, c. 91, commencing spring assizes 1839, and ending spring assizes 1844; also, a return, for the same period, of the long panel of the above county, from which petty juries are selected, HC 1844 (380), xliii, 161

Report from the select committee on legal education; together with the minutes of evidence, appendix and index, HC 1846 (686), x, 1

A return 'of all aggravated assaults; of all assaults endangering life; of all incendiary fires; of every demand or robbery of arms; of all cases of persons appearing armed; of all unlawful oaths administered or tendered; of all threatening notices or letters delivered or posted; of all malicious injuries to property; and of all firings into dwellings, in Ireland, since the 31st day of December 1845, up to the latest time, as specially reported by the police; specifying the time and place at which each of such offences was committed …', HC 1846 (369), xxxv, 181

Returns 'of the number of persons who have lost their lives in affrays with, or otherwise by, the constabulary in Ireland, in each year since the 1st day of December 1830, specifying the place where each homicide occurred; and also the nature of the warrant, if any, which the constabulary had to execute at the time of such homicide; and also stating what was in each case the verdict of the coroner's inquest, and in which of those cases bills of indictment were preferred, and the manner in which the same were disposed of …', HC 1846 (280), xxxv, 237

Homicides (Ireland). Extracts made by Colonel M'Gregor from the police reports, stating the particulars of the principal homicides in Ireland in the years 1845 and 1846, and forwarded to the home office by him, HC 1846 (179), xxxv, 261

A return 'of all murders that have been committed in Ireland since the 1st day of January 1842; specifying the county, and the barony of the county where such murder had been committed; the name and condition of the person so murdered; also, a return of the rewards offered in each such instance; where such rewards have been claimed; and where conviction has followed …', HC 1846 (220), xxxv, 293

Abstracts of the police reports of some of the principal outrages in the counties of Tipperary, Limerick, Clare, Leitrim, and Roscommon in the year 1845 [710], HC 1846, xxxv, 307

Report of George Wilkin, Esq., barrister-at-law, to the right honourable the lords commissioners of Her Majesty's Treasury, dated 6 July 1847, relating to the disposal of felons' property, HC 1847-8 (in 502), lii, 167

Return, showing how far crimes for which capital punishments have been abolished in this country are still capitally punished in the colonies and dependencies of Great Britain, HC 1850 (69), (738), xxxvi, 1, 27

Returns … of the number of persons tried by courts martial during the existence of military law in Cephalonia, and the sentences awarded, stating how many of those sentences have been carried out; also, the number of persons flogged in Cephalonia, in the year 1849, and by what tribunal sentenced, stating the greatest and the smallest number of lashes inflicted, and the total number of lashes inflicted, HC 1850 (215), xxxvi, 603

'Return of the number of persons, male and female, tried in the United Kingdom for murder, and attempts to murder, by the administration of poison, from the year 1839 to the year 1849, both inclusive …', HC 1850 (599), xlv, 447

A return 'of the jury panel in the criminal court at the last assizes for the county of Mayo, stating the names of the jurors empannelled and sworn in the case of The Queen *versus* Thadeus Derrig *and others; the order in which the persons on said panel were called; the names of those ordered on the part of the Crown to stand by, and the names of the counsel engaged in said prosecution'*, HC 1850 (235), l, 655

Papers relating to an investigation held at Castlewellan into the occurrence at Dolly's brae, on the 12th July, 1849 [1143], HC 1850, li, 331

Return 'from the clerks of the crown and clerks of the peace of the several counties in Ireland, of the number of bills of indictment sent up to the respective grand juries, between 20th day of February 1850 and the 5th day of April 1851; the number found, and the number ignored; and where such have not been found by reason of the non-attendance of witnesses, that the number be stated in the return', HC 1851 (328), l, 317

Copy of any report from the lord lieutenant of Ireland to the secretary of state for the home department, with reference to the late proclaiming of a district in the county of Down, under 11 & 12 Vict. c. 2, HC 1851 (250), l, 435

Report from the select committee on outrages (Ireland); together with proceedings of the committee, minutes of evidence, appendix and index, HC 1852 (438), xiv, 1

A return 'of the number of murders, waylayings, assaults, threatening notices, incendiary fires, or other crimes of an agrarian character reported by the constabulary, within the counties of Louth, Armagh, and Monaghan, since 1 Jan. 1849 [to 28 Mar. 1852], *distinguishing by name the persons murdered and waylaid; also stating the numbers arrested for each offence; whether informations have been sworn in the case, and the result of any trial of the same'*, HC 1852 (448), xlvii, 465

Return of the number of persons capitally convicted in England and Wales from the year 1838 to 1852, both inclusive; specifying the offences and sentences, and whether and how carried into effect by execution or otherwise, HC 1852–3 (386), lxxxi, 277

'Tabular returns of the number of committals for crime in Ireland, during each of the years from 1841 to 1852, inclusive; of the number of committals in England and Wales, for each year of the same period; and, in each case, of the number of accused persons unable to read or write, and their centesimal proportion to the whole', HC 1852–3 (338), lxxxi, 347

Copies of the several inquisitions removed from the Court of Queen's Bench in Ireland, in the month of January last, and transferred to the county of Clare ... in relation to any of the cases of homicide, riot, unlawful assembly or other criminal offence alleged to have been committed at the town of Sixmilebridge, in the month of July last, at the time of the general election ..., HC 1852–3 (313), xciv, 63

Return 'of the number of cases in which bills for murder or manslaughter against police, yeomen, or military, have been presented to grand juries in Ireland, since 1820, specifying in each case whether the bill was found true or ignored; and also specifying the locality in which the loss of life took place, and the number of persons killed; and also, whether the parties against whom bills have been found, have been convicted or acquitted by the petty jury', HC 1852–3 (475), xciv, 637

Report from the select committee on public prosecutors; together with the proceedings of the committee, minutes of evidence, appendix and index, HC 1854–5 (481), xii, 1

A return of the number of inquests held by the several coroners in Ireland, for each of the years 1843, 1844, and 1845, separately; and the sums presented each year as payment to those coroners, and also to medical witnesses; similar return for the years 1848, 1849, 1850, 1851, 1852, and 1853 ..., HC 1854–5 (332), xlvii, 371

Report from the select committee of the house of lords appointed 'to take into consideration the present mode of carrying into effect capital punishments'; and to report thereon to the house; together with the minutes of evidence, and appendix, HC 1856 (366), vii, 9

Lists of writs of error and appeals from courts of common law and equity in the United Kingdom of Great Britain and Ireland, distinguishing English, Scotch and Irish cases, which have been heard by this house, from the 1st January 1846 to the present time; distinguishing the cases affirmed, reversed, varied, and remitted, and showing the date of the sentence appealed from, and the date of the final judgment in each case, HC 1856, (272), l, 9

A report on criminal procedure to the lord chancellor; by Charles Sprengal Greaves, Esq., one of her majesty's counsel [456], HC 1856, l, 79

Report from the select committee on prosecution expenses; with the proceedings, minutes of evidence, appendix, and index, HC 1862 (401), xi, 1

Copy 'of the challenge to the array of the jury panel at the late Tyrone assizes, and of Mr Justice Christian's ruling when quashing the said panel, as returned by the sheriff', HC 1862 (232), xliv, 651

Returns 'stating the area and population of Geashill barony, in the King's County, Ireland; ... of the number of persons who have been summoned from said barony to serve as petty jurors at each assizes and quarter sessions respectively during the years 1857, 1858, 1859, 1860, 1861, and 1862; and also the number of persons from the said barony whose names have been returned on the jurors' books for those years', HC 1863 (337), l, 685

Return of the number of persons capitally convicted in Ireland for each of the last five years from the 1st day of January 1859 to the 1st day of January 1864; specifying the offences, and whether and how the sentences were carried into effect, by execution or otherwise; similar return for England and Wales; similar return for Scotland, HC 1864 (177), xlix, 5

Return of the number of persons in each of the last seven years, from 1857 to 1863 inclusive, committed in the United Kingdom for trial on the charge of murder; the number of such persons put on their trial; the number acquitted, distinguishing those acquitted on the ground of insanity; the number found insane on arraignment; number of such persons convicted of murder, the number of such persons convicted of manslaughter, and the number of concealment of birth; and number executed, HC 1864 (444), xlix, 515

A 'return showing, in each prison in the United Kingdom, on the 1st day of January 1864, the number of prisoners of each religious denomination, as entered on their caption … so far as relates to England and Wales', HC 1864 (150), xlix, 653

A 'return showing, in each prison in the United Kingdom, on the 1st day of January 1864, the number of prisoners of each religious denomination, as entered on their caption … so far as relates to Ireland and Scotland' , HC 1864 (150–I), xlix, 709

Return 'of the number of cases in Ireland, during the last twenty years, wherein persons accused of capital offences have been remanded to prison for re-trial, or have been set at large, in consequence of the inability of juries to agree to a verdict; specifying the name of the accused, the crime charged, the year in which the trial or re-trial took place, and the assize town in which it had been held; the return being made up to the 31st March 1865', HC 1865 (352), xlv, 323

Report of the capital punishment commission, together with the minutes of evidence, and appendix [3590], HC 1866, xxi, 1 (duke of Richmond, chairman)

Special report from the select committee on the Petit Juries (Ireland) Bill; with the proceedings of the committee, HC 1867–8 (390), x, 549

Minutes of proceedings of the select committee on the public prosecutors bill, HC 1870 (260), viii, 987

A bill to assimilate the law of trial by jury in Ireland to that of Scotland, HC 1871 (bill 47), vi, 473

Copy of a memorial addressed to the lord lieutenant by the coroners of Ireland, requesting that a measure on their behalf may be brought before parliament early in the present session, HC 1871 (86), lviii, 439

Report of the commissioners appointed by the lords commissioners of Her Majesty's Treasury to enquire into the condition of the civil service in Ireland on the Local Government Board, General Register Office, and general report: together with the minutes of evidence and appendices [C 789], HC 1873, xii, 1

First, second, and special reports from the select committee on juries (Ireland); together with the proceedings of the committee, minutes of evidence, and appendix, HC 1873 (283), xv, 389

Returns 'from the clerks of the crown in each county in Ireland, of the number of criminal cases in each county tried before a jury at the spring assizes of the years 1871, 1872, and 1873, with a description of the crime charged, and the result of the trial, specifying in each case whether the prisoner was found guilty (and, if so, of what offence) or acquitted, or the jury disagreed'; 'of the number of cases postponed on the application of counsel for the Crown, or in which nolle prosequi *was entered'; 'and, from the secretaries of the grand juries of Ireland respectively, of any resolutions adopted by any of the grand juries referring to the Juries Act (Ireland) of 1871'*, HC 1873 (220), liv, 359

Report from the select committee on jury system (Ireland); together with the proceedings of the committee, minutes of evidence, and appendix, HC 1874 (244), ix, 557

Return 'for each county in Ireland, of the amount expended at each assizes for the last three years in fees to counsel in criminal prosecutions (excluding the amount of fees paid to special counsel), and the number of cases in which such fees were paid'; 'and, similar return, for the same period, for each commission at Green-street for the county of Dublin and the county of the city of Dublin, and for the session of the city of Dublin held before the recorder', HC 1877 (40), lxix, 519

Return 'in tabular form as under, of the number of persons committed for trial in the several counties in Ireland, forming the six circuits in Ireland, awaiting their trial at assizes or quarter sessions on 1 Dec. 1876, and of the nature of the offences for which those persons were committed for trial', HC 1877 (121), lxix, 573

Report from the select committee of the house of lords on Irish jury laws; together with the proceedings of the committee, minutes of evidence, and appendix, HC 1881 (430), xi, 1

Reports of the law of foreign countries respecting homicidal crime [C 2849], HC 1881, lxxvi, 197

Further reports of the laws of foreign counties. Homicidal crime [C 2913], HC 1881, lxxvi, 267

'*Return of all persons in the United Kingdom convicted within the last five years of murder or manslaughter, whose sentences have been mitigated, or who have received a free pardon; together with a statement of the offences of which they were severally convicted*', HC 1881 (436), lxxvi, 369

Copy 'of report by Mr Richard Bourke, inspector of the Local Government Board, of the result of his inquiry into the circumstances connected with deaths of two children named Kavanagh, whose parents lived at Rhode, in the King's County, together with the minutes of evidence taken at the inquiry', HC 1882 (341), liv, 181

Copies 'of any documents (except official documents of a confidential and privileged character) in the nature of evidence or memorials, submitted for the consideration of the Irish executive, with reference to the alleged misconduct of members of the jury, the verdict, and the sentence, in the case of Francis Hynes, convicted of murder in the Dublin Commission Court on the 12th of August 1882, and executed in Limerick; and, of any letters written by the lord lieutenant with reference to such documents', HC 1882 (408), lv, 167

Copies 'of the report of the sentence passed by Mr Justice Lawson, in the Dublin Commission Court, on the 22nd day of August 1882, on Patrick Walsh, convicted of murder, as it appears in the transcript of the notes of the shorthand writer employed for the occasion by direction of the attorney general; and, of the official record of the sentence, as entered in the book of the clerk of the crown for the county and city of Dublin', HC 1882 (407), lv, 223

Copy 'of two letters of Mr Callan, MP, under date of the 25th or 26th days of August and the 31st day of August or the 1st day of September, addressed to his excellency the lord lieutenant of Ireland, and the reply thereto', HC 1883 (18), lvi, 97

Report of the committee appointed to inquire into the office of public prosecutor with minutes of evidence and appendix [C 4016], HC 1884, xxiii, 309

Report from the select committee of the house of lords on high sheriffs; together with the proceedings of the committee, minutes of evidence, and appendix, HC 1888 (257), xii, 209

Return of copy of rule for guidance of crown solicitors in Ireland in relation to the impanelling of jurors, HC 1894 (33), lxxii, 29

Report from the select committee on capital punishment together with the proceedings of the committee, and the minutes of evidence, taken before the select committee on capital punishment in 1929–1930, together with appendices and index, HC 1930–1 (15), vi, 1

Royal commission on capital punishment 1949–1953. Report [Cmd 8932], HC 1952–3, vii, 677

Returns of committals

Return of offenders committed to the different gaols [in Ireland] *for trial*, HC 1812 (246), v, 1005; HC 1812-13 (174), vi, 633; HC 1813–14 (264), xiii, 213; HC 1814–15 (331) (332), xi, 313, 359; HC 1824 (156), xxii, 1

Summary statements of the number of persons charged with criminal offences, who were committed to the different gaols in Ireland for trial at the assizes and sessions held in the several counties, cities, towns, and liberties therein, during the last seven years [1822–8] ..., HC 1829 (256), xxii, 427

Returns from clerks of the crown and clerks of the peace, of the several counties etc. in Ireland, of the number of persons committed to the different gaols thereof for trial, in the year 1830, HC 1830–1 (294), xii, 631

_____ , 1831, HC 1831–2 (299), xxxiii, 19

_____ , 1832, HC 1833 (61), xxix, 89

Returns from clerks of the crown, &c. of Ireland, of number of persons committed to the gaols, 1834, HC 1835 (295), xlv, 269

Returns from clerks of the crown of persons committed to the different gaols for trial, 1835, HC 1836 (97), xlii, 379

Returns from the clerks of the crown and clerks of the peace of the several counties in Ireland, of the number of persons committed to the different gaols thereof, in 1836, HC 1837 (158), xlv, 225

Returns from the clerks of the crown, and clerks of the peace, of the several counties, &c. in Ireland, of the number of persons committed to the different gaols thereof for trial, in the year 1837, HC 1837–8 (208), xlvi, 251

_____ , 1838, HC 1839 (78), xxxviii, 649

_____ , 1839, HC 1840 (42), xxxviii, 453

_____ , 1840, HC 1841 (101), xviii, 547

_____ , 1841, HC 1842 (91), xxxii, 435

_____ , 1842, HC 1843 (105), xlii, 181

_____ , 1843, HC 1844 (138), xxxix, 183

_____ , 1844, HC 1845 (44), xxxvii, 187

_____ , 1845, HC 1846 (46), xxxv, 1

_____ , 1846, HC 1847 (94), lvi, 89

_____ , 1847, HC 1847–8 (146), lvi, 131

_____ , 1848, HC 1849 (72), xliv, 9

_____ , 1849, HC 1850 (190), li, 245

_____ , 1850, HC 1852 (192), xlvii, 91

_____ , 1851, HC 1852–3 (340), lxxxi, 349

_____ , 1852, HC 1854 (138), lviii, 191

Inspectors of prisons reports

Prisons of Ireland. Report of inspectors general; 1823: with abstract from appendix of general observations on each prison, in the several districts, &c., HC 1823 (342), x

Prisons of Ireland. Report of inspectors general; 1824: with abstract from appendix of general observations on each prison, in the several districts, &c., HC 1824 (294), xxii

Prisons of Ireland. Eighth report of the inspectors general on the general state of the prisons of Ireland, 1830, HC 1830 (48), xxiv, 719 [figs for 1823–9]

Prisons of Ireland. Ninth report of the inspectors general on the general state of the prisons of Ireland: 1831, HC 1830–1 (172), iv, 269

Tenth report of the inspectors general on the general state of the prisons of Ireland, 1832: with appendices, HC 1831–2 (152), xxiii, 451

Eleventh report of the inspectors general on the general state of the prisons of Ireland, 1833: with appendices, HC 1833 (67), xvii, 307

Twelfth report of the inspectors general on the general state of the prisons of Ireland, 1834: with appendices, HC 1834 (63), xl, 69

Thirteenth report of the inspectors general on the general state of the prisons of Ireland, 1835, HC 1835 (114), xxxvi, 381

Fourteenth report of inspectors general on the general state of the prisons of Ireland, 1836: with an appendix, HC 1836 (118), xxxv, 431

Appendix [containing the criminal returns for 1835] *to the fourteenth report of the inspectors general on the general state of the prisons of Ireland; 1836*, HC 1836 (523), xxxv, 485

Fifteenth report of the inspectors general on the general state of the prisons of Ireland, 1836; with appendices HC 1837 (123), xxxi, 605

Sixteenth report of the inspectors general on the general state of the prisons of Ireland, 1837; with appendices HC 1837–8 (186), xxix, 475

Seventeenth report of the inspectors general on the general state of the prisons of Ireland, 1838; with appendices HC 1839 (91), xx, 403

Eighteenth report of the inspectors general on the general state of the prisons of Ireland, 1839; with appendices [240], HC 1840, xxvi, 165

Nineteenth report of the inspectors general on the general state of the prisons of Ireland, 1840; with appendices [299], HC 1841, xi, 759

Twentieth report of the inspectors general on the general state of the prisons of Ireland, 1841; with appendices [377], HC 1842, xxii, 117

Twenty-first report of the inspectors general on the general state of the prisons of Ireland, 1842: with appendices [462], HC 1843, xxvii, 83

Twenty-second report of the inspectors general on the general state of the prisons of Ireland, 1843: with appendices [535], HC 1844, xxviii, 329

Twenty-third report of the inspectors general on the general state of the prisons of Ireland, 1844: with appendices [620], HC 1845, xxv, 231

Twenty-fourth report of the inspectors general on the general state of the prisons of Ireland, 1845: with appendices [697], HC 1846, xx, 257

Twenty-fifth report of the inspectors general on the general state of the prisons of Ireland, 1846 with appendices [805], HC 1847, xxix, 151

Twenty-sixth report of the inspectors general on the general state of the prisons of Ireland, 1847: with appendices [952], HC 1847–8, xxxiv, 253

Twenty-seventh report of the inspectors general on the general state of the prisons of Ireland, 1848: with appendices [1069], HC 1849, xxvi, 373

Twenty-eighth report of the inspectors general on the general state of the prisons of Ireland, 1849: with appendices [1229], HC 1850, xxix, 305

Twenty-ninth report of the inspectors general on the general state of the prisons of Ireland, 1850: with appendices [1364], HC 1851, xxviii, 357

Thirtieth report of the inspectors general on the general state of the prisons of Ireland, 1851: with appendices [1531], HC 1852, xxv, 1

Tables of criminal offenders

Tables of number of criminal offenders committed for trial, or bailed for appearance at the assizes and sessions in each county, 1845; with the result of the proceedings [696], HC 1846, xxxv, 81

——, 1846 [822], HC 1847, xlvii, 189

——, 1847 [953], HC 1847–8, lii, 361

——, 1848 [1067], HC 1849, xliv, 129

——, 1849 [1271], HC 1850, xlv, 529

——, 1850 [1386], HC 1851, xlvi, 97

——, 1851 [1556], HC 1852–3, lxxxi, 71

——, 1852 [1654], HC 1852–3, lxxxi, 433

——, 1853 [1811], HC 1854, liv, 205

——, 1854 [1930], HC 1854–5, xlviii, 69

——, 1855 [2116], HC 1856, xlix, 71

——, 1856 [2248 sess. 2], HC 1857, xlii, 249

——, 1857 [2417], HC 1857–8, xlvii, 389

——, 1858 [2544 sess. 2], HC 1859, xix, 561

——, 1859 [2705], HC 1860, lvii, 723

——, 1860 [2863], HC 1861, lii, 209

——, 1861 [3035], HC 1862, xlvi, 1

——, 1862 [3220], HC 1863, xlix, 47

Judicial statistics

Judicial statistics 1863. Ireland: pt i, *Police, criminal proceedings, prisons;* pt ii, *Common law, equity, civil and canon law* [3418], HC 1864, lvii, 653

——, 1864 [3563], HC 1865, lii, 657

——, 1865 [3705], HC 1866, lxviii, 697

——, 1866 [3930], HC 1867, lxvi, 735

——, 1867 [4071], HC 1867–8, lvii, 737

_____ , 1868 [4203], HC 1868–9, lviii, 737

_____ , 1869 [C 227], HC 1870, lxiii, 753

_____ , 1870 [C 443], HC 1871, lxiv, 231

_____ , 1871 [C 674], HC 1872, lxv, 235

_____ , 1872 [C 851], HC 1873, lxx, 247

_____ , 1873 [C 1034], HC 1874, lxxi, 251

_____ , 1874 [C 1295], HC 1875, lxxxi, 259

_____ , 1875 [C 1563], HC 1876, lxxix, 273

_____ , 1876 [C 1822], HC 1877, lxxxvi, 261

_____ , 1877 [C 2152], HC 1878, lxxix, 265

_____ , 1878 [C 2389], HC 1878–9, lxxvi, 279

_____ , 1879 [C 2698], HC 1880, lxxvii, 251

_____ , 1880 [C 3028], HC 1881, xcv, 243

_____ , 1881 [C 3355], HC 1882, lxxv, 243

_____ , 1882 [C 3808], HC 1883, lxxvii, 243

_____ , 1883 [C 4181], HC 1884, lxxxvi, 243

_____ , 1884 [C 4554], HC 1884–5, lxxxvi, 243

_____ , 1885 [C 4796], HC 1886, lxxii, 233

_____ , 1886 [C 5177], HC 1887, xc, 241

_____ , 1887 [C 5495], HC 1888, cviii, 241

_____ , 1888 [C 5795], HC 1889, lxxxv, 241

_____ , 1889 [C 6122], HC 1890, lxxx, 253

_____ , 1890 [C 6511], HC 1890–1, xciii, 251

_____ , 1891 [C 6782], HC 1892, lxxxix, 253

_____ , 1892 [C 7189], HC 1893–4, ciii, 279

_____ , 1893 [C 7534], HC 1894, xcv, 105

_____ , 1894 [C 7799], HC 1895, cviii, 323

_____ , 1895, pt i [C 8616], HC 1897, c, 517

_____ , 1896, pt i [C 9492], HC 1899, cviii, pt ii, 1

_____ , 1897 [C 9493, C 9249], HC 1899, cviii, pt ii, 175

_____ , 1898 [Cd 225], HC 1900, civ, 1

_____ , 1899 [Cd 313], HC 1900, civ, 177

_____ , 1900 [Cd 725, 682], HC 1901, lxxxix, 463

_____ , 1901 [Cd 1208, 1187], HC 1902, cxvii, 395

_____ , 1902 [Cd 1746, 1676], HC 1903, lxxxiii, 403

_____ , 1903 [Cd 2218, 2149], HC 1904, cvii, 431

_____ , 1904 [Cd 2632, 2593], HC 1905, xcix, 417

_____ , 1905 [Cd 3112, 3050], HC 1906, cxxxv, 405

_____ , 1906 [Cd 3654, 3616], HC 1907, xcviii, 447

_____ , 1907 [Cd 4200, 3050], HC 1908, cxiii, 619

_____ , 1908 [Cd 4793, 4747], HC 1909, civ, 207

_____ , 1909 [Cd 5320, 5264], HC 1910, cxi, 359

_____ , 1910 [Cd 5866, 5848], HC 1911, cii, 367

_____ , 1911 [Cd 6419, 6329], HC 1912–13, cx, 703

_____ , 1912, pt i [Cd 7064], HC 1914, c, 349

_____ , 1913 [Cd 7536, 7600], HC 1914, c, 519

_____ , 1914 [Cd 8077, 8006], HC 1914–16, lxxxii, 451

3. OFFICIAL PUBLICATIONS

The statutes at large, passed in the parliaments held in Ireland: from the third year of Edward II, AD 1310, to the thirty-eighth year of George III, AD 1798, inclusive. With marginal notes, and a complete index to the whole, 18 vols (Dublin, 1799)

A collection of the public general statutes passed in ... the reign of King George IV ... (London, 1821–)

A collection of the public general statutes passed ... in the reign of King William IV ... (London, 1831–)

A collection of the public general statutes, passed ... in the reign of Her Majesty Queen Victoria ... (London, 1837–)

The public general acts passed ... in the reign of His Majesty Edward VII (London [1902–])

General valuation of rateable property in Ireland ... (Dublin, 1849–64) [There are collections in the National Library of Ireland, the library of Trinity College, Dublin, the National Archives, and the Public Record Office of Northern Ireland. Each collection is bound in a different way.]

Hansard's parliamentary debates: forming a continuation of the 'Parliamentary history of England, from the earliest times to the year 1803', 3rd series, 356 vols (London, 1831–91)

Rules and orders of the common law judges, and reserved cases, 1860–64 (Dublin, 1865)

The statutes revised. Northern Ireland ... ([1801–1920 covered by 7 vols], Belfast, 1956)

4. LAW REPORTS AND DIGESTS

Digests

Brunker, Thomas, *A digest of all the reported cases decided in the superior and other courts of common law in Ireland, and in the Court of Admiralty; from Sir John Davies' reports to the present time. With references to the statutes and general orders of court* (Dublin, 1865)

Murray, R.D., & G.Y. Dixon, *Digest of cases decided by superior courts of common law and equity, landed estates court, courts of admiralty, bankruptcy, probate and matrimonial causes, for crown cases reserved, and for land cases reserved; and by the Court of Appeal, and the several divisions of the High Court of Justice in Ireland. From the commencement of Hilary term, 1867, to the end of the Michaelmas sittings, 1893* (Dublin, 1899)

Maxwell, T. Henry (ed.), *A digest of cases decided by the superior and other courts in Ireland from the commencement of Hilary sittings, 1894, to the end of Michaelmas sittings, 1918 (including also the cases reported in volumes 16 & 17 Irish Common Law Reports)*, (Dublin, 1921)

Law Reports

Irish law reports, particularly of points of practice, argued and determined in the courts of Queen's Bench, Common Pleas, and Exchequer of Pleas, from Michaelmas term 1838–, 13 vols (Dublin, 1839–52)

Crawford, George, & Edward Spencer Dix, *Abridged notes of cases argued and determined in the several courts of law and equity in Ireland, during the years 1837 and 1838; with some decisions at nisi prius and on the circuits. A table of cases, and index to the principal matters* (Dublin, 1839)

_____ , *Reports of cases argued and ruled on the circuits, in Ireland, during the years 1839 and 1840; together with cases decided at the nisi prius sittings, and in the courts of criminal jurisdiction at Dublin, a table of cases, and an index to the principal matters* (Dublin, 1841)

_____ , *... during the years 1840, 1841, and 1842* (Dublin, 1843)

_____ , *... during the years 1843, 1844, 1845, and 1846, together with notes of cases decided at the nisi prius sittings in Dublin, and in the courts of municipal revision* (Dublin, 1847)

Cox, Edward W., *Reports of cases in criminal law, argued and determined in all the courts in England and Ireland*, 24 vols (London, 1843–1916)

Jebb, Robert, *Cases, chiefly relating to the criminal and presentment law, reserved for consideration, and decided by the twelve judges of Ireland, from May 1822, to November 1840* (Dublin, 1841)

_____ , & Richard Bourke, *Reports of cases argued and determined in the court of Queen's Bench, in Ireland, from Michaelmas to Trinity term, 5th Victoria (1841, 1842). With tables of the names of cases and principal matters* (Dublin, 1843)

_____ , & Arthur Symes, *Reports of cases argued and determined in the courts of Queen's Bench and Exchequer Chamber in Ireland, with tables of the names of the cases and the principal matters; vol. i, Containing the cases from Hilary term, 1 Victoria, to Trinity term, 2 Victoria (1838, 1839, inclusive* (Dublin, 1840)

_____ , vol. ii, *containing the cases from Michaelmas term, 3 Victoria, to Trinity term, 4 Victoria (1839, 1841) inclusive* (Dublin, 1842)

Reports of cases argued and determined on six circuits in Ireland taken during the assizes, in the years 1841, 1842, 1843 … (Dublin, 1843)

The Irish Jurist, 17 vols (Dublin, 1849-65)

Common law reports, of cases argued and determined in the courts of Queen's Bench, Common Pleas, Exchequer Chamber, and Court of Criminal Appeal, 17 vols (Dublin, 1852-67)

The Irish reports, published under the control of the Council of Law Reporting in Ireland, containing reports of cases argued and determined in the superior courts in Ireland [from Hilary term 1867 to Michaelmas term 1877], 11 vols (Dublin, 1868-79)

The law reports (Ireland), published under the control of the Council of Law Reporting in Ireland, containing reports of cases argued and determined in the Court of Appeal, the High Court of Justice, and the Court of Bankruptcy, in Ireland, 20 vols (Dublin, 1879-93)

The Irish reports (Dublin, 1894–)

5. NEWSPAPERS

Ballymena Observer   *Irishman*
Banner of Ulster   *Irish Law Times and Solicitors' Journal*
Belfast News Letter   *Irish Times*
Cork Examiner   *Mayo Examiner*
Dublin Evening Post   *Northern Standard*
Enniskillen Chronicle & Erne Packet   *Penny Despatch*
Galway Express   *Sligo Champion*
Impartial Reporter   *Tyrone Constitution*

6. CONTEMPORARY WORKS

A full report of the trial in the cause of The Queen at the prosecution of the attorney-general, versus Charles Gavan Duffy, Esq., proprietor of the Belfast Vindicator, on Monday, the 20th day of June, 1842, in the Court of Queen's Bench, with the speeches of the counsel for the prosecution and for the traverser, the charge of Chief Justice Pennefather at length. Compiled by a Law Student (Dublin, n.d. [1842])

A manual for articled clerks; or, guide to their examination & admission: containing courses of study in conveyancing, equity, bankruptcy, common law, special pleading, criminal law, etc.; a collection of questions, with references to works of authority in which answers may be found; and such other information as will tend to their successful examination and admission as attorneys of the courts …, to which is prefixed, A lecture on the study of the law by J.J.S. Wharton, Esq., S.C.L. (5th ed., London, 1847)

Alcock, John, *Observations concerning the nature and origin of the meetings of the twelve judges, for the consideration of cases reserved from the circuits* (Dublin, 1838)

Amos, Sheldon, *The science of law* (London, 1874)

Archbold's pleading and evidence in criminal cases: with precedents of indictments, &c. and the evidence necessary to support them (5th ed. by John Jervis, London, 1834); (20th ed. by William Bruce, London, 1886)

Armstrong, John Simpson, *A report of trials under a special commission for the county of Clare, held at Ennis, January 1848* (Dublin, n.d. [1849])

——, *A report of trials held under a special commission for the county of Limerick, held at Limerick, January 1848* (Dublin, n.d. [1849])

——, *Report of the trial of William Burke Kirwan, for the murder of Maria Louisa Kirwan, his wife, at the island of Ireland's Eye, in the county of Dublin on the 6th September, 1852, before the Hon. Judge Crampton and the Rt Hon. Baron Greene, at the Commission Court, Green Street, on the 8th and 9th December, 1852* (Dublin, 1853)

——, & Edward Shirley Trevor, *A report of the proceedings on an indictment for a conspiracy in the case of the Queen v. Daniel O'Connell, John O'Connell, Thomas Steele, Charles Gavan Duffy, Rev. Thomas Tierney, Rev. Peter James Tyrrell, Richard Barrett, John Gray, and Thomas Matthew Ray in Michaelmas term, 1843, and Hilary term, 1844* (Dublin, 1844)

Bailey, W.F., 'Magisterial reform: being some considerations of the present voluntary system, and suggestions for the substitution of an independent paid magistracy' in *Journal of the Statistical and Social Inquiry Society of Ireland of Ireland*, 8:63 (July 1885), 595–605

Bennett, John Hughes, *The mesmeric mania of 1851, with a philosophical explanation of the phenomena produced. A lecture* (Edinburgh, 1851)

Berry, James, *My experiences as an executioner*, ed. by H. Snowden Ward; with a new introduction and additional appendices by Jonathan Goodman (Newton Abbot, 1972)

Best, W.M., *A treatise on the principles of evidence and practice as to proofs in courts of common law; with elementary rules for conducting the examination and cross-examination of witnesses* (London, 1849)

Bodkin, Mathias M'D., *Recollections of an Irish judge: press, bar and parliament* (London, 1914)

[Boswell, John Knight], *The Kirwan case: illustrating the danger of conviction on circumstantial evidence, and the necessity of granting new trials in criminal cases* (Dublin, 1853)

Bridges, Frederick, *Phrenological-physiometrical characteristics of James Spollin, who was tried for the murder of Mr George S. Little, of the Broadstone terminus of the Midland Great Western Railway, on the 13 Nov., 1856, with an account of the author's interview with Spollin* (London, n.d. [1858])

Browne, George Joseph, *A report of the whole of the proceedings previous to, with a note of the evidence on, the trial of Robert Keon, Gent. for the murder of George Nugent Reynolds, Esq. and also of the charges of the judges thereon, together with the arguments and replies of counsel on the motion in arrest of judgment and the decision of the court thereon* (Dublin, 1788)

Brownrigg, Henry John, *Standing rules and regulations for the government and guidance of the constabulary force in Ireland; revised edition, as approved by his excellency the lord lieutenant* (Dublin, 1860)

——, *Examination of some recent allegations concerning the constabulary force in Ireland, in a report to his excellency the lord lieutenant* (Dublin, 1864)

Burge, William, *Commentaries on colonial and foreign laws generally, and in their conflict with each other, and with the law of England*, 4 vols (London, 1838)

Burke, Oliver J., *The history of the lord chancellors of Ireland from a.d. 1186 to a.d. 1874* (Dublin, 1879)

——, *Anecdotes of the Connaught circuit: from its foundation to close upon the present time* (Dublin, 1885)

Bussy, Frederick Moir, *Irish conspiracies: recollections of John Mallon (The Great Detective) and other reminiscences* (London, 1910)

Campion, William Bennett, *Memoir of William Bennett Campion serjeant-at-law* (Dublin, 1911)

Cherry, Richard R., *An outline of the criminal law as regards offences against individuals* (London, 1892)

Chitty, Joseph, *A practical treatise on the criminal law, comprising the practice, pleadings, and evidence, which occur in the course of criminal prosecutions whether by indictment or information: with a copious collection of precedents of indictments, informations …*, 4 vols (2nd ed., London, 1826)

Christian, E.B.V., *Leaves of the lower branch: the attorney in life and letters* (London, 1909)

Counsel, E.P.S., *Jurors and verdicts* (Dublin, 1887)

—— , *Jury packing* (2nd ed., Dublin, 1887)

Cox, Edward W., *The advocate: his training, practice, rights, and duties* (London, 1852)

Crane, C.P., *Memories of a resident magistrate 1880–1920* (Edinburgh, 1938)

Crilly, Daniel, *Jury packing in Ireland* (Dublin, 1887)

Croker, Rt Hon. John Wilson, *History of the guillotine* (London, 1853)

Croker, T. Crofton, *Researches in the south of Ireland, illustrative of the scenery, architectural remains, and the manners and superstitions of the peasantry: with an appendix, containing a private narrative of the rebellion of 1798* (London, 1824)

Curran, John Adye, *Reminiscences of John Adye Curran, KC, late county court judge and chairman of quarter sessions* (London, 1915)

Curran, William Henry, *Sketches of the Irish bar; with essays, literary and political*, 2 vols (London, 1855)

Daniel, W.T.S., *The history and origin of the law reports, together with a compilation of various documents shewing the progress and result of proceedings taken for their establishment, and the condition of the reports on the 31st December, 1883* (London, 1884)

Dickson, William Gillespie, *A treatise of the law of evidence in Scotland*, 2 vols (2nd ed. by John Skelton, Edinburgh, 1864)

Dixon, George Y., & W.L. Gilliland, *The law relating to sheriffs in Ireland with an appendix of statutes and forms* (Dublin, 1888)

E.P.S. Counsel, LL.D, TCD, *Jury packing* (2nd ed., Dublin, 1887)

Essays by a barrister (Reprinted from the Saturday Review), (London, 1862)

Faulkner, Brian, *Memoirs of a statesman*, ed. John Houston (London, 1978)

Fischel, Edward, *The English constitution*; translated from the 2nd German ed. by Richard Jenery Shee (London, 1863)

Foot, Charles H., *The grand jury laws of Ireland; comprising all the statutes relating to the powers and duties of grand juries, including orders in council relating to presentments and all matters connected therewith: to which are added copious notes, tables of cases reported under various acts, forms of procedure, criminal jurisdiction*, 2nd ed. rewritten and revised by John N. Gerrard and T.S.F. Battersby (Dublin, 1884)

Gabbett, Joseph, *A treatise of the criminal law; comprehending all crimes and misdemeanors punishable by indictment; and offences cognizable summarily by magistrates; and the modes of proceeding upon each*, 2 vols (Dublin, 1843)

Garsia, Marston, *Criminal law in a nutshell with a selection of questions at bar examinations* (London, 1922)

—— , *Evidence in a nutshell* (London, 1929)

Geoghegan, T.G., 'An account of a case of poisoning by monkshood, which formed the subject of a criminal trial; with observations' in *The Dublin Journal of Medical Science; exhibiting a comprehensive view of the latest discoveries in medicine, surgery, and the collateral sciences*, 19 (1841), 401–29

Greenleaf, Simon, *An examination of the testimony of the four evangelists, by the rules of evidence administered in courts of justice with an account of the trial of Jesus* (2nd ed., London, 1847)

Hamilton, Lord Ernest, *Forty years on* (London, n.d. [1922])

Hamilton, Lord Frederic, *The days before yesterday* (London, n.d. [1920])

Harrel, Sir David, Recollections and Reflections (typescript in Department of Early Printed Books, TCD; 25 copies produced 'for private circulation'; dated Apr. 1926)

Haughton, Samuel, 'On some experiments on the poisonous properties of strychnine and nicotine' in *Proceedings of the Royal Irish Academy*, 6 (1853–7), 420–3 (paper read 29 Nov. 1856)

—— , 'On nicotine considered as an antidote to strychnia' in *Proceedings of the Royal Irish Academy*, 7 (1857–61), 84–8 (paper read 28 June 1858)

—— , 'On the true height of the tide at Ireland's Eye on the evening of the 6th September, 1852, the day of the murder of Mrs Kirwan' in *Proceedings of the Royal Irish Academy*, 7 (1857–61), 511–13 (paper read 27 May 1861)

—— , 'On hanging, considered from a mechanical and physiological point of view' in *The London, Edinburgh, and Dublin Philosophical Magazine and Journal of Science*, 4th ser., 32:213 (July 1866), 23–34

Hayes, Edmund, *Crimes and punishments, or a digest of the criminal statute law of Ireland, alphabetically arranged, with ample notes, in which are discussed the powers and authorities of the several courts of criminal jurisdiction in Ireland; the duties, responsibilities, and privileges of magistrates, coroners, constables, and other officers, in bringing criminals to justice, and also the practice of the courts in punishing offences upon indictment*, 2 vols (2nd ed., Dublin, 1842)

Healy, Maurice, *The old Munster circuit: a book of memories and traditions* (London, 1939)

Hennessy, R.M., *The justice of the peace for Ireland: a treatise on the powers and duties of magistrates in Ireland, in cases of summary jurisdiction, and in other matters, founded partly on Molloy's Justice of the Peace; with an appendix of statutes* (Dublin, 1910)

Holthouse, Henry James, *A new law dictionary, containing explanations of such technical terms and phrases as occur in the works of the various law-writers of Great Britain; to which is added an outline of an action at law, and of a suit in equity. Designed expressly for the use of students* (London, 1839)

Houston, Arthur, 'Observations on trial by jury, with suggestions for the amendment of our present system' in *Journal of the Statistical and Social Inquiry Society of Ireland*, 3 (May 1861), 100–09

Huband, William G., *A practical treatise on the law relating to the grand jury in criminal cases the coroner's jury and the petty jury in Ireland* (Dublin, 1896)

Humphreys, Henry, *The Criminal Law and Procedure (Ireland) Act, 1887. 50 & 51 Vict., cap. 20 with a review on the general outline, scope, and provisions of the act; notes on the several sections, and offences to which is extended summary jurisdiction, with an appendix* (2nd ed., Dublin, 1887)

Jervis, John, *A practical treatise on the office and duties of coroners: with forms and precedents* (2nd ed. by W.N. Welsby, London, 1854)

Johnston, W.C., *Report of the trials at the Dublin Commission Court, April and May, 1883, of the prisoners charged with the Phoenix Park murder, the attempt to murder Mr Field, and the conspiracy to murder; before the Hon. Mr Justice O'Brien; reported by W.C. Johnston* (Dublin, 1883)

Joy, Rt Hon. Henry, *On the evidence of accomplices* (Dublin, 1836)

[Joy, Henry H.], *Letter to the Right Honorable Lord Lyndhurst, on the appointment of sheriffs in Ireland, under the earl of Mulgrave by a barrister* (London, 1838)

Joy, Henry H., *On the admissibility of confessions and challenge of jurors in criminal cases in England and Ireland* (Dublin and London, 1842)

—— , *On peremptory challenge of jurors, with the judgment of the Queen's Bench in the Queen v. Gray* (Dublin and London, 1844)

Kenny, Courtney Stanhope, *A selection of cases illustrative of English criminal law* (Cambridge, 1901)

—— , *Outlines of criminal law, based on lectures delivered in the University of Cambridge* (Cambridge, 1902)

Kingsley, Jeffries, *Preparations for the session of 1839: on the criminal returns of Ireland* (Dublin, 1839)

[Law Student], *The law student's question-book: containing all the questions propounded by the examiners from the commencement of the examination of articled clerks to the present time* (2nd ed., London, 1849)

—— , *The key to the examination questions, from 1835 to 1851, with full answers, by the editors of the* Law Student's Magazine. *Division V: criminal law* (2nd ed., London, 1851)

Lefroy, Thomas, *An analysis of the criminal law of Ireland, giving in alphabetical order all indictable offences, with their respective punishments and the statutes relating thereto, together with explanatory observations and notes; also an appendix of forms for the use of magistrates* (Dublin, 1849); 2nd ed. by Thomas Henry Barton (Dublin, 1862); 3rd ed. by Thomas Henry Barton (Dublin, 1865)

Levinge, Edward Parkyns, *The justice's manual, containing the justices' protection act, 1851, the summary jurisdiction act, 1851, the petty sessions act, 1851, and the law of evidence amendment act, with notes, comments, and copious index* (Dublin, 1853)

—— , *The game laws of Ireland* (Dublin, 1858)

——, *The justice of the peace for Ireland; comprising the practice in indictable offences, and the proceedings preliminary and subsequent to convictions; with an appendix of the most useful statutes, and an alphabetical catalogue of offences* (2nd ed., Dublin, 1862)

Lorrimer, James, *A hand-book of the law of Scotland* (2nd ed., Edinburgh, 1862)

McKenna, P.J., 'Observations on Lord Brougham's bill for the further amendment of the law of evidence, as well in criminal as in civil cases' in *Journal of the Dublin Statistical Society*, 2:8 (Jan. 1860), 362–8

MacKenzie, Thomas, *Studies in Roman law with comparative views of the laws of France, England, and Scotland* (Edinburgh and London, 1862)

Miller, James, *Surgical experience of chloroform* (Edinburgh and London, 1848)

Molloy, Constantine, 'Observations on the law relating to the qualification and selection of jurors, with suggestions for its amendment' in *Journal of the Statistical and Social Inquiry Society of Ireland*, 4:30 (July 1865), 186–93

——, *The justice of the peace for Ireland: a treatise on the powers and duties of magistrates in Ireland, in cases of summary jurisdiction, in the prosecution of indictable offences, and in other matters. Founded partly on Levinge's Justice of the Peace; with an appendix of statutes and notes and decisions thereon, and a catalogue of offences alphabetically arranged* (Dublin, 1890)

Mongan, James, *A report of the trial of William Kilfoyle, upon the charge of killing Mary Mulrooney at Newtownbarry, on the 18th of June, 1831; tried before the Hon. Baron Foster, at the spring assizes of Wexford, 1832* (Dublin, 1832)

——, *A report of the trials of John Kennedy, John Ryan, and William Voss, for the murder of Edmond Butler, at Carrickshock on the 14th December, 1831; tried before the Hon. Baron Foster, at the spring and summer assizes of Kilkenny, 1832* (Dublin, 1832)

——, *A report of trials before the Rt Hon. the Lord Chief Justice, and the Hon. Baron Sir Wm. C. Smith, bart at the special commission, at Maryborough, commencing on the 23rd May, and ending on the 6th June* [1832] (Dublin, 1832)

Morris, William O'Connor, *Memories and thoughts of a life* (London, 1895)

Nun, Richard, & John Edward Walsh, *The powers and duties of justices of the peace in Ireland, and of constables as connected therewith; with an appendix and statutes and forms* (Dublin, 1841)

O'Brien, Georgina, *The reminiscences of the Right Hon. Lord O'Brien (of Kilfenora) lord chief justice of Ireland*, edited by his daughter Hon. Georgina O'Brien (London, 1916)

O'Connor, James, *The Irish justice of the peace: a treatise on the powers and duties of justices of the peace in Ireland, and certain matters connected therewith* (Dublin, 1911)

Oulton, Andrew Norton, *Index to the statutes, at present in force in, or affecting Ireland, from the year 1310 to 1835, inclusive, to be continued by annual supplements* (Dublin, 1836)

Paterson, James, *A compendium of English and Scotch law stating their differences: with a dictionary of parallel terms and phrases* (Edinburgh, 1860)

Peake, Thomas, *A compendium of the law of evidence* (5th ed., London, 1822)

[Philander], *Capital punishment: is it defensible?* (London, 1865)

Pierrepoint, Albert, *Executioner: Pierrepoint* (Litton, n.d. [1978])

Pike, Luke Owen, *A history of crime in England illustrating the changes of the laws in the progress of civilization written from the public records and other contemporary evidence*, 2 vols (London, 1873, 1876). Vol. i, *From the Roman invasion to the accession of Henry VII* (1873). Vol. ii, *From the accession of Henry VII, to the present time* (1876)

Porter, Frank Thorpe, *Gleanings and reminiscences* (Dublin, 1875)

Priestly, W.O., & Horatio R. Storer (eds), *The obstetric memoirs and contributions of James Y. Simpson, MD FRSE*, 2 vols (Edinburgh, 1855)

Purcell, Theobald A., *A summary of the general principles of pleading and evidence, in criminal cases in Ireland: with the rules of practice incident thereto* (Dublin, 1849)

Rhadamanthus, *Our judges* (Dublin, 1890)

Lynch-Robinson, Sir Christopher, *The last of the Irish RMs* (London, 1951)

Roscoe, Henry, *A digest of the law of evidence in criminal cases* (2nd ed. by T.C. Granger, London, 1840)

Russell, Sir William Oldnall, *A treatise on crimes and misdemeanours*, 3 vols (4th ed. by Charles Sprengel Greaves, London, 1865)

Sewell, Richard Clarke, *A treatise of the law of sheriff with practical forms and precedents* (London, 1842)

Sheil, Richard Lalor, *Sketches, legal and political, by the late Right Honourable Richard Lalor Sheil*, ed. M.W. Savage (London, 1856)

Simmons, Thomas Frederick (continued by Thomas Frederick Simmons), *The constitution and practice of courts martial with a summary of the law of evidence as connected therewith; also some notice of the criminal law of England with reference to the trial of civil offences* (7th ed., London, 1875)

Smith, George Hill, *Forms of indictments (with special reference, where necessary to the requirements of Irish criminal laws)*, (Dublin, 1903)

Smythe, Hamilton, *Justice of the peace in Ireland* (Dublin, 1841)

Snow, John, *A letter to the Right Honourable Lord Campbell, lord chief justice of the court of Queen's Bench. On the clause respecting chloroform in the proposed prevention of offences bill* (London, 1851)

——, *On chloroform and other anæsthetics: their action and administration*, ed. with a memoir of the author, by Benjamin W. Richardson, MD (London, 1858)

Starkie, Thomas, *A practical treatise of the law of evidence, and digest of proofs in civil and criminal proceedings* (4th ed. by G.M. Dowdeswell & J.G. Malcolm, London, 1857)

Stephen, James Fitzjames, 'The relation of novels to life' in *Cambridge essays, contributed by members of the university, 1855* (London, n.d.), pp 148–92

——, 'The characteristics of English criminal law' in *Cambridge essays, contributed by members of the university, 1857* (London, n.d. [1857]), pp 1–63

——, *A general view of the criminal law of England* (London and Cambridge, 1863)

——, *The Indian evidence act (I. of 1872). With an introduction on the principles of judicial evidence* (Calcutta, Bombay, and London, 1872)

——, *A history of the criminal law of England*, 3 vols (London, 1883)

——, *A digest of the law of evidence*, 12th ed., revised by Sir Harry Lushington Stephen Bt., & Lewis Frederick Sturge (London, 1948)

——, & Herbert Stephen, *A digest of the law of criminal procedure in indictable offences* (London, 1883)

Sullivan, A.M., *Old Ireland. Reminiscences of an Irish KC* (London, 1927)

——, *Practice at the Irish bar: a reading delivered before the Honourable Society of the Middle Temple, Michaelmas 1936* (London, 1937)

——, *The last serjeant: the memoirs of Serjeant A.M. Sullivan, QC* (London, 1952)

Taylor, Alfred Swaine, *The principles and practice of medical jurisprudence* (London, 1865)

Taylor, John Pitt, *Treatise on the law of evidence as administered in England and Ireland with illustrations from the American and other foreign laws*, 2 vols (London, 1848)

The trials of George Robert Fitzgerald, Esq; and Timothy Brecknock, for the procurement of James Fulton and others, for the murder of Pat. Ran. M'Donnell and Charles Hipson. Also the trial of John Gallagher and others, for an assault on Geo. Rob. Fitzgerald, in the gaol of Castlebar ... (2nd ed., Dublin, 1786)

The wren of the Curragh; reprinted from the "Pall Mall Gazette" (London, 1867)

Thompson, John G., *The law of criminal procedure in Ireland* (Dublin, 1899)

Tomlins, Harold Nuttall, *A supplement to the crown circuit companion; containing adjudged cases, and precedents of indictments; together with all the statutes to the end of the last session of parliament, 6 George IV, 1823* (London, 1823)

Tomlins, Sir Thomas Edlyne, *The law-dictionary, explaining the rise, progress, and present state of the British law: defining and interpreting the terms or words of art, and comprising also copious information on the subjects of trade and government* 2 vols (4th ed., London, 1835)

—— , *A popular law-dictionary, familiarly explaining the terms and nature of English law; adapted to the comprehension of persons not educated for the legal profession, and affording information peculiarly useful to magistrates, merchants, parochial officers, and others* (London, 1838)

Trollope, Anthony, *The MacDermots of Ballycloran*, ed. Robert Tracy (Oxford, 1989)

Waters, Samuel, *A policeman's Ireland: recollections of Samuel Waters, RIC*, ed. Stephen Ball (Cork, 1999)

Wharton, J.J.S., *The law-lexicon, or dictionary of jurisprudence: explaining the technical words and phrases employed in the several departments of English law; including the various legal terms used in commercial transactions; together with an explanatory as well as literal translation of the Latin maxims contained in the writings of the ancient and modern commentators* (2nd ed., London, 1860)

Whishaw, James, *A new law dictionary; containing a concise exposition of the mere terms of art, and such obsolete words as occur in old legal, historical and antiquarian writers* (London, 1829)

Whiteside, James, *Italy in the nineteenth century, contrasted with its past condition*, 3 vols (London, 1848)

Wigram, W. Knox, *The justices' note-book* (London, 1880)

Wills, William, *An essay on the rationale of circumstantial evidence; illustrated by numerous cases* (London, 1838)

Wrottesley, Frederic John, *The examination of witnesses in court including examination in chief, cross-examination, and re-examination* (2nd ed., London, 1926)

Yielding, William, *Observations on the alleged 'discrepancies' between returns made to parliament, by the clerks of the crown and peace respectively, and by the inspectors general of prisons, of the number of persons committed for trial, and convicted on trial, in Ireland, and upon the constabulary returns made to the lord lieutenant of the number of offences committed there, alluded to in the debates on the earl of Roden's motion, on the 27th November, 1837 ...* (London, n.d. [1838])

7. WORKS OF REFERENCE

Ball, F. Elrington, *The judges in Ireland, 1221–1921*, 2 vols (London, 1926)

Ferguson, Kenneth, *King's Inns barristers 1868–2004* (Dublin, 2005)

O'Higgins, Paul, *A bibliography of Irish trials and other legal proceedings* (Abingdon, Oxon., 1986)

Thom's Irish almanac and official directory of the United Kingdom and Ireland (Dublin, 1845–)

8. PRINTED BROADSHEET BALLADS

White Ballad Collection (John Davis White, 1820–93, antiquary, solicitor, and editor of the *Cashel Gazette*), Dept of Early Printed Books, Trinity College, Dublin, OLS/X/1/530–2

9. MODERN WORKS

Allen, C.J.W., *The law of evidence in Victorian England* (Cambridge, 1997)

Bell, Robert Evan, 'The office of Director of Public Prosecutions for Northern Ireland' (PhD thesis, Queen's University, Belfast, 1989)

Bentley, David, *English criminal justice in the nineteenth century* (London and Rio Grande, 1998)

Bodkin, M. McDonnell, *Famous Irish trials* (Dublin, 1918)

Bonsall, Penny, *The Irish RMs: the resident magistrates in the British administration of Ireland* (Dublin, n.d.)

Bourke, Angela, *The burning of Bridget Cleary: a true story* (London, 1999)

Brady, J.C., 'Legal developments, 1801–79' in W.E. Vaughan (ed.), *A new history of Ireland*, v, *Ireland under the union I, 1801–70* (Oxford, 1989), pp 451–81

Brady, John, 'Irish interpreters at Meath assizes' in *Ríocht na Midhe*, 2:1 (1959), 62–3

Brennan, Karen, 'Beyond the medical model: a rationale for infanticide legislation' in *Northern Ireland Legal Quarterly*, 58:4 (winter 2007), 505–35

Brett, C.E.B., *Long shadows cast before: nine lives in Ulster, 1625–1977* (London, 1978)

Bridgeman, Ian, 'The constabulary and the criminal justice system in nineteenth-century Ireland' in *Criminal Justice History*, 15 (1994), 95–126

Brown, R. Blake, '"A delusion, a mockery, and a snare": array challenges and jury selection in England and Ireland, 1800–1850' in *Canadian Journal of History*, 39:1 (Apr. 2004), 1–26 (from http://www.findarticles.com (10 Aug. 2006)

Cairns, David J.A., *Advocacy and the making of the adversarial criminal trial, 1800–1865* (Oxford, 1998)

Carey, Tim, *Mountjoy: the story of a prison* (Cork, 2000)

Carroll-Burke, Patrick, *Colonial discipline: the making of the Irish convict system* (Dublin, 2000)

Casey, J.P., *The office of the attorney general in Ireland* (Dublin, 1980)

Chadwick, Roger, *Bureaucratic mercy: the Home Office and the treatment of capital cases in Victorian Britain* (New York and London, 1992)

Cockburn, J.S, & Thomas A. Green, (eds), *Twelve good men and true: the criminal trial jury in England, 1200–1800* (Princeton, NJ, 1988)

Coleman, Anne, *Riotous Roscommon. Social unrest in the 1840s* (Dublin and Portland, OR, 1999)

Conley, Carolyn A., 'No pedestals: women and violence in late nineteenth-century Ireland' in *Journal of Social History*, 28:4 (summer 1995), 801–18

—— , *Melancholy accidents: the meaning of violence in post-Famine Ireland* (Lanham, MD, 1999)

—— , 'Homicide in late-Victorian Ireland and Scotland' in *New Hibernia Review* (autumn 2001), 66–86

Connolly, S.J. (ed.), *Kingdoms United: Great Britain and Ireland since 1500: integration and diversity* (Dublin, 1999)

—— , 'Unnatural death in four nations: contrasts and comparisons' in Connolly (ed.), *Kingdoms United* (1999), pp 200–214

Corfe, Tom, *The Phoenix Park murders: conflict, compromise and tragedy in Ireland, 1879–1882* (London, 1968)

Costello, Kevin, 'A constitutional antiquity?-the Habeas Corpus (Ireland) Act, 1782 revisited' in *Ir Jur*, n.s., 23 (1988), 240–54

Crossman, Virginia, *Local government in nineteenth-century Ireland* (Belfast, 1994)

—— , *Politics, law and order in nineteenth-century Ireland* (Dublin, 1996)

Crowther, M. Anne, 'Crime, prosecution and mercy: English influence and Scottish practice in the early nineteenth century' in Connolly (ed.), *Kingdoms United* (1999), pp 225–38

Cunningham, John B., 'The investigation into the attempted assassination of ffolliot Warren Barton near Pettigo, on 31 October 1845' in *Clogher Record*, 13:3 (1990), 125–45

Dawson, N.M., Desmond Greer & Peter Ingram (eds), *One hundred and fifty years of Irish law* (Dublin and Belfast, 1996)

Dawson, N.M. (ed.), *Reflections on law and history: Irish Legal History Society discourses and other papers, 2000–2005* (Dublin, 2006)

Deale, Kenneth E.L., *Beyond any reasonable doubt? A book of murder trials* (Dublin, 1971)

De Blaghd, Earnan P., 'Tim Kelly guilty or not guilty?' in *Dublin Historical Record*, 25:1 (Dec. 1971), 12–24

Delany, V.H.T., *Christopher Palles, lord chief baron of Her Majesty's Court of Exchequer in Ireland 1874–1916: his life and times* (Dublin, 1960)

Doran, Sean, & John Jackson, 'The judicial role in criminal cases in Ireland' in Dawson, Greer, & Ingram (eds), *One hundred and fifty years of Irish law* (1996), pp 69–104

Duman, Daniel, *The judicial bench in England 1727–1875* (London, 1982)

Emsley, Clive, *Crime and society in England* (3rd ed., Harlow, 2005)

Evans, Richard J., *Rituals of retribution: capital punishment in Germany 1600–1987* (Oxford, 1996)

Farrell, Brian, *Coroners: practice and procedure* (Dublin, 2000)

Finnane, Mark, 'Irish crime without the outrage: the statistics of criminal justice in the later nineteenth century' in Dawson (ed.), *Reflections on law* (2006), pp 203–22

Flanagan, Kieran, 'The Chief Secretary's Office, 1853–1914: a bureaucratic enigma' in *IHS*, 24:94 (Nov. 1984), 197–225

Gamble, Charles, *Solicitors in Ireland 1607–1921: the Incorporated Law Society's work* (Dublin and London, 1921)

Garnham, Neal, *The courts, crime and the criminal law in Ireland 1692–1760* (Dublin, 1996)

—— , 'How violent was eighteenth-century Ireland?' in *IHS*, 30:119 (May 1997), 377–92

Gatrell, V.A.C., & T.B Hadden, 'Criminal statistics and their interpretation' in E.A. Wrigley (ed.), *Nineteenth-century society: essays in the use of quantitative methods for the study of social data* (Cambridge, 1972), pp 336–431

Gatrell, V.A.C., *The hanging tree: execution and the English people 1770–1868* (Oxford, 1994)

Geary, Laurence M., 'John Mandeville and the Irish crimes act of 1887' in *IHS*, 25:100 (Nov. 1987), 358–75

Greer, D.S., & N.M. Dawson (eds), *Mysteries and solutions in Irish legal history: Irish Legal History Society discourses and other papers, 1996–1999* (Dublin, 2001)

Greer, Desmond, *Compensation for criminal injury* (2nd ed., Belfast, 1990)

—— , 'Lawyers or politicians? The Irish judges and the right to vote, 1832–1850' in Caroline Costello (ed.), *The Four Courts: 200 years: essays to commemorate the bicentenary of the Four Courts* (Dublin, 1996), pp 126–58

—— , 'Crime, justice and legal literature in nineteenth-century Ireland' in *Ir Jur*, n.s., 37 (2002), 241–68

—— , 'A security against illegality? The reservation of crown cases in nineteenth-century Ireland' in Dawson (ed.), *Reflections on law* (2006), pp 163–202

Griffin, Brian, 'An agrarian murder and evictions in Rathcore' in *Ríocht na Midhe*, 9:1 (1994–5), 88–103

—— , *The Bulkies: police and crime in Belfast, 1800–1865* (Dublin, 1997)

—— , *Sources for the study of crime in Ireland, 1801–1921* (Dublin, 2005)

—— , 'Prevention and detection of crime in nineteenth-century Ireland' in Dawson (ed.), *Reflections on law* (2006), pp 99–125

Hannigan, Ken, 'A miscellany of murder: violent death in nineteenth-century Wicklow' in *Wicklow Hist Soc Jn*, 1:7 (1994), 22–34

Hart, A.R., *A history of the king's serjeants at law in Ireland: honour rather than advantage?* (Dublin, 2000)

Herlihy, Jim, *The Royal Irish Constabulary: a short history and genealogical guide. With a select list of medal awards and casualties* (Dublin, 1997)

—— , *The Royal Irish Constabulary: a complete alphabetical list of officers and men, 1816–1922* (Dublin, 1999)

—— , *The Dublin Metropolitan Police: a short history and genealogical table* (Dublin, 2001)

—— , *The Dublin Metropolitan Police: a complete alphabetical list of officers and men, 1836–1925* (Dublin, 2001)

—— , *Royal Irish Constabulary officers: a biographical dictionary and genealogical guide, 1816–1922* (Dublin, 2005)

Hickey, Éanna, *Irish law and lawyers in modern folk tradition* (Dublin, 1999)

Hogan, Daire, & W.N. Osborough (eds), *Brehons, serjeants and attorneys: studies in the history of the Irish legal profession* (Dublin, 1990)

Hogan, Daire, *The legal profession in Ireland 1789–1922* (Dublin, 1986)

—— , '"Vacancies for their friends": judicial appointments in Ireland, 1866–1867' in Hogan & Osborough (eds), *Brehons, serjeants and attorneys* (1990), pp 211–29

—— , '"Arrows too sharply pointed": the relations of Lord Justice Christian and Lord O'Hagan' in McEldowney & O'Higgins (eds), *The common law tradition* (1990), pp 61–83

—— , 'R.R. Cherry, lord chief justice of Ireland, 1914–1916' in Greer & Dawson (eds), *Mysteries and solutions* (2001), pp 161–92

Hostettler, John, *The politics of criminal law reform in the nineteenth century* (Chichester, 1992)

Ingram, Peter, 'Law and lawyers in Trollope's Ireland' in Dawson, Greer & Ingram (eds), *One hundred and fifty years of Irish law* (1996), pp 125–43

Ireland, Richard W., 'Putting oneself on whose country? Carmarthenshire juries in the mid-nineteenth century' in T.G. Watkin (ed.), *Legal Wales: its past, its future* (Welsh Legal History Society, vol. i, Cardiff, 2001), pp 63–87

Jackson, Claire, 'Irish political opposition to the passage of criminal evidence reform at Westminster, 1883–98' in McEldowney & O'Higgins (eds), *The common law tradition* (1990), pp 185–201

Jackson, J.D., 'In defence of a voluntariness doctrine for confessions: *The Queen v. Johnston* revisited' in *Ir Jur*, n.s., 31 (1986), 208–46

Jessop, W.J.E., 'Samuel Haughton: a Victorian polymath' in *Hermathena*, 116 (winter 1973), 5–26

Johnson, D.S., 'The trials of Sam Gray: Monaghan politics and nineteenth century Irish criminal procedure' in *Ir Jur*, n.s., 20 (1985), 109–34

—— , 'Trial by jury in Ireland 1860–1914' in *Journal of Legal History*, 17:3 (Dec. 1996), 270–93

Knelman, Judith, *Twisting in the wind. The murderess and the English press* (Toronto, Buffalo, London, 1998)

Kostal, R.W., 'Rebels in the dock: the prosecution of the Dublin fenians, 1865–6' in *Éire-Ireland*, 34:2 (summer 1999), 70–96

Laird, Heather, *Subversive law in Ireland 1879–1920* (Dublin, 2005)

Langbein, John H., *The origins of adversary criminal trial* (Oxford, 2003)

Lambert, Richard S., *When justice faltered: a study of nine peculiar murder trials* (London, 1935)

Leckey, John L., & Desmond Greer, *Coroner's law and practice in Northern Ireland* (Belfast, 1998)

Lowe, W.J., 'Policing Famine Ireland' in *Éire-Ireland*, 39:4 (1994), 47–67

Lynch, Pat, *They hanged John Twiss* (Tralee, 1982)

McArdle, Joseph, *Irish legal anecdotes* (Dublin, 1995)

McAree, Noel, *Murderous justice: a study in depth of the infamous Connemara murder* (London, 1990)

McAuley, Finbarr, *Insanity, psychiatry and criminal responsibility* (Dublin, 1993)

McCabe, Desmond, 'Magistrates, peasants and the petty sessions courts: Mayo, 1823–50' in *Cathair na Mart*, 5:1 (1985), 45–53

—— , '"The part that laws or kings can cause or cure": crown prosecution and jury trial at Longford assizes, 1830–45' in Raymond Gillespie & Gerard Moran (eds), *Longford: essays in county history* (Dublin, 1991), pp 153–72

—— , 'Open court: law and the expansion of magisterial jurisdiction at petty sessions in nineteenth-century Ireland' in Dawson (ed.), *Reflections on law* (2006), pp 126–62

McCracken, J.L., 'The fate of an infamous informer' in *History Ireland*, 9:2 (summer 2001), 26–30

MacDonagh, Oliver, *O'Connell: the life of Daniel O'Connell 1775–1847* (London, 1991)

McDowell, R.B., 'The Irish courts of law, 1801–1914' in *IHS*, 10:40 (Sept. 1957), 363–91

—— , *The Irish administration, 1801–1914* (London and Toronto, 1964)

McEldowney, John F., & Paul O'Higgins (eds), *The common law tradition: essays in Irish legal history* (Dublin, 1990)

McEldowney, John F., 'The case of *The Queen v. McKenna* (1869) and jury packing in Ireland' in *Ir Jur*, n.s., 12 (1977), 339–53

—— , 'Lord O'Hagan (1812–1885): a study of his life and period as lord chancellor of Ireland (1868–1874)' in *Ir Jur*, n.s., 14 (1979), 360–77

—— , '"Stand by for the Crown": an historical analysis' in *Criminal Law Review 1979*, 272–83

—— , 'Legal aspects of the Irish secret service fund 1793–1833' in *IHS*, 25:98 (1986), 129–37

—— , 'The appointment of sheriffs and the administration of justice in nineteenth-century Ireland' in Richard Eales & David Sullivan (eds), *The political context of law. Proceedings of the seventh British Legal History Conference Canterbury 1985* (London and Ronceverte, 1987), pp 119–34

—— , 'Crown prosecutions in nineteenth-century Ireland' in Douglas Hay & Francis Snyder (eds), *Policing and prosecution in Britain 1750–1850* (Oxford, 1989), pp 427–56

—— , 'Some aspects of law and policy in the administration of criminal justice in nineteenth-century Ireland' in McEldowney & O'Higgins (eds), *The common law tradition* (1990), pp 117–55

—— , 'Policing and the administration of justice in nineteenth-century Ireland' in Clive Emsley & Barbara Weinberger (eds), *Policing Western Europe: politics, professionalism, and public order, 1850–1940* (New York, Westport, CN, and London, 1991), pp 18–35

—— , 'Miscarriages of justice? The Phoenix Park murders, 1882' in *Criminal Justice History*, 14 (1993), 143–9

McGoff-McCann, Michelle, *Melancholy madness: a coroner's casebook* (Dublin, 2003)

McGrath, Declan, 'The accomplice corroboration warning' in *Ir Jur*, n.s., 34 (1999), 170–201

McGrath, Thomas, 'Fairy faith and changelings: the burning of Bridget Cleary in 1895' in *Studies*, 71 (summer 1982), 178–84

McMahon, Kevin, & Thomas McKeown, 'Agrarian disturbances around Crossmaglen, 1835–55' in *Seanchas Ardmhacha*, 9:2 (1979), 302–32; 10:1 (1981), 149–75; 10:2 (1982), 380–416

Maguire, W.A., *Captain Cohonny: Constantine Maguire of Tempo, 1777–1834* (Belfast, 2002)

Malcolm, Elizabeth, '"The reign of terror in Carlow": the politics of policing Ireland in the late 1830s' in *IHS*, 32:125 (May 2000), 59–74

—— , 'Investigating the "Machinery of Murder": Irish detectives and agrarian outrages, 1847–79' in *New Hibernia Review*, 6:3 (autumn 2002), 73–91

Murphy, Nancy, *Guilty or innocent? The Cormack brothers – trial, execution and exhumation* (Nenagh, Co. Tipperary, 1998)

Murtagh, Ann, *Portrait of Westmeath tenant community, 1879–85. The Barbavilla murder* (Dublin and Portland, OR, 1999)

O'Brien, Gerard, 'Capital punishment in Ireland' in Dawson (ed.), *Reflections on law* (2006), pp 223–58

O'Connell, Maurice R., 'Daniel O'Connell: income, expenditure and despair' in *IHS*, 17:66 (Sept. 1970), 200–220

O'Donnell, Ian, 'Unlawful killing past and present' in *Ir Jur*, n.s., 37 (2002), 56–90

O'Mahony, Paul (ed. with seven introductory essays), *Criminal justice in Ireland* (Dublin, 2002)

Osborough, W.N., 'Roman law in Ireland' in *Ir Jur*, n.s., 25–26 (1990–92), 212–68

—— , *Studies in Irish legal history* (Dublin, 1999)

—— , 'Law and the spread of literacy: millennial reflections on Boddington's plight': an inaugural lecture delivered at University College Dublin on 4 February 2000

—— , 'Bishop Dixon, the Irish historian and Irish law' in *Northern Ireland Legal Quarterly*, 57:2 (summer 2006), 235–45

Palmer, Stanley H., *Police and protest in England and Ireland, 1780–1850* (Cambridge, 1988)

Peers, Douglas M., 'Torture, the police, and the colonial state in the Madras presidency, 1816–55' in *Criminal Justice History*, 12 (1991), 29–56

Potter, Harry, *Hanging in judgment. Religion and the death penalty in England from the bloody code to abolition* (London, 1993)

Prior, Pauline M., 'Dangerous lunacy: the misuse of mental health law in nineteenth-century Ireland' in *Journal of Forensic Psychiatry & Psychology* (2003), 1–17

—— , 'Mad, not bad: crime, mental disorder and gender in nineteenth-century Ireland' in *History of Psychiatry*, 8 (1997), 501–16 (see also Ian O'Donnell & Finbarr McAuley (eds), *Criminal justice history: themes and controversies from pre-independence Ireland* (Dublin, 2003), pp 66–82)

——, 'Prisoner or patient? The official debate on the criminal lunatic in nineteenth-century Ireland' in *History of Psychiatry*, 15:2 (2004), 177–92

——, 'Murder and madness: gender and insanity defense in nineteenth-century Ireland' in *New Hibernia Review* (winter 2005), 19–36

Roughead, William, *Twelve Scots trials* (Edinburgh & London, 1913)

—— (ed.), *Trial of Oscar Slater*, 4th ed. (Edinburgh & London, 1950)

Sheehan, A.V., *Criminal procedure in Scotland and France: a comparative study, with particular emphasis on the role of the public prosecutor* (Edinburgh, 1975)

Sheils, Derek, 'The resident magistrates in Ireland, 1860–1922' in *International Association for the History of Crime and Justice Bulletin*, 15 (Feb. 1992), 39–53

Simpson, A.W. Brian, *Cannibalism and the common law* (Chicago, 1984)

Smith, Beverley A., 'The Irish General Prisons Board, 1877–1885: efficient deterrence or bureaucratic ineptitude?' in *Ir Jur*, n.s., 15 (1980), 122–36

Smith, K.J.M., *James Fitzjames Stephen. Portrait of a Victorian rationalist* (Cambridge, 1988)

Sweeney, Frank, *The murder of Conell Boyle, County Donegal, 1898*, Maynooth Studies in Local History, no. 46 (Dublin, 2002)

—— (ed.), *Hanging crimes* (Dublin, 2005)

Taylor, Howard, 'Rationing crime: the political economy of criminal statistics since the 1850s' in *Econ Hist Rev*, 51:3 (1998), 569–90

Vaughan, W.E., *Sin, sheep and Scotsmen: John George Adair and the Derryveagh evictions, 1861* (Belfast, 1983)

——, 'Ireland *c.*1870' in Vaughan (ed.), *A new history of Ireland*, v, *Ireland under the union I, 1801–70* (Oxford, 1989)

——, *Landlords and tenants in mid-Victorian Ireland* (Oxford, 1994)

Walker, David M., *The Oxford companion to law* (Oxford, 1980)

Waldron, Jarlath, *Maamtrasna: the murders and the mystery* (Dublin, 1992)

White, Philip, 'Homicide' in Monica A. Walker (ed.), *Interpreting crime statistics* (Oxford, 1995), pp 130–44

Wilbanks, William, 'Homicide in Ireland' in *International Journal of Comparative and Applied Criminal Justice*, 20:1 (spring 1996), 59–75

Index

*Acts of parliament are included in the body of the index and in
an addendum at pp 448–50.*

Executions for Murder Act 1836 (6 & 7
Will. IV, c. 30), 329
Exeter, defective gallows, 328

'facts', in issue, relevant, or introductory,
184; similar fact, 185
Fagan, Thomas, crown witness, 240
Fahy, Thomas, sentenced to death 1844,
249
Farrell and Moore (1848), a private
prosecution, 91
Farrell, John, exposed himself, 109
—, Robert, crown witness at Phoenix Park
murder trials, 232
—, sub-constable, 38
'father', senior barrister of circuit, 216
Faulkner, Brian, minister of home affairs,
NI (1959–63), 305
Fawcett, Sub-Inspector Robert (*recte*
Faussett), rebuked by Baron Deasy,
261
Fay (1872), change of venue, 125, 137–9,
164, 196, 371
felony, definition, 5–6. *See* misdemeanour
Fermanagh, county, 37, 87, 126, 131, 324,
330, 340
finger prints, 54
Finn, Phineas, tried for murder of
president of board of trade, 243
Firmount, near Blarney, 62
Fitt (1919), age of prisoner, 290
Fitzgerald, Francis, landlord, murdered,
39, 313, 343
—, Francis Alexander, baron of exchequer
(1859–82), 104, 251, 257–9, 261,
323–4; in *Cavendish* (1873), 223; in
Galvin (1865), 205; in *Johnston* (1864),
193; reserved *Gillis* (1866), 202; tried
McLoughlin, 243, 323; John Logue
mistook him for Judge Fitzgerald, 309;
resigned 1882 over prevention of
crimes bill, 262
—, John David, judge QB (1860–82), 50,
52, 79, 104, 157, 173, 214, 243, 252,
254, 259, 261–2, 265, 267, 284, 288,
292, 295; in *Fay* (1872), 137; in
Johnston (1864), 193; in *M'Eneany*
(1878), 138–9; defended his decision
in *M'Mahon* (1874), 158; in *Reardon*

(1873) and *Marshall* (1874), 50; tried
McCormick, 323; on prisoners at
inquests, 47; on social composition of
long panels, 125; on discharging
juries, 156; on setting aside, 156; on
when trial begins, 169; summing up at
Walsh's trial 1873, 254; reprimanded
Wexford grand jury, 262
—, Thomas, crown solicitor, Co. Donegal,
99
Fitzpatrick (1838), a challenge to the array,
136
Fitzpatrick, Michael, found guilty of
murder 1840, 101
—, Paddy, suggested as witness by
Kilkenny, 65
Flaherty, Mary, kept public house near
Ballymote, 178–9
Flanagan, P.A., catholic chaplain, attended
hanging at Sligo, 348
Fleet (1818), publication of *ex parte*
proceedings, 47
Fletcher, a dubious character, 81
Florence, 365
Foakes, John W., experiment at Ireland's
Eye, 370
Fogarty (1846), a challenge to the array,
136
Fogarty, Andrew, tried for poisoning wife,
216
—, Constable Patrick, 66
Foley, arrested on suspicion, 62
Follett, Sir William (1798–1845), English
barrister, died in sight of Woolsack,
216
Ford, a dubious character, 81
Forde, Robert, searched field for stolen
goods, 180
—, William Brownlow, JP, DL, MP for
Co. Down, (1857–74), 171–2
Forfeiture Act 1870 (33 & 34 Vict., c. 23),
293
Forgery, Abolition of Punishment of
Death Act 1832 (2 & 3 Will. IV, c.
123), 382
Forgery Act 1837 (7 Will. & 1 Vict., c. 84),
382
Forker, Margaret, murdered, 65
Forkill, Co. Armagh, 239–40, 342

The Irish Legal History Society

(www.irishlegalhistorysociety.com)

Established in 1988 to encourage the study and advance the knowledge of the history of Irish law, especially by the publication of original documents and of works relating to the history of Irish law, including its institutions, doctrines and personalities, and the reprinting or editing of works of sufficient rarity or importance.

Acts of Parliament